ROMANS & GALATIANS:
THE GOSPEL ACCORDING TO PAUL

Student Manual

by
Dr. Van Johnson, Dr. Quentin McGhee,
Rev. Edgardo Muñoz, and Dr. Steve Eutsler

Instructional Design by
Dr. Quentin McGhee, Senior Editor

PUT YOUR FAITH TO WORK!

Faith & Action Series

Faith & Action
637 Meadowview Ln
Chestnutridge, MO. 65630 U.S.A.

Photo Credits

	Figure #
Ken Berg	1.1; 2-apostle; 4.6b; 6.1
Bible History	1.3
DesignPics.com	3.13, 3.16; 4.3
Ralph W. Harris	1.7; 11.1
Imaginational	6.12; 7.3; 8.17-throne
Photos.com	1.5, 1.8, 1.18; 2.1, 2.3; 3.1, 3.2, 3.12, 3.15; 4.1, 4.6a; 5.2, 5.5, 5-key, 5.10; 6.7, 6.11; 7.1, 7.8, 7-warning, 7.13, 7.19, 7.22; 8.1, 8.9, 8.16; 9.2; 10.2-chariot, pitcher, pyramid; 10.9, 10.11, 10-children; 11.4, 11.8, 11.14
Tyndale	1.10
Lucinda Zilverberg	1.1b

Copyright Information

  **♥ Thank You ♥**

Special thanks to BGMC and LFTL for helping fund the Faith & Action Ministry.

First Edition 2012
Second Edition 2018

Faith & Action Series—Romans & Galatians, Second Edition
©2018 Faith & Action Team

Course # BIB2013
ISBN 978-1-60382-127-8
Item # 4412-21E0

Table of Contents

Chapter
Lesson

Unit One:
Sin and Our Need
for Righteousness (Romans 1:1–3:20)

Unit Two:
Justification—Righteousness God Provides for Us;
Pardon From the Penalty of Sin (Romans 3:21–5:21)

Unit Three:
Sanctification—Righteousness God Produces in Us;
Freedom From the Power of Sin (Romans 6–8)

Unit Four:
The Scope and Fruit of Righteousness (Romans 9–11)

Unit Five:
Relationships—The Fruit of Righteousness (Romans 12–16)

List of Figures

Faith & Action Series Overview

Bible	Theology	Church Ministries	General Education
Pentateuch	Systematic Theology: Articles in the Fire Bible (Life in the Spirit Bible)	Evangelism, Discipleship, & Church Planting	Survey of the New Testament
Historical Books	Theology 1: God, Bible, & Angels	Children's Ministry	Survey of the Old Testament
Major Prophets	Theology 2: Man, Sin, Christ, & Salvation	Pastoral Ministry	Wisdom Books (Introduction to Philosophy)
Minor Prophets	Theology 3: Holy Spirit, the Church, & Last Things	Leadership 1: Loving God & People	Homiletics: Preparing Biblical Messages
Synoptic Gospels: Life & Teachings of Christ	Hermeneutics 1: General Principles for Interpreting Scripture	Leadership 2: God's Love Crossing Human Boundaries (Conflict Resolution)	Principles of Teaching
Gospel of John: The Word Became Flesh	Hermeneutics 2: Interpreting Genres of Scripture	Biblical Counseling	Marriage & Family
Acts of the Holy Spirit		Introduction to Missions	Cross-Cultural Communications
Romans & Galatians: The Gospel According to Paul		Youth Ministry	The Bible & Science
First and Second Corinthians		Read the Light: Teaching Literacy	World Literature (Comparing the Holy Scriptures of Judaism, Christianity & Islam)
Prison Epistles: Ephesians, Colossians, Philippians & Philemon		Practicum 1: Preaching	Financial Management
Paul's Eschatological & Pastoral Epistles: 1 & 2 Thess., 1 & 2 Tim., Titus		Practicum 2: Evangelism, Discipleship, & Church Planting	
Hebrews		Practicum 3: Pastoral Ministry	
General Epistles: James—Jude		Practicum 4: Children's Ministry	
Revelation & Daniel (Eschatology)		Practicum 5: Youth Ministry	

Faith & Action
Four-Year Degree Plan (121 Credits)

First Year

First Semester

Course #	Course Title	Credits
BI 1013	Synoptic Gospels	3
TH 1013	Hermeneutics 1	3
BI 1023	Acts	3
GE 1013	Homiletics	3
MI 1013	Practicum 1: Preach 4 or more sermons on studies of this semester	3
		15

Second Semester

Course #	Course Title	Credits
BI 1033	Prison Epistles	3
MI 1023	Evan., Disc., & Church Planting	3
MI 1033	Practicum 2: Evan., Disc., & Church Planting	3
TH 1023	Pentecostal Doctrines + Fire Bible Articles	3
BI 1043	Ministerial Ethics + Pastoral Epistles	3
	AG Hist., Miss. & Gov. + Board Meetings	1
		16

Second Year

First Semester

Course #	Course Title	Credits
GE 2023	Old Testament Survey	3
GE 2033	New Testament Survey	3
TH 2033	Theology 1: God, Bible & Angels	3
BI 2053	Romans & Galatians	3
BI 2063	Introduction to Missions with Practice	3
		15

Second Semester

Course #	Course Title	Credits
BI 2173	Revelation & Daniel (Eschatology)	3
MI 2043	Leadership 1	3
MI 2053	Leadership 2 (Conflict Resolution)	3
MI 2063	Pastoral Ministry	3
MI 2073	Practicum 3: Pastoral Ministry	3
		15

Third Year

First Semester

Course #	Course Title	Credits
BI 3083	Pentateuch	3
MI 3083	Church Admin., Law & Finance with Practice	3
BI 3073	1 & 2 Corinthians	3
TH 3043	Theology 2: Humans, Sin, Christ & Salvation	3
TH 3053	Apologetics + Hermeneutics 2	3
		15

Second Semester

Course #	Course Title	Credits
MI 3093	Prayer, Worship & Practice	3
BI 3093	*Wisdom Books (Introduction to Philosophy)	3
GE 3043	Cross-Cultural Communications	3
GE 3053	*Marriage & Family	3
TH 3063	Theology 3: Holy Spirit, the Church, & Last Things	3
		15

Fourth Year

First Semester

Course #	Course Title	Credits
MI 4103	Children's Ministry	3
MI 4113	Practicum 4: Children's Ministry	3
MI 4123	Biblical Counseling with Practice	3
BI 4103	Hebrews	3
GE 4063 GE 4073	*The Bible & Science **or** *Financial Management	3
		15

Second Semester

Course #	Course Title	Credits
MI 4133	Youth Ministry	3
MI 4143	Practicum 5: Youth Ministry	3
BI 4113	John	3
BI 4123	General Epistles	3
GE 4083	*World Literature (Comparing the Holy Scriptures of Judaism, Christianity & Islam)	3
		15

Electives may be approved and substituted on a case by case basis.

Course letters: BI is Bible; TH is theology; MI is ministry; GE is general education.

Course numbers: The first number is the year of study; middle numbers show the sequence in a category; last number is the credits.

Example: BI1023 is a Bible course. The first 1 shows it is in the first year. 02 reveals this course is the second in the sequence of Bible courses. The final number, 3, shows the course is 3 credits.

About This Book

1. **The Lesson Headings** divide each chapter into several parts. Each of these lessons focuses on principles related to one theme. We number the lessons consecutively throughout the book.

2. **The Lesson Goals** are listed at the beginning of each chapter. Also, when a lesson begins, the goal for that lesson is printed there. You will find that there is at least one goal for each lesson.

3. **Key Words** are defined in a section called "Definitions" at the end of the book. The symbol * comes before all words that are defined. To help some students, we have also defined a few words that are not key words.

4. **Teaching Method:** These courses are designed for the *guided discovery* method of learning. This method focuses on the student, rather than the teacher. When this course is used in a classroom, lectures are not intended. Rather, most of the class time should be used for students to discuss the questions in the margins and related questions from the teacher and other students. At least 25% of the student's grade should be on how faithfully the student has tried to answer questions *before* class.

   It is VERY important for each student to own his or her book. We encourage Bible schools to require students to buy their texts at the time they pay tuition. It is a shame for students to leave school without their books, because they need them for a lifetime of ministry. Owning the book enables a student to write notes in it and underline important ideas. Also, when students own their books, they do not waste class time by copying things that are already written in the text. Rather, they spend their time discussing questions related to the Bible and ministry.

   In a classroom the teacher and students should discuss key questions together. The best teachers never answer their own questions. Some students will complain at first when the teacher requires them to think, read, and search for answers. But a good teacher knows that children who are always carried never learn to walk. And students who are always told the answer learn to memorize, but not to think and solve problems. In many ways, a good teacher is like a coach—guiding others to succeed.

   The questions in this course are like a path that leads straight to the goal. If the questions are too hard for a student, the teacher can ask easier questions that are like stairs toward harder questions. Also, the teacher should ask questions that guide students to apply the text to local issues. Often, a good teacher will add a story or illustration that emphasizes a truth for students.

5. **Schedule:** This *Faith & Action Series* course is for three credits. For a Bible school course, it is good to plan 40 contact hours between the teacher and students. This allows one lesson for a class hour.

6. **The Questions:** Most questions in the margins are identified by the hammer ⌐ and nail ⌐ symbols. Questions are steps toward a goal. As a student answers the questions, he or she is sure to reach the goals. The hammer introduces *content questions* and the nail precedes *application questions*. Our logo for this book includes the hammer hitting the nail. A student must grasp content before being able to apply it. The answers to all content questions are in the text, near the question. We encourage students to answer nail or application questions from their local settings.

   In some books there is the symbol of a shovel ⌐ before certain questions. Questions beside the shovel symbol are inductive questions. The word *induce* means "to lead." These questions lead students to discover truth for themselves.

7. *Sabio* is a Spanish word that means "wise man." This symbol ⌐ in the margin signifies a proverb or wise saying.

8. **The Illustrations**, such as stories and examples, are preceded by the candle symbol ⌐ .

9. **Figures** include pictures, photos, charts, and maps. We number the figures in order throughout the chapter. For example, the first three figures in chapter one are numbered 1.1, 1.2, and 1.3. There is a list of maps and charts near the front of the book.

10. **The Test Yourself** questions come at the end of each chapter and are indicated by the balance symbol ⚖. There are always ten of these questions. As a rule, there are two test questions for each goal in the chapter. If students miss any of these questions, they need to understand why they missed them. Knowing why an answer is right is as important as knowing the right answer.

11. **Essay Test Topics** are at the end of each chapter, indicated by the pencil symbol ✎. Note that these essay topics are the lesson goals of the chapter. A student should be able to summarize these goals, writing 50-100 words on each one. These essay topics test students at a much higher level than the multiple choice, Test Yourself questions.

12. **Sample Answers** to the hammer questions, some comments on the nail questions, and answers for the Test Yourself questions and Essay Topics are in the Teacher's Guide. Students should answer questions so they will grow and become strong in their mental skills.

13. **Bible quotations** are usually from the New International Version (NIV). We also use the New American Standard Bible (NASB) and the King James Version (KJV). We encourage students to compare biblical passages in several versions of the Bible.

14. **The Scripture List** includes key Scripture references in this course. It is located near the back of the book.

15. **The Bibliography** is near the endnotes page. It is a complete list of books the author refers to in this course. Some students will want to do further research in these books.

16. **Endnotes** identify the sources of thoughts and quotes. They are listed by chapter at the end of the book.

17. **The Unit Exams and Final Exam** are in the Teacher's Guide. In the Teacher's Guide there are also other useful items for the teacher and potential projects for the students.

18. **Course Description (BIB2013):** A thorough study of Romans and parallel passages in Galatians. The course begins with an analysis of Romans and Galatians: the cities, author, dates, readers, purposes, themes, special features, and outlines. The study continues with an exposition of each paragraph and section of Romans, with an emphasis on the two hermeneutical questions: What did the text mean to the first readers? How does it apply to us? Each lesson identifies timeless, cross-cultural principles. Interactive questions, case studies and illustrations guide students to apply these principles to the situations believers face today. (This course is designed for 3 credits, based on 16 class hours per credit.)

19. **Course Goals** for each chapter of this book:

F&A Chap.	Rom.	Goals
1–11	1–16	Value, apply, and live by the principles of Romans and Galatians.
1–11	1–16	Preach and teach the principles of Romans and Galatians.
1–11	1–16	Answer all of the questions Paul asks in Romans.
1–11	1–16	Analyze Paul's use of 60 Old Testament quotes and various allusions.
1	1:1-17	Analyze Romans: its city, author, date, readers, purpose, theme, special features, and outline. Analyze the background and purposes of Galatians in relation to Romans. Analyze 5 key words or phrases in Romans 1:16-17.
2	1:18–3:20	Explain why Gentiles and Jews need the righteousness God provides.
3	3:21–4:25	Compare and contrast justification and sanctification. Compare and contrast righteousness by faith and by the Law. Explain, illustrate, and apply seven principles of faith in Romans 4.
4	5:1-21	Relate justification to each of these: peace, hope, joy, inner and outer witnesses, assurance, and reconciliation. Contrast the results of Adam's disobedience and Christ's obedience.
5	6	Explain and illustrate three ways in which God and believers are holy. Explain, illustrate, and apply six keys to victorious living.

Continued on next page

Continued from previous page

F&A Chap.	Rom.	Goals
6	7	Interpret Paul's illustrations on: baptism, slavery, and marriage. Explain and illustrate five principles about law. Defend six reasons why we believe Romans 7:13-25 refers to a pre-Christian.
7	8	Identify and interpret key phrases and relationships in Romans 8:1-4. Contrast the values, characteristics, and destinies of those led by the flesh and those led by the Spirit. Analyze the conflict, fruit, and harvest of the flesh and of the Spirit in Galatians 5-6; compare this with parallel teachings in Romans 8. Outline the steps of restoration for a believer "caught" in a sin. Explain these concepts: suffering, predestination, assurance, super-victors.
8	9–11	Answer and explain: Did God's word to Abraham and Israel fail? Differentiate between election for service and for salvation; illustrate each. Explain how Jews and Gentiles may enjoy a right relationship with God. Explain the setting of Paul's teaching on the olive tree; interpret and apply it. Summarize Paul's glorious conclusion of Romans 9–11.
9	12:12	Analyze the sacrifice required of believers under the new covenant. Explain the relationship of Romans 12:1-2 and 12:3–15:13. Analyze and illustrate seven examples of spiritual gifts. Summarize the moral nature of *agape* love, and its expression in relationships.
10	13:1–15:13	Explain a believer's debts to government and society. Identify and illustrate guidelines for relationships between strong and weak believers.
11	15:14–16:27	Explain, illustrate, and apply values that guided Paul's ministry. Identify the two "bookends" of Romans, and terms common to both. Paraphrase the doxology of Romans.

20. Authors

Dr. Van Johnson is the Dean of Master's Pentecostal Seminary in Toronto. Dr. Johnson is the director of the MTS in Pentecostal Studies—a joint degree program of Tyndale Seminary and Master's. Van serves as adjunct faculty in New Testament at Tyndale and at Canadian Pentecostal Seminary. He is an ordained minister with the Pentecostal Assemblies of Canada, and serves on the pastoral staff at Agincourt Pentecostal Church. This pastoral role is part of the church-based model of Master's Seminary. Van previously taught at Eastern Pentecostal Bible College and Western Pentecostal Bible College. He has conducted chapels for the Montreal Expos, the Toronto Blue Jays, the Toronto Raptors, and the Toronto Argonauts. He wrote the commentary on Romans in the *Full Life Bible Commentary,* which was published by Zondervan Publishing House. Dr. Johnson contributed extensive notes for this course, and read through the manuscript, offering many helpful insights and suggestions. The combination of his pastoral and teaching experience with his own brand of humor contributes to his unique preaching style. His degrees include a B.A. in Sociology, McGill University (Montreal); M.Div., Trinity Evangelical Divinity School (Chicago); Th.D in New Testament, Wycliffe College, University of Toronto. His specialties are Pentecostal History, Luke, Romans, Jewish Apocalyptic, and Pastoral Theology.

Dr. Quentin McGhee is the founder, senior author, instructional designer, and an editor of the *Faith & Action Series*, a curriculum of 40 books at completion. He earned a B.A. in Biblical Studies from Southwestern College in Oklahoma City, and a B.S. in Math from Oral Roberts University (ORU). Later he completed his M.Div. at the Assemblies of God Theological Seminary, where he taught beginning Greek and was selected by the faculty for Who's Who Among Students. He earned a D.Min. from ORU in 1987 and in 2015 was inducted into the ORU Hall of Fame in the College of Science and Engineering.

Dr. McGhee and his wife, Elizabeth, pioneered a church in Oklahoma. They served as missionaries in Kenya for 15 years where they helped start many churches, developed an extension Bible school for full-time ministers, and assisted in curriculum development. Since 2005, Quentin and Elizabeth have served as Assemblies of God missionaries with the Latin America/Caribbean region. Dr. McGhee is developer and director of the *Faith & Action Series*, while Elizabeth assists with graphic design, desktop publishing, translations, and sales.

Edgardo Rolando Muñoz has an M.A. in Theology. Since 1981 he has served as pastor of Avance Cristiano Church in Temperley, Buenos Aires, Argentina. He has taught at Río de la Plata Bible Institute in Lomas de Zamora, Buenos Aires since 1981, and served there as Dean from 1985 to 1997. Since then, he has served as Assistant Director of that institution. From 1988 to 2003 he was a member of the Board of Directors of Christian Education Services. In 1996 he was named Secretary of Instituto de Superación Ministerial (ISUM), and continues in that position. Along with his duties as pastor, teacher, Assistant Director, and secretary, he presently serves as National President of the Christian Education Department of the Assemblies of God in Argentina (since 1998); National Director of the Bible Institutes in Argentina (since 1990); and Chief Editor of CONOZCA Magazine (since 1997).

Dr. Steve D. Eutsler has a rich ministerial background as a teacher, pastor, preacher, and writer. He serves as a mentor for students of Global University in the areas of Bible and Practical Theology. Also, he has served as adjunct professor at Central Bible College and Evangel University for 12 years, teaching courses on Bible, practical ministry, and preaching. Steve has pastored 18 years. He is the author of four books, *Light for the Darkened Heart, Clothing the Mind, Planning Pentecostal Preaching,* and *The Prison Epistles.* Steve is known for being an outstanding expository preacher. He has contributed sermons to *Preaching On-Line* and illustrations to *PreachingToday.com.* His sermon outlines often appear in *Enrichment Journal* and *Pulpit Helps.* Also, he serves as a Dale Carnegie trainer. He contributed significant research and notes for this *Faith & Action* course on *Romans & Galatians.* He earned his Doctor of Ministry degree at the Assemblies of God Theological Seminary in Springfield, Missouri, where he and his wife, Jackie reside. They have two grown children, Tabitha and Jeremy.

21. Contributors and Consultants

Dr. French L. Arrington's ministry includes involvement in evangelical and Pentecostal spheres around the world. Having served as a pastor and as director of the Department of Bible and Theology, professor of Greek New Testament and Pauline studies for 17 years at Lee University, has received the award for excellence in teaching. Speaking at seminars in Korea, Puerto Rico, Guatemala, the Philippines, Indonesia, Ecuador, the Virgin Islands, China, and Russia, he also ministers in seminars, conferences, and local churches. Dr. Arrington is an ordained bishop in the Church of God and served as professor of New Testament Greek and exegesis at Pentecostal Theological Seminary from 1981-2002. where he is now professor emeritus.

His academic achievements include Bachelor of Arts degrees from Lee College and the University of Chattanooga; a Master's Degree in Divinity and a Master's Degree in Theology from Columbia Theological Seminary; and a Ph.D. in Biblical Languages from Saint Louis University.

Dr. Arrington's published works include: *Paul's Aeon Theology in 1 Corinthians* and *New Testament Exegesis: Examples; Divine Order in the Church* (1 Corinthians), *The Ministry of Reconciliation* (2 Corinthians), and *Maintaining the Foundations* (1 Timothy). He contributed to the *Dictionary of Pentecostal and Charismatic Movements, The Complete Biblical Library,* and *The New International Dictionary of Pentecostal Charismatic Movements.* He served on the editorial board of *The Pentecostal Minister* magazine and as Greek editor of the four volumes: *A Biblical Theology of the Holy Spirit;* and contributed volume 4 of *Contemporary Issues in Pneumatology.* Hendrickson published his book *Acts of the Apostles: Introduction, Translation and Commentary.*

Arrington was a member of the editorial committee for the magazine: *The Pentecostal Minister* and for *The Full Life Study Bible* (subsequently named *Life in the Spirit Study Bible* and now *Fire Bible*). He served as the general editor of *Life in the Spirit New Testament Commentary.* He written works include study guides for the Global University courses: *Romans, 1 Corinthians* and *Prison Epistles.* Pathway Press published his three-volume work *Christian Doctrine: a Pentecostal Perspective.* His recent books include: *Encountering the Holy Spirit: Paths of Christian Growth and Service; Exploring the Declaration of Faith, Unconditional Eternal Security: Myth or Truth?; The Spirit-Anointed Jesus: A Study of Luke's Gospel* and *The Spirit-Anointed Church: A Study of Acts.* His latest work is a commentary published under the title: *The Greatest Letter Ever Written: A Study of Romans.*

Dr. George O. Wood contributed sermon manuscripts as a resource for this course. His insights and illustrations were vital to this course. He is co-author of the *Faith & Action* books *Acts of the Holy Spirit* and *First and Second Corinthians*. He is the son of missionary parents to China and Tibet. He completed his undergraduate degree from Evangel College (now Evangel University). Later, he earned a doctorate in theology from Fuller Theological Seminary, and a juris doctorate from Western State University College of Law. He was assistant district superintendent of Southern California for 4 years and pastored Newport-Mesa Christian Center in Costa Mesa for 17 years. Dr. Wood has authored a number of books including a college textbook on Acts. Dr. Wood served as General Secretary of the Assemblies of God from 1993, until he was elected as General Superintendent in 2007.

Dr. Stanley M. Horton approved this course for biblical and theological accuracy. His degrees include a B.S. from the University of California, an M.Div. from Gordon-Conwell Theological Seminary, an S.T.M. from Harvard University, and a Th.D. from Central Baptist Theological Seminary. He is Distinguished Professor of Bible and Theology Emeritus at the Assemblies of God Theological Seminary in Springfield, Missouri. Dr. Horton has written 400 articles and book reviews, and authored 46 books on topics such as Genesis, Amos, Matthew, John, Acts, First and Second Corinthians, Revelation, and the Holy Spirit.

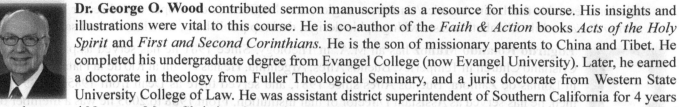

Rev. Larry Hatfield recently retired as senior pastor of Grand Assembly of God in Chickasha, Oklahoma. He and his wife, Helen, began pastoral ministry in 1963. They have lived by the principle, "Love God and love people." The Hatfields have served various Assemblies of God churches in Oklahoma, and also traveled throughout the Southwest as evangelists for 8 years. They ministered at youth camps in North Carolina and Oklahoma. Larry served as a hospital chaplain for 8 years at City Hospital in Tahlequah, Oklahoma. He studied at Oklahoma City Southwestern College, at East Central University, and Southwestern Assemblies of God University in Waxahachie, Texas. His articles have frequently been published in the *Pentecostal Evangel*. Larry supplied several illustrations for this course on *Romans & Galatians*. He broadcasts a 'Drive to Work' morning devotional radio program called "Coffee with the Pastor."

Dedication

This book on *Romans & Galatians* was made possible by a generous donation from Dr. Daniel T. and Bonnie Sheaffer.

Daniel Thomas Sheaffer was born November 29, 1929 to Reverend Gerald and Jeanette Sheaffer. Dan was named after his uncle, Daniel Thomas Muse, a bishop of the Pentecostal Holiness Church. Dan first began preaching at the age of 17. Like many Pentecostal pioneers, when he did not have a church in which to speak, he preached on street corners or used schools to hold revivals.

In 1950, at the age of 21, Dan married Bonnie Rose Benson, who became his faithful companion for the next 60 years. They conducted evangelistic meetings for several years, and Dan was ordained by the Assemblies of God Oklahoma District in 1958.

Dan and Bonnie pastored First Assembly in Miami, Oklahoma from 1961–1969. Then they accepted the pastorate of a small AG church in Oklahoma City. This proved to be a step of destiny into a ministry that would impact multitudes of people in many nations of the world. In the first 3 years, from 1969 to 1971, the small church grew from 42 to 1250 members, in a new building. Then in 1979 the Sheaffers led the congregation to build Crossroads Cathedral. Located on two major highways, this was one of the first and largest mega-churches in the Assemblies of God. It seated about 6,000 people each Sunday morning, contained more than 200,000 square feet, and was built debt free—partly because the Sheaffers founded a successful business to build homes and do general contracting to expand their ministry. Thousands of people came to Christ in this strategic mega-city church at the crossroads. But as Assemblies of God General Superintendent George O. Wood noted, Dan and Bonnie Sheaffer had a heart for Oklahoma City and the world. Their generosity is a legend. Here are a few of the projects made possible by their ministry and the millions of dollars they gave:

- The *Faith & Action* books *First and Second Corinthians* and *Romans & Galatians,* which more than three million students will study worldwide;
- Churches they founded and built in Liberia, Kenya, South Africa, Nigeria, Paraguay, Colombia, Jamaica, Chile, and Burundi;

Malawi, East Africa

- 1,000 churches they funded in Malawi, and sponsorhips that helped the Malawi Assemblies of God Church grow from 200 to 4,000 churches with 800,000 members;
- Malawi Assemblies of God School of Theology that trains students from across Africa;
- The Sheaffer Full Life Center at Southwestern Assemblies of God University in Waxahachie Texas. This building has 111,000 square feet, and contains a cafeteria, classrooms, offices, an athletic center, two gymnasiums, and a chapel;
- Participation in the construction of Bridges and Teeter Hall on the Southwestern Assemblies of God Univeristy campus;
- The financial undergirding of the Doctor of Ministry program at Assemblies of God Theological Seminary (AGTS) in Springfield, Missouri;
- The Assemblies of God Center for Holy Land Studies, funded during their final pastorate at Harvest AG;
- Initial funding for the Daniel T. Sheaffer Chair of Practical Ministry at AGTS.

Dan held degrees from Oklahoma City Southwestern College, Oklahoma City University, East Central State University, Tulsa University, Luther Rice Seminary, and Southwestern Assemblies of God University. Pastor Sheaffer and Bonnie hosted the popular Trinity Broadcasting Network program "The Answer" for 17 years and were frequent hosts and guests of TBN's "Praise the Lord" program. Dan authored two books of Bible questions and answers and a church growth book entitled, *Together We Grow*.

To Dan and Bonnie Sheaffer, we gratefully dedicate this book. Their legacy endures forever.

We express our thankfulness to their daughter, Terri, and her husband, Gary King; and their son, Mike, and his wife, Starla, who continue to fulfill the Great Commission as Dan and Bonnie cheer from heaven.

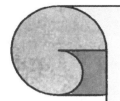

Unit One: Sin and Our Need for Righteousness
(Rom. 1:1–3:20)

Welcome to Romans, the gospel according to Paul. The *gospel* is a term that refers to *the good news of salvation* that the apostles preached and taught. As you study Romans you will discover that the gospel, or good news, is better than some people realize. Paul's letter to the Romans explains that his gospel of salvation spans from regeneration and adoption into God's family to glorification, when Jesus returns for us.

In this first Unit, we will study Romans 1:1–3:20. Here, Paul's gospel introduces the gospel and the problem. We have all sinned, and our sins have offended God and separated us from Him.

In Chapter 1, we will lay the foundation for our study. You will learn to:
- *Analyze Romans: its city, author, date, readers, purpose, special features, and outline.*
- *Analyze the background of Galatians and its relation to Romans.*
- *Explain the greater and lesser purposes of Galatians.*
- *State a principle about the gospel, in relation to each of these: the Old Testament, the Resurrection, obedience, and Galatians 1:6-9.*
- *Explain how Paul's desire to visit Rome affected his prayers and plans.*
- *Identify some spiritual gifts that Paul might have wanted to share.*
- *Explain the sense in which all believers are debtors.*
- *Analyze five key words or phrases in Romans 1:16-17.*

In Chapter 2, we come face to face with the problem of sin. By the time Paul finishes talking about sin, all who read Romans feel guilty and are ready for the righteousness God provides in Christ. As you study this second chapter of our book, we will enable you to:
- *Explain three reasons why Gentiles need the righteousness that God provides (Rom. 1:18-32).*
- *Identify the problem and three levels of sin in Romans 1:21-32.*
- *Contrast Paul's use of personal pronouns in Romans 1 and 2.*
- *Answer the questions that Paul asks in Romans 2:3-4 and 2:17-23.*
- *Give three examples how God will judge Jews the same as Gentiles.*
- *Relate the theme "God does not show favoritism" to each of these: Jews first, knowing versus doing, breaking the Law, trusting in symbols.*
- *Identify and answer the five key questions in Romans 3.*

Thank you for choosing to study Romans—the longest, most famous letter God gave us through Paul.

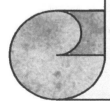

Chapter 1:
Romans: Paul's Longest, Most Famous Letter
(Romans 1:1-17)

Introduction

In Lomé, Togo, there is a market called the *Dead Yovo Market. Yovo* is the Ewe tribe's word for "white man." The market is filled with clothes from America—clothes given by family members of Americans who died. This is why the Ewe people call the market the *Dead Yovo Market!*

Figure 1.1
Christ's sacrifice on the cross provides us with a righteousness that is not our own (Rom. 10:3; Phil. 3:9).

The market is a great blessing to the local people. Many get expensive clothes at a price they can pay. Shirts, skirts, pants, dresses, and suits sell at low prices. If the *Dead Yovo Market* did not exist, they would not be able to afford such nice garments.

The president of a Bible school in Lomé stood beside his office. He noticed two students walking across the campus. They were wearing beautiful, expensive suits. "Wow," he said. "Those students are dressed as well as the president!" Another student explained, "That is because they went to the *Dead Yovo Market.*"

This story reminds us of what Jesus has done for us. He died on the cross to redeem us from sin. Now we are clothed with a righteousness that God gives us after a member of His family died (Rom. 10:3). By faith in Jesus we are clothed with a righteousness that is not our own (Phil. 3:9). The students who went to the *Dead Yovo Market* were dressed as well as the president. Romans reminds us that because Jesus died on the cross, we wear spiritual clothes provided by God Himself.[1]

Lessons:

Understanding Romans
Goal: *Analyze Romans: its city, author, date, readers, purpose, special features, and outline.*

The Relationship of Romans to Galatians
Goal A: *Analyze the background of Galatians and its relation to Romans.*
Goal B: *Explain the greater and lesser purposes of Galatians.*

Introduction to Romans—Part 1 (Rom. 1:1-7; Gal. 1:6-9)
Goal: *State a principle about the gospel in relation to each of these: the Old Testament, the Resurrection, obedience, and Galatians 1:6-9.*

Introduction to Romans—Part 2 (Rom. 1:8-17)
Goal A: *Explain how Paul's desire to visit Rome affected his prayers and plans.*
Goal B: *Identify some spiritual gifts that Paul might have wanted to share.*
Goal C: *Explain the sense in which all believers are debtors.*
Goal D: *Analyze 5 key words or phrases in Romans 1:16-17.*

Romans—people who lived in Rome, the capital of the Roman Empire

Galatians—probably refers to those in the southern towns of the province of Galatia, such as Lystra

gospel—the good news that Jesus died on the cross, arose from the dead, and ascended to the Father to deliver us from the penalty and power of sin, and restore us to a right relationship with God; He will come again to judge sinners, and rapture those of us who love Him so that we may live together with God forever.

righteousness—a right relationship with God

salvation—deliverance from the penalty and power of sin, and restoration to a right relationship with God

justification—a legal term that means right standing with God, and proclaims deliverance from the penalty of sin

sanctification—holiness; being set apart from sin to serve and worship God; freedom from the power of sin

faith—trust in God, shown by obeying the gospel and submitting to the Holy Spirit

---

Lesson

1

Understanding Romans

Goal: *Analyze Romans: its city, author, date, readers, purpose, special features, and outline.*

Many preachers and Bible teachers have praised the book of *Romans. Some say it is the most important writing in the world. Many Christians believe it is the most important book in the Bible. Martin Luther started the *Protestant Reformation of the church because of Romans 1:17. Luther did not think a person could read or study Romans too much. He also said that the more someone studies it, the more precious it becomes. Why is Romans so valuable? Because of all Paul's letters, Romans is the longest and most thorough explanation of the *gospel and how we live it.

**Figure 1.2
Martin Luther was saved as he studied Paul's letter to the Romans.**

A. The city of Rome

Rome was famous for several things.

- Rome was known for its size. It was the largest city of Paul's day, with over one million citizens.

- Rome was famous as the capital and symbol of the Roman Empire. To its citizens, and many others, Rome was the center of the world. The Roman kingdom was from 63 B.C. to A.D. 486.

- Rome was famous for its buildings like the Pantheon—a temple for its many false gods (Figure 1.4). Another famous building was the Colosseum, completed by A.D. 80 (Front cover, and Figure 1.5). In the Colosseum, Romans watched athletic contests and battles for life. In this arena, Romans watched Christians fight with wild animals. These believers had been condemned for their faith.

Q 1 *What are 5 reasons why Rome was famous?*

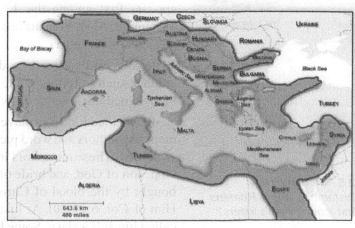

Figure 1.3 Boundary of the Old Roman Kingdom around modern nations

Figure 1.4   The Pantheon is a famous temple in Rome. It was first built in 27 B.C. and rebuilt in A.D. 120–124. Since A.D. 609, it has been used as a church.[2]

Figure 1.5   Many believers died in the Colosseum, an outdoor theater in Rome, where Roman citizens watched as believers and others fought wild beasts.

Q 2 ➤ *What was the Colosseum? (See Figure 1.5 and the cover photo.)*

Q 3 ➤ *In which 2 ways did the Roman government prepare the world for the gospel?*

Q 4 ➤ *What types of sins were common in Rome?*

- Rome was famous for its government. The government of the early Roman Republic has influenced the form of many democratic governments today.[3] And many Roman Caesars are still famous today (Figure 1.6). The Roman government brought peace on the earth. Also, the government built roads, like the Appian Way. Peace and roads helped spread the gospel.

- Rome was famous for its sin. Seneca said Rome was a *sewer of sin. The apostle John referred to Rome as a prostitute and the mother of all harlots (Rev. 17:1-18). Rome was known for sexual sins, slavery, greed, and idolatry.

Though Rome was famous, it was empty on the inside. This great city had a void that only the gospel could fill.

Caesar	Years of Rule	Comments
Augustus	31 B.C.–A.D. 14	He ruled the world when Jesus was born.
Nero	A.D. 54–68	He martyred Peter and Paul.
Vespasian	A.D. 69–79	He ruled when the temple in Jerusalem was destroyed.
Domitian	A.D. 81–96	He ordered people to worship him as the god, Jupiter. He ruled when John was exiled to Patmos.

Figure 1.6   Some Roman Caesars who are important in Church history

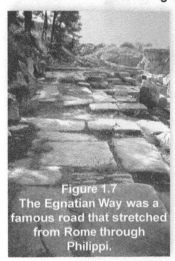

**Figure 1.7
The Egnatian Way was a famous road that stretched from Rome through Philippi.**

Q 5 ➤ *In the New Testament, why is Romans first among Paul's letters?*

Q 6 ➤ *In what ways do you think of yourself as a servant of Christ?*

B. The author of Romans

The apostle Paul puts his name at the beginning of Romans (Rom. 1:1), as he does in all of his 13 letters (Figure 1.9). Romans is the longest letter Paul wrote. It is also his most theological letter. Because of its length and theology, Romans appears first among the 13 letters Paul wrote in the New Testament. Also, Romans has influenced more people than any of Paul's other letters.

It was Paul's custom to dictate or speak his letters while another, such as Tertius, wrote for him (Rom. 16:22). Afterward, Paul signed the letter to show it was his (see 2 Thess. 3:17).

Paul called himself a slave or servant (Rom. 1:1). Paul used many metaphors and word pictures to describe our relationship with God. These metaphors included such pictures as slave of God, son of God, and bride of Christ. Paul, like all believers, belonged to Jesus. He was bought by the blood of Christ. Like Paul, we are all servants of God—we belong to Him (1 Cor. 6:19-20). At first it might have shocked the readers of Romans when Paul called himself a slave. Some historians estimate that the population of the entire Roman kingdom was 7.5 million. And of these, 3 million were slaves![4] But being a slave to God was not like being a slave to Rome, for God is a kind, loving, generous Master. "Slave of God" was a title of honor in biblical times, as it is now.[5]

**Figure 1.8
Stone carving of Nero, who ruled when Peter and Paul were martyred**

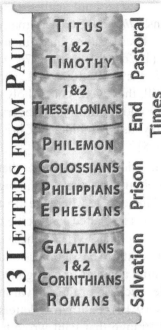

Figure 1.9 Paul's 13 Letters

Paul emphasizes that Christianity is more than a religion—it is a relationship.[6] Paul understood that, through the old covenant, God established a relationship with Abraham. That is, God established a relationship to create a people for Himself. God expected Israel to respond to Him with *faith, love, and obedience. Likewise, through the new covenant based on Jesus Christ, God establishes a relationship. Our part as believers is to respond with faith, love, and obedience. Paul's relationship with the God of the New Testament began on the road to Damascus. Paul's encounter with Jesus changed his life forever.

God called Paul to serve as an apostle—"one sent on a mission" (Rom. 1:1; also 1 Cor. 1:1). Paul's specific calling was to be an apostle to the *Gentiles—all people who were not Jews (Rom. 1:5; Gal. 1:15-16). Peter, John, and James recognized God's ministry to the Gentiles (Gal. 2:9). Still, many Jews, both inside and outside the Church, criticized Paul. They misunderstood the freedom in Christ that he preached. Paul's letter to the Romans helps all understand that Paul preached one message—for Jews and Gentiles.

Q 7 *When did Paul write Romans?*

C. The date of Romans

Paul wrote Romans about A.D. 57.[7] He stayed in Corinth for 3 months on his third missionary trip (Acts 20:2-3; see also Rom. 16:1, 23; 1 Cor. 1:14). The collection for the poor saints in Jerusalem was past (Rom. 15:25-28). And Paul would soon deliver that offering in Jerusalem. So it appears that Paul wrote Romans from Corinth, after writing 2 Corinthians (see 2 Cor. 8:1–9:15).

D. The first readers of Romans

Some Catholics claim that Peter started the church in Rome, but this is unlikely. If Peter was a leader in Rome, we would expect to find his name in the list of Romans 16. But Romans does not mention Peter.

The first believers in Rome may have been Jews converted on the Day of Pentecost (Acts 2:8-11).The church at Rome probably started like the church at Antioch. Common believers, filled with the Spirit, have started many churches (see Acts 11:19-21). Other believers might have been Paul's converts in Asia, Macedonia, and Greece (see Rom. 15:17-29). In its earliest days, the Roman church was probably mostly Jewish, but included some Gentiles who feared God.

Figure 1.10
Paul wrote to the Romans from Corinth, about A.D. 57.

Q 8 *How did the church in Rome begin?*

By the time Paul wrote to the Romans, the number of Gentiles in the house churches had increased greatly. The Roman Emperor Claudius expelled Jews from Rome (A.D. 49). Aquila and Priscilla were among the Jews that Claudius expelled (Acts 18:2). The law against Jews probably lapsed when Claudius died in A.D. 54. So many Jews may have returned to Rome by the time Paul wrote to the Romans about A.D. 57. Paul's letter shows a concern for the relationship between Gentiles and Jews (see especially Rom. 11:16-32; 14:1–15:13).

Q 9 *When Paul wrote to the Romans, were the house churches there filled with Jews or Gentiles? Explain.*

Paul reminds readers in Rome that God loves them and calls them all to be saints (Rom. 1:7). The word *saint* means "holy"—set apart *for* and *to* God. All believers are saints in God's sight. The blood of the Lamb cleanses us as we walk in the light

Q 10 *Are all true believers saints? Explain.*

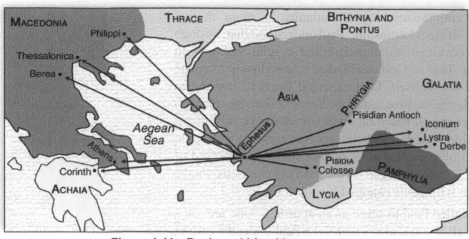

Figure 1.11   Paul used big cities as centers to evangelize and disciple the areas around them.

(1 John 1:7). Paul called the Corinthians *saints* (1 Cor. 1:2, many versions). These saints had many problems (1 Cor. 1:10; 5:1; 6:7, 18; 8:9; 11:17; 14:9, 20, 40; 15:12, and others). Still, they were saints (holy), set apart *for* and *to* God. As believers, we are holy as we abide in Christ (John 15:1-8).[8]

Paul's missionary work shows that God cares about Christians in the big cities. Paul liked to go where the most people lived. He visited large cities, such as Antioch in Syria, Ephesus, Philippi, Corinth, Thessalonica, and Rome—the center of the empire. Each city Paul visited became a center to evangelize and disciple the areas and small towns nearby.[9] For example, because of the revival in Ephesus, all of the province of Asia heard the gospel (Acts 19:10). Paul wrote letters to encourage and teach the saints in the cities. So it is not strange that Paul wrote to believers in Rome. He did not start their church. And Paul had not yet visited Rome when he wrote to the Romans. Paul cared about believers in Rome, because God cared about them. In Paul's day, Rome was the most strategic city in the world.

E. The purposes of Romans

Q 11 *What are 3 reasons why Paul wrote the book of Romans?*

Paul wrote to the Romans for three reasons:

- To impart a spiritual gift to strengthen Roman believers (Rom. 1:11). Paul wants believers at Rome to benefit from his apostolic ministry, which included teaching.
- To prepare the way for Roman believers to support his future ministry in Spain (Rom. 15:23-29). This is part of the reason why he explains the gospel he has preached for 25 years (Rom. 3:8; 6:1-2, 15). Believers should support ministries they know well. So Paul takes time, in Romans 1–16, to explain his gospel.
- To improve relationships between Jews and Gentiles on topics like *salvation, food, and special days (Rom. 2:1-29; 3:1, 9; 11:11-36; 14:1–15:13).

The gospel Paul preached offers a free pardon to all. But a pardon is only useful when people receive it. A pardon is a written, legal paper, stating that a person is forgiven and free. About 200 years ago President Andrew Jackson of the United States granted a pardon to prisoner George Wilson. Wilson had been sentenced to death by hanging. The pardon said he was free. But Wilson refused to accept the pardon. Was it legal to refuse the pardon? The Supreme Court met and decided that a pardon was only good if accepted. So Wilson was hanged. Likewise, about 2,000 years ago Jesus died on a cross to provide all a pardon for sin. But sinners must accept His offer. Otherwise, they will never receive forgiveness, and will face the judgment of God.[10]

F. Special features of Romans

Q 12 *What do you like the most about Romans? Explain.*

The apostle Paul includes some special features in his letter to the Romans:

- He uses a style of questions and answers (Figures 2.5, 3.7, 5.8, 8.3);
- He quotes the Old Testament about 60 times (See Figure 11.11);
- He emphasizes the *righteousness from God (Rom. 1:17; 3:21–5:21);
- He discusses our sin and the problem of the flesh (Rom. 6–7);
- He focuses on the Holy Spirit as the key to victory over sin and the flesh (Rom. 8);
- He explains the role of the Jews in God's plan of salvation (Rom. 9–11); and
- He applies the truths of the gospel to practical, daily living (Rom. 12–15).[11]

G. Outline showing the themes of Romans

The theme of Romans is righteousness. Our outline emphasizes five aspects of righteousness in Romans (Figure 1.12).

Theme	Romans
Introduction	**1:1-17**
A. Sin: Our Need for Righteousness	**1:18–3:20**
Gentile sin	1:18–2:16
Jewish sin	2:17–3:8
Everyone's sin	3:9-20
B. *Justification: God Provides Righteousness for Us—pardon from the penalty of sin	**3:21–5:21**
A summary of justification by faith	3:21-31
Abraham, an illustration of justification by faith	4:1-25
Blessings that come with justification by faith	5:1-11
Adam and Christ contrasted	5:12-21
C. *Sanctification: God Produces Righteousness in Us—freedom from the power of sin	**6–8**
Our union with Christ	6:1-23
The conflict of flesh and Spirit	7:1-25
The Spirit enables victory over sinful desires of the flesh	8:1-39
D. Election: God Offers Righteousness for Jews and Gentiles	**9–11**
Israel's past election: God's promises have not failed	9:1-29
Israel's present rejection: Not all Israelites have believed	9:30–10:21
Israel's future restoration: All Israel will be saved	11:1-36
E. Relationships: God Requires Righteousness <u>Among Us</u>—loving Him and others	**12:1–15:13**
The believer: a living sacrifice	12:1-2
The believer and others in the body	12:3-15
The believer and the government	13:1-7
The believer and the law of love	13:8–15:13
Conclusion and Greetings	**15:14–16:27**

Figure 1.12   Outline of Romans

Theme	Romans
A. Sin: _____	1:18–3:20
B. _____: Righteousness God Provides for Us	3:21–5:21
C. Sanctification: Righteousness God Produces in Us	_____
D. Election: _____	9–11
E. Relationships (practical): Righteousness in Action	_____

Figure 1.13   Practice identifying the five parts of Romans.

Q 13 *Read out loud the 5 main parts in the outline of Romans.*

Q 14 *Fill in the blanks in Figure 1.13 on the 5 parts of Romans.*

Lesson 2 **The Relationship of Romans to Galatians**

Goal A: *Analyze the background of Galatians and its relation to Romans.*
Goal B: *Explain the greater and lesser purposes of Galatians.*

A. Topics in both Romans and Galatians

The topics that are in both Romans and *Galatians have led many to study the two letters together. In this course, we will look at key passages in Galatians that shine light on Romans.

Topic	Romans	Galatians
Paul's calling to be an apostle	1:1, 5	1:1; 1:11–2:10

Q 15 *In this course, why will we study some passages in Galatians?*

Continued on next page

Continued from previous page

Topic	Romans	Galatians
Paul's gospel	1:2-4, 14-17	1:3-9
Righteousness by faith in Christ, not by works	1:16-17; 3:21–5:21	2:11–5:12; 6:12-16
Freedom from slavery to the Law and the flesh	6–7	5:16-21; 6:7-8
Freedom through life in the Spirit	8	5:16-26; 6:1, 7-10

Figure 1.14   Some topics in Roman and Galatians

B. Background of Galatians

In our Bibles, the order of Paul's letters is not based on the dates he wrote them. Rather, Paul's letters are listed from the longest to the shortest. Romans is the first of Paul's letters in our Bibles because it is the longest, with 7,101 words. Likewise, Philemon is the last of Paul's letters because it is the shortest, with 335 words.[12] The exceptions to this are the Pastoral Epistles: 1 & 2 Timothy and Titus. These are the only letters of Paul that are not listed according to length.

Group	Book Title	Book Sub-group	Date+	Author
1. Historical Books (5)	Matthew		55-70	Matthew
	Mark	Synoptic Gospels	50-68	Mark
	Luke		60	Luke
	John		85-95	John
	Acts		62	Luke
2. Paul's Epistles (13)	Romans		55-56	
	1 Corinthians	Salvation Epistles	55	
	2 Corinthians		56	
	Galatians		48-49	
	Ephesians		60-61	
	Philippians	Prison Epistles	61	
	Colossians		60-61	Paul
	Philemon		60-61	
	1 Thessalonians	Epistles about the future	50-51	
	2 Thessalonians		51	
	1 Timothy		63	
	2 Timothy	Pastoral Epistles	67	
	Titus		65	
3. Hebrews and the General Epistles (8)	Hebrews		65-70	Unknown
	James	Epistles to suffering believers	45-49	James
	1 Peter		63-65	Peter
	2 Peter		65-67	Peter
	1 John		85-90	John
	2 John	Epistles to correct false teachings	85-90	John
	3 John		85-90	John
	Jude		67-80	Jude
4. Prophecy	Revelation		90-95	John

Figure 1.15   Groups, sub-groups, dates, and authors of New Testament books

+ Bible scholars differ on the exact dates of New Testament books.

If we were studying Paul's letters according to dates, we would begin with Galatians. Paul wrote Galatians to the churches in the province of Galatia. He went to Southern Galatia on his first missionary journey (Acts 13:4–14:28). Recall that he ministered in the Galatian towns of Pisidian Antioch, Derbe, Lystra, and Iconium. Many Bible teachers think Paul wrote Galatians to believers in Southern Galatia about A.D. 49. This was just before the big Church Council in Jerusalem about A.D. 49 (Acts 15).

Q 16 *What are 3 churches in the province of Galatia?*

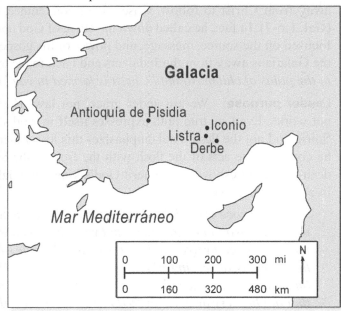

Figure 1.16 Map showing places Paul visited in Galatia

Recall that the Acts 15 Council was about the relationship between Jews and Gentiles. The Council concluded that Gentiles are saved by faith in Christ. Therefore, Jewish believers did not require Gentiles to keep the law of Moses. The main topic in Galatians was the main topic at the Jerusalem Council (Acts 15). The big question was: Are we saved by faith in Jesus alone, or must we obey some Old Testament laws? It appears that Paul wrote to the Galatians before he went to Jerusalem. Then, the Church took an official position on salvation through Christ alone.

Galatians is a strong defense of justification by faith. In Galatians, Paul emphasized that *"a man is not justified by observing the law, but by faith in Jesus Christ"* (Gal. 2:16). The Galatians had received the gospel. They had been justified by faith in Christ. But afterward, Jewish teachers known as *Judaizers were leading some astray. These false teachers said that believers must follow Jesus *and* Moses. That is, Judaizers were trying to require believers to follow certain Jewish practices for salvation.

Most of the first believers were Jewish. These early followers of Jesus continued their Jewish way of life. They attended the synagogues to worship and learn. They offered sacrifices in the temple. They celebrated the Jewish feasts. They obeyed the rules Moses gave them. So they circumcised their sons. And like all Jews, they lived separated from the Gentiles.

Then the Gentiles began to receive Christ. This forced the Jewish believers to face new questions. Should Gentiles be circumcised? Must Gentiles live like Jews to be saved? The meeting of Acts 15 was about these questions.

Judaizers taught that circumcision was necessary for salvation. But Paul reminded the Galatians of the basic truths of the gospel. We are saved by faith in Jesus, *not* by keeping the law of Moses. We have only one Savior, Jesus. Paul said that the Galatians had deserted Jesus and were following a useless gospel (Gal. 1:6-7). He said that those who were trying to keep the Law were under a curse (Gal. 3:10). He emphasized that salvation is by faith in Jesus alone. Under the new covenant, circumcision has no religious value (Gal. 5:6). In fact, Paul said that those who trusted in circumcision or other laws had *"fallen away from grace"* (Gal. 5:4).

Q 17 *Which 2 saviors did Judaizers claim we need?*

C. Purposes of Galatians

In Galatians, we see a greater purpose and a lesser purpose.

Q 18 *What is the main purpose of Galatians?*

Greater purpose: After a short greeting, Paul stated the major problem. He marveled that these Galatians had so quickly deserted his gospel of grace. They had turned away from Christ to follow Moses. Paul condemned the false teachers among them (Gal. 1:6-7). In fact, he called down the curse of God upon them (Gal. 1:8-9). Then Paul focused on the source, message, and power of his gospel. His main purpose was to turn the Galatians away from the Judaizers and back to the truth. As Paul put it, *"I am again in the pains of childbirth until Christ is formed in you"* (Gal. 4:19).

Q 19 *What is the lesser purpose of Galatians?*

Lesser purpose: We are under grace, not law. The basis of our salvation is faith, not works. Even so, true faith expresses itself in works. God requires us to walk in the Spirit, and not the flesh. Paul emphasizes this lesser theme in Galatians 5:16–6:1. Here, he contrasts the acts of the flesh with the fruit of the Spirit. Those who fulfill the evil desires of the flesh will not inherit God's kingdom (Gal. 5:19-21). Grace teaches us to live godly, holy lives.

> ¹¹*For the grace of God that brings salvation has appeared to all men.* ¹²*It teaches us to say "No" to ungodliness and worldly passions, and to live self-controlled, upright and godly lives in this present age,* ¹³*while we wait for the blessed hope— the glorious appearing of our great God and Savior, Jesus Christ,* ¹⁴*who gave himself for us to redeem us from all wickedness and to purify for himself a people that are his very own, eager to do what is good* (Titus 2:11-14).

Q 20 *What are the 3 parts in the outline of Galatians?*

D. Outline of Galatians

Galatians	Theme
1–2	**Personal:** (*Validation of Paul's apostleship*) Paul's testimony—the gospel revealed
3–4	**Doctrinal:** (*Justification*) The gospel explained
5–6	**Practical:** (*Sanctification*) The gospel applied

Figure 1.17   **There are three main parts in Galatians.**

In Lessons 1 and 2 of this chapter, we have studied the backgrounds and settings of Romans and Galatians. This gives us a good foundation to study all of Romans. And we will examine parts of Galatians that shine light on Romans.

Lesson 3

Introduction to Romans—Part 1 (Rom. 1:1-7; Gal. 1:6-9)

Goal: *State a principle about the gospel, in relation to each of these: the Old Testament, the Resurrection, obedience, and Galatians 1:6-9.*

Figure 1.18   **Romans 1:1-7 and Romans 16:25-27 are like two "Gospel Bookends"**
with five units or "books" between them that explain Paul's gospel.

Setting

The two "bookends" of Romans emphasize Paul's gospel to the nations: believe and obey Christ (Figure 1.18). Take time to read these two "bookends" at the introduction and conclusion of Romans. Notice the words and thoughts that are in both.

Q 21 ↖ *In your Bible underline the words or thoughts that appear in both "bookends" of Romans: gospel, God, prophets, grace, obedience, faith, glory, Jesus Christ, Gentiles (or nations, Greek: ethnos). See Figure 1.18.*

A. The Old Testament prophesies the gospel (Rom. 1:1-3).

Q 22 ↖ *Underline the words in Romans 1:1-3 that show the Old Testament prophesied the gospel.*

¹*Paul, a servant of Christ Jesus, called to be an apostle and set apart for the gospel of God—* ²*the gospel he promised beforehand through his prophets in the Holy Scriptures* ³*regarding his Son, who as to his human nature was a descendant of David* (Rom. 1:1-3).

The gospel was not a late thought that God had, or a second plan He made. Before the creation of the world, God planned to send Jesus to save us (1 Pet. 1:20; Rev. 13:8). The prophets predicted the coming of Christ for centuries (see Luke 1:70; 24:27; Gal. 3:8).

The Scripture foresaw that God would justify the Gentiles by faith, and announced the gospel in advance to Abraham: "All nations will be blessed through you" (Gal. 3:8; Gen. 12:3).

Q 23 ⤳ *Did God announce the gospel to Abraham? Explain.*

Abraham may not have understood how God would bless all nations through him. But looking back, we understand that the promise of Genesis 12:3 (Gal. 3:8) refers to Jesus, a son of Abraham. We will study this promise more later in this course. But for now, let us note that verses like Romans 1:3 and Galatians 3:8 remind us that the Old Testament prophesied the gospel—that the Son of David would come to save us. Jesus came through the lineage of David. Many verses in the Bible affirm that Jesus is a son of David (2 Sam. 7:12-16; Isa. 9:6-7; 11:1; Jer. 23:5-6; Matt. 1:1; see also Luke 3:23-37).

Scriptures often refer to Jesus, Son of David, as the Messiah. *Messiah* is a Hebrew word that means "anointed one" and *Christ* is a form of the Greek word that means "anointed one." So whenever we see the name *Christ,* as in Romans 1:1, we should remember that *Christ* is another word for *Messiah.* For centuries, the prophets foretold that the Messiah would come. Romans 1:1-3 emphasizes this great truth.

Q 24 ⤳ *How are the words "Christ" and "Messiah" related?*

Application: Two things about Romans 1:1-3 encourage us. *First,* God cared about us so much that, even before He created us, He planned to save us from our sins. *Second,* we can depend on the Scriptures. Many verses in the Old Testament prophesied about the Messiah, <u>before</u> He came. Then, He did come, and fulfilled the words God spoke through the prophets. No other book is like the Bible, predicting the future accurately. Prophecy that is fulfilled strengthens our belief in the Bible.

Q 25 ↖ *How does Romans 1:1-3 encourage you?*

B. The Resurrection confirms the Christ of the gospel (Rom. 1:4).

And who through the Spirit of holiness was declared with power to be the Son of God by his resurrection from the dead: Jesus Christ our Lord (Rom. 1:4).

The Holy Spirit declared Jesus to be the Son of God through His resurrection. During Christ's time on earth He seemed "weak" to some (see Matt. 27:32-44). But the Resurrection shows that Jesus is who He claimed to be—the Son of God! Jesus did not *become* the Son of God by the Resurrection; He was *already* the Son. But the Resurrection made a statement about Jesus. It announced to the world that Jesus is the Son of God. The *"Spirit of holiness"* is the Holy Spirit.[13] The Holy Spirit empowered Jesus to rise from the dead. Jesus is the only leader of a religion who conquered death. This adds authority to His teachings. The Resurrection testifies that Jesus is who He claims to be—the Son of God.

Q 26 ⤳ *What did the Resurrection announce? Explain.*

C. The gospel invites people to obey God by faith (Rom. 1:5).

⁵Through him and for his name's sake, we received grace and apostleship to call people from among all the Gentiles to the obedience that comes from faith. ⁶And you also are among those who are called to belong to Jesus Christ (Rom. 1:5-6).

Q 27 ➤ *What is grace?*

Grace is God's favor, presence, power, and love—that come to us through Jesus, by the Holy Spirit. Grace brings us mercy and forgiveness. It gives us the desire and the power to do God's will (John 1:16-17; Rom. 5:21; 12:3-8; 1 Cor. 15:10; 1 Tim. 1:15-16).[14] Grace enabled Paul to be an apostle and preach the gospel (Rom. 1:5). Likewise, God's grace enables all believers to share the gospel.

The gospel invites people to obey. Through the gospel, God calls all people to repent and believe in Jesus.

³⁰In the past God overlooked such ignorance [worshiping idols]*, but now he commands all people everywhere to repent. ³¹For he has set a day when he will judge the world with justice by the man he has appointed* [Jesus]. *He has given proof of this to all men by raising him from the dead* (Acts 17:30-31).

The faith that saves is the faith that obeys. Repenting and believing in Christ are the first steps on the path of obedience. Faith enables us to obey God and receive Christ into our hearts. Acts records that a large number of priests became obedient to the faith (Acts 6:7). Obedience is faith in action.

Romans begins and ends with obedience (Rom. 1:5 with Rom. 16:26). By accepting Christ, some in Rome became believers. God called them, and they obeyed by believing. Jesus became their Savior and new Master to obey. When we accept Christ as Savior, we also accept Him as Lord to obey (Rom. 1:5-6).[16]

Some who knew William thought he was crazy. He was a shoemaker—average, far below the best. Every night after work this shoemaker went home to study the biblical languages of Hebrew, Greek, and other languages. Also, he studied books on travel. Some thought he should have worked more and studied less. But this shoemaker was a serious young man. His study was a passion, not a hobby. His heart became more and more concerned about the lost who never heard the gospel of Christ. William wanted to do something to help them. Finally, God called this shoemaker to be a missionary. So William Carey went to India and shared the gospel. Thousands accepted Christ. The passion of this shoemaker inspired many to go into missions work. *Application:* God called one poor shoemaker by the name of William Carey to be a preacher. No one but God would have chosen him. But Carey obeyed the call. And multitudes have believed in Christ because he obeyed and preached the gospel. Otherwise, they might have never known the name of Jesus.[15] Likewise, God can call you, dear reader, to share the gospel with others, so they can obey God.

D. There is only one gospel (Rom. 1:6-9)

⁶And you also are among those who are called to belong to Jesus Christ. ⁷To all in Rome who are loved by God and called to be saints: Grace and peace to you from God our Father and from the Lord Jesus Christ. ⁸First, I thank my God through Jesus Christ for all of you, because your faith is being reported all over the world. ⁹God, whom I serve with my whole heart in preaching the gospel of his Son, is my witness how constantly I remember you (Rom. 1:6-9).

We will come to Paul's greatest words about the gospel in Romans 1:16-17, in the next lesson. But before leaving this lesson, let us note a principle that Galatians presents about the gospel (Gal. 1:6-9).

⁶I am astonished that you are so quickly deserting the one who called you by the grace of Christ and are turning to a different gospel— ⁷which is really no gospel at all. Evidently some people are throwing you into confusion and are trying to pervert the gospel of Christ. ⁸But even if we or an angel from heaven should preach a gospel other than the one we preached to you, let him be eternally condemned! ⁹As we have already said, so now I say again: If anybody is preaching to you a gospel other than what you accepted, let him be eternally condemned! (Gal. 1:6-9).

Q 28 ✎ *Complete Figure 1.19 by answering the questions in it.*

Gal.	Question	Answer
1.6	What amazed Paul?	
1:7	How many true gospels are there?	
1:7	How were false teachers confusing the Galatians?	
1:8	What judgment did Paul pray to come on those who changed the gospel message?	
1:6-9	What verse in Galatians 1:6-9 is repeated?	
1:6-9	Do you think Paul was too harsh? Explain.	

Figure 1.19   There is only one true gospel (Gal. 1:6-9).

Lesson 4

Introduction to Romans—Part 2 (Rom. 1:8-17)

Goal A: *Explain how Paul's desire to visit Rome affected his prayers and plans.*
Goal B: *Identify some spiritual gifts that Paul might have wanted to share.*
Goal C: *Explain the sense in which all believers are debtors.*
Goal D: *Analyze 5 key words or phrases in Romans 1:16-17.*

Setting

For many years Paul wanted to visit the Romans (Figure 1.20).

Q 29 ✎ *Complete Figure 1.20 by summarizing the Scriptures.*

Romans	Your summary
1:10	
1:11-12	
1:13	
1:15	
15:20-22	
15:23-24	
15:25-29	
15:31-32	

Figure 1.20   Verses in Romans that tell of Paul's desire to visit Rome

From Romans 1:8-17, we may state principles related to Paul's desire to visit Rome.

- Prayer draws people together (Rom. 1:8-10).
- Prayer and action go together (Rom. 1:8-10).
- Spiritual gifts strengthen the faith of believers (Rom. 1:11-13).
- Believers have a debt to pay to all people (Rom. 1:14-15).
- The gospel is God's powerful message to save everyone who believes (Rom. 1:16-17).

These are some of the reasons why Paul longed to go to Rome. Let us look at each of these five principles

A. Prayer draws people together (Rom. 1:8-10).

⁸First, I thank my God through Jesus Christ for all of you, because your faith is being reported all over the world. ⁹God, whom I serve with my whole heart in preaching the gospel of his Son, is my witness how constantly I remember you ¹⁰in my prayers at all times; and I pray that now at last by God's will the way may be opened for me to come to you (Rom. 1:8-10).

Explanation: We should pray to God the Father in the name of Jesus (Rom. 1:8; John 14:13-14; 15:16; 16:23-24, 26). And as we pray, we should give thanks (Rom. 1:8-10; Phil 4:6). Paul thanked God for the Roman believers as he prayed. Giving thanks and praying for believers was Paul's custom (Rom. 1:8; see also 1 Cor. 1:4; Eph. 1:16; Phil. 1:3; Col. 1:3; 1 Thess. 1:2; 2 Thess. 1:3; 2 Tim. 1:3; Phil. 1:4, and others).

The faith of the Roman Christians was known. So Paul prayed for these Christians he had never met. He knew that the church in Rome was strategic. Believers in Rome could affect the government, and this could help the Church. Paul prayed often for the Romans.

Q 30 ✎ *Complete Figure 1.21 by listing some people you should pray for, with their needs.*

Name	Need
1.	
2.	
3.	
4.	
5.	

Figure 1.21   Personal prayer list

Prayer draws people together. Prayer causes the love of God to fill our hearts. If we pray for someone, we will love that person more and want to help him.

B. Prayer and action go together (Rom. 1:8-10).

Paul put legs on his prayers. He was like the farmer who prayed for a good garden, as he hoed. So as Paul prayed to go to Rome, he made plans to go! The apostle said that he had been hindered from visiting Rome (Rom. 1:13). But he trusted that the door would open soon. So Paul wrote to prepare the way (Rom. 15:28). Too often Christians pray and then sit back and expect God to do everything for them. Faith without works is dead (James 2:26). We express faith as we make plans and take steps toward the goals of our prayers. The steps we take in the direction of our prayers may be small, but they are important.

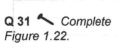

Q 31 ✎ *Complete Figure 1.22.*

- When you pray for rain, get your umbrella ready to use!
- Elijah built an altar *before* he prayed for God's fire to fall (1 Kings 18:30-38).
- As you pray for God to feed the hungry, take some food to a hungry person!

The goal you are praying to reach	The plan to reach the goal	The date to complete the goal
1. To read the whole Bible in a year	To read 3–5 chapters every day	December 31, _____
2.		
3.		

Figure 1.22   Spiritual goals for the next 12 months

Vern grew up in a rough neighborhood. His mother prayed often for him. Then God called him into the ministry. So he packed his things and went to Bible School. The only problem was that he had no money. But at the school, he received a scholarship that paid part of the costs. Also, Vern found a job that paid for some of his expenses. Prayer and action are a good combination!

C. *Spiritual gifts strengthen the faith of believers (Rom. 1:11-13).

[11]I long to see you so that I may impart to you some spiritual gift to make you strong— [12]that is, that you and I may be mutually encouraged by each other's faith. [13]I do not want you to be unaware, brothers, that I planned many times to come to you (but have been prevented from doing so until now) in order that I might have a harvest among you, just as I have had among the other Gentiles (Rom. 1:11-13).

Explanation: Paul states one of the reasons why he desires to visit the Romans: *"so that I may impart to you some spiritual gift to make you strong"* (Rom. 1:11). What kind of spiritual gift did Paul want to share with Roman believers? We do not know for sure. God gave the apostle Paul many gifts. And Paul himself was a gift to the Church. Consider some of the gifts that flowed through Paul:

- The gift of eternal life came to many through the preaching of Paul.
- The gift of being filled with the Spirit came to many, after they received Jesus as Savior, through Paul and other apostles (Acts 19:1-7; 8:14-17).
- Gifts of healing, miracles, deliverance, signs and wonders flowed through Paul (Acts 13:11-12; 14:3; 15:12; 16:16-18; 19:11-12; 20:7-12; 28:1-10; Rom. 15:19).
- The gifts of prophecy, serving, teaching, encouraging, giving, leading, and showing mercy were great blessings through Paul's ministry—in person and in his writings. Note that Paul mentions these seven gifts in Romans 12:6-8.
- Other gifts, such as the gift Timothy received, were *imparted as Paul and other elders laid on hands and prayed (2 Tim. 1:6).

Q 32 *Why did Paul want to visit the Romans?*

Q 33 *What are some spiritual gifts that flowed through Paul's ministry?*

Paul told the Corinthians that whenever they came together, they should seek to share spiritual gifts to edify, strengthen, and encourage others (1 Cor. 14:12). And we can be sure that Paul practiced what he preached. When Paul went to Rome, we can be sure that he was full of the Spirit and ready to share spiritual gifts with believers there. He wanted to plant some spiritual seeds in Roman believers so he could strengthen them and reap a harvest (Rom. 1:13).

Note: For a thorough study, please see "Spiritual Gifts for Believers" (1 Cor. 12) in the *Life in the Spirit Study Bible* or *The Full Life Study Bible*.

D. Believers owe a debt to all people (Rom. 1:14-15).

¹⁴*I am obligated both to Greeks and non-Greeks, both to the wise and the foolish.* ¹⁵*That is why I am so eager to preach the gospel also to you who are at Rome* (Rom. 1:14-15).

Explanation: Some translations use the word *debtor* instead of *obligated*. Paul saw himself in debt to Greeks, non-Greeks, the wise, and the foolish. He was in debt to everyone. Why? As a sinner, Paul deserved the wages of death (Rom. 3:23). Instead, God gave him the gift of eternal life, through Jesus Christ our Lord (Rom. 6:23). Then, God called Paul to share the gospel with others. So as Paul shared the gospel, he paid back a small part of the debt he owed to God. And as Paul preached to others, he fulfilled the debt of his calling.

Q 34 *Do you owe a debt to every sinner you meet? Explain.*

Application: Like Paul, we can never pay back to God all that we owe Him. We are like the servant who owed a king more than he could pay (Matt. 18:21-35). Still, as we pass on the love of God to others, we give some of what we can give! And we fulfill our responsibility of witnessing to others.

"Sir, I have come to pay you what I owe. As your debtor, it is time for me to pay. What I owe you is the message of God's love for us." These would be shocking words to use! So we do not often tell people that we are paying our debt to them. Still, we look for opportunities to show and tell the love of God to others. We owe it to them!

E. The gospel reveals that to be right with God, we must live by faith (Rom. 1:16-17).

Rom.	Topic	Words of Romans 1:16-17
1:16	The confidence in the gospel	*I am not ashamed of the gospel, because it is the power of God*
1:16	The purpose of the gospel	*for the salvation of everyone who believes:*
1:16	The sequence of the gospel	*first for the Jew, then for the Gentile.*

Continued on next page

Continued from previous page

1:17	The revelation of the gospel	*For in the gospel a righteousness from God is revealed,*
1:17	The essence of the gospel	*a righteousness that is by faith from first to last,*
1:17	The practice of the gospel	*just as it is written: "The righteous will live by faith."*

Figure 1.23   Expository chart on Romans 1:16-17, the key verses of Romans

[16]I am not ashamed of the gospel, because it is the power of God for the salvation of everyone who believes: first for the Jew, then for the Gentile. [17]For in the gospel a righteousness from God is revealed, a righteousness that is by faith from first to last, just as it is written: "The righteous will live by faith" (Rom. 1:16-17).

The two verses of Romans 1:16-17 are packed with meaning (see Figure 1.23). They summarize what Paul explains in Romans. To understand Romans 1:16-17 well, we must study the complete letter to the Romans! We will do this. Afterward, you will return to read Romans 1:16-17. Then, you will appreciate these verses more. For now, let us examine a few of the key words and phrases in these key verses.

- The word **gospel** means "good news." Some today limit the *gospel* to the justification God provides through faith in the life, death, resurrection, and ascension of Jesus. But the good news (Greek: *euangellion*) does not end with justification. For sure, the gospel centers on the person and ministry of Jesus Christ. But the good news about the salvation Jesus provides includes the past, present, and future.[17] In the past, Jesus lived on earth, died on the cross, rose from the dead, and ascended to the Father to deliver us from the penalty and power of sin, and to restore us to a right relationship with God. In the present, Jesus ministers today through the Holy Spirit, convicting of sin, imparting new life, filling believers with God's presence, and empowering us for victorious living and service. In the future, Jesus will come again to judge sinners, and to rapture those of us who trust, love, and obey Him so we may live together with God forever. The full gospel proclaims the past, present, and future ministry of Jesus.

- Rome was a powerful city. Roman Emperors had the power of death—the power to kill. Roman armies conquered the world. But Paul had the **power** of the gospel message of salvation—past, present, and future. Paul was not ashamed to preach the gospel in Rome or any other city.

- **Salvation** includes deliverance from the penalty *and* power of sin, and being restored to a right relationship with God. In Romans 1–8, Paul will explain aspects of salvation for Jews and Gentiles. These aspects of salvation span from adoption to glorification. In Romans 9–11, Paul will clarify how the Jews relate to God's plan of salvation. In Romans 12–15, he will emphasize practical principles of salvation for all believers.

- The gospel only helps those who **believe** it! The good news went first to the Jews. Some of them believed the message and became followers of Jesus. Next, the gospel went to the Gentiles—all who are not Jews. *"Anyone who trusts in him will never be put to shame"* (Rom. 10:11). Anyone!

- The gospel is about **righteousness**—being in a right relationship with God. Romans 1–3 teaches that we have all sinned. Sin separates people from God, and prevents them from having a right relationship with Him. Romans 4–5 emphasizes that Jesus died to pay the penalty for our sins. As we accept Jesus as God's sacrifice for sin, God justifies us—counts us righteous.

- To be right with God, we must **live by faith**—from first to last. That is, we begin to be righteous by faith as we accept Jesus and surrender our lives to Him as Savior and Lord. We continue to be righteous by faith as we follow Jesus, obey Him, and allow His Spirit to lead us. In Romans 6–8, Paul explains that living by faith means being led by the Spirit of Christ who lives in us. And in Romans 12–15, he emphasizes that living by faith causes us to relate rightly to believers and unbelievers.

Q 35   *Complete Figure 1.24.*

Word or Phrase	Your explanation of words in Romans 1:16-17
Gospel	
Salvation	
Believe	
Righteous	
Live by faith	

Figure 1.24   **There are at least five key words or phrases in Romans 1:16-17.**

Curt and Jeff stopped at a gas station. Curt noticed that the clerk inside had been crying. He soon learned that her name was Alma, and he asked her, "Has anyone told you today that Jesus loves you?" Jeff became embarrassed and walked away. Since no one else was inside, Curt took time to talk with Alma. She told about the hard time she was going through. After a few minutes, Curt shared the good news about Jesus with her. When they prayed together, Alma opened her heart and received Jesus as Savior and Lord. Her face was full of joy, instead of sorrow.

When Curt returned to the car, Jeff said, "Never do that again." "Do what?" Curt asked. Jeff answered, "You embarrassed that woman by witnessing to her in public. Did you see how upset she became?" Curt explained that it was only Jeff who was embarrassed. Alma was not embarrassed, but ready to accept Christ as her Savior. Then Curt took Jeff back inside to talk with Alma. Jeff was amazed to discover that Alma was completely changed.[18]

Application: Too often Christians are timid about sharing the gospel with strangers. We are too concerned about upsetting someone. We believers have what the world needs. So let us be bold to share our faith! We should not be ashamed of the gospel. It is God's powerful message to save people from sin, and become right with God! The Holy Spirit can give us boldness to share this powerful message. Many believers have learned to share the gospel at school, at work, and in other public places. They testify about Jesus when they ride buses, trains, and airplanes! There is so much bad news that many are ready to hear the good news!

Test Yourself: Circle the letter by the ***best*** completion to each question or statement.

1. Which was a built in Rome?
   a) The Parthenon
   b) The Temple of Diana
   c) The Acropolis
   d) The Colosseum

2. When did Paul write Romans?
   a) About 57 A.D.
   b) About 67 A.D.
   c) About 77 A.D.
   d) About 87 A.D.

3. Romans has 5 parts on the theme of
   a) holiness.
   b) election.
   c) righteousness.
   d) eschatology.

4. What was the main purpose of Galatians?
   a) To encourage those who were suffering
   b) To establish guidelines for deacons
   c) To restore peace among fighting members
   d) To correct errors caused by Judaizers

5. Parallel chapters to Romans 6–8 are
   a) Galatians 1–2
   b) Galatians 3–4
   c) Galatians 5–6
   d) Galatians 3–6

6. Which event declared that Jesus was the Son of God?
   a) The Incarnation
   b) The Temptation
   c) The Crucifixion
   d) The Resurrection

7. Romans 1 refers to Paul as
   a) an apostle and a prophet.
   b) a servant and a prisoner.
   c) a prisoner and an apostle.
   d) a servant and a debtor.

8. Which is a major reason why Paul wrote Romans?
   a) Future ministry
   b) Past conflicts
   c) Political concerns
   d) End-time doctrines

9. Which emphasizes a relationship?
   a) Born again
   b) Righteousness
   c) Grace
   d) Forgiveness

10. Romans 1 and 16 emphasize that faith brings
    a) repentance.
    b) salvation.
    c) obedience.
    d) grace.

Essay Test Topics: Write 50-100 words on each of these goals that you studied in this chapter.

- Analyze Romans: its city, author, date, readers, purpose, special features, and outline.
- Analyze the background of Galatians and its relation to Romans.
- Explain the greater and lesser purposes of Galatians.
- State a principle about the gospel, in relation to each of these: the Old Testament, the Resurrection, obedience, and Galatians 1:6-9.
- Explain how Paul's desire to visit Rome affected his prayers and plans.
- Identify some spiritual gifts that Paul might have wanted to share.
- Explain the sense in which all believers are debtors.
- Analyze 5 key words or phrases in Romans 1:16-17.

Chapter 2:
All Have a Great Need for Righteousness
(Romans 1:18–3:20)

Introduction

Figure 2.1
People may be infected, though symptoms are hidden.

María enrolled in her first year of college not knowing that she had a contagious disease. Her symptoms were like a common cold, so she did not go to a doctor.

During the first few months of classes no one was surprised that many students had colds in the classroom. But Estela, one of María's classmates, was put in the hospital because her cold was severe. After the doctor's tests, they identified the germs that caused the disease. Without treatment, this disease would lead to death. A few weeks later, Noemí, another classmate, was near death from the same germ, so she went to the hospital.

Finally, the college leaders decided to test all the students in the class. Among them was Daniel, who appeared to be in good health. When they told him the date for his test, Daniel asked himself: "Why should I be tested if I feel fine? My family is healthy, I eat and rest well. I even have all my shots to prevent diseases!"

The doctor explained to Daniel that some people carry a disease, but show no symptoms. Others feel only a little discomfort. But in other cases the signs of infection are clear. In other words, you cannot always measure a disease by its symptoms, or by how a person feels. Daniel agreed. And the tests revealed that the disease was hiding within him. So he received the same treatment as Estela and Noemí because he was infected.

Likewise, sin may be present, even when the symptoms are hidden. One does not need to appear as a murderer to need God's salvation. All are infected by sin, and need the cure God offers.

Lessons:

Gentiles Need the Righteousness God Offers in Christ (Rom. 1:18-32)
Goal A: *Explain 3 reasons why Gentiles need the righteousness that God provides (Rom. 1:18-32).*
Goal B: *Identify the problem and 3 levels of sin in Romans 1:21-32.*

Jews Need the Righteousness God Offers in Christ—Part 1 (Rom. 2:1-4)
Goal A: *Contrast Paul's use of personal pronouns in Romans 1 and 2.*
Goal B: *Answer the questions that Paul asks in Romans 2:3-4 and 2:17-23.*
Goal C: *Give 3 examples how God will judge Jews the same as Gentiles.*

Jews Need the Righteousness God Offers in Christ—Part 2 (Rom. 2:5-29)
Goal: *Relate the theme "God does not show favoritism" to each of these: Jews first, knowing versus doing, breaking the Law, trusting in symbols.*

Everyone Needs the Righteousness God Offers in Christ (Rom. 3:1-20)
Goal: *Identify and answer the 5 key questions in Romans 3.*

 Key Words

righteousness—a right relationship with God

Gentiles—ethnic groups or nations that are all non-Jews

wrath—vengeance, punishment, judgment for sin

favoritism—partiality; preference; showing favor to one over another

Lesson 5 — Gentiles Need the Righteousness God Offers in Christ (Rom. 1:18-32)

Goal A: *Explain 3 reasons why Gentiles need the righteousness that God provides (Rom. 1:18-32).*

Goal B: *Identify the problem and 3 levels of sin in Romans 1:21-32.*

Setting

In Romans 1:16-17 Paul introduced the gospel of salvation—how to be in a right relationship with God. He divides all people into two groups: *Jews (descendants of Abraham), and *Gentiles (all who are not Jews). In Romans 1:18–3:20, Paul explains why both Gentiles and Jews need the salvation that God provides. Let us examine three reasons why Gentiles need salvation.

Q 1 *Into which 2 groups does Paul divide all people (Rom. 1–3)?*

A. The *wrath of God is on all who practice sin (Rom. 1:18-20).

[18]*The wrath of God is being revealed from heaven against all the godlessness and wickedness of men who suppress the truth by their wickedness,* [19]*since what may be known about God is plain to them, because God has made it plain to them.* [20]*For since the creation of the world God's invisible qualities—his eternal power and divine nature—have been clearly seen, being understood from what has been made, so that men are without excuse* (Rom. 1:18-20).

Q 2 *Why is the gospel necessary (Rom. 1:18)?*

Speaker	Statement/Question	Romans
Paul	*I am not ashamed of the gospel,*	1:16
Student	Why not?	
Paul	*because it is the power of God for the salvation of everyone who believes:*	1:16
Student	How?	
Paul	*in the gospel a righteousness from God is revealed, a righteousness that is by faith...*	1:17
Student	Why is the gospel necessary?	
Paul	*the wrath of God is being revealed from heaven against all the godlessness and wickedness of men who suppress the truth by their wickedness,*	1:18

Figure 2.2   Chart on the discussion of Romans 1:16-18[1]

The Bible says that God is revealing His wrath now (Rom. 1:18). God's wrath means His anger against sin. God is the same yesterday, today, and forever. He always becomes angry when people sin, because He is righteous and holy. People get mad for various reasons. God becomes angry when people sin.

Q 3 *What makes God angry?*

- *In the past* God revealed His anger toward sin through the flood (Gen. 6–8). Likewise, He showed his anger toward sin: *when* He destroyed Sodom and Gomorrah with fire and brimstone (Gen. 18–19); *when* He sent ten plagues on Egypt (Exod. 7–12); *when* He punished the Israelites with deadly snakes (Num. 21:4-9); *when* He caused a generation to die in the wilderness (Num. 14:23; Ps. 95:10-11; Heb. 3:10-11); *when* He enabled Israel to conquer various nations (Joshua); *when* He sent nations to conquer Israel (Judges); *when* He sent Assyria to conquer the ten northern tribes of Israel (2 Kings 17); *when* He scattered Judah in Babylon (Lam. 4:16); *when* He allowed the Romans to wage war against, conquer, and rule Israel (Matt. 2); *when* He allowed the Romans to conquer and burn Jerusalem in A.D. 70. These are just a few examples from the past. They illustrate the principle that God shows His wrath against those who sin.[2]

Q 4 *In the past, what are some ways that God showed His anger?*

- *In the present* we see God's anger when He allows sinful people to become more sinful. His present wrath brings spiritual death to all who disobey Him (Rom. 6:23; Eph. 2:3). And at times He brings physical death, diseases, and destruction to those

Q 5 *Today, what are some ways that God shows His anger?*

who disobey Him. Not all problems on earth are signs of God's wrath. But many problems we have are a form of God's judgment.

Q 6 ↗ *In the future, how will God reveal His wrath?*

- ***In the future*** God will reveal His wrath: in the Great Tribulation (Rev. 6–19); on the day of judgment (Matt. 24:21; 2 Thess. 1:5-10); and by eternal punishment (Matt. 10:28; Rev. 14:11). God rejoices when people do what is right. But He gets upset when people choose evil.

God's wrath is slow but sure. He is never in a hurry to judge (see 2 Pet. 3:9). He is slow to anger and full of mercy (Neh. 9:17; Ps. 103:8; 145:8). God is patient, because He does not want any to perish, but all to repent (2 Pet. 3:9). But as a holy God, He must judge evil sooner or later.[3]

Q 7 ↖ *What is the difference between godlessness and wickedness?*

Romans 1:18 states that the Lord unveils His wrath against *godlessness* and *wickedness*. Little difference exists between these two words. *Godlessness* means "living like there is no God." *Wickedness* refers to evil deeds, such as *immorality.[4] God pours out His anger on both ungodliness and wickedness.

Q 8 ↗ *Why is everyone guilty, with no excuse for sinning against God?*

God's wrath is just (Rom. 1:19-20). Sinners are guilty and without an excuse that God will accept.

[19]*since what may be known about God is plain to them, because God has made it plain to them.* [20]*For since the creation of the world God's invisible qualities—his eternal power and divine nature—have been clearly seen, being understood from what has been made, so that men are without excuse* (Rom. 1:19-20).

People in every generation have some truth about God. Creation testifies that God exists. As artists reveal themselves in their art, God reveals Himself through His creation.

[1]*The heavens declare the glory of God; the skies proclaim the work of his hands.* [2]*Day after day they pour forth speech; night after night they display knowledge.* [3]*There is no speech or language where their voice is not heard.* [4]*Their voice goes out into all the earth, their words to the ends of the world* (Ps. 19:1-4).

People without the gospel have what theologians call *natural revelation*—the revelation of God in the physical world.[5] People who see God revealed in nature do not know enough to be saved. They cannot look at a tree, a cloud, or a rainbow and know how to be saved. But creation reveals that a Creator exists above all. Since creation testifies that God exists, humans have the responsibility of responding to Him. And all who rebel against the Creator are guilty—*"without excuse"* (Rom. 1:20).

All people have some sense of right and wrong. Yet people never live up to the truth they have. So their punishment is just. On the day of judgment, sinners will have no defense.[6]

The person who sins is like the man who jumped out of a window at the top of a tall building. He was 10 stories above the ground. When he dropped by the fifth floor, someone yelled out the window. "How are you doing?" He replied, "So far everything is going fine!" For a while, people living in sin may think they are doing fine. But life will end. Sudden judgment is ahead. Sooner or later, the wrath of God will condemn everyone who *falls* into sin.

Q 9 ↗ *When people reject the Creator, what do they worship?*

B. Those who reject the Creator become foolish enough to worship the creation (Rom. 1:21-23, 25).

Paul now summarizes the sinfulness of mankind. In the beginning, mankind knew God. As early as Eden, Adam and Eve knew God, but chose not to glorify and obey Him. They passed on the knowledge of God to Cain, Abel, and their other children. But humans continued to rebel against God. As one writer said, rebellion is the signature of humans apart from Christ.[7]

²¹*For although they knew God, they neither glorified him as God nor gave thanks to him, but their thinking became futile and their foolish hearts were darkened.* ²²*Although they claimed to be wise, they became fools* ²³*and exchanged the glory of the immortal God for images made to look like mortal man and birds and animals and reptiles* (Rom. 1:21-23).

²⁵*They exchanged the truth of* [about] *God for a lie, and worshiped and served created things rather than the Creator—who is forever praised. Amen* (Rom. 1:25).

Recall that Paul is explaining why Gentiles need *righteousness—the right relationship with God. His *first* reason was that God's wrath is on Gentiles because they are sinners. His *second* reason is about worship.

We are born with a need to worship. And creation guides us to worship the Creator. But if we turn away from God, the only direction we can go is down. So the slide down into sin goes like this:

- People know God exists because creation points toward a Creator;
- People reject God and are ungrateful for His gifts;
- People worship something in place of God.

Figure 2.3   Greek idols of Artemis and Hermes

In Paul's day, it was common for Gentiles to worship idols. Gentiles in Lystra worshiped idols of the Greek gods, such as Zeus and Hermes (Acts 14:11-13). The Gentiles at Athens had high education but worshiped many gods. The city was *"full of idols"* (Acts 17:16). Gentiles in Ephesus rioted when Paul told them that man-made gods are no gods at all. The whole city worshiped silver idols of the goddess Artemis or Diana (Acts 19:23-41). These Gentiles at Ephesus believed it was a fact that the image or idol of Artemis fell from heaven (Acts 19:35-36). Idolatry was common among Gentiles, whether they were uneducated or highly educated, poor or rich, young or old.

Romans teaches that those who reject God worship idols. To *worship* means to "praise, adore, honor, and lift up"—using actions, words, time, and wealth.

Some worship *dead* idols of gold, silver, stone, or wood. Idolatry is common in false religions. Hindus worship over 3 million gods, and Buddhists bow down to an idol of Siddhartha Gautama, whom they call the *Buddha, or *enlightened one*.

Others worship *living*, human idols, such as heroes, athletes, actors, leaders, the rich, or the beautiful.

Still others worship idols that are not physical, such as education, work, power, position, honor, pleasure, or self. Any form of greed—desiring something in the way that we should desire God—is idolatry (Col. 3:5).

Romans 1:25 contains a terrible warning. If we turn away from the truth, we will believe a lie. If we turn away from the light, we will walk in the darkness. Many people in cults and false religions once believed the truth. But when they rejected it, God allowed them to believe a lie. A stern principle says: Use it or lose it. But Romans 1:25 contains a sterner principle: If you refuse the truth, you will lose it and believe a lie. In Romans 1:21-25, Paul emphasizes that the Gentiles—the nations of the world—have lost the truth. They have rejected the truth about God, and now they believe lies. This is why there are so many false religions and cults in the world today.

Q 10 *What does Paul mean by righteousness?*

Q 11 *What are 2 reasons why Gentiles need the righteousness that God provides?*

Q 12 *What are some idols that people in your society worship?*

Q 13 *What is greed? Why are all forms of greed idolatry?*

Q 14 *What is worse than losing the truth?*

Q 15 ↖ *What is the third reason why Gentiles need righteousness?*

C. Those who reject the right relationship with God pervert other relationships (Rom. 1:24-32).

The Problem:

> [21]*For although they knew God, they neither glorified him as God nor gave thanks to him, but their thinking became futile and their foolish hearts were darkened.* [22]*Although they claimed to be wise, they became fools* [23]*and exchanged the glory of the immortal God for images made to look like mortal man and birds and animals and reptiles* (Rom. 1:21-23).

Q 16 ↗ *What problem does Paul summarize in Romans 1:21-32?*

In Romans 1:21-32, Paul summarizes the problem. When people turn away from God, He allows them to travel down the path they choose. This terrible path of rebellion goes from bad to worse, like steps going down (2 Tim. 3:13). Paul writes three descriptions of those who reject God. Each description begins with the words *"God gave them over,"* or *"he gave them over"* (Rom. 1:24, 26, 28). The three descriptions are like steps down into sin. Each description is worse than the one before it (Figure 2.4).

Q 17 ↖ *What are the 3 steps down into sin (Rom. 1:24-32)? Illustrate each.*

| **Level 1:** Sexual impurity, belief of lies, idolatry (Rom. 1:24-25) |
| **Level 2:** Homosexuality (Rom. 1:26-27) |
| **Level 3:** A depraved mind—with every kind of evil (Rom. 1:28-32) |

Figure 2.4   In Romans 1 Paul describes three levels going down into sin.

Description of Level 1 (48 words):   [24]*Therefore* <u>*God gave them over*</u> *in the sinful desires of their hearts to sexual impurity for the degrading of their bodies with one another.* [25]*They exchanged the truth of God for a lie, and worshiped and served created things rather than the Creator—who is forever praised. Amen* (Rom. 1:24-25).

Explanation: *"God gave them over"* to sinful desires of sexual impurity, to *degrade* their bodies (Rom. 1:24). God gives each person a body to use in a righteous and holy way. Those who reject God *degrade* their bodies—using them in unholy ways *beneath* God's plan. In this first picture, Paul mentions sexual sins, which may include fornication, adultery, prostitution, sexual abuse, and pornography.

Description of Level 2 (56 words):   [26]*Because of this,* <u>*God gave them over*</u> *to shameful lusts. Even their women exchanged natural relations for unnatural ones.* [27]*In the same way the men also abandoned natural relations with women and were inflamed with lust for one another. Men committed indecent acts with other men, and received in themselves the due penalty for their perversion* (Rom. 1:26-27).

Explanation: *"God gave them over"* to shameful lusts. This description focuses on homosexual sins, as in Sodom and Gomorrah (Gen. 19). When people reject their natural relationship with God, He allows them to reject their natural relationships of marriage. To many Jews, nothing was more repulsive, disgusting, or vile than homosexual relations.[8] To Paul, homosexual relations are a result of rejecting God and rejecting the relationships the Creator planned for creation (Lev. 18:22; 1 Cor. 6:9-10).[9]

Description of Level 3 (109 words):   [28]*Furthermore, since they did not think it worthwhile to retain the knowledge of God,* <u>*he gave them over*</u> *to a depraved mind, to do what ought not to be done.* [29]*They have become filled with every kind of wickedness, evil, greed and depravity. They are full of envy, murder, strife, deceit and malice. They are gossips,* [30]*slanderers, God-haters, insolent, arrogant and boastful; they invent ways of doing evil; they disobey their parents;* [31]*they are senseless, faithless, heartless, ruthless.* [32]*Although they know God's righteous decree that those who do such things deserve death, they not only continue to do these very things but also approve of those who practice them* (Rom. 1:28-32).

Explanation: God *"gave them over"* to a depraved mind. A depraved mind is twisted and perverted. It calls evil good. This darkest description includes 23 types of sin that occur as people push God out of their thoughts. Sin breeds sin and multiplies. These verses describe slaves who are *filled full* of sin.[10] In the first step of rebellion, people reject God and choose one evil thought. At the bottom of the stairs, their minds always think evil. Paul lists more than 20 sins that characterize those who persist in rejecting God. (For other lists of sins see Rom. 13:13; 1 Cor. 5:10-11; 6:9-10; 2 Cor. 12:20-21; Gal. 5:19-21; Col. 3:5-8; and Rev. 21:8.)

Conclusion: We may view Romans 1:21-32 as a problem followed by three levels of judgment.[11] One step in sin leads down to another. For emphasis, each description is darker, and uses more words, than the description before it. Each description begins with: *"God gave them over."* God judges rebels by permitting them to go all the way down to the place that the path of sin leads.

Q 18 *How do the 3 steps down into sin compare to each other?*

The journey away from God goes from bad to worst. Rebels choose the first step down toward hell. Most people do not intend to go farther and farther into sin. But one step down leads to another, and people become slaves of sin. As Sabio said,

> "SIN WILL TAKE YOU FARTHER THAN YOU WANT TO GO.
> SIN WILL KEEP YOU LONGER THAN YOU WANT TO STAY.
> SIN WILL COST YOU MORE THAN YOU WANT TO PAY."

When people do not give God His glory, He does not give them theirs.[12] Rebellion leads to ruin.

While Nero was emperor of Rome, he was known for his godlessness. He had an affair with a woman named Poppaea Sabina. She asked Nero to divorce his wife so he could marry her. But Nero's mother, Agrippina, opposed Poppaea's plans. So Poppaea nagged Nero to kill his mother. He tried to have his mother drowned at sea. When she survived, he had four of his men beat her to death.[13] Once people begin to sin, who knows what they will do? At one time Nero would have never thought of killing his mother. But even family members are not safe when sin rules its slaves (Mark 13:12).

Q 19 *Give an example of someone whose sins got worse and worse.*

Paul has stated three reasons why Gentiles need to be in a right relationship with God.

- God's wrath is on them because they have rejected Him.
- Those not wise enough to worship the Creator become foolish enough to worship the creation.
- Those who reject the right relationship with God pervert other relationships.

Q 20 *What are the 3 reasons why Gentiles need the righteousness that God provides?*

The Jews agreed with what Paul said about Gentiles. But next, Paul will explain that the Jews need salvation as much as the Gentiles need it.

 Lesson **Jews Need the Righteousness God Offers in Christ—Part 1 (Rom. 2:1-4)**

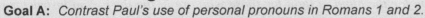
⟨6⟩ **Goal A:** *Contrast Paul's use of personal pronouns in Romans 1 and 2.*
Goal B: *Answer the questions that Paul asks in Romans 2:3-4 and 2:17-23.*
Goal C: *Give 3 examples how God will judge Jews the same as Gentiles.*

Setting

In Romans 1:18-32, Paul wrote as a Jew about Gentiles. So his style was in the *third* person, using the pronouns: they, them, themselves, and their. (See question 23.)

Q 21 *In Romans 1:18-32, why does Paul use pronouns like "they" instead of "we"?*

Q 22 ⬉ *Read Romans 1:19-32, and underline pronouns in the third person (they, them, their, themselves).*

[19]*since what may be known about God is plain to them, because God has made it plain to them* (Rom. 1:19).

[21]*For although they knew God, they neither glorified him as God nor gave thanks to him, but their thinking became futile and their foolish hearts were darkened.* [22]*Although they claimed to be wise, they became fools* (Rom. 1:21-22).

[24]*Therefore God gave them over in the sinful desires of their hearts to sexual impurity for the degrading of their bodies with one another.* [25]*They exchanged the truth of God for a lie...* (Rom. 1:24-25).

[26]*Because of this, God gave them over to shameful lusts. Even their women exchanged natural relations for unnatural ones.* [27]*In the same way the men also abandoned natural relations with women and were inflamed with lust for one another. Men committed indecent acts with other men, and received in themselves the due penalty for their perversion* (Rom. 1:26-27).

Q 23 ⬈ *How many pronouns in the third person are there in Romans 1:19-32?*

[28]*Furthermore, since they did not think it worthwhile to retain the knowledge of God, he gave them over to a depraved mind, to do what ought not to be done.* [29]*They have become filled with every kind of wickedness, evil, greed and depravity. They are full of envy, murder, strife, deceit and malice. They are gossips,* [30]*slanderers, God-haters, insolent, arrogant and boastful; they invent ways of doing evil; they disobey their parents;* [31]*they are senseless, faithless, heartless, ruthless.* [32]*Although they know God's righteous decree that those who do such things deserve death, they not only continue to do these very things but also approve of those who practice them* (Rom. 1:28-32).

Q 24 ⬈ *In Romans 2, why do Paul's pronouns shift from "they" to "you"?*

In Romans 2 Paul turns from the Gentiles to his fellow Jews. His writing style shifts from the third person (they) to the second person (you). Writing directly to a Jew, Paul used the pronouns: you, your, and yourself. (See question 26.)

Q 25 ⬉ *Read Romans 2:1-5 and 2:17-24, and underline pronouns in the second person (you, your, yourself).*

[1]*You, therefore, have no excuse, you who pass judgment on someone else, for at whatever point you judge the other, you are condemning yourself, because you who pass judgment do the same things.* [2]*Now we know that God's judgment against those who do such things is based on truth.* [3]*So when you, a mere man, pass judgment on them and yet do the same things, do you think you will escape God's judgment?* [4]*Or do you show contempt for the riches of his kindness, tolerance and patience, not realizing that God's kindness leads you toward repentance?* [5]*But because of your stubbornness and your unrepentant heart, you are storing up wrath against yourself for the day of God's wrath, when his righteous judgment will be revealed* (Rom. 2:1-5).

[17]*Now you, if you call yourself a Jew; if you rely on the law and brag about your relationship to God;* [18]*if you know his will and approve of what is superior because you are instructed by the law;* [19]*if you are convinced that you are a guide for the blind, a light for those who are in the dark,* [20]*an instructor of the foolish, a teacher of infants, because you have in the law the embodiment of knowledge and truth—* [21]*you, then, who teach others, do you not teach yourself? You who preach against stealing, do you steal?* [22]*You who say that people should not commit adultery, do you commit adultery? You who abhor idols, do you rob temples?* [23]*You who brag about the law, do you dishonor God by breaking the law?* [24]*As it is written: "God's name is blasphemed among the Gentiles because of you"* (Rom. 2:17-24).

Q 26 ⬈ *How many pronouns in the second person are there in Romans 2:1-5 and 2:17-24?*

Now you are aware of the contrast between Romans 1:18-32 and Romans 2. In Romans 1, Paul wrote to show that Gentiles are sinners who need the righteousness that God provides in Christ. In Romans 2, he writes to convince the Jews that, like the Gentiles, they are sinners who need the righteousness that Jesus provides.

Style of Questions and Answers (Rom. 2–11). Throughout the rest of Romans, Paul uses questions and answers. Paul's questions help readers focus on key topics. We want to guide you to notice Paul's questions, meditate on them, and be able to answer them. In fact, a good test for Romans would be to see if students can answer the questions that Paul asks. For if you can answer Paul's questions in Romans, you deserve an A for this course. So we will identify Paul's questions and guide you to learn the answers he gives.

Q 27 ⟋ *What grade does a student deserve who can answer Paul's questions in Romans?*

Q 28 ⟍ *Write the answers—in your own words—to Paul's questions in Romans 2–3 (Figure 2.5).*

Rom.	Questions From a Jewish View	Answers/Responses	Rom.
2:3-4	When you judge others, *and yet do the same things, do you think you will escape God's judgment?* ⁴*Do you show contempt for God's kindness, tolerance, and patience, not realizing that God's kindness leads you toward repentance?*		2:1-2, 5-16
2:17-23	You who call yourself a Jew—who teach spiritual babies, ...²¹do you not teach yourself? ²¹*You who preach against stealing, do you steal?* ²²*You who say that people should not commit adultery, do you commit adultery?* *You who abhor idols, do you rob temples?* ²³*You who brag about the law, do you dishonor God by breaking the law?*		2:24-29

Figure 2.5   Questions and answers in Romans 2

A. God does not show *favoritism—He judges all who break His laws (Rom. 2:1-4).

We can study all of Romans 2 looking at the theme: God does not show favoritism. He judges all, both Gentiles and Jews, by His laws about right and wrong. Sometimes a writer puts his main point first and *then* explains or illustrates it. But in these verses, Paul's main point is last, in Romans 2:11—*"God does not show favoritism"*—and he puts his illustrations first. Let us examine the paragraphs in Romans 2 and see the one big theme that Paul emphasizes.

Romans 2:1-4. ¹*You, therefore, have no excuse, you who pass judgment on someone else, for at whatever point you judge the other, you are condemning yourself, because you who pass judgment <u>do the same things</u>. ²Now we know that God's judgment against those who do such things is based on truth. ³So when you, a mere man, pass judgment on them and yet <u>do the same things</u>, do you think you will escape God's judgment? ⁴Or do you show contempt for the riches of his kindness, tolerance and patience, not realizing that God's kindness leads you toward repentance?* (Rom. 2:1-4).

Q 29 ⟋ *What is the main theme of Romans 2:1-4?*

If you are not careful, you might think the theme of Romans 2:1-5 is judging others. In other verses, such as Matthew 7:1-5, the Bible warns against criticizing and judging others. But in Romans 2:1-5, Paul is not warning the Jews against judging. Rather, he is saying they are guilty *because* they *"do the same things"* that they condemn in others (Rom. 1:2). It was right for the Jews to condemn the sins of the Gentiles. But it was wrong for the Jews to commit the same sins that they condemned!

The words *"do the same things"* in Romans 2:1 and 2:3 are important. Recall that after idolatry (Rom. 1:23), Paul gave three descriptions of the sins of the Gentiles—three levels of sin (Rom. 1:24-28). Gentile sins included *first*: sexual sins between men and women; *second,* homosexual sins; *third,* a depraved mind that resulted in all kinds of sins.

Paul accuses the Jews of committing <u>these same sins</u>. Let us examine some sins of the Jews.

1. Idolatry: Few Jews worshiped idols of metal, wood, or stone. The fiery trial of 70 years as captives in Babylon purified them from bowing to idols made by human hands. But some, like Zacchaeus and Matthew (tax collectors), *worshiped* the idol of wealth. And some, like the Pharisees, *worshiped* the idols of position and honor. Still others, to advance or be accepted in society, worshiped idols in the Roman cults.

Recall the meaning of *worship.* We worship what we value most. We worship what means the most to us. What did the Pharisees worship or value most? They worshiped the honor and praise that came from other humans. This human attention meant more to them than God's favor! They did not pray, fast, or give to worship God. Rather, they did religious acts so men would praise them (Matt. 6:5).

Jesus said this about the Pharisees:

⁵*"Everything they do is done for men to see: They make their *phylacteries wide and the tassels on their garments long;* ⁶*they love the place of honor at banquets and the most important seats in the synagogues;* ⁷*they love to be greeted in the marketplaces and to have men call them 'Rabbi'"* (Matt. 23:5-7).

"How can you believe if you accept praise from one another, yet make no effort to obtain the praise that comes from the only God?" (John 5:44).

Gentiles worshiped idols made by human hands. But some Jews worshiped idols of position and honor.

2. Sexual sins: We are examining the words *"do the same things"* (Rom. 2:1, 3). Gentiles were known for sexual sins, such as adultery, fornication, homosexual sins, and prostitutes in temple worship (1 Cor. 6:15-20). In contrast, Jews had a better reputation for avoiding sexual sins. Still, some Jews committed sexual sins. Jesus reminded them that God looks at the heart. It is likely that many Jews committed sexual sins through the lust of their thoughts (Matt. 5:27-30).

3. Sins of a depraved mind: Recall that Paul listed over 20 sins in Romans 1:28-32. This was his third description of Gentile sins. All of these sins came as the result of a depraved, darkened mind. Gentiles turned away from God, from light to darkness. Paul wrote to Jews, *"you ... do the same things"* (Rom. 2:1, 3). From Paul's long list of sins, some of the most common sins among the Jews were:

- **Greed**—because of greed, Jews cheated Jews at the temple when changing money (Matt. 21:12-13).
- **Envy**—Pilate knew that the Jewish leaders hated Jesus because they envied Him (Matt. 27:18).
- **Murder**—Jews stoned the prophets and crucified the Messiah (Matt. 23:37).
- **Strife**—there was great division between the Pharisees and the Sadducees (Acts 23:6-10).
- **Arrogance, pride, and boasting**—Paul exposes these sins in Romans 2:19-20).
- **Unbelief**—one of the greatest sins of the Jews was their unbelief in Jesus (John 6:36; 12:37-38; Rom. 11:20, 30-32; Heb. 3:18-19).
- **Unkindness**—Jesus often accused the Jewish leaders of lacking mercy (Matt. 12:7; 23:23).

The Jews sinned by doing *"the same things"* as the Gentiles. And God does not show favoritism. He judges whomever sins—Gentiles or Jews. As Romans 2:2 says, *"God's*

Q 30 ⬿ *Did Jews commit the same sins as Gentiles? Give 3 examples.*

Q 31 ⬿ *Why did Paul say that God would judge the Jews?*

judgment against those who do such things is based on truth." God's judgment is based on truth, not race!

Lesson 7 — Jews Need the Righteousness God Offers in Christ—Part 2 (Rom. 2:5-29)

Goal: *Relate the theme "God does not show favoritism" to each of these: Jews first, knowing versus doing, breaking the Law, trusting in symbols.*

A. <u>God does not show favoritism</u> toward those who call themselves Jews (Rom. 2:5-11).

Like a carpenter hammering a nail, Paul hammers the truth: *God does not show favoritism.* God was patient with Jews. He did not want to judge their sins. But Jews misunderstood God's patience. His kindness was for the purpose of leading them to repent, to avoid judgment. God and most human leaders made in His image prefer to be gentle with others. But when people misinterpret kindness, those in authority must use force. Paul warned the Jews to repent of their sins. Notice what Paul emphasizes: God will judge without partiality or favoritism.

> ⁵*But because of your stubbornness and your unrepentant heart, you are storing up wrath against yourself for the day of God's wrath, when his righteous judgment will be revealed.* ⁶*God "will give to each person according to what he has done."* ⁷*To those who by persistence in doing good seek glory, honor and immortality, he will give eternal life.* ⁸*But for those who are self-seeking and who reject the truth and follow evil, there will be wrath and anger.* ⁹*There will be trouble and distress for every human being who does evil: first for the Jew, then for the Gentile;* ¹⁰*but glory, honor and peace for everyone who does good: first for the Jew, then for the Gentile.* ¹¹*For God does not show favoritism* (Rom. 2:5-11).

Q 32 ✎ *Underline the words in Romans 2:5-11 which emphasize that God shows no favoritism.*

Jews first. God judges all by the same standards. He judges *"each person"* (Rom. 2:6) and *"every human"* (Rom. 2:9) by His truth about good and evil. Jews thought they were God's favorite people. And it is true that God chose them for a purpose—to be a light to all nations (the Gentiles). But Romans 2:9 states a shocking truth. God will judge the Jews first! Privilege does not excuse us from being judged. Rather, privilege brings responsibility. On judgment day, when God pours out His wrath, those who have been given the most will be judged first. That is why Capernaum will be judged more harshly than Sodom (Matt. 11:20-24), and Jews will be judged before Gentiles.

Q 33 ✎ *What is Paul's purpose in Romans 2:6-11?*

God is a fair judge. He will give eternal life to all who practice doing good; He will *give* eternal life (Rom. 2:7). Paul will soon conclude that no one practices good without Christ. Later in Romans, he will show that we can practice good *only* as we depend on God's Spirit within us. But in Romans 1–3, Paul's purpose is to show that all need the salvation that God offers. He is a fair judge who will pour out wrath on all who sin—and both Gentiles and Jews sin.

Q 34 ✎ *Is it possible for someone without Christ to practice doing only good? Explain.*

B. <u>God does not show favoritism</u> toward those who know right, but do not do it (Rom. 2:12-16).

Paul continues to hammer the same nail: God does not show favoritism. He judges *each* person by his actions, not his race. God will condemn all who sin (Gentiles and Jews).

Many of the Pharisees and Sadducees came to where John was baptizing. He called them the children of snakes (Matt. 3:7). Paul warned them: *"Do not think you can say to yourselves, 'We have Abraham as our father'"* (Rom. 3:9). God does not judge by genealogies, family trees, or lineage. Whoever lives like a snake will be judged like a snake. Repent, and bring forth fruit to match your repentance. *"Every tree that does not*

produce good fruit will be cut down and thrown into the fire" (Matt. 3:10). Every tree! No exceptions. In a fair government, even policemen who break the law will be judged. And God's government is fair. He shows no partiality. God shows NO favoritism. Judges who sentence others will be judged if they break God's Law. Scribes who write copies of God's Law will be judged if they break it. Moses wrote down the Ten Commandments, but God still judged him when he disobeyed. Nadab and Abihu were sons of Aaron, the high priest. But God struck them dead when they broke the Law (Lev. 10:1-2). Uzzah meant well when he touched the ark to steady it on the way to Jerusalem. But God struck him dead because his actions disobeyed the Law (2 Sam. 6:1-6). Preachers, Bible school teachers, missionaries, evangelists, Sunday school teachers, deacons, parents, choir members, and Bible school students—all will be judged if they break God's Law. God judges all by His standards—Jews and Gentiles, kings and beggars, men and women, boys and girls, educated and illiterate, famous and unknown, clever and common, beautiful and pitiful, handsome and homely, tall or short, old or young, fat or thin, black or white—God judges sin wherever He finds it.

> ¹²*All who sin apart from the law will also perish apart from the law, and all who sin under the law will be judged by the law.* ¹³<u>*For it is not those who hear the law who are righteous in God's sight, but it is those who obey the law who will be declared righteous.*</u> ¹⁴*(Indeed, when Gentiles, who do not have the law, do by nature things required by the law, they are a law for themselves, even though they do not have the law,* ¹⁵*since they show that the requirements of the law are written on their hearts, their consciences also bearing witness, and their thoughts now accusing, now even defending them.)* ¹⁶*This will take place on the day when God will judge men's secrets through Jesus Christ, as my gospel declares* (Rom. 2:12-16).

The Jews thought they had eternal life because they had the Scriptures. As Jesus told the Jews: *"You diligently study the Scriptures because you think that by them you possess eternal life"* (John 5:39). But they were mistaken. We cannot excuse our sins by knowing Scripture or quoting Scripture. God shows no favoritism. Under the Old Testament, God forbade judges to show favoritism for any reasons, neither for bribes nor for friends (Lev. 19:15; Deut. 1:17; Prov. 24:23). Likewise in the New Testament, God forbids favoritism (James 2:1-9). And God does not practice what He forbids! He makes no exceptions; He shows no favoritism. His face is against all ungodliness, sin, rebellion, disobedience, wrong, and evil doing. Fire shows no favorites. It burns whatever fire will burn. Likewise God shows no favoritism. His wrath is toward all sin.

Knowing versus doing. Paul emphasizes that having the Law is not a blessing in itself. *"For it is not those who hear the law who are righteous in God's sight, but it is those who obey the law who will be declared righteous"* (Rom. 2:13).

Q 35 ✎ *How did Jesus contrast knowing and doing (Matt. 7:24-27)?*

Paul is teaching what Jesus taught. God does not show favoritism. He justifies those who *do* right, not those who *know* right.

> ²⁴*"Therefore everyone who hears these words of mine and puts them into practice is like a wise man who built his house on the rock.* ²⁵*The rain came down, the streams rose, and the winds blew and beat against that house; yet it did not fall, because it had its foundation on the rock.* ²⁶*But everyone who hears these words of mine and does not put them into practice is like a foolish man who built his house on sand.* ²⁷*The rain came down, the streams rose, and the winds blew and beat against that house, and it fell with a great crash"* (Matt. 7:24-27).

Scriptures reveal sin and do not cover it. Some have the Bible, but all have a conscience—an inner voice that testifies to good and evil. Everyone knows some things that are right and wrong. And God will judge people on that basis. The problem is, without Christ, no one practices all the right he knows. Paul is emphasizing that God does not show favoritism. He judges all who sin. Things are dark in Romans 1:18–3:20. But be encouraged. First, Paul emphasizes the problem that we are all sinners under God's wrath. Then, he will show us the solution! After he makes us thirsty, he will offer us a drink of cool water.

C. God does not show favoritism toward those who break the Law (Rom. 2:17-24).

Breaking the Law. Paul continues to hammer the truth: *God does not show favoritism.* He judges anyone who breaks His laws. The Jews thought they had a good relationship with God because they had the Law. They thought that *knowing* the Law and *teaching* it made them righteous. But notice how Paul identifies their sin.

Q 36 ✎ *Why was it a mistake for Jews to trust in the Law?*

> ¹⁷*Now you, if you call yourself a Jew; if you rely on the law and brag about your relationship to God;* ¹⁸*if you know his will and approve of what is superior because you are instructed by the law;* ¹⁹*if you are convinced that you are a guide for the blind, a light for those who are in the dark,* ²⁰*an instructor of the foolish, a teacher of infants, because you have in the law the embodiment of knowledge and truth—* ²¹*you, then, who teach others, do you not teach yourself? You who preach against stealing, do you steal?* ²²*You who say that people should not commit adultery, do you commit adultery? You who abhor idols, do you rob temples?* ²³*You who brag about the law, do you dishonor God by breaking the law?* ²⁴*As it is written: "God's name is blasphemed among the Gentiles because of you"* (Rom. 2:17-24).

The Jews had the Law, but they did not practice it! And God's Law only helps those who obey it. Paul emphasizes that Jews, as well as Gentiles, need help. Without Christ, none of us walks in the light that God has given us. Without God's help, Gentiles disobey their consciences, and Jews break the law of Moses.

D. God does not show favoritism toward those who trust in symbols (Rom. 2:25-29).

Trusting in symbols. Different hammer, same nail: *God does not show favoritism.* He does not excuse the sins of people who are circumcised. The Jews had two great symbols of the covenant: the Law and circumcision.¹⁴ Paul has shown that having the Law does not cover sin. Now he explains that circumcision, in itself, does not provide righteousness. Rather, circumcision was only an outward sign that God gave the Jews to show that they were in a right relationship with Him. If the relationship with God is wrong, the outward symbol has no value.

Q 37 ✎ *Which 2 symbols did God intend to show a right relationship with Him?*

> ²⁵*Circumcision has value if you observe the law, but if you break the law, you have become as though you had not been circumcised.* ²⁶*If those who are not circumcised keep the law's requirements, will they not be regarded as though they were circumcised?* ²⁷*The one who is not circumcised physically and yet obeys the law will condemn you who, even though you have the written code and circumcision, are a lawbreaker.* ²⁸*A man is not a Jew if he is only one outwardly, nor is circumcision merely outward and physical.* ²⁹*No, a man is a Jew if he is one inwardly; and circumcision is circumcision of the heart, by the Spirit, not by the written code. Such a man's praise is not from men, but from God* (Rom. 2:25-29).

Paul emphasizes that the condition of our heart is what matters to God. Our Heavenly Judge does not show favoritism. He judges on the basis of the heart, not on outward symbols. He will judge anyone who sins, whether or not they have the Law or are circumcised. Is there value in wearing a soldier's uniform if a person is not in the army? Is there value in wearing a wedding ring if a person is not being faithful in a marriage relationship? Will carrying a Bible help a person who does not obey it? Will wearing a

Q 38 ✎ *Do you know people who trust in religious symbols? Give examples.*

cross, or having a Christian name, help slaves of sin? Will singing hymns, raising your hands in church, or taking communion deliver sinners from God's judgment? Outward symbols only have value to the person who has a right heart and relationship. God has a special name for those who pretend to be righteous, but are evil—He calls them *hypocrites*! Jesus condemned hypocrites with strong words of judgment (Matt. 23).

Paul is leading all people to repent. **All of us**—Jews and Gentiles—have sinned. As slaves of sin, we know what is right, but we fail to do it. We are guilty and need God to help us. Paul beats this drum in Romans 1:18–3:20. He wants everyone to feel the guilt of sin, and the need for God's help.

Lesson 8

Everyone Needs the Righteousness God Offers in Christ (Rom. 3:1-20)
Goal: *Identify and answer the 5 key questions in Romans 3.*

Q 39 *Why does a wise preacher emphasize the problem before offering the solution?*

In Romans 1:18-32 Paul describes the sins of the Gentiles. All of them are guilty and under sin. In Romans 2, Paul emphasizes that Jews are also sinners. God is a judge who does not show favoritism. He pours out His wrath on all of who sin—Gentiles and Jews. All are guilty and need help. So in Romans 1:18–2:29, Paul has made his readers thirsty. He has preached everyone under conviction of sin. Like every good preacher, he has emphasized and illustrated the problem until people felt it was their problem. He has plowed the ground. Soon he will sow the seed of the solution.

In Romans 3:1-20, Paul is almost ready to offer us a solution—a cool drink of water. But first, he must be sure that everyone is thirsty and ready to drink. Paul is like a shepherd leading sheep to drink water. He wants all of the sheep to come as a group. He does not want to leave even one or two sheep astray, apart from the flock. He does not want any of his readers to be thinking about questions that he has not answered. Every preacher knows that before you offer people the solution, you must answer their questions and objections. Otherwise, at the invitation they will not be ready. So in Romans 3:1-20, the Holy Spirit leads Paul to ask and answer five questions that people might still be asking. Read the five questions in Figure 2.6. Then, fill in the answers to these questions as you study Romans 3:1-20.

Q 40 *Complete Figure 2.6 on the 5 questions and answers in Romans.*

Rom.	Questions	Paul's Answer	Rom.
3:1	1. *What advantage, then, is there in being a Jew?*		3:2
3:3	2. *What if some [Jews] did not have faith? Will their lack of faith nullify God's faithfulness [to Jews who believe and obey]?*		3:4
3:5	3. If our unrighteousness makes God look more righteous, is God unjust for pouring wrath on us?		3:6
3:7-8a	4. If my sinning makes God look more holy, why not say (as some slanderously report we say), *"Let us do evil that good may result?"*		3:8b
3:9a	5. Are we Jews any better than Gentiles?		3:9b-20

Figure 2.6   Five questions and answers in Romans 3

A. Question 1: What early advantage did Jews have over Gentiles?

¹What advantage, then, is there in being a Jew, or what value is there in circumcision?

Answer: *²Much in every way! First of all, they have been entrusted with the very words of God* (Rom. 3:1-2).

Explanation: Paul has said that Jews are as guilty as Gentiles. Instead of thinking about his guilt, some Jew might be asking a question that leads him away from the problem and the solution. So Paul mentions that God did give the Jews an advantage—the light of the Scriptures. Paul lists more advantages of Jews in Romans 9:4-5. But they did not use the blessings God gave them. They did not walk in the light He shined on their path. They did not take advantage of their advantage!

B. Question 2: If some Jews did not have faith, will this cancel God's faithfulness?

³What if some did not have faith? Will their lack of faith nullify God's faithfulness?

Answer: *⁴Not at all! Let God be true, and every man a liar. As it is written: "So that you may be proved right when you speak and prevail when you judge"* (Rom. 3:3-4).

Explanation: God does not change when people refuse to believe and obey. Paul says elsewhere, *"If we are faithless, he will remain faithful, for he cannot disown himself"* (2 Tim. 2:11-13). The character of God is fixed. He does not change (James 1:17). People may choose to walk away from Him, but He remains on the side of truth and righteousness.

Some Jews did not believe and obey God. As Romans 3:4 says, God is the righteous judge of all who disobey. Still, God continues to be faithful to the covenant He gave Abraham. As Paul will explain in Romans 4, Abraham is the father of all who believe. Thus we see that God is faithful to His promises, even if some do not inherit them because of unbelief.[15]

God's faithfulness appears in different ways. His faithfulness is like a mirror—it reflects our actions. If we are faithful to obey God, He is faithful to reward us forever. If we are unfaithful to God, He is faithful to judge us.

Paul emphasizes the faithfulness of God in 1 Corinthians 10:1-13. God was faithful to deliver Israel from the bondage of Egypt. He was faithful to provide for them. But when they sinned, He was also faithful to righteousness, so He had to judge them.

¹For I do not want you to be ignorant of the fact, brothers, that our forefathers were all under the cloud and that they all passed through the sea. ²They were all baptized into Moses in the cloud and in the sea. ³They all ate the same spiritual food ⁴and drank the same spiritual drink; for they drank from the spiritual rock that accompanied them, and that rock was Christ. ⁵Nevertheless, God was not pleased with most of them; their bodies were scattered over the desert.

⁶Now these things occurred as examples to keep us from setting our hearts on evil things as they did. ⁷Do not be idolaters, as some of them were; as it is written: "The people sat down to eat and drink and got up to indulge in pagan revelry." ⁸We should not commit sexual immorality, as some of them did—and in one day twenty-three thousand of them died. ⁹We should not test the Lord, as some of them did—and were killed by snakes. ¹⁰And do not grumble, as some of them did—and were killed by the destroying angel.

¹¹These things happened to them as examples and were written down as warnings for us, on whom the fulfillment of the ages has come. ¹²So, if you think you are standing firm, be careful that you don't fall! ¹³No temptation has seized you except what is common to man. And God is faithful; he will not let you be tempted beyond what you can bear. But when you are tempted, he will also provide a way out so that you can stand up under it (1 Cor. 10:1-13).

C. Question 3: If our sin makes God look more holy, is it wrong for God to judge us?

⁵But if our unrighteousness brings out God's righteousness more clearly, what shall we say? That God is unjust in bringing his wrath on us? (I am using a human argument.)

Q 41 *In what sense is God's faithfulness like a mirror?*

Q 42 *In 1 Corinthians 10:1-13, what are some ways that God is faithful?*

Q 43 *Does sin make God look better? Explain.*

Answer: *⁶Certainly not! If that were so, how could God judge the world?* (Rom. 3:5-6).

Explanation: God is our Creator, but He gives us a free will. The thought of accusing God of being unrighteous causes Paul to disclaim: *"I am using a human argument"* (Rom. 3:5). Paul wants some distance between himself and those who accuse God of being unrighteous.

God's apostle knew that God *is* righteous, and appears righteous, whether people choose good or evil. Darkness may make light appear brighter. But in truth, light is light, and darkness does not increase or decrease it.

Some may think God looks better because He forgives our sin. But in truth, our sin can never make God look better. When God's people sin, it gives God's enemies an opportunity to defame God—an occasion to mock God's deliverance (2 Sam. 12:14). *Ghandi said his problem was not with Christ, but with Christians. Paul quoted from Isaiah 52:5—*"God's name is blasphemed among the Gentiles because of you"* (Rom. 2:24). Our sin can never make God look better, but it makes Him look worse in the eyes of unbelievers.

The suggestion that God is unjust alarms Paul. This is so unthinkable that he spends little time discussing it.

D. Question 4: Should we do evil so God will look better?

⁷Someone might argue, "If my falsehood enhances God's truthfulness and so increases his glory, why am I still condemned as a sinner?" ⁸Why not say—as we are being slanderously reported as saying and as some claim that we say—"Let us do evil that good may result"?

Answer: *Their condemnation is deserved* (Rom. 3:7-8).

Explanation: Note that question 4 repeats part of question 3 above.¹⁶ Paul's enemies accused him of saying that grace is like a coat that covers the sins a person practices (Rom. 3:8; see Gal. 2:17-18). Paul has more to say about this false accusation in Romans 6:1-14. But in Romans 3:8, his answer is that people who think they can hide the practice of sin under grace deserve the condemnation God will give them. So Romans 3:8 is an illustration of Paul's big theme: God does not show favoritism—He judges sin wherever He finds it. We may summarize three things Paul has said about God's judgment on sinners:

- **God will judge Gentiles who practice sin** (Rom. 1:18-32). Even if they do not have the Law, they have the voice of conscience to guide them. Ignorance does not pardon those who practice sin.
- **God will judge Jews who practice sin** (Rom. 2:1-29). The Law and circumcision are only outward symbols. They will not excuse those who sin against God. The Law does not pardon those who break it—it condemns them.
- **God will judge those who practice sin and try to hide under the banner of grace** (Rom. 3:8). Grace is not a coat to cover us as we continue to practice sin. Rather, it is a *pardon* that forgives our sin, and a *power* that frees us from sin. Grace is a teacher that guides and enables us to live a holy life (Titus 2:11-13). Grace pardons no one who continues to be a slave of sin (Rom. 3:8; Rom. 8:13; 1 Cor. 6:9-11; Gal. 5:19-21; Rev. 21:6-8).

¹¹For the grace of God that brings salvation has appeared to all men. ¹²It teaches us to say "No" to ungodliness and worldly passions, and to live self-controlled, upright and godly lives in this present age, ¹³while we wait for the blessed hope— the glorious appearing of our great God and Savior, Jesus Christ (Titus 2:11-13).

God does not show favoritism—He judges all who sin. Neither ignorance, the Law, circumcision, nor grace will pardon those who practice sin.

Q 44 ✎ *Does the blood of Jesus prevent God from seeing and judging those who practice sins? Explain.*

Q 45 ✎ *Does grace cover and hide our present sins from God? Explain.*

Q 46 ✎ *What does Titus 2:11-13 teach about the relationship of grace to sin?*

Paul has gathered all the sheep into a flock. He has led us through a dry desert of sin. Now we are almost ready to drink. As we move toward the solution, Paul summarizes the problem with one final question (Rom. 3:9-20).

E. Question 5: Are Jews any better than Gentiles (Rom. 3:9-20)?

[9] *What shall we conclude then? Are we any better?*

Answer: *Not at all! We have already made the charge that Jews and Gentiles alike are all under sin* (Rom. 3:9).

Q 47 Is it better to be a Jew or a Gentile? Explain.

Explanation: Paul concludes that Gentiles and Jews are both *under* sin (Rom. 3:9). This is a major thought in Paul's theology. Men and women do not merely sin; they are *under the power* of sin.[17] Paul quotes at least six Scriptures to confirm this point. This is the longest string of references Paul uses in any of his letters.[18] These six passages emphasize that all of us are sinners who need God to save us.

Read Romans 3:9-18, then complete Figure 2.7.

[9] *What shall we conclude then? Are we any better? Not at all! We have already made the charge that Jews and Gentiles alike are all under sin.* [10] *As it is written: "There is no one righteous, not even one;* [11] *there is no one who understands, no one who seeks God.* [12] *All have turned away, they have together become worthless; there is no one who does good, not even one."* [13] *"Their throats are open graves; their tongues practice deceit." "The poison of vipers is on their lips."* [14] *"Their mouths are full of cursing and bitterness."* [15] *"Their feet are swift to shed blood;* [16] *ruin and misery mark their ways,* [17] *and the way of peace they do not know."* [18] *"There is no fear of God before their eyes"* (Rom. 3:9-18).

Q 48 Complete Figure 2.7 on Romans 3:9-18.

Parts of the Body	Explanation, in Your Own Words	Rom.	Old Testament Reference
Minds and hearts	No one understands or seeks God.	3:10-12	Ps. 14:1-3; 53:1-3; [Eccl. 7:20]
Throats and tongues		3:13	Ps. 5:9
Lips		3:13	Ps. 140:3
Mouths		3:14	Ps. 10:7
Feet		3:15-16	Isa. 59:7-8
Eyes		3:18	Ps. 36:1

Figure 2.7   Practice chart on Romans 3:10-18

[19] *Now we know that whatever the law says, it says to those who are under the law, so that every mouth may be silenced and the whole world held accountable to God.* [20] *Therefore no one will be declared righteous in his sight by observing the law; rather, through the law we become conscious of sin* (Rom. 3:19-20).

The word *law* in Romans 3:19 refers to the quotes in Romans 3:10-18. These quotes are from Psalms and Isaiah. So Paul is saying that the Old Testament laws speak to the Jews, who are under the Law. But in Romans 3:19, what is the connection between *"those under the law"* (Jews) and *"the whole world"* (Gentiles and Jews)? All agreed that the Gentiles were guilty of sin (Rom. 1:18-32). The Gentiles were *most* of the world. Paul used the Law to show that the Jews are also guilty. Thus, the whole world, Gentiles and Jews, are guilty of sin (Rom. 3:19). Jews had the greatest advantage or opportunity to live a righteous life (Rom. 3:1-2). Yet they failed to obey the Law well enough to be counted righteous.

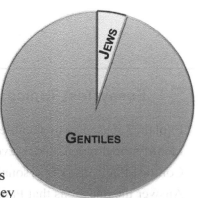

**Figure 2.8
The whole world includes Gentiles and Jews.**

Paul has brought the whole world into God's courtroom. Job thought he would have much to say to God. But in God's presence, Job put his hand over his mouth (Job 40:4). Likewise, the whole world must be silent before the Heavenly Judge. We are guilty under the power of sin.

Test Yourself: Circle the letter by the ***best*** completion to each question or statement.

1. What does Romans 1 say God pours on sinners?
a) Wrath
b) Grace
c) Mercy
d) Sickness

a) Jews do not worship idols.
b) Jews commit fewer sins than Gentiles.
c) Jews commit the same sins as Gentiles.
d) Jews commit more sins than Gentiles.

2. What happens now to those who reject the Creator?
a) They do not worship anything.
b) They lose the desire to worship.
c) They worship God and others.
d) They worship the creation.

7. Which symbol did many Jews of Paul's day trust?
a) Circumcision
b) The Star of David
c) The ark of the covenant
d) Roman government

3. What does Romans 1:24-32 describe?
a) God allows people to choose their own paths.
b) God has mercy on all who seek Him.
c) God chooses some to be saved.
d) God's mercy is limited to the elect.

8. What advantage do the Jews have?
a) The sign of circumcision
b) The Aaronic High Priest
c) The sacrifices
d) The words of God

4. Why does Paul shift from *they* to *you* (Rom. 2)?
a) He turns from believers to sinners.
b) He changes from impersonal to personal.
c) He returns to addressing friends.
d) He turns from Gentiles to Jews.

9. What did Paul tell those who misuse grace?
a) They should learn the truth.
b) They should repent at once.
c) Their condemnation is deserved.
d) Their conscience has been seared.

5. Why will God judge Jews who sin?
a) God does not show favoritism.
b) Jews have more light than Gentiles.
c) Jews are still God's chosen people.
d) God disciplines all of His children.

10. Are Jews any better than Gentiles (Rom. 3)?
a) Yes
b) Sometimes
c) Maybe
d) No

6. Which of the following is TRUE?

 Essay Test Topics: Write 50-100 words on each of these goals that you studied in this chapter.

• Explain 3 reasons why Gentiles need the righteousness that God provides (Rom. 1:18-32).

• Identify the problem and 3 levels of sin in Romans 1:21-32.

• Contrast Paul's use of personal pronouns in Romans 1 and 2.

• Answer the questions that Paul asks in Romans 2:3-4 and 2:17-23.

• Give 3 examples how God will judge Jews the same as Gentiles.

• Relate the theme "God does not show favoritism" to each of these: Jews first, knowing versus doing, breaking the Law, trusting in symbols.

• Identify and answer the 5 key questions in Romans 3.

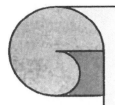

Unit Two: Justification—Righteousness God Provides for Us; Pardon From the Penalty of Sin (Rom. 3:21–5:21)

Like every good preacher, Paul presents the problem before the solution. He plows the ground before he sows the seed. He makes us thirsty before he offers us a drink. Reading Romans 1:18–3:20 is like walking through a desert. It makes us very thirsty. Paul lists sins of many types. And he shines a light on every kind of sinner—Gentiles and Jews, young and old, rich and poor.

²At dawn he [Jesus] appeared again in the temple courts, where all the people gathered around him, and he sat down to teach them. ³The teachers of the law and the Pharisees brought in a woman caught in adultery. They made her stand before the group ⁴and said to Jesus, "Teacher, this woman was caught in the act of adultery. ⁵In the Law Moses commanded us to stone such women. Now what do you say?" ⁶They were using this question as a trap, in order to have a basis for accusing him. But Jesus bent down and started to write on the ground with his finger. ⁷When they kept on questioning him, he straightened up and said to them, "If any one of you is without sin, let him be the first to throw a stone at her." ⁸Again he stooped down and wrote on the ground. ⁹At this, those who heard began to go away one at a time, the older ones first, until only Jesus was left, with the woman still standing there (John 8:2-9).

When Jesus finished writing sins in the dust, every listener felt guilty and left. Likewise, Paul talks about sin until every mouth is silent, and every head is bowed in shame. Then he offers us a pardon from God.

Chapter 3 is like an oasis at the edge of a desert we have just walked through. As you study this chapter you will discover how to:
- *Explain what Paul means by "sinned" and "glory of God" in Romans 3:23.*
- *Contrast justification and sanctification.*
- *Identify and explain eight key words in Romans 3:21-26.*
- *Contrast righteousness by faith and by the Law.*
- *On the theme of righteousness, explain four principles relating faith and law (Rom. 3:21-31).*
- *Answer Paul's five questions in Romans 3:21–4:24.*
- *Explain the basis on which God justifies (Rom. 4).*
- *Identify the true children of Abraham (Rom. 4).*
- *Contrast faith in God with faith in someone or something else (Rom. 4).*
- *Clarify faith in relation to facts (Rom. 4:18-25).*
- *Explain how faith strengthens itself (Rom. 4:18-25).*
- *Illustrate the principle: "Faith affirms what God says" (Rom. 4:18-25).*
- *Explain and illustrate why our faith must embrace both halves of the gospel (Rom. 4:25).*

Chapter 4 of our book continues to celebrate justification—a glorious declaration. Justification is the Judge's proclamation. It announces a glorious part of Paul's gospel. All who trust in Jesus are no longer guilty, but free from the penalty of sin. As you study this good news you will learn to:
- *Relate justification to each of these blessings: peace, hope, joy (Rom. 5:1-4).*
- *Summarize the inner and outer witnesses of justification by faith (Rom. 5:5-8).*
- *Relate justification to the blessings of assurance and reconciliation (Rom. 5:9-11).*
- *Analyze the results of Adam's sin and yours (Rom. 5:12-19).*
- *Contrast spiritual and physical death (Rom. 5:12-19).*
- *Complete Figure 4.4, contrasting Adam's disobedience and Christ's obedience (Rom. 5:12-21).*

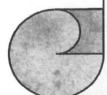

Chapter 3:

Righteousness Is by Faith in Jesus Christ

Romans 3:21–4:25

Introduction

Europe suffered misery during World War 2. Money was devalued. The harvest was ruined. Enemy soldiers threatened to invade on every side.

Most governments taxed families by drafting males once they were old enough to carry a rifle. Often local, hungry soldiers robbed houses they found along their way. Europe looked like it would be a disaster for several decades. There seemed to be no hope for the younger generations.

Figure 3:1 The price Jesus paid provides everything we need for salvation.

People no longer thought of buying land or a new home. The little money that people saved was used to make a trip to the New World—far from the smell of gunfire. One Italian man saved coins until he was able to travel third class, the lowest level on a ship. He did not carry any luggage except a small bag of hard cheese for the trip of 20 days.

Some fellow passengers told him his meals were included in the fare he had paid. During the first few days he listened to the bells that called people to lunch and dinner. But he thought that only first and second-class passengers had access to the dining room. After 10 days, his cheese was gone. Feeling very hungry, he walked to the dining room to beg for scraps. To his surprise the chief waiter asked him, "Why are you asking me for the leftovers? Your meals are included in the fare you paid."

The poor traveler had not believed his friends. If he had believed what they said, he would have had plenty of food to eat.

Likewise, faith in the gospel brings benefits. The price Jesus paid for us includes full sonship and salvation. We only need to believe that God's grace is sufficient for the forgiveness of our sins and for eternal life.

Lessons:

Righteousness Is by Faith in Jesus Christ—Part 1 (Rom. 3:21-31)

Goal A: *Explain what Paul means by "sinned" and "glory of God" in Romans 3:23.*
Goal B: *Contrast justification and sanctification.*
Goal C: *Identify and explain 8 key words in Romans 3:21-26.*
Goal D: *Contrast righteousness by faith and by the Law.*

Righteousness Is by Faith in Jesus Christ—Part 2 (Rom. 3:21-31)

Goal: *On the theme of righteousness, explain 4 principles relating faith and law (Rom. 3:21-31).*

Seven Principles About Faith—Part 1 (Rom. 4:1-25)

Goal A: *Answer Paul's 5 questions in Romans 3:21–4:24.*
Goal B: *Explain the basis on which God justifies (Rom. 4).*
Goal C: *Identify the true children of Abraham (Rom. 4).*
Goal D: *Contrast faith in God with faith in someone or something else (Rom. 4).*

Seven Principles About Faith—Part 2 (Rom. 4:1-25)

Goal A: *Clarify faith in relation to facts (Rom. 4:18-25).*
Goal B: *Explain how faith strengthens itself (Rom. 4:18-25).*
Goal C: *Illustrate the principle: "Faith affirms what God says" (Rom. 4:18-25).*
Goal D: *Explain and illustrate why our faith must embrace both halves of the gospel (Rom. 4:25).*

righteousness—justice; a right relationship with God

justification—righteousness that God provides for us and credits to us through the Cross (Rom. 3:21–5:21)

sanctification—righteousness that God produces in us by His Spirit (Rom. 6–8)

sinned—disobeyed God's Law or commands (Rom. 3:23)

glory of God—the glory God intends for us (Rom. 3:23)

faith—trusting in Jesus Christ, believing in Him, and obeying Him

justified—credited as righteous by faith in Jesus Christ; forgiven and brought into a right relationship with God

grace—the love, mercy, kindness, and favor God shows us in Christ

redemption—buying back a slave; making him or her free by paying a ransom

sacrifice of atonement—Jesus offering Himself to pay the penalty for our sins and to remove them

---

Lesson 9

Righteousness Is by Faith in Jesus Christ—Part 1 (Rom. 3:21-31)

Goal A: *Explain what Paul means by "sinned" and "glory of God" in Romans 3:23.*
Goal B: *Contrast justification and sanctification.*
Goal C: *Identify and explain 8 key words in Romans 3:21-26.*
Goal D: *Contrast righteousness by faith and by the Law.*

Setting/Problem

*Justification and *sanctification are different aspects of the *righteousness God provides. *Justification* is a legal term that refers to our standing or position in Christ. Justification is righteousness that God provides *for us* through the Cross, and *credits to us* as we trust in the sacrifice of Jesus (Rom. 3:21–5:21). Likewise, *sanctification* is righteousness that God produces *in us* by His Spirit (Rom. 6–8). Sanctification is something we experience. It is righteousness that we receive as we partake of the Spirit at the new birth. And sanctification is righteousness we reflect in our attitudes and our character. As a coin only exists with both sides, justification and sanctification always exist together.

In Romans, justification and sanctification are together, side by side, in one letter. Justification is instantaneous. We are *justified in Christ—counted and credited as 100 percent righteous the moment we believe. In contrast, sanctification is progressive. The righteousness of sanctification increases as we grow in *grace. Sanctification begins the moment we are born again, and it increases throughout life. As Paul said, *"We, who with unveiled faces all reflect the Lord's glory, are being transformed into his likeness with ever-increasing glory, which comes from the Lord, who is the Spirit"* (2 Cor. 3:18).

In Romans 1:18–3:20, Paul has explained the *problem:* All have sinned, and the wrath of God is upon us. God created Adam and Eve to live *above* sin in a close relationship with Him. But when they chose to disobey God, sin entered the world (Rom. 5:12). People became *"under sin"* (Rom. 3:9), that is, under the power of sin. *Under sin* emphasizes that people do not just *sin*. Rather, they are *under the power* of sin. They need more than forgiveness—they need deliverance![1]

Figure 3.2 As a coin has two sides, there are two sides to righteousness: justification (what God does for us) and sanctification (what God does in us).

Q 1 ➤ *What are the 2 sides of righteousness? Explain each.*

Q 2 ➤ *On what basis can God justify us—count us 100 percent righteous?*

Q 3 ➤ *When does sanctification begin? When is it complete?*

Q 4 ➤ *Summarize the problem Paul presents in Romans 1:18–3:20.*

Romans 3:23 states that *"all have sinned and fall short of the glory of God."* It is important to understand what Paul means by *sinned and *glory of God. Let us examine these closely before we study righteousness, the main topic of Romans 3:21-26.

Q 5 ⟋ Why is it unwise to ask Moses what Paul means by "sin"?

"All have sinned." *Hermeneutics, the study of interpreting the Bible, teaches us to allow a biblical writer to explain the words he uses. For example, it is good to allow Paul to tell us what he means by *"sin"* or *"sinned"* in Romans 1:18–3:20. It would be unwise to ask a writer of the Old Testament (such as Moses) to explain what Paul means by *sin.* Likewise, it would be unwise to ask a writer of the New Testament (such as John) what Paul means by *sin.* The rules of interpreting Scripture teach us to search for meaning within the context of a writer. Paul does not leave us to guess what he means by *sin.* Later, in Romans 6–8, Paul will use the word *sin* in various ways. He will refer to *sin* as an act of disobedience (Rom. 6:1), a power that deceives (Rom. 6:11), a master that rules (Rom. 6:12-14), and a law or principle that wars against inner, godly desires (Rom. 7:23; 8:2). And as we noted above, Paul says that Gentiles and Jews are *under sin*—that is, under the power of sin (Rom. 3:9). But in Romans 3:23, *sinned* means "disobeyed" God's law or commands. In Romans 1:18-32, we studied many examples of *sin* (disobedience) that Paul wrote about, such as idolatry, sexual sins, greed, pride, murder, gossiping, slander, and hating God. All of these *sins* are examples of disobedience—breaking God's laws.

Q 6 ⟍ What does Paul mean by "sinned" in Romans 3:23?

Application: Some writers do not follow the rules of interpreting the Bible when they interpret Romans 3:23. They define *sin* in a different way than Paul defines *sin.* For example, some lead people astray by teaching that *sin* is falling short of God Himself. As humans, we will always be less than God Almighty. We fall short of God in every way, and always will. We worship Him because He is God and we are humans! We are created in His image, and we seek to be *like* Him. God has predestined or chosen us to be conformed to the image of His Son (Rom. 8:29).We imitate God's attitudes toward people (Rom. 15:7; Matt. 5:48; Eph. 5:1). But the laws and standards that God gives us are far beneath the level on which He lives. Imagine if God required humans to be as righteous as He is. That would be like requiring a gnat to be as strong as an elephant! Would God condemn a candle because its light is less in quality and quantity than the light of the sun? No! God does not require us to be as righteous as He is! Rather, God gives us laws that are fitting for humans.

Q 7 ⟍ Does sin mean "to fall short of God"? Explain.

Adam and Eve did not sin by being less righteous than God. Rather, they sinned by breaking the <u>only</u> law that God gave them. Likewise, Gentiles and Jews did not sin by being less than God. We sinned by breaking God's laws. For Paul, <u>sin is disobeying the laws God gives in writing or in the conscience.</u>

Q 8 ⟋ If sin meant being less than God, could Romans 6:15-18 be true? Explain.

Those who define *sin* as being less than God commit two errors. *First,* they teach against the Bible. For if it were a sin to fall short of God, than we would always be sinners—slaves of sin (Rom. 6:15-16). But the Bible teaches that believers are no longer slaves of sin. We will study Romans 6–8 later. There, Paul teaches that we used to be slaves of sin, but we become slaves of righteousness in Christ by the power of the Holy Spirit (Rom. 8:5-9). *Second,* it is an error to teach believers that they are slaves of sin, because what we believe affects the way we live. If you teach a child that he cannot succeed, he will believe you and fail. If you teach people that they cannot support themselves, they will depend on others to care for them. And if you teach believers that they cannot live a life of victory over sin, they will live as slaves of sin. Let us not be content to scratch like sparrows when God made us to soar like eagles![2] Let us expect to grow in Christ and live above sin, not under its dominion.

Q 9 ⟍ What happens when we teach believers that they are sinners and slaves of sin?

"The glory of God." What does Paul mean in Romans 3:23, *"for all have sinned and fall short of the glory of God."* The *"glory of God"* refers to the glory that God intends for us. He created us in His image, to reflect His glory. The moon reflects the

Q 10 ⟍ What does Paul mean when he says that we all fall short of the glory of God (Rom. 3:23)?

glory of the sun. Likewise Moses reflected the glory of God, after being in His presence (Exod. 34:29-30). God's plan is for us to reflect His glory, spiritually, through our *relationship* with Him. But as Romans 1–3 teaches, man rejected God and sank lower and lower into sin. Because all have sinned, all fall short of the glory that God planned for us.[3] Sin separates us from God and from being the glorious people He desires us to be. When we refuse to give God the glory He deserves (Rom. 1:21), we fall short of the glory God intends us to reflect.

In the future, God will reveal great glory in us (Rom. 8:18; 1 Cor. 15:43). Even now, Paul says we are increasing in glory as we obey God.

> [18]*And we, who with unveiled faces all reflect the Lord's glory, are being transformed into his likeness with ever-increasing glory, which comes from the Lord, who is the Spirit* (2 Cor. 3:18).

Sin causes us to fall short of the glory that God intends for us. But obedience causes us to increase in glory, little by little, as we grow in grace. We reflect God's glory as we show things such as righteousness, holiness, goodness, love, gentleness, kindness, patience, self-control, and mercy. This fruit of the Spirit is the life and glory of God shining through us (Gal. 5:22-23).

Q 11 ↖ *What does the glory of God look like as it shines through us (Gal. 5:22-23)?*

We have reviewed the terrible *problem:* all have sinned. We have all fallen short of the glory that God intends for us. God's wrath is upon us (Rom. 1:18–3:20). But Romans 3:21-31 is a major change in topics. Paul turns from the *problem* to the *solution*. We agree with the preacher who said that in all of Scripture, there are no words more wonderful than the two words in Romans 3:21 *"But now"*. These two words introduce a great change—from the old age when sin ruled, to the new era of salvation.[4] We may study Paul's theme of righteousness by examining *four* relationships (A–D) between faith and the Law. (We will also consider parallel passages from Galatians 3.) The first relationship between faith and law is a contrast.

Q 12 ↗ *Which 2 words in Romans 3:21 signal a great change? Explain.*

A. Righteousness from God is by *faith* in Jesus Christ, apart from the Law (Rom. 3:21-26).

> [21]*But now a righteousness from God, apart from law, has been made known, to which the Law and the Prophets testify.* [22]*This righteousness from God comes through faith in Jesus Christ to all who believe. There is no difference,* [23]*for all have sinned and fall short of the glory of God,* [24]*and are justified freely by his grace through the redemption that came by Christ Jesus.* [25]*God presented him as a sacrifice of atonement, through faith in his blood. He did this to demonstrate his justice, because in his forbearance he had left the sins committed beforehand unpunished—* [26]*he did it to demonstrate his justice at the present time, so as to be just and the one who justifies those who have faith in Jesus* (Rom. 3:21-26).

Q 13 ↖ *Do we attain or maintain righteousness by obeying the Law? Explain.*

Paul wrote three chapters to explain the problem. Then he summarizes the solution in only 11 verses. But these verses are packed full of important words related to salvation. So let us examine several key terms in the order they appear in Romans 3:21-26.

Q 14 ↖ *Complete Figure 3.3.*

Rom.	Key Words	Explanation in your own words
3:21	*Righteousness*	
3:22	*Faith*	
3:23	*Sinned*	
3:24	*Justified*	
3:24	*Grace*	
3:24	*Redemption*	
3:25	*Sacrifice of atonement*	
3:25-26	*Justice*	

Figure 3.3   Practice explaining key words about salvation in Romans 3:21-26.

Righteousness—right relationship with God. There are two sides to righteousness: justification (*imputed) and sanctification (*imparted). (See Figure 3.2.)

Faith—trusting in Jesus Christ, believing in Him, and obeying Him. Biblical faith always has an object. It focuses on God.

Sinned—disobeyed God's commands; broke His Law.

Justified—credited as righteous by faith in Jesus Christ; forgiven and brought into a right relationship with God.

Grace—in Romans 3:24, *grace* refers to the love, mercy, kindness, and favor that God shows us in Christ. The word *grace* appears 155 times in the New Testament. Paul loves the word *grace* and uses it about 100 times in his letters, including 26 times in Romans.[5]

Redemption—in the beginning, redemption meant the buying back of a slave, making him free by paying a ransom.[6] On the cross, Jesus paid the price that satisfied God's justice. His death freed us from being slaves of sin, and bought us to be slaves of righteousness and slaves of God (Rom. 6:16-22).

Q 15 ✎ *What does "atone" mean? How did Jesus atone for our sins?*

Sacrifice of atonement—these words translate one Greek word *hilasterion*, the lid of the ark or mercy seat in the Holy of Holies. Under the old covenant, the High Priest sprinkled blood on the ark. He did this once each year on the Day of Atonement. The blood was to atone or pay for the sins of the nation (Lev. 16). Likewise, Jesus shed His *blood* to atone for our sins.[7] To *atone* means "to pay the penalty for" our sins and remove them. Under the old covenant, God allowed the Jews to kill an animal, which died instead of the guilty person. The animal was the *substitute for the guilty people. Likewise, Jesus was our substitute. He died to take the penalty for our sins. As one song says, "I should have been crucified. ... But Jesus, God's Son took my place."[8] This is the heart of the gospel.

The Jews asked, "How can a holy God forgive a person who is guilty? How can God make a relationship 'right' without a payment for sin? Is it just to call the guilty innocent?" The Jews were quick to ask, "Where is justice?" Christ's death on the cross is God's answer. It shows how God satisfied justice. Jesus paid the penalty for our sins.

But God demonstrates his own love for us in this: While we were still sinners, Christ died for us (Rom. 5:8).

He himself bore our sins in his body on the tree, so that we might die to sins and live for righteousness; by his wounds you have been healed (1 Pet. 2:24).

God made him who had no sin to be sin for us, so that in him we might become the righteousness of God (2 Cor. 5:21).

Q 16 ✎ *How could God be righteous without judging the past sins of Israel? Explain.*

Justice—righteousness. Both justice and righteousness are used to translate the same Greek word (*dikaiosune*), as in Romans 3:25b and 3:26.[9] God sent Jesus to die for us to show that He was a *just* and *righteous* judge–of *past* and *present* sinners. In the *past*, God accepted temporary animal sacrifices. As Romans 3:25 states, God left sins of the past unpunished. That is, He did not fully punish people for their sins. The animal sacrifices were a symbol of Jesus—God's permanent sacrifice for us (Heb. 10:1-10). In the *present*, believing in the death and blood of Jesus is the only way to be forgiven and brought into a right relationship with God.

Righteousness with God is a relationship. We are *justified*—brought into the right relationship with God,[10] through faith in Christ. Sin separated us from God and made Him angry with us. But Jesus died on the cross to pay the debt we owed. Only Christianity teaches the way to be right with God. All other religions, such as Hinduism, Islam, and Buddhism, teach that people can come to God through their own good works and sacrifices. But Jesus is the *way*, the *truth*, and the *life*, and no one can come to the Father except through Him (John 14:6). "Without the *way* there is no going; without the *truth* there is no knowing; without the *life* there is no living."[11] Elsewhere, Paul said that God overlooked much ignorance that people had about Him (Acts 17:30). But now, He commands all to repent and accept Jesus as Savior and Lord (Acts 17:31; Rom. 3:25-26). Jesus alone makes righteousness possible. Only Jesus enables us to be in a right relationship with God.

> THE DOCTRINE OF JUSTIFICATION EMPHASIZES THAT JESUS DIED AS OUR SUBSTITUTE.

The doctrine of justification emphasizes that Jesus died as our substitute. Spurgeon said this teaching should be as common as salt and bread on the table.[12] Jesus died as our substitute—this is the soul of the gospel. For each person must either stand before God and be cursed, or accept the sacrifice Jesus made on the cross. Christ suffered, the just for the unjust, that He might bring us to God (1 Pet. 3:18). Jesus redeemed us from the curse (judgment) of the Law by being made a curse for us on the cross (Gal. 3:13). If you remove from the Bible the truth that Jesus died for our sins, there is no good news left in the gospel.[13]

Q 17 *In what sense is justification the soul of the gospel?*

A group of students sat in a classroom with a strict teacher. When it was time for lunch, Big Jake, the largest boy, discovered that part of his food was gone. One of the students had stolen it. The teacher was very angry and began to question each student. In time, the smallest, poorest, weakest boy—Johnny—confessed. He was feeling hungry, and he had no food to eat. The teacher called little Johnny to the front of the room. He told Johnny to remove his shirt and prepare for a beating. Just then, Big Jake stepped forward and asked, "Teacher, I know that someone must be punished for this crime. Is it possible for me to take the beating, even though I am the one who was wronged?" The teacher agreed and gave the beating to Big Jake. Afterward, Jake shared his lunch with Johnny that day, and the days to come. The teacher's heart was touched, for the event reminded him of the love of Christ. Jesus was the One who was offended, but He took the beating we deserved.

In Galatians 3, Paul also contrasts law and faith on the theme of righteousness. There, he explains that the Law was temporary. Its purpose was to make us aware of our sin. The Law tells us what is right, but it does not give us any power to *do* what is right. When we realize that we cannot keep the Law in our own strength, the wise turn away from it and look for a better solution. So in a sense, the Law leads us away from itself to seek a Savior.

Q 18 *How does the Law help lead some to Christ?*

> [21]*Is the law, therefore, opposed to the promises of God? Absolutely not! For if a law had been given that could impart life, then righteousness would certainly have come by the law.* [22]*But the Scripture declares that the whole world is a prisoner of sin, so that what was promised, being given through faith in Jesus Christ, might be given to those who believe.* [23]*Before this faith came, we were held prisoners by the law, locked up until faith should be revealed.* [24]*So the law was put in charge to lead us to Christ that we might be justified by faith.* [25]*Now that faith has come, we are no longer under the supervision of the law* (Gal. 3:21-25).

Lesson

10 Righteousness Is by Faith in Jesus Christ—Part 2 (Rom. 3:21-31)

Goal: *On the theme of righteousness, explain 4 principles relating faith and law (Rom. 3:21-31).*

We are studying Paul's theme of righteousness by examining *four* relationships (principles) on faith and the Law. The first principle between faith and law revealed a contrast. We saw that:

A. Righteousness from God is by *faith* in Jesus Christ, apart from the Law (Rom. 3:21-26).

Now let us move on to Paul's second principle relating faith and law.

B. The Law and the Prophets testify about righteousness that comes by faith in Christ (Rom. 3:21-24).

Paul wants his readers to understand what he thinks about the Law. On the one hand, salvation is *"apart from law"* (Rom. 3:21). God does not count us righteous because we obey the Law. All have sinned—broken God's laws.

Q 19 ➤ *In Romans 3:21 the Law refers to _____, and the Prophets refer to _____?*

On the other hand, *"the Law and the Prophets"* testify about being righteous by faith.[14] It was common for the Jews to refer to the entire Old Testament as the Law and the Prophets. The Law refers to the Pentateuch—the five books of Moses. The Prophets refers to all the rest of the Old Testament.[15] We could study many testimonies of the Law and the Prophets about righteousness by faith. But this course is on Romans and Galatians. So it is best for us to see what Paul says in these two books. Paul uses several verses in Romans and Galatians to show that the Law and the Prophets testify about righteousness by faith.

Q 20 ➤ *Whom does Paul use to show that the Law testifies about righteousness by faith (Rom. 4)? Explain.*

In Romans 4, Paul uses Abraham to show that the Law testifies about righteousness by faith. We will study Romans 4 in the next lesson. But for now, let us note a key testimony that Moses wrote in the Law: *"What does the Scripture say? 'Abraham believed God, and it was credited to him as righteousness'"* (Rom. 4:3; Gen. 15:6).

Q 21 ➤ *Whom does Paul use to show that the Prophets testify that righteousness is by faith (Rom. 4)? Explain.*

Also, in Romans 4 Paul quotes from David to show that the Prophets (the Old Testament books after the Law) testify to righteousness by faith.

4Now when a man works, his wages are not credited to him as a gift, but as an obligation. 5However, to the man who does not work but trusts God who justifies the wicked, his faith is credited as righteousness. 6David says the same thing when he speaks of the blessedness of the man to whom God credits righteousness apart from works: 7"Blessed are they whose transgressions are forgiven, whose sins are covered. 8Blessed is the man whose sin the Lord will never count against him" (Rom. 4:4-8; Ps. 32:1-2).

In Galatians 3, Paul uses several verses to show that the Law and the Prophets testify to righteousness by faith:

Consider Abraham: "He believed God, and it was credited to him as righteousness" (Gal. 3:6; Gen. 15:6).

The Scripture foresaw that God would justify the Gentiles by faith, and announced the gospel in advance to Abraham: "All nations will be blessed through you" (Gal. 3:8; Gen. 12:3).

Q 22 ✎ *Complete Figure 3.4.*

Clearly no one is justified before God by the law, because, "The righteous will live by faith" (Gal. 3:11; Hab. 2:4).

Old Testament Scripture	New Testament Scripture	Explanation about righteousness by faith, in your own words
Gen. 12:3	Gal. 3:8	
Gen. 15:6	Rom. 4:3	
Ps. 32:1-2	Rom. 4:4-8	
Hab. 2:4	Gal. 3:11	

Figure 3.4   Practice explaining that the Law and the Prophets testify about righteousness by faith.

The prophet Isaiah wrote these words, 800 years *before* Jesus became a sacrifice to atone for our sins:

4Surely he took up our infirmities and carried our sorrows, yet we considered him stricken by God, smitten by him, and afflicted. 5But he was pierced for our transgressions, he was crushed for our iniquities; the punishment that brought us peace was upon him, and by his wounds we are healed. [6]We all, like sheep, have gone astray, each of us has turned to his own way; and the Lord has laid on him the iniquity of us all (Isa. 53:4-6).

We may compare sin to the rays of some evil sun, shining all over the earth. But on the cross, God focused all of these rays of sin on Jesus.[16] God justifies—counts righteous—all who believe in Jesus as Savior and Lord.

Paul wants his readers to understand the relationship of the Law to righteousness. God does not count us righteous because we obey the Law. But the Law and the Prophets *testify* to the righteousness that comes by faith. This is a big theme in Romans and Galatians.

C. No one who is righteous by faith can brag about it (Rom. 3:27-30).

[27]*Where, then, is boasting? It is excluded. On what principle? On that of observing the law? No, but on that of faith. [28]For we maintain that a man is justified by faith apart from observing the law. [29]Is God the God of Jews only? Is he not the God of Gentiles too? Yes, of Gentiles too, [30]since there is only one God, who will justify the circumcised by faith and the uncircumcised through that same faith* (Rom. 3:27-30).

This is our third principle on the relationship of law and faith to righteousness.

First, Paul wrote that righteousness is apart from the Law. The only way that God counts people righteous is through faith in Jesus Christ. To believe in Jesus means to trust and obey Him.

Second, Paul wrote that the Law and the Prophets testify to righteousness by faith alone. Paul illustrates righteousness by faith in Romans 4 through Abraham.

Third, if righteousness came by obeying the Law, people would have something to brag about. But since righteousness is by faith in Jesus, no one can boast about being righteous by his own efforts. Even Abraham, the father of the Jews, could not brag about the way that he was counted righteous. God counted Abraham righteous because he believed God, *before* he was circumcised (Rom. 4:1-12).

It offends God when humans boast in His presence. Should a poor man brag about his wealth in the presence of a king? Should a lame man boast about how fast he can run when he is in the presence of a great athlete? Should a human boast about his righteousness in the presence of God?

Jesus told a parable to show that God will condemn all those who trust in their own deeds of righteousness.

[9]*To some who were confident of their own righteousness and looked down on everybody else, Jesus told this parable:* [10]*"Two men went up to the temple to pray, one a Pharisee and the other a tax collector.* [11]*The Pharisee stood up and prayed about himself: 'God, I thank you that I am not like other men—robbers, evildoers, adulterers—or even like this tax collector.* [12]*I fast twice a week and give a tenth of all I get.'* [13]*But the tax collector stood at a distance. He would not even look up to heaven, but beat his breast and said, 'God, have mercy on me, a sinner.'* [14]*I tell you that this man, rather than the other, went home justified before God. For everyone who exalts himself will be humbled, and he who humbles himself will be exalted"* (Luke 18:9-14).

At one time, believers in Corinth were going astray. They were beginning to trust in worldly values like wealth, education, or the ability to speak well. Paul reminded them that faith in Jesus Christ leads us to boast only in Him.

Q 23 ↖ *Why does God prefer to use the foolish, the weak, the lowly, and the despised?*

[26]Brothers, think of what you were when you were called. Not many of you were wise by human standards; not many were influential; not many were of noble birth. [27]But God chose the foolish things of the world to shame the wise; God chose the weak things of the world to shame the strong. [28]He chose the lowly things of this world and the despised things—and the things that are not—to nullify the things that are, [29]so that no one may boast before him. [30]It is because of him that you are in Christ Jesus, who has become for us wisdom from God—that is, our righteousness, holiness and redemption. [31]Therefore, as it is written: "Let him who boasts boast in the Lord" (1 Cor. 1:26-31).

Paul also writes, *"May I never boast except in the cross of our Lord Jesus Christ"* (Gal. 6:14). Paul may have been thinking of the words of the prophet Jeremiah. [23]*"Let not the wise man boast of his wisdom or the strong man boast of his strength or the rich man boast of his riches, [24]but let him who boasts boast about this: that he understands and knows me, that I am the LORD..."* (Jer. 9:23-24).

Q 24 ↖ *Why did God want Gideon to send most of his army home?*

[1]Early in the morning, Jerub-Baal (that is, Gideon) and all his men camped at the spring of Harod. The camp of Midian was north of them in the valley near the hill of Moreh. [2]The Lord said to Gideon, "You have too many men for me to deliver Midian into their hands. In order that Israel may not boast against me that her own strength has saved her, [3]announce now to the people, 'Anyone who trembles with fear may turn back and leave Mount Gilead.'" So twenty-two thousand men left, while ten thousand remained (Judges 7:1-3).

Peter recognized that the Lord was responsible for a net full of fish (John 21:1-12). Let us recognize that it is the Lord alone who is responsible for our success, and our righteousness. O Lord, there is none like You!

Q 25 ↖ *How is our righteousness like the light of the moon?*

God resists the proud, but gives grace to the humble (James 4:6). By His grace God enables us to live a righteous life and bear fruit for Him. We must be careful to give Him the credit for any good we do. The moon should never boast about how beautiful it appears, for it only reflects the light of the sun. Likewise, any good in us is the glory of God shining through. Salvation by faith guides us to boast only about our Father, our Lord and Savior, and the Spirit He freely gives us.

[8]For it is by grace you have been saved, through faith—and this is not from yourselves, it is the gift of God— [9]not by works, so that no one can boast (Eph. 2:8-9).

Q 26 ↖ *Complete Figure 3.5.*

"Nothing in my hand I bring, only to the cross I cling."[17]

Scripture	Summary of teaching about boasting
Luke 17:10	
Jer. 9:23-24	
Rom. 3:27-28	
1 Cor. 1:31	
Gal. 6:14	
Eph. 2:8-9	
James 4:8	

Figure 3.5   Practice explaining verses about boasting.

D. The *righteous living* that the Law requires is fulfilled in those who live by faith (Rom. 3:31; 8:4; 13:8-10).

Do we, then, nullify the law by this faith? Not at all! Rather, we uphold the law (Rom. 3:31).

Q 27 ↖ *In your own words, summarize principles A-C on the relationship of faith and law.*

We are examining the relationship of *faith* and the *Law* to righteousness. The Law explains what God considers good and evil. The Law teaches us what it means to live a righteous life. The problem is that, in our own strength, we are not able to do what the Law commands. All have sinned; all have broken God's laws.

We were guilty and deserved to be punished. God is a just judge, who must punish sin. But God loved us so much that He sent Jesus to be our substitute. In this way, God remained just. Jesus bore the penalty for our sins. He suffered to redeem us. His sacrifice paid the debt we owed for breaking God's law.

Now we are saved by grace, and free from the Law. Consider these questions:

- Does grace guide us to ignore the Law?
- Does faith in Christ allow us to live any way that we please?
- Do believers choose between doing what the Law says is right, and following Christ?
- Has God changed His mind about how we should live to please Him?
- Under grace, does God count us righteous when we commit such sins as idolatry, adultery, murder, stealing, or lying?

The answer to all of these questions is NO! Faith does not nullify or do away with the Law. Faith upholds the Law (Rom. 3:31). That is, through faith in Christ, God enables us to live the righteous way that the Law introduced.

One purpose of the Law is to explain the actions and attitudes that God considers right. The Law tells us how to live rightly in relation to God and others. There are hundreds of laws, but it is easy to summarize them in one or two sentences.

Q 28 ✎ *Complete Figure 3.6.*

Scripture	Summary of the relationship between law and love
Micah 6:8	
Matt. 7:12	
Matt. 22:37-40	
Rom. 8:1, 4	
Rom. 13:8-10	

Figure 3.6   Practice explaining how faith in Christ leads us to fulfill God's law through love.

Micah summarized how God's law teaches us to live:

He has showed you, O man, what is good. And what does the Lord require of you? To act justly and to love mercy and to walk humbly with your God (Micah 6:8).

Jesus taught that all of the Law and the Prophets are easy to summarize:

"So in everything, do to others what you would have them do to you, for this sums up the Law and the Prophets" (Matt. 7:12).

[25]*On one occasion an expert in the Law stood up to test Jesus. "Teacher," he asked, "what must I do to inherit eternal life?"* [26]*"What is written in the Law?" he replied. "How do you read it?"* [27]*He answered, "'Love the Lord your God with all your heart and with all your soul and with all your strength and with all your mind;' and, 'Love your neighbor as yourself.'"* [28]*"You have answered correctly," Jesus replied. "Do this and you will live"* (Luke 10:25-28).

Paul summarizes the relationship of faith in Christ and fulfilling the Law:

[2]*...through Christ Jesus the law of the Spirit of life set me free from the law of sin and death...* [4]*in order that the righteous requirements of the law might be fully met in us, who do not live according to the sinful nature but according to the Spirit* (Rom. 8:2, 4).

[8]*Let no debt remain outstanding, except the continuing debt to love one another, for he who loves his fellowman has fulfilled the law.* [9]*The commandments, "Do not commit adultery," "Do not murder," "Do not steal," "Do not covet," and whatever other commandment there may be, are summed up in this one rule: "Love your neighbor as yourself."* [10]*Love does no harm to its neighbor. Therefore love is the fulfillment of the law* (Rom. 13:8-10).

God is not unreasonable. His laws do not frustrate us. He is not like a father who is impossible to please. Under the new covenant of grace, God writes His laws in our hearts (Jer. 31:31-34; Heb. 8:8-12; 10:16-18). The heart is the source of desires. So when God's laws are in our heart, we desire and delight to please Him. Under the new covenant, by the Holy Spirit, believers receive a new nature, a heart free from the bondage of sin, a heart that knows God's will, and the power to do God's will.[18] As John wrote, His commands are not a burden for us to obey. Rather, because we love Him, we obey Him.

This is love for God: to obey his commands. And his commands are not burdensome (1 John 5:3).

In Romans 8, Paul will have much to say about living a righteous life by the power of the Holy Spirit. So we will study this great truth more thoroughly when we examine Romans 6–8.

Summary: In Romans 3:21-31 we looked at four principles relating faith and law to the theme of righteousness. Our four principles are:
- Righteousness from God is by *faith* in Jesus Christ, apart from the *Law* (Rom. 3:21-26).
- The Law and the Prophets testify about righteousness that comes by *faith* in Christ (Rom. 3:21-24).
- No one who is righteous by *faith* can brag about it (Rom. 3:27-30).
- The *righteous living* that the Law requires is fulfilled in those who live by *faith* (Rom. 3:31; 8:4).

Q 29 ✎ *If Paul emphasizes salvation by faith, then why, in 1 Corinthians 7:19, does he emphasize that "Keeping God's commands is what really matters"?*

Lesson 11

Seven Principles About Faith—Part 1 (Rom. 4:1-25)

Goal A: *Answer Paul's 5 questions in Romans 3:21–4:24.*
Goal B: *Explain the basis on which God justifies (Rom. 4).*
Goal C: *Identify the true children of Abraham (Rom. 4).*
Goal D: *Contrast faith in God with faith in someone or something else (Rom. 4).*

Review and overview

Q 30 ✎ *Write the answers, in your own words, to Paul's questions in Romans 3–4 (Figure 3.7).*

Rom.	Questions	Answers/Responses	Rom.
3:27a	Is boasting excluded by keeping the Law?		3:21-26, 27b-28
3:29a	Is God the God of Jews only, or is He the God of both Jews and Gentiles?		3:29b-30
3:31a	Do we then nullify the Law by this faith?		3:31b (8:4)
4:1, 3a	What did Abraham, our forefather, discover about boasting and justification? What does the Scripture say?		4:3b-8
4:9a, 10a	Is this blessedness of being justified by faith for Jews, known for circumcision, or also for Gentiles, who are not known for circumcision? Was Abraham justified after or before circumcision?		4:9b, 10b–24

Figure 3.7   Questions and answers in Romans 3:21–4:24

Q 31 ⚒ *Whom does Paul use to illustrate that faith excludes boasting?*

Setting

Figure 3.8 shows that Paul introduces three topics in Romans 3:27-31 and explains them in Romans 4:1-25.[19]

	Romans 3:27-31 introduces three topics	Romans 4 explains and illustrates the three topics of Romans 3:27-31	
3:27a	Faith excludes boasting.	Abraham had no right to boast.	4:1-2
3:27b-28	A person is justified by faith, not works of the Law.	Abraham was justified by faith, not works.	4:3-8
3:27-31	Faith unites the circumcised and the uncircumcised under God.	The circumcised and uncircumcised are children of Abraham through faith.	4:9-17

Figure 3.8   Romans 3:21-27 introduces topics that Romans 4 explains and illustrates.

In Romans 4, Paul uses Abraham to show that the old covenant teaches salvation by faith.[20] Every Jew honored Abraham, the father of the Jews. So it was powerful and persuasive to use Abraham as an example of righteousness by faith. Genesis 15:6 says that Abraham believed God, and *it was credited to him as righteousness.* Paul waves this verse like a banner, referring to it at least five times in Romans 4 (Rom. 4:3, 5, 9, 22, 23).

Faith is the topic of every paragraph in Romans 3:27–4:25.[21] So let us examine seven principles about faith in relation to Abraham.

A. Faith enables God to justify—to credit a person as righteous (Rom. 4:1-3, 5-9, 18-25).

Romans 4 explains and applies one verse: *"Abraham believed God, and it was credited to him as righteousness"* (see Gen. 15:6; Rom. 4:3). This verse illustrates the doctrine of justification by faith. Romans 4:3 contains two key words we must examine: *believed* and *credited.*[22]

Q 32 *Which verse does all of Romans 4 explain and apply?*

Abraham *believed* God. That is, he trusted God to do what only God could do. Biblical faith is believing that God will do for us what we cannot do for ourselves. Abraham believed God to give him a multitude of children or descendants. Only God could do this, because both Abraham and Sarah were too old to have any children.

Q 33 *What does this mean: "Abraham believed God"?*

God *credited* Abraham as righteous. Jewish tradition taught that Abraham was righteous, because he was faithful. They taught that Abraham deserved to be called righteous. But Paul says Abraham was counted righteous because of *faith,* not faithfulness. Abraham trusted God to do what only God could do. This pleased God, so God counted Abraham righteous. Abraham did not deserve to be counted righteous. He did not receive righteousness as a reward or wages. Righteousness came to Abraham through his faith, by God's grace. We could say that Abraham did not pay for his righteousness. Rather, he got it on credit. Abraham wanted righteousness. He wanted to please God and be in a right relationship with Him. But Abraham was unable to pay for the righteousness he wanted. In fact, all the money in the world is not enough to buy a right relationship with God. So God told Abraham, "If you will trust me, I will credit you with righteousness. I will give you credit that you cannot pay now, and you can never repay. If you will trust me, I will give you righteousness as a free gift in exchange for your trust, because I love you." Abraham was no fool. He knew a bargain when he saw it. *"Abraham believed God, and it was credited to him as righteousness"* (see Gen. 15:6; Rom. 4:3). Faith enables God to justify—to credit a person with righteousness.

Q 34 *Did God count Abraham righteous as a reward for his faithfulness? Explain.*

To put it another way, Abraham was still a sinner when God counted him righteous. God *"justifies the wicked"* (Rom. 4:5)! These words shock us! Like the Jews, we tend to believe that God justifies the righteous and condemns the wicked. But the doctrine of justification by faith teaches that while we were yet sinners, Christ died for us—the godly for the ungodly. It is true that sanctification follows justification. That is, *after* God counts us righteous by faith in Christ, He makes us righteous, little by little, as we grow in grace. Paul will write about this in Romans 6–8. But our righteousness with God is based on our relationship with Christ, not our own good deeds. *"He who has the Son has life; he who does not have the Son of God does not have life"* (1 John 5:12).

Q 35 *In what sense does God justify "the wicked"?*

Dear reader, let the truth of Romans 4:3 (Gen. 15:6) sink deep into your heart. God counts us righteous because we put our trust in Jesus Christ, not because of the good deeds we do. In Romans, and all of Paul's letters, he has much to say about how those who are saved from sin must live. But always remember that our salvation is on the shoulders of Jesus, not our own. The hope of our salvation rests on the same shoulders that carried the cross for us. Our trust is in Jesus Christ who saved us, and not ourselves.

Q 36 Complete Figure 3.9.

He saved us, not because of righteous things we had done, but because of his mercy (Titus 3:5).

Religious Group	Belief About Salvation
Evangelicals	
Catholics	Faith in Christ + works (such as suffering in purgatory)
Hindus	
Muslims	
Jews of Luke 18:9-14	

Figure 3.9   Practice contrasting beliefs about salvation.

*Evangelicals include groups such as Pentecostals, Charismatics, Baptists, and others. Evangelicals teach that saving faith receives salvation from God as a *free gift*, not *wages* we deserve. Muslims teach that a person is saved by keeping the five pillars: praying, giving, fasting, memorizing the Koran, and traveling to Mecca. But Jesus taught that we are saved by God's mercy, not our good deeds.

4Now when a man works, his wages are not credited to him as a gift, but as an obligation. 5However, to the man who does not work but trusts God who justifies the wicked, his faith is credited as righteousness. 6David says the same thing when he speaks of the blessedness of the man to whom God credits righteousness apart from works: 7"Blessed are they whose transgressions are forgiven, whose sins are covered. 8Blessed is the man whose sin the Lord will never count against him" (Rom. 4:4-8).

Hindus and Catholics teach that God does not forgive our sins by grace alone. They teach that we must pay the penalty for our own sins after death. Catholics teach that people must pay for their sins in purgatory, after they die. Likewise, Hindus teach that one person lives and dies many times. They say that each time a person is reborn, he is paying for sins in his past life. But the Bible does not mention purgatory. And the Scriptures teach that each person dies only once before the final judgment. Romans emphasizes that righteousness and forgiveness are free gifts. Jesus paid a debt He did not owe, to give us freedom that we do not deserve. As Luther taught, we are saved by *sola fide*—in Latin this means *faith alone!*

9To some who were confident of their own righteousness and looked down on everybody else, Jesus told this parable: 10"Two men went up to the temple to pray, one a Pharisee and the other a tax collector. 11The Pharisee stood up and prayed about himself: 'God, I thank you that I am not like other men—robbers, evildoers, adulterers—or even like this tax collector. 12I fast twice a week and give a tenth of all I get.' 13But the tax collector stood at a distance. He would not even look up to heaven, but beat his breast and said, 'God, have mercy on me, a sinner.' 14I tell you that this man, rather than the other, went home justified before God. For everyone who exalts himself will be humbled, and he who humbles himself will be exalted" (Luke 18:9-14).

Q 37 Explain: Good deeds are always the fruit, but never the root, of salvation.

Figure 3.10
Faith alone saves us, but saving faith is never alone. As a fruit tree bears good fruit, saving faith produces good deeds, such as obedience to God. Paul's gospel reveals that good deeds are always the fruit, but never the root, of salvation.

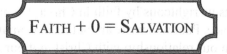

Faith + 0 = Salvation

B. Faith pleases God, wherever He finds it (Rom. 4:9-12).

⁹*Is this blessedness only for the circumcised, or also for the uncircumcised? We have been saying that Abraham's faith was credited to him as righteousness.* ¹⁰*Under what circumstances was it credited? Was it after he was circumcised, or before? It was not after, but before!* ¹¹*And he received the sign of circumcision, a seal of the righteousness that he had by faith while he was still uncircumcised. So then, he is the father of all who believe but have not been circumcised, in order that righteousness might be credited to them.* ¹²*And he is also the father of the circumcised who not only are circumcised but who also walk in the footsteps of the faith that our father Abraham had before he was circumcised* (Rom. 4:9-12).

Q 38 ✎ *What enables God to credit a person as righteous?*

Righteousness by faith in Christ is for Jews and Gentiles. Abraham is the father of all who believe—whether or not they are circumcised. The Jews emphasized being the *physical, outward* children of Abraham. They taught that the only children of Abraham were those with Abraham's blood in them. And they emphasized physical, outer circumcision as the sign of the covenant God gave Abraham. But Paul is concerned about Abraham's *spiritual* children. He says that all who believe—in every nation— are Abraham's children. And the only circumcision that matters is inner, spiritual circumcision of the heart:

Q 39 ✎ *What is the difference between Abraham's physical children and his spiritual children?*

No, a man is a Jew if he is one inwardly; and circumcision is circumcision of the heart, by the Spirit, not by the written code. Such a man's praise is not from men, but from God (Rom. 2:29).

Is God the God of Jews only? Is he not the God of Gentiles too? Yes, of Gentiles too (Rom. 3:29).

Paul was reflecting the teachings of Jesus. True children of Abraham live by faith.

Q 40 ✎ *Does it matter to God what nation we are from? Does God care if a man is circumcised? Explain.*

"Abraham is our father," they answered. "If you were Abraham's children," said Jesus, *"then you would do the things Abraham did"* (John 8:39).

Q 41 ✎ *Sabio asks: "Was Abraham a Gentile, a Jew, or both?*

God loves all of the people in the world. And He loved the Gentiles before the first Jew was born. Think about it. Abraham is the father of the Jews. But the father of the Jews was a Gentile when God justified him!

Q 42 ✎ *Complete Figure 3.11.*

Reference	Your summary of what these verses teach about faith and salvation
Acts 10:34-35	
Rev. 7:9-17	
Gal. 3:6-9	

Figure 3.11   Practice summarizing verses about salvation.

Peter was at the household of Cornelius, a Roman. While there, Peter learned a great lesson:

³⁴...*"I now realize how true it is that God does not show favoritism* ³⁵*but accepts men from every nation who fear him and do what is right"* (Acts 10:34-35).

The apostle John wrote that God accepts people everywhere who put their trust in Jesus Christ.

⁹*After this I looked and there before me was a great multitude that no one could count, from every nation, tribe, people and language, standing before the throne and in front of the Lamb. They were wearing white robes and were holding palm branches in their hands.* ¹⁰*And they cried out in a loud voice: "Salvation belongs to our God, who sits on the throne, and to the Lamb."* ¹¹*All the angels were standing around the throne and around the elders and the four living creatures. They fell down on their faces before the throne and worshiped God,* ¹²*saying: "Amen! Praise and glory and wisdom and thanks and honor and power and*

strength be to our God for ever and ever. Amen!" [13]*Then one of the elders asked me, "These in white robes—who are they, and where did they come from?"* [14]*I answered, "Sir, you know." And he said, "These are they who have come out of the great tribulation; they have washed their robes and made them white in the blood of the Lamb.* [15]*Therefore, they are before the throne of God and serve him day and night in his temple; and he who sits on the throne will spread his tent over them.* [16]*Never again will they hunger; never again will they thirst. The sun will not beat upon them, nor any scorching heat.* [17]*For the Lamb at the center of the throne will be their shepherd; he will lead them to springs of living water. And God will wipe away every tear from their eyes"* (Rev. 7:9-17).

Q 43   *In what way is Abraham the father of many nations, spiritually?*

The Bible recognizes Abraham as a key person who believed. God made him *a father of many nations* (Rom. 4:17). In Galatians, Paul also explains that all who believe are children of Abraham.

[6]*Consider Abraham: "He believed God, and it was credited to him as righteousness."* [7]*Understand, then, that those who believe are children of Abraham.* [8]*The Scripture foresaw that God would justify the Gentiles by faith, and announced the gospel in advance to Abraham: "All nations will be blessed through you."* [9]*So those who have faith are blessed along with Abraham, the man of faith* (Gal. 3:6-9).

When Gene was a youth, he and his mother went to a friend's house for dinner. There Gene met Miss Addie, a black servant who helped fix the meal. He noticed that she did not eat at the table with them. On the way home, Gene asked his mother "Why didn't Miss Addie eat with the family and guests?" His mother said that the lady of the house did not believe people of different races should eat together at the same table. Gene felt badly about what had just happened. A few days later, Gene came home and found his mother cooking dinner. She told him they were having a guest, Miss Addie. That evening, Gene's mother became his hero. God is like Gene's mother, only better. Through faith, everyone is welcome at His table. God offers His righteousness to whoever believes— every person of every race and every color.[23]

Q 44   *In your own words, what do principles A and B teach? Summarize them.*

C. Faith is only as good as its focus (Rom. 4:17).

Q 45   *Explain: Everyone has faith in something.*

All people have faith in something. Some believe in various world religions. Others believe in education or science. Many believe only in themselves. Some, such as members of Christian Science [Church of Christ, Scientist], believe in mind over matter. These have faith in faith. But all have faith in something. Even the demons have a type of faith (James 2:19). Everyone believes in someone or something.

Faith is only as good as its object—what it focuses on. Abraham believed *God* (Rom. 4:16). *"He is our father in the sight of God, <u>in whom he believed</u>"* (Rom. 4:17). The only faith that saves is faith in God.

Q 46   *In the verses that follow, underline the focus of faith.*

Over and over, the Bible guides us to believe in God—to focus our faith on Him.

"Do not let your hearts be troubled. Trust in God; trust also in me" (John 14:1).

"So keep up your courage, men, for I have faith in God that it will happen just as he told me" (Acts 27:25).

Therefore, holy brothers, who share in the heavenly calling, fix your thoughts on Jesus, the apostle and high priest whom we confess (Heb. 3:1).

Let us fix our eyes on Jesus, the author and perfecter of our faith, who for the joy set before him endured the cross, scorning its shame, and sat down at the right hand of the throne of God (Heb. 12:2).

Faith is only as valuable as what it trusts in. Faith in anything less than God is *worthless* for salvation. But faith in God is *priceless*.

Faith trusts in God to fulfill His promises. Some people say, "On my knees, I pray as if everything depends on God. But on my feet, I work as if everything depends on me." We understand that God expects us to hoe, after we pray for a good harvest. But we should have the same attitude when we are on our feet that we have on our knees. In other words, even when we work, we should depend on the Spirit to help us. Paul asked the Galatians, ²*"...Did you receive the Spirit by observing the law, or by believing what you heard? ³Are you so foolish? After beginning with the Spirit, are you now trying to attain your goal by human effort?"* (Gal. 3:2-3). Only God can fulfill the promises He gives us. We should remind ourselves of this often. There is the danger for us to think too seriously about ourselves—to depend on our own efforts, instead of the Spirit. What promises has God given to you? What visions or dreams has He put in your heart? Are you, like Abraham, waiting on God and depending on Him? Remember, Jesus did not say that from our inner being we would pump rivers of living water. Rather, He said that rivers of living water would flow from us, by the Spirit (John 7:38). May God deliver us from trying to fulfill by the flesh, what is possible only by trusting in the Spirit.

Paul asked common believers in Galatia, *"Does God give you his Spirit and work miracles among you because you observe the law, or because you believe what you heard?"* (Gal. 3:5). John Wesley recorded over two hundred healings and miracles in his journal. He said that the gifts of the Spirit have at times been lost through unbelief, but that the Church can regain them through faith in God. As we trust in God, we can see the supernatural works of God in our generation, just as the early church saw them. All things are possible to those who believe in God (Mark 11:22-24). Miracles are for today—for those who believe God today.

Q 47 ✎ *As you think about your ministry, what is the focus of your trust, plans, dreams, and hopes?*

Those who honor leaders get what human authority has to offer—and authority is ordained by God (Rom. 13:1). Those who value education get what wise teachers have to offer—and God gives teachers (Eph. 4:11). Those who respect power get what human strength has to offer—and this may be profitable. Those who appreciate money get what riches have to offer—and we all need funds. Those who seek research get what books and programs have to offer—and God values study. But those who trust in God get what heaven has to offer—and we need God's help to do God's work. A verse we should often remember is: *"Not by might nor by power, but by my Spirit says the L*ORD *Almighty"* (Zech. 4:6).

Lesson 12

Seven Principles About Faith—Part 2 (Rom. 4:1-25).

Goal A: *Clarify faith in relation to facts (Rom. 4:18-25).*
Goal B: *Explain how faith strengthens itself (Rom. 4:18-25).*
Goal C: *Illustrate the principle: "Faith affirms what God says" (Rom. 4:18-25).*
Goal D: *Explain and illustrate why our faith must embrace both halves of the gospel (Rom. 4:25).*

We are studying seven principles of faith. In Lesson 11 we examined principles A–C:

A. Faith enables God to justify—to credit a person as righteous (Rom. 4:1-3, 5-9, 18-25).

B. Faith pleases God, wherever He finds it (Rom. 4:9-12).

C. Faith is only as good as its focus (Rom. 4:17).

Now in Lesson 12, let us continue with principles **D–G**.

D. Faith faces the facts—without weakening or wavering (Rom. 4:19-20).

¹⁹*Without weakening in his faith, he faced the fact that his body was as good as dead—since he was about a hundred years old—and that Sarah's womb was also*

dead. ²⁰*Yet he did not waver through unbelief regarding the promise of God, but was strengthened in his faith and gave glory to God* (Rom. 4:19-20).

Some mislead people today by telling them to ignore or deny the facts. These say we should not admit it when we are sick. They tell us not to confess it, if we have needs. This is really a form of a false religion called Christian Science. Members of Christian Science believe that whatever the mind focuses on affects the facts.

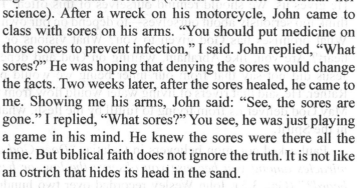

A student named John was in a math class that I taught in secondary school. He was trying to follow the teachings of Christian Science (which is neither Christian nor science). After a wreck on his motorcycle, John came to class with sores on his arms. "You should put medicine on those sores to prevent infection," I said. John replied, "What sores?" He was hoping that denying the sores would change the facts. Two weeks later, after the sores healed, he came to me. Showing me his arms, John said: "See, the sores are gone." I replied, "What sores?" You see, he was just playing a game in his mind. He knew the sores were there all the time. But biblical faith does not ignore the truth. It is not like an ostrich that hides its head in the sand.

Q 48 \ *Have you heard of false teachers who say we should ignore the facts? Give examples.*

Figure 3.12
There is an old story about an ostrich that ignored the facts. It hid its head in the sand when it saw a lion coming. It was pretending that the enemy did not exist. What do you think happened to the ostrich that ignored the facts?

Abraham faced the facts. He did not deny the fact that his body was 100 years old, and as good as dead for producing children. Likewise, he faced the fact that Sarah was 90, and that her womb was dead—too old to have children (Rom. 4:19-20). The father of the Jews faced the facts. But he did not stumble over the facts. He did not allow the facts to weaken his faith. How could he continue to believe, when the facts opposed the promise? This brings us to the next point.

Q 49 \ *What were some facts that Abraham faced about himself, Sarah, and the seven nations of Canaan?*

Q 50 \ *How does faith respond to facts that discourage?*

E. Faith strengthens itself by magnifying God (Rom. 4:17-21).

Faith faces the facts, but it does not stare at the facts. Faith considers the circumstances, but it does not meditate on the circumstances. Instead, faith turns from the facts to the Father. Faith elevates God above facts and circumstances. Faith invites the facts to the back seats of the banquet, but faith gives the front seat to God.

Our faith is not in ourselves, but in our God. Our faith does not change the present or create the future. But our God does. Faith reminds itself that God has the power to do what He has promised (Rom. 4:21). All believers must walk by faith, not by sight (Rom. 1:17; Hab. 2:4; Gal. 3:11; Heb. 10:38). Often, we must focus on the unseen, not the seen (2 Cor. 4:18).

Doubt magnifies the seen. Israel stumbled over the seen—they fell over the facts. The walls of Canaan were tall and the giants were big. Ten of the spies faced these facts, and meditated on them. Unbelief led them to magnify the facts. They turned the facts over and over in their minds, like a person turns a piece of candy in his mouth. These ten spies buried the promise, and bowed to the facts. The more they thought about the giants, the bigger the giants seemed. The giants were only a little taller than the warriors of Israel. But as unbelief magnified the facts, the Israelites seemed as small as grasshoppers (Num. 13:31-33). Imagine a man no taller than the sole of a sandal! Unbelief magnifies the facts until they look like a mountain—too steep and tall to climb over.

Q 51 \ *What mistake did the ten spies make about the facts of Canaan?*

Faith magnifies the Lord. A magnifying glass makes something look bigger. Likewise, doubt magnifies facts that discourages. On the edge of Canaan, doubt magnified the giants until they were so tall that the Israelites seemed like grasshoppers.

Q 52 \ *How does faith in God overcome facts that discourage?*

But faith magnifies God—it makes God so big that His enemies look like grasshoppers (Isa. 40:22). Faith meditates on chapters like Isaiah 40. (Take a few minutes to read Isaiah 40:6-31 and worship our God.) Compared to Him, all the nations are like *a drop in a bucket.*

Faith magnifies God—it enlarges Him to fill the place He deserves. To faith, who God is and what He says mean everything. Abraham knew that *God* gave him a promise. Nothing in the facts or circumstances encouraged him. Everything around him frowned on the promise. Experience was against it. Common sense was against it. And yet Abraham did not stagger or stumble.[24] He looked at the facts like they were as small as grasshoppers. And He thought of God as a giant who stood tall above them. Abraham believed GOD.

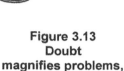

**Figure 3.13
Doubt
magnifies problems,
but faith
magnifies God.**

Problems

Q 53 ✎ *Complete Figure 3.14.*

F. Faith says what God says (Rom. 4:17-21).

Reference	Your summary of what these verses teach about faith
Rom. 4:17a	
Judges 6	
Matt. 9:23-25	
Gal. 3:6-9	
Rom. 4:17b	

Figure 3.14   Practice summarizing verses that emphasize God's ability to see the future, and declare it as the present.

Abraham steadied himself on the promise of God. He leaned on it like a weak man leans on a cane. He rested in the promise like a person rests in a comfortable chair. He relaxed in the promise like a person relaxes in the shade on a hot day. He magnified God! In the day he walked in the sand and said, "God said that my children will be as many as the sand of the sea—and I believe what God said." At night he looked up at the heavens and declared, "God said that my children will be as many as the stars—and I believe it." When people asked him his name, although he had no children, he said, "My name is Abraham—which means 'father of many nations.'" Abraham magnified God. He repeated what God told him. He held the promise close to him, like he would hold the son God promised to give him. Abraham said, like the apostle Paul, *"I have faith in God that it will happen just as he told me"* (Acts 27:25). Likewise, Joshua and Caleb spoke words of faith in God about Canaan. While ten spies spoke doubt, two said what God said.

Only God can see the future as we see the present. This enables God to make promises—to call the things that are not as though they already are.

God said to Abraham, *"I have made you a father of many nations"* (Rom. 4:17a). Notice that the verse does NOT say, "I will make." Rather, Romans 4:17 is in the past tense. It says, *"I have made you a father of many nations."* The point is that *God calls the things that are not as though they were* (Rom. 4:17b). Faith takes hold of a promise like this, and affirms that what God says is true. *"God...calls things that are not as though they were"* (Rom. 4:17b). Faith repeats what God says.

God called Gideon a *"mighty warrior"* while he was a frightened farmer (Judges 6). Gideon agreed, and walked forward with steps of faith. He became the mighty warrior whom God said he was. *"God...calls things that are not as though they were"* (Rom. 4:17b). Faith says what God says.

Jesus saw the daughter of Jairus alive in the future, while she was dead in the present. Looking at the future He said, *"She is not dead but asleep"* (Luke 8:52). Jairus agreed with God. He put his trust in what Jesus said. And the dead girl sat up. *"God...calls things that are not as though they were"* (Rom. 4:17b). Faith affirms what God says.

Jesus spoke about Lazarus as though he were alive (John 11:11). He called to Lazarus as though a dead man could still hear (John 11:43). Someone believed Jesus and rolled away the stone—and Lazarus lived! *"God...calls things that are not as though they were"* (Rom. 4:17b). Faith believes and acts upon what God says.

We are the righteous, living children of Abraham. While we were sinners, God called us righteous—the moment we trusted in Jesus (Rom. 4:5). He calls the things that are not as though they were. We agree with Him, and affirm His Word. We call ourselves saints instead of sinners. Our faith enables God to clothe us with the righteousness of Christ. He puts His Spirit within us, and begins to change us from glory to glory. He credits us with righteousness the instant we believe. And He transforms us to become like Jesus, little by little. We grow in grace. And all that He says we are, we become by faith in Him. *"God...calls things that are not as though they were"* (Rom. 4:17b). Faith agrees with God and says what God says.

Do not try to create your own promise. Do not put your faith in yourself. Do not try to change yourself or your circumstances through the power of your own words. Rather, pray and seek the Lord. Receive the promises that God gives to you. Affirm God and His Word, although He calls the things that are not as though they were. Be patient, and repeat what God says:

³*"For the revelation awaits an appointed time; it speaks of the end and it will not prove false. Though it linger, wait for it; for it will certainly come and will not delay. ⁴See, he is puffed up; his desires are not upright—but the righteous will live by his faith* (Hab. 2:3-4).

G. Faith embraces both the Cross and the Resurrection (Rom. 4:25).

He was delivered over to death for our sins
and was raised to life for our justification (Rom. 4:25).

This verse contains two part, Romans 4:25a and 4:25b.

The first part is about death: *"He was delivered over to death for our sins"* (Rom. 4:25a). These words reflect Isaiah 53:12 in the Septuagint (LXX), the Greek translation of the Old Testament—*he was handed over because of our iniquities* (Isa. 53:12).[25] On the cross, Jesus paid the price for our sins. He took our place. At Calvary was the day Jesus wore my crown! He bore my sins on His shoulders. Through my union with Christ, the penalty of my sins is paid on the cross.

Q 54 *What emphasizes our victory over sin, the Crucifixion or the Resurrection? Explain.*

The second part is about life. It links justification to the Resurrection—*"and was raised to life for our justification"* (Rom. 4:25b). The Resurrection reveals a shift from death to new life. The Cross shows Jesus dead, bearing guilt. The Resurrection shows Him alive, having overcome sin and the grave.

There is a theological connection between justification and the Resurrection (see Rom. 5:10). On the cross, Jesus provided the sacrifice of atonement for our sins. The Crucifixion provided the basis for God to justify us. And at the Resurrection, God showed that He approved Christ and His sacrifice. At the Resurrection, God freed Christ forever from the sin He bore. Likewise for us, the resurrection of Christ provides power over sins as we are in union with Christ.[26] In Romans 6–8, Paul will emphasize that justification without holy living is fiction. As God raised Christ from being under the penalty and power of sin, He raises us through our union with Christ.

Romans 4 introduces the thought that God raises the dead. Paul gives three examples of God's resurrection power in Romans 4–8.

The body of Abraham was *"as good as dead."* And *"Sarah's womb was also dead"* (Rom. 4:19). But because Abraham believed, God raised him up to be the father of many nations.

He [Jesus] was delivered over to death for our sins and was raised to life for our justification (Rom. 4:25).

Those who identify with Christ die to sin and are raised to new life in Christ (Rom. 6:11; 8:10-11)

In the same way, count yourselves dead to sin but alive to God in Christ Jesus (Rom. 6:11).

[10]But if Christ is in you, your body is dead because of sin, yet your spirit is alive because of righteousness. [11]And if the Spirit of him who raised Jesus from the dead is living in you, he who raised Christ from the dead will also give life to your mortal bodies through his Spirit, who lives in you (Rom. 8:10-11).

As we have said, Romans 4 introduces the thought that God raises the dead. We will study this glorious truth more in Romans 6–8. There Paul emphasizes that believers have been raised with Christ, from slaves of sin to servants of righteousness. For now, let us note that salvation by faith embraces the Cross and the Resurrection.

Q 55 *What happens in a church that emphasizes only the first half of the gospel?*

Sometimes the church has emphasized only the Cross. Society knows Jesus died on the cross. After all, He is hanging from the cross on every crucifix around us. We see Jesus hanging on the cross in the entrance of houses, from the mirrors in cars, on the front of some churches, and even on necklaces people wear. The death of Jesus on the cross is not news to many!

Visit any cathedral on Good Friday, the day Jesus died on the cross. Thousands of people surround cathedrals on the day Jesus died on the cross! Millions know the message of forgiveness and pardon—through the death of Jesus on the cross.

Q 56 *Why is it important to preach the full gospel, not just the first half of it?*

But the Cross is only one aspect of the gospel. We should always connect the Cross with the good news of Easter—the Resurrection. If by His death I am saved from sin, then by His life I am saved from sinning! There is pardon through Christ's death on the cross. But God can do more with sin than forgive it. God's plan is not to leave us as slaves of sin. We do not need to keep repeating the cycle of sin, confession, and forgiveness. The message of Easter is good news—Jesus lives. And

**Figure 3.15
Many churches show Jesus on the cross.**

because He lives, we can have new life that overcomes our sinful nature!

There is **pardon** for sin—this is an important part of the gospel (Rom. 3:21–5:21). But there is also **power** over sin—this is also a vital part of the gospel (Rom. 6–8). There is **forgiveness** for sin, but there is also **freedom** from sin. Both of these are important parts of the gospel—along with other parts of the gospel, such as the Second Coming of Christ, and our glorification!

In society, consider the need to preach both the Cross and the Resurrection. When we emphasize only the Cross, the man is forever weak. Why? Because his role model, the Jesus he knows, is weak, dying on the cross or lying dead in the lap of His mother. Males who relate to a dead Jesus tend to be weak.

**Figure 3.16
The Resurrection is the good news that Jesus lives!**

Then one day a man grasps another part of the gospel message—Jesus is Risen! He is no longer the weak and dying one, but He is the Conqueror of death, the Risen One, the Overcomer, the one who triumphs over the tomb. Now the male has a new model—one who is strong, who does not need to sink into the mud of sin. Because Jesus lives, we live also! And we see the new man, filled with resurrection life. He takes his place in the home and in society—strong, Spirit-filled, an overcomer—because Christ *lives* in his heart by faith![27]

So as we proclaim the faith in our churches, our witness, and our daily lives, let us be sure we emphasize both the Cross and the Resurrection (Rom. 4:25).

Test Yourself: Circle the letter by the *best* completion to each question or statement.

1. In Romans 3:23, what does *sinned* mean?
a) Lived less holy than God lives
b) Missed the target they aimed at
c) Behaved less than ideal
d) Disobeyed God's Law

2. Of what have we fallen short (Rom. 3:23)?
a) The glory of God Himself
b) The glory God intended for us
c) The glory of the First Adam
d) The glory of the Final Adam

3. Which term refers to freedom from the power of sin?
a) Regeneration
b) Justification
c) Sanctification
d) Glorification

4. What does the word *atone* mean?
a) To cover or conceal
b) To pay the penalty for
c) To accept payment for
d) To cancel or nullify

5. Which describes the relationship of the Law to faith?
a) Law was an early form of righteousness by faith.
b) Law is the path to righteousness by faith.
c) Law testifies to the righteousness by faith.
d) Law is an example of righteousness by faith.

6. When was Abraham justified?
a) Before circumcision
b) After circumcision
c) In route to Canaan
d) In Egypt

7. Who are Abraham's true children?
a) Jews of his lineage
b) Jews who believe
c) Gentiles of his lineage
d) All who believe

8. Evangelicals believe
a) Faith + works = salvation
b) Faith + 0 = salvation
c) Faith + purgatory = salvation
d) Faith + 5 pillars = salvation

9. How does faith strengthen itself?
a) By ignoring the problem
b) By denying the facts
c) By magnifying God
d) By shouting louder than doubt

10. Which emphasizes freedom from sin?
a) The Crucifixion
b) The Resurrection
c) The Ascension
d) The Glorification

 Essay Test Topics: Write 50-100 words on each of these goals that you studied in this chapter.

- Explain what Paul means by "sinned" and "glory of God" in Romans 3:23.
- Contrast justification and sanctification.
- Identify and explain 8 key words in Romans 3:21-26.
- Contrast righteousness by faith and by the Law.
- On the theme of righteousness, explain 4 principles relating faith and law (Rom. 3:21-31).
- Answer Paul's 5 questions in Romans 3:21—4:24.
- Explain the basis on which God justifies (Rom. 4).
- Identify the true children of Abraham (Rom. 4).
- Contrast faith in God with faith in someone or something else (Rom. 4).
- Clarify faith in relation to facts (Rom. 4:18-25).
- Explain how faith strengthens itself (Rom. 4:18-25).
- Illustrate the principle: "Faith affirms what God says" (Rom. 4:18-25).
- Explain and illustrate why our faith must embrace both halves of the gospel (Rom. 4:25).

Chapter 4:
God Has Provided Righteousness for All
(Romans 5:1-21)

Introduction

Romans 5:2 says we have *"gained access by faith into this grace in which we now stand."* Note that grace is not a result of justification by faith. Rather, grace describes God's dealings with us from start to finish. It was by His grace or graciousness that He saved us. And grace continues to be the basis of our relationship with Him. As John said, *"From the fullness of his grace we have all received one blessing after another"* (John 1:16).

Faith in Christ enables us to gain *"access...into this grace in which we now stand"* (Rom. 5:2). To the Jew, gaining access into the presence of God would suggest going behind the heavy curtain in the temple. This curtain was like a cloth wall between common people and God. And to the Greek, gaining access would lead them to think of the palace. A person only gained access to the king through grace. Then, a servant led the visitor into the presence of the king. Surely Jesus is the one who has opened the veil to the presence of God. And He is the One who introduces us to the King![1]

Figure 4.1   Through Christ, God has pulled away the curtain that separated common people from Him, and He has invited us into His presence (Heb. 10:19-21).

Lessons:

Righteousness by Faith Brings Many Blessings (Rom. 5:1-5)

Goal A: *Relate justification to each of these blessings: peace, hope, joy (Rom. 5:1-4).*

Goal B: *Summarize the inner and outer witnesses of justification by faith (Rom. 5:5-8).*

Goal C: *Relate justification to the blessings of assurance and reconciliation (Rom. 5:9-11).*

Righteousness Came by Jesus as Judgment Came by Adam (Rom. 5:12-21)

Goal A: *Analyze the results of Adam's sin and yours (Rom. 5:12-19).*

Goal B: *Contrast spiritual and physical death (Rom. 5:12-19).*

Goal C: *Complete Figure 4.4, contrasting Adam's disobedience and Christ's obedience (Rom. 5:12-21).*

 Lesson ### Righteousness by Faith Brings Many Blessings (Rom. 5:1-5)

Goal A: *Relate justification to each of these blessings: peace, hope, joy (Rom. 5:1-4).*

Goal B: *Summarize the inner and outer witnesses of justification by faith (Rom. 5:5-8).*

Goal C: *Relate justification to the blessings of assurance and reconciliation (Rom. 5:9-11).*

Setting

In Romans 4, Paul shows that Abraham was credited with righteousness because of believing. He found favor with God through faith, not works. Paul concludes that God will credit us with righteousness as we trust in Jesus (Rom. 4:24-25).

Romans 5:1-11 contains three parts (Figure 4.2). The parts on the far left and right mention several benefits of justification by faith. The middle part states the basis of our benefits—the reason why God's blessings come to us.

Benefits of justification (5:1-5)	The basis of benefits (5:6-8)	Benefits of justification (5:9-11)

Figure 4.2   Romans 5:1-11 contains three parts.[2]

Take a few minutes to read Romans 5:1-11 once or twice. Then we will study these verses by examining seven principles about the benefits of justification by faith.

[1]Therefore, since we have been justified through faith, we have peace with God through our Lord Jesus Christ, [2]through whom we have gained access by faith into this grace in which we now stand. And we rejoice in the hope of the glory of God. [3]Not only so, but we also rejoice in our sufferings, because we know that suffering produces perseverance; [4]perseverance, character; and character, hope. [5]And hope does not disappoint us, because God has poured out his love into our hearts by the Holy Spirit, whom he has given us. [6]You see, at just the right time, when we were still powerless, Christ died for the ungodly. [7]Very rarely will anyone die for a righteous man, though for a good man someone might possibly dare to die. [8]But God demonstrates his own love for us in this: While we were still sinners, Christ died for us. [9]Since we have now been justified by his blood, how much more shall we be saved from God's wrath through him! [10]For if, when we were God's enemies, we were reconciled to him through the death of his Son, how much more, having been reconciled, shall we be saved through his life! [11]Not only is this so, but we also rejoice in God through our Lord Jesus Christ, through whom we have now received reconciliation (Rom. 5:1-11).

A. Justification by faith brings peace with God (Rom. 5:1-2).

The Old Testament records times of war and peace. To possess Canaan, Israel fought against seven nations. Later, in the period of the judges, Israel was often at war with nations like Moab, Amon, Edom, and Philistia. Later, in the time of the kings, Israel fought with nations like Egypt, Syria, Assyria, and Babylon. All of these were *horizontal wars—between two nations on the earth. But Paul introduces the thought of a *vertical war—a conflict between earth and heaven.

Q 1 *What does "peace with God" mean?*

Paul has shown that God is angry with all sinners. God is angry with those who break His commands. Like a king at war, the wrath of God is upon His enemies—those who sin. But Jesus Christ made a treaty of peace between us and God. Now, since we have been justified by faith, we have peace with God—a peaceful relationship with God.[3] Hallelujah! And this vertical peace also results in inner peace. We no longer fear Him, because He is our Father and we are His children.

A traveler spent a night in a Chinese temple. When she awoke, her eyes saw moonlight shining through the window. They lit up the faces of the pagan idols in the temple. She noticed that each god had a snarl or a sneer. Each god was angry with its worshipers. There was no peace in that pagan temple.[4]

THE TRUE GOD LOVES PEOPLE SO MUCH THAT HE GAVE HIS SON TO DIE FOR US.	The gods of false religions do not love their followers. But the true God loves people so much that He gave His Son to die for us. God's justice demanded a payment for sin. His love offered the sacrifice on the cross. Now, we are justified by faith. And this justification brings peace with God. Those *without* faith in Christ stand under God's wrath. But those *with* faith in Christ have peace, standing in the grace of God (Rom. 5:2).

Q 2 ✎ *In Christ, how is our hope related to glory?*

B. Justification by faith brings hope in the glory of God (Rom. 5:2b).

A second blessing that faith in Jesus brings is hope—the theme of Romans 5:2-10. Note that our hope is in the glory of God. Earlier, we studied the phrase *"glory of God"* in Romans 3:23. *"All have sinned and fall short of the glory of God."* That is, because of sin, we fail to receive and reflect the glory God intends for us. But through Christ's death on the cross, we receive hope. Our hope is that the glory mankind lost in Eden will be fully restored to us. In Romans 8:18-39, Paul will have much to say about the glory that God will reveal in us.[5] Even now, God restores His glory in us as we grow in grace. This process is called *sanctification,* which relates to our next point (Rom. 5:3-5).

C. Justification by faith brings joy in suffering (Rom. 5:3-5).

Q 3 ✎ *For what purpose does God use our sufferings?*

All people suffer. Suffering may include such things as discouragement, fear, loneliness, conflict at home or at work, financial problems, sickness, weakness, and persecution. Unbelievers and believers suffer with these problems.

But after we are in a right relationship with God, He uses our suffering for a purpose. God uses suffering to perfect us. Suffering produces perseverance—the inner strength that stands firm during trials. Perseverance is what a runner needs to stay

Figure 4:3
Both believers and unbelievers suffer.

in a long race. It enables us to run our race, all the way to the finish line (Heb. 12:1). Perseverance produces character—the quality of being approved. And character strengthens hope. For hope is like a muscle; we must use it to make it strong. As we exercise hope during suffering, our hope does not get weaker, but stronger.

Q 4 ➢ *How is hope like a muscle?*

Paul mentions hope before and after the topic of suffering (Rom. 5:2b-5). There is a strong relationship between hope and suffering. Our hope (belief) is that God will restore His glory in us. Hope increases as we suffer, because godly character shows He is already restoring His glory in us.[6]

Q 5 ✎ *Does your church teach that suffering may have value? Explain.*

Pentecostal theology declares the power of God to deliver us from troubles. We emphasize that by the Spirit's power we can cast out demons, heal the sick, and even raise the dead. Small faith the size of a mustard seed can move the biggest mountain. These are biblical truths, and Pentecostals have done well to proclaim them. But let us also declare that the same God gives power to deliver and power to endure. Faith enables some to remove mountains, and others to climb them. Suffering is a normal part of the Christian life. God always delivers us from evil. But sometimes He delivers us through it, rather than from it.

Q 6 ✎ *Why did Paul delight in weakness, insults, hardship, and persecution (2 Cor. 12:7-10)?*

Q 7 ✎ *Why did James tell believers to rejoice in trials (James 1:2-3)?*

D. Justification by faith brings an inner witness of God's love for us (Rom. 5:5).

*God has **poured out** his love into our hearts by the Holy Spirit* (Rom. 5:5).

The Spirit himself testifies with our spirit that we are God's children (Rom. 8:16).

One of the greatest benefits of justification by faith is *love* (Rom. 5:5; 8:16).

Q 8 ✎ *What inner proof does God give that we are in a right relationship with Him?*

Paul's enemies, and ours, say that justification by faith is legal fiction—a declaration of a right relationship with God, but lacking proof.[7] They say that justification by faith affects no change and requires no change in a person. Later in Romans, Paul will explain that justification by faith brings a big change in the way people live (Rom. 6–8). And in Romans 5:5, he gives proof that a change has occurred: *"God has poured out his love into our hearts by the Holy Spirit"* (Rom. 5:5).

The love of God in our hearts is emotional proof, but it is real. All believers have the inner witness of the Holy Spirit (Rom. 8:15-16; Gal. 4:6). At the moment of the new birth, God's Spirit enters us. This Spirit within us fills our hearts with the love of God. We know that our relationship with God is right, because we can *feel* His great love within us. Outwardly, we can point to the cross as proof that we are right with God. And inwardly, we can testify of God's love in our hearts.

The moment of the new birth may be the first time that a person feels the love of God. The Holy Spirit is the person who fills us with this *blessed assurance* of salvation. And Pentecostals testify that after being born again, there is a deeper experience in the love of God. We refer to this as the baptism in the Holy Spirit. One believer named Quentin testified the night he was filled and spoke in tongues, "It was like a baptism in pure love." He had been following Jesus for at least 10 years. That year in college, he spent one hour every morning in Bible study and worship. The love of God in him was easy to see. But on the evening he was filled with the Spirit, it felt like love filled him on the inside and surrounded him on the outside. He was nearly drunk with love. He smiled at strangers, and hugged every brother he saw. Paul says that *"God has **poured out** [Greek ekcheo] his love into our hearts by the Holy Spirit"* (Rom. 5:5). It is no wonder that this verb, poured out, causes Pentecostals to link this to verses in which the Holy Spirit is poured out on those who are already believers.[8]

> *"I will **pour out** my Spirit on all people"* (Joel 2:28).

> [15] *"These men are not drunk, as you suppose. It's only nine in the morning!* [16]*No, this is what was spoken by the prophet Joel:* [17]*'In the last days, God says, I will **pour out** my Spirit on all people'"* (Acts 2:15-17).

> [45]*The circumcised believers who had come with Peter were astonished that the gift of the Holy Spirit had been **poured out** even on the Gentiles.* [46]*For they heard them speaking in tongues and praising God* (Acts 10:45-46).

God pours out His love in our hearts at conversion, and later, at the baptism in the Holy Spirit. These experiences give us an inner assurance of God's love and our future glory.[9]

E. Justification by faith is based on an outer witness of God's love for us (Rom. 5:6-8).

> [6]*You see, at just the right time, when we were still powerless, Christ died for the ungodly.* [7]*Very rarely will anyone die for a righteous man, though for a good man someone might possibly dare to die.* [8]*But God demonstrates his own love for us in this: While we were still sinners, Christ died for us* (Rom. 5:6-8).

Paul has said that our hope in God will not cause us to be ashamed (Rom. 5:5). The inner proof of God's love in our hearts assures us that we will not be ashamed when we stand in God's presence. But the outer proof, Christ's death on the cross, is even greater. The highest form of human love is to die for another. In rare cases, a person's love is so strong that he will freely die for someone close—perhaps a wife or child. But God's love for us is greater than this. While we were still sinners—hopeless, helpless, and powerless—Christ died for us. Paul emphasized this grace and love in Romans 3:21-26. Our hope is based on strong evidence. The cross proves that God loves us more than we can imagine.

Q 9 *What outward proof did God give to show that He loves us?*

We recognize a person's love for us in many ways. We see love when someone gives us a card, a letter of thanks, or a small gift. We discern people's love when they give blood for us, or even a part of the body. For example, a husband loved his wife so much that he gave her one of his kidneys when both of hers stopped working. Children recognize the love of their parents, who sacrifice time, energy, and money to serve them.

But the greatest possession and gift that people can give is life. Do we recognize how much God loved us when He gave His only Son so that we could become His children?

For God so loved the world that he gave his one and only Son, that whoever believes in him shall not perish but have eternal life (John 3:16).

F. Justification by faith brings assurance about our future (Rom. 5:9).

Q 10 ✎ *How do we know that our future with God is safe?*

We are sure our future is secure. God gave His Son to die for us when we were His enemies. Surely He will care for us now that we are His children! We have a deep assurance that we are safe from the wrath of God, and living in the love of God.

God has already given us the most. Surely He will give us the least.

He who did not spare his own Son, but gave him up for us all—how will he not also, along with him, graciously give us all things? (Rom. 8:32).

Joseph's brothers sold him into slavery. Later, they trembled before him when he became a powerful ruler in Egypt. Joseph was kind to them and blessed them in many ways. But in time, their father Jacob died.

[15]When Joseph's brothers saw that their father was dead, they said, "What if Joseph holds a grudge against us and pays us back for all the wrongs we did to him?" [16]So they sent word to Joseph, saying, "Your father left these instructions before he died: [17]'This is what you are to say to Joseph: I ask you to forgive your brothers the sins and the wrongs they committed in treating you so badly.' Now please forgive the sins of the servants of the God of your father." When their message came to him, Joseph wept (Gen. 50:15-17).

Joseph wept when his brothers doubted that he had forgiven them and loved them. Imagine how it grieves God when His children doubt that He has forgiven us, and that He loves us. Believer, rest assured that God will never punish you for the sins of which you have repented. God poured out His wrath on His own Son on the cross so that we can be free. If you sin, ask God to forgive you. He may discipline and train you to become more mature. Discipline is for sons (Heb. 12:4-11), but wrath is for God's enemies. Rest in the assurance that His banner over you is love, not wrath. As Paul writes:

Wait for his Son from heaven, whom he raised from the dead—Jesus, who rescues us from the coming wrath (1 Thess. 1:10).

For God did not appoint us to suffer wrath but to receive salvation through our Lord Jesus Christ (1 Thess. 5:9).

We are safe. Our salvation is past, present, and future. As John Wesley said, "I am saved, I am being saved, and I will be saved." We are saved from our past sins. We are being saved from the evil of this world. And we will be saved forever when Jesus returns. Our future is as bright as the love of God.

G. Justification by faith brings reconciliation to God (Rom. 5:10-11).

Q 11 ✎ *What does it mean to say, "We are reconciled to God"?*

From Romans 3:21–5:9 Paul wrote about justification through the blood of Jesus. *Justification* is a legal term. It pictures the judge in court declaring that the believer is innocent. But in Romans 5:10, Paul introduces the words *reconcile* and *reconciliation*. These are not legal terms. Rather, they speak about personal relationship.[10]

To reconcile means "to bring together" or "to make peace between those who were separated as enemies." In Christ, God reconciled the world to Himself (2 Cor. 5:19). Outside of Christ, people are God's enemies. But in Christ, we are a part of God's family. Other religions have little or nothing to say about reconciliation. They seldom speak of a personal relationship between God and humans. But Christianity emphasizes reconciliation. Once, we were rebels—sinners who were hostile to God. And because of our disobedience, God was angry with us.

Jesus is our peace and our peacemaker. He reconciled us to God.

¹As for you, you were dead in your transgressions and sins, ²in which you used to live when you followed the ways of this world and of the ruler of the kingdom of the air, the spirit who is now at work in those who are disobedient. ³All of us also lived among them at one time, gratifying the cravings of our sinful nature and following its desires and thoughts. Like the rest, we were by nature objects of wrath. ⁴But because of his great love for us, God, who is rich in mercy, ⁵made us alive with Christ even when we were dead in transgressions—it is by grace you have been saved. ⁶And God raised us up with Christ and seated us with him in the heavenly realms in Christ Jesus, ⁷in order that in the coming ages he might show the incomparable riches of his grace, expressed in his kindness to us in Christ Jesus. ⁸For it is by grace you have been saved, through faith—and this not from yourselves, it is the gift of God— ⁹not by works, so that no one can boast (Eph. 2:1-9).

In Romans, forms of the Greek word *kauchaomai* are translated as *brag, boast,* and *rejoice.* Paul wrote that no one can rejoice or boast about being called righteous by works (Rom. 2:17, 23; 3:27; 4:2-3). But we do rejoice in our hope and our sufferings. And we rejoice or boast *"in God through our Lord Jesus Christ, through whom we have now received reconciliation"* (Rom. 5:11). We rejoice or boast in the Lord.¹¹ *"As it is written: 'Let him who boasts, boast in the Lord'"* (1 Cor. 1:31). For no matter how much we rejoice or boast about God's love for us, we can never rejoice enough!

Lesson 14 **Righteousness Came by Jesus as Judgment Came by Adam (Rom. 5:12-21)**

Goal A: *Analyze the results of Adam's sin and yours (Rom. 5:12-19).*
Goal B: *Contrast spiritual and physical death (Rom. 5:12-19).*
Goal C: *Complete Figure 4.4, contrasting Adam's disobedience and Christ's obedience (Rom. 5:12-21).*

Setting

Romans 5:12-21 contrasts the ways that Adam and Jesus affect all people. Some readers might ask, "Can the life of one man affect all others?" Paul shows that Adam and Jesus affect everyone, for better or for worse. Figure 4.4 summarizes the ways that Adam and Jesus affect people. Note that the words *all* and *many* are synonyms in Romans 5:12-19.

Q 12 ↗ *What great contrast is in Romans 5:12-21?*

¹²Therefore, just as sin entered the world through one man, and death through sin, and in this way death came to all men, because all sinned— ¹³for before the law was given, sin was in the world. But sin is not taken into account when there is no law. ¹⁴Nevertheless, death reigned from the time of Adam to the time of Moses, even over those who did not sin by breaking a command, as did Adam, who was a pattern of the one to come. ¹⁵But the gift is not like the trespass. For if the many died by the trespass of the one man, how much more did God's grace and the gift that came by the grace of the one man, Jesus Christ, overflow to the many! ¹⁶Again, the gift of God is not like the result of the one man's sin: The judgment followed one sin and brought condemnation, but the gift followed many trespasses and brought justification. ¹⁷For if, by the trespass of the one man, death reigned through that one man, how much more will those who receive God's abundant provision of grace and of the gift of righteousness reign in life through the one man, Jesus Christ. ¹⁸Consequently, just as the result of one trespass was condemnation for all men, so also the result of one act of righteousness was justification that brings life for all men. ¹⁹For just as through the disobedience of the one man the many were made sinners, so also through the obedience of the one man the many will be made righteous (Rom. 5:12-19).

Q 13 ✎ *How can you measure your success in this lesson?*

Q 14 ✎ *Complete Figure 4.4 on contrasts between Adam and Christ.*

Most verses in Romans 5:12-21 contrast the lives of Adam and Christ. To help you learn these contrasts, we have created a chart (Figure 4.4). Complete this chart as you work through this lesson. Review it from time to time. You can measure your success in this lesson by the chart. By the end of the lesson, if you can complete this chart from memory, you have done well.

Rom.	Adam's disobedience...	Christ's obedience...
5:12-15	brought the wages of sin—death to all.	
5:16	brought judgment and condemnation to all.	
5:17	enabled death to reign through sin.	
5:18	brought judgment to all.	
5:19	led all into sin.	
5:20	caused sin to increase.	
5:21	enabled death to reign over all.	

Figure 4.4   Most verses in Romans 5:12-21 contrast Adam's disobedience and Christ's obedience.

We will study Romans 5:12-21 in two parts.

A. Adam's disobedience opened the door to sin, death, and judgment (Rom. 5:12-19).

Review the column about Adam in Figure 4.4. Romans 5:12-21 reviews all that Paul has said in Romans 1–5. In Romans 1–3, Paul emphasized that all have sinned. Romans 5:12-19 reviews the history of sin, which began in Eden. Paul begins the history of sin with: *"Just as sin entered the world through one man"* (Rom. 5:12). Then he takes time to explain some things about sin. Later, in Romans 5:18-19, Paul completes the comparison that he started in Romans 5:12. Let us look at *three principles* about sin related to Adam's disobedience (Rom. 5:12-19).

Q 15 ✎ *What affect did Adam's sin have on all humans?*

1. Adam opened the door for sin to rule on earth.   There is a connection between Adam's sin and ours. Everyone did not sin when Adam sinned (Rom. 5:14-15).[12] But Adam's sin opened the door for sin to enter our world. As a result, each of us is born into a sinful world. And sin in our world is so powerful that no one but Jesus has been able to resist it.[13] God created Adam as a free man, with sin locked behind a prison door. But since Adam opened the door, sin makes people its slaves. Even small children have a tendency toward sinning. As God said, the desires of our heart tend to be evil, even from childhood (Gen. 8:21).

Imagine a prison in Eden. The prison has no windows, so inside it there is total darkness. The one door to the prison is metal, and it is locked. Inside the prison is sin, evil, death, condemnation, pain, suffering, sickness, poverty, and every bad thing in the world. Adam and Eve have seen the prison. But they cannot see all the evils behind the locked door. In fact, they are very innocent to the evils in the prison. God gives them the key to the prison. And He warns them: "Do not open that door, or what comes out will kill you." All goes well for a time. Adam and Eve enjoy the beauty of Eden and fellowship with God. But in time, they begin to get bored with blessings. Several times a day one question repeats itself: "What is behind the prison door?" Paradise surrounds them. God has given them every good thing. And He has imprisoned every enemy of mankind. But one day, they turn away from all of God's blessings. Together, they use the key of disobedience to unlock the door. As Adam opens the prison, every possible evil escapes to curse mankind. Through one act of disobedience, Adam opened the door for sin to rule the world.

Q 16 ✎ *Will God judge you and me for Adam's sin? Explain.*

2. Each of us is responsible for his own sins.   *"Death came to all men, because all sinned"* (Rom. 5:12). God does not judge us because of Adam's sin. Rather, He judges us because of our own sins.

Throughout history, people have sinned, and then blamed others. Adam blamed Eve for his sin, and Eve blamed the serpent (Gen. 3:12-13). Aaron blamed the people for his sin (Exod. 32:22-24). And when King Saul sinned, he blamed the soldiers (1 Sam. 15:15, 20). Likewise, the Israelites once complained that God was judging them for the sins of their parents. But Ezekiel wrote:

"What do you people mean by quoting this proverb about the land of Israel: 'The fathers eat sour grapes, and the children's teeth are set on edge?'" (Ezek. 18:2).

Today, some blame Satan, saying, "The devil made me do it." For sure, Satan tempts people to sin (Matt. 4:1-11). And some cause others to stumble (Matt. 18:6-9). God will judge those who sin by leading others into sin. But it does not help us to blame Adam, another person, or even Satan for our sins. Each of us is responsible for his own disobedience. God's says *"The soul who sins is the one who will die"* (Ezek. 18:4).

Q 17 *What is spiritual death? Explain its root and fruit.*

3. Adam's sin brought spiritual and physical death into the world (Rom. 5:12-19). In the Bible, life for humans is more than a beating heart, and death is more than the absence of breath. Life is living in a close relationship with God. Death is being separated from God.[14] When Paul says we were *"dead"* in our sins and transgressions (Eph. 2:1-2), he means that we were separated from God. Likewise, to become *alive* means to come into a right relationship with God. Satan's first lie, and his most common lie, is that disobeying God will not separate us from God (Gen. 3:4).[15] Yet the Bible teaches us that all who practice disobedience die in their relationship to God (Gen. 2:17; Rom. 6:23).

Q 18 *In what sense is spiritual death present now, but not yet complete?*

Q 19 *Sabio asks: Can a person be dead and alive at the same time? Explain.*

⁴But because of his great love for us, God, who is rich in mercy, ⁵made us alive with Christ even when we were dead in transgressions—it is by grace you have been saved (Eph. 2:4-5).

Q 20 *Complete Figure 4.5.*

Scripture	Explanations of the words *die, dead, death, alive,* and *lives*
Gen. 2:17	
Matt. 8:21-22	
Luke 15:32	
John 11:25-26	
1 Tim. 5:6	
Rom. 5:17	

Figure 4.5   Practice explaining the meaning of spiritual death and life.

"But you must not eat from the tree of the knowledge of good and evil, for when you eat of it you will surely die" (Gen. 2:17).

²¹Another disciple said to him, "Lord, first let me go and bury my father." ²²But Jesus told him, "Follow me, and let the dead bury their own dead" (Matt. 8:21-22).

³²"But we had to celebrate and be glad, because this brother of yours was dead and is alive again; he was lost and is found" (Luke 15:32).

²⁵Jesus said to her, "I am the resurrection and the life. He who believes in me will live, even though he dies; ²⁶and whoever lives and believes in me will never die. Do you believe this?" (John 11:25-26).

But the widow who lives for pleasure is dead even while she lives (1 Tim. 5:6).

For if, by the trespass of the one man, death reigned through that one man, how much more will those who receive God's abundant provision of grace and of the gift of righteousness reign in life through the one man, Jesus Christ (Rom. 5:17).

Romans 5 emphasizes spiritual death that brought physical death into the world. Today, even when sins are forgiven, believers still die physically. But we rejoice to be alive in our relationship with God.

Sin results in death, whether laws are absent or present. Sin is easier to recognize when there are laws against it (Rom. 5:13-14). But sin was present long before the law of Moses. The Bible records the sin of Adam in Eden.

Q 21 ➤ *Does the absence of law prevent death from ruling? Explain.*

[13]*for before the law was given, sin was in the world. But sin is not taken into account when there is no law.* [14]*Nevertheless, death reigned from the time of Adam to the time of Moses, even over those who did not sin by breaking a command, as did Adam* (Rom. 5:13-14).

The words *"sin is not taken into account when there is no law"* do not mean that there is no sin or guilt without written law. Paul has already explained that those without written law sin against conscience (Rom. 2:12-15). But where there is law, sin is judged by the standard of law, as well as by conscience.

The Law was a teacher to bring people to Christ (Gal. 3:24-25). That is, the Law explained what sin is—it taught people what is right and wrong. The Law convinces us that *"the whole world is a prisoner of sin"* (Gal. 3:22). The Law is like a flashlight shining on sin that is in the dark. After the Law exposes sin, people realize they need a Savior. Thus the Law brings us to Christ. We will study more about the role of the Law when we reach Romans 7:7-12.

Adam was a *"pattern"* or type of Christ, *"the one to come"* (Rom. 5:14). That is, there are some comparisons and contrasts between Adam and Jesus.[16] As Adam was a pioneer in the history of sin, Jesus is the author of salvation. As Adam opened the door to sin, Jesus opened the door to salvation. We have studied three principles about sin, related to Adam's disobedience. Let us now examine *two truths* related to Christ's obedience.

B. Christ's obedience opens the door to a gift—life and justification for all (Rom. 5:15-21).

1. Christ's obedience offers gifts we do not deserve.   Romans 5:15-19 contrasts wages and gifts. Adam received the wages of sin he deserved—death and judgment (Rom. 3:23). And since all sinned, all deserve God's judgment as wages. In contrast, Jesus took the wages and penalty we deserved.

Q 22 ➤ *In which 2 ways does Jesus offer Himself as a gift?*

Notice that Christ gives *Himself* as a gift in two ways. *First,* He gave Himself as a gift on the cross. His life was a gift—a sacrifice for our sins. *Second,* Christ gives Himself in a relationship that imparts righteousness—a right relationship with God. Count the number of times the word *gift* appears in Romans 5:15-17. Underline or circle the word *gift* in these verses. In Romans 5:15-16, *gift* refers to the sacrifice Jesus gave—His life. But in Romans 5:17, Paul refers to righteousness as a *gift*—a gift that results from our relationship with Christ.[17] Meditate on this truth. The righteousness we receive is *in Christ.* Apart from Jesus, we have no justification, no right relationship with God. For Jesus Christ *is* our righteousness. As Paul wrote elsewhere, *"Christ Jesus…has become for us wisdom from God—that is, our righteousness, holiness and redemption.* [31]*Therefore, as it is written: 'Let him who boasts boast in the Lord'"*(1 Cor. 1:30-31). A glorious theme in Scripture is that God *gives* Himself to His people. The Father, Son, and Holy Spirit *give* Themselves to us. God becomes our God, and we become His people (Gen. 17:1-8; Lev. 26; Jer. 24:7; 32:38; 2 Cor. 2:1; 6:16; Heb. 8:10; 10:16; Rev. 21:3). Hallelujah! What a glorious inheritance and privilege. God gives Himself to us. He becomes our Father, and we become His children (Rom. 8:17; Gal. 4:6). *"Thanks be to God for his indescribable gift"*—the gift of Himself! (2 Cor. 9:15). Let us always show respect and honor for God, living in holiness and obedience. Let us always remind ourselves that we do not deserve the gifts of redemption and relationship that come to us *in Christ.*

The heat from a fire is in the fire. Without the fire, the heat does not exist. The life that a tree or vine offers is through the connection of branches to the stem or trunk. Likewise, the gifts of righteousness and eternal life exist only in Christ. It is impossible to separate righteousness and eternal life from Christ. The gifts are *in the Son* (1 John 5:11). *"He who has the Son has life; he who does not have the Son of God does not have life"* (1 John 5:12). In Scripture, eternal life is always through a relationship with God, just as eternal death results in separation from God. If we unplug a machine from the source of electricity, the power stops flowing. Likewise, justification and life flow through our *connection* with Jesus. The gifts God provides are always *in Christ*.

Q 23 *Is it possible to be separated from Christ, yet be justified? Explain.*

All people stand with one of two leaders: Adam or Jesus. Those with Adam will receive the wages sinners deserve—death and judgment. Those with Jesus Christ receive the gifts of righteousness and eternal life (Rom. 5:17, 21).

ADAM
and his followers receive the wages of death and judgment.

JESUS
and His followers receive the gift of righteousness.

Figure 4.6 All people stand with one of two leaders: Adam or Jesus.

Paul also emphasizes the number of sins related to Adam and Jesus. With Adam, judgment followed *one sin*. This is what we would expect. One sin led to one judgment. But with Christ, one act of obedience has the power to cleanse the many sins of all the ages. This is amazing! The obedient gift Jesus gave on the cross was much more powerful than Adam's disobedience. This brings us to Paul's great conclusion.

2. Christ's obedience caused grace to increase more than sin increased (Rom. 5:20-21).

Q 24 *Explain: "Where sin increased, grace increased more."*

In Romans 5:18-21 Paul completes the comparison he began in Romans 5:12.

One man led the world into sin, and one Man redeemed it.[18] The gift of Christ *far surpasses* the damage Adam caused. By one sin, Adam set the world on fire—burning with death and judgment. But by His gift, Jesus rescues His followers to life and justification. Christ's grace exceeds Adam's sin like a mighty rain puts out a small fire.

Consider a man who falls from a ship in the midst of the sea. He struggles for his life. His only hope is for someone to help him. Left to himself, he will drown. Hindus tell him he deserves to drown—it is his *karma. Buddhists tell him to deny his desire to live, then he will die peacefully. Muslims tell him to save himself by his own efforts. This is like saying, "Swim to shore." But the man is too weak and the shore is too far. Christianity says God will save you if you call out to Jesus. God is willing to save anyone. How far does God's grace reach? Always far enough to include a sinner who repents. (For more on "Faith and Grace," see *The Full Life Study Bible,* Romans 5:21 article.)

The apostle Paul met grace face to face. In Romans he wrote: *"Where sin increased, grace increased all the more"* (Rom. 5:20). Paul also wrote, [13] *"Even though I was once a blasphemer and a persecutor and a violent man, I was shown mercy because I acted in ignorance and unbelief.* [14]*The grace of our Lord was poured out on me abundantly"* (1 Tim. 1:13-14; see Acts 8:1; 9:1-6). Paul called himself *"the worst"* of sinners (1 Tim. 1:15). He liked to testify that the grace Jesus offers is greater than the sin Adam welcomed into the world. Since the Lord saved Paul, the worst of sinners, He can save anyone. He drove seven demons out of Mary Magdalene and filled her with the Spirit (Luke 8:2). He even forgave King Manasseh who led Israel into sin for over 50 years (2 Chron. 33:11-13). The grace of God can save the worst of sinners.

John Newton captured slaves in Africa and sold them in America. After years of such sin, he repented, and God saved him. Soon afterward, Newton wrote a famous song. The first verse is "Amazing grace, how sweet the sound, that saved a wretch like me; I once was lost, but now I'm found; was blind, but now I see." Praise the Lord for grace that is greater than all our sin! Where sin increased, grace increased more!

Q 25 *From memory, try to complete Figure 4.7 on contrasts between Adam and Christ.*

Rom.	Adam's disobedience...	Christ's obedience...
5:12-15	brought the wages of sin—death to all.	
5:16	brought judgment and condemnation to all.	
5:17	enabled death to reign through sin.	
5:18	brought judgment to all.	
5:19	led all into sin.	
5:20	caused sin to increase.	
5:21	enabled death to reign over all.	

Figure 4.7   Most verses in Romans 5:12-21 contrast Adam's disobedience and Christ's obedience.

Test Yourself: Circle the letter by the *best* completion to each question or statement.

1. *Peace with God* refers to
a) an event.
b) a status.
c) a relationship.
d) an effect.

2. What helps give joy in suffering?
a) Knowing that sinners suffer
b) Knowing that other believers suffer
c) Knowing that our sufferings are limited
d) Knowing the purpose of our sufferings

3. How is hope like a muscle?
a) It supports parts of the body.
b) It needs exercise to become strong.
c) It weakens with age.
d) It may be injured.

4. Which is a Scripture on the inner witness?
a) Romans 3:23
b) Romans 5:1
c) Romans 8:16
d) Romans 10:4

5. Which word is the theme of the outer witness?
a) Forgiveness
b) Justification
c) Mercy
d) Love

6. Which is a result of justification?
a) Regeneration
b) Adoption
c) Reconciliation
d) Conversion

7. What resulted from Adam's sin?
a) A guilty conscience for all
b) Death for all
c) Total depravity for all
d) An increase of hope

8. Who caused an increase of sin on earth?
a) Adam
b) Eve
c) Demons
d) Satan

9. Another phrase for spiritual death is
a) physical death.
b) eternal punishment.
c) separation from God.
d) bondage to sin.

10. Christ caused grace to increase
a) as much as sin increased.
b) more than sin increased.
c) before sin increased.
d) at the same time that sin increased.

 Essay Test Topics: Write 50-100 words on each of these goals that you studied in this chapter.

• Relate justification to each of these blessings: peace, hope, joy (Rom. 5:1-4).

• Summarize the inner and outer witnesses of justification by faith (Rom. 5:5-8).

• Relate justification to the blessings of assurance and reconciliation (Rom. 5:9-11).

• Analyze the results of Adam's sin and yours (Rom. 5:12-19).

• Contrast spiritual and physical death (Rom. 5:12-19).

• Complete Figure 4.4, contrasting Adam's disobedience and Christ's obedience (Rom. 5:12-21).

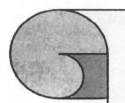

Unit Three: Sanctification—Righteousness God Produces in Us; Freedom From the Power of Sin (Romans 6–8)

Paul's gospel teaches that grace brings aspects of a right relationship with God—such as the aspects of justification and sanctification.

- *Justification* is a narrow, legal term about our *position* in Christ—like a status God writes in a book or ledger in heaven. Justification refers to *right standing* with God. It emphasizes freedom from the *penalty of sin*. Through our faith in Christ, God justifies us—He declares us guiltless, holy, and righteous. At justification, God credits us with the righteousness of Christ Himself. We are justified through faith in Christ, not by our own good deeds. Theologians refer to this as *imputed righteousness*—righteousness that God credits to us. Paul emphasizes this *imputed righteousness,* justification, in Romans 3:21–5:21. Justification is an important part of Paul's gospel of salvation.

- *Sanctification* is a broad word that means "holiness." Sanctification emphasizes freedom from the *power of sin*. Our right relationship with God begins with justification and adoption into God's family. As God's new children, we begin by grace to practice right living—a major theme of sanctification. Justification involves God's proclamation that we are righteous, and not guilty. But sanctification involves a transformation. This new transfer of holiness begins at regeneration as we partake of God's nature (2 Pet. 1:4). And our holiness increases as we grow in grace and are conformed to the image of Christ (Rom. 8:29; 2 Cor. 3:18; 7:1). Sanctification is possible through the Holy Spirit, a living Person and power who enables us to be holy and act holy—to do what is right. Most of Romans 6–8 is about right living. In Paul's gospel, justification is always joined together with sanctification—righteousness in holy living.

With the gospel of grace comes a great danger—a danger as real for the 21st century as it was for the 1st century. The danger is that those under grace may forget that sin is a deadly enemy. Sin kills people spiritually. Some may think, "If God forgives our sins, then we do not need to avoid and overcome sin." But as Paul emphasizes, those in Christ must wear new clothes and walk new paths. For the evil desires of the flesh lead away from God to sin and spiritual death. But the Holy Spirit leads God's children in a different direction—into a right relationship with God, and into the eternal life that results (Rom. 6–8).

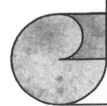

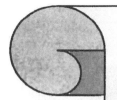

In Chapter 5 (Romans 6), Paul emphasizes that justification (right standing) is linked to sanctification (right living). As you study this chapter, we will guide you to:
- *Explain three ways in which God is holy. Give examples.*
- *Explain three ways in which believers are holy. Give examples.*
- *Explain the triangle of holiness, and how its sides relate to each other.*
- *Answer the two questions Paul asks in Romans 6.*
- *Explain what it means to be united to Christ in His life and death. Apply this.*
- *Explain how water baptism illustrates our death and life with Christ.*
- *Explain the importance of resisting sin, and explain ways we do this.*
- *Contrast offering ourselves for bad and good purposes. Give examples.*
- *Explain: All people are slaves to something.*
- *Defend this statement: The bad get worse and the good get better.*
- *Contrast the results of serving sin and serving righteousness.*

In Chapter 6 (Romans 7), Paul contrasts living under the law of Moses and living under the grace of Jesus. In this chapter, you will learn to:
- *Summarize Paul's teachings in each illustration: baptism, slavery, and marriage (Rom. 6–7).*
- *Answer the three questions Paul asks about the Law (Rom. 7:1-13).*
- *Explain and illustrate five principles about law in Romans 7:7-13.*
- *Refute three reasons why others think Romans 7:13-25 refers to a Christian.*
- *Explain six reasons why we believe Romans 7:13-25 refers to a pre-Christian.*

In Chapter 7 we find that Romans 8 is glorious. Paul emphasizes that the Holy Spirit gives us all the power and help we need to live in a righteous and holy relationship with God. This holy living is a wonderful aspect of Paul's gospel of salvation. In this chapter, you will rejoice as you discover how to:
- *Analyze the words: "no condemnation" and "in Christ" (Rom. 8:1).*
- *Interpret seven key phrases in Romans 8:1-3.*
- *Identify four relationships in Romans 8:1-4.*
- *Analyze: The law of God is not over, under, or behind us—it is in us.*
- *Explain how we are able to fulfill the righteous requirements of the Law (Rom. 8:4).*
- *Contrast the values of those led by the flesh and those led by the Spirit (Rom. 8:5).*
- *Contrast the spiritual states of those led by the flesh and those led by the Spirit (Rom. 8:6, 13).*
- *Identify characteristics of God's enemy and God's family (Rom. 8:7-17).*
- *Analyze the conflict in believers between the flesh and the Spirit (Gal. 5:13-18).*
- *Explain and illustrate the fruit of the flesh, and their results (Gal. 5:19-21).*
- *Explain and illustrate the fruit of the Spirit, and their results (Gal. 5:22-26).*
- *Describe God's plan for a believer "caught" in a sin (Gal. 6:1-5).*
- *Summarize and illustrate God's law of harvest (Gal. 6:7-10).*
- *Summarize some New Testament verses that link suffering and glory.*
- *Contrast our present sufferings with our future glory (Rom. 8:18).*
- *Explain three types of groaning that express hope (Rom. 8:19-27).*
- *Interpret and illustrate Romans 8:28.*
- *Explain God's purpose in working all things for our good (Rom. 8:29).*
- *Explain five steps in the sequence of our salvation (Rom. 8:29-30).*
- *Explain and illustrate four reasons why we are super-victors in whatever we must face (Rom. 8:31-39).*

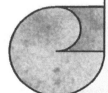

Chapter 5:
Freedom From Slavery to Sin
(Romans 6)

Introduction

Spurgeon was a famous preacher who emphasized justification by faith. A section adapted from one of his sermons follows:

Q 1 *Is it possible to be justified without righteous living? Explain.*

Holy living is always present in guests at the King's banquet. For without holy living no man will see the Lord (Heb. 12:14). Many false Christians claim they possess *imputed* righteousness (*justification, Rom. 3–5). Such hypocrites care little about the sanctifying work of the Holy Spirit (Rom. 6–8). These fake followers of Christ refuse to put on the garment of obedience. They reject the white linen that is the righteous acts of the saints (Rev. 19:8). Thus they reveal their self-will, their enmity to God, and their lack of submission to His Son. Such people talk about justification by faith and salvation by grace, but they are rebels at heart. Like

Figure 5.1   Charles Spurgeon, Preacher

the self righteous, they do not wear a wedding garment (Matt. 22:11). The fact is that if we want the blessings of grace, we must submit to the rules of grace—without picking and choosing. It is foolish to argue whether the wedding garment is faith, love, righteous deeds, or holy living. For all the graces of the Spirit are together in the new covenant. No one ever had the imputed righteousness of Christ (justification) without receiving the *imparted* righteousness (*sanctification)—which comes as we submit to the Holy Spirit. Justification by faith is not contrary to the fruit of good works: God forbid. The faith by which we are justified is the faith that produces holy living. And those whom God justifies by faith, He sanctifies and delivers from the love of *sin in this life.[1]

Lessons:

The Meaning of Sanctification—God Is Holy
Goal: *Explain 3 ways in which God is holy. Give examples.*

The Meaning of Sanctification—We Are Holy
Goal A: *Explain 3 ways in which believers are holy. Give examples.*
Goal B: *Explain the triangle of holiness, and how its sides relate to each other.*

Keys to Right Living: Sanctification—Part 1 (Rom. 6:1-11)
Goal A: *Answer the 2 questions Paul asks in Romans 6.*
Goal B: *Explain what it means to be united to Christ in His life and death. Apply this.*
Goal C: *Explain how water baptism illustrates our death and life with Christ.*

Keys to Right Living: Sanctification—Part 2 (Rom. 6:12-14)
Goal A: *Explain the importance of resisting sin, and explain ways we do this.*
Goal B: *Contrast offering ourselves for bad and good purposes. Give examples.*

Keys to Right Living: Sanctification—Part 3 (Rom. 6:15-23)
Goal A: *Explain: All people are slaves to something.*
Goal B: *Defend this statement: The bad get worse and the good get better.*
Goal C: *Contrast the results of serving sin and serving righteousness.*

imputed righteousness—right standing (justification) that God credits to us as we trust in Jesus as Savior and Lord

imparted righteousness—holiness we experience (sanctification) as we partake of the nature of God at regeneration, and as we grow in the likeness of Christ (Rom. 8:29)

sanctification—right living; holiness of position, actions, and condition

antinomianism—lawlessness; anti-law; rebellious and against law

sin—disobeying God; following the evil desires of the flesh, and resisting the Holy Spirit

flesh—the human enemy of the Spirit. Fleshly life is pursuing one's own desires, independent of God or His law, not submitting to Jesus as Lord, and hostile to the Holy Spirit. Living in the flesh is pleasing self, ignoring God, and rebelling against Him (Rom. 8:1-15; Gal. 5:16–6:10).

Lesson
15

The Meaning of Sanctification—God Is Holy

Goal: *Explain 3 ways in which God is holy. Give examples.*

Setting

Salvation is a relationship with God, and not just the event of justification—being declared righteous. Salvation is a holy *way* of living, not just an *intersection* on a road. When we come to Christ, God justifies us—counts us righteous by faith in a moment. With this beginning, life changes, and He empowers us to live right.

Figure 5.2 A rowboat moves forward by human effort, but a sailboat uses the power of the wind.

There is the temptation to see justification (*right* standing) as an act of grace, but view sanctification (*right* living) as something we do alone. In contrast, Romans 6 teaches that *right living* is a *reality* through union with Christ. And Romans 8 emphasizes that *right living* is a *reality* through submission to the Holy Spirit.[2] Romans teaches that we must depend on God's grace for *both* justification and sanctification. All aspects of our salvation are like being in a sailboat, not a rowboat. We depend on God for the wind that blows the sail. But it is our responsibility to raise the sail and choose to stay in the boat. God requires us to cooperate with the Spirit of grace.

Q 2 *How is our salvation like being in a sailboat, not a rowboat (Figure 5.2)?*

Q 3 *What responsibilities does a believer have in right living?*

Sanctification means "holiness." Figure 5.3 shows three common words related to holiness.

Greek Word	Times in New Testament	Meaning	Examples
Hagios (adjective)	245	Holy; saints	Rom. 1:2 The *Holy* Scriptures Rom. 1:7 loved by God, called *holy* (saints) Rom. 5:5 The *Holy* Spirit, who is given to us (Rom. 7:12; 8:27; 9:1; 11:16; 12:1, etc.)
Hagiazo (verb)	30	To make holy; sanctify	Rom. 15:16 *sanctified* by the Holy Spirit

Continued on next page

Continued from previous page

Hagiasmos (noun)	10	Holiness; sanctification	Rom. 6:19 offer the parts of your body in slavery to righteousness leading to *holiness*. Rom. 6:22 Now that you have been set free from sin and become slaves of God, the benefit you reap leads to *holiness*.

Figure 5.3   Forms of the word *holy* appear about 300 times in the New Testament and 23 times in Romans.

Q 4 ✎ *According to Romans 8:29, what is God's plan for believers?*

Holiness or sanctification is the work of the Holy Spirit in us to make us more and more like Jesus (Rom. 8:29).[3]

For those God foreknew he also predestined to be conformed to the likeness of his Son, that he might be the firstborn among many brothers (Rom. 8:29).

In this lesson we will focus on the meaning of *holiness* or *sanctification*. Let us begin with the question, What do we mean when we say that God the Father, Son, and Spirit are holy?

Q 5 ↗ *What are 3 ways in which God is holy (A–C)?*

The Scriptures teach that God is holy in three ways. Like a diamond, holiness is beautiful as you look at it from different views. Let us enjoy admiring God's holiness from three perspectives.

A. God is holy in His position.

Q 6 ✎ *What are some characteristics linked to God's holiness in Revelation 15:4-5?*

Q 7 ↗ *In what sense is God holy in His position? Illustrate this.*

In this sense, *holy* is the opposite of *common*. We say that God is holy because He is separate—high above all else. In His position, God is holy—Lord, divine, supreme, exalted, glorious above all creation (Rev. 4). This holiness of position makes people tremble and nations dread (Exod. 15:11-18; 1 Sam. 6:20; Ps. 68:35; 99:1-3).[4] In His position as Lord above all, at the top, God alone is holy, for He alone is God (Rev. 15:4). There is none holy like Him (1 Sam. 2:2). [English speakers, for an inspiring song on God's holiness, visit http://www.youtube.com/watch?v=9zl6Sf3Rt0s]

[1]*The Lord reigns, let the nations tremble; he sits enthroned between the cherubim, let the earth shake.* [2]*Great is the Lord in Zion; he is exalted over all the nations.* [3]*Let them praise your great and awesome name—he is holy* (Ps. 99:1-3).

God requires humans to respect His holiness of position. He is Lord—the Ruler of all in heaven and earth. How do we show that we respect God as holy—the Lord and God over all? Through our obedience we acknowledge that God is holy, high above all. But those who disobey God fail to recognize Him as holy. God told Moses to *speak* to the rock in the desert so water would come forth for Israel to drink. But Moses disobeyed God and struck the rock. By his disobedience, Moses showed that he did not think God was holy—worthy of obedience. Note God's response:

Q 8 ✎ *How does a person acknowledge that God is holy?*

Q 9 ✎ *Why is disobedience a sin against God's holiness?*

[9]*So Moses took the staff from the Lord's presence, just as he commanded him.* [10]*He and Aaron gathered the assembly together in front of the rock and Moses said to them, "Listen, you rebels, must we bring you water out of this rock?"* [11]*Then Moses raised his arm and struck the rock twice with his staff. Water gushed out, and the community and their livestock drank.* [12]*But the Lord said to Moses and Aaron, "Because you did not trust in me enough to honor me as holy in the sight of the Israelites, you will not bring this community into the land I give them."* [13]*These were the waters of Meribah, where the Israelites quarreled with the Lord and where he showed himself **holy** among them* (Num. 20:9-13).

Q 10 ✎ *Why will some who say Jesus is Lord (the Holy One over all) be sent to hell (Matt. 7:21-23; Luke 6:46-49)?*

To honor God as holy means to obey Him—to show in our actions that God is high and exalted above all. When Moses disobeyed God, this servant acted like *he* was in charge—like *he* was the one who gave the commands. Disobedience to God is rebellion against His holy position as Lord and God of the universe.

Q 11 ✎ *Who is blessed more, Mary, as the mother of Jesus, or those who obey the teachings of Jesus (Luke 11:28)? Explain.*

God requires us to acknowledge His holiness with our words *and* actions. Those who disobey God, by their actions, deny that He is holy.

B. God is holy in His actions—holy in all He does.

His mighty acts, judgments, laws, and decrees are completely holy—altogether just, righteous, and true.

Q 12 *In what sense is God holy in His actions? Illustrate this.*

> [4]*The King is mighty, he loves justice—you have established equity; in Jacob you have done what is just and right.* [5]*Exalt the Lord our God and worship at his footstool; he is holy* (Ps. 99:4-5).

Mary's song emphasizes that God is *holy* in all He *does*. She sings about God's holy and righteous actions as Savior and Judge.

Q 13 *How many actions does Mary mention as she emphasizes that God our Savior is holy?*

> [46]*And Mary said: "My soul glorifies the Lord* [47]*and my spirit rejoices in God my Savior,* [48]*for he has been mindful of the humble state of his servant. From now on all generations will call me blessed,* [49]*for the Mighty One has done great things for me— holy is his name.* [50]*His mercy extends to those who fear him, from generation to generation.* [51]*He has performed mighty deeds with his arm; he has scattered those who are proud in their inmost thoughts.* [52]*He has brought down rulers from their thrones but has lifted up the humble.* [53]*He has filled the hungry with good things but has sent the rich away empty.* [54]*He has helped his servant Israel, remembering to be merciful* [55]*to Abraham and his descendants forever, even as he said to our fathers"* (Luke 1:46-55).

C. God is holy in His nature—His being.

Holiness is one of the attributes or qualities of God. His being and essence are fully holy. He is holy in His ethics—the principles that govern His actions. His nature and character are 100 percent pure—unmixed with any trace of evil.

Q 14 *In what sense is God holy in His nature—His being? Illustrate this.*

Light illustrates God's holiness. *"God is light; in Him there is no darkness at all"* (1 John 1:5). Jesus revealed Himself to Paul as a light brighter than the sun at noon (Acts 9). Later, Paul wrote that God dwells in the light that no one can approach (1 Tim. 6:16). And the apostle John saw Jesus, blazing like the sun in all its brightness (Rev. 1:16). Later, he compared the Father's appearance to the stones of jasper and carnelian—which look like coals of fire (Rev. 4:3). In Scripture, darkness is often linked to evil. But light is a characteristic of God's holiness.

In a vision John saw four living creatures worshiping God on His throne.

> *"Day and night they never stop saying: 'Holy, holy, holy is the Lord God Almighty, who was, and is, and is to come"* (Rev. 4:8). This verse emphasizes the holiness of God. We may not be sure why the word *holy* occurs three times in this verse. But let it remind us that God is holy in three ways—holy in His position, actions, and nature. *"Holy, holy, holy is the LORD Almighty; the whole earth is full of his glory* (Isa. 6:3).

Q 15 *In which 3 ways is God holy? Illustrate each.*

Lesson 16

The Meaning of Sanctification—We Are Holy

Goal A: *Explain 3 ways in which believers are holy. Give examples.*
Goal B: *Explain the triangle of holiness, and how its sides relate to each other.*

A. We are holy in our position—our standing in Christ.

Dr. Horton wrote, "Positional sanctification is necessary before we can begin to live a holy life."[5] This is why the base of the triangle in Figure 5.4 is holiness of position. Holiness of position in Christ is the foundation for holy actions and holy character.

Holiness of position includes justification and regeneration. These two aspects of salvation are *simultaneous—they occur at the same time. The moment we believe, we are justified. At justification, God declares us holy in Christ—He counts us righteous and free from guilt. Justification refers to initial, *imputed* holiness.[6] To impute means to "credit with, attribute to, or ascribe to." The holiness that God credits to us, the holiness of Christ, is the same for each believer. This aspect of holiness is 100 percent perfect the moment of belief. In regard to imputed, credited holiness, the youngest believer is as holy as the oldest apostle. Still, our justification is not final until we reach heaven (Rom. 8:23-25).

Holiness of position includes justification (*imputed* holiness), and also regeneration (*imparted* holiness). At the new birth, we experience holiness. Our position changes from being outside of Christ to being in Christ.

In our position in Christ, we are justified, holy members of God's family. Through the cross, God makes our position of holiness possible. Without Christ's sacrifice on the cross, we would be unjustified—guilty, with the wrath of God upon us. And apart from Christ, we would be separated from God's presence—and separated from the divine power we need to live a holy life. So we thank God for our holiness of position, which includes justification and regeneration.

God justifies us as He welcomes us into His family. He seals us with His Spirit—a sign that He owns us (Eph. 1:13-14). Still, we must abide in Christ, walk in the Spirit, and run the race before us with patience. So at the end of our days, God will welcome us into His presence in heaven, forever! Then we will attain the holiness and righteousness for which we now believe, hope, and await. *"But by faith we eagerly await through the Spirit the righteousness for which we hope"* (Gal. 5:5). We are not home yet, but we are on the right road.

Like God, believers are holy in three ways. (Figure 5.4 Triangle).

In Christ

Glorification

B. Our Actions (Doing)   C. Our Condition (Being)

Holiness

A. Our Position (Standing)

Aspect of Holiness	Explanation	Scriptures
A. Our Position (Where we *stand* in Christ)	The cross is the key to our positional sanctification.[7]	1 Cor. 1:30 *You are in Christ Jesus, who has become for us wisdom from God—that is, our righteousness, holiness and redemption.* (Compare Rom. 1:22)
B. Our Actions (What we *do*)	Holiness means living separated *from* sin *to* God.	2 Cor. 7:1 *Let us purify ourselves from everything that contaminates body and spirit, perfecting holiness out of reverence for God.* Rom. 12:1 *Therefore, I urge you, brothers, in view of God's mercy, to offer your bodies as living sacrifices, holy and pleasing to God—this is your spiritual act of worship.* 1 Pet. 1:15-16 *Be holy in all you do.*
C. Our Condition (What we *are*)	This aspect of holiness focuses on our purity and character. Christ imparts this holiness to us by the Spirit. This is holiness we experience. It increases in us from the new birth to the new body, from regeneration to glorification.	1 Thess. 5:23 *May God himself, the God of peace, sanctify you through and through.* Rom. 6:19 (see 6:22) *Just as you used to offer the parts of your body in slavery to impurity and to ever-increasing wickedness, so now offer them in slavery to* [ever increasing] *righteousness leading to holiness* [of actions and condition].[8] 2 Cor. 3:18 *And we, who with unveiled faces all reflect the Lord's glory, are being transformed into his likeness with ever-increasing glory, which comes from the Lord, who is the Spirit.*

Figure 5.4   **Holiness (sanctification) includes three aspects: our position, our actions, and our condition.**

Q 16 ⟋ *What are 3 aspects or sides of our holiness (A–C)?*

Q 17 ⟋ *What does it mean to be holy in our position?*

OUR POSITION EMPHASIZES THAT WE ARE HOLY IN OUR STANDING. JESUS DIED FOR OUR SINS, FORGAVE US, AND IMPARTED NEW LIFE. WE ARE HOLY THROUGH *HIS* DEATH, BLOOD, AND SACRIFICE ON THE CROSS. WHEN JESUS SAID, *"IT IS FINISHED"* AND DIED, HE PAID THE PENALTY FOR OUR SINS, ONCE AND FOR ALL (HEB. 10:10). AND THROUGH THE NEW COVENANT OF HIS BLOOD, HE PROVIDED THE WAY FOR US TO BE JUSTIFIED AND BORN INTO HIS FAMILY—HOLY IN POSITION.

Here are some verses about holiness of position:

- *"To all in Rome who are loved by God and called to be saints"* (Rom. 1:7).
- *"It is because of him that you are in Christ Jesus, who has become for us wisdom from God—that is, our righteousness, holiness and redemption"* (1 Cor. 1:30).
- *"And this is what some of you were. But you were washed, you were sanctified, you were justified in the name of the Lord Jesus Christ and by the Spirit of our God"* (1 Cor. 6:11).
- *"We have been made holy through the sacrifice of the body of Jesus Christ once for all"* (Heb. 10:10).

Holiness of position emphasizes a *derived* holiness—a holiness that comes from a relationship. This means that things, people, places, and angels are holy in relation to a Holy God.

- The ground Moses walked on was holy because the Holy God was there (Exod. 3:5).
- The dishes and objects in the temple were holy because they were related to the Holy God.
- The Jerusalem on earth is called the holy city because it is the city where Jesus ministered, died, and rose from the dead (Matt. 4:5).
- The heavenly Jerusalem is holy because it is associated with the Holy God (Rev. 21:2).
- Israel was a holy nation because of belonging to God.
- Feast days and Sabbaths are holy because they are a part of God's calendar and decrees.
- Believers are called saints, holy ones, because we belong to God.

We are holy in our *position* because we are God's holy *possession*. We are holy because we belong to God. He has bought us, separated us from *sin and common things—for His special purposes. Nothing is holy in itself, but it becomes holy, sacred, and uncommon when related to God.[9]

The light of the moon is *derived* light. It is light that is possible only because the sun shines on it. Likewise, we are not the source of our holiness. We have this holiness only *in Christ* because He shares it with us. Take a few moments to reflect on your holy position. Be filled with wonder that the Holy God of the universe has redeemed you to be His holy child, forever. Give thanks for your holy position in Christ. Rejoice that you have been separated from all that is vile, common, and unclean, to fellowship with the Holy God and be filled with the Holy Spirit. Holiness is not just dutiful, it is beautiful. What a glory, honor, and privilege to be called God's holy people. Holiness of position is awesome!

B. We are holy in our actions—what we *do* as we serve Christ and others.

The base of the triangle affects all above it. Being holy in our position affects our actions, choices, ethics, character, lifestyle, and service. As *holy* people we hate and turn from what is wrong (Rom. 12:9). We choose to love, embrace, and practice what is right. Thus we fellowship with the Holy God and are able to serve others.

Q 18 ⟋ *Explain: The base of the triangle affects the two sides above it.*

Holiness of position emphasizes our standing. We are the justified, holy children of God. Holiness of actions emphasizes what Jesus does *with and through us*. Holy actions grow. Our holiness increases as we study and meditate on God's Word. Our holy actions and attitudes mature as we fellowship with the Holy God, are filled with the Holy Spirit, and walk in the Spirit. We begin at regeneration as infants in Christ. As children grow, they may look more and more like their parents. Likewise, as we grow in Christ, we become more like Him in holiness. At glorification, our holiness will be complete. For then we will be conformed to the likeness of Christ (Rom. 8:29).

Q 19 ⟋ *How does holiness in our actions differ from holiness in our position?*

Positional holiness is God's gift to us, through Christ. But as one writer notes, the gift of holiness becomes the task![10] God gives us holiness, but commands us to practice holy living. Holy actions—what we think, say, and do—are our task and response to God (Rom. 12:1). We practice holy living as we yield to and depend on His Holy Spirit in us. To be holy in our actions means to become like Jesus in all we do (Rom. 8:29). To be holy in our actions means to present our bodies as *living sacrifices,* and not conform any longer to the pattern of the world, but to be *transformed* by the renewing of our minds (Rom. 12:1-2a). This holy lifestyle is our gift to God. God gave us the gifts of justification and sonship—holiness of position. In response, we offer to God the thanksgiving of holy living. Holy living is our spiritual worship to God (Rom. 12:1-2a).

> [1]*Therefore, I urge you, brothers, in view of God's mercy, to offer your bodies as living sacrifices,* **holy** *and pleasing to God—**this is your spiritual act of worship**.* [2]*Do not conform any longer to the pattern of this world, but be transformed by the renewing of your mind* (Rom. 12:1-2a).

Q 20 ✎ *In the triangle of holiness, what do the bottom two corners emphasize?*

Our position of holiness begins in a moment at conversion, justification, and regeneration. But holiness is not just a fact, an act, or an event—it is a *way* of life. Those who are holy in position are those, and only those, who are also holy in their actions. Those who are washed and sanctified are the same ones who practice resisting the desires of the *flesh and submitting to the leadership of the Spirit. The promise of being cleansed by the blood of Jesus is only for those who walk in the light (1 John 1:6-7). When is it true that we are *dead to sin* (Rom. 6)? In practice, we are only dead to sin as we die to sin daily. Death to sin begins in a moment, when we are converted. But death to sin is a lifestyle. We are only dead to sin as we refuse sinful desires and are obedient to a higher power. So Christianity is always a combination of gift and task. In the triangle of holiness, the corners intersect. Our position is connected to both our actions and our condition. To be holy in our position, we must practice being holy in our actions. In Romans 6–8, Paul emphasizes that holy people live holy lives!

Q 21 ✎ *How does Paul in 1 Corinthians 6:9-10 compare with Spurgeon on Hebrews 12:14?*

Here are some verses about holiness in our actions. Note that these verses do **not** emphasize *justification*—what Christ provided *for* us on the cross. Rather, these verses emphasize an aspect of *sanctification*—holy living that Christ produces *through us,* as we submit to Him as our holy Lord, and walk in the Spirit.

- *"Let us purify ourselves from everything that *contaminates body and spirit,* **perfecting holiness** *out of reverence for God"* (2 Cor. 7:1).
- *"Offer your bodies as living sacrifices,* **holy** *and pleasing to God—this is your spiritual act of worship"* (Rom. 12:1).
- *"Follow after* **holiness**..." (Heb. 12:14, KJV).
- *"Be* **holy** *in all you do..."* (1 Pet. 1:15-16).
- *"If a man* **cleanses himself** [sanctifies himself] *from the latter, he will be an instrument for noble purposes, made holy, useful to the Master and prepared to do any good work"* (2 Tim. 2:21).

Q 22 ✎ *How would you respond to a person who said: "Holiness in me is God's responsibility, not mine"?*

All these five verses on holiness refer to our actions—our responsibility. They stress that we must turn away from what is wrong, and turn toward what is right. Scripture commands us to present ourselves as a living sacrifice, *holy* and pleasing to God (Rom. 12:1). Our holiness is based on what Jesus did *for* us on the cross, but it includes what we allow Jesus to do *in and through us.* Holiness includes living uprightly.

Q 23 ➚ *Contrast the ways sin and holiness affect us.*

Sin is the enemy of holiness. Sinners are children of the devil, but saints (the holy) are children of God. Understanding what sin does guides us to holiness. Sin destroys all of our senses. Sin decreases sight and pulls toward blindness. Sin numbs hearing and makes men deaf. Sin perverts the taste, causing men to confuse the sweet with the bitter. Sin hardens the touch and leads us to being "past feeling." All these are biblical comparisons. Sin blocks and chokes the senses of the spirit. Sin causes us to be insensitive and unable to fellowship with God. Sin creates calluses, and makes us unaware of our dangerous condition.[11]

In contrast, holiness does the opposite of what sin does. Holiness enhances all our senses. It enables us to see, hear, and taste well. Holiness enables us to feel the leading of God's Spirit. Holiness opens the senses of the spirit. It makes it possible for us to discern right from wrong, and live close to God.

C. We are holy in our condition—what we are in Christ.

The holiness of our *position* emphasizes that God justified us and made us His holy children. But holiness of *action* is about what Jesus does with and through us. In contrast, the holiness of our *condition* is what Jesus does *in* us. The New Testament explains that we participate in the divine nature (2 Pet. 1:4), and we *"share in his holiness"* (Heb. 12:10). Our condition of holiness begins at the new birth and is completed at glorification. Our nature is being changed into His image and likeness (Rom. 8:29).

Being is more important than doing. Our condition of holiness is more vital than witnessing, evangelizing, giving, and every other form of service. God wants us to *be* holy, not just *do* good deeds. For only as we become like Jesus can we do what brings glory to God.[12] A holy heart is like a spring that bubbles all the holy actions of life (Prov. 4:23; compare Matt. 15:10-20).

Being holy in our condition means conforming to God's nature (Rom. 8:29).[13] John Wesley wrote a lot about entire sanctification (also called perfect holiness, complete holiness, and Christian perfection). Wesley taught that perfect holiness is possible on earth, *instantaneously*, through an experience with God *after* being born again. In contrast, we believe that holiness begins in an instant at the new birth, but is *progressive* throughout life on earth. We are changed into the likeness of Christ little by little on earth, not all at once (2 Cor. 3:18). Although we do not agree with John Wesley on the timing of perfect holiness, his descriptions of holiness are helpful. Wesley taught that when we are completely holy, the *quality* of our love for God and man will not increase. If a person is completely holy, every thought, word, and deed is guided by pure love. Wesley helps us understand that being holy in our condition refers to the *quality* of our love, values, attitudes, and character.

Holiness of position is about our standing. Holiness of action is about doing. Holiness of condition is about being.

What is a holy person like within? When we say that we are holy in our condition, we mean that our hearts are pure. We mean that our nature is like Christ (Rom. 8:29). To be holy means to have attitudes, values, motives, and desires that are unselfish, pure, and unmixed. When we pray, "Father, help me to be more like you," we are asking God to make us more holy in our actions and in our hearts. Becoming more holy in our condition means becoming more like God.

How do we become more holy? Men refine metals like gold and silver to purify them. For example, gold, in its natural state, is mixed with rock that has no value. To refine gold, men put it in big metal pots and build a hot fire under it. As the fire melts the gold, impurities rise to the top. Then men skim them off. The metal that results from this process is *pure* gold, of great value. As fire refines gold, trials refine our faith (1 Pet. 1:7). Likewise, God refines our holiness through the trials of life, and through discipline or training (Heb. 12:10). He also makes us more holy through studying and meditating on the Bible, prayer, worship, and fellowship with other believers. The more time a person spends in a garden of flowers, the more he or she smells like flowers. And the more time we spend in God's presence, the more holy we become like Him. As standing in the presence of God caused Moses to glow, living in the presence of God causes us to reflect His holiness.

Q 24 ⟩ *How does holiness of condition differ from holiness of position?*

Q 25 ⟩ *Describe the heart of a holy person.*

Q 26 ⟩ *How does God purify us to be more holy?*

Q 27 ➤ *As a condition, holiness is the opposite of _____, as _____ is the opposite of _____.*

Q 28 ✎ *Which aspect of our holiness is perfect, and will never increase?*

Q 29 ✎ *Which aspects of our holiness increase as we grow in grace?*

Q 30 ✎ *What does the top corner of the triangle of holiness emphasize? Explain and illustrate this truth.*

Q 31 ✎ *How does holiness of position affect holiness in actions? Give examples.*

Q 32 ✎ *How does holiness of position affect holiness of condition? Give examples.*

As a condition, holiness is the opposite of sinfulness. As darkness represents sinfulness, light represents holiness. God is holy—He is light in whom there is no darkness at all. At conversion, God delivered us from the kingdom of darkness and brought us into the kingdom of the light. As God's children, we are in His kingdom of light and holiness.

Healthy children grow. The holiness of our *condition* is progressive—it grows. Our holy condition does not end at the new birth—it only begins there! The Corinthians had been sanctified, at the new birth, when they were justified. In their position, in Christ, they had perfect holiness. But Paul called the Corinthians mere infants in Christ. That is, their *condition* did not match their *position*.[14] They needed to grow and mature in grace and holiness. In heaven, when our holiness is complete, pure love will govern all our thoughts, words, motives, and deeds. We look forward to the day when our love for God and mankind will be wholly holy—unmixed with selfish desires. Meanwhile, we practice walking in the Spirit and submitting to Him. God enables us to please Him and become more holy, like Jesus (Rom. 8:29; 2 Cor. 3:18).

D. Our three aspects of holiness are connected

As the sides of the triangle connect at the corners, aspects of holiness are connected.

1. Our holy position in Christ is connected to our holy actions and holy nature.

As we said earlier, the base of the triangle affects all above it. Who we are affects what we do, and what we are. Holiness in actions and condition are not options for Christians. Holiness in *doing* and *being* prove that we are justified and in Christ. We know a tree by its fruit. As P. C. Nelson said, holiness of *condition* is the fruit of our *position* in Christ.[15] In contrast to the holy, Paul warned that the wicked, those who rebel like the devil, *"will not inherit the kingdom of God'* (Gal. 5:21; 1 Cor. 6:9). Therefore, we must cooperate with the Holy Spirit, and *"make every effort…to be holy"* (Heb. 12:14). As we submit to the Holy Spirit, He produces holy actions and holy attitudes.

[22] *"But the fruit of the* [Holy] *Spirit is love, joy, peace, patience, kindness, goodness, faithfulness,* [23]*gentleness and self-control* (Gal. 5:22-23a). (Those who show the fruit of the Holy Spirit are holy and godly, *like* God.)

Perfect holiness is the aim of saints on earth and the reward of saints in heaven.[16] Holiness of position inspires us to pursue holy actions and holy character.

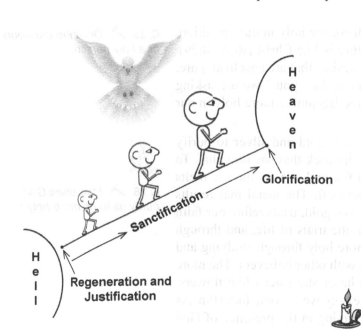

Regeneration and Justification — Sanctification — Glorification — Heaven — Hell

Figure 5.5   Romans 3:21–5:21 emphasizes justification—holiness and righteousness of position that God imputes (credits to us) through faith in Christ (see the base of the holiness triangle in Figure 5.4). Likewise, Romans 6–8 emphasizes sanctification—holiness and righteous doing and being (see the sides of the holiness triangle in Figure 5.4).

Romans 6–8 stresses the process of growing in the likeness of Christ. The imparted holiness of sanctification begins at regeneration, and reaches its highest level at glorification. In between the new birth and the new body, we perfect holiness—we increase in holy actions, holy attitudes, and holy character.

Some children of righteousness are babies in Christ, while others have grown to be more mature. Our glorious destiny is to become completely holy, like God the Son! Even now, the Spirit enables us to become more and more like our Savior (Rom. 8:29; 2 Cor. 3:18).[17]

Hebrews 12:14 says *"make every effort…to be holy; without holiness no one will see the Lord."* This verse emphasizes the top sides of the holiness triangle. About this verse Spurgeon said: "You will not gain holiness by standing still. Nobody ever grew holy without consenting, desiring, and agonizing to be holy. Sin will grow without sowing, but holiness requires hoeing. Follow holiness; for it will not run after you (Heb. 12:14). You must pursue it with determination, with eagerness, with perseverance, as a hunter pursues his prey."[18] Our holiness of position leads to holiness in actions and condition.

> SIN WILL GROW WITHOUT SOWING, BUT HOLINESS REQUIRES HOEING.

2. Our holy actions affect our holy nature.

In the triangle of holiness, two sides join together at the top. This reminds us that there is a close relationship between doing and being—between outer holiness and inner holiness.

Doing affects being. What we *do* affects what we *are*. Holy actions shape our hearts and character. For example, 2 Corinthians 7:1 tells us to *perfect holiness*. This verse emphasizes our actions. It teaches us to separate ourselves from evil, and purify ourselves from all that contaminates (defiles) body and spirit. Holiness in actions means choosing friends that are holy. It means separating ourselves from sinful relationships and evil entertainment. This holiness is continued consecration[19] of self, and it improves our *condition* of holiness.

Doing validates our standing. Holy actions prove that we have a holy position. Faith without works is dead (James 2:17). Holy actions prove that our faith is alive, and we are truly justified, holy in position.

3. Our holy nature affects our holy actions and our holy position.

Being affects doing. The heart is the wellspring of life (Prov. 4:23). The heart is the source of actions (Matt. 15:19). The more holy we are at heart, the more holy our actions become. A holy heart is a fountain and source of holy actions. As a good tree produces good fruit, a holy heart produces holy deeds (Matt. 12:33).

Being assures standing. The right side of the triangle affects the base. Our condition affects our position. Peter encouraged believers to increase in inner qualities of character. He promised that as we become more and more like God, we make our calling and election certain, and will never fall. In contrast, evil finds an easy entrance into the lazy and the lukewarm.[20] But growing in holiness of condition keeps us in holiness of position (2 Pet. 1:4-11). We cannot go two directions at the same time. Moving upward prevents sliding downward. Growing in grace and the likeness of Christ ensure safety. Nurturing our holy character and condition is one way we *keep ourselves in God's love* (Jude 21). Holiness of condition maintains holiness of position. 'Forward ever' assures 'backward never.'

> [4]*Through these he has given us his very great and precious promises, so that through them you may participate in the divine nature and escape the corruption in the world caused by evil desires.* [5]*For this very reason, make every effort to add to your faith goodness; and to goodness, knowledge;* [6]*and to knowledge, self-control; and to self-control, perseverance; and to perseverance, godliness;* [7]*and to godliness, brotherly kindness; and to brotherly kindness, love.* [8]*For **if you possess these qualities in increasing measure**, they will keep you from being ineffective and unproductive in your knowledge of our Lord Jesus Christ.* [9]*But if anyone does not have them, he is nearsighted and blind, and has forgotten that he has been cleansed from his past sins.* [10]*Therefore, my brothers, be all the more eager to make your calling and election sure. **For if you do these things, you will never fall**,* [11]*and you will receive a rich welcome into the eternal kingdom of our Lord and Savior Jesus Christ* (2 Pet. 1:4-11).

Q 33 *What effect do holy actions have on our holy nature and position? Illustrate this.*

Q 34 *How does our holy condition affect our holy actions?*

Q 35 *How do a holy heart and holy character affect our standing?*

Practice on the lesson:

Q 36 ✎ *Put each word or phrase in the proper column (or columns) below. Justification, imparted righteousness, godly character, imputed righteousness, consecration, glorification, right living, right standing, purity of heart, regeneration, sanctification.*

A. Holy Position	B. Holy Actions	C. Holy Condition

Figure 5.6   Practice matching theological words and phrases with three aspects of holiness (sanctification). Note: The purpose of this practice is not to memorize answers, but to analyze aspects of holiness. Various answers are correct. You will grow in understanding holiness as you explain your answers and discuss the answers with other students.

Q 37 ✎ *Put each verse in the proper column or columns below. Many of these verses belong in more than one column. So be ready to defend your choices. Matt. 5:8; 1 Thess. 4:3-4; Rev. 21:27; Heb. 12:10; 1 Pet. 1:15-16; Rom. 12:1; Rev. 22:11; 2 Cor. 3:18; Rom. 8:4; Eph. 4:24; Rom. 6:19; Rom. 1:2, 7; 2 Cor. 7:1; Heb. 10:10; 2 Tim. 2:21; Eph. 1:4; 1 Cor. 1:30; Gal. 5:16; Gal. 5:22-23.*

A. Holy Position	B. Holy Actions	C. Holy Condition

Figure 5.7   Practice matching Scriptures with three aspects of holiness (sanctification).

Conclusion: God is holy in three ways. *First*, He is holy in position, high above His creation. *Second,* He is holy in all His actions. And *third,* He is holy in His nature.

Likewise, we are holy in our position, actions, and condition.

The three sides of a triangle are connected to each other. The three aspects of our holiness affect each other.

Through His Word, His Spirit, and the ministry of His body (the Church), God lifts us into fellowship with Him, and gives Himself to us. As a result we grow in holiness, in His likeness (Eph. 4:15; 2 Cor. 3:18).[21]

We have studied three aspects of holiness. Together, these three aspects give us a balanced understanding of what it means to be sanctified and holy. To inherit the kingdom of God we must live in a holy relationship to the holy King.

Holiness of position, especially *justification,* is the theme of Romans 3:21–5:21.

Holy living, *sanctification,* is the theme of Romans 6–8.

Lesson **Keys to Right Living: Sanctification—Part 1 (Rom. 6:1-11)**

17

Goal A: *Answer the 2 questions Paul asks in Romans 6.*
Goal B: *Explain what it means to be united to Christ in His life and death. Apply this.*
Goal C: *Explain how water baptism illustrates our death and life with Christ.*

Setting

Q 38 ✎ *For a review and overview of Romans 6, complete Figure 5.8.*

In Romans 6–8, Paul continues to use a style of questions and answers. All of Romans 6 centers around two questions (Figure 5.8). Please read Romans 6 and answer the two questions. Then we will look closer at them in the three lessons that follow.

Rom.	Questions	Answers	Rom.
6:1	Shall we go on sinning so God can give more grace?		6:2 6:2-14
6:15	*Shall we sin because we are not under law but under grace?*		6:15-16 6:15-23

Figure 5.8   Two questions and answers in Romans 6

In Romans 6:1 Paul asks the question: Shall we go on sinning so God can give more grace? Then, he answers the question in Romans 6:2-14.

God's enemies practice *antinomianism, which is lawlessness. *Anti* is a Greek word that means "against." *Nomia* is a Greek word for "law." Anti-nomians are anti-law. They do not submit to God's law, rule, or authority. Antinomians are led by selfish, fleshly desires. And Paul's critics claimed he approved of antinomians. They claimed Paul taught that grace eliminates the need to obey God's laws about right and wrong.

Q 39 *What big question does Paul answer in Romans 6:1-14? Explain the answer.*

Paul emphasized that we are saved by grace, not law (Rom. 5:20-21). But Paul did not say that grace encourages us to sin more. Rather, Paul wrote that grace teaches us to stop sinning:

> [11]*For the grace of God that brings salvation has appeared to all men.* [12]*It teaches us to say "No" to ungodliness and worldly passions, and to live self-controlled, upright and godly lives in this present age* (Titus 2:11-12).

Romans 6 is about sanctification—righteous, holy living. In Romans 6, Paul explains six principles to help us live holy lives. These six principles are keys to help us succeed, not clubs to beat us down with guilt. Much of Romans 6 is about right thinking, which leads to right living. As we study these six keys to right living, we will relate them to the triangle of holiness. We want to move the truth of the triangle from your head to your heart. Now, let us study the first key—a mental key that leads to holy living.

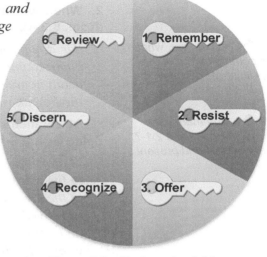

A. Holy Living Key 1: Remember that spiritually we are united to Jesus Christ—in His death and life (Rom. 6:1-11).

Figure 5.9   Six keys to right living in Romans 6

In Romans 6:1-2, Paul responds to his critics. They said he taught that grace leads us to sin more. Since Paul emphasized grace instead of law, his critics claimed that his message encouraged people to sin. Paul replied:

> [1]*What shall we say, then? Shall we go on sinning so that grace may increase?* [2]*By no means! We died to sin; how can we live in it any longer?* [3]*Or don't you know that all of us who were baptized into Christ Jesus were baptized into his death?* (Rom. 6:1-3).

Romans 6:1-3 emphasizes our holy position in Christ. According to Paul it is *impossible* for a believer to continue to live in sin. Why? Because we are united to Christ in His death and life. Let us examine these two aspects of our union with Christ—death and life.

1. When we united with Christ, we died to sin. Romans 6:1-14 emphasizes our relationship with Christ, which began at conversion. At the moment of conversion, we were born again, and baptized by the Spirit into the body of Christ. At the moment of conversion, we became one with Christ. The closer two people become, the more they share life.[22] A husband and wife become so close, so joined together, that the Bible describes them as one flesh. Likewise, in Christ, we are joined to Him spiritually and become *"members of his body"* (Eph. 5:30). As Paul writes, our union with Christ is *"a profound mystery"* (Eph. 5:32). Romans 6:1-14 emphasizes our new identity, united with Christ.

Q 40 *At water baptism, what does going down into the water illustrate? Explain.*

Paul says, *"We died to sin"* (Rom. 6:2). These words describe a change. Before Christ, we lived *alone,* without Christ, in sin. In sin we were separated from Christ, *"without hope and without God"* (Eph. 2:12). But when we received Christ as Savior and Lord and became His children, we died to sin and our old ways of sinful living. In our new position and relationship with Christ, we have our face toward what is right, and our backs to sin.

Q 41 *In Luke 6:32-36, with whom does Jesus contrast His followers? Explain.*

Some today teach that followers of Jesus are sinners—those who go on sinning. But Paul says, *"We died to sin."* One of the greatest contrasts possible is between sinners and followers of Jesus. Those who follow Jesus died to sin and become slaves of righteousness. Read Luke 6:32-34. With whom does Jesus contrast His followers three times?

32"If you love those who love you, what credit is that to you? Even 'sinners' love those who love them. 33And if you do good to those who are good to you, what credit is that to you? Even 'sinners' do that. 34And if you lend to those from whom you expect repayment, what credit is that to you? Even 'sinners' lend to 'sinners,' expecting to be repaid in full (Luke 6:32-34).

Sinners practice sin. But those united to Christ died to sin.

2. When we united with Christ, God raised us up to live a new life spiritually (Rom. 6:3-4).

Q 42 *At baptism, what does coming up out of the water illustrate? Explain.*

3Or don't you know that all of us who were baptized into Christ Jesus were baptized into his death? 4We were therefore buried with him through baptism into death in order that, just as Christ was raised from the dead through the glory of the Father, we too may live a new life [now] (Rom. 6:3-4).

At the moment we died to sin, we were born again, and we began to live a new, righteous life in Christ.

Q 43 *Summarize the contrast in Ephesians 2:1-7 about our past and present.*

*1As for you, you were dead in your transgressions and sins, 2in which you **used to live** when you followed the ways of this world and of the ruler of the kingdom of the air, the spirit who is now at work in those who are **disobedient**. 3All of us also **lived among them at one time**, gratifying the cravings of our sinful nature and following its desires and thoughts. Like the rest, we were by nature objects of wrath. 4But because of his great love for us, God, who is rich in mercy, 5made us **alive with Christ** even when we were dead in transgressions—it is by grace you have been saved. 6And God **raised us up** with Christ and seated us with him in the heavenly realms in Christ Jesus, 7in order that in the coming ages he might show the incomparable riches of his grace, expressed in his kindness to us in Christ Jesus* (Eph. 2:1-7).

Q 44 *What is the difference between freedom from the penalty of sin and freedom from the power of sin?*

Before we united with Christ, we were like slaves, prisoners of sin. Picture a slave, locked in prison and bound with chains. This slave has no freedom. The bars prevent him from leaving his cell. The chains make it impossible for the slave to be free. This picture illustrates our slavery to sin. Before Christ, we had no options, no choices, no freedom. We were powerless. Sin was our master. Then Jesus, our Saviour, came. He opened the door of our prison. He released us from our chains. For the first time in our lives, Jesus enabled us to be free, to serve righteousness instead of sin. Now, a new power rules us. God has given us a new nature, and new spiritual life.

Freedom from the power of sin is the theme of Romans 6–8. In Romans 3:21–5:21 Paul focused on justification, freedom from the *penalty* of sin. But in Romans 6–8 Paul emphasizes sanctification, freedom from the *power* of sin. Through our union with Christ, and the power of the Spirit, God enables us to live a victorious life—doing what is right, and avoiding what is wrong.

Q 45 *How does water baptism illustrate our death and life with Christ?*

3. Water baptism illustrates our death and life with Christ. It shows that we are united to His *death* and resurrection *life*.

As Romans 6:10 says, *"The death he died, he died* [in relation] *to sin once for all."* On the cross, Jesus died once and for all in relation to sin and its influence. He will not bear sin again. Likewise, when we went down into the water at baptism, this represented going into a grave and dying with Christ to sin. Now, we are united to Christ, and dead to the past life of sin.

And *"just as Christ was raised from the dead through the glory of the Father, we too may live a new life"* (Rom. 6:4). Earlier in Romans, we read that Abraham believed in God *"who gives life to the dead"* (Rom. 4:17). We also believe that God gives life to the dead, because He has given life to us. [4] *"...God, who is rich in mercy,* [5] *made us alive with Christ even when we were dead in transgressions—it is by grace you have been saved.* [6] *And God raised us up with Christ* (Eph. 2:4-6).

Each believer is united with the death and resurrection of Jesus. The *death* of Jesus provides justification (right standing) for us. And His resurrection *life* flows through us and enables sanctification (right living, Rom. 5:10).[23] Later, in Romans 8, Paul will talk about future glory. God will reveal this glory in us at the Resurrection (Rom. 8:18-30). But throughout Paul's writing we find an overlap of the present and the future. Theologians call this overlap the *already/not yet. Already* we have died with Christ to sin. We have *not yet* received a new, glorious body. But *already* His resurrection power flows through us in *glory,* giving us power to live a new, holy life (Rom. 6:4).[24] Jesus said that at His Second Coming *"the righteous will shine like the sun in the kingdom of their Father"* (Matt. 13:43). We have *not yet* reached that level of glory. But *already* we are the light of the world (Matt. 5:14). And *even now* we have received a measure of His glory. For the followers of Jesus live differently than sinners. Sinners are characterized by darkness, but we live as *children of light* (Eph. 4:17–5:20). *Already* we shine like stars as blameless and pure, *"children of God without fault in a crooked and depraved generation"* (Phil. 2:15). Our destiny is to be completely changed into the likeness and image of Christ (Rom. 8:29). But *already* and *even now* we are being changed into His likeness, from glory to glory (2 Cor. 3:18). Through our union with Christ, we die to sin and *"put on the new self, created to be like God in true righteousness and holiness"* (Eph. 4:24). Paul will emphasize this truth more in Romans 8:29. But our holy living is so glorious that he introduces it in Romans 6:4.

Water baptism gives us a picture. It shows that we are *united* to Christ. We died with Christ to sin, and went down into a watery grave with Him. Then we arose with Him to live a new, holy life. This *holy union* inspires, compels, and enables us to stop sinning— to leave our old ways behind and live a holy life, now.

> [5]*If we have been united with him like this in his death, we will certainly also be united with him in his resurrection* [now]. [6]*For we know that our old self was crucified with him so that the body of sin* [sins of the body] *might be done away with, that we should no longer be slaves to sin—* [7]*because anyone who has died has been freed from sin.* [8]*Now if we died with Christ, we believe that we will also live with him* [now, daily]. [9]*For we know that since Christ was raised from the dead, he cannot die again; death no longer has mastery over him.* [10]*The death he died, he died to sin once for all; but the life he lives, he lives to God.* [11]***In the same way****, count yourselves* ***dead*** *to sin but* ***alive*** *to God in Christ Jesus* [now] (Rom. 6:5-11).

In Romans 6, Paul stresses holy actions based on our union with Christ. Holy thinking is a key to victory. Let us remind ourselves often of our holy position. We are united with Christ—one with Him, spiritually. As He died to sin, we died to sin. As He rose to a new life, we rise to live a new life in Him, today. Our union with Christ enables and guides us to be faithful to Him, our Lord and Savior. The Lordship of Christ demands that we serve *Him* rather than the old life of *sin.*[25]

> ╔══════════════════╗
> ║ SALVATION IS   ║
> ║ LIKE MARRIAGE IN ║
> ║ SEVERAL WAYS.   ║
> ╚══════════════════╝

Salvation is like marriage. Marriage begins with an event—a special time when two people choose to live together for life. Marriage follows a decision, and includes a ceremony. This ceremony is a public announcement of a big change. After deciding to marry, two people make

Q 46 How does our union with Christ affect the way we live now? Give examples.

Q 47 How is our union with Christ like marriage? Explain.

vows to each other. They promise to turn away from other lovers, and be faithful to each other. Marriage customs vary in each culture. But all who marry do things to remind themselves that they are married. Some exchange rings to wear the rest of their lives. Many join their names together as Mr. and Mrs. _____, as the wife exchanges her last name for the last name of her husband. Often, those who marry take photos or give gifts. It is important for married people to remind themselves that they are united, because being married demands a new style of living. Likewise, salvation begins with the decision to receive Christ. We are converted and united to Christ. We commit to live by His teachings, and submit to His Spirit within us. And soon after conversion is the public ceremony of water baptism.

Orlando married, after a history of sinful living. Soon, an old girlfriend saw him in town. She went to him, smiled, and said, "I have not been with you in a long time. Let us spend some time together." "No," he replied. "Now I am married. I cannot live like I lived in the past. Marriage requires me to be faithful to my wife." Then he turned and walked away from his old friend.

Q 48 *How does this first key, principle A, help us to live a holy life?*

It is important for us believers to remind ourselves that we are "married" to Christ. We are united to him in a special relationship for life. In Romans 7:1-6, Paul will write more about our *marriage* to Christ. Also, in other passages, he uses marriage to illustrate our relationship to Christ (1 Cor. 6:17; 2 Cor. 11:2; Eph. 5:22-23). Paul often writes that we are *in Christ* and *with Christ*. Our salvation, our forgiveness, our holy living, and our eternal life are possible because we are united with Christ. Let us remind ourselves often that we are united with Christ.

> RIGHT THINKING HELPS ENABLE RIGHT LIVING.[26]

Q 49 *What does the lesson about Napoleon illustrate?*

Napoleon was a famous general in France. One night, he could not sleep and was walking around the camp of soldiers. He came to a soldier who was sleeping during his time to guard. Napoleon guarded for him, beside the sleeping soldier. Later, when the soldier awoke, Napoleon (who could call 10,000 people by name) asked, "Soldier, what is your name?" The sleepy soldier replied, "My name is Napoleon, the same as your name." The stern general replied, "Soldier, change your conduct, or change your name." Likewise, we are called Christians, united with Christ. This must affect the way we live.

> *God's solid foundation stands firm, sealed with this inscription: "The Lord knows those who are his," and, "Everyone who confesses the name of the Lord must turn away from wickedness"* (2 Tim. 2:19).

Remember often that you are married to Jesus, spiritually—dead to sin and alive in Christ. Right thinking leads to right living. That we are dead to sin is not a fixed, static fact. Rather, we are only dead to sin and alive to God as we choose to resist sinful desires and obey God's Spirit.[27]

Q 50 *How is "self-talk" related to right living?*

Self-talk should be a holy action. The way we talk to ourselves is powerful. The Psalmist often spoke to his soul: *"Why are you downcast, O my soul?"* (Ps. 42:5). Then, he guided his soul to trust in God. Likewise, Paul told believers to talk to themselves. We must remind ourselves often that we are dead to sin and alive in Christ. We are united with Christ. We live hand in hand with Him. This union and bold

> THE WAY WE TALK TO OURSELVES IS POWERFUL.

declaration of truth helps us rise above temptations to sin. Right actions flow from right thinking. Turn your back to temptation and your face to Jesus. If temptation knocks at the door, take Jesus with you to answer it. Include Him in all you do. Abide in Him. Live *in Christ*. And remind yourself often of your holy position. We are united to Jesus Christ and are never alone.

Keys to Right Living: Sanctification—Part 2 (Rom. 6:12-14)

Goal A: *Explain the importance of resisting sin, and explain ways we do this.*
Goal B: *Contrast offering ourselves for bad and good purposes. Give examples.*

Q 51 *What key question is Paul answering in Romans 6:1-14?*

Rom.	Questions	Answers	Rom.
6:1	Shall we go on sinning so God can give more grace?		6:2 6:2-14

We are studying six keys to righteous living. In Lesson 17 we studied the first key:

A. Holy Living Key 1: Remember that spiritually we are united to Jesus Christ—in His death and life (Rom. 6:1-11).

Now let us continue with the second key or principle for living in a righteous relationship with God.

B. Holy Living Key 2: Resist sin, temptations, and the devil—so you can remain free (Rom. 6:12).

Do not let sin reign in your mortal body so that you obey its evil desires (Rom. 6:12).

Romans 6:12 emphasizes holiness in action. Resisting is active, not passive. Paul continues to talk about our responsibilities—things we must do. He is giving us keys to live holy, but we must use the keys. We are saved by grace, but we must *"stand fast therefore in the liberty by which Christ has made us free"* (Gal. 5:1 NKJV).

Is the nation you live in free? Or is it a slave, conquered by others? If your nation is free, its citizens must resist those who want to conquer it. Free nations only remain free as they protect their borders, guard their government, and care for the rights of their citizens. There are always greedy people who want to conquer others. The price of freedom is resisting those who want to make us slaves.

Each believer is in a spiritual war to remain free. Satan and sin want to make us slaves again. Even though we are freed from sin, we live in a sinful world. Even though we are God's children, we must guard against sinful desires of the flesh and the world. Romans declares that we *"have been set free from sin"* (Rom. 6:22). We died with Christ, as water baptism showed. And *"anyone who has died has been freed from sin"* (Rom. 6:7). Sin is not our master any longer (Rom. 6:14). We are free in Christ, and called to serve Him. But we must protect our freedom. To remain free, we must resist evil. Peter warns:

[8]*Be self-controlled and alert. Your enemy the devil prowls around like a roaring lion looking for someone to devour.* [9]*Resist him, standing firm in the faith* (1 Pet. 5:8-9).

How does sin work? It seeks to conquer as much territory as possible. As a Christian, picture your heart as a battlefield. Is all of it free? Have you stopped the enemy at the borders? Sin is an enemy that will attack at any weak point. Sin will try to enter through doors of fear, anger, bitterness, unforgiveness, greed, or lust. As believers, we must resist sin. Hospitality is good to practice with friends. But we should not open the door to sin and welcome it into our lives. The Bible teaches us to resist the devil and resist evil.

Submit yourselves, then, to God. Resist the devil, and he will flee from you (James 4:7).

Resist evil thoughts that are temptations to sin. Temptation is not sin. Even Jesus was tempted, but He did not sin. Sin occurs when we welcome temptation and agree to it. If a person likes a piece of candy, he will turn it over and over in his mouth. If he does not

Q 52 *What are the first 2 keys to right living (Rom. 6)?*

Q 53 *What must free nations and Christians do to remain free (Rom. 6)?*

Q 54 *Since sin is not our master, does it leave us alone (Rom. 6)? Explain.*

Q 55 How should
believers respond to
temptation?

like it, he will spit it out. Treat sinful thoughts like a piece of candy you do not like. Love what God loves and hate what He hates. When an evil thought comes to you, do not turn it over and over in your mind—like a piece of candy in your mouth. Spit it out! You cannot prevent a bird from flying over your head. But you can prevent it from building a nest in your hair. Do not submit to evil. Resist it, and you will remain free. Resist evil through the blood of Jesus, the Word of God, the grace of God, prayer, and the power of the Spirit. Resist sin as Joseph resisted Potiphar's wife. Say "No" to sin. Do not shake hands with sin and talk with it. Resist it. Hate sin. Run from it.

Paul resisted evil by holding *"weapons of righteousness in the right hand and in the left"* (2 Cor. 6:7). He used such weapons as purity, understanding, patience, kindness, living in the Holy Spirit, love, truthful speech, and the power of God (2 Cor. 6:6-7; see also Eph. 6:10-18).

Nehemiah and those with him rebuilt the walls of Jerusalem in 52 days. This was possible because God gave them grace, and they resisted evil.

[15]*When our enemies heard that we were aware of their plot and that God had frustrated it, we all returned to the wall, each to his own work.* [16]*From that day on, half of my men did the work, while the other half were equipped with spears, shields, bows and armor. The officers posted themselves behind all the people of Judah* [17]*who were building the wall. Those who carried materials did their work with one hand and held a weapon in the other,* [18]*and each of the builders wore his sword at his side as he worked. But the man who sounded the trumpet stayed with me* (Neh. 4:15-18).

[21]*So we continued the work with half the men holding spears, from the first light of dawn till the stars came out.* [22]*At that time I also said to the people, "Have every man and his helper stay inside Jerusalem at night, so they can serve us as guards by night and workmen by day."* [23]*Neither I nor my brothers nor my men nor the guards with me took off our clothes; each had his weapon, even when he went for water* (Neh. 4:21-23).

Q 56 What lesson should
we learn from the camel
illustration?

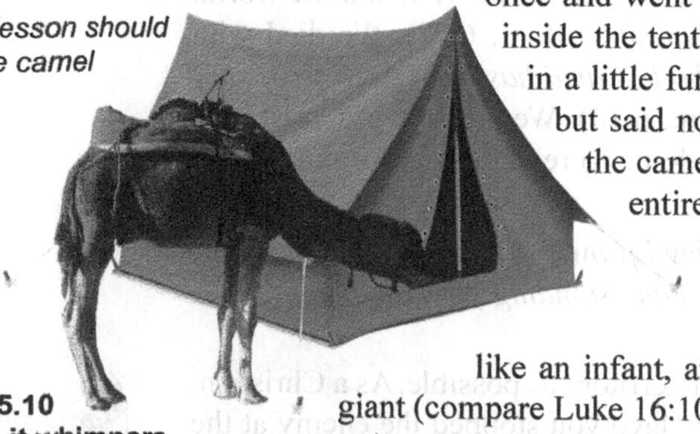

On a cold night, a camel looked for a warmer place. He stuck his nose in a tent. The owner resisted, and yelled "Get out, camel! This tent is not for you." The camel left at once and went on to the next tent. Slowly, it poked only its nose inside the tent. No one rebuked it. So the camel pushed its head in a little further, until its eyes were in the tent. Some noticed, but said nothing, thinking it was cute. Slowly, little by little, the camel kept pushing its way into the tent. In the end, the entire tent fell down. Allow sin to take an inch, and it will take a mile. Give sin a centimeter, and it will take a kilometer. Resist sin in its smallest forms and earliest stages. Resist sin when it whimpers like an infant, and you will conquer it later, though it roars like a giant (compare Luke 16:10). Practice being righteous in the little temptations, and your character will become righteous for the big temptations.

Figure 5.10
**Resist sin when it whimpers
like an infant, and you will
conquer it later, though it
roars like a giant.**

As a man and wife walked away from their home, their small dog followed them. The wife smiled and said sweetly to the dog, "Go home, we do not want you to follow." The little dog wiggled its tail, and then sat down, as if it did not understand. She petted it and said in a soft voice, "You cute little puppy, go back to the house." Then they turned and walked away, but the little dog followed. Suddenly, the husband turned and yelled in a loud voice "Get!" At once the dog turned and ran home. When you resist sin, do not smile at it, pet it, and whisper in kind words that it should leave. Speak to sin in angry words of authority, and mean what you say.

Resisting evil is an important skill and attitude for success. Do you have a garden? You must resist the things that will destroy it, such as weeds, birds, and wild animals. Do you have money, a job, a privilege, or possessions? You must resist the temptation to be lazy or you will lose many things of value (Prov. 10:4). Do you live in a home? Resist thieves, or they will steal your possessions (Matt. 24:43). Are you a young man or woman who is a virgin? Guard your virginity as a gift for the one you marry, and resist those who want to steal it. Are you free from sin and alive in Christ? You must resist sin, or it will conquer you, make you a slave, and steal your inheritance. What did Samson think would happen when he laid his head in Delilah's lap (Judges 16)? Do your small part. Resist evil and depend on God. Then He will enable you to stand firm and remain free.

Q 57 *Is resisting enemies and evil a part of life? Give illustrations.*

Resist evil. *"**Do not** let sin reign in your mortal body so that you obey its evil desires"* (Rom. 6:12).

C. Holy Living Key 3: <u>Offer</u> the parts and abilities of your body to God— not to sin (Rom. 6:13-14).

Paul continues to talk about holy actions.

Q 58 *What are the first 3 keys to right living in Romans 6?*

[13]*Do not offer the parts of your body to sin, as instruments of wickedness, but rather offer yourselves to God, as those who have been brought from death to life; and offer the parts of your body to him as instruments of righteousness.* [14]*For sin shall not be your master, because you are not under law, but under grace* (Rom. 6:13-14).

These verses contrast instruments (tools) of wickedness, and tools of righteousness. A tool is neutral—neither bad nor good. We may use a tool for a bad purpose or a good purpose. We may use a hammer to build a house, or break into a house. A pencil is an instrument or tool—neither bad nor good. We may use a pencil to write words of criticism, or words of encouragement. Likewise, the parts and abilities of the body are living tools. We may use them to do bad or good.

Many have offered the parts and abilities of their bodies for evil. Adam and Eve used their hands to pick fruit that God forbade. Cain used his strength to kill his brother. Canaan used his eyes as tools to look at his naked father. Lot's wife used her eyes to gaze at Sodom. Lot's daughters used their minds to plan evil, and their bodies to commit sexual sin with their father. Balaam used the insights God gave him to cause Israel to stumble. Samson used his body to have sex with Delilah. David used his eyes to lust after Bathsheba, his mind to plan her husband's death, his hands to write an order to kill Uriah, and his body to commit adultery. The Bible records many examples of those who used the parts and abilities of their bodies for evil.

Q 59 *Complete Figure 5.11.*

Scripture	People	Explanation of using the parts or abilities of the body for evil
Matt. 14	Herodias	
John 12:6		
Matt. 28:11-15		
1 Cor. 5:1		
Your choice		

Figure 5.11 **Practice giving examples of those who offered themselves for evil purposes.**

In contrast, the Scriptures tell of many who used their body parts and abilities for good. Noah used his hands to build an ark. Abraham used his hands to build altars to God. Moses used his small talents and abilities so God could lead a nation to freedom. Gideon used his strength to tear town an idol and defeat an enemy. David used his skill to kill a giant.

Q 60 *Complete Figure 5.12.*

Scripture	People	Explanation of using the parts or abilities of the body for good
Acts 1:8		
Acts 9:36-40		
Acts 21:10-11		
Your choice		
Your choice		

Figure 5.12   Practice giving examples of those who offered themselves for good purposes.

Each person must choose. We either offer ourselves to serve sin or Jesus Christ.

A rich man was drowning. A poor man jumped into the water and pulled the rich man to safety. To show his thanks, the rich man offered the poor man a small coin. May none of us be like that rich man. Jesus has brought us *"from death to life"* (Rom. 6:13). Let us show that we are grateful by offering Him our bodies and abilities to serve Him.

Q 61 *Complete Figure 5.13.*

Scripture	Explanation
Job 31:1	
Matt. 22:37-38	
Rom. 12:1-2	
Gal. 5:16	
2 Tim. 2:20-21	

Figure 5.13   Scriptures about offering ourselves for good purposes

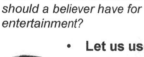

Romans 6:13 commands us:

Do not offer the parts of your body to sin, as instruments of wickedness, but rather offer yourselves to God, as those who have been brought from death to life; and offer the parts of your body to him as instruments of righteousness.

Q 62 *What does offering ourselves as a living sacrifice to God include?*

Q 63 *What standards should a believer have for entertainment?*

To offer our bodies as a living sacrifice means to give all of ourselves to God. This includes what we see, hear, touch, think, feel, and choose. Let us offer to God every aspect of our lives.

- **Let us use our <u>eyes</u>** to read the Bible, see the lost and those in need, watch entertainment that glorifies God and edifies the soul, enjoy the beautiful and holy things God has created. Let us turn our eyes away from evil people and evil entertainment (Job 31:1). Set holy standards for yourself and your family. Refuse to watch anything that has nudity or profanity (1 Pet 2:11).

- **Let us use our <u>ears</u>** to listen to godly music, Scripture, good conversations, and wholesome discussions. Let us close our ears to worldly music, gossip, and vile entertainment.

- **Let us use our <u>hands</u>** to help those in need, pick up the Bible and helpful books, pray for the sick, and do good deeds. Let us never use our hands in a way that shames God or causes someone to stumble.

- **Let us use our <u>minds</u>** to think about Scripture, love, forgiveness, worship, and blessing. Let us use our minds to hate what is wrong and love what is right. Let us never use our minds to plan evil, or meditate on evil.

- **Let us use our <u>heart</u>** and emotions to worship God and celebrate experiences that are holy.

- **Let us use our <u>wills</u>** to choose thoughts, actions, and relationships that honor God.

Response: Choose a song you know about offering yourself completely to God. Sing it and worship the Lord. Offer yourself to Him anew today. The decision to glorify God with our bodies and abilities is something we should do each day. The longer we serve Him, the more we love Him.

Lesson 19 — Keys to Right Living: Sanctification—Part 3 (Rom. 6:15-23)

Goal A: *Explain: All people are slaves to something.*
Goal B: *Defend this statement: The bad get worse and the good get better.*
Goal C: *Contrast the results of serving sin and serving righteousness.*

Q 64 ➘ *For a review and overview of Romans 6, complete Figure 5.14.*

Rom.	Questions	Answers	Rom.
6:1	Shall we go on sinning so God can give more grace?		6:2 6:2-14
6:15	*Shall we sin because we are not under law but under grace?*		6:15-16 6:15-23

Figure 5.14   Paul answers two questions in Romans 6.

Q 65 ➘ *Complete Figure 5.15 on 6 keys for holy living in Romans 6. (Write the first word of the principle, then state the whole principle.)*

We have studied the first three keys (A–C) for living in a right relationship with God. In this lesson we will look at the last three keys (D–F) in Romans 6.

D. Holy Living Key 4: <u>Recognize</u> that each person is a slave—of sin or righteousness (Rom. 6:15-18).

15What then? Shall we sin because we are not under law but under grace? By no means! 16Don't you know that when you offer yourselves to someone to obey him as slaves, you are slaves to the one whom you obey—whether you are slaves to sin, which leads to death, or to obedience, which leads to righteousness? 17But thanks be to God that, though you used to be slaves to sin, you wholeheartedly obeyed the form of teaching to which you were entrusted. 18You have been set free from sin and have become slaves to righteousness (Rom. 6:15-18).

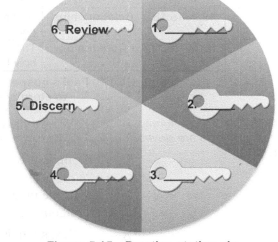

Figure 5.15   Practice stating six keys to right living (Rom. 6).

The Bible often divides people into two groups: those for Christ, and those against Him (Matt. 12:30); the wise virgins and the foolish virgins (Matt. 25:1-13); faithful servants and unfaithful servants (Matt. 25:14-30); the sheep and the goats (Matt. 25:31-46); slaves of sin and slaves of righteousness (Rom. 6:15-18).

Paul divides people into two groups with the metaphor (comparison) of slavery. Some say that 85 percent of the people in Rome were slaves or children of slaves.[28] So Paul's readers were familiar with slavery. But it must have shocked them when he wrote that even the free are a type of slave.[29]

For Paul, the *gospel* refers to all he preached and taught. As Guthrie says, the gospel includes the moral and ethical teachings of the Law (1 Tim. 1:8-11).[30] Fee notes that the gospel is the *"source and measure"* of healthy teaching.[31] Bruce affirms that the gospel message includes the Second Coming of Christ to judge the world and complete His saving work.[32] The *gospel* does not end with Romans 5! It includes Romans 6–16, and *all* doctrines of the New Testament.

Q 66 ➘ *Sin leads to _____, but obedience leads to _____ (Rom. 6:16).*

Q 67 ➚ *Was slavery common in the Roman Empire? Explain.*

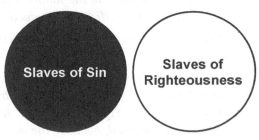

**Figure 5.16
There are only two types of people on earth:
slaves of sin and
slaves of righteousness.**

In Romans, Paul explains several topics of his gospel (Figure 5.17).

Romans	Topic of Paul's Gospel	Teaching of Paul's Gospel	Romans
		Romans: The Gospel According to Paul	
1:1-17	Introduction	Paul's gospel reveals the power of God for salvation, for all who believe—those who live by faith from start to finish.	1:16-17
1:18–3:20	Sin	All have sinned—disobeyed God. As sinners, both Jews and Gentiles are objects of God's wrath.	2:5; 3:9
3:21–5:21	Justification	In Christ, God provides righteousness <u>for us</u>—pardon from the *penalty* of sin.	
6–8	Sanctification	In Christ, God produces righteousness <u>in us</u>—freedom from the power of sin. True children of God are controlled by the Spirit, not the flesh. Those who love God are predestined to become more and more like Jesus, including glorification—perfection in heaven.	6:1-2, 11-14, 15-23; 8:4, 9 8:28-30
9–11	Election	God *chooses* all Jews and Gentiles who respond to His call of salvation in Christ. Anyone who trusts in Him will never be ashamed.	9:33; 10:11
12:1–15:13	Relationships	God requires righteousness <u>among us</u>—living holy lives, loving Him and others.	12:1-2
15:14–16:27	Conclusion	Through the gospel we become an offering acceptable to God, made holy by the Holy Spirit who fills and guides us.	15:16

Figure 5.17   Paul's gospel spans from God's decision to save us (before Creation, Eph. 1:4) to eternity in heaven or hell (Rom. 2:7-11; 2 Thess. 1:5-10).

Q 68 ↖ *Do you agree that all people are slaves? Explain.*

We are slaves to the one we obey. In the past, we were all slaves of sin. We *"used to be slaves of sin"* (Rom. 6:17). Back then, we had no choice. We were born sinners—slaves of sin. But we chose to obey the gospel and receive Jesus as Savior and Lord. Now, we *"have been set free from sin and have become slaves to righteousness"* (Rom. 6:18). To continue practicing sin is to return to bondage all over again.[33] But we remain slaves of righteousness as we obey Jesus Christ.

Jesus taught that we are slaves to the one we obey.

Q 69 ↖ *How can we recognize a person's master?*

[31]*To the Jews who had believed him, Jesus said, "If you hold to my teaching, you are really my disciples.* [32]*Then you will know the truth, and the truth will set you free."* [33]*They answered him, "We are Abraham's descendants and have never been slaves of anyone. How can you say that we shall be set free?"* [34]*Jesus replied, "I tell you the truth, everyone who sins is a slave to sin.* [35]*Now a slave has no permanent place in the family, but a son belongs to it forever.* [36]*So if the Son sets you free, you will be free indeed"* (John 8:31-36).

The apostle John divided people into two groups: those who serve sin, and those who serve Christ.

Q 70 ↖ *Do followers of Christ live like sinners— slaves of sin? Explain.*

[6]*No one who lives in him keeps on sinning. No one who continues to sin has either seen him or known him.* [7]*Dear children, do not let anyone lead you astray. He who does what is right is righteous, just as he is righteous.* [8]*He who does what is sinful is of the devil, because the devil has been sinning from the beginning. The reason the Son of God appeared was to destroy the devil's work.* [9]*No one who is born of God will continue to sin, because God's seed remains in him; he cannot go on sinning, because he has been born of God.* [10]*This is how we know who the children of God are and who the children of the devil are: Anyone who does not do what is right is not a child of God; nor is anyone who does not love his brother* (1 John 3:6-10).

Encourage yourself. Remember that you are a slave of righteousness and Jesus Christ. *"No one can serve two masters"* (Matt. 6:24). Right thinking about our holy calling leads to holy actions and holy character.

E. Holy Living Key 5: <u>Discern</u> that the bad get worse and the good get better (Rom. 6:19).

Just as you used to offer the parts of your body in slavery to impurity and to ever-increasing wickedness, so now offer them in slavery to righteousness leading to holiness (Rom. 6:19).

All people are works in process. No one stands still for long. We are either moving forward or backward, up or down. The bad become worse and the good get better. Let us examine the two parts of this principle.

Slaves of sin get worse. Sinners will become worse tomorrow than they are today. Paul wrote that sinners are slaves of *"ever-increasing wickedness"* (Rom. 6:19). As a log decays little by little and becomes more and more rotten, a sinner sinks lower and lower in sin.

Q 71 ↖ *Give 3 illustrations of the principle: Slaves of sin get worse.*

People do not fall into sin, like a man falls off a cliff. Rather, Jesus said people walk to destruction one step at a time on the broad road (Matt. 7:13). Do you see an alcoholic—a slave of alcohol? He began with one drink. Do you know a person addicted to drugs? He began on a different level, with one smoke of marijuana, one pill, one drink, or one needle. Have you seen a person dying from sexual diseases? There was a time when he was strong and healthy. Sin is a cruel master. It will take you farther than you want to go, keep you longer than you want to stay, and charge you more than you want to pay. Sinners are like people on stairs—each step takes them down one more level. Review Romans 1:21-32. Sin is a stairway whose steps lead down into deeper darkness and bondage. The good become better, but the bad become worse.

Judas is an example of what sin does to a person. At first Judas sinned only a little. Perhaps he stole just one coin from the purse he carried. But like yeast, sin increases. Like a cancer, it spreads. As time went on, stealing changed from an event to a habit for Judas (John 12:6). Sin became bolder. It moved from a private place to a public place—from a secret sin to a meeting to sell Jesus. Sin began in the shadows, but ended in the street. At first, there was only a little room for sin in the heart of Judas. But in the end, Satan himself filled the heart of Judas (Luke 22:3; John 13:27). People should discern that those who choose the beginning of a road choose its end.

Slaves of righteousness get better. In contrast to a sinner, a saint (any person following Christ) increases in righteousness. As a healthy child grows in size, a healthy child of God grows in grace. Believers are not perfect. One wise person said, "God is not finished with me yet." Another said, "He is still working on me." As believers, we do not claim to be all we should be. We do not know as much as we ought to know (1 Cor. 8:2). And we do not behave as well as we could behave. Believers may sin from time to time. At such times God forgives us as we confess our sins, repent, and turn from sin to God (1 John 1:9). If any believer sins, we have an *advocate—one who speaks in our defense—with the Father (1 John 2:1). It is possible for a weak believer to get entangled in a sin. Paul wrote: *"Brothers, if someone is caught in a sin, you who are spiritual should restore him gently. But watch yourself, or you also may be tempted"* (Gal. 6:1).

No follower of Jesus is perfect. But all who follow Him are growing in grace. We are *"perfecting holiness out of reverence for God"* (2 Cor. 7:1). Believers are being *"built up,"* growing and maturing unto the *"whole measure of the fullness of Christ"* (Eph. 4:12-13) Paul tells us to offer the parts of our body *"in slavery to righteousness <u>leading to</u> holiness"* (Rom. 6:19). Obeying Romans 6:19 leads us to live a life that is more holy. As slaves of righteousness, we are growing in grace. Consider these Scriptures that describe spiritual growth:

- [3]*"...we also rejoice in our sufferings, because we know that suffering produces perseverance; [4]perseverance, character; and character, hope"* (Rom. 5:3-4).

- *"For those God foreknew he also predestined to be conformed to the likeness of his Son"* (Rom. 8:29). God is changing us to be more and more like Jesus. The good become better.

- [2]*"Consider it pure joy, my brothers, whenever you face trials of many kinds, [3]because you know that the testing of your faith develops perseverance. [4]Perseverance must finish its work so that you may be mature and complete, not lacking anything"* (James 1:2-4).

- [5]*"For this very reason, make every effort to add to your faith goodness; and to goodness, knowledge; [6]and to knowledge, self-control; and to self-control, perseverance; and to perseverance, godliness; [7]and to godliness, brotherly kindness; and to brotherly kindness, love. [8]For if you possess these qualities in increasing measure, they will keep you from being ineffective and unproductive in your knowledge of our Lord Jesus Christ"* (2 Pet. 1:5-8).

Q 72 *Does Romans 6:19 encourage you? Whose slave are you?*

Encourage yourself with the truth of Romans 6:19. As you follow Jesus, you will grow in grace and holy living. We become slaves to habits. Each time we give in or submit to sin, it gets harder to say "No" the next time. And each time we say "No" to sin and "Yes" to righteousness, living right becomes easier. We become slaves to whom we obey—for better or for worse.

"And we, who with unveiled faces all reflect the Lord's glory, are being transformed into his likeness with ever-increasing glory, which comes from the Lord, who is the Spirit" (2 Cor. 3:18). John Wesley taught that *righteousness* is conforming to God's will. And *holiness* (sanctification; right living) is conforming to God's nature or character.[34]

The law of the harvest is to reap more than you sow. Sow an act, and you reap a habit; sow a habit, and you reap a character; sow a character, and you reap a destiny.[35]

No believer on earth is perfect. But as we follow Jesus, He saves us from our sins— and we increase in right living. (Review Figure 5.5.) The angel told Joseph: *"She will give birth to a son, and you are to give him the name Jesus, because he will save his people from their sins"* (Matt. 1:21). Romans declares that we used to be slaves of sin, but Jesus has freed us! His name is called Jesus (Savior) because He saves us from our sins.

If Jesus saves us from our sins, we are not still in them. If you save a drowning person from water, he is not still in the water. If you save a man from fire, he is not still in the fire. If you save a man from prison, he is not still in prison. If you save a person from cancer, he is not still in sickness. If Jesus saves a person from sin, that person is not still in sin.

Dare to come to Jesus in the full meaning of His name—Savior. Will you daily commit yourself to being one of His people? If so, He will break every chain of sin that enslaves you. Though seven demons bind you, as they did Mary Magdalene, He will set you free. Through Moses, God delivered the children of Israel from the bondage of Egypt. Through Jesus, God delivers His people from the bondage of sin. This is His most important concern for His people in this life.

Jesus saves us from the *penalty* of sin, and gives us *right standing* (justification) before God. Jesus saves us from the *power* of sin, and gives us the power for *right living* (sanctification) before God.

Q 73 *Is it possible to be justified, but not sanctified? Explain.*

"Believe and behave!" Believing brings us into a relationship with God. Behaving proves our relationship with God.[36] If we are not sanctified, there is no reason to believe we have been justified.[37] Augustine said, "Love God and do what you want." He meant that if we love God, we will only want to do what pleases Him.

F. Holy Living Key 6: <u>Review</u> the results of serving sin and serving righteousness (Rom. 6:20-23).

²⁰*When you were slaves to sin, you were free from the control of righteousness.* ²¹*What **benefit** did you reap at that time from the things you are now ashamed of? Those things **result** in death!* ²²*But now that you have been set free from sin and have become slaves to God, the **benefit** you reap leads to holiness, and the **result** is eternal life.* ²³*For the wages of sin is death, but the gift of God is eternal life in Christ Jesus our Lord* (Rom. 6:20-23).

A wise method for making right choices uses a chart with two columns. To use this method, draw a line in the middle of a blank sheet of paper, from top to bottom. Above the left column, write "Results of Choice A." Above the right column, write, "Results of Choice B." In Romans 6:20-23, Paul guides us to contrast the choices of serving sin and serving righteousness (Figure 5.17). When tempted to sin, each believer should ask himself the question: ²⁰*"When you were slaves of sin...* ²¹*What benefit did you reap at that time from the things you are now ashamed of?"* (Rom. 6:20-21).

Q 74 ✎ *What contrast does Paul make in Romans 6:20-23?*

Q 75 ✎ *In your words, summarize the method of weighing choices (Rom. 6:20-23).*

Q 76 ✎ *Review Figure 5.18. Summarize the results of serving sin. Then summarize the results of serving righteousness.*

Rom.	Results of Choice A: Serving Sin	Results of Choice B: Serving Righteousness	Rom.
1:18; 2:5	God's wrath	God's praise	2:29
1:21, 26	Inner darkness and shame	Glory, honor, immortality; eternal life God's Spirit within	2:7 8:9
1:24	Sexual impurity	The new way of the Spirit	7:6
1:25	Believing a lie	The truth of God	1:16, 25
1:28	A depraved mind	Perseverance, character, hope, love	5:3-4
2:15	A guilty conscience	Peace with God	5:1
2:1; 3:9-20	Condemnation	Justification No condemnation	5:1; 3:9-20 8:1
6:17	Slavery to sin	Slavery to righteousness	6:18
6:19	Increasing wickedness	Increasing holiness	6:22
6:23	Eternal death (separation from God)	Eternal life (a relationship with God)	6:23

Figure 5.18 **To make right choices, list the results of each choice in a column as we did above. Seeing the results of each choice enables us to decide wisely.**

Q 77 ✎ *Review Figure 5.18. Could you use this method to help yourself or someone make a wise decision? Explain.*

An evil king called one of his servants. He asked him, "What do you do?" The man replied, "I am a blacksmith." So the king told him to make a heavy chain 3 meters long. When the blacksmith came back, the king told him to make it twice as long—6 meters. The third time he returned, the king said to double it again, making it 12 meters long. Finally, the blacksmith returned again. This time the king told other servants to bind the blacksmith with the chain he had made. Then the king had them throw the blacksmith bound into a furnace of fire. This was the wages for doing what the evil king commanded.

The devil commands sinners to make their own chains. He instructs them to keep making their chains longer. Some sinners work on their chains 10, 20, 50 years or more. In the end, these chains will bind their makers forever in the lake of fire.

In contrast, God sets believers free. He does not give us what we deserve. God gives us what He wants us to have. Both God and the devil give according to their natures. One is good. The other is evil. We decide if we get the wages we deserve or the gift God offers us.³⁸ Which do you choose: the wages of sin or the gift of righteousness (Rom. 6:23)?

Q 78 ⬟ *Complete Figure 5.19 on 6 keys for holy living.*

| Key 1: _____ |
| _____ |
| _____ |
| Key 2: _____ |
| _____ |
| _____ |
| Key 3: _____ |
| _____ |
| _____ |
| Key 4: _____ |
| _____ |
| _____ |
| Key 5: _____ |
| _____ |
| _____ |
| Key 6: _____ |

Figure 5.19   Practice stating six keys to right living (Rom. 6).
(Your summaries of the full principles)

Test Yourself: Circle the letter by the *best* completion to each question or statement.

1. God is "high above all else" refers to
a) holiness of position.
b) holiness of action.
c) holiness of condition.
d) holiness of disposition.

2. Our holiness includes how many aspects?
a) 1
b) 2
c) 3
d) 4

3. Purity of heart refers to holiness of
a) position.
b) action.
c) condition.
d) direction.

4. In the holiness triangle, which sides touch at the top?
a) Action and condition
b) Position and action
c) Condition and position
d) Action and direction

5. Another word for holiness is
a) regeneration.
b) justification.
c) conversion.
d) sanctification.

6. In Romans 6, what is the answer to Paul's first question?
a) Yes, now and then.
b) By no means!
c) If possible.
d) No, never!

7. What is the first key to victorious living?
a) Remember, Christ died for us.
b) Remember, grace covers all our sins.
c) Remember, we are united to Christ.
d) Remember, Christ rose from the dead.

8. Which is a key to victorious living?
a) Use your will to resist sin.
b) Put all the responsibility on God.
c) Know that all future sins are forgiven.
d) Look for temptations to conquer.

9. Which statement is TRUE?
a) The bad become better.
b) Some remain the same for years.
c) All people have a degree of freedom.
d) Each person is a slave.

10. Which is a key to victorious living?
a) Discern that some sins are worse than others.
b) Remember that we are all slaves of sin.
c) Contrast the results of sin and righteousness.
d) Recognize that victory belongs to the victor.

 Essay Test Topics: Write 50-100 words on each of these goals that you studied in this chapter.

• Explain 3 ways in which God is holy. Give examples.
• Explain 3 ways in which believers are holy. Give examples.
• Explain the triangle of holiness, and how its sides relate to each other.
• Answer the two questions Paul asks in Romans 6.
• Explain what it means to be united to Christ in His life and death. Apply this.
• Explain how water baptism illustrates our death and life with Christ.
• Explain the importance of resisting sin, and explain ways we do this.
• Contrast offering ourselves for bad and good purposes. Give examples.
• Explain: All people are slaves to something.
• Defend this statement: The bad get worse and the good get better.
• Contrast the results of serving sin and serving righteousness.

Chapter 6:
Freedom From Struggling Under the Law
(Romans 7)

Introduction

Q 1 ⟋ *What are 2 types of misguided teachers that Paul confronted in Romans? Explain each.*

Figure 6.1
In Romans and Galatians, Paul battles two types of false teachers—both legalists (A and B).

False teaching A: Some Pharisees and Sadducees said people were saved by obeying the law of Moses. (Paul refutes this in Romans 7.) These Jews accused Paul of teaching salvation by grace without law. They said Paul taught that grace permits believers to live as sinners, ignoring the Law. (Paul refutes this accusation in Romans 6.)

False teaching B: Judaizers taught salvation by Moses *plus* Jesus (Acts 15:1-31). Paul refutes this in several letters. He emphasizes that to be saved by the Law, a person must keep all of it—which is impossible (Gal. 3:10; 5:3; Rom. 2:25; 3:20; 10:4-5). Salvation does not depend on circumcision or observing special days (Gal. 3–4; Col. 2:16-17). Salvation is through Jesus alone, not Moses plus Jesus.

Paul's gospel: God's apostle taught salvation by faith in Christ, who by the Spirit enables us to fulfill the law of love (Rom. 8).

Lessons:

Truths About the Law (Rom. 7:1-13)

Goal A: *Summarize Paul's teachings in each illustration: baptism, slavery, and marriage (Rom. 6–7).*
Goal B: *Answer the 3 questions Paul asks about the Law (Rom. 7:1-13; Figure 6.4).*
Goal C: *Explain and illustrate 5 principles about law in Romans 7:7-13.*

Failure to Obey the Law Without Christ (Rom. 7:13-25)

Goal A: *Refute 3 reasons why others think Romans 7:13-25 refers to a Christian.*
Goal B: *Explain 6 reasons why we believe Romans 7:13-25 refers to a pre-Christian.*

 Key Words

condemnation (a judicial term)—a judgment that comes down from the court of heaven. God *condemns* those who practice sin.

law of sin—the authority or rulership of sin. Being a prisoner of the law of sin means that sin is a person's master or lord.

flesh—the human enemy of the Spirit. Fleshly life is pursuing one's own desires, independent of God or His law, not submitting to Jesus as Lord, and hostile to the Holy Spirit. Living in the flesh is pleasing self, ignoring and rebelling against God (Rom. 8:1-15; Gal. 5:16–6:10).

under law—being under the old covenant

under grace—being under the new covenant

Lesson **Truths About the Law (Rom. 7:1-13)**

20 **Goal A:** *Summarize Paul's teachings in each illustration: baptism, slavery, and marriage (Rom. 6–7).*
Goal B: *Answer the 3 questions Paul asks about the Law (Rom. 7:1-13; Figure 6.4).*
Goal C: *Explain and illustrate 5 principles about law in Roman 7:7-13.*

Setting

Romans	Salvation Theme	Galatians
1:18–3:20	Condemnation: the need for righteousness	
3:21–5:21	Justification: righteousness in our standing; freedom from the guilt of sin	3–4
6–8	Sanctification: righteousness in holy living; freedom from the power of sin	5–6
9–11	Election: righteousness for Jews and Gentiles	
12–15	Relationships: righteousness with God and others	

Figure 6.2 Aspects of righteousness in Romans and Galatians

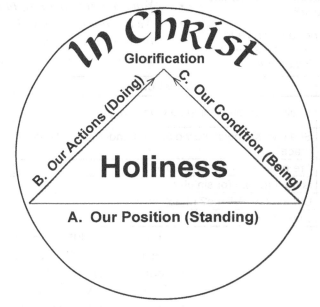

Figure 6.3   There are three aspects or sides of holiness in Christ. (Review the chart in Figure 5.4.)

Romans and Galatians are letters about salvation (soteriology). In these letters, Paul teaches aspects of salvation, including condemnation (Rom. 1:18–3:20), justification (Rom. 3:21–5:21), and sanctification (Rom. 6–8), see Figure 6.2.

Justification relates to the *penalty* of sin. Justification is a legal term. We have been justified—declared not guilty, declared righteous and holy because Jesus took our place at Calvary. He was our substitute. On the cross Christ received the penalty for our sins. He died as our sacrifice so we could be free from the guilt and penalty of sin (Rom. 8:3). This is the theme of Romans 3:21–5:21 and Galatians 3–4. Justification and regeneration form the base of the triangle of holiness (Figure 6.3).

Sanctification is a broad word that means "holiness." It includes justification, and stresses salvation from the *power* of sin. Sanctification emphasizes what Jesus does with, through, and in us, as we live holy lives.

The outline in Figure 6.2 helps us understand the main sections of Romans and Galatians. Many teachers emphasize that *justification* is the theme of Romans 3:21–5:21 and Galatians 3–4. Likewise, *sanctification* is the main theme of Romans 6–8 and Galatians 5–6. Outlines are helpful. They enable us to review the main parts of a letter. But recall that justification and regeneration are the beginning of our holiness (sanctification). The base of the holiness triangle is holiness of position. Our holy position in God's family includes justification and regeneration. Without these, we have no holiness, and no basis for holy actions and holy condition. So in a broad sense, it is important to understand that justification is a vital part of sanctification. Let us keep this in mind as we emphasize aspects of sanctification such as holy actions and a holy heart.

Romans 7 is the middle chapter of Romans 6–8, a **unit** about sanctification—being holy like God in daily living.

Q 2 ⟩ *Which chapters in Galatians are parallel to Romans 6–8?*

Q 3 ⟩ *In your own words, what is justification? Explain it.*

Q 4 ⟩ *Justification relates to the _____ of sin, and sanctification relates to the _____ of sin.*

Q 5 ⟩ *Why is it important to understand that justification is a part of sanctification?*

Q 6 ⟍ *What is the big contrast in Romans 6–8?*

The key to understanding Romans 6–8 is recognizing the contrast: *under law* and *under grace*.

Under law means being under the old covenant. **Under grace** means being under the new covenant.

Q 7 ⟋ *Which 3 verses contrast being under law and under grace?*

Several key verses in Romans 6–8 contrast being *under law* and being *under grace*:
- *"You are not under law, but under grace"* (Rom. 6:14).
- *"We are not under law, but under grace"* (Rom. 6:15).

Q 8 ⟍ *For a review and overview of Romans 6–7, complete Figure 6.4.*

- *"We have been released from the law so that we serve in the new way of the Spirit, and not in the old way of the written code [law]"* (Rom. 7:6).

Rom.	Questions	Answers	Rom.
6:1	Shall we go on sinning so God can give more grace?		6:2 6:2-14
6:15	Shall we sin because we are not under law but under grace?		6:15-16 6:15-23
7:1	Are believers under the Law?		7:2-6
7:7	Is the Law sin (or sinful)?		7:7-12
7:13	Did the Law kill me? (If not, what did?)		7:13-23
	Does 7:14-25 refer to a Christian?		7:14-25

Figure 6.4   Questions and answers in Romans 6–7

In Romans 7, Paul defends the Law. He has already mentioned the law of Moses several times (Rom. 3:19-20, 27-28; 4:13-15; 5:13-14, 20).[1] Paul does not want believers in Rome, or anywhere, to think that his gospel of grace is against law. So he takes the time to explain the Law's place in the history of salvation. In this lesson we will examine three questions related to the Law (Rom. 7:1-13, see Figure 6.4).

A. Question: Are believers under the Law? (Rom. 7:1)

Q 9 ⟍ *Are believers under the Law? Explain.*

Answer: No, believers died to the Law and are now married to Christ (Rom. 7:1-6).

Paul often uses figurative language—illustrations, pictures, and comparisons—to explain our relationship with Christ.

Q 10 ⟍ *What are 3 illustrations that Paul gives of believers? Explain each.*

In Romans 6 he used *water baptism* as a picture of dying and rising with Christ. With this picture, Paul taught that we died to sin with Christ and arose to live a new holy life in Him (Rom. 6:1-14).

Also in Romans 6, the apostle used the illustration of *slavery*. This illustration shows that we *were* slaves of sin, but Jesus freed us to be slaves of righteousness (Rom. 6:17-18; 8:2).

In Romans 7:1-6, Paul uses the metaphor of *marriage*. Death ends a marriage. A wife is released from her husband at death. Likewise, we died with Christ. He represented us on the cross. This illustration teaches that through this death with Christ, we are released from marriage to the Law so that we might belong to a new husband—Jesus Christ (Rom. 7:4).

These three pictures—baptism, slavery, and marriage—help us understand our relationship to the past, and to Jesus Christ. Take time to read Paul's illustration about marriage in Romans 7:1-6.

¹Do you not know, brothers—for I am speaking to men who know the law—that the law has authority over a man only as long as he lives? ²For example, by law a married woman is bound to her husband as long as he is alive, but if her husband dies, she is released from the law of marriage. ³So then, if she marries another man while her husband is still alive, she is called an adulteress. But if her husband dies, she is released from that law and is not an adulteress, even though she marries another man. ⁴So, my brothers, you also died to the law through the body of Christ, that you might belong to another, to him who was raised from the dead, in order that we might bear fruit to God. ⁵For when we were controlled by the sinful nature [the flesh], *the sinful passions aroused by the law were at work in our bodies, so that we bore fruit for death. ⁶But now, by dying to what once bound us, we have been released from the law so that we serve in the new way of the Spirit, and not in the old way of the written code* (Rom. 7:1-6).

In Galatians 3:23-25, Paul uses another illustration to contrast life under the Law and life in Christ. He says that under the Law, believers of the Old Testament were like children under a tutor. Paul's readers understood this well. The Greek word for *tutor* is *paidagogos.* It means "schoolmaster, supervisor, or guardian."² This tutor was usually a slave, put in charge of his master's son. The boy was under the care of the slave from the age of 6 to 16 years. The slave taught the boy good manners, and even punished him if necessary. The slave walked with the boy to school, and carried his bag. There was a special place in the school for such slaves to wait. At the end of the day, the guardian walked home with the boy, asked him questions about the lessons, and guided him to recite his memory work. The guardian shaped the boy for the future. Likewise, the role of the Law was to teach us that by the Law salvation is impossible, and to bring us to Christ.³

Q 11 Which 2 kinds of fruit does Romans 7:4-6 contrast?

Q 12 In what sense was the Law like a tutor (Gal. 3:23-25)?

Q 13 Read Galatians 4:21-31 and answer the 5 questions in Figure 6.5.

Paul uses Hagar and Sarah to contrast those under law and those under grace (Gal. 4:21-31).

Gal.	Your summary of what this illustration teaches on law and grace
4:21	Why did Paul use the illustration of Hagar and Sarah?
4:22-23	Which two types of birth does Paul contrast?
4:24-27	Which two covenants do Hagar and Sarah represent?
4:25-26	Which children are slaves, and which are free?
4:31	What is Paul's main point? Those under law are slaves, and those with faith in Christ are _____.

Figure 6.5   Practice answering five questions about Hagar and Sarah (Gal. 4:21-31).

Q 14 Complete Figure 6.6.

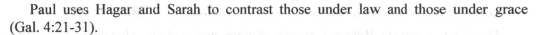

Illustration	Scripture	Your summary of what each illustration teaches on law and grace
Baptism	Rom. 6:1-14	
Slavery	Rom. 6:17-18; 8:2	
Marriage	Rom. 7:1-6	
A child under a tutor	Gal. 3:21–4:7	
Hagar and Sarah	Gal. 4:21–31	

Figure 6.6   Practice explaining illustrations Paul uses to contrast being under law and under grace.

Recognize Paul's purpose in Romans 7:1-6. He is emphasizing that life has changed. We used to be slaves of sin under the Law. Back then, our fruit was bad. But Christ has freed us to live holy lives and bear good fruit. Paul states the main point of Romans 7 in 7:6.⁴

Q 15 In Romans 7:1-6, what does Paul do before he reviews living under the Law (Rom. 7:13-25)?

But now, by dying to what once bound us, we have been released from the law so that we serve in the new way of the Spirit, and not in the old way of the written code (Rom. 7:6).

Romans 8 will emphasize our *new way* of life in the Spirit. But first, Paul wants to review what it was like living under the law of Moses. To refute the false teachings of his opponents, there are more things he must say about *"the old way"* of the law—*"the written code"* (Rom. 7:6). In Romans 7:7-25, Paul reminds believers that under the Law it was impossible to please God.

Q 16 Which 2 ways of living does Romans 7:6 contrast?

B. Question: Is the Law sin (or sinful) (Rom. 7:7-12)?

Answer: *"Certainly not! ...The law is holy, and the commandment is holy, righteous and good"* (Rom. 7:7, 12).

Q 17 Is the Law sinful (Rom. 7:7-12)? Explain.

Q 18 *What did Paul's enemies say he taught about the relationship of grace and law?*

Paul's enemies said he did not respect the law of Moses. They falsely accused Paul of disregarding the Law. They slandered Paul, claiming he said, *"Let us do evil that good [grace] may result"* (Rom. 3:8). They said Paul criticized the law of Moses and turned people away from it (Acts 21:21; 23:29). In contrast, Paul said, *"I believe everything that agrees with the Law and that is written in the Prophets"* (Acts 24:14). Earlier, Paul wrote that grace does not abolish or do away with law, rather grace *upholds* law (Rom. 3:31). And in Romans 7:7-25, Paul defends the Law.[5] But he puts the blame on sin.

Romans 7:7-12 begins with the question: *"Is the law sin?"* That is, "Is the law evil?" This passage ends with the complete answer: *"So then, the law is holy, and the commandment is holy, righteous and good"* (Rom. 7:12).

As we study Romans 7:7-12, let us look at five main points or principles that Paul states.[6]

Principle 1: God's law reveals sin (Rom. 7:7).

Q 19 *In what sense is the Law like a flashlight, revealing sin?*

What shall we say, then? Is the law sin? Certainly not! Indeed I would not have known what sin was except through the law. For I would not have known what coveting really was if the law had not said, "Do not covet" (Rom. 7:7).

God's law is not sin. Rather, it reveals, defines, and explains what sin is. Law shines a light on sin so we can see it clearly.

Opinions vary on what is right and wrong. Some cultures say lying and stealing are only wrong if you get caught. Some say that sex before marriage is good—just a part of learning. Some say abortion is wrong, but others say it is helpful. On every topic, there are many points of view. One person's conscience accuses, while another's conscience excuses. So how do we know what is wrong and what is right?

> GOD'S LAW REVEALS WHAT IS RIGHT AND WHAT IS WRONG.

God's law reveals what is right and what is wrong. Since God is the Judge of all, He is the only One who can make the rules. In the end, it will not matter what each person said was wrong. As Paul wrote, under the old covenant God gave Israel the rules or laws by which to live. Moses wrote these laws so the people would know what pleased God and what made Him angry.

Q 20 *Under grace, how do we fulfill the spirit of the Law? Give examples.*

Application: The law of the New Testament does *not require* obeying *the letter of the Old Testament law*—such as animal sacrifices, physical circumcision, earthly priests, death by stoning, or rigid rules about feasts and the Sabbath. Rather, under the New Testament we fulfill the *spirit* of the law by practicing the law of love. Paul wrote:

> [8]*Let no debt remain outstanding, except the continuing debt to love one another, for he who loves his fellowman has fulfilled the law.* [9]*The commandments, "Do not commit adultery," "Do not murder," "Do not steal," "Do not covet," and whatever other commandment there may be, are summed up in this one rule: "Love your neighbor as yourself."* [10]*Love does no harm to its neighbor. Therefore love is the fulfillment of the law* (Rom. 13:8-10).

In Romans 7:14-25, Paul will explain that we cannot obey God's law in our own strength. And in Romans 8, he will explain that through Christ and the Holy Spirit, God enables us to live in a way that pleases God.

Q 21 *Would we be better off without laws? Explain.*

Laws are helpful. Imagine what it would be like if the government had laws but did not tell us what they are. The police could punish us for paying too little tax, driving too fast, or not honoring the government. This would not be fair, since we did not know the laws. It is very helpful to know the laws by which we will be judged.

Paul respected the laws of man and government. Still, he knew that in the end there is only one Judge.

> [3]*I care very little if I am judged by you or by any human court; indeed, I do not even judge myself.* [4]*My conscience is clear, but that does not make me innocent. It is the Lord who judges me* (1 Cor. 4:3-4).

All of us will one day be judged by God. Let us give thanks that He has told us what is right and wrong. For His laws and commands are as helpful as a flashlight in the dark. His laws show the wrong path and the right path. Law reveals sin.

A young girl thought the kitchen was clean. Her mother smiled and wiped a wet, white cloth across the table. The child was shocked to see that the white cloth had become dirty! Likewise, law reveals sin, where people did not see it.

Principle 2: Sin used God's law for a bad purpose—to bring death (Rom. 7:8-11).

Q 22 *What surprising thing did sin use to defeat us? Explain.*

Is God's law sin or sinful? No, but sin used God's law for a sinful purpose—to kill us spiritually.

> [8]*But sin, seizing the opportunity afforded by the commandment, produced in me every kind of covetous desire. For apart from law, sin is dead.* [9]*Once I was alive apart from law; but when the commandment came, sin sprang to life and I died.* [10]*I found that the very commandment that was intended to bring life actually brought death.* [11]*For sin, seizing the opportunity afforded by the commandment, deceived me, and through the commandment put me to death* (Rom. 7:8-11).

In Romans 7:8, Paul uses *personification.* That is, he refers to sin as an evil person, force, or power. In Romans 7:8, the Greek word translated *opportunity* is *aphorme.* This word often referred to a *military base.*[7]

Sin was like an enemy commander who needed a military base to work from. Sin was like a power that wanted to conquer. But it needed a starting point—a military base or headquarters. Sin needed an opportunity through which to work. Sin wanted to make slaves out of all humans. But how could sin find a way to defeat us? We might think that sin would choose the most sinful thing it could find for its evil purpose. But to our surprise, sin chose something holy and good to defeat us. Sin chose God's holy law!

> *But sin, seizing the opportunity* [Greek: *aphorme*] *afforded by the commandment, produced in me every kind of covetous desire. For apart from law, sin is dead* (Rom. 7:8).

How did sin use the commandment to defeat us? Sin used the Law to awaken sinful desires in us.

Law is like the man who woke up a sleeping dog, named evil. While sleeping, the dog was quiet. But when awake, the dog was mean and bit people. Evil desires may sleep within us. But we do not like rules or limits. When someone gives us a rule, it awakens a sinful desire to break the rule.

Q 23 *If law points to the best, how does it bring out the worst in us?*

> *For when we were controlled by the sinful nature, the sinful passions **aroused by the law** were at work in our bodies, so that we bore fruit for death* (Rom. 7:5).

Law arouses or awakens sinful desires. The Law is good. But sin uses the Law to awaken sinful desires.

Although law points to the best, it may bring out the worst in us (Rom. 7:7-11). Consider Adam and Eve. Life was sweet for them until sin misused the law of God. In Eden, sin used one rule to awaken the sleeping dog of rebellion in them (Gen. 3:1-6). Awakened by the commandment, sinful desires said: "What? Do you forbid us to eat the fruit of one tree in the Garden? Then we must eat it! Is there something that God forbids us to have? Then we must have it." As Paul says, the command, *" 'Do not covet,'...produced in me every kind of covetous desire"* (Rom. 7:7-8). Tell a child not to touch a hot stove, and something inside the child wants to touch it. Is the speed limit 30? Then we want to go 35. Is it wrong to walk on the grass? Then we want to put at least one foot on it. Does the sign say, "Wet paint, do not touch?" Then something in us wants to touch it! Law works that way. It stirs up rebellion and sinful desires—especially in unspiritual people.

Romans 7:9-11 reminds us of Adam and Eve. They were alive before the commandment came. They were happy in paradise. Then the rule came. Soon they disobeyed. *"Sin sprang to life"* and they died—in their relationship to God. For disobedience results in separation from God. Likewise, even though God's law and commandments are good, they stir up rebellion, which brings death.

James describes the process of how the power of sin brings death to us. When fleshly people know something is wrong, they have sinful desires to do it.

> [14]*Each one is tempted when, by his own evil desire, he is dragged away and enticed.* [15]*Then, after desire has conceived, it gives birth to sin; and sin, when it is full-grown, gives birth to death* (James 1:14-15).

Many things in life have two sides. Money can be used to bless or to bribe, to buy good things or bad. Likewise, a knife can be used to help or to hurt. And law can be used to commend or condemn. Sin used law for a bad purpose—to stir up evil desires in us.

Principle 3: Law is good (Rom. 7:12).

Is law sin or sinful? Certainly not (Rom. 7:7). For the Law reflects the holy God who gave it.[8] God's law is good because God is good (Rom. 7:12, 14, 16, 22; see Matt. 19:17). It tells us what is right and wrong. The Law is like a helpful sign that points in the right direction, or warns of danger. Paul defends the Law in Romans 7:7-12. He says law is not the problem. Our trouble does not come from God's holy law, but from sin and evil fleshly desires.

Q 24 \ *Did the Law kill me? If not, who did?*

C. Bridge Question: Did the Law kill me (Rom. 7:13)?

Answer: No, do not blame the Law for your spiritual death. Sin is the killer.

> *Did that which is good, then, become death to me? By no means! But in order that* **sin** *might be recognized as* **sin**, *it* [sin] *produced death in me through what was good* [law], *so that through the commandment* **sin** *might become* [appear to be] *utterly* **sinful** (Rom. 7:13).

Romans 7:13 is like a bridge that connects Romans 7:7-12 and 7:14-25. It relates to both of these passages.

In relation to Romans 7:7-12 we may understand Romans 7:13 to contain two principles:

Principle 4: God let sin misuse law for an evil purpose so that we will discern the evil character of sin (Rom. 7:13).

Q 25 \ *What are some examples of sin using good things for bad purposes?*

Application: God gave the Law for a good purpose—to show us how to please Him. For God desires to bless us. And if we please Him, He is able to fulfill all His wonderful plans for us. But sin is so evil that it used God's holy law for an evil purpose. The way sin misused God's law reveals how evil sin is (Rom. 7:13).

Christian, beware of sin. Sin has no conscience. It has no shame. There is nothing so holy that sin will not misuse it for an evil purpose. There is no level too low for sin to stoop. There is no lie sin will not tell. There is no soul sin will not sell. There is never a penny it does not hope to gain. There is nothing holy it will not profane.

- Sin will twist a father against his own holy daughter and seduce him to incest.
- Sin will lead a pastor to steal a holy offering that widows sacrifice to give for God's work.

- Sin will entice a great king like David to use his sacred position to murder a loyal soldier and commit adultery with this soldier's wife.
- Sin will slaughter innocent children without a tear.
- Sin will distort a holy honor, like that given to Mary, and lead a multitude to worship her, instead of the Savior she bore.
- Sin will misquote holy Scripture to lead believers astray.
- Sin will pervert the calling to be an apostle, like Judas, into using the position to get money.
- Sin will tempt leaders to misuse their position for selfish, evil purposes.

Follower of Christ, see sin for what it is—a hideous, immoral, 100 percent evil power of hell. Sin used God's holy law to deceive mankind out of paradise, away from God, toward eternal destruction.

Figure 6.7
One type of wasp lays eggs
in the body of a caterpillar.

One type of wasp lays as many as 80 eggs in the body of a caterpillar. Two weeks afterward, the eggs hatch into grubs that burst through the caterpillar's skin. But despite its injuries, the caterpillar remains alive as a prisoner. The enslaved caterpillar stays near the hatched grubs as they spin their cocoons and later turn into adults. The caterpillar never crawls away, and it never eats. All it does is swing its head when something nearby moves. Thus it serves as an enslaved guard of the wasp that conquered it. After the new wasps grow and fly away, the caterpillar will die.[9] Likewise, sin lays its eggs in a victim. When they hatch, the sinning person becomes a slave of sin. In the end, sin lives on, but the person dies.

Principle 5: The Law causes sin to become even more sinful (Rom. 7:13).

Q 26 *How does the Law make sinning more sinful?*

When people sin, this is bad, even if they do not know they are sinning. Sin is evil, whether people recognize it or not. But when the commandments of God come, people become aware of what sin is. Then, if they choose to disobey God, their sin is even worse.

Jesus taught the principle that deliberate sin is worse than innocent sin. Judgment will be in proportion to what a person knows about God.

[47]*"That servant who knows his master's will and does not get ready or does not do what his master wants will be beaten with many blows.* [48]*But the one who does not know and does things deserving punishment will be beaten with few blows. From everyone who has been given much, much will be demanded; and from the one who has been entrusted with much, much more will be asked"* (Luke 12:47-48).

Likewise, Peter wrote that rejecting God's truth increases responsibility and punishment:

[21]*It would have been better for them not to have known the way of righteousness, than to have known it and then to turn their backs on the sacred command that was passed on to them.* [22]*Of them the proverbs are true: "A dog returns to its vomit," and, "A sow that is washed goes back to her wallowing in the mud"* (1 Pet. 2:21-22).

Q 27 ⟍ *State Paul's
5 principles about law in
Romans 7:7-13. Explain and
illustrate each to a friend.*

Privilege increases responsibility. Those who neglect revelation increase their guilt. Deliberate sin is worse than sins of ignorance. Thus God will judge Capernaum more severely than Sodom (Matt. 11:20-24). Sodom had no Bible, and no prophet. But Jesus taught and did many miracles in Capernaum. So the guilt of Capernaum is greater than the guilt of Sodom. Knowledge of God's Word increases the sinfulness of sin. The revelation of God's law makes sin utterly sinful (Rom. 7:13).

Principle	Your summary of Paul's principles about law (Rom. 7:7-13)	Rom.
1.		7:7
2.		7:8-11
3.		7:12
4.		7:13
5.		7:13

Figure 6.8   Practice stating and explaining five principles about law (Rom. 7:7-13).

Lesson 21 — Failure to Obey the Law Without Christ (Rom. 7:13-25)

Goal A: *Refute 3 reasons why others think Romans 7:13-25 refers to a Christian.*
Goal B: *Explain 6 reasons why we believe Romans 7:13-25 refers to a pre-Christian.*

Overview. We are making progress studying the big sections of Romans:

Romans 1:18–3:20 showed that all have sinned—all need a Savior.

Romans 3:21–5:21 shows that we are justified by faith in Christ. Jesus died as our substitute. God declares us holy as we repent of our sins, put our faith in Christ, and submit to Him.

Romans 6–8 emphasizes holy living.

Romans 6 teaches that under law, sin was our master. But we do not go on sinning now that we are under grace (Rom. 6:1, 14).

Romans 6:15-18 says people are slaves to whatever they serve—sin or righteousness. We used to be slaves of sin, but through Christ, we become slaves of righteousness (Rom. 6:15-18).

In **Romans 7:1-6** Paul stresses that believers are no longer under the Law. We died with Christ, and are now united with Him.

In **Romans 7:7-13** Paul defends the Law. He explains that although the Law is good, sin used God's law for a bad purpose—to kill us spiritually.

In **Romans 7:14-25** Paul continues to defend the Law. And he explains how sin was able to kill us. Our defeat to sin came through evil desires of our flesh. Law communicated well—showing us what was wrong, and shining a light on the right path. But law gave us no help to overcome our evil desires. Law pointed in the right direction, but it did not pull us in that direction. Law told us what to do, but gave us no power to do it.

Paul's enemies accused him of rejecting God's law. So Paul is careful to show that he believes the Law is holy and good. Our problem is not God's law. Rather, our problem is sin that results from the evil desires of our flesh.

There are two interpretations of Romans 7:14-25. We will examine *both* views in this lesson. Others think these verses describe the struggles of a Christian. But we believe these verses describe the slavery of a non-Christian. The authors of this course, like leaders of the Church for the first 3 centuries,[10] believe Romans 7:14-25 is about a pre-Christian, unregenerate person living under the Law. Take a few minutes to study Figure 6.9. It contrasts the old way of living under law and the new way of living under grace (Rom. 6–8).

Q 28 ↖ *Of the 11 contrasts in Figure 6.9, which 3 encourage you the most? Explain.*

Rom.	Living Under Law (Old Testament) (Slaves of Sin, Controlled by the Flesh)	Living Under Grace (New Testament) (Slaves of Righteousness, Led by the Spirit)	Rom.
5:21	*Just as **sin reigned** in death,*	*so also **grace might reign** through righteousness...*	5:21
6:1	***Shall we go on sinning?** [as slaves of sin do]...*	*²**We died to sin**; how can we live in it any longer? ⁶...our old self was crucified with him...that we should no longer be slaves to sin... ¹⁴For **sin shall not be your master**, because **you are not under law, but under grace**.*	6:2, 6, 14
6:16	*slaves to sin, which leads to death...*	*slaves...to obedience, which leads to righteousness.*	6:16
6:17	***You used to be** slaves to sin, ...*	***You have been set free** from sin and have become slaves to righteousness.*	6:18
6:20-21	*²⁰**When you were** slaves of sin, ... ²¹...Those things result in death!*	*But **now** that you have been set free from sin and have become slaves to God, the benefit you reap leads to holiness, and the result is eternal life.*	6:22
7:5	*When we were controlled by the sinful nature, the sinful passions aroused by the law were at work in our bodies, so that we bore fruit for death.*	*But **now**, by dying to what once bound us, we have been released from the law so that we serve in the new way of the Spirit, and not in the old way of the written code [law].*	7:6
7:8	*Sin...produced in me every kind of covetous desire.*	*But **now**, by dying to what once bound us, we have been released from the law so that we serve in the new way of the Spirit, ...*	7:6
7:14-15	*¹⁴...the law is spiritual; but I am unspiritual, sold as a slave to sin. ¹⁵...what I want to do I do not do... what I hate I do.*	*Through Christ Jesus the law of the Spirit of life **set me free** from the law of sin and death.*	8:2
7:18-20, 23-24	*¹⁸...I have the desire to do what is good, but I cannot carry it out. ¹⁹...The evil I do not want to do—this I keep on doing. ²⁰...sin living in me... does it. ²³...[I am] **a prisoner** of the **law of sin**... ²⁴...Who will rescue me from this body of death?*	*²⁵Thanks be to God—through Jesus Christ our Lord!... Therefore, there is **now** no condemnation for those who are in Christ Jesus, ²because **through Christ Jesus the law of the Spirit of life set me free from the law of sin and death**.*	7:25; 8:1-2
8:5, 8	*⁵Those who live according to the sinful nature have their minds set on what that nature desires;*	*but those who live in accordance with the Spirit have their minds set on what the Spirit desires.*	8:5
8:8	*Those controlled by the sinful nature cannot please God.*	*You, however, are controlled not by the sinful nature but by the Spirit, if the Spirit of God lives in you. And if anyone does not have the Spirit of Christ, he does not belong to Christ.*	8:9
8:13	*For if you live according to the sinful nature, you will die [spiritually]...*	*¹³...but if by the Spirit you put to death the misdeeds of the body, you will live [spiritually], ¹⁴because those who are led by the Spirit of God are sons of God.*	8:13-14

Figure 6.9   Eleven contrasts of living under the old way of the Law, and the new way of the Spirit (Rom. 6–8)

Thank you for studying Figure 6.9. It is a good way to review the context and key verses of Romans 6–8. Now take a few minutes to read Romans 7:13-25 two or three times. (We have included Romans 7:13 because it is a bridge between two passages.)

A. There are three main reasons why <u>others</u> believe Romans 7:14-25 refers to a Christian.

Let us examine these **three reasons**, and explain why we reject each of them.

1. First reason of others: Some teach that Paul is giving his personal testimony as a Christian, because he is using the present tense.   The verbs of Romans 7:7-13 are in the past tense. But most of the verbs of Romans 7:14-25 are in the present tense. Thus some say Paul is describing his present experience, because he uses the present tense.

Q 29 ↖ *Why does Paul use some verbs in the present tense in Romans 7:14-25?*

Our response: Those who call attention to the verb tense in Romans 7:14-25 defeat themselves. For in Romans 7:24-25, the tense that refers to help from Jesus is the *future tense.* Paul says, *"Who will rescue me from this body of death?"* The person struggling in Romans 7:14-25 has not gotten help from Jesus yet. But this pre-Christian person hopes for help from Jesus in the future. In contrast, when Paul describes Christians in

Q 30 ↖ *Has the person in Romans 7:14-25 been rescued from the slavery of sin yet?*

Q 31 *Have believers been rescued from the slavery of sin yet? Give references.*

Romans 6 and 8, he uses the perfect tense, past tense, and present tense to show that Jesus has already set us free from the Law and from sin. (See the verb tenses in the right column of Figure 6.9.) The verb tenses of Romans 6–8 show that as Christians, Christ has *already* rescued us from the struggle with sin under the Law, and we find help even now as we walk in the Spirit. But the unconverted is like a person drowning in sin, hoping that someone will hear his cries and will come to help in the future.

Why use the present tense of verbs in Romans 7:14-25? In 7:7-13, Paul used the past tense because he was summarizing what rules did to people in the past, from Eden forward. But in 7:14-25, Paul uses the present tense to show that even today, anyone seeking salvation through the Law faces the same struggles and defeat as those who failed earlier.[11]

A reporter named John believed that those who speak in tongues are confused or deceived. So he set out to prove their error. He searched the favorite Scriptures of Pentecostals and Charismatics, and studied these verses. He attended their church services, heard their sermons, and watched them worship. He interviewed many, and was amazed as they told about the way their lives had been filled with more of God. In the end, John Sherrill was baptized in the Holy Spirit and began to speak in tongues himself. Research is risky. Sincere searching with an open heart led him to the opposite conclusion he expected. Likewise, those who study the verb tenses of Romans 6–8 with an open mind and heart may discover that followers of Jesus do not struggle to keep the Law, for we have already died to it (Rom. 7:1-6). They may discover Paul taught that followers of Jesus are not slaves of sin, but we have already been set free from sin's prison and sin's chains (Rom. 6:22). And Paul insisted that even now it is our privilege and obligation to resist the lusts of the flesh, and to submit to the joyful, victorious leading of the Holy Spirit (Rom. 8:12-14).

Q 32 *How do people live if you teach them that they are slaves of sin?*

What a person believes is very important, because it affects behavior. A lion was locked in a large cage. Day after day, year after year, it walked back and forth, from one end of the cage to the other. Then one day people decided to free the lion. They carried the cage out of the city and opened the door. At last the lion was free to go anywhere it wanted. But alas, it did not believe the door was open. To the amazement of the people, it continued to walk back and forth in its cage, right past the open door. Likewise, Jesus Christ has freed us from being slaves of sin. But only those who believe this live free, victorious over sin's power. Pastors and teachers, minister the full truth of Romans 6–8 so your people can enjoy the freedom that the death and resurrection of Jesus Christ make possible.

Romans 7:14-25 may have been Paul's testimony *before* he met Christ. But in Christ, Paul was free from the power of sin. (Review the illustration on Paul's testimony, just before the test at the end of this chapter.)

2. Second reason of others: Only those who are born again *"delight in God's law."* The person in Romans 7:14-25 delights in God's law (7:22), seeks to obey God's law (7:15-20), and desires to serve God's law (7:25). The unregenerate do not seek after God (Rom. 3:11). Therefore, since the person in Romans 7:14-25 does these things, this person must be a Christian.

Q 33 *Did some Jews under the Old Testament delight in God's law? Explain.*

Our response: It is an error to say that all Jews under the Law did not delight in God's law. It is true that some who claim to be Jews did *not* love God's law. *But* Psalm 19 and Psalm 119 show us that some Jews loved God's law and delighted in it. Paul says *"For I can testify about them that they* [Jews] *are zealous for God"* (Rom. 10:2). Paul believed that many Jews were sincere and delighted in God's law. The rich young ruler who came to Christ had a delight and respect for God's law. And his testimony, like the person of Romans 7:22, was that he delighted in God's commandments and obeyed them (Matt. 19:20). Likewise, Paul, before his conversion, from a Jewish point of view loved God's law and sought to obey it (Phil. 3:4-6). Looking back, Paul understood that he failed to keep the Law. But many unconverted Jews delighted in God's law in the *inner person*—that Godward, immortal, spiritual aspect of a person.[12]

3. Third reason of others: Romans 7:25b mentions the struggle, *after* Romans 7:24-25a has already mentioned deliverance through Christ.   Therefore, the person struggling in these verses has already been saved.

Q 34 ✎ *Why does Paul mention the struggle with sin in Romans 7:25b?*

Our response: As we already noted, the salvation mentioned in Romans 7:24 is future. *"Who **will** rescue me"* is future tense. The person struggling in Romans 7:14-25 is a Jew trying to keep God's law, crying out for help that has not yet come.

So why does Romans 7:25b mention the struggle with sin, after Jesus was already mentioned in 7:25a? The final verse of Romans 7 *summarizes the problem* of Romans 7:7-24. Then, in Romans 8, Paul will give the solution to the problem. The best writers and preachers summarize the problem *just before* they offer the solution.

We have looked at three reasons why <u>others</u> believe Romans 7:14-25 refers to a Christian. And we have explained why we reject these reasons. Now, let us look at six reasons why <u>we</u> believe Romans 7:14-25 is the testimony of a pre-Christian, unconverted, unregenerated person struggling to keep the Law.

B. Six reasons why <u>we</u> believe Romans 7:14-25 describes a pre-Christian, struggling under the Law. [13]

1. The person in Romans 7:14-25 is controlled by the *"flesh"* (or as the NIV says, the *sinful nature*).   To interpret Romans 6–8, we need a clear understanding of what Paul means by *flesh*. The Greek word for flesh is *sarx*, which appears about 150 times in the New Testament, and about 90 times in Paul's writings.[14] For a quick overview of *sarx* in Romans 6–8 turn to Figure 7.9. Also, the chart below shows four ways Paul uses the word *flesh, sarx*.

Q 35 ✎ *What are 4 different meanings of flesh in the New Testament?*

Meaning of Flesh	Verses	Reference
1. That which covers bones	*A man is not a Jew if he is only one outwardly, nor is circumcision merely outward and physical* [in flesh].	Rom. 2:28;
	All flesh is not the same flesh...men...animals... birds...fish	1 Cor. 15:39
2. Earthly relationships	*For I could wish that I myself were cursed and cut off from Christ for the sake of my brothers, those of my own race* [relatives according to the flesh]	Rom. 9:3
3. Human	*Brothers, think of what you were when you were called. Not many of you were wise by human* [fleshly] *standards;*	1 Cor. 1:26
4. Rebellion to God; self-centered; independent of God	*in order that the righteous requirements of the law might be fully met in us, who do not live according to the sinful nature* [flesh] *but according to the Spirit.*	Rom. 8:4-8, 13;
	Rather, clothe yourselves with the Lord Jesus Christ, and do not think about how to gratify the desires of the sinful nature [flesh].	Rom. 13:14;
	The acts of the sinful nature [flesh] *are obvious....*	Gal. 5:19-21

Figure 6.10   Some meanings of the word *flesh* in Paul's writings[15]

Definition of flesh in Romans 6–8: Writers of the New Testament use the word *flesh* in various ways. The best explanation of flesh in Romans 6–8 is to say *flesh* is the human enemy of the Spirit. Fleshly life is pursuing one's own desires, independent of God or His law, not submitting to Jesus as Lord, and hostile to the Holy Spirit. Living in the flesh is pleasing self, ignoring and rebelling against God.[16]

Q 36 ✎ *What does Paul mean by 'flesh' in Romans 6–8?*

Paul says that *"when we **were controlled by the sinful nature** [flesh], the sinful passions aroused by the law were at work in our bodies, so that we bore fruit for death"* (Rom. 7:5). Scholars agree that this verse refers to those controlled by the flesh, under the Law, *before* they met Christ.

Q 37 ✎ *What is the first reason why we believe Romans 7:14-25 refers to a pre-Christian?*

Q 38 ✎ *Is a slave of the flesh a child of God? Explain.*

The Law is spiritual (Greek: *pneumatikos*), but the person in Romans 7:14 is unspiritual (Greek: *sarkikos*, fleshly). In contrast, even among the Galatian Christians, many were spiritual (*pneumatikos*) (Gal. 6:1).

- In Romans 8:7-8, Paul explains that those controlled by the flesh cannot please God.
- In Galatians 5:19-21 Paul lists the acts of the sinful nature (flesh). He explains that no one who lives controlled by the flesh has any inheritance in God's kingdom. A person like the one in Romans 7:14-25 is controlled by the flesh, and has not yet become a child of God—one controlled by the Spirit (Rom. 8:9).

Q 39 *Why does Romans 7:14-25 not mention the Spirit's help and victory?*

2. The person in Romans 7:14-25 struggles alone, by himself.   Note that he says *"I myself"* (Rom. 7:25). In the conflict of Romans 7:14-25, the Holy Spirit is never mentioned. This is the testimony of a person without Christ. In contrast, the person in Christ has the Holy Spirit, who is mentioned 18 times in Romans 8! In Christ, we are never alone in our struggles. Jesus never leaves us, and the Spirit is always present to help us. But the person in Romans 7:14-25 is alone, without the Spirit's help.

Q 40 *What wages must a slave of sin receive?*

Q 41 *What does 1 Corinthians 6:9-11 say about slaves of sin?*

Q 42 *Will slaves of sin go to heaven (Gal. 5:19-21)?*

3. The person in Romans 7:14-25 is a *"slave to sin"* (7:14b).   In contrast, Paul says that followers of Jesus have been set free from sin. Review what Paul writes so clearly about those who are born again:

- *"Shall we go on sinning?... ²By no means. We died to sin, how can we live in it any longer?"* (Rom. 6:1-2).
- ⁶*"For we know that our old self was crucified with him so that the body of sin might be done away with, that we should no longer be slaves to sin— ⁷because anyone who has died has been freed from sin"* (Rom. 6:6-7).
- *"In the same way, count yourselves dead to sin but alive to God in Christ Jesus"* (Rom. 6:11).
- *"You have been set free from sin and have become slaves to righteousness"* (Rom. 6:18).
- ²⁰*"When you were slaves to sin, you were free from the control of righteousness. ²¹What benefit did you reap at that time from the things you are now ashamed of? Those things result in death! ²²But now that you have been set free from sin and have become slaves to God, the benefit you reap leads to holiness, and the result is eternal life. ²³For the wages of sin is death, but the gift of God is eternal life in Christ Jesus our Lord"* (Rom. 6:20-23).

> THOSE WHO ARE SLAVES OF SIN EARN THE WAGES OF ETERNAL DEATH.

Those who are slaves of sin earn the wages of eternal death. In contrast, slaves of God and righteousness receive the gift of eternal life. The person in Romans 7:14-25 is a slave of sin, a non-Christian, under the sentence of eternal death.

Q 43 *How does a believer differ from a prisoner of the law of sin (Rom. 7:23; 8:2)?*

4. The person in Romans 7:14-25 is a *"prisoner of the law* [authority] *of sin"* (Rom. 7:23).   That is, this person is a slave of sin. Being a *"prisoner of the law of sin"* means that sin is a person's master or lord. Whenever this person wants to do good, sin overrules. In contrast, Paul says that *"through Christ Jesus the law of the Spirit of life set* [us] *free from the law of sin and death"* (Rom. 8:2).

5. The person in Romans 7:14-25 is completely defeated by sin—time after time.   All believers can identify with the struggles of Romans 7:15-20. None of us is perfect. None of us does all the good we would like to do. All of us, at times, say or do things that lead us to repentance. And all of us face temptations.

Temptation. Some falsely teach that we lose our *fleshly desires* or *sinful nature* at the new birth. But all believers continue to live in a body of flesh! And as Dr. George O. Wood notes, we may cast a demon out of an unbeliever, but we cannot cast the flesh out of a believer.[17] The desires of flesh do not leave us at the new birth. For sure, God's plan of salvation affects spirit, soul, and body (1 Thess. 5:23). Paul urges all believers to offer our bodies as living sacrifices, holy and pleasing to God (Rom. 12:1). Regeneration and justification have a sanctifying effect on the desires of our bodies. Still, believers may continue to be tempted through fleshly desires, from time to time. James (the brother of Jesus, and leader of the church in Jerusalem) wrote about the temptations that come through fleshly desires.

> [13]*When tempted, no one should say, "God is tempting me." For God cannot be tempted by evil, nor does he tempt anyone;* [14]*but each one is tempted when,* <u>*by his own evil desire*</u>*, he is dragged away and enticed.* [15]*Then, after desire has conceived, it gives birth to sin; and sin, when it is full-grown, gives birth to death* (James 1:13-15).

James reveals that it is not a sin to be tempted through the desires of our flesh. Even Jesus was tempted, but He did not sin (Matt. 4:1-11; Heb. 4:15). Sin occurs if we submit to temptations, rather than resist them. We cannot prevent all temptations, but we can prevent some temptations by turning away from them. You cannot prevent a bird from flying over your head. But you can prevent it from building a nest in your hair!

Q 44 *Is it a sin to be tempted with fleshly desires? Explain.*

We must keep in mind that Paul and John may use the word *flesh* in different ways. Yet it is helpful to compare the writers of the New Testament. John wrote that the *"cravings"* of flesh (Greek: *sarkos*), the *"lust"* of the eyes, and the *"boasting"* of what a person has and does come *"not from the Father but from the* **world***"* (1 John 2:16). Yet recall that John says all who are born of God have overcome the world (1 John 5:4). Often, John contrasts those of the world and those in Christ (1 John 2:15-17; 3:1, 13; 4:1-5; 5:4-5, 19). John sees two groups. In one group John sees children of the devil, led by the flesh, loving the world, and walking in the darkness. In the other group John sees those born of God, led by the Spirit, who do not love the world, and who walk in the light. God is Spirit, and we are being conformed to His spiritual likeness. At the moment we become children of God, He frees us from being slaves of the flesh.

In the past, sin commanded us with a loud voice. We lacked the power to resist sin. Without Christ, it was impossible to say "No" to sin. Jesus Christ frees us to choose between good and evil. The flesh still whispers and sometimes yells, suggesting evil thoughts and sinful deeds. But the Spirit of God wants to rise up with power within us. And the Spirit is always present to lead us away from evil to bear good fruit. Before Christ, law *pointed* to good, but sin *pulled* us the opposite direction. So before Christ, we were totally defeated by sin, like the person of Romans 7:14-25. But in Christ, the Spirit *pulls* us toward what is right. Now, we may at times feel the struggle between what is right and wrong. This is a part of spiritual warfare. Believers may sin from time to time, although sin is more common in believers who are immature or weak, rather than among the spiritual (Gal. 6:1-2). But the theology of Paul and the New Testament does not allow Romans 7:14-25 to be the story of a person in Christ. As Christians, we may not win every spiritual battle, but we are not like the slave of Romans 7:14-25, who was totally defeated by sin in every contest.

Young or weak Christians struggle more with the flesh than mature believers—who are strong in Spirit—struggle (Gal. 6:1). Even the apostles grew in grace. As a *young* apostle, John was called a Son of Thunder (Mark 3:17). In those early days of following Christ, John's fleshly desires wanted to destroy the Samaritans with fire from heaven (Luke 9:54). And as a young Christian, John desired to be the greatest on earth (Mark 9:33-34) and the most respected in heaven (Matt. 20:20-28). But as an old apostle, John was known for humility, love, and kindness (2 John 1-6). The longer John followed Jesus, the better his *fruit for God* became.

Q 45 *Is it possible for believers to sin? Explain.*

Q 46 *In Galatians 6:1, what contrast does Paul make between a spiritual and a weak believer?*

A new convert swore—using the Lord's name in vain. He was surprised and ashamed at what he heard come out of his own mouth. So he quickly repented. Within a few days, the Spirit helped him overcome this old habit.

Desires of the flesh are like small fires. Turn away from them, and they will burn down. Feed them, and they will grow. So Peter urged believers: *"Dear friends, I urge you, as aliens and strangers in the world, to abstain from sinful desires, which war against your soul"* (1 Pet. 2:11).

Q 47 ⬉ *What makes fleshly desires stronger or weaker? Explain.*

A man in Christ was tempted by lust. His eyes were pulled toward a beautiful woman, who dressed in a worldly way that seduced men. The Spirit reminded him that he was looking at her in the wrong way. Although his flesh protested, the Spirit led him to turn away from her. He obeyed, and chose to sing a chorus of worship. Soon, the voice of the flesh faded into silence. For the flesh is like a small child being weaned from milk. At first, the child cries and screams as if it will die from hunger. But in a short time, the child's diet changes, and it learns that other foods satisfy. Likewise, we must wean the flesh from indulging in evil desires, and train ourselves to eat food that nourishes the spirit. As we obey the Spirit, we grow in grace. We become less fleshly and more spiritual—less like the first Adam and more like the Last Adam (1 Cor. 15:45). Paul does not teach that we are perfect and unable to sin. But he guides us to resist sin, confess sin, repent if we stumble, turn from our old, fleshly life—and to be led by the Spirit to bear good fruit. Walking in the flesh, we are able to sin. But walking in the Spirit, we are able not to sin.

Q 48 ⬉ *Is it possible for believers not to sin? Why or why not?*

> [5]*Put to death, therefore, whatever belongs to your earthly nature: sexual immorality, impurity, lust, evil desires and greed, which is idolatry.* [6]*Because of these, the wrath of God is coming.* [7]*You used to walk in these ways, in the life you once lived.* [8]*But now you must rid yourselves of all such things as these: anger, rage, malice, slander, and filthy language from your lips.* [9]*Do not lie to each other, since you have taken off your old self with its practices* [10]*and have put on the new self, which is being renewed in knowledge in the image of its Creator* (Col. 3:5-10).

The authors of this course are not asking you to deny that you still have struggles with the flesh. And we are not asking you to claim that you are perfect. But we urge you to see the difference between the weakest Christian and the person in Romans 7:14-25 (who is completely defeated by sin). For whoever is a slave of sin, and a prisoner of the law of sin, has not yet been saved from sin.

Q 49 ⬉ *Does a follower of Christ struggle to keep the Law? Explain.*

6. The person in Romans 7:14-25 is a Jew who struggles to obey the law of Moses. In contrast, Paul has proclaimed that we believers are no longer under the Law (Rom. 6:14; 7:4-6). We are saved by faith in Christ, not by keeping the Law. Those seeking to be justified by law have either fallen from grace (Gal. 5:4), or have not yet known grace (Rom. 7:14-25).

In Romans 7:14-25, Dr. George O. Wood reviews Paul's terrible condition under the Law.[18] Consider five characteristics of Paul's testimony *before* he met the Savior on the road to Damascus.

Q 50 ⬉ *What are 5 points of the person's testimony in Romans 7:14-25?*

- **Under the Law** Paul was **bound**. He was sold under sin—a captive, with no freedom (Rom. 7:14).
- **Under the Law** Paul was **perplexed.** He was confused—unable to understand himself. He said, "I do not understand my own actions" (Rom. 7:15). Perplexed.
- **Under the Law** Paul was **disgusted**. He was frustrated. "I do not do what I want. I do the very thing I hate" (Rom. 7:15).
- **Under the Law** Paul was **powerless**. He desired to do good, but could not (Rom. 7:15). He was unable to serve God. He was too weak to be an example to anyone, or to serve God.

- **Under the Law** Paul was *"wretched."* The word describes a failure—one who is miserable, defeated, unable to help himself. In total despair, as the chief of sinners (1 Tim. 1:15), Paul cried out:

What a wretched man I am. Who will rescue me from the body of this death? (Rom. 7:24).[19]

If we accept Romans 7:14-25 as a description of Paul *after* he was converted, we are saying that a normal Christian is **bound, perplexed, disgusted, powerless,** and **wretched**.

In contrast Romans teaches that we are **free, at peace, victorious, empowered, justified,** and **sanctified!**

Q 51 *How is the testimony of a believer different from the person in Romans 7:14-25?*

- **Romans 5:1,** *"We have peace with God."*
- **Romans 5:3** says we have **joy.** *"We also rejoice in our sufferings."*
- **Romans 5:16** declares we are **justified**, and there is no condemnation. We have been set **free** from condemnation. But Paul's description in Romans 7:14-25 overflows with condemnation.
- **In Romans 5:21** Paul says grace is now reigning through **righteousness**. Grace is king.
- **In Romans 6:4** he says we are now **walking in newness of life** (NASB). There is a spring to our step. Our behavior is right.
- **In Romans 6:13** he says, *"Do not offer the parts of your body to sin."*
- **Romans 6:16** says, *"You are slaves to the one whom you obey."*
- **Romans 6:18** says we are *"slaves to righteousness,"* and we are to yield our members to righteousness.

Do you see the contradiction of saying the person in Romans 7:14-25 is born again, set free from sin? Those whose testimony is Romans 7 cannot do what they want. So why would Paul tell such people, "Offer your members to righteousness" (Rom. 6:11-14)? *If* Romans 7:14-25 describes Christians who have no power to do what is right, why are there any commands in the New Testament? But God does not frustrate us. He does not command us to do what we have no power to do. Romans 7:14-25 describes an unregenerate, unsaved, fleshly person under law, who is crying out for a Savior.

Q 52 *Does Romans 7:14-25 describe a person following Jesus? Explain.*

Figure 6.11   In a game called "tug of war," each group tries to pull others a certain direction.

Figure 6.12   The struggle between law and flesh is unlike tug of war. Although the flesh pulls us toward sin, the Law only points toward righteousness.

There is a game called *tug of war.* People divide into two teams that face each other. Everyone holds onto a long rope. The teams pull opposite directions. Each team tries to pull the other across a line. It is a good contest, *if* the teams are even.

Before he met Christ, Paul was unspiritual—like all slaves of sin. But what a difference Jesus made in Paul's life.

Q 53 *Give 3 examples of how Paul's testimony as a Christian differed from the person of Romans 7.*

- **Before Christ,** Paul was full of covetousness (Rom. 7:8). But in Christ, Paul was free from covetousness. He said, *"I have not coveted anyone's silver or gold or clothing"* (Acts 20:33-35).
- **Before Christ,** Paul was a prisoner of his thoughts (Rom. 7:14-23). But in Christ, Paul made thoughts his prisoners. He said, *"We take captive every thought to make it obedient to Christ"* (2 Cor. 10:5).
- **Before Christ,** Paul was a slave to his body (Rom. 7:24). But in Christ, Paul made his body his slave (1 Cor. 9:27).

Q 54 *What is your testimony? Are you like the slave of sin in Romans 7:14-25, or has Christ set you free from sin's dominion?*

Before Christ, all people are sinners, and thus unspiritual. But when we receive Jesus as Savior, we are born again. Hallelujah! He forgives our sins, washes them away, and sets us free from them. No wonder the angel told Joseph,

"You are to give him the name Jesus [Savior]*, because he will save his people from their sins"* (Matt. 1:21).

Test Yourself: Circle the letter by the *best* completion to each question or statement.

1. Which word relates to the penalty of sin?
a) Conversion
b) Justification
c) Regeneration
d) Sanctification

2. Which chapters of Romans are a unit?
a) 1–4
b) 3–5
c) 6–8
d) 8–12

3. A contrast in Romans 7 is
a) law and grace.
b) law and promise.
c) law and Spirit.
d) law and flesh.

4. Are believers today under the Law?
a) No
b) Yes
c) Yes and no
d) At times

5. Under the old covenant, what killed people?
a) The Law
b) Conscience
c) Sin
d) The flesh

6. Which illustration shows that we died to the Law?
a) Baptism
b) Slavery
c) Marriage
d) The vine

7. Which statement is NOT true?
a) God's law reveals sin.
b) Sin used law for a bad purpose.
c) Law is good.
d) Without law there is no sin.

8. Increased privilege brings increased
a) judgment.
b) responsibility.
c) reward.
d) sin.

9. The person of Romans 7:14-25 is controlled by
a) law.
b) flesh.
c) conscience.
d) Spirit.

10. The person in Romans 7:14-25 is completely defeated by
a) Satan.
b) self.
c) law.
d) sin.

 Essay Test Topics: Write 50-100 words on each of these goals that you studied in this chapter.

- Summarize what Paul teaches in each illustration: baptism, slavery, and marriage (Rom. 6–7).
- Answer the 3 questions Paul asks about the Law (Rom. 7:1-13).
- Explain and illustrate 5 principles about law in Romans 7:7-13.
- Refute 3 reasons why others think Romans 7:13-25 refers to a Christian.
- Explain 6 reasons why we believe Romans 7:13-25 refers to a pre-Christian.

Chapter 7:
Freedom Through the Spirit-led Life
Romans 8

Introduction

Here are some praises people have sung about Romans 8:

- "Romans 8 is my favorite chapter in the whole Bible. It is the most inspiring, most assuring, most enlightening, and most glorious!"
- "If we compare the book of Romans to a ring, then Romans 8 is the diamond on it."
- "Romans 8 is the grandest chapter, in the grandest book of the Bible."
- "Romans 8 is like the tree of life in the Garden of Eden."[1]
- "Romans 8 is the highest peak in a range of mountains."

All of God's Word is precious to us. But Romans 8 is special, because it emphasizes that the Holy Spirit leads us in daily victory over sin and the flesh. May the Spirit inspire you as you study this famous chapter of Scripture.

Figure 7.1   Romans 8 is like the highest peak in a range of mountains.

Q 1 ⬿ *For a review and overview of Romans 6–8, complete Figure 7.2 as you study this chapter.*

Rom.	Questions	Answers	Rom.
6:1	Shall we go on sinning so God can give more grace?		6:2 6:2-14
6:15	*Shall we sin because we are not under law but under grace?*		6:15-16 6:15-23
7:1	*Do you not know, brothers, ...that the law has authority over a person only* [while he is alive]?		7:2-6
7:7	*Is the Law sin* (or sinful)?		7:7-12
7:13	Did the Law kill me? (If not, what did?)		7:13-23
7:14-25	Does 7:14-25 refer to a Christian?		7:14-25
7:24	Who will rescue me from the sinful desires of my flesh?		7:23 8:1-17
	What are 3 types of groaning Paul mentions?		8:19-27
	What are 5 steps God takes in His plan of salvation?		8:28-30
8:31-35	[31]...*If God is for us, who can be against us?* [32]*He who did not spare his own Son, but gave him up for us all—how will he not also, along with him, graciously give us all things?* [33]*Who will bring any charge against those whom God has chosen? It is God who justifies.* [34]*Who is he that condemns?* [35]*Who shall separate us from the love of Christ? Shall trouble or hardship or persecution or famine or nakedness or danger or sword?*		8:37-39

Figure 7.2   Practice answering questions in Romans 6–8.

Lessons:

Freedom From the Guilt and Power of Sin—Part 1 (Rom. 8:1-4)
Goal A: *Analyze the words "no condemnation" and "in Christ" (Rom. 8:1).*
Goal B: *Interpret 7 key phrases in Romans 8:1-3.*

Freedom From the Guilt and Power of Sin—Part 2 (Rom. 8:1-4)
Goal A: *Identify 4 relationships in Romans 8:1-4.*
Goal B: *Analyze: The law of God is not over, under, or behind us—it is in us.*
Goal C: *Explain how we are able to fulfill the righteous requirements of the Law (Rom. 8:4).*

In the Flesh or in the Spirit?—Part 1 (Rom. 8:5-17)
Goal: *Contrast the values of those led by the flesh and those led by the Spirit (Rom. 8:5).*

In the Flesh or in the Spirit?—Part 2 (Rom. 8:5-17)
Goal A: *Contrast the spiritual states of those led by the flesh and those led by the Spirit (Rom. 8:6, 13).*
Goal B: *Identify characteristics of God's enemy and God's family (Rom. 8:7-17).*

In the Flesh or in the Spirit?—Part 3 (Gal. 5:13–6:10)
Goal A: *Analyze the conflict in believers between the flesh and the Spirit (Gal. 5:13-18).*
Goal B: *Explain and illustrate the fruit of the flesh, and their results (Gal. 5:19-21).*
Goal C: *Explain and illustrate the fruit of the Spirit, and their results (Gal. 5:22-26).*
Goal D: *Describe God's plan for a believer "caught" in a sin (Gal. 6:1-5).*
Goal E: *Summarize and illustrate God's law of harvest (Gal. 6:7-10).*

The Agony and the Glory (Rom. 8:18-27)
Goal A: *Summarize some New Testament verses that link suffering and glory.*
Goal B: *Contrast our present sufferings with our future glory (Rom. 8:18).*
Goal C: *Explain 3 types of groaning that express hope (Rom. 8:19-27).*

Predestined for Glory (Rom. 8:28-30)
Goal A: *Interpret and illustrate Romans 8:28.*
Goal B: *Explain God's purpose in working all things for our good (Rom. 8:29).*
Goal C: *Explain 5 steps in the sequence of our salvation (Rom. 8:29-30).*

More Than Conquerors (Rom. 8:31-39)
Goal: *Explain and illustrate 4 reasons why we are super-victors in whatever we must face (Rom. 8:31-39).*

 Key Words

condemnation, a judicial term—a judgment that comes down from the court of heaven. God *condemns* those who practice sin.

law of the Spirit—the authority, rule, or power of the Holy Spirit. The power of the Spirit sets us free from the powers of sin and death.

law of sin and death—the rule, authority and power of sin and death; being under these laws means that a person is a slave of sin, under the sentence of physical and spiritual death.

sinful nature—the flesh (Greek: *sarx*); the human enemy of the Spirit. Fleshly life is pursuing one's own desires, independent of God or His law, not submitting to Jesus as Lord, and hostile to the Holy Spirit. Living in the flesh is pleasing self, ignoring and rebelling against God (Rom. 8:1-15; Gal. 5:16–6:10).

foreknowledge—knowledge *before* something happens. God *foreknows* the events of earth and the choices of people. He knows in advance what will happen.

predestined—planned for a destiny. Those who choose Christ, God *predestines* or plans to become like Christ.

called—God wants all to be saved. The *called* are those who respond and agree to God's invitation, conditions of salvation, and Lordship of Jesus.

justified—declared righteous and not guilty through faith and obedience to Jesus

glorified—restored to the glory, honor, and destiny that God intends for us. Glorification begins at regeneration, increases as we grow in grace, and reaches a new height when Jesus returns for us.

Figure 7.3

God's law has always pointed in the right direction. And some in every generation have desired to obey God's law and please Him. But without Christ, all people are slaves of sin. Because the flesh is weak with sinful desires, sin is able to capture people and pull them in the wrong direction, away from God. So God sent a Savior to help us. When we repent and put our faith in Jesus, God forgives our sins, and we become His children. God writes His moral laws in our hearts, and imparts His Spirit to strengthen us, guiding us to fulfill the Law through love, from the inside out. As God's children, we are no longer slaves of sin. All God's children are led by the Spirit and are slaves (servants) of doing what is right and pleasing to God (Rom. 6–8, 12–13).

Lesson 22 · Freedom From the Guilt and Power of Sin—Part 1 (Rom. 8:1-4)

Goal A: *Analyze the words "no condemnation" and "in Christ" (Rom. 8:1).*
Goal B: *Interpret 7 key phrases in Romans 8:1-3.*

Setting

Q 2 *Do we lose our fleshly desires when we are born again? Explain.*

Moving from Romans 7 to Romans 8 is like escaping from a dark, prison dungeon into the glorious light of freedom. A cloud of despair hung over most of Romans 7. But the cloud suddenly disappears with the first verse of Romans 8! Recall the cry of desperation: *"What a wretched man I am! Who will rescue me from this body of death?"* (Rom. 7:24). This was the cry of one outside of Christ and under the Law. It was the cry of a prisoner, under the law of sin and death (Rom. 8:2). This cry of desperation and defeat receives a response. And this plea for help fades away as Paul declares that there is freedom for those who are in Christ. Yes, there is life in the Holy Spirit—now and forever![2]

Q 3 *How does Romans 8 differ from Romans 7? Describe the contrast.*

The word *therefore* in Romans 8:1 connects Romans 5–7 with Romans 8. In Romans 8:1-17, Paul continues the explanation that grace does not bury righteousness. Rather, the Holy Spirit makes righteous living possible in the life of believers. The power of the Holy Spirit enables believers to actualize, realize, experience, and live what Jesus made possible on the cross. The cross gives us *imputed,* credited righteousness. And the Spirit gives us *imparted,* actualized righteousness. The cross gives us righteousness in the bank of heaven. And the Spirit gives us righteousness in our souls and our steps.

What a glorious difference between the captive of Romans 7 and the delivered person in Romans 8! No wonder so many believers delight in Romans 8. To begin studying this famous chapter, let us look at four relationships in Romans 8:1-4. (We will label these A–D.)

A. The relationship of believers to God in Christ (Rom. 8:1).

Principle: There is now no condemnation to those who are in Christ Jesus.

The word **condemnation* involves heaven and earth. Condemnation is a judicial term—a judgment that comes down from the court of heaven. God condemns those who practice sin.

Q 4 ➤ *What is condemnation? Define it.*

We can see condemnation from God in the past, present, and future.

- *Past* acts of condemnation include the Flood, the destruction of Sodom and Gomorrah, the judgment of the seven nations of Canaan, the judgment of the Northern and Southern Kingdoms of Israel, and the destruction of Jerusalem.

Q 5 ↖ *Give some biblical examples of past, present, and future condemnation.*

- *Present* examples of condemnation by God are in Romans 1:18–3:20. Present condemnation from heaven may be less dramatic than the Flood, but just as deadly. *"The wrath of God is being revealed from heaven against all the godlessness and wickedness of people, who suppress the truth by their wickedness"* (Rom. 1:18).

  This present form of condemnation includes separation from God in this life—living without God and without hope. As God exiled Adam from Eden for sin, He exiles all now who choose to live in Adam's rebellion. Present condemnation includes reaping a harvest of shame and sorrow for sin now, such as sexual diseases, addictions, and the sorrows that come with *"the pleasures of sin for a season"* (Heb. 11:25, KJV). God gives people over to sin and sinful desires so that they sink into sin, one level at a time (review Rom. 1:18-32).

- In the *future,* condemnation will take the form of sudden judgment and final, eternal punishment. Jesus will return with vengeance. *"He will punish those who do not know God and do not obey the gospel of our Lord Jesus"* (2 Thess. 1:8). Revelation describes sinners trying to hide in caves and under rocks as Jesus returns to judge those who have lived in rebellion against His Lordship (Rev. 6:15-17). Condemnation is a terrible fate. It is a fearful and *"dreadful thing to fall into the hands of the living God"* (Heb. 10:31).

On earth, living in condemnation includes aspects mentioned above, plus the personal feelings of blame, guilt, criticism, fear, and judgment. Sinners deserve condemnation. But saints, those who live in a right relationship with Christ, escape condemnation—now and forever.

There is no condemnation to those in Christ.   Condemnation can be *like* a messenger of Satan sitting on a believer's shoulder. The accuser says: "You are not worthy. You are guilty and do not deserve forgiveness. You are a failure! What makes you think you will ever make it to heaven? God is upset with you. You try, but never hard enough. Just wait, you will be ashamed when you stand before God."

Q 6 ↖ *What are some reasons why believers may feel condemnation over their past sins?*

Troubled hearts may result from lost opportunities and broken relationships. Condemnation! It is like a flashing sign that reads, "Failure! Guilty! Worthless!"

Then Jesus comes. He announces, "I have met all of God's demands. I have satisfied the Law. I have erased every accusation against you." *"Therefore, there is now no condemnation for those who are in Christ Jesus"* (Rom. 8:1).

This message from heaven does not say, "Some condemnation, not much condemnation, or a little condemnation." Rather, Romans 8:1 declares, *"There is now **no** condemnation to those who are in Christ Jesus!"* When Jesus said, *"It is finished,"* He erased the condemnation and guilt of our past sins. Why then do some believers struggle with guilt?

Some believers feel that Romans 8:1 is too good to be true. Perhaps these children of God committed many sins for many years. So they think they deserve to be punished. It is true that we all deserve to be punished. Even those who have committed few sins and

Q 7 ↖ *Are some sins harder for God to forgive than other sins? Explain.*

small sins deserve God's wrath. But Jesus died for small sinners and big sinners, young sinners and old sinners. He died for the least sinner and the worst sinner. The Son of God died as our substitute. And the price Jesus paid was enough to forgive all the sins of people in a million worlds. Imagine the value of the blood of God. Jesus paid enough for your forgiveness and mine! No matter how great or how terrible the sin, the blood of Jesus can wash it away. When all who come to Jesus have been forgiven, there will still be enough power left in His blood to forgive everyone a billion times more. Do not underestimate the blood of Jesus, or the price He paid. Believe that it is enough to wash your sins away forever. God said so. There is no condemnation to those who are in Christ Jesus (Rom. 8:1).

Q 8 *What are the 2 types of people on earth? Which group is condemned?*

> THERE ARE ONLY TWO TYPES OF PEOPLE: THOSE IN CHRIST AND THOSE OUTSIDE OF CHRIST.

There are only two types of people: those in Christ—led by the Spirit, and those outside of Christ—led by the flesh. So how can a person tell if he is in Christ or outside of Him? Paul will explain this in Romans 8:1-17. Those outside of Christ are led by the flesh. The wrath of God is upon them. They must repent and submit to the Savior, or perish. But those in Christ submit to His Lordship, and are led by the Spirit. For these in Christ, there is no condemnation—not any! His forgiveness is complete. His love knows no limits. But let us always remember that the love of God is in Christ Jesus our Lord (Rom. 8:39).

Q 9 *What does it mean to be " in Christ"?*

"In Christ:" This is one of Paul's favorite phrases. The words *in Christ, in Christ Jesus, in him,* or *in the Lord* appear 160 times in Paul's writings. *In Christ* means that the believer now lives, abides, acts, and rests in the realm of Jesus Christ. *In Christ* is a place—an environment, a state of living. *In Christ* describes a union with Jesus, our Savior and Lord. *In Christ* believers have a conscious communion with the Savior. *In Christ* a believer's life reflects the life of Jesus within. This fellowship with Christ is the most important thing in Christian experience. The Bible contrasts our new life *in Christ* with our old, unregenerate life *outside* of Christ—in Adam. The old life was known for disobedience, sin, condemnation, and death. In contrast, our new life *in Christ* is known for salvation, life in the Spirit, abundant grace, righteousness, holiness, and eternal life (see Rom. 5:12-21; 6:8; 8:1-17; 14:17-19; 1 Cor. 15:21-22, 45-49; Phil. 2:1-5; 4:6-9).[3]

A prostitute knelt at the feet of Jesus. Repenting, she wept for her many sins and washed His feet with her tears. The Pharisees were angry because Jesus let her touch Him. But He rebuked them and forgave her many sins (Luke 7:36-50). Another time the Pharisees criticized Jesus for eating with tax collectors—the most hated sinners of their day. Jesus told them the reason why He came to earth was to find sinners and help them. *"It is not the healthy who need a doctor, but the sick. I have not come to call the righteous, but sinners"* (Mark 2:17). Jesus made helping sinners His priority. Matthew was a Jew, and a national traitor. He padded his pockets with tax money that he collected for the Roman government. But Jesus forgave him and called him to be an apostle. Likewise, Saul called himself the 'chief of sinners' (1 Tim. 1:15). Before he met Jesus, Saul put Christians in prison—both men and women. He forced many to blaspheme the name of Christ, and helped murder those who would not deny Jesus. So Jesus went looking for Saul and found him. The Savior led him to repent, and made him an apostle to help others. There is no condemnation to those who are in Christ. He forgives sex offenders, national traitors, murderers, drug dealers, and the worst sinners you can ever imagine.

Raymond was a sinful man. Although he received Christ, he continued to struggle with guilt over past deeds. Raymond's pastor took him to the edge of the ocean. He gave Raymond a stick and told him to write in the sand all of the sins he had done. Afterward, they walked away. The next day they returned to the same spot, but there were no sins written in the sand. The ocean had risen during the night and erased all the sins that Raymond wrote. The pastor explained that God's grace is greater than the ocean. God casts our sins into the sea.

> [18]*Who is a God like you, who pardons sin and forgives the transgression of the remnant of his inheritance? You do not stay angry forever but delight to show mercy.* [19]*You will again have compassion on us; you will tread our sins underfoot and hurl all our iniquities into the depths of the sea* (Mic. 7:18-19).

There is no reason for believers to feel condemnation after we repent and turn away from sins. God forgives us, and washes our sins away. Believers should not allow the past to ruin the present or the future. *"Therefore, there is now no condemnation for those who are in Christ Jesus"* (Rom. 8:1).

Pharisees brought a woman to Jesus. Somehow they had caught her in the act of adultery. They wanted to stone the woman. Jesus invited anyone without sin to throw the first stone. One by one, from the oldest to the youngest they left. Jesus asked her, *"Woman, where are they? Has no one condemned you?"* [11]*"No one, sir,"* she said. *"Then neither do I condemn you,"* Jesus declared. *"Go now and leave your life of sin"* (John 8:10-11). Jesus did not come to condemn us, but to save us (John 3:16-21). There is no condemnation to those who are in Christ. They walk in the Light, and live in Him. Condemnation is only for those who walk in darkness.

Some believers feel condemned because they condemn themselves. Jimmy felt discouraged. He had played hard in the game, but his team lost. Michael felt ashamed. His business had failed. Ann felt embarrassed when she burned the dinner a little. Sondra practiced her song for several days. But at church she felt bad because her voice cracked on one note. To all of these believers Jesus says: "It is not Me that makes you feel that way." There is no condemnation to those in Christ Jesus (Rom. 8:1). Is your earthly father or mother difficult to please? Be encouraged. Jesus is easy to please. Did you have a teacher who looked for the chance to scold you? Be encouraged. Jesus looks for the opportunity to praise you. He especially likes your righteousness—a gift He gives you (Phil. 3:9).

B. The relationship of believers to sin (Rom. 8:2-3)

Principle: Christ has set us free from the power sin had over us.

> [1]*Therefore, there is now no condemnation for those who are in Christ Jesus,* [2]*because through Christ Jesus the* <u>law of the Spirit of life</u> *set me free from the* <u>law of sin and death.</u> [3]*For* <u>what the law was powerless to do</u> *in that it was* <u>weakened by the sinful nature</u> [flesh], *God did by sending his own Son in the* <u>likeness of sinful man</u> *to be a* <u>sin offering.</u> *And so* <u>he condemned sin in sinful man</u> [flesh] (Rom. 8:1-3).

Please read Romans 8:1-3 at least three times. This passage is like a suitcase full of clothes—it is packed. As we unpack it, there are at least seven phrases to explain. We have underlined these seven phrases above. Now let us examine them one by one

1. *"Law of the Spirit of life"* (Rom. 8:2). Paul uses the word *law* several ways in Romans. In Romans 8:3 *law* refers to the law of Moses. In Romans 7:1-20, Paul refers to the law of Moses at least 11 times. But in Romans 8:2, the word *law* means "power" or "authority that controls." The **law of the Spirit of life* refers to the *power* of the Spirit of life. In other words, Romans 8:2 means: through Jesus Christ, the *power* of the Holy Spirit of life set me free from the power of sin and death. Sin and death ruled over mankind until a greater *power* set us free.[4]

Q 10 ✎ *Does Jesus keep a record of past sins that He has forgiven? Explain.*

Q 11 ✎ *Why do some believers condemn themselves? What is the solution?*

Q 12 ✎ *How does the* <u>penalty</u> *of sin differ from the* <u>power</u> *of sin? Contrast these.*

Q 13 ✎ *What does "law" mean in Romans 8:3? What is the meaning of "law" in Romans 8:2?*

Q 14 ✎ *According to Romans 8:2, what has the power of the Holy Spirit done for believers?*

Q 15 *What does Paul mean by "the law of sin and death"?*

Q 16 *Before we met Christ, what did the law of sin do to us?*

Q 17 *In what sense was the law of Moses powerless to help us?*

Q 18 *In what way was the flesh stronger than the Law?*

Q 19 *Why does Paul use the word "likeness" in Romans 8:3?*

Q 20 *In Romans 8:3, what does Paul mean by "sin offering"? Explain this concept.*

Q 21 *How does Paul compare sin to an evil person?*

Q 22 *What does it mean: "God condemned sin"?*

Q 23 *How would you help a believer who said, "My freedom depends on Jesus, not on my choices"?*

2. *"Law of sin and death" (Rom. 8:2): This law refers to the *power* of sin and death. The power of sin brings men and women into slavery. In Romans 8:2, Paul is using the word *law* the same way he used *law* in Romans 7:23.

> *But I see another law* [power] *at work in the members of my body, waging war against the law* [power/authority] *of my mind, and making me a prisoner of the law* [power] *of sin* (Rom. 7:23).

3. *"What the law was powerless to do" (Rom. 8:3): The law of Moses lacked the power to deliver us from sin. Law pointed in the right direction, but law did not pull, push, lead, or enable us. Law lacked the ability to break the power sin had over us. Law lacked the power to impart life (Gal. 3:21).

4. *"Weakened by the *sinful nature" [flesh] (Rom. 8:3): The law of Moses pointed for us to walk on the right path. But the sinful desires of the flesh pulled us off the path. If we could follow the law of Moses, we would arrive at the right place. But the Law was weak, and failed to help us, because the flesh was strong.

5. *"Likeness of sinful man" (Rom. 8:3): Paul wants to avoid the thought that Jesus became sinful when He became flesh. So Paul says Jesus came in the *likeness* of sinful man. Jesus was fully man, but He was without sin, just as God created Adam in Eden (compare Heb. 4:15). And since Jesus had no sin of His own, He was able to be a substitute for the guilty.

6. *"Sin offering" (Rom. 8:3): As the perfect, sinless Lamb of God, Jesus gave His life as an offering for our sin (John 1:29). Under the old covenant, priests sacrificed sheep, goats, and bulls. These animals died as substitutes, instead of the guilty people. Such animal sacrifices were temporary—until Jesus came to die for our sins.

> *And he died for all, that those who live should no longer live for themselves but for him who died for them and was raised again* (2 Cor. 5:15).

> *We have been made holy through the sacrifice of the body of Jesus Christ once for all* (Heb. 10:10).

> *Christ died for sins once for all, the righteous for the unrighteous, to bring you to God* (1 Pet. 3:18).

7. *"He condemned sin in sinful man" [flesh] (Rom. 8:3): By offering His life for our sins, Jesus condemned the power of sin. As a judge sentences a criminal, so Jesus judged, condemned, sentenced, and stopped the reign of sin. Notice that Paul is referring to sin as if it were a person. This is a literary style or method called *personification*. Through His sacrifice for us, Jesus broke the power sin had over us. What the law of Moses lacked the power to do, Jesus did for us. He freed us from the power of sin. As a righteous general defeats and judges an evil ruler, Jesus ended the reign of sin over His children. (As we will study in point D, through Christ, God sends us the Spirit, who gives us power to overcome.)

It is vital for Christians to believe that Jesus breaks the power of sin in our lives. Right doctrine is the foundation of right living. Jesus does not ask us to save ourselves. He does not expect us to break our own chains. But as Paul emphasizes, we are to be active, not passive. We become free and remain free as we cooperate with God. In Romans 6, we studied six keys to practice to be free:

- **Holy Living Key 1:** Remember that spiritually we are united to Jesus Christ—in His death and life (Rom. 6:1-11).
- **Holy Living Key 2:** Resist sin, temptations, and the devil—so you can remain free (Rom. 6:12).
- **Holy Living Key 3:** Offer the parts and abilities of your body to God—not to sin (Rom. 6:13-14).

- **Holy Living Key 4:** Recognize that each person is a slave—of sin or righteousness (Rom. 6:15-18).
- **Holy Living Key 5:** Discern that the bad get worse and the good get better (Rom. 6:19).
- **Holy Living Key 6:** Review the results of serving sin and serving righteousness (Rom. 6:20-23).

Our part is to make an effort to practice these six keys. This practice involves a believer's mind, will, and actions. We do not save ourselves. But remember, we are never more free than we want to be.

His name is *Jesus* because He came to save us from sin itself (Matt. 1:21)! His goal was not to save us from sin's *penalty,* but leave us prisoners of sin's *power*!

He came to save His people *from* their sins, not *in* them.

Q 24 *Do you need Jesus to free you from sin in any area of your life? Explain.*

- **If you save** a drowning person *from* water, you do not leave that person *in* the water.
- **If you save** a person *from* fire, you do not leave that person *in* the flames.
- **If you save** a person *from* prison, you do not leave that person *in* the cell.
- **If you save** a person *from* cancer, that person does not remain *in* sickness.
- **If Jesus saves** a person *from* sin, He does not leave that person *in* sin.

The Bible does not teach that believers never struggle with sin. But Scriptures teach that Jesus saves us from <u>both</u> the *penalty* and *power* of sin, now, in this life. What is your testimony? What sins has Jesus already delivered you from? Rejoice for this deliverance. What other sins do you want Jesus to save you from? Do you struggle with any of these sins: anger, worry, gossip, overeating, unforgiveness, lust, adultery, pornography, greed, other addictions, envy, homosexuality? Millions of believers rejoice and testify that Jesus has saved them from these sins!

Q 25 *What should we learn from Peter's great mistake (Luke 5:8)?*

Bring your sins to Jesus—the One who died and lives to save us from our sins. Do not make the mistake that Peter made. Jesus borrowed one of Peter's boats at a lake. The Lord sat down in the boat and taught a crowd of people that gathered on the shore near the boat. When Jesus finished teaching, He told Peter to put his nets into the lake to catch some fish. Peter and the others had fished all night and caught nothing. Still, Peter did the right thing; He obeyed the Lord. Soon, they caught so many fish that they filled the net! Then came one of Peter's many mistakes. The big fisherman said, *"Go away from me, Lord; I am a sinful man!"* (Luke 5:8). Peter's long list of mistakes included such things as: rebuking Jesus face to face (Matt. 16:22), honoring Moses and Elijah the same as Jesus (Matt. 17:4), thinking that seven times is the most we should forgive anyone (Matt. 18:21), proudly rejecting the Lord's prophecy that all the apostles would desert Him (Matt. 26:33), cutting off a man's ear at Gethsemane (John 18:10), three times denying that he knew the Lord (Matt. 26:69-75), and being a hypocrite at Antioch, Syria (Gal. 2:11-21). Peter, like all of us, made many mistakes. But one of Peter's greatest mistakes was his statement: *"Go away from me, Lord; I am a sinful man!"* Jesus loves sinners. The mission and heartbeat of Jesus is to save sinners from their sins. So when the Spirit of God makes us aware of our sins, let us say, "Come close to me, Lord, I am a sinful man!" Should a starving man tell a friend with food to depart? Should an illiterate person tell a reading teacher to leave? Should a sick person tell a doctor to go away? Should a sinful person tell the Savior of sinners to go away, or come near?

Q 26 *Is it God's will for believers to live in freedom and victory above all sins <u>now</u>? Explain.*

Dare to approach Jesus in the full meaning of His name. Will you daily commit yourself to being one of His people? If so, He will break every chain of sin that enslaves you. Although seven demons bind you as they did Mary Magdalene, He will set you free.[5] Through Moses, God delivered His people from the bondage of Egypt. Through Jesus, God delivers His people from the bondage of sin. Saving us from sin is the

Savior's main goal for His people in this life. Jesus can do more than forgive sin. He can save us from it. He can deliver us from sin's power. His name is our invitation, NOW!

In Romans 8:5-17, Paul will have more to say about our relationship with sin and evil desires of the flesh. Paul insists that true believers are those led by the Spirit, not the flesh (Rom. 8:13-14). It is possible for those in Christ to sin, from time to time. But thank God it is possible for those in Christ *not* to sin. For those *in Christ* are no longer the slaves of sin. Jesus sets us free. We will return to this truth in point D.

Lesson 23	**Freedom From the Guilt and Power of Sin—Part 2 (Rom. 8:1-4)**

Goal A: *Identify 4 relationships in Romans 8:1-4.*
Goal B: *Analyze: The law of God is not over, under, or behind us—it is in us.*
Goal C: *Explain how we are able to fulfill the righteous requirements of the Law (Rom. 8:4).*

We are looking at four relationships (A–D) in Romans 8:1-4. In the previous lesson we looked at:

A. The relationship of believers to God (*"There is now no condemnation to those in Christ"* Rom. 8:1.)

Q 27 ✎ Complete Figure 7.4.

B. The relationship of believers to sin (See Figure 7.4 below.)

Phrase in Romans 8:2-3	Your Explanation
1. *Law of the Spirit of life*	
2. *Law of sin and death*	
3. *What the law was powerless to do*	
4. *Weakened by the sinful nature* [flesh]	
5. *Likeness of sinful man*	
6. *Sin offering*	
7. *He condemned sin in sinful man* [flesh].	

Figure 7.4   Review and practice explaining seven key phrases in Romans 8:2-3.

In this lesson we will explore two more relationships (C and D) in Romans 8:1-4.

C. The relationship of believers to the Law (Rom. 8:4)

Principle: The law of God is not over, under, or behind us—His law is in us.

¹Therefore, there is now no condemnation for those who are in Christ Jesus, ²because through Christ Jesus the law of the Spirit of life set me free from the law of sin and death. ³For what the law was powerless to do in that it was weakened by the sinful nature, God did by sending his own Son in the likeness of sinful man to be a sin offering. And so he condemned sin in sinful man, ⁴in order that the righteous requirements of the law might be fully met in us, who do not live according to the sinful nature but according to the Spirit (Rom. 8:1-4).

Some misunderstand God. They think He made harsh laws in the Old Testament, but converted to love and grace in the New Testament. But God does not change (Num. 23:19; Mal. 3:6; James 1:17). Jesus did not come to abolish the Law but to fulfill it (Matt. 5:17-19). A Jewish teacher answered correctly that the Law instructs us to love God and neighbors. Jesus told him, *"You are not far from the kingdom of God"* (Mark 12:34). There is law in God's kingdom! The New Testament teaches us four truths about the relationship of believers to God's law.

Q 28 ➶ *Is law over believers, like a husband or a master? Explain.*

1. Law is not *over* us—as a husband, master, judge, or savior.

Law was once a husband over us. But we died with Christ to that relationship, and now we are married to Christ (Rom. 7:1-6).

Law is not a *master* who imposes his will on us. ... *"We are not under law but under grace"* (Rom. 6:15). We have only one Master, Jesus Christ, who is altogether kind and good.

Neither is law a *judge* who accuses and hands down a sentence of condemnation on us. *"There is now no condemnation for those who are in Christ Jesus"* (Rom. 8:1). *"Who will bring any charge against those whom God has chosen? It is God who justifies"* us in Christ (Rom. 8:33). No one can condemn those in Christ—neither law, human enemies, nor Satan (which means "Accuser" in Hebrew, Rev. 12:10). Paul teaches that Christ has cancelled the role of the Law as judge (Col. 2:14). Therefore, we should not let anyone judge us by laws about eating, drinking, feasts, or even the Sabbath day (Col. 2:16). Christ abolished the ritual laws that made Jews and Gentiles unclean (Eph. 2:15; see the NIV Study Bible). Law is not a judge over believers.

Nor is law a *savior,* reaching down to lift us up. Some in the early church wanted to require Gentiles to seek salvation through circumcision and the law of Moses (Acts 15:5). But the apostles rebuked the Judaizers and affirmed that Jews and Gentiles are saved by grace (Acts 15:11). We are saved by Christ alone, not Christ and Moses. Law is not a ladder we can climb to heaven. For no one will be declared righteous by keeping the Law (Rom. 3:20). Law saves no one, under the Old Testament or the New Testament. Paul emphasized having a righteousness that we do not produce—rather, it is the righteousness that comes through faith in Christ (Phil. 3:9). Thank God, law is not over us—as a husband, master, a judge, or a savior.

2. Law is not *under* us. Believers are not above the Law. We do not trample God's laws under our feet, and live like rebels—as though law does not apply to Christians. We are not like God's fleshly, hostile enemies who do not submit to His law (Rom. 8:7).

Jesus rebuked teachers who debated small rules but *ignored* big laws—like *"justice, mercy and faithfulness"* (Matt. 23:23; see Amos 5:15; Mic. 6:8; Zech. 7:9). He said they strained out a gnat, but swallowed a camel.

There is law in God's kingdom! For lawlessness—disobeying the Law—is the essence of sin (1 John 3:4). Romans emphasizes that obedience to God's rule, authority, and law over us is a major part of Paul's gospel (Rom. 1:5; 2:8; 6:16; 15:18; 16:26). Paul rebukes those who use grace as a cloak to cover their sins. Some accused Paul of encouraging sinning, so God could give more grace (Rom. 6:1). But Paul says of those who twisted his words, *"Their condemnation is deserved"* (Rom. 3:8).

In some countries, government officials say they are above the law, and that certain laws do not apply to them. Likewise, some who call themselves followers of Christ claim they are above the Law—that in grace, law does not apply to us. Theology calls this *antinomianism—against the law. At the final judgment, Jesus will say to all workers of *lawlessness* (Greek: *a-nomian*), *"I never knew you. Away from me, you evildoers"* (Matt. 7:23). Law is not something that believers treat with contempt, and step on. Law is not beneath us.

3. Law is not *behind* us. It is not something we can ignore. Even though we are under the New Testament, this does not mean that we have outgrown the Law. Jesus did not fulfill the Law so we could turn our backs on it. We have not graduated from law, as a student moves from one grade to the next. Law is not outdated. It is not a thing of the past. We no longer sacrifice animals or depend on earthly priests. But law is not obsolete. Paul practiced forgetting those things that were behind him (Phil. 3:13). But he did not forget God's law, because it is not something that the New Testament left behind (Acts 22:3; 23:1-5; 24:14, 16; 25:8; 28:23). So if God's law is not over, under, or behind us, where is it?

Q 29 *Which verses show that law is not over us like a judge who condemns?*

Q 30 *Is law like a ladder that people can climb to heaven? Explain.*

Q 31 *Although we are not saved by law, can we ignore it? Explain.*

Q 32 *Which aspects of the law of Moses are obsolete?*

Q 33 ➤ Who prophesied that, under the New Testament, God would write His law on our hearts?

Q 34 ➤ Why are God's laws helpful to those saved by faith in Christ?

Q 35 ✎ In Romans, how does Paul say we fulfill God's law?

Q 36 ✎ In our relationship with God, "the only thing that counts is _____ that expresses itself through _____" (Gal. 5:6).

Q 37 ✎ Complete Figure 7.5.

4. Law is *in* us. Hallelujah! This is the promise Jeremiah foretold. It is part of the new covenant that the writer of Hebrews emphasized (Jer. 31:31-34; Heb. 8:10; 10:16). Under the new covenant, God writes His laws in our hearts. Law was *"added"* to show how sinful we were without Christ (Rom. 5:20; see also Rom. 3:19–21). Law served *"to lead us to Christ that we might be justified by faith"* (Gal. 3:24). But law does more than show us we were sinful. It teaches us what pleases and displeases our Father. As His children, we delight to please Him. In our inner being we love what His law declares is right. We hate and abhor what His law says is wrong. God's law is in us, because the lawmaker is in us. And *"the righteous requirements of the law"* are *"fully met in us, who do not live according to the sinful nature but according to the Spirit"* (Rom. 8:4).

Faith and grace do not bury law. Rather, they enable us to fulfill it. As Paul wrote earlier, *"Do we, then, nullify the law by this faith? Not at all! Rather, we uphold the law"* (Rom. 3:31).

How is the law of the Old Testament summarized in the New Testament? The New Testament does *not require* obeying *the letter of the Old Testament law*—about animal sacrifices, physical circumcision, earthly priests, death by stoning, or rigid rules about feasts and the Sabbath. Rather, under the New Testament we fulfill the *spirit* of the law by practicing love. In Romans, Paul echoed Christ when he wrote:

8Let no debt remain outstanding, except the continuing debt to love one another, for he who loves his fellowman has fulfilled the law. 9The commandments, "Do not commit adultery," "Do not murder," "Do not steal," "Do not covet," and whatever other commandment there may be, are summed up in this one rule: "Love your neighbor as yourself." 10Love does no harm to its neighbor. Therefore love is the fulfillment of the law (Rom. 13:8-10).

Reference	Questions to answer about the relationship of believers to the Law
Matt. 7:12	How did Jesus summarize the Law and the Prophets in one short sentence?
Matt. 22:37-40	Which two commandments summarize the essence of the Law?
Rom. 13:8-10	How did Paul say we can fulfill the Law?
Gal. 5:13-14	What problem was Paul addressing in these verses? What solution does he give?

Figure 7.5   Guided practice relating law in the Old Testament to law in the New Testament

Q 38 ✎ How are believers like Maria?

Maria was married to a harsh man. He wrote a list of 10 things for her to do each day. Then he nailed the list to the door in the kitchen. Each night, when he came home, he checked to see if she had done all he commanded. Otherwise, he would threaten or beat her. Maria became bitter. She only did the things he wanted because he forced her. She worked as little as possible—just enough to avoid trouble. This poor woman felt like she had become a slave. In time her husband died. Maria took down his list and put it in a drawer. Later she married another man, who was loving, kind, generous, and thoughtful. She enjoyed cooking his breakfast and doing things at home to please him.

One day Maria found the old list of rules. She discovered that she was doing all those things and more for her new husband. Love had led her beyond the place that fear had driven her.[6]

D. The relationship of believers to the Holy Spirit (Rom. 8:4)

Principle: The power of the Holy Spirit enables us to obey the law of love.

Q 39 ➤ According to Romans 8:4, how are we able to obey the law of love?

1Therefore, there is now no condemnation for those who are in Christ Jesus, 2because through Christ Jesus the law of the Spirit of life set me free from the law of sin and death. 3For what the law was powerless to do in that it was weakened by the sinful nature, God did by sending his own Son in the likeness of sinful man to be a sin offering. And so he condemned sin in sinful man, 4in order that the righteous requirements of the law might be fully met in us, who do not live according to the sinful nature [flesh] ***but according to the Spirit*** (Rom. 8:1-4).

Romans 8:4b reveals the way that we are able to fulfill the righteous requirements of the Law. Note that Paul did not say the righteous requirements of the Law were met in us when Christ died on the cross. Rather, the righteous requirements of the Law are met in us as we live *"according to the Spirit"* (Rom. 8:4b). On the cross, Jesus sentenced and condemned the rule of sin in those who follow Him (Rom. 8:3). On the cross, Christ paid the price for our freedom. And Paul says victory belongs to those who resist sinful desires of the flesh, and live *"according to the Spirit"* (Rom. 8:4b). In Lesson 24 that follows, we will contrast living in the flesh and living in the Spirit. For now, as a foundation for Lesson 24, let us review ministries of the Spirit. In the New Testament, writers emphasize different ways the Spirit helps us. Review Figure 7.6. It contrasts the ministries of the Spirit that Luke, John, and Paul emphasize.

Q 40 ⟋ *In whom are the righteous requirements of the Law fully met?*

Q 41 ⟋ *Does Luke emphasize the role of the Spirit in victorious living? Explain.*

Q 42 ⟋ *Who teaches most about the role of the Spirit in victorious living: John or Paul? Give references.*

Writer	Ministry of the Holy Spirit	Selected Scriptures
Luke	1. Service (The Spirit enables us to serve unbelievers and believers.)	1. Luke 1:15-17, 39-56, 67-80; 2:25-38; 3:21-22; 4:18-19; 11:5-13; 24:45-49 (Acts 1:8 and all other references to the Spirit in Acts)
John	1. Regeneration (The Spirit draws the lost to Christ, convicts of sin, and imparts spiritual life at the new birth.)	1. John 12:32; 16:8-11; 3:5-8; 20:21-22
	2. Victorious living (The Spirit counsels, guides into truth, encourages us, and enables us to bear fruit.)	2. John 14:15-27;15:16-17; 1 John 2:20
	3. Service (The Spirit is the source of power to witness through words, deeds, and lifestyle.)	3. John 1:32; 7:37-39; 14:12-27; 15:26-27
Paul	1. Regeneration	1. Rom. 8:9, 15-16, 23; 1 Cor. 6:11; 12:13; 2 Cor. 1:22; 2 Thess. 2:13; Titus 3:5
	2. Victorious living (The Spirit enables us to live a holy life that pleases God.)	2. Rom. 8:1-14; 15:13; 2 Cor. 3:17-18; Gal. 5:22-26; Eph. 5:18; Titus 3:6
	3. Service (The Spirit empowers us to minister through gifts, deeds, and fruit.)	3. Rom. 12:3-8; 15:19; 1 Cor. 12:4-11; Gal. 5:22-26
	4. Resurrection/Glorification	4. Rom. 8:11, 29-30

Figure 7.6 The Spirit's ministry, according to Luke, John, and Paul

In the next lesson, we will explore what Paul says about the way the Spirit enables us to overcome sinful desires of the flesh.

A 747 jet plane seems too heavy and big to rise above the ground. But the power of its engines enables it to fly. This airplane can fly 35,000 feet above the earth, at 600 miles per hour (about 900 kph). Gravity tries to pull the airplane down. But the power of the engines lift this "jumbo jet," which may fly weighing almost 1 million pounds (440,000 kgs).[7] The engine and design of a plane enable it to overcome the law of gravity. Likewise, *"through Christ Jesus the law of the Spirit of life set me free from the law of sin and death"* (Rom. 8:2).[8] Christ empowers believers to rise above sin, and fulfill God's law of love. We can never obey God's law in our own strength. But the Spirit gives us power to rise above the downward pull of the flesh.

Figure 7.7 The powerful engines of a 747 "jumbo jet" enable it to fly 35,000 feet above the earth.

Lesson

24

In the Flesh or in the Spirit?—Part 1 (Rom. 8:5-17)

Goal: *Contrast the values of those led by the flesh and those led by the Spirit (Rom. 8:5).*

Background

Romans 8:4-17 contrasts living in the flesh and living in the Spirit. As we approach this passage, let us review two principles that emphasize the Spirit's ministry to believers.

Q 43 ⬦ *Why does Paul refer to the Holy Spirit as the "Spirit of sonship"?*

- **The Holy Spirit brings new life at the new birth (Rom. 8:15).**   Paul refers to the Holy Spirit as the Spirit of sonship.

  ¹⁵For you did not receive a spirit that makes you a slave again to fear, but you received the Spirit of sonship. And by him we cry, "Abba, Father." ¹⁶The Spirit himself testifies with our spirit that we are God's children (Rom. 8:15-16).

  The moment we turn from our sins and invite Christ into our hearts by faith, the Holy Spirit enters us—and assures us that we are God's children. Paul refers to the Holy Spirit as the *Spirit of Christ* (Rom. 8:9). God's apostle explains that the presence of Christ is in us, through the Holy Spirit—the same Spirit who raised Christ from the dead (Rom. 8:10-11). This same Spirit, *of* and *from* Christ, brings us life and gives us the inner witness that we are God's children (Rom. 8:16). Thus Paul refers to the Holy Spirit as the *Spirit of sonship* (Rom. 8:15).

  We cannot fully understand the Trinity. But we know that the Father, Son, and Holy Spirit have the same purpose, same nature, same essence, and same characteristics. Jesus said that whoever has seen Him has seen the Father (John 14:9). For the Son is the exact representation of the Father (Heb. 1:3). Likewise, Christ and the Spirit are so equal and united, that Jesus said, *"I will not leave you as orphans; I will come to you"*—through the Spirit of truth (John 14:15-18).

  When the Holy Spirit enters us at the new birth, we receive God's nature (2 Pet. 1:4). This does not mean that we become gods. But it does mean that at the new birth God begins the process of transforming us into the likeness of Christ (Rom. 8:29). The power of the *Spirit of life* enters us at regeneration (Rom. 8:2).

Q 44 ⬹ *How are our needs for physical and spiritual food alike?*

- **The Spirit brings new power and godliness, as He fills and refills us—over and over (Rom. 8:4-17; Eph. 5:18).**   All believers receive the Holy Spirit at the new birth. But this is not the end of the Spirit's ministry to us—it is only the beginning! Did you fill your stomach with food yesterday? Did that food give you strength to work and enjoy life? We hope so. But yesterday's food is not enough for today. That is why the Lord taught us to pray, *"Give us **this** day our daily bread."* Likewise, yesterday's spiritual food is not enough for today's spiritual battles.

Q 45 ⬦ *How often should we seek to be filled with the Spirit? Explain.*

  God does not want us to fight today's battles with yesterday's power. So Paul commands us: *"be filled with the Spirit"* (Eph. 5:18). This is a command in the present tense! Paul is not saying, "Be filled with the Spirit last year, last month, last week, or even yesterday." Ephesians 5:18 emphasizes being filled today, right now! The apostles were filled with the Spirit on the Day of Pentecost (Acts 2:1-4). As an outward sign of their filling, they spoke in new languages (Acts 2:4). But this was not the last time they were filled with the Spirit. They were filled again and again (Acts 4:8, 31). Acts is the story of how the Church spread from Jerusalem to Rome by the power of the Holy Spirit. Acts emphasizes, at least 10 times, the importance of staying filled with the Spirit (Acts 2:4; 4:8, 31; 6:3, 5; 7:55; 9:17; 11:24; 13:9, 52).

Q 46 ⬦ *Which is more important, the first time you were filled with the Spirit or the most recent time? Explain.*

  The early church did not look for deacons who had the reputation that they were once *filled* with the Spirit, in the past. No! They chose men who were *full* the day the church needed them (Acts 6:3, 5; 7:55). The question is not, Were you once filled with the Spirit? The question is, Are you full of the Spirit now? (Acts 11:24). It appears that Paul was filled with the Spirit when Ananias prayed for him (Acts 9:17). But Paul was either refilled or still full of the Spirit in a spiritual battle that blinded Elymas (Acts 13:9-11). Paul stayed so full of the Spirit that he prayed in tongues more than all the Corinthians (1 Cor. 14:18). Likewise, Paul led some disciples to be filled with the Spirit (Acts 19:1-7). How much gasoline you have in the tank today is more important than knowing the date you last filled it!

Caution: Do not expect to overcome the desires of the flesh with *only* the strength you received the day you were born again. The victorious life we will study in Romans 8:4-17 is possible to those who live filled with the Spirit. We hope that all of our readers are born again. And we hope that, like Paul and the other apostles, you have been filled with the Spirit and have prayed in a heavenly language. But our main concerns are: Are you filled with the Spirit today? Are you praying in tongues today? Is the fruit of the Spirit (Gal. 5:22-23) in your life today? Are you winning the battle over the flesh, the world, and the devil today?

Q 47 ⬟ *Why are some believers defeated by sin and the world? Explain.*

Let us not be like the five foolish virgins who were content with lamps half full of oil. They began well, but failed! The demands of life were more than they expected, and their lamps went out. In contrast, let us seek to be *filled* with the Spirit day by day, and hour by hour (Eph. 5:18).

We are taking time to emphasize the continuing ministry of the Spirit. Why? Paul prayed that believers *"may be filled to the measure of all the fullness of God"* (Eph. 3:19). All believers receive the Holy Spirit at the new birth. But we need the continuing ministry of the Spirit, lest we lack the power to resist and overcome the sinful desires of the flesh. In one nation, a recent statistic states that half of the men who attend church watch pornography.[9] The world is screaming "Look," and the flesh agrees. But the Spirit whispers, "Look away from the sinful attractions of the flesh and the world…Look up to Jesus." Fix your eyes on Jesus—*"the pioneer and perfecter of our faith"* (Heb. 12:2). Keep your heart and your thoughts on things above, not on earthly things (Col. 3:1-2). As we are filled with the Spirit, we hear Him speak to us and let Him lead us to please God. Is it possible that some think Romans 7:14-25 refers to believers because they do not live filled with the Spirit? Following Jesus is a spiritual journey. Let us hunger for God as we begin our day, and throughout the day. Let us walk softly before Him, depend on Him, and receive as much of His presence and power as He wants to give us. It is easier to *walk* in the Spirit when we are *filled* with the Spirit (Rom. 8:4)!

Q 48 ⬟ *How much of the Spirit did Paul want believers to live with? Explain.*

> IT IS EASIER TO *WALK* IN THE SPIRIT WHEN WE ARE *FILLED* WITH THE SPIRIT (ROM. 8:4).

Action Steps: How can I stay filled with the Spirit? Here are some guidelines to help all believers obey the wise counsel God gave through Paul: *"Be filled with the Spirit"* (Eph. 5:18).

1. To stay filled, be sure you are filled the first time. After you were born again, has the Spirit filled you as He filled the apostles and all the 120 on the Day of Pentecost? If not, seek this biblical filling. You may study more about this initial filling in the *Faith & Action Series* book, *Acts of the Holy Spirit*.

Q 49 ⬈ *What is the first step toward staying filled with the Spirit?*

2. Practice spiritual activities that increase the Spirit's presence in your life. Here are some examples. When you wake up in the morning, invite the presence of God by singing a chorus or hymn. Worship, sing to the Lord, pray in your native language and in tongues, even before you get out of bed, and as you prepare for the day. Listen to God, because He delights to talk with you. Begin your day with devotions. Throughout the day sing to yourself and to God with spiritual songs (Col. 3:16). Meditate on God and your favorite Scriptures. Thank God for who He is, and what He does for you and others. Praise Him for His goodness and faithfulness. Listen to spiritual music. Attend church, home Bible studies, and gospel concerts. Spend time with other believers. Minister to others. One of the reasons why God fills us is so there will be something to overflow for others. Practicing spiritual activities like these increases the Spirit's presence, and *fans into flame* spiritual gifts within you (2 Tim. 1:6).

Q 50 ⬟ *What are some activities that help us stay filled with the Spirit?*

3. Avoid things that quench the Spirit (1 Thess. 5:19). As the NIV states, *"Do not put out the Spirit's fire"* (1 Thess. 5:19). The main meaning of 1 Thessalonians 5:19 is about having an attitude of respect toward spiritual gifts, such as prophecy. Paul

Q 51 ⬟ *What are some things to avoid because they decrease the Spirit's presence in our lives?*

wrote this because spiritual gifts were common in worship services of the early church. Showing contempt for spiritual gifts is one way to decrease the Spirit's presence in our lives. Other ways to quench the Spirit include participating in activities that dishonor and offend God, such as viewing pornography, refusing to forgive, watching worldly entertainment, using drugs, and choosing to sin. The fire of the Spirit goes out when people throw water on it.

Q 52 *How can a believer make his body a slave, rather than a master?*

4. Make your body your slave, not your master. The body makes a good servant, but a poor boss. Paul testified that he made his body his slave (1 Cor. 9:27). Paul did not abuse his body, but neither did he indulge it. He lived a life of self discipline, and practiced self denial. He did not give the flesh all that it asked for. The Bible warns about indulging the flesh by eating too much (gluttony), sleeping too much (laziness), or sitting around too much (idleness). A good diet, good exercise, and practicing self discipline quiet the voice of the flesh.

Q 53 *Do you practice making the Spirit your master? Give examples.*

5. Make the Spirit your master. Submit to Him when He whispers to you. Obey the Scriptures. Practice things that please the Lord. Live with a clean conscience.

Let us make habits out of these five guidelines so we can live filled with the Spirit. Before a vessel can overflow with living water to refresh others, it must first be filled (John 7:38-39).

Overview

Q 54 *What big contrast is in Romans 7:21–8:17?*

Walking in the flesh or in the Spirit? This is the big contrast in Romans 7:21 through 8:17.

Romans 7:24 asks the <u>key question</u>: *"Who will rescue me from this body of death?"* In other words, Paul is asking, "Who will deliver me from slavery to the evil desires of rebellion—fleshly desires that result in spiritual death?" Paul has already given short answers to this question in Romans 6 and 7. Romans 6:6 said that *"our old self was crucified with him, so that the **body of sin** [evil desires of the flesh] might be done away with, that we should no longer be slaves to sin."* Likewise, Romans 7:25 affirms that we are rescued *"through Jesus Christ our Lord!"*

Romans 8:1-4 also answers the question: Who will deliver me from the sinful desires of my flesh?

Q 55 *What is the Greek word for "flesh"? How many times did Paul write it in Romans 8?*

Q 56 *Why is it sad that some translations do not use the word "flesh" in Romans 8?*

Some translations, like the New International Version (NIV), are usually helpful. At other times, as in Romans 8:1-17, the NIV blurs the contrast between *flesh* and *Spirit*. In the Greek text in Romans 8, the word *Spirit* occurs 21 times; and of these 21 times, all but two (8:15a and 8:16b) refer to the Holy Spirit.[10] These are easy to see in Romans 8 because the NIV *always* translates the Greek word *pneuma* as Spirit (or spirit). But in Romans 8, the Greek word *sarx* [flesh] appears 17 times. Yet the NIV "translates" *sarx* (or a form of it) <u>seven different ways</u>! As Figure 7.8 shows, in Romans 6–8, the NIV <u>never</u> translates *sarx* as flesh, but translates *sarx* as: *natural selves, sinful nature, unspiritual, sinful man, sinful mind, that nature,* and *it*. We can appreciate the translators emphasizing that our struggle is not with flesh or skin itself. Rather, we struggle with the **evil desires of our flesh**—or body. But as we study Romans 7–8, let us keep in mind that the big contrast is between the flesh (*sarx*) and the Spirit (*pneuma*). When we see clearly the contrast between *flesh* and *Spirit* in Romans 8, we understand that the person led by the flesh in Romans 7:14-25 was non-Christian.

Q 57 *How many different ways does the NIV translate "sarx"?*

Romans	Greek	NIV translations of *sarx* (or a form of *sarx*)
6:19	*sarx*	You are weak in your **natural selves**.
7:5	*sarx*	When we were controlled by the **sinful nature**,
7:14	*sarkinos*	The law is spiritual [*pneumatikos*]; but I am **unspiritual** [fleshly, *sarkinos*],
7:18	*sarx*	Nothing good lives in me, that is, in my **sinful nature**.

Continued on next page

7:25	*sarx*	*...but in the **sinful nature** a slave to the law of sin.*
8:3	*sarx*	*It was weakened by the **sinful nature**,*
8:3	*sarx*	*Sending his own Son in the likeness of **sinful man**...*
8:3	*sarx*	*And so he condemned sin in **sinful man**.*
8:4	*sarx*	*...of the law might be fully met in us, who do not live according to the **sinful nature** but according to the Spirit.*
8:5	*sarx*	*Those who live according to the **sinful nature** have their minds set on what that nature desires;*
8:6	*sarx*	*The mind of **sinful man** is death,*
8:7	*sarx*	*The **sinful mind** is hostile to God. It does not submit to God's law...*
8:8	*sarx*	*Those controlled by the **sinful nature** cannot please God.*
8:9	*sarx*	*You, however, are controlled not by the **sinful nature** but by the Spirit,*
8:12	*sarx*	*Therefore, brothers, we have an obligation—but it is not to the **sinful nature**, to live according to **it**.*
8:13	*sarx*	*For if you live according to the **sinful nature**, you will die; but if by the Spirit you put to death the misdeeds of the body, you will live,*

Figure 7.8   As you study Romans 7–8, keep in mind that over and over, Paul emphasizes the contrast between the <u>flesh</u> and the <u>Spirit</u>.

In Romans 8:4, Paul wrote that we fulfill the righteous requirements of the Law as we walk, not in the *flesh*, but in the *Spirit*. In Romans 8:5-17, Paul explains this contrast between flesh and Spirit. Let us examine four aspects or characteristics of the theme: in the flesh or in the Spirit?

A. Values: Are you guided by the flesh or the Spirit? (Rom. 8:5)

Those who live according to the sinful nature [flesh] have their minds set on what that nature [flesh] desires; but those who live in accordance with the Spirit have their minds set on what the Spirit desires (Rom. 8:5).

1. Problem: Those led by the flesh live by the selfish values of the world (Rom. 8:5a).   The New Testament uses the word *flesh* in various ways. The word *flesh* may mean the same as *human*. John says, *"The Word became flesh..."* (John 1:14). John means: the Son of God became human—the Son of Man. Likewise, Paul wrote that *"flesh and blood cannot inherit the kingdom of God"* (1 Cor. 15:50). Paul means that humans who perish and decay cannot inherit the eternal.[11] A different meaning of *flesh* appears in Romans 9:3. There, Paul refers to the Jews, his kinsman according to the flesh. He means that the Jews are his people, his ethnic group by blood. But in most of Romans, such as Romans 7–8, the word *flesh* refers to our evil fleshly desires. Likewise in Galatians, Paul describes the evil deeds of *the flesh:*

> [19]*The acts of the sinful nature [flesh] are obvious: sexual immorality, impurity and debauchery;* [20]*idolatry and witchcraft; hatred, discord, jealousy, fits of rage, selfish ambition, dissensions, factions* [21]*and envy; drunkenness, orgies, and the like. I warn you, as I did before, that those who live like this will not inherit the kingdom of God (Gal. 5:19-21).*

To be led by the flesh, rather than the Spirit of God, means to think like the world thinks. To be led by the flesh means to serve self, rather than others, or God. Although they might not say it, the actions of fleshly, carnal people show that they believe "I am my own god." Those in the flesh follow the lust of the flesh, the lust of the eyes, and the pride of life (1 John 2:16). Those led by the flesh say, "I want to get all I can of pleasure, money, power, prestige, recognition, comfort, and such." Favorite words of the flesh are: I, me, my, mine, and myself. The fruit of Galatians 5:19-21 reveals the root of the flesh.

In a letter to Timothy, Paul describes those led by the flesh:

> [1]*But mark this: There will be terrible times in the last days.* [2]*People will be lovers of themselves, lovers of money, boastful, proud, abusive, disobedient to their parents, ungrateful, unholy,* [3]*without love, unforgiving, slanderous, without self-*

Q 58 ↗ *What does Paul mean by "flesh" in Romans 8 and Galatians 5?*

Q 59 ↖ *What are some characteristics of those led by the flesh?*

control, brutal, not lovers of the good, ⁴treacherous, rash, conceited, lovers of pleasure rather than lovers of God (2 Tim. 3:1-4).

In a letter to the Ephesians, Paul contrasted those in the flesh and those in the Spirit:

²⁹*Do not let any unwholesome talk come out of your mouths, but only what is helpful for building others up according to their needs, that it may benefit those who listen.* ³⁰*And do not grieve the Holy Spirit of God, with whom you were sealed for the day of redemption.* ³¹*Get rid of all bitterness, rage and anger, brawling and slander, along with every form of malice.* ³²*Be kind and compassionate to one another, forgiving each other, just as in Christ God forgave you.* ¹*Be imitators of God, therefore, as dearly loved children* ²*and live a life of love, just as Christ loved us and gave himself up for us as a fragrant offering and sacrifice to God.* ³*But among you there must not be even a hint of sexual immorality, or of any kind of impurity, or of greed, because these are improper for God's holy people.* ⁴*Nor should there be obscenity, foolish talk or coarse joking, which are out of place, but rather thanksgiving.* ⁵*For of this you can be sure: No immoral, impure or greedy person—such a man is an idolater—has any inheritance in the kingdom of Christ and of God.* ⁶*Let no one deceive you with empty words, for because of such things God's wrath comes on those who are disobedient.* ⁷*Therefore do not be partners with them* (Eph. 4:29–5:7).

Those led by the flesh want to push God off the throne and sit on it themselves. They reject His Law and His Lordship. For a few Old Testament examples of those led by the flesh, review the stories of Adam and Eve, Cain, Lamech, people just before the Flood, Achan, Samson, the sons of Samuel, Saul, David and Bathsheba, Solomon, the Israelites whom God delivered from Egypt, Balaam, Nadab and Abihu, Ahab and Jezebel. And in the New Testament, review accounts of Herod, Pilate, the High Priests, Pharisees, Sadducees, Herodians, the rich young ruler, Herodias and Salome, Judas, Ananias and Sapphira, Saul of Tarsus, and a multitude of others. Examples of those led by the flesh are easy to find. Because without Christ, every human is an example of a fleshly, sinful person—from the crib to the tomb. Some led by the flesh are more violent and obvious. But all without Christ are fleshly, unspiritual, prisoners of sin—slaves of fleshly desires.

Q 60 Who are some biblical examples of people led by the flesh?

2. Solution: Those led by the Spirit live by the values of God (Rom. 8:5b).

But those who live in accordance with the Spirit have their minds set on what the Spirit desires (Rom. 8:5a).

To live in the Spirit, we must focus our minds on what the Spirit desires. We must value what God values.

Galatians 5:17-18 is a parallel passage to Romans 7:17-24. It describes a person trying to live in his own strength, under the Law. Paul urges such people to stop living like they are under law. Rather, the key to overcoming the desires of the flesh is depending on the Holy Spirit.

Q 61 What is the key to overcoming selfish desires of the flesh?

¹⁶*So I say, live by the Spirit, and you will not gratify the desires of the sinful nature* [flesh]. ¹⁷*For the sinful nature* [flesh] *desires what is contrary to the Spirit, and the Spirit what is contrary to the sinful nature* [flesh]. *They are in conflict with each other, so that you do not do what you want.* ¹⁸*But if you are led by the Spirit, you are not under law* (Gal. 5:16-18).

Those depending on the Law and living under it will fail. Law commands us to stop sinning, but it cannot deliver us from sin's power.

Q 62 Does the conflict between flesh and Spirit end at the new birth? Explain.

The solution. *"Live by the Spirit, and you will not gratify the desires of the sinful nature* [flesh]*"* (Gal. 5:16). The conflict between flesh and Spirit does not go away when we are born again. But at the new birth, we receive the Spirit and the freedom to follow Him. Slaves of sin have no choice; they are prisoners to a stronger power. But when we receive the Spirit, He begins to lead us away from darkness and bondage into a new way of life. Thus Paul refers to *"the new way of the Spirit"* (Rom. 7:6). Led by the Spirit, our desires change. *"Those who live in accordance with the Spirit have their minds set on what the Spirit desires"* (Rom. 8:5b). Listening to the Spirit, we learn to value the things God values. This happens because God changes our hearts, and we partake of God's nature. God lives within us, and this influences what we love and what we hate.

Led by the Spirit, we value Scripture, obedience, prayer, worship, holiness, righteousness, fellowship with God and His people, forgiveness, compassion, pleasing God, and serving others.

Q 63 *As the Spirit leads us, what are some things we learn to value?*

In a letter to the Colossians, Paul describes the <u>process</u> of being led by the Spirit.

¹*Since, then, you have been raised with Christ, set your hearts on things above, where Christ is seated at the right hand of God. ²Set your minds on things above, not on earthly things. ³For you died, and your life is now hidden with Christ in God. ⁴When Christ, who is your life, appears, then you also will appear with him in glory. ⁵Put to death, therefore, whatever belongs to your earthly nature: sexual immorality, impurity, lust, evil desires and greed, which is idolatry. ⁶Because of these, the wrath of God is coming. ⁷You used to walk in these ways, in the life you once lived. ⁸But now you must rid yourselves of all such things as these: anger, rage, malice, slander, and filthy language from your lips. ⁹Do not lie to each other, since you have taken off your old self with its practices ¹⁰and have put on the new self,* **which is being renewed in knowledge in the image of its Creator** (Col. 3:1-10).

Q 64 *Is being led by the Spirit an event or a process? Explain.*

Read Colossians 3:10 again. At the new birth, God is not finished with us yet. Paul tells us to aim for perfection (2 Cor. 13:11). To be as perfect as Christ is our aim, our goal, and our destiny. Let us practice keeping this goal before us. But let us also remember that we are not perfect yet. As we will study in Romans 8:29, God's plan is to transform us into the likeness of Jesus. Encourage yourself. There is no perfection in Christ, yet, on this earth. But neither is there any condemnation in Christ (Rom. 8:1)! We may still have our faults and failures, but we are facing the right direction! We are on the right road! Hallelujah! Our values are better than they used to be. Our thoughts and actions are improving. We are becoming more holy, more godly, more like Christ. The Spirit is leading us onward and upward! We are *"being renewed in knowledge in the image of [our] Creator"*—Jesus Christ (Col. 3:10; John 1:1).

Q 65 *What encouragement does Colossians 3:10 give you? Summarize this verse.*

Q 66 *How have your values changed since the Spirit began to lead you?*

Lesson 25

In the Flesh or in the Spirit?—Part 2 (Rom. 8:5-17)

Goal A: *Contrast the spiritual states of those led by the flesh and those led by the Spirit (Rom. 8:6, 13).*

Goal B: *Identify characteristics of God's enemy and God's family (Rom. 8:7-17).*

We are examining four aspects or characteristics of the theme: in the flesh or in the Spirit? In Lesson 24 we looked at the first aspect:

A. Values: Are you guided by the flesh or the Spirit (Rom. 8:5)?

Now let us study three more aspects (B–D), contrasting flesh and Spirit.

B. Spiritual pulse: Are you dead or alive? (Rom. 8:6, 13)

The mind of sinful man [flesh] *is* **death**, *but the mind controlled by the Spirit is* **life** *and peace* (Rom. 8:6).

For if you live according to the sinful nature [flesh], *you will* **die**; *but if by the Spirit you put to death the misdeeds of the body, you will* **live** (Rom. 8:13).

Q 67 *What does "death" mean in Romans 8:6, 13?*

Q 68 ⟍ *Is it possible for a person to die spiritually? Explain.*

1. Problem: Those led by the flesh die spiritually (Rom. 8:6a, 13).   Death knocks on every door. Physical death comes to Christians and non-Christians. But Romans 8:6 and 8:13 refer to spiritual death. Those led by the flesh die spiritually—both now and forever. God warned Adam that if he ate of the forbidden fruit in the garden, he would die (Gen. 2:17). Years after his disobedience, Adam died physically. But Adam died spiritually the day he disobeyed God.

Spiritual death refers to our relationship with God. God is holy, and we who relate to Him must seek to be holy in all we do (1 Pet. 1:13-16). For practicing sin kills our relationship with God.

Note that Romans 8:13 does NOT say, "If you live according to the flesh, you were never born of the Spirit." And it does NOT say, "If you live according to the flesh, you can never die." Some falsely teach that those who follow the flesh *never* knew God. And they also teach that those born of the Spirit can never die spiritually. But Romans 8:13 is written to believers. It warns those who are spiritually alive. If we follow the sinful desires of the flesh, this leads to eternal death. Two roads are ever before us (much like Figure 7.11; Gal. 6:7-10). Those who choose to follow the desires of the flesh walk in darkness, and separate themselves from God—for He is Light. Those who claim to fellowship with God, but walk in darkness, are liars (1 John 1:6). Following the flesh leads away from God into darkness and destruction. Walking in sin results in condemnation and spiritual death now. As Paul wrote, a person who lives to please the flesh is dead, even while living—dead spiritually while living physically (1 Tim. 5:6). And at the end of this life, God will separate from Himself, forever, those who followed their fleshly desires. He will cast them into the lake of fire that was prepared for the devil and his angels. Scripture refers to this judgment as *"the second death"* (Rev. 20:14).

Paul reminded the Ephesians that sin caused their spiritual death before they met Christt:

> [1]*As for you, you were **dead** in your transgressions and sins,* [2]*in which you used to live when you followed the ways of this world and of the ruler of the kingdom of the air, the spirit who is now at work in those who are disobedient.* [3]*All of us also lived among them at one time, gratifying the cravings of our sinful nature* [flesh] *and following its desires and thoughts. Like the rest, we were by nature objects of wrath.* [4]*But because of his great love for us, God, who is rich in mercy,* [5]*made us **alive** with Christ even when we were **dead** in transgressions—it is by grace you have been saved* (Eph. 2:1-5).

Q 69 ⟍ *What causes spiritual death?*

In Romans, Paul refers many times to the spiritual death linked to following the flesh (Rom. 6:13, 16, 21, 23; 7:5, 10-11, 13, 24; 8:6, 13).

2. Solution: Those led by the Spirit have spiritual life and peace (Rom. 8:6a, 13).

The mind of sinful man [flesh] *is **death**, but the mind controlled <u>by the Spirit</u> is **life** and peace* (Rom. 8:6).

For if you live according to the sinful nature [flesh], *you will **die**; but if <u>by the Spirit</u> you put to death the misdeeds of the body, you will **live*** (Rom. 8:13).

By the Spirit. To avoid despair, frustration, and failure, we must pay attention to the words *"by the Spirit"* (Rom. 8:6, 13). We live in bodies of flesh and daily face temptations. Sin is bold. It increases and seduces every day. Jesus prophesied, *"Because of the increase of wickedness, the love of most will grow cold"* (Matt. 24:12). However, God does not expect us to pick up a cross each day and go looking for sins to crucify. Let us not focus too much on the problem, but emphasize God's solution to temptation. We overcome *"by the Spirit"* (Rom. 8:6, 13). Only by the Spirit can we live as *"aliens and strangers in the world"* and turn away from fleshly desires, *"which war against"* our souls (1 Pet. 2:11). The flesh pulls one way, but the Spirit pulls another. So let us practice responding to and depending on the Spirit. What is impossible in our own strength is easy in the Spirit.

> SOME SEEM TO THINK WE ARE SAVED FROM OUR PAST SINS BY GRACE, BUT OVERCOME OUR PRESENT TEMPTATIONS BY OUR OWN EFFORTS.

Some seem to think we are saved from our past sins by grace, but overcome our present temptations by our own efforts. In contrast, Paul teaches that we overcome as we allow the Spirit to control us. Those who depend on themselves are insecure. They live in constant fear of failure. But we did not save ourselves from past sins, and we are not alone in our struggles with temptation. In ourselves, we lack the power to defeat sin. Yet *"by the Spirit"* we *"put to death the misdeeds of the body"* (Rom. 8:13). The Spirit within us gives us power to conquer and to live! Our victory over sin is by the Spirit. This is that same Spirit who enters believers at the new birth. He is the same Spirit of Christ who fills believers with power to witness and enables us to speak in tongues. He is the same Spirit who enables us to abound in the fruit of the Spirit (including self control). This is that same Spirit who enables us to crucify the hostile desires of the flesh, die daily, take up a cross, deny ourselves, and follow Jesus (Gal. 5:22-25). This is the same Spirit we need to fill and refill us each day. Every moment of our success depends on listening to and submitting to the Spirit within us.

Q 70 *Contrast those who depend on themselves with those who depend on the Spirit.*

A young man was walking down the road. An attractive woman walked toward him. Desires of the flesh pulled him to look toward the left, at the woman. But the Spirit whispered, look toward the right and give thanks for your godly mother, sisters, and the wife I will give you. The young man allowed the Spirit to control him, and he walked forward in freedom.

Q 71 *Has the Spirit helped you overcome a sin or temptation? Explain.*

A husband became angry with his wife. They were arguing about money. The Spirit whispered to him, "Lower your voice, and practice being gentle. Remember the Scripture, *"Husbands, love your wives and do not be harsh with them"* (Col. 3:19). The husband obeyed, and soon, his anger cooled, and his mind became clear.

Miriam and Suzy were close friends, until Suzy was offended. In her anger, Suzy began to say hateful things to others about Miriam. These unkind words, like seeds, produced a harvest. For in time, some of Miriam's friends told her the hateful things Suzy was saying. Miriam talked to Suzy to try to repair their relationship, but Suzy was unwilling. Still, Miriam knew she should forgive Suzy. Time after time Miriam chose to forgive. She told herself, told God, and told others that she had forgiven Suzy. Yet even though Miriam was willing to forgive, and tried to forgive, feelings of bitterness remained in her heart. So day after day Miriam brought Suzy to the throne of grace in prayer. And she continued to ask the Father to heal her bitterness toward Suzy. For although Miriam was willing, she could not free herself from this bitterness. Then one day as Miriam prayed, it seemed as if the finger of God reached down and touched her heart. In that moment, she was free from her bitterness toward Suzy. Likewise, our part is to bring our faults, hurts, and sins to God. And God's part is to save us from our sins *by the Spirit*. We must use our will and our freedom to choose. But *only God* can give us the power we need to rise above temptations and sins *by the Spirit*.

The contrast between the Spirit's gifts and fruit: The flesh produces *death*, but the Spirit produces *life*. The Spirit in us does not just lead us toward life. Rather, the Spirit *produces* life in and through us. Too often, when we think of the Spirit, we think of the gifts He manifests. The presence of the Spirit brings to us the gift of eternal life. We receive this gift in a moment at the new birth. Likewise, the baptism in the Spirit is a gift Father promised (Acts 1:4). We receive this Pentecostal baptism of the Spirit in a moment. Likewise, the gifts of the Spirit in 1 Corinthians 12–14 are quick, sudden bursts

Q 72 *How is bearing a fruit different from receiving a gift?*

of the Spirit's power. For example, a gift of healing or a miracle may be as fast as the flash of a camera.

In contrast, Romans 8:4-17 emphasizes a relationship and a *process* of living by the Spirit. We do not want believers to choose between the gifts and the fruit of the Spirit. We want both! But consider the *process* of bearing the fruit of the Spirit. For example, consider the spiritual fruit of gentleness. Gentleness is not like a gift that the Spirit hands to us. It is *not something we receive*. Rather, gentleness is *something we become*.[12] Ponder this encouraging, amazing truth. God's plan is to make us like Jesus (Rom. 8:29). He is the most gentle of all people. Our Savior, Lord, and Example is so gentle that He will not break a bruised reed, or quench a smoking wick of a candle (Matt. 12:20). Jesus is our model for gentleness. And through His Spirit within us, we partake of the nature of Christ. The Spirit produces the fruit of gentleness in us. The more we grow in Christ, the more we become gentle, like Jesus.

Q 73 ✎ *Explain: Fruit is the outer evidence of an inner nature.*

The government cannot write laws that require trees to bear fruit. And the Church cannot preach laws that will produce spiritual fruit in believers. Fruit is the outer evidence of an inner nature. A banana tree produces bananas because of its nature. Man can help by pruning and using fertilizer. But the fruit of a tree depends on the nature of the tree. Likewise, we must depend on the Spirit within us to produce the fruit of a victorious life.

> [22]*But the fruit of the Spirit is love, joy, peace, patience, kindness, goodness, faithfulness,* [23]*gentleness and self-control. Against such things there is no law.* [24]*Those who belong to Christ Jesus have crucified the sinful nature with its passions and desires.* [25]*Since we live by the Spirit, let us keep in step with the Spirit* (Gal. 5:22-25).

Look again at the fruit of the Spirit (Gal. 5:22-25). As we submit to the Spirit, we live and have this fruit in our lives. And with this living fruit, we will overcome every temptation of the world. For temptations and sins of the world are one direction, and the fruit of the Spirit is the opposite direction. Those led by the flesh walk away from God to death, but the Spirit leads us to closer fellowship with Jesus. He produces life everlasting in us, and ministry that refreshes others.

Q 74 ✎ *How does John 7:37-39 emphasize the Spirit in a relationship, rather than just an event?.*

> [37]*"If anyone is thirsty, let him come to me and drink.* [38]*Whoever believes in me, as the Scripture has said, streams of living water will flow from within him."* [39]*By this he meant the Spirit, whom those who believed in him were later to receive* (John 7:37-39).

Q 75 ✎ *How is living in the Spirit related to remaining in Christ?*

> *"Remain in me, and I will remain in you. No branch can bear fruit by itself; it must remain in the vine. Neither can you bear fruit unless you remain in me"* (John 15:4).

C. Status: Are you one of God's enemies or in His family?

1. Problem: Those led by the flesh are God's enemies (Rom. 8:7-8).

Q 76 ✎ *Did the person in Romans 7:14-25 live like God's enemy or a member of His family? Explain.*

> [7]*The sinful mind* [flesh] *is hostile to God. It does not submit to God's law, nor can it do so.* [8]*Those controlled by the sinful nature* [flesh] *cannot please God* (Rom. 8:7-8).

Those led by the Spirit have *peace* with God (Rom. 8:6). But those led by the flesh are hostile to God—they are God's enemies. Paul wrote about God's enemies earlier in Romans:

Q 77 ✎ *What are some characteristics of God's enemies?*

> [8]*But for those who are self-seeking and who reject the truth and follow evil, there will be wrath and anger.* [9]*There will be trouble and distress for every human being who does evil: first for the Jew, then for the Gentile* (Rom. 2:8-9).

In 2 Thessalonians, Paul warns that God will one day judge His enemies—those who do not submit to His Law, Lordship, and rule:

⁶God is just: He will pay back trouble to those who trouble you ⁷and give relief to you who are troubled, and to us as well. This will happen when the Lord Jesus is revealed from heaven in blazing fire with his powerful angels. ⁸He will punish those who do not know God and do not obey the gospel of our Lord Jesus. ⁹They will be punished with everlasting destruction and shut out from the presence of the Lord and from the majesty of his power ¹⁰on the day he comes to be glorified in his holy people and to be marveled at among all those who have believed (2 Thess. 1:6-10).

Those who rebel against the Spirit and choose to follow the sinful desires of the flesh choose to be God's enemies. These, like Esau, forfeit the blessings Father planned for them. Like the Israelites who rejected God and Moses, they choose the curses of disobedience, rather than the blessings of obedience (Deut. 28).

2. Solution: Those led by the Spirit are God's family (Rom. 8:9-17).

⁹You, however, are controlled not by the sinful nature [flesh] but by the Spirit, if the Spirit of God lives in you. And if anyone does not have the Spirit of Christ, he does not belong to Christ. ¹⁰But if Christ is in you, your body is dead because of sin [dead to the cause of serving sin—see Rom. 6:11], *yet your spirit is alive because of righteousness* [alive to serve righteousness—see Rom. 6:11]. *¹¹And if the Spirit of him who raised Jesus from the dead is living in you, he who raised Christ from the dead will also give life to your mortal bodies through his Spirit, who lives in you. ¹²Therefore, brothers, we have an obligation—but it is not to the sinful nature [flesh], to live according to it. ¹³For if you live according to the sinful nature [flesh], you will die; but if by the Spirit you put to death the misdeeds of the body, you will live, ¹⁴because those who are led by the Spirit of God are sons of God. ¹⁵For you did not receive a spirit that makes you a slave again to fear, but you received the Spirit of sonship [adoption]. And by him we cry, "Abba, Father." ¹⁶The Spirit himself testifies with our spirit that we are God's children. ¹⁷Now if we are children, then we are heirs—heirs of God and co-heirs with Christ, if indeed we share in his sufferings in order that we may also share in his glory* (Rom. 8:9-17).

We could spend a whole lesson on this passage, but we lack the space. But note some of the characteristics of God's children, as you stand on the mountaintop of Romans 8:

- **Relationships bring responsibilities.** God's children have an *obligation* to honor Him. In contrast, we should not expect those led by the flesh to obey and honor God (Rom. 8:12). He is not their Father.

- **God's children are led by the Spirit (Rom. 8:14).** In contrast, the devil's children are led by the flesh (John 8:44). We recognize God's children because they obey God and do His will.

    ⁴⁶While Jesus was still talking to the crowd, his mother and brothers stood outside, wanting to speak to him. ⁴⁷Someone told him, "Your mother and brothers are standing outside, wanting to speak to you." ⁴⁸He replied to him, "Who is my mother, and who are my brothers?" ⁴⁹Pointing to his disciples, he said, "Here are my mother and my brothers. ⁵⁰For whoever does the will of my Father in heaven is my brother and sister and mother" (Matt. 12:46-50).

- **God's children have a close relationship with Him.** His Spirit in us fills us with love for Him, and enables us to call Him *Abba*—the Aramaic word for *father* (Rom. 8:15). *"God has poured out his love into our hearts by the Holy Spirit, whom he has given us"* (Rom. 5:5). Consider the contrast between God's enemies and His beloved children! As a father holds his child on his lap, God delights to hold us close to him.

Q 78 *How can we recognize a member of God's family?*

- **God's children have an inner assurance that we belong to Him.** *"The Spirit himself testifies with our spirit that we are God's children"* (Rom. 8:16).

    People in many religions do not know where they will spend eternity. Good Muslims pray five times a day, and fast during the month of Ramadan. Yet they are not sure what the future holds. And many who read the Bible and attend church 'now and then' have only a faint hope of reaching heaven. In contrast, Paul wrote that God's true children know for certain that God is their father (Rom. 8:16). As John Wesley's father told him, every person should seek the inner witness of the Spirit to be sure of peace with God.[13] Eternity is too long to leave to chance.

- **God's children are co-heirs with Christ.** As Jesus told the disciples, *"Do not be afraid, little flock, for your Father has been pleased to give you the kingdom"* (Luke 12:32). An earthly father delights to share all he has with his children who please him. Likewise, God delights to share the riches of heaven with us, forever.

Q 79 *What truth does Romans 8:16 declare? Memorize this verse.*

In the Flesh or in the Spirit?—Part 3 (Gal. 5:13–6:10)

Lesson 26

Goal A: *Analyze the conflict in believers between the flesh and the Spirit (Gal. 5:13-18).*
Goal B: *Explain and illustrate the fruit of the flesh, and their results (Gal. 5:19-21).*
Goal C: *Explain and illustrate the fruit of the Spirit, and their results (Gal. 5:22-26).*
Goal D: *Describe God's plan for a believer "caught" in a sin (Gal. 6:1-5).*
Goal E: *Summarize and illustrate God's law of harvest (Gal. 6:7-10).*

Our study of Romans includes parallel passages in Galatians. We have seen that the big contrast in Romans 8 is being led by the *flesh* or being led by the *Spirit*. Galatians 5:13–6:10 gives another great contrast between *flesh* and *Spirit*. We will explore five principles that Paul presents in this section:

A: The flesh and the Spirit oppose each other (Gal. 5:13-18).
B: Those led by the flesh will not inherit the kingdom of God (Gal. 5:19-21).
C: Those led by the Spirit enjoy total freedom (Gal. 5:22-26).
D: If a believer is trapped in a sin of the flesh, those led by the Spirit should gently restore him (Gal. 6:1-5).
E: Each person reaps what he sows (Gal. 6:7-10).

Let us take a closer look at each of these five principles.

A. The flesh and the Spirit oppose each other (Gal. 5:13-18).

Congratulations! You have completed six chapters in this *Faith & Action* book. Now you are in chapter 7, **Freedom Through the Spirit-led Life.** Keep this in mind as you read Galatians 5:13-18:

> *[13]You, my brothers, were called to be free. But do not use your freedom to indulge the sinful nature [flesh]; rather, serve one another in love. [14]The entire law is summed up in a single command: "Love your neighbor as yourself." [15]If you keep on biting and devouring each other, watch out or you will be destroyed by each other. [16]So I say, live by the Spirit, and you will not gratify the desires of the sinful nature [flesh]. [17]For the sinful nature [flesh] desires what is contrary to the Spirit, and the Spirit what is contrary to the sinful nature [flesh]. They are in conflict with each other, so that you do not do what you want. [18]But if you are led by the Spirit, you are not under law* (Gal. 5:13-18).

Q 80 *What are some examples of indulging the flesh?*

Under the Law, people were prisoners of the flesh—slaves of fleshly desires (Gal. 5:18; Rom. 6:17; 7:5, 18-20). But when we become God's children, Christ *frees* us from being slaves of sin and the flesh (Rom. 5:13; Rom. 6:18; 7:6; 8:1-4). As one song proclaims, "My chains are gone, I've been set free. My God, my Savior has ransomed me!"[14]

Freedom is a great privilege. But we can misuse any privilege. Hophni and Phineas were priests, sons of Eli. But they abused and misused their freedom for a sinful purpose. *"They slept with the women who served at the entrance to the Tent of Meeting"* (1 Sam. 2:22). Many misuse their freedom. So Paul warns believers: *"Do not use your freedom to indulge the sinful nature* [flesh]*"* (Gal. 5:13).

The battle between the flesh and the Spirit does not end at the new birth. The new life and presence of the Spirit in us does not at once destroy the old desires of the flesh. So long as we live on this earth in "this age," the *flesh* remains a force within us, ready to rebel against the *Spirit* at any moment.[15] Recall that by the word *flesh* Paul is not referring to what covers human bones. Rather, *flesh* refers to the aspect or domain of each person that tends to resist, oppose, and fight against the Holy Spirit. NIV sometimes translates *flesh* as sinful nature. Non-theologians refer to *flesh* as the base or dark side of humanity. At conversion and regeneration, Christ sets us free from being prisoners of the *flesh*. However, even as followers of Christ, the *flesh* remains as a part of our humanity, as long as we dwell in a body of flesh. Believers are no longer prisoners of the *flesh,* but we must still overcome *fleshly* temptations and suggestions toward evil. In Romans 6 we studied six keys or principles Paul wrote to help believers overcome the flesh and live in the Spirit. And in Romans 8 we examined several principles for walking in the Spirit, not the flesh. Likewise, in Galatians 5:16-18 Paul wrote to believers. He said that the *flesh* and the *Spirit* are in conflict with each other. The *flesh* leads one direction, and the *Spirit* leads a different direction. The *flesh* leads us to serve only ourselves. The *Spirit* leads us to love our neighbor <u>as</u> ourselves (Gal. 5:14).

- **The bad news is:** Even the most mature, Spirit-filled believers can testify that the struggle between *flesh* and *Spirit* continues through all of life on earth.
- **The good news is:** The more we practice being led by the *Spirit,* the less influence the *flesh* has on us.

There is an old story about a man who had two dogs—one was dark and the other light. The dogs often fought against each other, and people bet money on which dog would win. This story is about a cruel sport, and we are thankful that in most places today it is illegal to have contests where dogs fight. But the interesting thing in the *old story* is that the owner could always predict which dog would win the fight. Sometimes the owner knew the dark dog would prevail. Other times he knew the lighter dog would be the victor. A friend asked the owner, "How are you always sure which dog will overcome the other?" The owner replied, "That is easy. The winner is always the one that I feed that day." And so it is in the struggle between the *flesh* and the *Spirit.* We *feed* the spiritual part of us with daily devotions, an attitude of prayer without ceasing, meditation on Bible verses, and practicing good thoughts. We feed our spirit-being as we enjoy spiritual songs, worship, thanksgiving, and wholesome entertainment. We feed the *inner man* as we turn away from evil and turn toward things that are righteous, edifying, and pleasing to God. As we allow the Spirit to lead us in this *lifestyle,* the voice of the *flesh* becomes as weak as a whisper, and often unheard. With this use of our *freedom,* the new way of the Spirit crowds out the old dominion of the *flesh.* In contrast, some believers *indulge the flesh* (Gal. 5:13). They nurse bitterness and review past offenses they have never forgiven. In time, a root of bitterness in them grows into a small tree. Or they feed the *flesh* by meditating on evil thoughts of lust and pornography. They *indulge the flesh* by approving entertainment that would cause a holy person to blush. They grieve the Holy Spirit by abusing their freedom to choose. Thus they sow to the flesh and must reap a harvest of destruction (Gal. 6:7-10). So let us always discern that the *flesh* and the *Spirit* oppose each other. Let us obey Paul's warning, *"do not use your freedom to indulge the sinful nature* [flesh]*"* (Gal. 5:13). *"Let us live by the Spirit,"* and we *"will not gratify the desires of the sinful nature* [flesh]*"* (Gal. 5:16).

Q 81 ↖ *When does the struggle between flesh and Spirit end?*

Q 82 ↖ *What is the lesson in the story of the two dogs? Illustrate this principle.*

Q 83 ❮ *Does a person who practices sexual sins have any inheritance in the kingdom of Christ (Gal. 5:21; Eph. 5:5)? Explain.*

B. Those led by the flesh will not inherit the kingdom of God (Gal. 5:19-21).

Some believers deceive themselves. They think grace is a robe that covers a lifestyle of sinful living. These mistaken believers say that because of grace and the blood of Christ, God does not see the sins a believer commits. But notice what Paul wrote about those led by the flesh, instead of the Spirit:

[19]*The acts of the sinful nature are obvious: sexual immorality, impurity and debauchery;* [20]*idolatry and witchcraft; hatred, discord, jealousy, fits of rage, selfish ambition, dissensions, factions* [21]*and envy; drunkenness, orgies, and the like. I warn you, as I did before, that **those who live like this will not inherit the kingdom of God*** (Gal. 5:19-21).

As we noted earlier, the notion of justification <u>without</u> sanctification is fiction. Those led by the flesh will not inherit heaven. Not everyone who talks about heaven is going there.

In other letters Paul mentions other sins, such as: murder, deceit, malice, pride, disobedience, coarse talk, lying, stealing, lusting, greed, gossip, slander (Rom. 1:28-32; Eph. 4:25–5:5; Col. 3:5). But in Galatians 5:19-21 Paul lists 15 deeds or fruits of the flesh. Study these in Figure 7.9, and practice giving examples of each. Seeing these evil deeds in Scripture, and recalling examples of those who sinned, helps steer us away from destruction and toward eternal life (Gal. 5:21; 6:7-10; Eph. 4:5-6).

Q 84 ❮ *Write the names that follow with the fruit of the flesh they illustrate in Figure 7.9. The first name, Diotrephes, we have written for you. (Some of the names can be in more than one box, and some do not belong in the chart. Add examples you think of yourself.) Diotrephes (3 John 9); Samson (Judg. 14–16); Cain (Gen. 4); Corinthian believers (1 Cor. 3:1-4; 11:17-19); Noah (Gen. 9:21); Paul (Rom. 9:1-3); Jewish chief priests (Matt. 27:18); Zimri and Cozbi (Num. 25:6, 14-15); Euodia and Syntyche (Phil. 4:2); Simon (Acts 8:18-19); Ahab (1 Kings 21); Israelites (Exod. 32:6; 1 Cor. 10:7); Pharisees (Matt. 15:1-20); the sinful believer (1 Cor. 5:1, 9); godless men (Jude 4, 11-12); homosexuals of Sodom (Gen. 19:4-9; 2 Pet. 2:7-8); sinners of Revelation 21:8; Moses (Num. 20:10-12); false prophets (2 Thess. 2:2); greedy people (Col. 3:5)*

Sins of the Flesh	Greek Word	Definitions and Explanations	Example and References
1. Sexual immorality	*porneia*	Sexual activity outside the marriage union. The word *pornography* is based on *porneia*. So sexual immorality includes pornographic pictures and films.	
2. Impurity	*a-katharsia*	The opposite of pure or clean; refers to sexual sins, evil deeds, and attitudes—including thoughts and desires of the heart (Eph. 5:3; Col. 3:5).	
3. Debauchery	*aselgeia*	Sensuality; unbridled or uncontrolled lust; following one's passions or desires without shame or public respect (2 Pet. 2:7; Rom. 13:13)	
4. Idolatry	*eidololatria*	To trust, serve, love, or worship anyone or anything in a manner that only God deserves (1 Cor. 10:7)	
5. Witchcraft	*pharmakeia*	Sorcery, spiritism, black magic, worship of demons, and the use of drugs in seeking spiritual experiences	
6. Hatred	*echtra*	Hostile thoughts, feelings, and acts; extreme dislike or enmity	
7. Discord	*eris*	Quarreling, arguing, fighting	
8. Jealousy	*zelos*	Fear of losing someone or something that a person values. Herod was jealous (over-protective) of his throne (Matt. 2). He killed family members and even infants who threatened what he wanted for himself. He did not want a better king to reign.	
9. Fits of rage	*thumos*	Anger that explodes with harmful words or deeds (Col. 3:8)	
10. Selfish ambition	*eritheia*	Unrighteous desire for power or position	Diotrephes (3 John 9)
11. Dissensions	*dichostasia*	Divisive and unbiblical teachings (Rom. 16:17)	

Continued on next page

12. Factions	*hairesis*	Groups or cliques that destroy the unity in a church. These groups may result from quarreling, jealousy, status, ethnicity, and such	
13. Envy	*phthonos*	Covetousness; wanting something another has, such as beauty, wealth, power, abilities, or status	
14. Drunkenness	*methe*	A shameful state of stupor, delusion, or impairment caused by drinking alcohol	
15. Orgies	*komos*	Wild parties involving sex, feasting, drinking, dancing, and drugs	

Figure 7.9   Paul lists 15 fruits of the flesh—a harvest of destruction (Gal. 5:19-21).

C. Those led by the Spirit enjoy total freedom (Gal. 5:22-26).

²²But the fruit of the Spirit is love, joy, peace, patience, kindness, goodness, faithfulness, ²³gentleness and self-control. Against such things there is no law (Gal. 5:22-23).

There is no law against the fruit of the Spirit! No restrictions against these actions! Believers have total and unlimited freedom to practice being led by the Spirit! Life in the Spirit provides maximum freedom.

Q 89 ✎ *Write the names that follow with the fruit of the Spirit they illustrate in Figure 7.10. The first name, Job, we have written for you. (Some of the names can be in more than one box, and some do not belong in the chart. Add examples you think of yourself.) Job (James 5:11); Salome (Matt. 14:6-11); Moses (Num. 12:3); the opposite of Amnon (2 Sam. 13); Paul (2 Cor. 7:4); John Mark (Acts 13:13); believers of Hebrews 12:1; the man who obeys Proverbs 23:2; Moses (Heb. 3:5); God in Romans 2:4; the Samaritan (Luke 10:30-35); the stewards of Matthew 25:14-23; Paul (1 Cor. 9:27-28); Jesus (Matt. 21:5); the person who obeys Isaiah 26:3*

Q 85 ✎ *How did Phineas show he was as zealous for God's honor as God was zealous (Num. 25:10-11)?*

Q 86 ✎ *How did God reward Phineas? Does God still reward those who are zealous for His honor? Explain.*

Q 87 ✎ *Who has total freedom? Explain.*

Q 88 ✎ *What type of struggles with the flesh do you see behind Paul's statement in 1 Corinthians 7:27-28?*

Fruit of the Spirit	Greek Word	Explanation	Examples and References
1. Love	*agape*	Seeking the best for others, without desiring personal gain (Rom. 5:5 ; 13:8-10); the cornerstone of all other virtues	
2. Joy	*chara*	Gladness based on God's love, grace, promises, and presence—that belong to those in Christ (Rom. 14:17; 15:13)	
3. Peace	*eirene*	Rest of heart and mind, with freedom from turmoil or anxiety—based on knowing that all is well in our relationship with the Father (Rom. 15:33; Phil. 4:7). Peace is tranquility—being calm in any storm.	
4. Patience	*makrothumia*	Endurance, perseverance; remaining steadfast through delays, hard work, and trials	Job (James 5:11)
5. Kindness	*chrestotes*	Considerate, understanding, loving, gracious, generous	
6. Goodness	*Agathosune*	Love for what is right and hate for what is wrong (Rom. 15:14); the opposite of evil, badness, sinfulness, or unrighteousness	
7. Faithfulness	*Pistis*	Steadfast loyalty in a relationship—based on commitment, promise, trust, perseverance, and honesty (Rom. 3:3)	
8. Gentleness	*prautes*	Tamed strength, like a stallion that a small child can ride in safety	
9. Self-control	*egkrateia*	Mastering our desires, emotions, thoughts, words, actions, and reactions; the opposite of uncontrolled or undisciplined; the capstone of all virtues	

Figure 7.10   Practice illustrating the fruit of the Spirit (Gal. 5:22-23).

D. If a believer is trapped in a sin of the flesh, those led by the Spirit should gently restore him (Gal. 6:1-5).

Brothers, if someone is caught in a sin, you who are spiritual should restore him gently. But watch yourself, or you also may be tempted (Gal. 6:1).

In Galatians 6:1, Paul continues to contrast those led by the flesh and those led by the Spirit. The one *"caught in a sin"* is a person who was led by the flesh. In contrast, in Galatians 6:1, *"you who are spiritual"* refers to believers led by the Spirit. Note that

Q 90 ✎ *How can we recognize those who are spiritual (Gal. 6:1)?*

Paul expects *most* believers to be spiritual—led by the Spirit. He contrasts one person *caught or trapped in a sin* with many believers led by the Spirit (*"you [plural] who are spiritual"*).

Q 91 ＼ *What does Paul mean by "caught" in a sin?*

What kind of situation was Paul thinking of when he wrote *"if someone is caught in a sin"* (Gal. 6:1)? Scholars agree that this person was not searching for a way to sin. The sin of Galatians 6:1 was a false step,[16] not a conscious or deliberate sin.[17] Rather, the word *caught* refers to someone not alert, not on guard, seized by a trap, web, or snare. In the Old Testament, sins of ignorance illustrate this unintended sin (Lev. 4:2; Heb. 9:7). The flesh pulled this person into sin, suddenly, when the believer was not walking in the Spirit. A biblical example of this might be Acts 23:1-5. Paul's anger flared when someone suddenly slapped him in the face. At once he rebuked the high priest. But Paul repented just as quickly, when he realized he was talking to a leader of God's people.

Q 92 ＼ *What types of sin will God forgive?*

The grace of God amazes us when we consider what our Heavenly Father is willing to call a *sin of ignorance,* or a sin that people get *caught* in. *Caught* in a sin does not always mean the sin was unintentional. Consider the merciful and gracious words of Jesus from the cross, *"Father, forgive them, for they do not know what they are doing,"* (Luke 23:34). On the one hand, they *knew* what they were doing when they handed Christ over to Pilate. They were *paying attention* when they whipped His back, plucked His beard, slapped His face, crammed the thorns on His head, and hammered the nails in His hands and feet. They *intended* to hurt His feelings when they mocked Him as He hung naked in public on the cross. Their *aim* was to deface, humiliate, torture, and kill Christ. The crucifixion and events before it were not an accident. So on the one hand, they were not just *caught* in these sins the day they murdered God's Son in broad daylight. On the other hand, behold the grace of God! Jesus said, *"They do not know what they are doing."* That is, they did not *fully* know the extent of their terrible sin. The God who makes the rules was willing to say, "they were *caught* in a sin of ignorance."[18] Likewise, after the Day of Pentecost, Peter reflects God's gracious offer of forgiveness and restoration to mankind's most terrible sins. Preaching the good news to those who crucified Christ, Peter kindly says:

> [15]*"You killed the author of life, but God raised him from the dead. We are witnesses of this.* [16]*By faith in the name of Jesus, this man whom you see and know was made strong. It is Jesus' name and the faith that comes through him that has given this complete healing to him, as you can all see.* [17]<u>*Now, brothers, I know that you acted in ignorance, as did your leaders.*</u> [18]*But this is how God fulfilled what he had foretold through all the prophets, saying that his Christ would suffer.* [19]*Repent, then, and turn to God, so that your sins may be wiped out, that times of refreshing may come from the Lord,* [20]*and that he may send the Christ, who has been appointed for you—even Jesus* (Acts 3:15-20).

Q 93 ＼ *How was the Greek word for "restore" used?*

Sins vary. Some sins are only between a believer and God. Other sins may be handled by two believers, or quietly in a small group (Matt. 18:15-19). A few sins require church discipline, or even a time of excommunication (1 Cor. 5). But it is *always* God's will for those led by the Spirit to be <u>gentle, humble, and loving</u> as we seek to restore a brother or sister who is *caught* in a sin. The Greek word for *restore* in Galatians 6:1 often referred to "mending a net, setting a broken bone, or bring factions together."[19]

Q 94 ＼ *What are some guidelines for those who seek to restore one who was caught in a sin?*

Paul warns those who seek to restore the sinner: *"Watch yourself, or you also may be tempted"* (Gal. 6:1).

Let us restore those who sin as gently as we would like a doctor to restore a broken bone in our own body. And let us be watchful, knowing that all of us have weaknesses and face the same temptations. We are all made from the same dirt.

E. Each person reaps what he sows (Gal. 6:7-10).

⁷*Do not be deceived: God cannot be mocked. A man reaps what he sows.* ⁸*The one who sows to please his sinful nature* [flesh], *from that nature* [flesh] *will reap destruction; the one who sows to please the Spirit, from the Spirit will reap eternal life.* ⁹*Let us not become weary in doing good, for at the proper time we will reap a harvest if we do not give up.* ¹⁰*Therefore, as we have opportunity, let us do good to all people, especially to those who belong to the family of believers* (Gal. 6:7-10).

Q 95 ➚ *What is the law of harvest? State it.*

Eternal Life

Spirit

Thoughts and Deeds Are Seeds ⟶

Flesh

Destruction

Figure 7.11   The law of harvest: A man reaps what he sows (Gal. 6:7-8).

Figure 7.12   We reap what we sow, for better or for worse.

Believers are not under the law of Moses. But all people are under God's natural and spiritual laws. God uses these laws, like the *law of gravity, to govern the world.

Paul refers to the law of sowing and reaping. Farming was common in Galatia. So Galatian believers knew God's natural law about harvest: We reap what we sow. If we plant wheat, we reap wheat. If we sow tares, we reap these ugly, unwelcome weeds (Matt. 13). Paul teaches the spiritual side of the law of harvest. *"The one who sows to please his sinful nature* [flesh], *from that nature* [flesh] *will reap destruction; the one who sows to please the Spirit, from the Spirit will reap eternal life"* (Gal. 6:8).

Paul has already summarized sowing and reaping to the flesh (Gal. 5:19-21).

And he has summarized the fruit we harvest as we sow to the Spirit (Gal. 5:22-23).

To govern the world, God has put laws over mankind—such as the law of harvest. We may do bad things that people do not know about. And we may do good things that people do not appreciate. But the response of people to our lives is secondary. The primary thing to understand is that bad and good deeds are seeds we sow. And whether or not people know, God's law of harvest applies to all actions. We reap what we sow. People can sneak across borders without the police knowing. And people can pay tithes that no human knows about. But the Judge of the world set up laws to punish or reward every deed. We reap what we sow, from bad seed or good seed. God's law of harvest is as consistent and certain as the sunrise.

Sowing to the flesh may not produce a harvest of eternal destruction *at once*. Nor do we reap the full benefits of eternal life each time we sow to the Spirit. Nevertheless, every act of sowing to the flesh is destructive and has harmful results. For example, indulging anger may not kill a person, but it is harmful to the human body, destroying peace, hurting a person's reputation, damaging relationships, and causing physical problems such as: high blood pressure, headaches, insomnia, tooth decay, and stomach problems. Likewise, while sowing to the Spirit, we remain citizens of two places, earth and heaven. Eternal life is ours *even now*, but *not yet* complete. At the end of the path of sowing to the Spirit, we will enjoy eternal life in a new body, and be with the Lord forever. And even now, as we sow to the Spirit, we enjoy the sweet, satisfying fruit of the Spirit (Gal. 5:22-23).

God's natural and spiritual laws enable us to know the results of some actions. A parent may warn a child, "Do not put your hand on the hot stove, or it will burn you."

Q 96 ↖ *In what sense are all people under law? Illustrate this.*

Q 97 ↖ *What harvest or fruit comes from sowing to the flesh (Gal. 5:19-21)?*

Q 98 ↖ *What harvest or fruit comes from sowing to the Spirit (Gal. 5:22-23)? Give examples.*

Q 99 ↖ *How is the harvest of sowing to the flesh "even now, but not yet" (Gal. 5:19-21; 6:8)? Explain.*

Q 100 ↖ *In what sense do those who sow to the Spirit enjoy the fruit of eternal life even now (Gal. 5:19-21; 6:7-8)? Explain.*

Q 101 *Does God need a policeman to enforce the law of harvest? Explain.*

This illustrates a natural law. Hand on stove results in burn (compare Prov. 6:28)! Day or night, parent present or absent, a hand on a hot stove will burn. In such a case, the parent cannot be mocked. If the child disobeys, the result is certain. Likewise, God has created laws to punish or reward actions. *⁷Do not be deceived: God cannot be mocked. A man reaps what he sows. ⁸The one who sows to please his sinful nature* [flesh], *from that nature* [flesh] *will reap destruction; the one who sows to please the Spirit, from the Spirit will reap eternal life.* (Gal. 6:7-8).

We win or lose by the seeds we choose. *"The one who sows to please his sinful nature* [flesh], *from that nature* [flesh] *will reap destruction; the one who sows to please the Spirit, from the Spirit will reap eternal life."* Galatians 6:8 is a two edged sword. It discourages those led by the flesh and encourages those led by the Spirit.

The following refers to both bad and good seeds. God gives us the free will to choose what we sow.

* Sow a thought and you reap an action;
* Sow an act and you reap a habit;
* Sow a habit and you reap a character;
* Sow a character and you reap a destiny.[20]

Figure 7.13
Martin Luther

At first thought, it might shock us that Paul says eternal life is a *harvest* that results from what we *sow*. In Romans, Paul presents eternal life as a *gift*, contrasted with the wages of sin people earn (Rom. 6:23). Great teachers like Martin Luther loved Paul's teachings on salvation by faith, not deeds. Luther did not like the emphasis that James places on good deeds. Recall that James says *"faith without deeds is useless"* (James 2:20). Likewise, James wrote that *"a person is justified by what he does and not by faith alone"* (James 2:24). In other words, James says that *barren faith* is not the type of faith that saves. Referring to *barren or fruitless faith*, James asks, *"Can such faith save him?"* (James 2:14). Many have contrasted James 2:24 with Romans 3:28 or Ephesians 2:8-9. But as we compare Romans 3:28 with Galatians 6:7-10, we are not comparing James and Paul, but Paul and Paul! For sure, Paul emphasizes that we are justified by faith in Christ, and not by our own good works.

Q 102 *Is eternal life like a gift or a harvest? Explain.*

Paul says that eternal life is a *gift* (Rom. 6:23). Yet this same apostle says that eternal life is a *harvest* we reap from what we sow (Gal. 6:8-10). So let us remind ourselves that eternal life is both a gift and a harvest. We do not work to earn eternal life. Jesus already paid for it on the cross. We receive eternal life as a gift, through faith in Jesus Christ. Yet the faith Paul knows *always* expresses itself in obedience and good deeds. People may imagine many paths to heaven and define faith in many ways. But as Paul wrote, *"The only thing that counts is faith expressing itself through love"* (Gal. 5:6). As we resist evil desires of the flesh and sow to the Spirit, we live a life of love, and will reap eternal life (Gal. 6:8; 5:16; Rom. 8:4). And as we sow to reap eternal life, let us give thanks that all good gifts come from God—including the ability to live, sow, and reap.

Q 103 *What big theme is in Romans 8 and Galatians 5–6?*

In Romans 8, over and over Paul contrasts being led by the flesh and being led by the Spirit. We noted that in Romans 8 the Greek word *sarx* (flesh) appears 17 times—in contrast to the Greek word *Pneuma* (Spirit), which appears 21 times. So in Romans 8, over and over Paul contrasts pleasing the flesh and pleasing the Spirit. Those who follow fleshly desires walk away from God to eternal destruction. But those led by the Spirit walk with God toward eternal life. In Galatians 6:7-10, Paul's illustration on the law of harvest illustrates what he teaches in Romans 8. Those who sow to please the flesh reap destruction. Those who sow to please the Holy Spirit reap the harvest of eternal life.

Good crops do not happen by accident. A harvest depends on hard work, such as plowing, sowing, hoeing, and reaping. So the Scripture encourages: *"Let us __not become__*

weary in doing good, for at the proper time we will reap a harvest if we do not give up" (Gal. 6:9). Let us be patient as we wait to harvest eternal life, as the farmer waits for a valuable crop (see James 5:7-8). We do good as we respond to the Spirit and cultivate the fruit of love, joy, peace, patience, kindness, goodness, faithfulness, gentleness, and self-control (Gal. 5:22-23). Furthermore, God gives us a priority as we sow good deeds. Paul says, *"Let us do good to all people, especially to those who belong to the family of believers"* (Gal. 6:10). Love begins at home, in the family of God, and spills over to outsiders.[21] Let us encourage ourselves and be patient as we sow to the Spirit. For the law of the harvest is steadfast, unfailing, dependable.

A young man chose to sow seeds that pleased his sinful, fleshly desires. He satisfied his flesh with all kinds of evils, such as sexual sins, drunkenness, smoking, and other drugs. After many years, he repented and chose to follow Christ. He asked a friend named Sabio, "Will God forgive me, and heal my diseases?" Sabio replied, "God always forgives the sins of those who repent, but our bodies seldom forgive."[22] Sometimes God does miracles. But most of the time, the law of harvest rules over the actions of people. God forgave King David for his adultery with Bathsheba (2 Sam. 11–12). As the prophet Nathan said, *"The Lord has taken away your sin"* (2 Sam. 12:14). But there was still a harvest of the evil seeds David sowed (2 Sam. 12:7-14). The child conceived from David's sin died, even though David fasted and prayed for it to live. The sword that David used to kill Uriah never departed from David's household. He reaped rebellion and murder year after year. And David has continued to reap a harvest of shame for 3,000 years. The wise recognize that we reap what we sow—for better or for worse. So let us choose our seeds with care.

Q 104 *Why do those who sow good seed need encouragement?*

Q 105 *Although God forgave King David, what harvest did he reap for his sexual sin (2 Sam. 11–12)?*

Lesson 27

The Agony and the Glory (Rom. 8:18-27)

Goal A: *Summarize some New Testament verses that link suffering and glory.*
Goal B: *Contrast our present sufferings with our future glory (Rom. 8:18).*
Goal C: *Explain 3 types of groaning that express hope (Rom. 8:19-27).*

Setting

In Romans 8:1-17, Paul contrasts two ways: living in the flesh, and living in the Spirit. Those led by the Spirit are God's children and co-heirs with Christ. Romans 8:17 is a bridge. It introduces the connection between sonship, suffering, and glory. In Romans 8:18-27 Paul emphasizes the theme of hope, as we endure suffering. Take a few minutes to study Figure 7.14.

Let us consider three great truths as we study Romans 8:17-25.

A. The New Testament links suffering and glory (Rom. 8:17-18).

Scripture often links things in pairs. In people, we see pairs like man and wife, father and son, mother and daughter. In topics, we see pairs like knowledge and wisdom, faith and hope, grace and truth, honor and glory. All of these pairs seem like a proper match. But in Romans 8:18-27, we see an odd couple: suffering and glory. Linking these together seems as strange as joining hurt and hallelujah. Suffering and glory—what an unusual marriage! Yet the New Testament links these two topics in many passages:

Figure 7.14
Romans 8:17-27 emphasizes the theme of hope, as we endure suffering in the present and wait for glory in the future.

Q 106 *Which surprising topics does Paul link in Romans 8:17-18?*

*²And we rejoice in the hope of the **glory** of God. ³Not only so, but we also rejoice in our **sufferings**, because we know that suffering produces perseverance; ⁴perseverance, character; and character, hope. ⁵And hope does not disappoint us, because God has poured out his love into our hearts by the Holy Spirit, whom he has given us* (Rom. 5:2-5).

*Now if we are children, then we are heirs—heirs of God and co-heirs with Christ, if indeed we share in his **sufferings** in order that we may also share in his **glory*** (Rom. 8:17).

*I consider that our present **sufferings** are not worth comparing with the **glory** that will be revealed in us* (Rom. 8:18).

*⁶In this you greatly rejoice, though now for a little while you may have had to **suffer** grief in all kinds of trials. ⁷These have come so that your faith—of greater worth than gold, which perishes even though refined by fire—may be proved genuine and may result in praise, **glory** and honor when Jesus Christ is revealed* (1 Pet. 1:6-7).

*And the God of all grace, who called you to his eternal **glory** in Christ, after you have **suffered** a little while, will himself restore you and make you strong, firm and steadfast* (1 Pet. 5:10).

*²⁵He said to them, "How foolish you are, and how slow of heart to believe all that the prophets have spoken! ²⁶Did not the Christ have to **suffer** these things and then enter his **glory**?"* (Luke 24:25-26).

In Christianity, suffering must come before glory, as surely as the cross precedes the crown.

B. Our sufferings in the present do not compare with our glory in the future (Rom. 8:18).

Q 107 *Why is our present suffering not worth comparing to our future glory?*

Paul links suffering with glory. But he is quick to say that they are a mismatch. People use a balance scale to compare the weight of two things. If the weight of two objects is similar, they are worth comparing. But if one thing is much heavier than the other, they are not worth comparing. Imagine comparing the weight of a bicycle to the weight of a bus. These two weights are not worth comparing. Likewise, Paul says:

*I consider that our present **sufferings** are <u>not worth comparing</u> with the **glory** that will be revealed in us* (Rom. 8:18).

This truth of future glory takes the sting out of suffering. It provides courage to face today. Future glory offers strength to handle hardships. Paul throws the rope of faith into the future. He ties it around our future glory—and pulls believers toward it day by day. The sufferings of earth and glories of heaven are an inspiring contrast.

Q 108 *What are some ways that all people suffer?*

Believers suffer in <u>two</u> ways. *First,* we suffer like all humans. Both Christians and non-Christians suffer alike in many ways. The rain falls on the just and the unjust. Likewise, the troubles of earth befall the righteous and the unrighteous. Since sin entered the world through Adam, all mankind suffers.

Life is not easy. Work is hard. Jobs end. Relationships sour. Investments go bad. Tragedies strike. Accidents happen. Sickness scourges. Disease deforms, cripples, and kills. Health fails. Natural disasters such as earthquakes and famines destroy. Nations war. People fight. Thieves steal. Crooks cheat. Friends disappoint us. Satan hinders. Sin deceives. Hopes dim. Moths eat. Rust corrodes. Inflation devalues. No one is immune. Everyone on earth suffers because we live in a fallen world.

Second, in addition to common trials of earth, believers suffer persecution. Because we love Christ, the world hates us. As Cain persecuted Abel, unbelievers persecute believers. *"In fact, everyone who wants to live a godly life in Christ Jesus will be persecuted"* (2 Tim. 3:12).

- **Do you believe** that God created the heavens and the earth? Some people will ridicule you.
- **Do you believe** that sex before marriage is a sin? Many will say you are narrow-minded.
- **Do you believe** it is possible to live a life of victory over sin? Most will say you are a hypocrite.
- **Do you believe** that Jesus is the only way to heaven? People will criticize you for lacking tolerance.
- **Do you believe** the A, B, C's of the Bible? Unbelievers will mock you, reject you, laugh at you, slander you, and persecute you.

Q 109 *How do the sufferings of believers differ from the sufferings of sinners?*

A student is not above his teacher, and a servant is not above his master. If unbelievers hated Jesus, they will hate his followers. Do not think He came to bring peace on earth. He did not come to bring peace, but a sword. Unbelievers will betray believers in their family. Parents will betray their children. Children who do not believe will betray parents who believe. Brothers and sisters will imprison family members who believe. Men will beat, crucify, and murder those who follow Jesus Christ (Matt. 10).

The bad news is that *"in this world you will have trouble."* But take heart! The good news is that Jesus has *"overcome the world"* (John 16:33). And our future looks glorious! What does Paul mean by *"the glory that will be revealed in us"* (Rom. 8:18)? Figure 7.14 shows four aspects of our future glory. Romans 8:29 summarizes our future glory: We will be *"conformed to the likeness of his Son."* Hallelujah! This is the top of the ladder! Imagine God's children, in new bodies, shining and radiating the glory of God Himself! This future glory of heaven is not worth comparing to the sufferings of earth!

Q 110 *What does Paul mean by "the glory that will be revealed in us" (Rom. 8:18)?*

C. Three types of groaning express hope as we suffer (Rom. 8:19-27).

Characteristics of biblical hope: To the world, *hope* is just a wish or an expectation, without confidence or assurance. Non-Christians hope for things, but they do not know whether their hopes will be fulfilled.

In contrast to worldly hope, let us consider seven characteristics of biblical hope.

Q 111 *In your own words, summarize 7 aspects of biblical hope (Figure 7.16).*

Characteristics of biblical hope	Your explanation and illustration
1. Akin to faith	
2. Dependable	
3. Supernatural	
4. God-centered	
5. Present	
6. Future	
7. A gift	

Figure 7.15   Practice summarizing seven characteristics of biblical hope.

- **Biblical hope is akin (similar) to faith.** It is a trust and expectation (Rom. 4:18), and at times a synonym of faith (Ps. 25:1-3). Hope is a sister of faith, and sometimes a twin.
- **Biblical hope is dependable.** The Bible compares our hope to an anchor in a storm. Our hope is firm and secure. *"We have this **hope** as an **anchor** for the soul, firm and secure"* (Heb. 6:19; Rom. 5:4).
- **Biblical hope is supernatural.** Unlike hope of the world, biblical hope is a supernatural, living hope—something God creates in us.

*³Praise be to the God and Father of our Lord Jesus Christ! In his great mercy he has given us new birth into a **living hope** through the resurrection of Jesus Christ from the dead, ⁴and into an inheritance that can never perish, spoil or fade—kept in heaven for you* (1 Peter 1:3-4).

- **Biblical hope focuses on God.** Hope, like faith, has an object—God. We do not hope in hope itself. Rather, we hope in God. Furthermore, our hope is not in a distant God, but in a God whose presence we experience and enjoy within us. Paul describes our hope as *"Christ in you, the hope of glory"* (Col. 1:27). Those of the world hope in earthly money, power, and ability. Scripture says hope in anything but God is like trusting *"in a spider's web"* (Job 8:13-14). But those who hope in Christ will never be disappointed or ashamed (Rom. 9:33).

- **Biblical hope is something we have in the present.** Our hope begins when we are born again. *"For in this hope we were saved"* (Rom. 8:24).

- **Biblical hope looks toward the future.**

  ²⁴...But hope that is seen is no hope at all. Who hopes for what he already has? ²⁵But if we hope for what we do not yet have, we wait for it patiently (Rom. 8:24-25).

  *¹¹For the grace of God that brings salvation has appeared to all men. ¹²It teaches us to say "No" to ungodliness and worldly passions, and to live self-controlled, upright and godly lives in this present age, ¹³while we wait for **the blessed hope—the glorious appearing of our great God and Savior, Jesus Christ,** ¹⁴who gave himself for us to redeem us from all wickedness and to purify for himself a people that are his very own, eager to do what is good* (Titus 2:11-14).

- **Biblical hope is a gift to us by the power of the Holy Spirit.** God does not expect us to create our own hope. We are not the author of our own faith or hope. God is both the object and the source of our hope, by the power of the Holy Spirit.

  May the God of hope fill you with all joy and peace as you trust in him, so that you may overflow with hope by the power of the Holy Spirit (Rom. 15:13).

Our biblical hope is as certain as the character and promises of the God who saves and keeps us.

In Romans 8:18-27, Paul says that hope expresses itself in **three types of groaning**.

Q 112 *What are 3 types of groaning that express hope?*

Q 113 *In what way does Paul liken creation to a person?*

1. Creation groans in hope of deliverance from the curse (Rom. 8:19-22). God cursed the earth when Adam and Eve sinned (Gen. 3:17-19).

Read Romans 8:19-22. Paul refers to creation like it is a person. We call this type of writing *personification*. Of course creation is not a person who can groan. But Paul uses this figurative language as a reminder. He wants us to remember what life was like in Eden before sin entered the world. When sin came, it changed God's beautiful plan. God planned that there would be a wonderful relationship between the earth and humans. But sin changed this.

One writer compared all of the earth to a bride—including the trees, plants, and animals. Before Adam sinned, the earth was like a bride in her wedding dress, waiting for the bridegroom (Adam). Then Adam sinned against God. As a result, Adam left the earth, standing in her bridal dress with tears in her eyes. And she is still waiting for the relationship that God planned.²³

Paul reminds us that God's plan of salvation includes redeeming creation. As Peter wrote, God will create a new heaven and a new earth. *"But in keeping with his promise we are looking forward to a new heaven and a new earth, the home of righteousness"* (2 Pet. 3:13) . Until then, Paul describes creation as a person, waiting for *"the glorious freedom of the children of God"* (Rom. 8:21), when Jesus returns and we are glorified. Note that this is not a groaning of despair. Rather, creation groans like a pregnant woman groans as she gives birth—hoping and looking forward to the birth of her child (Rom. 8:22).

Q 114 *Complete Figure 7.16 on the ways creation groans with hope.*

Rom.	Aspects of Hope	Your Explanation
8:19	Creation longs for revelation	
8:20-21	Creation hopes for liberation	
8:22	Creation groans in expectation	

Figure 7.16   Creation suffers in hope until the Millennium.[24]

2. Believers groan as we endure in hope, awaiting our full adoption as sons (Rom. 8:23-25).

[23]*Not only so, but we ourselves, who have the firstfruits of the Spirit, groan inwardly as we wait eagerly for our adoption as sons, the redemption of our bodies.* [24]*For in this hope we were saved. But hope that is seen is no hope at all. Who hopes for what he already has?* [25]*But if we hope for what we do not yet have, we wait for it patiently* (Rom. 8:23-25).

Q 115 *What are "firstfruits"? Give an example.*

All believers have *"the firstfruits of the Spirit."* The concept of *firstfruits* is common in the Old Testament. Firstfruits was not the full harvest. Rather, it referred to the first, small part of a harvest. The 12 spies brought grapes from Canaan. These illustrate the concept of firstfruits.[25]

Q 116 *Explain the Feast of Firstfruits. How did Jesus fulfill it?*

In the Old Testament, the Feast of Firstfruits was on Sunday, the day after the Sabbath that followed Passover (Lev. 23:11). It celebrated the barley harvest. Jews planted the barley seeds in the fall, and these seeds rose and matured in the spring. But before the full harvest, they took a sheaf of barley grain to the priest. He waved it to the Lord as the "firstfruit." Then, the full harvest was acceptable to God and certain to man.

Jesus fulfilled the Feast of Firstfruits. He rose from the dead on Sunday, the exact day of the Feast of Firstfruits.[26] Thus Paul refers to Him as *"the firstfruits of those who have fallen asleep,"* and the assurance that we *"all will be made alive"* or resurrected (1 Cor. 15:20, 22). The firstfruits preceded and guaranteed the harvest for Israel. Likewise, the resurrection of Jesus, the firstfruits of those who rose from the dead, precedes and guarantees our resurrection.

Q 117 *Why does Paul compare the Spirit in us to the firstfruits of our inheritance?*

Firstfruits of the Spirit (Rom. 8:23). Paul says that we have received *"the firstfruits of the Spirit."* In other words, God has put His Spirit in us as a small taste and assurance of the glory ahead. Sometimes, in special moments of prayer and worship as God's Spirit fills us, it seems as though we will burst with glory. But this presence of the Spirit in us is only the firstfruits—only the small beginning of the glory that God has planned for us. The rest and the best is yet to come!

Q 118 *What are some things we have tasted that make us groan for our full inheritance (compare Heb. 6:4-5)?*

Adoption as sons (Rom. 8:23). We as believers groan in hope. We long for our full *"adoption as sons"* (Rom. 8:23). Earlier, Paul wrote that God has adopted us as sons (Rom. 8:15). We became God's children at the new birth. At that time He put His Spirit in us, and we call Him *Abba (Father). But the new birth was just the beginning of our adoption. One writer compares us to children at an orphanage who have been adopted. The legal papers have been signed. But the parents have not yet taken the children to their new home. Likewise, we are legally adopted as God's children. He has written our names in the book of life. He has justified us. He has given us the firstfruits of His Spirit. And yet the best part of our adoption is still in the future. Jesus has prepared a place for us in Father's house (John 14:2). When Jesus returns, He will take us home with Him forever! Hallelujah! At that time we will receive *"the redemption of our bodies"* (Rom. 8:23; 1 Cor. 15:51-52; 2 Cor. 5:2, 4). No more aches and pains. No more beatings and stripes like Paul and so many believers receive. No more blind eyes and crippled limbs. No more sickness, disease, or death. No more sin! And best of all, we will be *"conformed to the likeness of His Son"* (Rom. 8:29). No wonder theologians call this doctrine *glorification*! Truly, *"our present sufferings [the sufferings of this present age] are not worth comparing with the glory that will be revealed in us"* (Rom. 8:18). In our hardest times, and those time when we overflow with God's presence, we groan in hope, looking forward to our full adoption, eternal inheritance, and unending fellowship with our Holy God!

Q 119 *What are some ways and times that the Spirit may groan for us?*

3. The Holy Spirit groans in prayer for believers (Rom. 8:26-27).

²⁶...the Spirit helps us in our weakness. We do not know what we ought to pray for, but the Spirit himself intercedes for us with groans that words cannot express. ²⁷And he who searches our hearts knows the mind of the Spirit, because the Spirit intercedes for the saints in accordance with God's will (Rom. 8:26-27).

There are many times that we as believers do not know what to pray. For example, Paul prayed for God to remove his thorn, but this was not God's will (2 Cor. 12:7-9).[27] When believers do not know what to pray, the Holy Spirit prays for and through us with groans. These groans might be like those of the Israelites under bondage in Egypt (Acts 7:34).[28] This groaning of the Spirit may include speaking in tongues (1 Cor. 14:2).[29] Or the Spirit may be praying directly to God, without our involvement.

On earth, we will never know all the times and all the ways that the Spirit groans and prays for us. Nevertheless, it encourages us to know that the Spirit in us participates in our struggles. In our most difficult times, the Holy Spirit prays for us. *"And he who searches our hearts knows the mind of the Spirit, because the Spirit intercedes for the saints in accordance with God's will"* (Rom. 8:27). Likewise, Jesus, at the Father's right hand, intercedes for us (Rom. 8:34). With this kind of help we are going to make it!

A machine broke down in an office. The owner called the repair shop. But he soon discovered that he was unable to describe the problem well. He did not know the names of the parts in the machine, or how they worked. So the repair shop sent out a person to fix the machine. While working on the machine, the repairman called the shop. He knew how to describe the problem, and he knew the names of the parts he needed to fix it. Likewise, the person at the shop understood him and sent the parts he needed. In the same way, the Holy Spirit knows how to talk to heaven. He understands the problems believers face. And God understands the Spirit and sends the help we need.[30]

Q 120 *Which of the ways in Figure 7.18 has the Holy Spirit helped you? Have you thanked Him today?*

Praise the Lord for the help of the Holy Spirit. Take a few minutes to study Figure 7.17. It summarizes the powerful ministries of the Holy Spirit mentioned in Romans 8.

The Powerful Ministry of the Holy Spirit (Romans 8)	Rom.
He provides power to live free from condemnation.	8:1-2
He provides power to daily fulfill God's moral law.	8:4
He provides power to control our thoughts and desires.	8:5
He provides power to live in peace with God and please Him.	8:6-8
He provides power to resist and overcome evil desires of the flesh.	8:9
He provides power to rise from the dead.	8:11
He provides power to live spiritually, and not die.	8:13
He provides power to walk on this earth as sons of God.	8:14
He provides power (an inner witness) to know we are children of God.	8:15-16
He provides power to endure in hope until our full adoption as sons.	8:23
He provides power to pray in God's will.	8:26-27

Figure 7.17   The Holy Spirit provides power in the life of believers (Rom. 8).

There is a song, "No More Night," about God making all things new. Part of the lyrics are in the endnotes, plus where to locate them.[31]

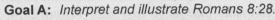

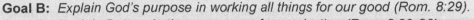

Lesson
28

Predestined for Glory (Rom. 8:28-30)

Goal A: *Interpret and illustrate Romans 8:28.*

Goal B: *Explain God's purpose in working all things for our good (Rom. 8:29).*

Goal C: *Explain 5 steps in the sequence of our salvation (Rom. 8:29-30).*

Setting

Romans 8:28-30 celebrates the certainty of salvation for those who abide in Christ. Jesus climbed a mountain with Peter, James, and John (Matt. 17). There, they enjoyed the presence of God as Jesus was transformed. *"There He was transfigured before them. His face shone like the sun, and his clothes became as white as the light"* (Matt. 17:2). Likewise, studying Romans 8:28-39 brings us into the glory of God's presence. As Paul describes our security in God's great love for us, our hearts overflow with worship. This passage is so precious, that like Peter, we may want to build some shelters and stay here for a few days. On this top of this holy mountain of Scripture, some turn from worshiping to arguing. These want to debate Calvinism and Arminianism, and matters like predestination, election, and eternal security. We wonder if some will still be arguing at the Marriage Supper of the Lamb! Paul wrote this passage to inspire us, not to divide us. Arguing over this passage is like starting a fight at a feast! We must examine key terms in these verses. But let us maintain an attitude of worship as we study.

Romans 8:28-30 is like a seed of corn. It sprouts, buds, and then blossoms. In other words, this is one of those passages that unfolds and explains itself as the reader continues. Like Romans 8:1-4, these verses have many concepts packed together. We will examine each of these concepts as we progress through the lesson, including the five steps in the sequence of salvation (Figure 7.20). We will study Romans 8:28-30 by looking at three key principles.

A. Principle 1: In all things God works for the good of those who love Him (Rom. 8:28).

And we know that in all things God works for the good of those who love him, who have been called according to his purpose (Rom. 8:28).

Many believers love Romans 8:28, but they miss its connection with Romans 8:29. So they are like people who needed to ride three buses to reach a destination. They ride the first bus, but fail to make the second connection, or the third. In this first principle, we will ride the first bus. Then, in the second and third principles, we will continue the journey to our eternal destiny.

Q 121 ➤ *How are Romans 8:28, 8:29, and 8:30 like three bus connections to one destination?*

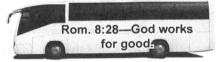
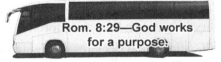

Figure 7.18 **We may compare Romans 8:28-30 to riding three buses that take us from earth to glory.**

For now, let us examine part of Romans 8:28: *"And we know that in all things God works for the good."* This is a wonderful part of Romans 8:28. Paul wants his readers to know that even when we suffer, God is working in our lives. *"In all things"* God is doing something good for us. This does not mean that all things are good. For example, our sins are not good. Accidents, sickness, and disease are not good. War, famine, and crime are not good. Temptations and trials are not good. We live in a fallen world, so many bad things happen. Satan, demons, sin, and sinful people are the sources of many bad things. Yet Romans 8:28 gives us assurance. It proclaims that *"in all things"* God is working for a good purpose.

Q 122 ➤ *Does Romans 8:28 say everything that happens to us is good? Explain.*

Q 123 ➤ *What assurance does Romans 8:28 give us?*

It was bad when Joseph's brothers sold him as a slave. The brothers meant it for evil, but God used it for good (Gen. 37). It was a bad thing when some of the Israelites rejected Moses and said, *"Who made you ruler and judge over us?"* (Exod. 2:14; Acts 7:35). Moses fled to the wilderness and stayed there 40 years. But God used those 40 years for a good purpose—to shape Moses into a powerful leader. It was a bad thing when a mob of unbelieving Jews shouted for the crucifixion of Jesus Christ. But God used this evil thing for a good purpose, as the Lamb of God died to take away the sins of the world. It was a bad thing when unbelieving Jews chased believers from Jerusalem (Acts 8:1). These early saints lost their homes, possessions, and family connections. But God used this persecution for good. For everywhere these believers fled, they spread the gospel of freedom to the slaves of sin. We know that *"in all things"* God works for the good. God is always at least one step ahead of the devil.

Q 124 *Does God work all things for good for all people? Explain.*

Notice for whom God is working good—for *"those who love him"* (Rom. 8:28). God wants to work good for everyone. But those who rebel against Him reject His plans. God was not able to work good for people such as Cain, Balaam, Achan, or Judas. God does not force His blessings on anyone. He requires us to cooperate. The promise of Romans 8:28 is for those—and only those—who love Him. God has chosen to allow all people to have free wills. He allows all people to choose. But Romans 8:28 declares good news for those who choose to love God. For *"those who love him,"* God works all things toward a good purpose. In Romans 6–8, Paul puts two choices before us. Those who reject Jesus as Lord are led by the flesh. These refuse to love God, and cannot please Him (Rom. 8:8). But those who choose Christ become God's children (Rom. 8:17). Our Father pours out His love in our hearts by the Spirit (Rom. 5:5). He gives us a new heart that loves Him. He writes His laws on our hearts, and enables us to love and obey Him (Rom. 8:1-17). Those of us in Christ love God, and we know He is working *"in all things"* for His purpose. We might say that *purpose* is the name of the second bus. Romans 8:28 mentions God's purpose, and Romans 8:29 explains it.

Q 125 *In Romans 8:29, what is the purpose to which God has called us?*

B. Principle 2: God is working 'good' for a purpose—to conform us to the likeness of His Son (Rom. 8:29).

28And we know that in all things God works for the good of those who love him, who have been called according to his purpose. 29For those God foreknew he also predestined to be conformed to the likeness of his Son, that he might be the firstborn among many brothers (Rom. 8:28-29).

Q 126 *Through Christ, what is God restoring that was distorted and damaged in Eden?*

God plans ahead. He works 'good' for a purpose. His purpose is to transform us into the likeness of Jesus. In the beginning, God created man in His own image and likeness. Like God, man was without sin and ruled over creation. Through sin, mankind fell. But Jesus came to restore everything Adam lost, and more.

> GOD'S PURPOSE IS TO TRANSFORM US INTO THE LIKENESS OF JESUS.

Q 127 *How does the process of being conformed to Christ relate to sanctification? Explain.*

At justification, God declares us righteous. We call this side of salvation *imputed righteousness.* But at regeneration (the start of sanctification), God begins the process of *making* us righteous—conforming us to the likeness of Jesus. At the new birth, we partake of the divine nature (2 Pet. 1:4). We refer to this side of salvation as *imparted righteousness.* At *justification,* God credits us with the righteousness of Jesus. Through *sanctification* (from regeneration to glorification), God transforms us into the likeness of Christ. Take a few minutes to rejoice in God's glorious plan for us. God's purpose includes more than just justifying sinners. He transforms sinners into children who are like Jesus—completely holy and righteous. Our relationship with God begins as adopted sons. But the longer we are in the family, the more we grow in grace—and the more of God's nature we reflect. At the last trumpet, we will be changed to be like Jesus forever (1 Cor. 15:51-58).

Romans 8:29b states the reason why God wants us to be conformed to Jesus—*"that he might be the firstborn among many brothers."* In other words, God wants a family that looks like Jesus, acts like Jesus, and honors Jesus. Next to the father, the firstborn held the highest position in the family. So in this comparison, Scripture compares Jesus to the firstborn son. And it is our destiny to be like Him in righteousness and holiness, and to share His inheritance (Eph. 4:24; Rom. 8:17)! Hallelujah! If Romans 8:29 does not inspire you to worship, check your heartbeat!

Q 128 ✎ *Complete Figure 7.19.*

Ref.	Your Explanation of God's Purpose for Us
Rom. 8:29	
Eph. 4:24	
Col. 3:10	
2 Cor. 3:17-18	
1 John 3:2-3	

Figure 7.19
Many verses in the New Testament emphasize that God's purpose is to conform us to the likeness of Christ.

Romans 8:29 introduces the key theological words *foreknew* and *predestined*. We will look at these in point C.

C. Principle 3: Paul identifies five steps of God in the sequence of our salvation (Rom. 8:29-30).

Take a minute to read and review Romans 8:28-29. Underline the five steps in Romans 8:29-30.

> ²⁸*And we know that in all things God works for the good of those who love him, who have been called according to his purpose.* ²⁹*For those God foreknew he also predestined to be conformed to the likeness of his Son, that he might be the firstborn among many brothers.* ³⁰*And those he predestined, he also called; those he called, he also justified; those he justified, he also glorified* (Rom. 8:28-30).

- Romans 8:28 declares that *"in all things"* God is working for good, for those who love Him, and are called for His purpose.

- Romans 8:29 explains that God's purpose is to make us like Jesus.

- Romans 8:29-30 lists five steps through which God fulfills His purpose (Figure 7.20).

The five steps in Romans 8:29-30 contain important theological terms. Let us briefly examine each of the five.

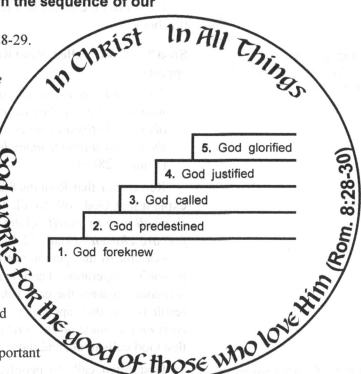

Figure 7.20   Romans 8:29-30 describes five steps God takes in His plan of salvation.

Step 1:   God *foreknew those who would believe in Jesus as Savior and Lord (Rom. 8:29). To *foreknow* means "to know something <u>before</u> it happens." Humans are *finite—we are limited in knowledge, wisdom, and length of life. We are limited to being in one place at one time. And we are limited to the realm of time. Our lives on earth have a beginning and an end. In contrast, God is *infinite. He has no limits that He does not want. God has no limits on His knowledge, wisdom, location, or life. He has no beginning and no end. A human may sit on a hill and look down on a town. However, God sits on His throne and looks down on time. No events on earth are hidden from God. He sees the present as well as He sees the past and the future. We are amazed that God sees the future. He told Abraham that his descendants would be slaves in Egypt 400 years. God enabled Isaiah to prophesy the birth of Christ 800 years before

Q 129 ✎ *What are the 5 steps God took in Romans 8:29-30? Underline them in the passage above.*

Q 130 ✎ *How is God able to foreknow the decisions of people?*

it happened. Nothing surprises God, because He *foreknows*. Thus we say that God is *omniscient—He knows everything: past, present, and future. As one person said, what happens on earth is like a movie that God has already seen. God allows people to make choices. He does not force people to choose anything. But He knows what they will choose, before they choose. This is *foreknowledge. God has it, but we do not. We will discuss foreknowledge more in Romans 9. God *foreknew* those who would believe in Jesus.

Q 131 *What destiny did God plan for those who choose to follow Jesus (Rom. 8:29)?*

Step 2: God *predestined those who chose Christ to become like Him (Rom. 8:29). To *predestine* means "to plan a destiny." God does not force anyone toward the destiny of heaven or hell. John 3:16 tells us that God loves everyone and gave His Son so that whoever believes in Him might not perish, but have eternal life. And other verses declare that it is not God's will for any to perish, but for all to repent (Matt. 18:14; 2 Pet. 3:9).

Also, let us remember that Romans 8:18-39 says nothing about the lost. These verses all focus on those who have chosen to submit to God. Our Father does <u>not</u> predestine anyone to hell or heaven. But for those of us who choose to trust in Christ and be led by the Spirit, God has planned or predestined for us to become like Jesus. *"For those God foreknew he also predestined to be conformed to the likeness of his Son"* (Rom. 8:29).

For more on election and predestination, see the illustration that opens chapter 8 of this book.

Q 132 *What is needed for God's call to be completed?*

Step 3: God *called. Read Romans 8:28-30 again, and underline the two times *called* appears.

> ²⁸*And we know that in all things God works for the good of those who love him, who have been called according to his purpose.* ²⁹*For those God foreknew he also predestined to be conformed to the likeness of his Son, that he might be the firstborn among many brothers.* ³⁰*And those he predestined, he also called...* (Rom. 8:28-30).

Remember that Romans 8:28-39 refers *only* to believers. Other verses in the Bible explain that God *calls* to all. Jesus said, *"When I am lifted up from the earth, [I] will draw **all** men to myself"* (John 12:32). Likewise, Jesus said that *"many are called, **but few are chosen"*** (Matt. 22:14 NASB). You may call someone on the phone, but you cannot talk to that person until he or she answers. A completed phone call requires a person's cooperation. There is a sender and a receiver. A phone call is incomplete until someone answers the call. Likewise, God calls, but many do not answer. So the end result is that they appear "uncalled." As Romans 10:12-13 explains, *"Everyone who calls on the name of the Lord will be saved"* (Rom. 10:13). This is another way to say that God calls to all, and those who respond connect with Him and are saved.

Q 133 *What are some ways that God calls to everyone?*

God often calls to people, but they refuse to respond. *"...concerning Israel he [God] says, 'All day long I have held out my hands to a disobedient and obstinate people'"* (Rom. 10:21). Again, Jesus said of Israel, *"How often I have longed to gather your children together, as a hen gathers her chicks under her wings, but you were not willing"* (Matt. 23:37). God calls through creation, the witness of believers, apostles, prophets, evangelists, pastors, and teachers. He calls through gospel TV, radio, Internet, and other forms of media that present the gospel. He calls through visions, dreams, and conscience. And because God knows all, even before He calls, He knows those who will respond. God calls to all, but most do not answer. Some do not recognize His voice. Others are led away from Him by the flesh, the world, and the devil.

Q 134 *In Romans 8:28-30, does "called" refer to all people? Explain.*

In contrast, Romans 8:28-30 describes those who answer "Yes" when God calls. These are *the called* in the sense that they respond and agree to God's invitation, conditions, and Lordship.

Step 4:   God *justified. God calls people for a purpose—to become like Jesus (Rom. 8:28-30). What a glorious purpose and destiny God has for those who respond to His call. We come to God as sinners and put our trust in Christ. In that moment, He *justifies* us.

Several Greek words relate to justification.

- The Greek verb *dikaioo* means "to declare just or righteous."
- Likewise, the Greek word *dikaioma* means "justification" (Rom. 5:16).
- And the Greek word *dikaiosune* is translated "righteousness" over 35 times in Romans.

So in Greek, *justification* and *righteousness* are "members of the *dikaios* family."[32] They are all related.

In Greek, *justified* and *righteous* sound alike, since they are forms of the same word *dikaioo*. To justify (Greek *dikaioo*) is to declare just or righteous.[33] So whatever language you study, keep in mind that a justified person is one whom God declares just—righteous. Romans teaches that God justifies us, not because we earn it, but because we believe in Jesus. God does not count us righteous because of our good deeds, but because of the good life of Jesus offered for us on the cross.

> *For the wages of sin is death, but the gift of God is eternal life in Christ Jesus our Lord* (Rom. 6:23).

Because we trust in Jesus Christ as our Savior and Lord, God gives us the free gift of justification—righteousness. Hallelujah! Through our faith in Christ, the Judge of the universe declares us just, and righteous!

When Martin Luther trusted in his own righteous deeds, he was afraid. God was a source of fear to him. Then one glorious day, Luther understood the gospel. He saw that justification is by faith in Christ. At once, Luther's relationship with God changed. Instead of being a source of fear, God became a mighty fortress. Because of Christ, we run *to* God, rather than *from* Him.[34]

Step 5:   God *glorified. *"And those he predestined, he also called; those he called, he also justified; those he justified, he also glorified"* (Rom. 8:30).

In theology *glorification* most often refers to the event at the second coming of Christ. When Jesus returns, we will be caught up in the air to meet Him. The dead in Christ will rise from the graves, and believers alive on earth will be transformed (1 Thess. 4:14-17). In the twinkling of an eye, all who have trusted in Christ will receive new bodies (1 Cor. 15:52). At this final level of glorification, God will complete His plan to conform us to be like Jesus. This is our destiny, and the glory ahead. Great glory *"will be revealed in us"* (Rom. 8:18). This future glory is so certain in God's plan that He states it as past tense—already done!

But let us keep in mind that glorification, like adoption, has both *now*, and *not yet* aspects. In Romans 8:15, Paul reminds us that we received the Spirit of sonship or adoption. We are adopted as God's children *even now*. Yet in Romans 8:23, Paul says we, *"who have the firstfruits of the Spirit, groan...as we wait eagerly for our adoption, ...the redemption of our bodies."* We are adopted *even now*, but our adoption is *not yet* complete. Likewise, we are glorified *even now*. Jesus said that He gave His followers glory that we might be one (John 17:22). Elsewhere, Paul writes about stages of glory in the salvation process:

> *And we, who with unveiled faces all reflect the Lord's glory, are being transformed into his likeness with ever-increasing glory, which comes from the Lord, who is the Spirit* (2 Cor. 3:18).[35]

Take a few minutes to give glory to God. Worship Him for the way He has glorified you by living in you through the Spirit. And thank Him for the assurance of the glory He

Q 135   *In what sense does God justify those who respond to His call?*

Q 136   *What are the "even now" and "not yet" aspects of our glorification? Describe them.*

will reveal in you when Jesus returns. Under the old covenant, the glory of God filled the old temple. Under the new covenant, His glory fills us, the new temple!

The five steps of our salvation are certain:

> [28]*And we know that in all things God works for the good of those who love him, who have been called according to his purpose.* [29]*For those **God foreknew** he also **predestined** to be conformed to the likeness of his Son, that he might be the firstborn among many brothers.* [30]*And those he predestined, he also **called**; those he called, he also **justified**; those he justified, he also **glorified*** (Rom. 8:28-30).

Lesson 29

More Than Conquerors (Rom. 8:31-39)

Goal: *Explain and illustrate 4 reasons why we are super-victors in whatever we must face (Rom. 8:31-39).*

Setting

Q 137 ⟋ *What is the Greek word translated "we are more than conquerors"?*

In all these things we are more than conquerors through him who loved us (Rom. 8:37).

The Greek verb *nikao* means "I conquer, I win, I overcome." And the Greek noun *nike* means "victory." In modern times, Nike is a famous brand of sports equipment.

Figure 7.21 The Romans conquered many nations in New Testament times, and Rome ruled the world.

In Romans 12:21, Paul uses a form of the verb *nikao* twice. *"Do not be overcome by evil, but overcome evil with good."* And in Romans 8:37 Paul uses a form of *nikao*. The words *"we are more than conquerors"* translate one Greek word *huper-nikomen. Huper* means "super, above, over, beyond, even more than."[36] Paul says that we believers are super-conquerors, super-victors, super-winners, beyond overcomers—*"through him who loved us"* (Rom. 8:37).

Q 138 ⟋ *What are some comparisons Paul made to Roman soldiers and warfare?*

People in New Testament times understood the word *conqueror* well. At the time of Christ, Rome had conquered the Jewish nation, and many other nations. In Paul's letters, he often compares Christians and our spiritual battles to the Roman soldiers and warfare. Paul said we should *"put on the full armor of God"* and stand firm in our spiritual battles (Eph. 6:10-18). He gave thanks to God the Father who, like a conquering general, always leads us in a victory parade—a procession of triumph (2 Cor. 2:14-16). And at the end of his life Paul wrote, *"I have fought the good fight"* (2 Tim. 4:7).

As we study Romans 8:31-37, the highest peak in the mountains of Paul's writings, let us examine four reasons why we are super-victors in whatever we must face (Rom. 8:37).

A. We are more than conquerors because God is for us (Rom. 8:31).

Q 139 ⟋ *In Romans 8:31, to what does "this" refer?*

Paul asks: *"What, then, shall we say in response to this?"* (Rom. 8:31). Every student should ask: In response to what? Paul has just affirmed the certainty of our salvation *in Christ*. He has said that God is working all things for good to those called to His purpose. God foreknew us, predestined us to be like Jesus, called us, justified us, and glorified us (Rom. 8:28-30). *"What, then, shall we say in response to this?"* (Rom. 8:31). Paul answers: *"If God is for us, who can be against us?"* (Rom. 8:31).

Q 140 ⟋ *How do we know that God is for us?*

God is for us. He has forgiven our sins, and justified us in Christ. God is for us. He has poured out His love in our hearts by the Holy Spirit. God is for us. He has put His Spirit in us so that we call Him *Abba*—Father (Rom. 8:15). God is for us. We have become members of His family—His beloved children. God is for us. We are co-heirs with Christ! *"What, then, shall we say in response to this?"* (Rom. 8:31). Hallelujah! Our salvation and future are settled because God is for us!

If God were against us, we would be without hope. God was against Satan, one of the most powerful angels. Jesus saw what happened: *"I saw Satan fall like lightning from heaven"* (Luke 10:18). There is no hope for those whom God is against. God was against the sinful society of Noah's day. He judged His enemies with the Flood (Gen. 6). God was against Pharaoh, and Egypt, the most powerful nation on earth. Remember who won that contest? When the battle was over, the land of Egypt was ruined, and Pharaoh's army was at the bottom of the Red Sea (Exod. 14). God is against all who reject Jesus as Savior and Lord. The Almighty sent His only Son to be a sacrifice for the sins of the world. Those who refuse God's love offering and sow to the flesh are God's enemies. He is against these. They must appear before Him at the final judgment. It is a fearful and terrible thing to have God against you.

But God is for us. The One with all power and authority is for us. The Creator of heaven and earth is on our side. Review Hebrews 11. It lists some of those whom God has been with in ages past. The Judge of the whole earth has adopted us as His children. Hallelujah! God is for us. No one can stand against us.

Q 141 *What happens to those whom God is against? Give examples.*

Q 142 *How does it make you feel to know that God is for us?*

B. We are more than conquerors because God is not going to change (Rom. 8:32).

He who did not spare [withhold] *his own Son, but gave him up for us all—how will he not also, along with him, graciously give us all things?* (Rom. 8:32).

God is not going to change His mind about us. He did not bring us this far to leave us. He did not lift us up to let us down. What He has started, He will finish. *"He who began a good work in you will carry it on to completion until the day of Christ Jesus"* (Phil. 1:6).

In Romans 8:32, Paul reasons from the greater to the lesser. He says that God did not spare or withhold the *greater* part. He has already sacrificed His own Son so we could become His children. God has already loved us so much that He sacrificed the greatest treasure of heaven for us. Consider the way earthly parents love their only child. Nothing else in the home, the bank, or the world compares to the value the parents place on their only child. They would die for the child.

God once tested Abraham's love for Him. Abraham had one special son named Isaac. Through this one son, God promised to give Abraham a nation of children. Nothing on earth was as dear to Abraham as this one son, Isaac. Then one day came the terrible test. Would Abraham sacrifice his *greatest* possession to please God? Would the Father of the Jews withhold his greatest treasure—his special son Isaac? Abraham passed the test on Mount Moriah. He gave what he valued most—his only son. So God knew He could trust Abraham with anything.

Q 143 *How can we be sure that God is not going to change His mind about us?*

> [15]*The angel of the Lord called to Abraham from heaven a second time* [16]*and said, "I swear by myself, declares the Lord, that because you have done this and* **have not withheld your son, your only son,** [17]*I will surely bless you and make your descendants as numerous as the stars in the sky and as the sand on the seashore. Your descendants will take possession of the cities of their enemies,* [18]*and through your offspring all nations on earth will be blessed, because you have obeyed me"* (Gen. 22:15-18).

This event on Mount Moriah was prophetic. Years later, God sacrificed *His* only Son on Mount Calvary. Many scholars believe this was the same mountain where God tested Abraham. God gave the greatest gift that heaven could offer. *"Thanks be to God for his indescribable gift"* (2 Cor. 9:15). And since He has given the *greatest* part needed for our salvation, is there any doubt that God will give us the *lesser* things we need?

Q 144 ✎ What does the illustration about the buyer's deposit show?

When a buyer wants to purchase a piece of land or a home, he puts down a deposit. This money is just a small percentage—perhaps only five percent or less of the total price. Nevertheless, this small commitment by the buyer assures the seller that the buyer will not change his mind. But imagine how certain the seller would be if the buyer gave a deposit of 95 percent of the total cost. And yet this is what God has done. For, the price He has already paid to redeem us was His only Son. So we are absolutely certain that God is not going to change His mind!

C. We are more than conquerors because God is the final Judge (Rom. 8:33-34).

33Who will bring any charge against those whom God has chosen? It is God who justifies. 34Who is he that condemns? Christ Jesus, who died—more than that, who was raised to life—is at the right hand of God and is also interceding for us (Rom. 8:33-34).

Q 145 ✎ Why is it a waste of time for anyone to accuse us? Explain.

Satan, demons, and humans may accuse us, and they often do. The word *Satan* means "accuser" in Hebrew (Rev. 12:9-10). But God is the only Judge of the universe. And He is the One who has already justified us in Christ.

Q 146 ✎ How do the Father, Son, and Holy Spirit work together for our salvation?

The Word of God says *"there is now no condemnation for those who are in Christ Jesus"* (Rom. 8:1). Whoever accuses those in Christ is wasting time and effort. God is for us. He is not going to change. And He is the Judge of judges. There is no place to appeal God's decision. The court of heaven is the supreme court of the universe.

John 5 says, *" 22...the Father judges no one, but has entrusted all judgment to the Son, 23that all may honor the Son just as they honor the Father"* (John 5:22-23). This verse reveals that God the Father and God the Son have the same standards and conclusions about judgment. Through his writings, John emphasizes that the Father and the Son are one. What the Father says about us, the Son says about us. For the Trinity works together in our salvation. The Father sent His Son to be our peacemaker and sacrifice. The Son gave His life for us on the cross. The Spirit enters our hearts at the new birth, bringing the presence of Jesus to us. And the Spirit encourages and empowers us to live a life of victory. Our relationship with God the Judge assures and comforts our hearts.

In addition, Paul emphasizes three encouraging things about Jesus. *"Who is he that condemns? Christ Jesus, who died—more than that, who was raised to life—is at the right hand of God and is also interceding for us"* (Rom. 8:34). Jesus not only died for us, He rose from the grave, and now intercedes for us. Earlier, Paul wrote that the Holy Spirit intercedes for us (Rom. 8:26-27). And in Romans 8:34, Paul writes that Jesus is praying for us. Whenever you need encouragement and assurance about your salvation, read Romans 8. Imagine the heavenly scene. The Father and Son are united—one in nature, one in their standards and opinions. They sit together on thrones, side by side. And when the Son lifts His hands to pray for us, the Father sees the nail prints in them. Meanwhile, on earth, the Holy Spirit prays for us. How much assurance of salvation do you need? In Romans 8, there is more than enough for any occasion. The Godhead is on our side! We are super-victors, soon to be crowned.

Q 147 ✎ How is Zechariah 3:1-5 parallel to what God has done for us?

1Then he showed me Joshua the high priest standing before the angel of the LORD, and Satan standing at his right side to accuse him. 2The LORD said to Satan, "The LORD rebuke you, Satan! The LORD, who has chosen Jerusalem, rebuke you! Is not this man a burning stick snatched from the fire?"3Now Joshua was dressed in filthy clothes as he stood before the angel. 4The angel said to those who were standing before him, "Take off his filthy clothes." Then he said to Joshua, "See, I have taken away your sin, and I will put rich garments on you." 5Then I said, "Put a clean turban on his head." So they put a clean turban on his head and clothed him, while the angel of the LORD stood by. 6The angel of the LORD gave this charge to Joshua: ⁷*"This is what the* LORD *Almighty says: 'If you will walk in my ways and keep my requirements, then you will govern my house and have charge of my courts, and I will give you a place among these standing here* (Zech. 3:1-7).

Christians, let us be encouraged. God has taken away our filthy garments and clothed us with the righteousness of Christ. As we follow the Spirit, He leads us on the path of obedience, upward to heaven. And we do not need to defend ourselves against evil accusations. The Lord Himself will rebuke those who accuse us!

D. We are more than conquerors because nothing can separate us from the love of God in Christ Jesus our Lord (Rom. 8:31-39).

Romans 8 begins with *no condemnation* in Jesus Christ (Rom. 8:1). And it ends with *no separation* in Jesus Christ (Rom. 8:39). Praise the Lord! What an awesome chapter.

Q 148 ⚲ *How does Romans 8 begin and end for those in Christ?*

**Figure 7.22
Nothing can separate us from the love of God, in Jesus Christ our Lord.**

Throughout Romans 6–8, Paul has made it clear that those who follow the flesh will die. But those of us led by the Spirit will live forever. When Jesus Christ is *our Lord,* the present is anchored in hope and surrounded by love. And the future is glorious and certain.

Paul gives *two lists* of things we face on earth. These are some of the *all things* that God uses for good, for those who love God (Rom. 8:28).

Who shall separate us from the love of Christ? (Rom. 8:35a).

Q 149 ⚲ *Which of the things on Paul's lists have you battled?*

First list: ³⁵*Shall trouble or hardship or persecution or famine or nakedness or danger or sword?* ³⁶*As it is written: "For your sake we face death all day long; we are considered as sheep to be slaughtered."* ³⁷*No, in all these things we are more than conquerors through him who loved us* (Rom. 8:35b-37).

Second list: ³⁸*For I am convinced that neither death nor life, neither angels nor demons, neither the present nor the future, nor any powers,* ³⁹*neither height nor depth, nor anything else in all creation, will be able to separate us from the love of God that is in Christ Jesus our Lord* (Rom. 8:38-39).

FOR PAUL, LIFE WAS A SERIES OF BATTLES. HE FOUGHT WITH BEASTS AT EPHESUS (1 COR. 15:32). HE FOUGHT WITH ACADEMIC PRIDE AND INTELLECTUALISM AT ATHENS (ACTS 17). HE FOUGHT WITH DECEPTION, RELIGIOUS BUSINESS, AND INJUSTICE AT PHILIPPI (ACTS 16). HE FOUGHT WITH PHYSICAL ILLNESS AND PERSECUTION IN GALATIA (ACTS 14; GAL. 4:13). HE FOUGHT WITH DIVISION, SLANDER, AND FALSE APOSTLES AT CORINTH (1 & 2 COR.).

Q 150 ⚲ *How does the form of the second list differ from the first list?*

The *first list* has <u>seven</u> things and is arranged like a ramp. It begins with our lightest trial, *trouble,* and ends with the most severe, *the sword* (Rom. 8:35). Throughout history, the earth has been soaked with the blood of righteous people (Matt. 23:35). Especially in New Testament times, God's people have been killed—like sheep for the slaughter (Rom. 8:36; Ps. 44:22). Tradition records that all of the apostles were martyred. And from these first followers of Jesus to the last, believers overcome by the blood of the Lamb and their testimony—and they do not love their lives, but are willing to die for Christ (Rev. 12:11). The apostle John saw a vision of *"a great multitude that no one could count, from every nation, tribe, people and language."* These saints came out of the Great Tribulation (Rev. 7:9-17). Most evangelical scholars believe they were martyred. But as believers, we do not fear being martyred. For death is not an enemy that can separate us from the love of God. Rather, death is just the last door between us and our Father.

Paul's second list includes <u>four</u> pairs of extremes. It begins where the first list ended, with the sword or death. And the list ends with *"nor anything else in all creation"* —anything you can imagine (Rom. 8:39). It is like a "fill in the blank" sentence. Put whatever troubles you the most in this final category of *"nor anything else."* Nothing, absolutely nothing we face, can *"separate us from the love of God that is in Christ Jesus our Lord."*

Q 151 ✎ *What were some things Paul fought and conquered?*

Throughout his ministry, Paul fought to overcome cold, hunger, and nakedness. He fought to conquer beatings, stripes, chains, and imprisonment. He fought to survive thieves and robbers. He used spiritual *weapons* to win over false teachers, false doctrines, and every thought that exalted itself against Christ (2 Cor. 10:1-6). He beat his own fleshly desires into submission and made his body his slave (1 Cor. 9:27). He fought to overcome enemies who misrepresented him, hated him, and stoned or abused him in every city. He fought *"with weapons of righteousness in the right hand and in the left"* (2 Cor. 6:7). Paul saw the Christian life as a fight! And yet, with a thorn in his flesh and war scars on his body, Paul could write: *"In all these things we are more than conquerors through him who loved us"* (Rom. 8:37).[37]

Q 152 ✎ *Was Romans 8:31-39 prophetic to Roman believers? Explain.*

Paul's words about suffering were prophetic to the Roman Christians. He wrote his letter to the Romans about 57 A.D. Within 6 years, Nero, a Roman Caesar, began murdering Christians in Rome. There was a great fire in Rome, and many blamed Nero. To shift the guilt, Nero blamed the Christians for starting the fire. This evil Caesar convicted a great multitude of Christians and began to punish them. They were guilty, not of starting a fire, but of refusing to worship Nero, or other Roman gods. So Nero hated them. Some he put to death with the sword. Others, he covered with hides of beasts and put in an arena. People cheered as wild dogs tore the Christians to death. Many were crucified. Others were set on fire to serve as human lights at night. Nero opened his gardens to display the burning Christians. And this was just the beginning of persecution in Rome that lasted for about 200 years.[38]

Q 153 ✎ *For what reason do many believers suffer today?*

Application: Christians today need to face the facts about suffering, pain, and spiritual warfare. In the Old Testament, except for Job, God's people suffered mostly for disobedience. When the Israelites sinned, God sent enemies to take away their land and afflict them. But in the New Testament, we find God's people suffering for doing what is right. This year, unbelievers will martyr about 160,000 believers.[39] Most believers do not face death by martyrdom. And we are delivered from the wrath of God. Still, all believers face the fury of Satan and unbelievers.

Q 154 ✎ *Did Paul promise that as conquerors we escape suffering? Explain.*

> PAUL DID NOT SAY THAT *ALL THINGS BECOME EASY TO THOSE IN CHRIST.*

Paul did not say that *all things become easy to those in Christ.* He does not write that God wipes our tears away now. He does not tell us that if we follow Christ, our bodies will not hurt, and our souls will not ache. He says nothing about a smooth road—with no groaning. Paul does not promise that death will fold its dark wings and fly away. He says none of these things. Rather, he says the opposite. As followers of Christ, we must face everything that unbelievers face, and more. Because our spirits are alive and sensitive, the injustice and sins of the world will vex us more. Because we love Christ, the world will hate us. Because we will not conform to sinful ways, the world will exclude us and persecute us.

But what we see in Romans 8:31-39 is a Christian facing the worst that life can bring—and triumphing over all these things in Christ![40] Paul speaks from experience. He recalls the things that have tried to separate him from the love of God. And he asks **the question**:

[35]*Who shall separate us from the love of Christ? Shall trouble or hardship or persecution or famine or nakedness or danger or sword?* [36]*As it is written: "For your sake we face death all day long; we are considered as sheep to be slaughtered"* (Rom. 8:35-36).

Paul's answer to the question is *NO person or thing* (Rom. 8:37-39). He had already been through most of these trials. And he could testify, from personal experience and with authority, *"No, in all these things we are more than conquerors through him who loved us"* (Rom. 8:37).

Life is a mixture of joy and sorrows, laughter and tears, pleasure and pain. From day to day we do not know what we will face. Life is uncertain. The sun may shine today, and it may be raining tomorrow. But believers can count on our relationship with God. Whatever comes, our salvation is secure and steadfast in Christ.

Q 155 *What assurance is in Romans 8:31-39?*

There is a song, "Still," that reflects these verses in Romans. Part of the lyrics are in the endnotes, plus where to locate them.[41]

Conclusion

In Romans 8:28-30, Paul reminds us that God works all things together for good, to those who love God and are called to fulfill God's purpose. We have studied that God's purpose is to have a family of believers who think, act, and live like Jesus. We noted the five steps in the sequence of salvation. God foreknew us, predestined us, called us, justified us, and glorified us.

Application: In Romans 8:31 Paul asks, *"What, then, shall we say in response to this?"* We have studied Paul's response in Romans 8:31-39. His response is filled with faith, optimism, worship, thanksgiving, and affirmation.

But what is your response to all that God has done and planned for us? Do you go through life with your head down? Do you spend your days grieving over yesterday, whining about today, and worrying about tomorrow? Do you see life like a mirror or a window? Do you see yourself and your own concerns in almost everything you look at? Or when you look around, do you see a world full of people who need your testimony, your help, and all the faith you can inspire them to have? Are you like the ten spies who were filled with cowardice and fear, after God had delivered them from Egypt and drowned an army of enemies? Or are you like Joshua and Caleb who were filled with faith and confidence in God? We have studied Paul's response. But what is your response to all that God has done for us?

Our response is important. For as we think on the right things, the peace of God fills our hearts and minds (Phil. 4:6-8). And as we think on the right things, the love of God radiates from us to others. As we focus on who our Father is and all He has done and planned for us, our hearts are filled with faith and overflow with love, joy, and worship. A proper response to who we are in Christ encourages us and uplifts others. May our response to all that life can bring—the best and the worst—be like Paul's response. May we see ourselves as more than conquerors—super-victors—for four reasons:

- We are super-victors because **God is for us**.
- We are super-victors because **God is not going to change**.
- We are super-victors because **God is the final Judge**.
- We are super-victors because **nothing can separate us from the love of God in Christ Jesus**.

Test Yourself: Circle the letter by the ***best*** completion to each question or statement.

1. There is no condemnation for those who
a) have been born again.
b) have been baptized.
c) are led by the Spirit.
d) are awaiting glorification.

2. What was law powerless to do?
a) Reveal the will of God to us
b) Break sin's power over us
c) Inform the conscience
d) Condemn those who sinned

3. What is a believer's relationship to law?
a) Law is over us
b) Law is under us
c) Law is behind us
d) Law is in us

4. How do we fulfill the righteous requirements of the Law (Rom. 8:4)?
a) Through Christ's death on the cross
b) Through walking in the Spirit
c) Through justification
d) Through glorification

5. In the Greek text of Romans 7–8, how many times do the words *flesh* and *Spirit* each occur?
a) Less than 5
b) Less than 10
c) More than 15
d) More than 20

6. Which is TRUE of all God's human enemies?
a) They do not pray to Jesus.
b) They do not read the Bible.
c) They are led by the flesh.
d) They are proud of sinning.

7. When does the battle between flesh and Spirit end?
a) At the moment of the new birth
b) When a believer is filled with the Spirit
c) When a believer becomes mature
d) At the moment of death

8. Why does God work all things for our good?
a) Because He loves us
b) So we will become super-conquerors
c) To conform us to the image of Christ
d) For the purpose of defeating Satan

9. The second of five steps in Romans 8:28-30 is
a) God predestined
b) God elected
c) God foreknew
d) God adopted

10. Why are we more than conquerors?
a) Human enemies cannot kill us.
b) God is the final Judge.
c) Satan is too weak to defeat us.
d) Life on earth is only for a season.

Essay Test Topics: Write 50-100 words on each of these goals that you studied in this chapter.

- Analyze the words: *"no condemnation"* and *"in Christ"* (Rom. 8:1).
- Interpret 7 key phrases in Romans 8:1-3.
- Identify 4 relationships in Romans 8:1-4.
- Analyze: The law of God is not over, under, or behind us—it is in us.
- Explain how we are able to fulfill the righteous requirements of the Law (Rom. 8:4).
- Contrast the values of those led by the flesh and those led by the Spirit (Rom. 8:5).
- Contrast the spiritual states of those led by the flesh and those led by the Spirit (Rom. 8:6, 13).
- Identify characteristics of God's enemy and God's family (Rom. 8:7-17).
- Analyze the conflict in believers between the flesh and the Spirit (Gal. 5:13-18).
- Explain and illustrate the fruit of the flesh, and their results (Gal. 5:19-21).
- Explain and illustrate the fruit of the Spirit, and their results (Gal. 5:22-26).
- Describe God's plan for a believer *"caught"* in a sin (Gal. 6:1-5).
- Summarize and illustrate God's law of harvest (Gal. 6:7-10).
- Summarize some New Testament verses that link suffering and glory.
- Contrast our present sufferings with our future glory (Rom. 8:18).
- Explain 3 types of groaning that express hope (Rom. 8:19-27).
- Interpret and illustrate Romans 8:28.
- Explain God's purpose in working all things for our good (Rom. 8:29).
- Explain 5 steps in the sequence of our salvation (Rom. 8:29-30).
- Explain and illustrate 4 reasons why we are super-victors in whatever we must face (Rom. 8:31-39).

Unit Four: The Scope and Fruit of Righteousness (Romans 9–11)

Moving from Romans 8 to Romans 9 is jarring—like a shift from celebration to lamentation. In Romans 1–8 Paul has discussed how God has made it possible for Jews and Gentiles to be in a right relationship with Him. Then, in Romans 9–11 Paul focuses on the nation of Israel in relation to God's plan of salvation. Why does Paul focus on Israel in Romans 9–11 when he has already applied his gospel to them in Romans 1–8? Because Jews were lagging behind Gentiles in response to the gospel of salvation. The poor response of Jews to the gospel raised questions. If the Jews are God's chosen people, then why have they rejected God's chosen Messiah? Why are many Gentiles coming into God's kingdom, while few Jews enter it? And does Israel's rejection of the gospel cast a shadow of doubt on God's promises to Abraham and his descendants? Has God's righteousness toward Israel failed? Has God failed to provide salvation for Jews?

Questions like those above affected how people received Paul and his gospel message of salvation. Paul was the main apostle to the Gentiles. Some Jews accused Paul of forsaking his own race, the Jews. Likewise, they claimed Paul taught Jews and Gentiles to ignore the signs of God's covenant with Israel—sacred signs such as circumcision and food laws. Some Jews thought the reason why many Gentiles were accepting the gospel was because Paul made it too easy for them. Many Jews thought Paul was a threat and a traitor.

So Paul takes time to clarify and defend his gospel of salvation. In Romans 9–11 he will explain that God's promises to Israel have not failed. Paul will show that from the beginning, God's plan was to reach all nations. And that the true children of Israel are those who respond to God by faith in Christ. Paul will show that in the end, God will use the salvation of the Gentiles to draw all Israel back to Him. And Paul will warn Gentiles to beware of pride, lest like thousands of Israelites, they fall short of inheriting the promises God intended for them. For as Paul's gospel of salvation declares at the beginning of Romans, the just must live by faith, from first to last—from the start of the race to its finish (Rom. 1:17).

In this chapter, as you work through Romans 9–11, we will guide you to:
- *Summarize and apply Paul's attitude toward the Jews (Rom. 9:1-5).*
- *Answer and explain: Did God's word (promise) to Abraham and Israel fail (Rom. 9:6–13)?*
- *Explain and illustrate: Privileges do not guarantee personal salvation (Rom. 9:4-5).*
- *Interpret and apply: Not all who are descended from Israel are Israel (Rom. 9:6b).*
- *Explain four principles about election to serve.*
- *Summarize two principles about election to salvation.*
- *Explain and illustrate: Humans and God have the freedom to choose.*
- *Explain and illustrate: God is patient with those who rebel against Him (Rom. 9:22-29).*
- *Answer the key questions in Romans 9:30–10:21.*
- *Explain and illustrate three reasons why some do not find righteousness.*
- *Identify six passages that show how anyone can find a right relationship with God (Rom. 9:30–10:13).*
- *Review the five steps that lead to salvation, illustrating failures and successes of each step.*
- *Answer the key questions in Romans 11.*
- *Explain and illustrate: We find grace when we look where God tells us to look (Rom. 11:1-10).*
- *Analyze the role of envy in drawing the lost to Christ (Rom. 11:11-16).*
- *Explain five truths Paul teaches in relation to the olive tree (Rom. 11:16b-25).*
- *Summarize Paul's glorious conclusion of Romans 9–11.*

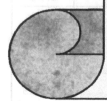

Chapter 8:
The Width of Righteousness: Israel in God's Plan of Salvation
(Romans 9–11)

Introduction

    *Election and *predestination are important topics in Romans 9–11. To understand these two doctrines, consider a great ship on its way to heaven. The ship represents the Church. God has chosen (elected) the ship. And He bought it to be His own possession. Christ is the Captain of the ship. No one can pay to ride this ship. But all are welcome free. The only condition to come onto the ship is to be a friend of the Captain. As people develop a personal relationship with the Captain, they are chosen (elected) to come onto the ship. As long as people are on the ship, in a good relationship with the Captain, they are

Figure 8.1
An illustration about a great ship helps us understand the doctrines of election and predestination.

among the elect—the chosen. But if they choose to abandon the ship and its Captain, they cease to be part of the elect. Election is always in connection with the Captain and His ship. Predestination tells us about the ship's destination and what God has prepared for those who remain on it. God invites everyone to come onto the ship, through faith and submission to the Captain.[1]

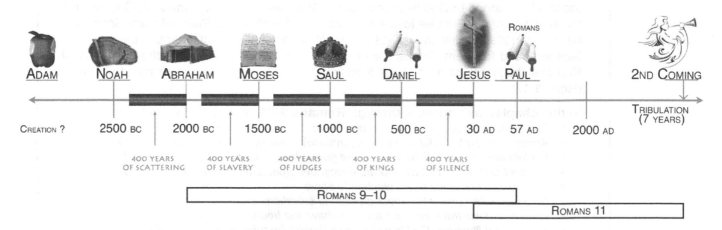

Figure 8.2   Romans 9–11 examines Israel in God's plan of salvation, from Abraham to Christ's return.

Q 1 ↖ *To review Romans 9–11, complete Figure 8.3 as you study this chapter.*

Rom.	Questions	Answers	Rom.
9:1-5	What was Paul's attitude toward the Jews?		9:1-5
9:6	Did God's word (promise) to Abraham fail (Gen. 12:3; 22:18)?		9:6-29
9:14	*Is God unjust* (for using Isaac, Jacob, and even Pharaoh for His purposes)?		9:15-21
9:22	Why is God patient with those who rebel against Him?		9:23-29

Continued on next page

9:30-32a	Why did *Israel fail to obtain righteousness?		9:32-33
10:14-15a	*How? How? How? How? How!* Which 5 steps make salvation possible?		10:15b-17
10:18a	Did Israel not all hear (God's message)?		10:18b
10:19a	*Did Israel not understand (God's message)?*		10:19-21
11:1a	*Did God reject his people?*		11:1-10
11:1a	*Did God reject his people?*		11:1-10
11:11a	Did Israel stumble and fall beyond recovery?		11:11-32
11:34-35	*Who has known the mind of the Lord?* *Who has been his counselor?* *Who has ever given to God, that God should repay him?*		11:33, 36

Figure 8.3   Key questions and answers in Romans 9–11

Lessons:

Israel's Past Election, a Blessing to the Nations—Part 1 (Rom. 9:1-29)

Goal A: *Summarize and apply Paul's attitude toward the Jews (Rom. 9:1-5).*
Goal B: *Answer and explain: Did God's word (promise) to Abraham and Israel fail (Rom. 9:6-13)?*
Goal C: *Explain and illustrate: Privileges do not guarantee personal salvation (Rom. 9:4-5).*
Goal D: *Interpret and apply: Not all who are descended from Israel are Israel (Rom. 9:6b).*

Israel's Past Election, a Blessing to the Nations—Part 2 (Rom. 9:1-29)

Goal A: *Explain 4 principles about election to serve.*
Goal B: *Summarize 2 principles about election to salvation.*
Goal C: *Explain and illustrate: Humans and God have the freedom to choose.*
Goal D: *Explain and illustrate: God is patient with those who rebel against Him (Rom. 9:22-29).*

Israel's Present Rejection—Unbelief Toward the Gospel (Rom. 9:30–10:21)

Goal A: *Answer the key questions in Romans 9:30–10:21 (Figure 8.8).*
Goal B: *Explain and illustrate 3 reasons why some do not find righteousness.*
Goal C: *Identify 6 passages that show how anyone can find a right relationship with God (Rom. 9:30–10:13).*
Goal D: *Review the 5 steps that lead to salvation, illustrating failures and successes of each step.*

Israel's Future Restoration—An Awakening Is Coming (Rom. 11:1-36)

Goal A: *Answer the key questions in Romans 11 (Figure 8.12).*
Goal B: *Explain and illustrate: We find grace when we look where God tells us to look (Rom. 11:1-10).*
Goal C: *Analyze the role of envy in drawing the lost to Christ (Rom. 11:11-16).*
Goal D: *Explain 5 truths Paul teaches in relation to the olive tree (Rom. 11:16b-25).*
Goal E: *Summarize Paul's glorious conclusion of Romans 9–11.*

     Key Words

Israel—sometimes refers to physical descendants of Abraham; other times refers to spiritual descendants of Abraham, that is, those who live by faith

remnant—those physical descendants of Abraham whom God saved, as they chose to live by faith

election—choosing for a purpose, whether service or salvation; God elects all who choose and obey Jesus to be saved.

mercy—kindness, love, and compassion that God desires to give each and every person

Israel's Past Election, a Blessing to the Nations—Part 1 (Rom. 9:1-29)

Lesson 30

Goal A: *Summarize and apply Paul's attitude toward the Jews (Rom. 9:1-5).*
Goal B: *Answer and explain: Did God's word (promise) to Abraham and Israel fail (Rom. 9:6-13)?*
Goal C: *Explain and illustrate: Privileges do not guarantee personal salvation (Rom. 9:4-5).*
Goal D: *Interpret and apply: Not all who are descended from Israel are Israel (Rom. 9:6b).*

Setting

Q 2 ✎ *To review Romans 9:1-29, complete Figure 8.4 as you study Lesson 30.*

Rom.	Questions	Answers	Rom.
9:1-5	A. What was Paul's attitude toward the Jews?		9:1-5
9:6	B. Did God's word (promise) to Abraham fail?		9:6-29
9:14	C. *Is God unjust* (in choosing Isaac, Jacob, and even Pharaoh for His purposes)?		9:15-21
9:22	D. Why is God patient with those who rebel against Him?		9:23-29

Figure 8.4   Four questions on Romans 9:1-29 that we will examine in Lesson 30

As Figure 8.4 shows, we will examine and answer four questions in Lesson 30.

Q 3 ✎ *As an apostle to the Gentiles, did Paul lose his love for Jews? Explain.*

A. Question: What was Paul's attitude toward the Jews (Rom. 9:1-5)?

Jews and Gentiles asked: "Had Paul forsaken his own people, the Jews?" Some Jews felt that Paul was a traitor to Israel. For even though Paul was a Jew, he was an apostle to the Gentiles (Rom. 11:13). Early in Paul's ministry (about A.D. 49), Paul wrote that Gentiles did not need to follow Jewish customs, such as circumcision, to be saved (Gal. 2:12). At a council in Jerusalem, the apostles discussed the relationship of Jewish and Gentile believers. The apostles agreed with Paul (Acts 15). Still, many Jews had hard feelings toward Paul. Recall Paul's visit to Jerusalem, after years of ministry:

Q 4 ➚ *Why did many Jewish believers have hard feelings toward Paul?*

¹⁷When we arrived at Jerusalem, the brothers received us warmly. ¹⁸The next day Paul and the rest of us went to see James, and all the elders were present. ¹⁹Paul greeted them and reported in detail what God had done among the Gentiles through his ministry. ²⁰When they heard this, they praised God. Then they said to Paul: "You see, brother, how many thousands of Jews have believed, and all of them are zealous for the law. ²¹They have been informed that you teach all the Jews who live among the Gentiles to turn away from Moses, telling them not to circumcise their children or live according to our customs. ²²What shall we do? They will certainly hear that you have come" (Acts 21:17-22).

Many rumors spread about Paul. It was not true that Paul taught Jews to turn away from Moses. Paul wrote:

Q 5 ✎ *Was it true that Paul taught Jews to turn away from Moses? Explain.*

²⁰To the Jews I became like a Jew, to win the Jews. To those under the law I became like one under the law (though I myself am not under the law), so as to win those under the law. ²¹To those not having the law I became like one not having the law (though I am not free from God's law but am under Christ's law), so as to win those not having the law. ²²To the weak I became weak, to win the weak. I have become all things to all men so that by all possible means I might save some (1 Cor. 9:20-22).

Paul did not teach Jewish believers to abandon their customs. And when he was with Jews, he showed respect for their beliefs. But Paul taught Gentiles that they did not need to follow Jewish customs. And much of Paul's success was among Gentiles.

Paul's pattern was to preach to Jews first in cities he visited (Acts 14:1; 18:5-8). Many Jews received Christ as Paul preached. But often, Jewish leaders rejected Paul and hated him for preaching Jesus. Unbelieving Jews stirred up the people against Paul (Acts 14:2). In Lystra, unbelieving Jews from Antioch and Iconium won the crowd.

They persuaded the multitude to stone Paul. Some dragged him outside the city, and thought he was dead (Acts 14:19). Wherever he went, Paul faced persecution from Jews who rejected Jesus. How did all the rumors, misunderstandings, and hate among the Jews affect Paul?

What was Paul's attitude toward the Jews (Rom. 9:1-5)?

Answer: Paul's heart overflowed with God's love for the Jews.

[1]I speak the truth in Christ—I am not lying, my conscience confirms it in the Holy Spirit— [2]I have great sorrow and unceasing anguish in my heart. [3]For I could wish that I myself were cursed and cut off from Christ for the sake of my brothers, those of my own race, [4]the people of Israel... (Rom. 9:1-4).

Principle: God's love for the lost inspires us believers to love others (Rom. 9:1-4).

Paul affirms his love for the Jews. In the flesh, people may desire for their enemies to be punished. But Paul was led by the Spirit. He did not wish the Jews ill, but good.[2]

When Paul looks at Christ, he celebrates. He worships as he declares that nothing can separate those in Christ from the love of God (Rom. 8:31-39). But when Paul looks at Israel, he cries (Rom. 9:1-2).[3] And he is willing to be separated from Christ, *if* it would save the Jews. Paul appeals to Christ, his conscience, and the Holy Spirit to confirm his truthfulness. Paul loved the Jews so much that he was willing to be accursed—forever lost—as a substitute for his brothers. But of course, this was not possible. Paul knew that only Christ could become a curse for sin (Gal. 3:13).[4] Still, the love Paul felt for the Jews was an example of the love Jesus Christ feels for the lost. [7]*"Very rarely will anyone die for a righteous man, though for a good man someone might possibly dare to die. [8]But God demonstrates his own love for us in this: While we were still sinners, Christ died for us"* (Rom. 5:7-8).

Paul loved like Moses, who prayed: *"Oh, what a great sin these people have committed! They have made themselves gods of gold. [32]But now, please forgive their sin—but if not, then blot me out of the book you have written"* (Exod. 32:31-32). Paul loved like Stephen, who forgave those who stoned him (Acts 7:60). Paul loved like Jesus, who forgave those who mocked Him as He died for them on the cross (Luke 23:34). Who are *we* trying to love into the Kingdom? What type of things are we doing to show our love for the lost?

B. Question: Did God's word (promise) to Abraham and Israel fail (Rom. 9:6-13)?

We will answer the question of B above. But first, let us review some of the privileges that God gave the Israelites. Paul wrote:

[4]...Theirs is the adoption as sons; theirs the divine glory, the covenants, the receiving of the law, the temple worship and the promises. [5]Theirs are the patriarchs, and from them is traced the human ancestry of Christ (Rom. 9:4-5).

Let us look briefly at each of the eight privileges Paul lists.

- *Adoption*. God adopted the nation of Israel as His son (Exod. 4:22-23; Deut. 14:1-2; Jer. 31:9; Hos. 11:1).
- *Glory*. God revealed His glory to and through Israel (Exod. 16:7, 10; Lev. 9:6, 23; Num. 16:19).
- *Covenants*. God made a covenant with Abraham (Gen. 15:17-21; 17:1-8). This covenant was expanded through Moses (Exod. 19:5; 24:1-4). The Israelites confirmed the covenant at Moab (Deut. 29:1-15), at Mount Ebal and Mount Gerizim (Josh. 8:30-35), and at Shechem (Josh. 24:1-27). Likewise, God renewed the covenant with David (2 Sam. 7). Thus God's covenant with Abraham appears in many forms, but there is one covenant at the core. And when God made a new covenant, He

Q 6 ✎ *Summarize Paul's attitude toward the Jews (Rom. 9:1-5).*

Q 7 ✎ *Which lost people do you love the most? How do you show your love for them?*

Q 8 ✎ *Which of the eight privileges to Israel stand out the most to you? Explain.*

Q 9 ➤ *How many covenants with Israel were there in the Old Testament?*

announced it first to Israel, and included Israel first among the nations of the covenant (Jer. 31:31-40). But notice that even in the promise of God's covenant with Abraham, God mentions all the nations of the world (Gen. 12:1-3).

- *Law.* God gave the Law to Israel through Moses, on Mount Sinai (Exod. 19–24). As Paul has shown, the Law is holy, righteous, and good—because it reflects the God who gave it (Rom. 7:7-12).
- *Temple worship.* Worship began in the tabernacle (Exod. 40), and continued through the temple Solomon built (1 Kings 5–9).
- *Promises.* God's promises to Israel first appear in His word to Abraham (Gen. 12:1-3). Although the promises to Israel are many, they are all rooted and fulfilled in Jesus Christ, the Messiah.
- **Patriarchs.* Abraham, Isaac, Jacob and his sons.
- *Christ.* The list of privileges ends with the fact that Christ is a son of Abraham. Thus Paul emphasizes the paradox—the problem. Jesus is the Alpha and Omega of Israel's privileges. He is the beginning and the end of all privileges. He is the source of all blessings—yet most Jews have rejected Him![5] Does this mean that God's promises to the Jews have failed (Rom. 9:6)?

Q 10 Why did God choose Abraham? What was God's plan?

To know if God's word to the Jews has failed, we must understand God's plan and purpose. Why did God choose Abraham? What was God's plan? Let us review God's first promise to Abraham.

> [1]*The LORD had said to Abram, "Leave your country, your people and your father's household and go to the land I will show you.* [2]*I will make you into a great nation and I will bless you; I will make your name great, and you will be a blessing.* [3]*I will bless those who bless you, and whoever curses you I will curse;* **and all peoples on earth will be blessed through you**" (Gen. 12:1-3).

When God first talked to Abraham, there were no Jews—only Gentiles. In fact, Abraham himself was a Gentile. From verses such as John 3:16, we understand that God loves everyone. Our Heavenly Father wants all to become His children. And even in Genesis 12:3, we see the reason why God chose Abraham. The Lord had a plan to bless all nations. God's word to Abraham focused on His plan and purpose: *"and all peoples on earth will be blessed through you"* (Gen. 12:3). Abraham became the father of the Jews. And through the Jewish nation, God sent the Savior of all nations.

The Scripture foresaw that God would justify the Gentiles by faith, and announced the gospel in advance to Abraham: *"All nations will be blessed through you"* (Gal. 3:8).

Q 11 Does God love Jews more than Gentiles? Explain.

God has no favorites. He loves both Jews and Gentiles the same. In Romans 1, Paul declared that God offers righteousness to all who live by faith—Jews and Gentiles.

> [1]*Paul, a servant of Christ Jesus, called to be an apostle and set apart for the gospel of God—* [2]*the gospel he promised beforehand through his prophets in the Holy Scriptures* [3]*regarding his Son, who as to his human nature was a descendant of David....*[16]*I am not ashamed of the gospel, because it is the power of God for the salvation of everyone who believes:* **first for the Jew, then for the Gentile**. [17]*For in the gospel a righteousness from God is revealed, a righteousness that is by faith from first to last, just as it is written: "The righteous will live by* **faith**" (Rom. 1:1-3, 16-17).

Since Eden, *faith* has been the only path of salvation. Hebrews 11 lists examples of the righteous who lived by faith, including Abel, Enoch, Noah, Abraham, Isaac, Jacob, Moses, and the Israelites (Heb. 11).

Q 12 What was God's promise to Abraham (Gen. 12:1-3)?

Answer: God's Word has not failed. But people have failed to live by God's Word. God has done as He planned. God chose a man, Abraham, to be the father of a nation.

And through that nation, God sent the Savior of all people who *choose* to live by faith in God. This was God's plan from the beginning. Neither His plan nor His word has failed. Jews and Gentiles who relate to God by faith find salvation and righteousness.

Q 13 *Did God's word (promise) to Abraham and Israel fail (Rom. 9:6-13)? Explain.*

God's word to the Jews has not failed (Rom. 9:6). Let us look at two lesser principles related to this big theme of Romans 9–11.

1. Privileges do not guarantee personal salvation. In Romans 9:4-5 we studied eight privileges that God gave to Israel. Yet many Jews will fall short of heaven. Jesus was amazed at the faith of a Gentile centurion. Then He said:

Q 14 *What lasting benefit did most Jews receive from the eight privileges of Romans 9:4-5?*

> [10] *"I tell you the truth, I have not found anyone in Israel with such great faith.* [11] *I say to you that many will come from the east and the west, and will take their places at the feast with Abraham, Isaac and Jacob in the kingdom of heaven.* [12] *But the* subjects *[Greek, sons] of the kingdom will be thrown outside, into the darkness, where there will be weeping and gnashing of teeth"* (Matt. 8:10-12).

In Matthew 8:12 the NIV, unlike other versions, translates the Greek word *huioi* as *subjects* instead of *sons,* the common translation of *huioi* throughout the New Testament. *Huioi* is the same Greek word that the NIV translates as *sons* in Romans 8:14 and 8:19. The Jews were the first *adopted* sons of the Kingdom (Rom. 9:4). But no privilege, not even sonship, guarantees salvation. Paul will write about this in Romans 11. He will remind us that Jewish branches were *broken off* the vine because of unbelief. And Paul will warn that Gentiles may be *cut off* through unbelief (Rom. 11:20-22). Despite all the privileges listed in Romans 9:4-5, many Jews will be lost forever.

Q 15 *What are 2 examples that show we may be adopted as God's sons, but afterward be lost forever?*

Likewise, Jesus rebuked the Jews and Gentiles of Capernaum. They had the privilege of seeing about 70 percent of His miracles.

Q 16 *What privileges has God given you? What do these guarantee?*

> [23] *"And you, Capernaum, will you be lifted up to the skies? No, you will go down to the depths. If the miracles that were performed in you had been performed in Sodom, it would have remained to this day.* [24] *But I tell you that it will be more bearable for Sodom on the day of judgment than for you"* (Matt. 11:23-24).

Application: Have you received the privilege of hearing the gospel? Have you been blessed to receive biblical teaching, good preaching, and gospel music? Be a good steward of your privileges. God requires more from those who receive more (Luke 12:35-48; James 3:1). Privileges ensure giving an account. But as Israel can testify, privileges do not guarantee salvation.

2. God's only children are those born through His promises. *"Not all who are descended from Israel are Israel"* (Rom. 9:6b). This proverb means that there is a smaller group of "true Israelites" within the larger nation of Israel. Paul illustrates this truth with two pairs of brothers: Isaac and Ishmael were both sons of Abraham. But Abraham's descendants were counted through Isaac, not Ishmael. Likewise, Jacob and Esau were twin sons of Isaac and Rebekah. But the promises of God came through Isaac, not Esau. These brothers illustrate that true Jews come only through promise, not a human bloodline.

Q 17 *Are all Abraham's descendants his children? Explain.*

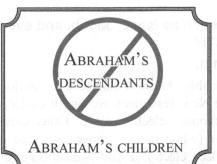

ABRAHAM'S DESCENDANTS

ABRAHAM'S CHILDREN

John the Baptist warned the Pharisees and Sadducees not to base their relationship with God on their lineage. Rather, only those who repent and bear good fruit are acceptable to God (Matt. 3:7-10). Likewise, Jesus told His followers that Abraham's descendants and Abraham's true children are two different groups.

Paul made this same point about *true Jews* earlier in Romans.

Q 18 How can we recognize a true Jew?

[28] *"A man is not a Jew if he is only one outwardly, nor is circumcision merely outward and physical.* [29]*No, a man is a Jew if he is one inwardly; and circumcision is circumcision of the heart, by the Spirit, not by the written code. Such a man's praise is not from men, but from God"* (Rom. 2:28-29; Deut. 30:6). True children of Abraham experience a spiritual change within. As they receive God's Word, the Holy Spirit gives them a new heart—a new birth. As James said, *"He [God] chose to give us birth through the word of truth"* (James 1:18). And as Peter wrote, through God's promises, we partake of the divine nature (2 Pet. 1:3-4). True children of Abraham are also called God's children (Rom. 9:8). But we do not become God's children through the blood of our earthly parents. Christians do not give birth to other Christians. God has no grandchildren. His only children are those born of the Spirit, by faith in His Word (John 1:12). Thus Paul explains that Abraham is the father of all who believe God's promises (Rom. 4:11, 16-25). This is why Jesus told Nicodemus, a Jew, [5]*"No one can enter the kingdom of God unless he is born of water and the Spirit.* [6]*Flesh gives birth to flesh, but the Spirit gives birth to spirit.* [7]*You should not be surprised at my saying, 'You must be born again'"* (John 3:5-7).

Q 19 What evidence shows that God's word to the Jews has not failed?

God's word to the Jews has not failed. He promised to make Abraham into a great nation. And Paul explains that all who live by faith are Abraham's children (Rom. 4:16-17). Likewise, God promised that through Abraham, He would bless all the nations of the earth. And that is just what God has done and is doing. All who walk with God by faith are true children of Abraham and of God. *"He redeemed us in order that the blessing given to Abraham might come to the Gentiles through Christ Jesus, so that by faith we might receive the promise of the Spirit"* (Gal. 3:14).

God's promise to Abraham and his spiritual children has not failed. But the promise was bigger and broader than Abraham ever imagined!

Lesson 31

Israel's Past Election, a Blessing to the Nations—Part 2 (Rom. 9:1-29)

Goal A: *Explain 4 principles about election to serve.*
Goal B: *Summarize 2 principles about election to salvation.*
Goal C: *Explain and illustrate: Humans and God have the freedom to choose.*
Goal D: *Explain and illustrate: God is patient with those who rebel against Him (Rom. 9:22-29).*

Q 20 To review Romans 9:1-29, complete Figure 8.5 as you study Lesson 31.

Rom.	Questions	Answers	Rom.
9:1-5	A. What was Paul's attitude toward the Jews?		9:1-5
9:6	B. Did God's word (promise) to Abraham fail?		9:6-29
9:14	C. *Is God unjust* (in choosing Isaac, Jacob, and even Pharaoh for His purposes)?		9:15-21
9:22	D. Why is God patient with those who rebel against Him?		9:22-29

Figure 8.5   Four key questions on Romans 9:1-29

In Lesson 30 we covered the first two questions of Figure 8.5 Now, in Lesson 31 we continue with the last two questions, C–D.

C. Is God unjust to choose (elect) people such as Isaac, Jacob, and even Pharaoh for His purposes (Rom. 9:10-21)?

Answer: *"Is God unjust? Not at all!"* (Rom. 9:14).

Q 21 What are some synonyms of the verb "elect"?

Election is a word that causes some to stumble. *Election* can be a mysterious word. But as we study forms of this word in the New Testament, we find it easier to understand. The Greek verb *eklegomai* means "choose, select, or elect." Other Greek forms (cognates) of this word are the noun *eklogen* (which means "chosen, selected, or elected"), and the adjective *eklektos* ("chosen, select, elect").[6] Figure 8.6 shows a few verses in the New Testament where a form of the Greek word for *elect* appears. Study these to get a better understanding of this word, *elect*. (Note: You can study any word in the Bible using a concordance. Use a Strong's Concordance to look up *election*. In Strong's, the number beside election, 1589, guides you to a list at the back of Strong's. This list contains verses which use the Greek word translated *election*.)

Q 22 ⬐ *In the New Testament, are _elect_ and _election_ always "theological" words? Explain.*

New Testament	Verse containing the verb *elect* or the noun *election*
Luke 6:13	*He called his disciples to him and **chose** (elected) twelve of them.*
Luke 10:42	*"Mary has **chosen** (elected) what is better, and it will not be taken away from her."*
Luke 14:7	*When he noticed how the guests **picked** (chose, elected) the places of honor at the table, he told them this parable:*
John 6:70	*"Have I not **chosen** (elected) you, the Twelve? Yet one of you is a devil!"*
Acts 6:5	*They **chose** (elected) Stephen, a man full of faith and of the Holy Spirit; also Philip…*
Rom. 8:33	*Who will bring any charge against those whom God has **chosen** (selected, elected)?*
Rom. 9:11	*Yet, before the twins were born or had done anything good or bad—in order that God's purpose in **election** (choosing, selecting) might stand:*
Rom. 11:5	[4]*…"I have reserved for myself seven thousand who have not bowed the knee to Baal."* [5]*So too, at the present time there is a remnant **chosen** (selected, elected) by grace.*
Rom. 16:13	*Greet Rufus, **chosen** (elected) in the Lord, and his mother, who has been a mother to me, too.*
1 Cor. 1:27	*But God **chose** (elected) the foolish things of the world to shame the wise; God **chose** the weak things…*
James 2:5	*Has not God **chosen** (elected) those who are poor in the eyes of the world to be rich in faith and to inherit the kingdom he promised those who love him?*
1 Pet. 2:6	*"See, I lay a stone in Zion, a **chosen** (elect) and precious cornerstone, and the one who trusts in him will never be put to shame."*
2 Pet. 1:10	[10]*Therefore, my brothers, be all the more eager to make your calling and **election** (selection) sure. For if you do these things, you will never fall,* [11]*and you will receive a rich welcome into the eternal kingdom of our Lord and Savior Jesus Christ.*
Rev. 17:14	*They will make war against the Lamb, but the Lamb will overcome them because he is Lord of lords and King of kings—and with him will be his called, **chosen** (elected) and faithful followers.*

Figure 8.6   Some verses in the New Testament that contain a form of the verb *elect* or the noun *election*.

Now you have a better understanding of the word *elect*, which means "to choose or select."

There are two types of election: election for *service*, and election for *salvation*. Let us look at some principles related to these two types of election (Rom. 9:6-29).

Q 23 ⬈ *What are 2 different types or purposes of election?*

1. Principles about election to serve:

- **Election to serve is public.** The broad election to serve relates to God's plans for the earth. Jesus chose (elected) 12 apostles to serve (Luke 6:13). This election was for public ministry. Likewise, God chose Abraham, Isaac, and Jacob for a public ministry. He *elected* them to be the forefathers of a nation. And through this nation of Israel, God sent the Savior of the world—the public.

Q 24 ⬐ *Do you know someone elected (chosen) to serve the public? Give an example.*

- **Election to serve is based on God's foreknowledge and wisdom.** God's choices are not *arbitrary—they are not illogical, uninformed, or by chance. In the days of Samuel, priests poked a fork with three prongs into a pot of boiling meat. Whatever the fork pulled out belonged to the priest. With this random *method of chance*, the priest did not know what he would get (1 Sam. 2:14). In contrast, God does not choose like this. God chooses on the basis of His foreknowledge.[7] God knows everything. He chooses a person who is best suited for a purpose. God's purpose was to build a nation and send the Savior of the world through that nation. Jacob was a better choice than Esau for this purpose. Jacob looked farther ahead than Esau. He saw the value of his father's blessing. In contrast, Esau lived for the moment. He was led by impulse, fleshly desires, and passion.[8] Likewise, Jacob showed a hunger for the spiritual that Esau never displayed. So God chose Jacob instead of Esau. This does not mean Jacob was more worthy, but

Q 25 ⬐ *Does God elect or choose by chance? Explain.*

rather, more suitable. Is a church unjust for choosing a pastor, or a deacon who is most qualified? Is an employer unjust in selecting the best person for a position? Certainly not. And God is not unjust in choosing the best people to fulfill His will. Romans 9:13 says, *"Jacob have I loved, but Esau have I hated"* (KJV). By His foreknowledge, God loved or preferred Jacob for the task at hand. He loved Jacob as the best to serve as an ancestor of Christ.

Q 26 ✎ *Why did God love Jacob more than Esau? What affected God's choice?*

Romans 9:13 with *figurative* language says, *"Jacob I loved, but Esau I hated."* Likewise, with *figurative* language, Luke 14:26 uses extreme contrasts to make a point: *"If anyone comes to me and does not hate his father and mother, his wife and children, his brothers and sisters—yes, even his own life—he cannot be my disciple."* Other verses teach us to love our family members. But Luke's point is that our *love* for God must be greater than our love for family members and greater than our love for self. To put it another way, our love for God must be so great that our love for family and self is as distant as *hate* (see Matt. 22:37-40; Eph. 5:25). God wants our love for Him to be first. And whatever is in second place, He wants it to be far away from our love for Him—as far as hate is from love. Likewise, for the purpose of service, God loved Jacob *more* than Esau (Rom. 9:13). Still, other verses show that God loved and cared for Esau and his children (Deut. 2:1-6).

Application: God has a purpose for you. Take heed. The sight and smell of tasty food seduced Esau away from his birthright. Beware, lest you trade the unseen and eternal for a moment of satisfaction or pleasure. See to it that you do not sell your inheritance for a single meal (Heb. 12:16).

Q 27 ✎ *Did God choose Pharaoh to serve forever? Explain.*

- **Election to serve is temporal.** God chooses people to serve on earth for a few years. He chose Cyrus to serve as king of Persia. He chose Pharaoh to serve as the leader of Egypt. He chooses some to serve as pastors, missionaries, or Bible teachers. And there is a sense in which God chooses all believers to serve in their circumstances (1 Cor. 7:17). All choices to serve are temporal—for a few years on earth.

Q 28 ✎ *Does election to serve determine election to salvation? Give examples.*

- **Election to serve does not determine election for salvation.** God elected the nation of Israel to serve. He chose Israel as the nation through whom He blessed all nations. Yet only a *remnant of the chosen Israelites was saved (Rom. 9:27). Likewise, Jesus chose 12 apostles to serve. But one was lost. And God chose Paul to serve. But Paul was careful to maintain his *personal election to salvation.* Otherwise, after serving others, it was possible for him to be lost (1 Cor. 9:27).

Election to serve is a different matter than election to eternal salvation. God elected King Manasseh to serve as king of Judah. He failed in this public service, and was the worst king in the history of Judah. We might say that he lost that election. But at the end of his life he repented and was elected to eternal salvation. In free nations, people may elect someone to serve. But this does not determine a person's eternal destiny. An election to service does not determine election to salvation.

2. **Principles on election to salvation:**

Q 29 ➚ *How many voters are in the election for salvation? Explain.*

- **Responding to election for salvation is private and personal.** Each person decides his or her personal election. A wise man said that in an election for personal salvation, there are only three voters: God, Satan, and an individual. God votes for all to be saved. It is not God's will *"that any should perish, but that all should come to repentance"* (2 Pet. 3:9 KJV). In contrast, the devil votes for all to be lost. Like the thief, his desire is to steal, kill, and destroy (John 10:10). So the third vote, the vote of each person, determines the election. If a person votes (chooses) to be saved, he is elected by a two-thirds majority. But if a person votes to be lost, he is elected to hell.

Salvation is a personal matter. Neither Ishmael, Esau, nor Pharaoh was chosen for the same service as Jacob. But each person is free to choose the election of salvation. God did not choose Rahab the Canaanite, Ruth the Moabite, nor Uriah the Hittite to be born as Jews. But they all chose to love and obey the God of Abraham. So as they 'voted' they were elected to salvation. Your election depends on your vote.

The Spirit and the bride say, "Come!" And let him who hears say, "Come!" Whoever is thirsty, let him come; and whoever wishes, let him take the free gift of the water of life (Rev. 22:17).

- **Election to salvation is eternal.** Men, women, youth, and children have eternal souls. We will live or die forever somewhere. An election for service on earth is for a short time. But the election to salvation is eternal.

Conclusion: *Both humans and God have the freedom to choose or elect.* People value the freedom to make personal choices. Some nations give their citizens more freedom than other nations give. But God allows each person in every nation to choose or reject salvation. God never violates a person's freedom—his free will. He never forces anyone to choose right or wrong. Rather, God allows each person to choose.

Likewise, God has the right and freedom to choose. It is God's right to choose whom He wants to show *mercy. But His choices are not arbitrary—they are not made without a standard. Rather, God's choices are based on His holiness and righteousness. God chooses to have mercy on those who relate to Him with humility, repentance, faith, and obedience. God is just to show mercy on those who ask for it. And He is just to pour out wrath on those who reject His mercy.

Was God *unjust* to harden Pharaoh's heart? Not at all. God hardens a heart by leaving it alone. As the rain keeps the soil moist, the presence of God keeps the heart soft and the soul sensitive. When God backs away from people, their hearts begin to dry up and harden. (Review the phrase *God gave them over* in Romans 1:24, 26, 28.) God did not harden Pharaoh's heart *until* Pharaoh chose, many times, to harden his own heart (Exod. 7:13, 22; 8:19; 9:7). So God hardened Pharaoh's heart—by *giving him over to his own sinful desires.*

God did use Pharaoh's stubbornness for His purpose—*"that I might display my power in you and that my name might be proclaimed in all the earth"* (Rom. 9:17). God gave Pharaoh the free will to harden his own heart. Still, God had the right to use Pharaoh to fulfill His purposes. As a result, Egypt and the nations nearby learned of God's power (Exod. 9:16). And today, nations all over the earth read about God's victory over Pharaoh. God lets people choose the road they will travel. But God chooses what is at the end of each road.

God's *national* judgment on Pharaoh did not prevent some Egyptians from choosing *personal* salvation with the God of Israel (Exod. 12:38). As a wise man said, God has designed things so that He does not violate our free will; and our free will does not cancel His free will. Both God and humans have the freedom to choose or elect.[9]

D. Why is God patient with those who rebel against Him (Rom. 9:22-29)?

These verses continue to emphasize that God's word to Abraham and his true children has not failed (Rom. 9:6). In Romans 8 the key words *flesh* and *Spirit* occur many times. In Romans 9:15-29 the key word is *mercy*, which occurs six times. Similar words in this passage are *compassion, patience,* and *love.* God is Sovereign—free to do whatever He desires. Do not be mistaken. Have no doubts about it. God alone decides those to whom He will show mercy. But the good news is that God delights to show mercy to all. Mercy,

Q 30 *Did God want Esau and Pharaoh to be saved? Explain.*

Q 31 *Was God unjust to harden Pharaoh's heart? Explain.*

not wrath, is God's first choice. Why is God so patient with rebels? The **answer** amazes us: Because He delights to show mercy.

Q 32 *How are rebels prepared or fitted for God's wrath? Give examples.*

Paul speaks of *"the objects of God's wrath—prepared for destruction"* (Rom. 9:22). He contrasts these with *"the objects of his mercy, whom he prepared in advance for glory"* (Rom. 9:23). Some translations, like the NIV, have the word *prepared* in both Romans 9:22-23. But the Greek text has two separate words. In Romans 9:22, the Greek word translated *prepared* means "fit together" or "restore." This Greek word *katarizo* does not mean "to predestine." Rather, it shows that rebels, like Pharaoh, *are fitted and shaped* to receive God's wrath. Little by little, one sin at a time, they forge the chains that will bind them (Rom. 1–2). Each act of rebellion makes them into the type of people that a just God must punish.[10]

Q 33 *Would God rather show wrath or mercy? Explain.*

Principle: God delights to show mercy, not wrath.

We humans are often quick to be angry and slow to show mercy. But God's patience amazes us. James and John wanted to call fire down from heaven on the Samaritans who rejected Jesus. But our Lord explained that such an attitude of revenge was far from God (Luke 9:54-55). Unbelieving Jews killed the prophets that God sent them. Then they hated Jesus and rejected His miracles and ministry. His response? He wept over Jerusalem because they would not receive God's love and mercy (Matt. 23:37; Luke 19:41).

> GOD'S LOVE AND MERCY ARE BEYOND OUR UNDERSTANDING.

The prophet Hosea preached not only through his words, but also through his life. God called Hosea to marry a harlot named Gomer. She represented Israel—who was unfaithful to God. Hosea and Gomer had three children: Jezreel, Lo-Ruhamah (not loved), and Lo-Ammi (not my people) (Hos. 1:4-9). Then Gomer was unfaithful to Hosea, and became a slave. Later, God told the prophet to buy her back and show his love to her again. God said: *"Love her as the LORD loves the Israelites, though they turn to other gods"* (Hos. 3:1). An earthly husband may divorce his wife at the first sign of unfaithfulness. But the Northern Kingdom of Israel did not have one godly king in their history of 250 years. Still, God continued to love them all of these years! This kind of love and mercy is almost unbelievable. As Paul says, God's love and mercy are beyond our understanding. God's love *"surpasses knowledge"* (Eph. 3:19).

In Romans 9:25 Paul quotes from Hosea 2:23. This passage in Hosea prophesied that God would once again love Israel, and they would again be His people. Paul uses this passage to illustrate that God's patience is to show mercy—on Jews and Gentiles (Rom. 9:24-26).

Likewise, Paul writes that only the mercy of God prevented Israel from being destroyed like Sodom and Gomorrah (Rom. 9:29). Most people never change, no matter how patient God is. But because God is patient and merciful, some change from the group Lo-Ruhamah (not loved) to Ruhamah (loved); and they move from Lo-Ammi (not my people) to Ammi (my people)—and *"sons of the living God"* (Rom. 9:25-26). Give thanks to the Lord for He is good, His love endures forever.

A husband and wife had a son who was precious to them. But when he became a teenager, he rebelled against his parents. The boy dropped out of school. He chose bad friends. Once, in the middle of the night, the boy came home drunk. His mother slipped out of bed. Later the father got up. He thought his wife was in the kitchen crying. Instead, the father found her in their son's bedroom. The mother was sitting on their son's bed, stroking his hair as he slept. The father asked his wife what she was doing. The mother said, "Our son won't allow me to love him any other time." God is like that mother. He steps into people's darkness to show them His love. God loves people even when they do not want Him to love them. God's love causes Him to wait for people to turn their lives over to Him. And because of God's love and patience, He will save at least a remnant of people.[11]

Review of Romans 9:1-29:

Rom. 9	People	Key concepts	Principles
9:1-3	I (Paul)	Love for the lost	God's deep desire to save the lost should fill our hearts.
9:4-5	Israel	Privileges	Group privileges do not guarantee personal salvation.
9:5	Christ	Seed of Abraham	God sent the Savior of the world through Abraham's lineage.
9:6-29	God	God's eternal purpose	God promised to bless all nations of the earth through the Seed of Abraham (Gen. 22:18; Gal. 3:8, 16).
9:6-9	Isaac/(Ishmael)	Children of promise	God's children are those born through His promise. Abraham is the father of all who believe (Rom. 4:11).
9:10-13	Jacob/Esau	Love/hate	God is free to choose whomever He desires to fulfill His plans.
9:14-24	Moses/Pharaoh	Patience/wrath	God is free to make the rules for His mercy and judgment.
9:25-26	Hosea	Jews and Gentiles	In His mercy, God reaches out in love to those who have rejected Him—both Jews and Gentiles.
9:27-29	Isaiah	Remnant	In His mercy, God saves a remnant of Jews (and Gentiles).

Figure 8.7   Key people and principles showing God's word (plan/promise) has not failed (Rom. 9:1-29)

God's word to Abraham has not failed (Rom. 9:6). Because of His mercy, there is a remnant that walks with God by faith, and receives Jesus as Savior and Lord.

There is the song "Forever God Is Faithful" by Michael W. Smith, based on Psalm 136.[12]

Israel's Present Rejection—Unbelief Toward the Gospel (Rom. 9:30–10:21)

Lesson 32

Goal A: *Answer the key questions in Romans 9:30–10:21 (Figure 8.8).*

Goal B: *Explain and illustrate 3 reasons why some do not find righteousness.*

Goal C: *Identify 6 passages that show how anyone can find a right relationship with God (Rom. 9:30–10:13).*

Goal D: *Review the 5 steps that lead to salvation, illustrating failures and successes of each step.*

Paul's letter to the Romans contains five big parts—five units.

Unit 1 describes the problem—our need for righteousness (Rom. 1:1–3:20). This unit emphasizes that all have sinned. Both Jews and Gentiles deserve God's judgment. All sinners are under God's wrath. We all fall short of what God requires. We all need God to provide righteousness for us.

Unit 2 emphasizes the solution—we receive righteousness by faith in Christ (Rom. 3:21–5:21). Abraham was among the first to receive righteousness through believing—through trusting God. He is like a spiritual father or forefather of all who seek a relationship with God through faith and trust.

Unit 3 reveals the key to living a life of victory and holiness (Rom. 6–8). These chapters contrast the desires of the flesh and the desires of the Spirit. Under the Law, people often failed to please God. For although the Law pointed the right way, the flesh pulled the wrong way. But under the new covenant, God frees us from the bondage of sin. And He empowers righteous living by His Spirit. As we submit to His Spirit within us, and resist evil desires of the flesh, we walk in freedom and please God. His powerful Spirit enables us to live a life of love, which summarizes and fulfills the Law (Rom. 8:4).

Unit 4 examines Israel in God's plan of salvation (Rom. 9–11). We are studying this unit in three parts: Israel's past election (Rom. 9:1-29), Israel's present rejection (9:30–10:21), and Israel's future restoration (Rom. 11).

Unit 5 gives practical applications for righteous living (Rom. 12–16).

Q 34 ✎ *What are the 5 big parts of Romans?*

Q 35 ↖ *To review Romans 9–11, complete Figure 8.8 as you study this chapter.*

Rom.	Questions	Answers	Rom.
9:1-5	What was Paul's attitude toward the Jews?		9:1-5
9:6	Did God's word (promise) to Abraham fail (Gen. 12:3; 22:18)?		9:6-29
9:14	*Is God unjust* (for using Isaac, Jacob, and even Pharaoh for His purposes)?		9:15-21
9:22	Why is God patient with those who rebel against Him?		9:23-29
9:30-32a	Why did Israel fail to obtain righteousness?		9:32–10:13
10:14-15a	*How? How? How? How? How!* Which 5 steps make salvation possible?		10:15b-17
10:18	Did Israel not all hear (God's message)?		
10:19a	*Did Israel not understand* (God's message)? What was Israel's problem?		10:19-21
11:1a	*Did God reject His people?*		11:1-10
11:11a	Did Israel stumble and fall beyond recovery?		11:11-32
11:34-35	*Who has known the mind of the Lord? Who has been his counselor? Who has ever given to God, that God should repay him?*		11:33, 36

Figure 8.8   Key questions and answers in Romans 9–11

Setting and Introduction

Figure 8.9   Many Jews stumbled over Christ, who was like the big cornerstone of a building, laid in the middle of the main street in Jerusalem (Rom. 9:32-33; Isa. 8:14; 28:16). Some stones in Herod's temple were as big as a bus. The largest stone in Herod's temple was 44 feet by 11 feet by 16 feet and weighed about 500 tons. But most stones in Herod's temple were about 2.5 by 3.5 by 15 feet (about 28 tons).[13]

Q 36 ↗ *On which path was Jesus a stumbling stone? Explain.*

A. Question: Why did Israel fail to obtain righteousness (Rom. 9:30)?

Answer: They sought righteousness by their own works, rather than by faith in Christ (Rom. 9:32-33).

1. First problem: Some stumble over Christ.

Imagine that you were a Jew living in Jerusalem at the time of Christ. Early each morning you looked toward the temple. You gave thanks as the smoke of the morning sacrifice ascended to heaven. Throughout the day you quoted verses from the Law. You sang Psalms of praise from time to time. And in the evening, you once again looked toward the temple. You prayed as the smoke of the evening sacrifice rose to God.

Then one morning you saw something that shocked you. As you looked toward the temple, you could hardly believe your eyes. For in the night, someone had been digging in the middle of the main street. There were piles of dirt from the hole that someone dug. It was a large hole, big enough to put several sheep in it. But the hole was not empty. For in it was a large stone. Most of the stone was down in the hole. Only a few inches of it showed. This was no ordinary stone. It was not just a round boulder that had rolled down the mountain. No! The stone was flat on the sides and the top. It was a cornerstone—the kind that workers chiseled to prepare. This was a precious stone of a foundation. It was level on the top, and straight on the sides. This stone was the corner of a new building! Someone was planning to build a big, new building—right in the middle of Jerusalem! Unbelievable! It was in the middle of the street that led to the temple. Only a little of it was showing. But there it was. Strange! Unexpected! Confusing! This stone would be a problem. For Jews with their eyes on the temple would stumble over this cornerstone. And sure enough, this is what happened—many stumbled. Paul wrote:

> *They stumbled over the "stumbling stone."* [33]*As it is written: "See, I lay in Zion a stone that causes men to stumble and a rock that makes them fall, and the one who trusts in him will never be put to shame"* (Rom. 9:32b-33).

Paul quotes Isaiah 8:14 and 28:16 about the cornerstone. It was God who laid the stone in Jerusalem, also called Zion. Isaiah wrote these words about 800 years before Christ. Note that Isaiah used figurative language. His words about a cornerstone are a picture. Jesus Christ is *like* the cornerstone of a new temple (Eph. 2:20-21). Peter refers to these same two passages, Isaiah 8:14 and 28:16. Peter compares Jesus to a living cornerstone, and believers to living stones in a temple (1 Pet. 2:4-8). Both Peter and Paul teach that all who disobey God and reject the gospel shape their own destiny— to stumble and fall (1 Pet. 2:8). Let us take a closer look at why Paul says the Jews stumbled.

2. Second problem: Some seek to establish their own righteousness (Rom. 10:3).

Righteousness is a key word in Romans 9:30–10:21. It appears at least seven times in these verses. Several verses in this section emphasize why some Israelites did not obtain *righteousness*. Why did they miss the bus to heaven?

Q 37 ➤ *Why did many Israelites miss the only bus going to heaven? Explain.*

Israel got sidetracked. They got off the path. They tried to use the Law *from* heaven as a ladder *to* heaven. Like those who built the tower of Babel, they tried to establish a name for themselves. They sought to impress God with their own good deeds. They wanted to *earn* God's favor—and make God their debtor. They thought that obeying some laws causes us to *deserve* God's blessings.[14] What a mistake!

Earning God's favor was never part of God's plan. The just live by faith *in God*— not faith in themselves (Rom. 1:17; Hab. 2:4). Earlier, Paul wrote that what we deserve is God's judgment and wrath. The wages we have *earned* are eternal death (Rom. 1:1–3:20). Paul emphasized that Jews and Gentiles are justified *only* by faith (Rom. 3:21–5:21). And in Romans 9:30–10:21, Paul explains that many Jews are not on the faith bus—the *only* bus going to heaven. Paul summarized it this way:

Q 38 ➤ *Did God ever plan for the Law to be a ladder to heaven? Explain.*

> [31]*Israel, who pursued a law of righteousness, has not attained it.* [32]*Why not? Because they pursued it not by faith but as if it were by works* (Rom. 9:31-32).

Israel pursued a *law of righteousness.* That is, they sought righteousness through keeping the Law, not by faith in God. Earlier, Paul wrote that the Law was not our problem. Israel was not wrong in trying to obey the Law. Obeying the Law was a proper response of love and faith—although the Law was too hard to keep perfectly (Rom. 10:5). But Israel's biggest error was in letting law crowd God out of the picture. The Law is good. It reveals what God likes, and what God hates. But as the years went by, Jewish leaders shifted the focus from the *God* of the Law to the *law* of God. They turned from the unseen God to the tablets He gave them. And they added hundreds of laws to the ones God gave. Some rabbis added the law that on the Sabbath, no one could lift anything heavier than two dried figs. Jesus rebuked the Pharisees for tying heavy loads on men's shoulders. These loads were the hundreds of laws Jewish teachers added (Matt. 23:4). Imagine this: The God who gave the Law became a man and was born in Israel. But some Jews were so focused on the Law that they did not even recognize the God who gave the Law to them! Good things can blind good people.

Q 39 ➤ *In what sense did the Law crowd God out of the picture?*

Q 40 ✎ *What did Paul mean when he said that some Jews have zeal without knowledge?*

3. Third problem: Those seeking to establish their own righteousness have zeal without knowledge (Rom. 10:2-3).

Unbelieving Jews had zeal without knowledge. Paul wrote:

> [2]*I can testify about them that they are zealous for God, but their zeal is not based on knowledge.* [3]*Since they did not know the righteousness that comes from God and sought to establish their own, they did not submit to God's righteousness* (Rom. 10:2-3).

Paul himself was once a Jew who had zeal without knowledge. Paul had great zeal in those pre-Christian days. He used his time, money, and energy to persecute followers of Christ (Acts 9:1-3).

Zeal is good, if it is based on knowledge. In Romans Paul writes, *"Never be lacking in zeal"* (Rom. 12:11). But zeal is not a good substitute for knowledge. One must get on the right bus to reach the right location. No amount of zeal will make up for getting on the wrong bus. And no amount of religious deeds will earn salvation. The just live by faith in God, not their own deeds.

People in many religions have zeal without knowledge. Muslims do many good deeds, such as praying, fasting, and giving. Some even give their lives for the cause of Islam. But their zeal is without the knowledge of Christ. They are trying to establish their own righteousness through good deeds. Meanwhile, like unbelieving Jews, *"they [do] not know the righteousness that comes from God."* So they refuse to submit to the only righteousness that God accepts (Rom. 10:3). Likewise, Hindus, Buddhists, and some Catholics do many religious deeds, such as sacrificing, giving, fasting, and attending religious meetings. But all who seek to establish their own righteousness have zeal without knowledge. They exalt themselves, not God. Imagine someone singing to God: "I Did It My Way," or "How Great I Am." Ridiculous!

Q 41 ✎ *Do you know people who have zeal without knowledge? Explain.*

> [9]*To some who were confident of their own righteousness and looked down on everybody else, Jesus told this parable:* [10]*"Two men went up to the temple to pray, one a Pharisee and the other a tax collector.* [11]*The Pharisee stood up and prayed about himself: 'God, I thank you that I am not like other men—robbers, evildoers, adulterers—or even like this tax collector.* [12]*I fast twice a week and give a tenth of all I get.'* [13]*But the tax collector stood at a distance. He would not even look up to heaven, but beat his breast and said, 'God, have mercy on me, a sinner.'* [14]*I tell you that this man, rather than the other, went home justified [righteous] before God. For everyone who exalts himself will be humbled, and he who humbles himself will be exalted"* (Luke 18:9-14).

Application: We can make the same mistake that some Israelites made. We can shift our focus from God to ourselves. Under the old covenant, Jews sought to obey the Law. And they trusted God to forgive their sins through the sacrifices. The Old Testament plan was to trust God while seeking to live in ways that pleased Him. The New Testament plan is like the old plan. We must trust God to save us, although we do not deserve salvation. The animal sacrifices pointed to Christ, the Lamb of God who takes away our sins. So faith in Christ is the basis of our justification—our righteousness. Still, we delight to obey God's laws, because we know this makes God happy. But our confidence must not be in our obedience, our building houses of worship, education, success, worship, giving, singing, church attendance, prayers, sacrifices, knowledge of Scripture, or other good deeds. Rather, we must trust in God, who is loving and gracious. We must not let works we can see become an idol we exalt. Let us not seek to establish our own righteousness (Rom. 10:3). May we never let the good things of God replace the God of good things. Let us never forget the one reason why God will welcome anyone into heaven.

B. Solution: God counts all righteous who trust in Jesus Christ (Rom. 9:30–10:13).

Over and over Paul emphasizes the solution to the human problem. We cannot earn our own righteousness. But God will give righteousness to all who seek it by faith in Christ. May each student, like the authors of this course, worship with tears of joy and a heart overflowing with thanksgiving as you study these verses.

Q 42 ✎ *How does Jesus end or fulfill what the Law started (Rom. 10:4)?*

Q 43 ✎ *Does God ask us to do the impossible (Rom. 10:6-10)? Explain.*

Q 44 ✎ *What does trusting Jesus look like in daily living (Rom. 10:11)?*

Rom.	Verses that emphasize righteousness by faith in Christ	Old Testament
9:30	*What then shall we say? That the Gentiles, who did not pursue righteousness, have obtained it, a righteousness that is by faith.* **Note:** We Gentiles did not pursue righteousness under the old covenant. But many of us Gentiles seek a right relationship with God by faith, and find it.	
9:33	*"See, I lay in Zion a stone that causes men to stumble and a rock that makes them fall, and the one who trusts in him will never be put to shame."*	Isa. 8:14; 28:16
10:4	*Christ is the end [fulfillment] of the law so that there may be righteousness for everyone who believes.* **Note:** Jesus fulfilled the Law. He completed what the Law started. The Law showed people how to be in a right relationship with God. Jesus obeyed all of the Law. As we believe in Him, God credits us with His righteousness. Then He writes the Law in our hearts and enables us to fulfill it by love, through the Spirit. Thus Jesus enables us to live in a right relationship with God. Let us always remember that our righteousness—our right relationship with God—is based on what Jesus does for us and in us, not what we do for Him.[15]	
10:6-10	*⁶But the righteousness that is by faith says: "Do not say in your heart, 'Who will ascend into heaven?'" (that is, to bring Christ down) ⁷"or 'Who will descend into the deep?'" (that is, to bring Christ up from the dead). ⁸But what does it say? "The word is near you; it is in your mouth and in your heart," that is, the word of faith we are proclaiming: ⁹That if you confess with your mouth, "Jesus is Lord," and believe in your heart that God raised him from the dead, you will be saved. ¹⁰For it is with your heart that you believe and are justified, and it is with your mouth that you confess and are saved.* **Note:** Moses first spoke these words to Israel. He emphasized that what God was asking them to do was not hard, but easy. Likewise, God does not ask us to do the impossible. We do not need to bring Christ down from heaven—He has already come down and died for us. And we do not need to raise Christ up from the grave. He has already resurrected and ascended for us. We only need to repent, confess that He is our Savior and Lord, believe in our hearts, and daily enjoy a relationship with Him by faith.	Deut. 30:12-14
10:11	*"Anyone who trusts in him will never be put to shame."* **Note:** This is the gospel in a short sentence. What a glorious promise! Hallelujah! Anyone! Note that the present tense *"trusts"* emphasizes a present relationship.	Isa. 28:16
10:12-13	*¹²For there is no difference between Jew and Gentile—the same Lord is Lord of all and richly blesses all who call on him, ¹³for, "Everyone who calls on the name of the Lord will be saved."* **Note:** Praise the Lord! All who call! Everyone!	Joel 2:32

Figure 8.10 Key verses that emphasize: God counts all righteous who trust in Christ (Rom. 9:30–10:13)

Both hell and heaven will contain the best and the worst of sinners. Hell will be the eternal home of a mixture of people. It will contain the best of sinners—those who tried to climb to heaven on the ladder of their own good deeds. But they discovered that their ladder was too short! So they fell into the lake of fire. Examples of the best sinners include devout Muslims, some Pharisees (Acts 15:5), sincere Hindus, some Protestants, and some Catholics who expect to pay for their sins in purgatory. Likewise, hell will contain the worst of sinners—thieves, liars, sex offenders, addicts, and murderers—who never asked Christ to forgive and save them. Who are the worst sinners you have read about or know personally?

In contrast, heaven will be the eternal home of a variety of people. It will contain those who were once the best of sinners. These committed few sins and trusted in Christ at an early age. And heaven will also house some who were among the most sinful people who ever lived. Some prostitutes like Rahab will be there. Some who committed sexual sins, like David, will be there. Some thieves, like the one crucified beside Jesus, will be in heaven. Some who once murdered, like Paul, will be there.

Q 45 ↖ *What is the one reason why God will open the gates of heaven for anyone?*

All who try to earn a right relationship with God will perish. But everyone who calls on the name of the Lord Jesus for mercy will be saved. What is your story? What is the basis for your hope of salvation? If you stand at the gates of heaven and an angel asks, "Why should I open the gates for you?", what will your answer be?

C. Review question: What are five steps that lead to the privilege of salvation for Jews and Gentiles?

In Romans 10 Paul is considering the question: Why are some Jews not saved? He has stated that all who call on the name of the Lord will be saved (Rom. 10:13). But many Jews are not being saved. Why? Paul knows that calling on the Lord is the fifth step that comes after four earlier steps. He examines steps 1–4 to find the reason why many Israelites are not being saved. Paul retraces the steps of salvation in reverse order from the last step to the first step (Figure 8.11).

Step 5: [13]*"Everyone who calls on the name of the Lord will be saved."*

Step 4: [14]*How, then, can they call on the one they have not believed in?*

Step 3: *And how can they believe in the one of whom they have not heard?*

Step 2: *And how can they hear without someone preaching to them?*

Step 1: [15]*And how can they preach unless they are sent? As it is written, "How beautiful are the feet of those who bring good news!"* (Rom. 10:13-15).

---

5. **God saves** all who call on Him (Rom. 10:13).

4. **Sinners call** on the Christ as they believe in Him (Rom. 10:14).

3. **Sinners believe** in Christ as they hear the good news (Rom. 10:14).

2. **Sinners hear** the good news as believers preach it (Rom. 10:14).

1. **God sends** believers to preach the good news (Rom. 10:15).
   (Note that other believers partner with God to send these preachers to the lost.)

Figure 8.11   Five steps in the privilege of salvation

Q 46 ↖ *On which step of the salvation process does Paul find a problem? Explain the problem.*

Paul finds no problem in the early steps of the gospel. *Step 1* is fine. Paul and others have preached the gospel to the Jews. And *Step 2* is also fine. The Jews have heard the gospel. But Paul finds a problem on *Step 3*, believing. For as Paul kindly says, *"not all the Israelites accepted the good news"* (Rom. 10:16). He quotes Isaiah 53:1, *"Lord, who has believed our message?"* (Rom. 10:16). Please turn to Isaiah 52:13–53:12 and read it. This is a famous prophecy about the Messiah. It is often called "the gospel in the Old Testament." Writers of the New Testament quote this passage more than any other passage of the Old Testament.[16] Faith comes to people as they hear the message. This faith enables people to believe. But some Jews refused to believe. So Paul quotes Isaiah 53:1.

One man owns a business that cleans rugs. To show customers the need, he visits their home. After an explanation, he turns down the lights. Then the businessman turns on a special light he has that causes stains to glow in the dark. This allows people to see all the stains in their home. One customer begged, "Turn off your light. I cannot stand to see all these ugly stains anymore. Please clean my home!" Likewise, God's Word and Spirit reveal the stains of our lives! The knowledge of sin is painful at first. But the forgiveness of sin leaves a person feeling clean within.[17]

Paul has identified the main problem: unbelief. And he has explained that Israel has zeal without knowledge. Still, he continues to look for other reasons why some Israelites have not been saved.

Question: *"Did they not hear?"* (Rom. 10:18).

Answer: Paul returns to Step 2, *hearing*. He affirms again that the Israelites have heard the message. Paul quotes the same verse he quoted earlier (Rom. 1:20; 10:18; Ps. 19:4). Paul uses Psalm 19 to show a parallel. As creation testifies to all about God, Paul and others have testified to the Jews about God. So the problem is not that the Jews have not heard the gospel.

Question: *"Did Israel not understand?"* (Rom. 10:19).

To answer this question, Paul quotes Moses: *"I will make you angry by a nation that has no understanding"* (Deut. 32:21). Paul's point is that the Gentiles, who have little or no understanding of God, have understood the gospel and believed it. So if those with little spiritual insight have understood the gospel, then surely the Jews have understood it. Neither a lack of hearing nor a lack of understanding the gospel is the cause of Israel's unbelief.

Conclusion: Why did Israel fail to obtain righteousness (Rom. 9:30-31)?

Boom! Paul ends the discussion in one sentence. He puts the blame on the shoulders of the Israelites. The root of Israel's unbelief is their stubborn hearts. Isaiah described it this way:

All day long I have held out my hands to a disobedient and obstinate people (Isa. 65:2; Rom. 10:21).

Take a moment to read Isaiah 65:1-7. You will need a tissue or handkerchief, because this passage will make you cry.

"All day long I have held out my hands to a disobedient and obstinate people" (Rom. 10:21). Paul is quoting Isaiah 65.

1*"I revealed myself to those who did not ask for me; I was found by those who did not seek me. To a nation that did not call on my name, I said, 'Here am I, here am I.'* 2*All day long I have held out my hands to an obstinate people, who walk in ways not good, pursuing their own imaginations—* 3*a people who continually provoke me to my very face, offering sacrifices in gardens and burning incense on altars of brick;* 4*who sit among the graves and spend their nights keeping secret vigil; who eat the flesh of pigs, and whose pots hold broth of unclean meat;* 5*who say, 'Keep away; don't come near me, for I am too sacred for you!'"* (Isa. 65:1-5).

Year after year God reached out to the Jews. Time after time He offered them the privilege of salvation. He sent prophets to preach God's offer of forgiveness and salvation. But the Jews rejected God's messengers and their message. Some Jews would not accept God under the Old Testament, and they would not accept Him under the New Testament. Jesus wept as He described the rejection of Israel:

37*"O Jerusalem, Jerusalem, you who kill the prophets and stone those sent to you, how often I have longed to gather your children together, as a hen gathers her chicks under her wings, but you were not willing.* 38*Look, your house is left to you desolate.* 39*For I tell you, you will not see me again until you say, 'Blessed is he who comes in the name of the Lord'"* (Matt. 23:37-39).

All day long the loving, patient, merciful God of heaven has reached out His hands to the Jews. But many have rejected His love.

Note that the Spirit led Paul to apply Isaiah 65:1 to the Gentiles, and Isaiah 65:2 to the Jews. Paul's first readers understood that God reached out to stubborn Jews *before*

Q 47 ⬿ *To what does Paul compare the voice of God's messengers (Rom. 10:18)?*

Q 48 ⬿ *How does Paul prove that Israel understood the gospel (Rom. 10:18)? Explain his logic.*

Q 49 ⬿ *To whom does Paul apply Isaiah 65:2?*

Q 50 ⬿ *What caused most Israelites redeemed from Egypt to lose their inheritance and relationship with God?*

Q 51 ⬿ *What things amaze you in Isaiah 65:1-5? Give examples.*

He reached out to stubborn Gentiles. It is amazing that humans are so rude to God Almighty. But what is even more amazing is that God continues to reach out to those who show Him such disrespect. Read Isaiah 65:1 again. God is like an unwanted lover, following after an unfaithful spouse. He revealed Himself to Israel saying, *"Here am I, here am I."* But Israel's response was, *"Keep away; don't come near me, for I am too sacred for you!"* (Isa. 65:5). Century after century, decade after decade, year after year, all day long God revealed Himself to those who did not seek Him. How sad. But encourage yourself with this thought. If God loves people so much that He will reveal Himself to those who *do not seek* Him, how much more will He reveal Himself to those who *do seek* Him?

Application: What about you and me? God has given us the privilege of salvation. He has sent preachers. They have made the message clear. We have felt the Holy Spirit pulling us away from the fires of hell, toward the God who gave His Son for us. How do we respond? Are we among those who say "Thank You," or those who say "Go away"?

Israel's Future Restoration—An Awakening Is Coming (Rom. 11:1-36)

Lesson 33

Goal A: *Answer the key questions in Romans 11 (Figure 8.12).*
Goal B: *Explain and illustrate: We find grace when we look where God tells us to look (Rom. 11:1-10).*
Goal C: *Analyze the role of envy in drawing the lost to Christ (Rom. 11:11-16).*
Goal D: *Explain 5 truths Paul teaches in relation to the olive tree (Rom. 11:16b-25).*
Goal E: *Summarize Paul's glorious conclusion of Romans 9–11.*

Q 52 *What are the 3 parts of Romans 9–11?*

Q 53 *To review Romans 9–11, complete Figure 8.12 as you study this chapter.*

Romans 9–11 has three parts:

- Israel's past election (Rom. 9:1-29),
- Israel's present rejection (Rom. 9:30–10:21), and
- Israel's future restoration (Rom. 11).

Romans 11 includes a few key questions (Figure 8.12). Read Romans 11 at least twice. As you read, look for the answers to the key questions.

Rom.	Questions	Answers	Rom.
9:1-5	What was Paul's attitude toward the Jews?		9:1-5
9:6	Did God's word (promise) to Abraham fail (Gen. 12:3; 22:18)?		9:6-29
9:14	*Is God unjust* (for using Isaac, Jacob, and even Pharaoh for His purposes)?		9:15-21
9:22	Why is God patient with those who rebel against Him?		9:23-29
9:30-32a	Why did Israel fail to obtain righteousness?		9:32-33
10:14-15a	*How? How? How? How? How!* Which 5 steps make salvation possible?		10:15b-17
10:18	Did Israel not all hear (God's message)?		
10:19a	*Did Israel not understand* (God's message)?		10:19-21
11:1a	*Did God reject His people?*		11:1-10
11:11a	Did Israel stumble and fall beyond recovery?		11:11-32
11:34-35	*Who has known the mind of the Lord? Who has been his counselor? Who has ever given to God, that God should repay him?*		11:33, 36

Figure 8.12   Key questions to answer in Romans 9–11

Setting

In this lesson we will help you answer the key questions in Figure 8.12 Also, we will guide you to discover five principles about grace in Romans 11. (Note: The big theme of Romans is *righteousness*—being in a right relationship with God. But note that it is God's grace that makes our right relationship with Him possible.)

A. Question: Did God reject His people (Rom. 11:1-10)?

Answer: No, God has always chosen a remnant of Jews by grace (Rom. 11:1-6). Paul gives three examples of Jews whom God has chosen by grace.

- God chose Paul by grace (Rom. 11:1).
- God chose Elijah and 7,000 other Jews by grace (Rom. 11:2-4).
- God chose a remnant of Jews by grace in Paul's day (Rom. 11:5).

The question of Romans 11:1 reminds us of Romans 9:6. God's promises to Abraham have not failed. God does all He planned through the remnant of Jews who believe—those He foreknew. Those who believe are the true children of Israel (Rom. 9:6b). Did God reject His people? No; but let us discern that "God's people" are those who believe His promises (Rom. 9:6-9). In Romans, Paul links God's *foreknowledge* to the remnant that believe and obey Him (Rom. 8:29; 11:2).

Romans 11:1-10 divides Jews into two groups: those who received grace and those who did not. What made the difference? Why did God choose some by grace, but give others eyes that could not see? These questions lead us to a principle.

Principle 1: We find grace when we look where God tells us to look (Rom. 11:1-10). In Romans 9 we stated that God is not arbitrary.

A general in a war captured 10 soldiers. To decide their fate he put 10 beans in a leather hat. Five of the beans were brown, and five were red. An officer held the hat above the soldiers so they could not see inside it. Each soldier was told to reach his hand into the hat and pull out one bean. If the bean was brown, the soldier lived. But if the bean was red, the soldier was put to death. The general who used this method was arbitrary. He did not base his decision on character, truth, merit, or guilt. His only standard was the color of beans. God is not like this general. He is not arbitrary. He offers salvation to all who choose to trust in Jesus Christ as Savior and Lord. In His foreknowledge, God knows which decisions people will make. But His desire is for all to choose salvation. He has enough brown beans for each person to choose one! Jesus draws all people to Himself. His Spirit pulls them toward salvation (John 12:32). God offers grace to all.

Success in finding grace, for Jews or Gentiles, increases as we seek God. The promises of God are to those who ask, seek, and knock (Matt. 7:7-8). Consider the two types of Jews that Paul mentions in the days of Elijah (Rom. 11:2-4). One group killed God's prophets, tore down God's altars, and worshiped idols (Rom. 11:3). The other group honored God and refused to bow the knee to Baal. Which group found grace? Grace is easier to find in a church than it is in a bar. What we find depends on where we look.

God does not hide grace from people. He wants to give grace to everyone. Look at the two groups of Jews in Romans 11:5-10. One group believed the gospel. This group received grace as Jews accepted Jesus as Lord and Savior. The other group rejected Jesus. As time went by, their minds became dull, their eyes became dim, and their hearts became hard. Does it surprise you which group of Jews found grace?

As the gospel came to the Jews, thousands found grace. On the Day of Pentecost when the 120 spoke in tongues, Jews *"from every nation under heaven"* were present (Acts 2:5). About 3,000 Jews believed that day and were baptized (Acts 2:41). As early as Acts 4, the number of Jewish men who believed had grown to about 5,000 (Acts 4:4). Acts 6:7 reveals that *"a large number of priests became obedient to the faith."* (Note that as heat is always with fire, obedience is always with saving faith.) And wherever Paul preached, some Jews believed the gospel, trusted in Christ, and committed to live

Q 54 *What are 3 examples of Jews chosen by grace (Rom. 11:1-6)?*

Q 55 *Who are "God's people"?*

Q 56 *Why do some find grace, and others not find it?*

Q 57 *In Elijah's day, which group found grace?*

Q 58 *Does God hide grace? What is the key to finding grace?*

by His teachings. James reminds Paul of *"how many thousands of Jews have believed"* (Acts 21:20). Multitudes of Jews found grace, as they looked for it.

God gives a measure of grace to all. *"He causes his sun to rise on the evil and the good, and sends rain on the righteous and the unrighteous"* (Matt. 5:45). Jesus gave these examples to illustrate the fact that God pours out love and grace on everyone. Still, God watches and expects us to be good stewards of His grace (1 Pet. 4:10). A big principle in Scripture is that God adds to the diligent, but subtracts from the negligent (Matt. 13:11-15; 25:28-30). Privilege brings responsibility. Thus those who misused grace were *hardened* and lost their ability to think clearly, see well, and hear God's voice (Rom. 11:7-8). Paul emphasized this in Romans 1:18-32. In time, after people did not respond to the grace God gave, He *"gave them over"* to evil (Rom. 1:24, 26, 28). "What did you do with what God gave you?" John Wesley says God will judge every person by this question.[18] Grace is free, but we must use it or lose it. And God will judge us on the basis of what He gave us, whether little or much.

Genesis 6:8 says, *"Noah found favor (grace) in the eyes of the Lord."* Genesis 6:9 says, *"Noah was a righteous man, blameless among the people of his time, and he walked with God."* Does it surprise you that Noah found grace on the path he walked with God? Does it surprise you that those who followed evil, but refused to walk with God, found judgment rather than grace? Grace is always easy to find if we look where God tells us to look.

Q 59 ✎ *What helped Noah find grace?*

Before he met Christ, Paul was like many Israelites. He had zeal without knowledge. He was sincere, but he was wrong. Paul rejected Jesus and persecuted Christians. Jesus called the Pharisees hypocrites several times (Matt. 23). Unlike Paul, they were not sincere. Even before he met Christ, Paul was sincere. He was trying to please God, even though he was mistaken. Paul wrote to Timothy:

Q 60 ✎ *What guidance does Romans 10:13 give for finding grace?*

> [13]*Even though I was once a blasphemer and a persecutor and a violent man, I was shown mercy because I acted in ignorance and unbelief.* [14]*The grace of our Lord was poured out on me abundantly, along with the faith and love that are in Christ Jesus* (1 Tim. 1:13-14).

Before Christ, Paul acted *"in ignorance"* (1 Tim. 1:13). As Fee explains, Paul did not realize that he was doing wrong. His sin was not intentional. Rather, he was among those who err without knowing it (Num. 15:22-31).[19] Paul was among the thousands of Jews who found grace. When Paul understood that Jesus is the Messiah, he repented and received Him as Lord. The key to finding grace is kneeling before Jesus. All find grace who look for it in Jesus Christ. Everyone who calls on the name of the Lord will be saved (Rom. 10:13).

God did not reject His people, ever. He continues to reach forth His hands, even to those who refuse Him (Rom. 10:21). None of us deserves God's grace, even when we seek it. And sometimes we may sin on purpose, even when we know sin is wrong. It is hard to find grace if our backs are toward God. But whenever we turn our faces toward the Father, repent, and ask for grace, He delights to give it. There is joy in heaven when one sinner repents—no matter what he or she has done (Luke 15). No matter what! And finding this amazing grace is as easy as kneeling!

B. Question: Did Israel stumble and fall beyond recovery (Rom. 11:11a)?

Is God through with Israel? Did He mark them off His list? Is there any hope for the children of Abraham?

These are important questions, because their answer affects not only Jews, but all of us. For if there is still hope for Israel after her long list of sins, then there is still hope for anyone.

Answer: *"Not at all!"* **(Rom. 11:11).** Paul explains this answer in Romans 11:11b-32. Let us examine his explanation by looking at Principles 2, 3, and 4.

1. God justifies Abraham by faith, and promises to bless all nations through his Seed (Gen.). →	2. Jesus the Messiah appears, and reveals Himself first to Jews. →	3. Many Israelites stumble in unbelief, and reject Christ. →	4. Israel's sin of unbelief results in the salvation of the Gentiles, who find righteousness by faith in Christ. →	5. Jews envy God's blessings on Gentiles; Jews believe in Christ, and are restored to righteousness.

Figure 8.13   Sequence in the history of redemption as God reveals and fulfills His Word

Principle 2: God draws unbelievers to Himself as they see the blessings of grace and envy them (Rom. 11:11-16).

Q 61 How do God's blessings on Gentiles attract Jews to Him?

Paul continues to explain that although Israel has fallen, God's word to the Jews has not failed (Rom. 9:6).

The gospel was for the Jews *first* (Rom. 1:16). Jesus came first to the Jews. He was born of Jewish parents—*"born under law, to redeem those under law"* (Gal. 4:4-5). In His ministry on earth, Jesus went first and foremost to the Jews (Matt. 10:6; 15:24). Likewise, the 12 apostles were Jews who went first to the Jews. Jerusalem, the capital of Israel, was the center of the early church. And in Rome, Paul went to Jews first, which was his method (Acts 28:23-28). As we noted earlier, thousands of Jews believed in Jesus Christ.

Still, from the outpouring of the Spirit at Pentecost, *not all* Jews accepted the good news (Rom. 10:16). The early church was a Jewish church. It grew for a few years in Jerusalem. Then persecution from unbelieving Jews scattered the believers.

God used this Jewish unbelief to spread the gospel beyond the Jewish community. Philip, full of the Spirit, took the gospel to the Samaritans. Recall that Samaritans were part Jewish—born when Jews and Assyrians married. This occurred after Assyria conquered the Northern Kingdom and took captives to Assyria in 722 B.C. Many Samaritans were blessed, as a result of Jewish unbelief. And Philip also took the gospel to an African from Ethiopia. Likewise, God led Peter to preach the gospel to Cornelius, a Roman. This was an amazing step since the Romans were Gentiles who had conquered the Jews! The riches of the gospel continued to overflow from Jerusalem to other tribes, peoples, and nations, as a result of Jewish unbelief. Believers were scattered at Stephen's death in Jerusalem (Acts 8:4). Luke records that *"some ...began to speak to Greeks also, telling them the good news about the Lord Jesus."* Thus in Antioch, Syria, *"a great number of people* [Gentiles] *believed and turned to the Lord* (Acts 11:20-21). So we see that God used Jewish unbelief to extend the gospel to the Gentiles. But this does not mean that God is through with Israel.

From the days of Paul to the present, God draws Jews to grace as they see His blessings on the Gentiles, and envy them (Rom. 11:11-16). God's blessings are like a magnet that attracts people. Flowers attract bees. God's blessings attract people. People want to participate in good things. The gospel announces many blessings. God invites us to exchange guilt for forgiveness, turmoil for peace, loneliness for His presence, exile for sonship, condemnation for justification, our sins for the righteousness of Christ, hell for heaven. The gospel is good news. Its blessings attract people.

When David became king of Israel, he tried to move the ark in a cart to Jerusalem. An ox pulling the cart stumbled. Without thinking, Uzzah touched the ark to steady it. Because of Uzzah's lack of respect for God, he died at once. This caused David to fear, and he left the ark at the home of Obed-Edom, a Gittite—that is, a person who lived in Gath, a city of the Philistines.[20]

Q 62 What stirred up David to return the ark to Jerusalem? Apply this.

[11]*The ark of the Lord remained in the house of Obed-Edom the Gittite for three months, and the Lord blessed him and his entire household.* [12]*Now King David*

was told, *"The Lord has blessed the household of Obed-Edom and everything he has, because of the ark of God." So David went down and brought up the ark of God from the house of Obed-Edom to the City of David with rejoicing"* (2 Sam. 6:11-12; see also 1 Chron. 15:11-28).

Figure 8.14   The ark of the covenant had rings on it for poles to pass through. God commanded the Israelites not to touch the ark, but to carry it with poles.

God blessed the household of Obed-Edom, who lived in a Gentile city. These blessings stirred up David, Israel's king, to want what Obed-Edom had. The blessings also inspired Obed-Edom to move from Gath to Jerusalem. King David brought the ark and Obed-Edom to Jerusalem! Obed-Edom became a doorkeeper for the ark in Jerusalem. God's blessings stir up righteous envy that draws people to Him.

A chaplain came to the side of a soldier wounded in battle. He stayed with the soldier while the rest of the troops retreated. In the heat, the chaplain gave him water from his own bottle. At night, he covered the soldier with his own coat. In time the wounded man asked the chaplain, "Are you a Christian?" "I try to be one," the chaplain answered. "Then I want to be one, too. Whatever makes a man do what you have done for me, I want." The chaplain's example made the wounded soldier envy his faith.[21] Do our lives attract others to God? Because of us, do people turn away from God or toward Him?

Q 63 *Complete Figure 8.15 on verses that explain ways that make the gospel attractive or unattractive.*

Ref.	What do these verses teach about attracting others to God?
2 Sam. 12:14	
Matt. 5:13	
Matt. 5:14-16	
Mark 5:18-20	
John 4:39	
John 13:34-35	
Rom. 12:17-21	
Eph. 5:8-11	
Phil. 1:27	
James 2:14-17	
1 Pet. 3:1-2	
1 Pet. 3:13-16	

Figure 8.15   Many verses emphasize that God attracts unbelievers through the grace believers reflect.

2. Some Gentile branches were grafted in by faith (Rom. 11:17b).

5. Some fallen Jewish branches will be grafted in by faith (Rom. 11:23).

4. Some Gentile branches may be cut off by unbelief and pride (Rom. 11:22).

1. Some Jewish branches were broken off by unbelief (Rom. 11:17a).

3. Jewish roots support the tree, the Church (Rom. 11:18).

Figure 8.16   Paul used an olive tree to teach five truths about Gentiles and Jews.

Conclusion: The gospel came to the Jews first, and many received it. Yet many Jews did not believe. This unbelief opened the door of the gospel to the Gentiles. Still, God's blessings on the Gentiles in Christ attract Jews to the Savior. Then, they experience new life, as those raised from the dead (Rom. 11:15). God pulls the lost to Himself through the grace they see in believers.

Principle 3: Pride beguiles and misleads some believers from grace to wrath (Rom. 11:16b-25).

In Romans 11:16-25 Paul is concerned about pride among the Gentiles. There is only one Jewish race. The rest of the world is Gentile. For each Jew in the world today, there are over 500 Gentiles.[22] So there are many more Gentiles than Jews in the Church. The book of Revelation contrasts 144,000 Jewish believers with a multitude of Gentiles that no one can number (Rev. 7).

In Paul's day, the large number of Gentile believers could cause Gentiles to feel arrogant. Perhaps they were tempted to think that God was through with the Jews. Some Gentile believers may have felt that they were God's favorite people. Paul is concerned that Gentiles do not fall into the sin of pride, as some Jews fell. Recall that some Jews fell because they trusted in their own works and position, rather than in God. Earlier, Paul rebuked the Jews for bragging about their relationship with God (Rom. 2:17; see Matt. 3:9). Pride is an enemy that kills faith. The proud trust in themselves, not God. Pride lures us from looking out the window at all God has created, to looking in the mirror. *"Pride goes before destruction, a haughty spirit before a fall"* (Prov. 16:18). Pride was one of the things that led to the fall of the Jews. And pride among the Gentiles was bad for two reasons: their own spiritual well being, and their relationship with the Jews.

Paul wants Gentiles to have a humble attitude about themselves. He warns that as Jewish branches were broken off, Gentile branches can be cut off (Rom. 11:22). And he wants Gentiles to appreciate, love, and pray for Jews—both the saved in house churches at Rome and the unsaved.

Application: We need balance in our theology about God. Paul's illustration of an olive tree contrasts the kindness and the sternness of God. God showed His kindness by grafting Gentiles into the olive tree. But God showed His sternness by breaking off Jewish branches because of unbelief. These two sides of God, kindness and sternness, are always there. Some today want to talk only about the love and kindness of God. These unbalanced teachers tell believers "Nothing you ever do will change God's attitude toward you." Wrong! God's attitude toward the Jews changed when they showed their unbelief through disobedience. Suddenly, branches that were on the tree were on the ground! It was the people whom God had chosen and delivered that He broke off! Likewise, Jesus warned that branches of a vine that do not abide in Him and bear fruit, God will cut off and cast into the fire (John 15). Paul said, *"Consider, therefore, the kindness and sternness of God"* (Rom. 11:22). Consider both! For any doctrine of God that ignores His kindness *or* His sternness is unbalanced. So if you must

Q 64 ✎ *Explain the olive tree in Figure 8.16 to a friend. Ask him or her questions to test understanding.*

Q 65 ✎ *What might have caused Gentile believers to feel proud of themselves?*

Q 66 ✎ *In Romans 11:22, what warning does Paul give Gentile believers?*

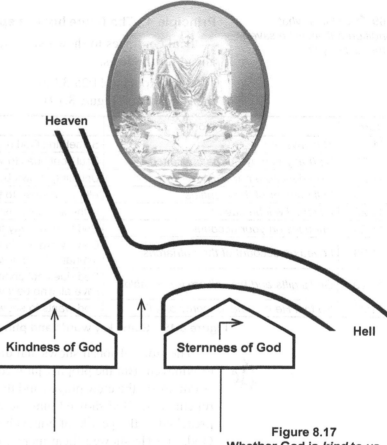

Figure 8.17 Whether God is *kind* to us or *stern* with us depends on how we relate to Him (Rom. 11:22-24).

Q 67 ✎ *What determines whether God is kind or stern to us (Rom. 11:22)? Give examples.*

talk of unconditional love (a phrase not in the Bible), speak also about unconditional sternness. Throughout Church history, people have erred in two ways. Some paint God too kind. Others paint Him too stern. The best painters reveal both sides of God.

"So, if you think you are standing firm, be careful that you don't fall!" (1 Cor. 10:12). Has God blessed your nation, your tribe, and your family? Give Him thanks. But do not forget that God loves Jews as much as He loves Gentiles. And He loves all others as much as He loves you. Israel has not fallen beyond recovery. And we should walk humbly in faith, lest we fall.

Q 68 *Complete Figure 8.18 on verses that warn about the danger of pride.*

Ref.	What do these verses teach about the danger of pride?
Isa. 14:12-15	
Ezek. 28:1-10	
Luke 10:18	
Prov. 16:5	
James 4:6	

Figure 8.18   Many verses emphasize that pride is an enemy of faith.

Q 69 *Under what condition will Jews be saved in the last days?*

Principle 4: The future holds a special time of grace for Israel (Rom. 11:25-32).

Paul continues to show that Israel has not fallen beyond recovery. A great revival is ahead for the Jews.

Read Romans 11:25-32 two or there times. As you read, note some key phrases and their meanings (Figure 8.19).

Rom.	Biblical words	Comments on meaning
11:25	This mystery	Something God hid in the past, but has now revealed
11:25	So that you may not be conceited	Paul continues to warn the Gentiles to beware of pride.
11:25	Experienced a hardening	Unbelief, shown by disobedience, always hardens the heart.
11:25	Full number of the Gentiles	All who choose to trust and follow Christ
11:26	All Israel will be saved.	In the last days, Israel as a whole will trust in Christ.
11:28	Enemies on your account	God turned away from unbelieving Jews to save Gentiles who will believe.
11:28	Loved on account of the patriarchs	God's word to Abraham and others has not failed. He is faithful to save the remnant that believe.
11:29	God's gifts and his call are irrevocable.	God does not change His mind. He will fulfill His purpose with Israel, and save all who believe in Christ.
11:32	So that He may have mercy on all	God wants to show mercy on all who disobey Him.

Figure 8.19   Some key words and phrases in Romans 11:25-32

The story of Jonah shows that disobedience can lead to mercy. God told Jonah to go to Nineveh. But the prophet jumped in a boat and went the opposite direction. When a storm arose, the crew prayed and then threw Jonah overboard. Inside the big fish, Jonah repented; so God showed him mercy. After the fish spit Jonah out on dry land, Jonah preached to the people of Nineveh in Assyria. They repented for their disobedience to God, and He showed them mercy. Both Jonah the prophet and the people of Nineveh disobeyed God. But when they repented, He delighted to give them mercy. Mercy is one of God's favorite words. If we will allow Him, He always prefers to show kindness rather than sternness.

Principle 5: There is none like our God, who delights to give grace (Rom. 11:33-36).

Q 70 *What causes Paul to burst into praise and worship?*

Q 71 *As you look over the past, present, and future, what inspires you to worship God now?*

Paul ended Romans 8 with a burst of praise. Likewise, he concludes Romans 11 with his face turned upward and both hands raised in worship to our Heavenly Father. Paul has looked back over 20 centuries. He has quoted verses that scan from God's promise to Abraham to their fulfillment in Christ. And He has looked forward at least 20 more centuries to a great revival in Israel in the last days. The Spirit has guided God's apostle to consider God's great plan of salvation for Jews and Gentiles. And Paul has quoted from the Old Testament about 60 times (Figure 11.11). His heart is full and overflowing! He can hardly contain the wonder and awe He feels toward the God of the heavens.

There is none like our God! As the heavens are high above the earth, His ways are high above us. When God wants to see a counselor, He looks in the mirror. God does not ask for advice; He gives it. And He does not make mistakes. But He is willing to forgive ours. God knows all the answers to all the questions. God owes nothing to anyone, but to Him we owe everything.

Worship with Paul as you read his *doxology of Romans 9–11. This is his hymn of praise, his worship to God for saving Jews and Gentiles.

33Oh, the depth of the riches of the wisdom and knowledge of God! How unsearchable his judgments, and his paths beyond tracing out! 34"Who has known the mind of the Lord? Or who has been his counselor?" 35"Who has ever given to God, that God should repay him?" 36For from him and through him and to him are all things. To him be the glory forever! Amen (Rom. 11:33-36).

Test Yourself: Circle the letter by the *best* completion to each question or statement.

1. What was Paul's attitude toward the Jews?
a) Condemnation
b) Bitterness
c) Pity
d) Love

2. Did God's promise to Israel fail?
a) Yes, because of unbelief
b) No, God saves all who believe.
c) We do not yet know the outcome.
d) That promise has been replaced.

3. Which is NOT a true statement?
a) Some Jews are not Abraham's children.
b) Some Gentiles are children of Abraham.
c) Abraham was a Jew before he was a Gentile.
d) God has no grandchildren.

4. Why did Israel fail to obtain righteousness?
a) Sin
b) Unbelief
c) Election
d) Temptation

5. Which is a synonym of *elected*?
a) Predestined
b) Foreknown
c) Determined
d) Chosen

6. In what sense was the nation of Israel elected?
a) Elected to service
b) Elected to condemnation
c) Elected to salvation
d) Elected to favoritism

7. What is the 5th step in God's plan of salvation (Rom. 10)?
a) Sinners call on Christ as they believe in Him.
b) God saves all who call on Him.
c) Sinners hear the good news as believers preach.
d) God glorifies those He has chosen.

8. What helps people find grace for salvation?
a) Election to salvation
b) Predestination to glorification
c) Looking in the right places
d) Nothing except God's choice

9. In Romans 11 the broken branches represent
a) Jews who lost their relationship with God.
b) Gentiles who were grafted into the tree.
c) Loss of reward, but not loss of sonship.
d) Discipline that resulted in good behavior.

10. How does Paul end his discussion of Israel (Rom. 11)?
a) With his head down, crying
b) With his head up, worshiping
c) With his eyes looking ahead, focusing
d) With his palms up, questioning

Essay Test Topics: Write 50-100 words on each of these goals that you studied in this chapter.

- Summarize and apply Paul's attitude toward the Jews (Rom. 9:1-5).
- Answer and explain: Did God's word (promise) to Abraham and Israel fail (Rom. 9:6-13)?
- Explain and illustrate: Privileges do not guarantee personal salvation (Rom. 9:4-5).
- Interpret and apply: Not all who are descended from Israel are Israel (Rom. 9:6b).
- Explain 4 principles about election to serve.
- Summarize 2 principles about election to salvation.
- Explain and illustrate: Humans and God have the freedom to choose.
- Explain and illustrate: God is patient with those who rebel against Him (Rom. 9:22-29).
- Answer the key questions in Romans 9:30–10:21 (Figure 8.8).
- Explain and illustrate 3 reasons why some do not find righteousness.
- Identify 6 passages that show how anyone can find a right relationship with God (Rom. 9:30–10:13).
- Review the 5 steps that lead to salvation, illustrating failures and successes of each step.
- Answer the key questions in Romans 11 (Figure 8.12).
- Explain and illustrate: We find grace when we look where God tells us to look (Rom. 11:1-10).
- Analyze the role of envy in drawing the lost to Christ (Rom. 11:11-16).
- Explain 5 truths Paul teaches in relation to the olive tree (Rom. 11:16b-25).
- Summarize Paul's glorious conclusion of Romans 9–11.

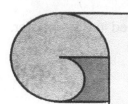

Unit Five: Relationships—The Fruit of Righteousness (Romans 12–16)

We have come to the fifth and final part of Paul's gospel of salvation. The theme of Romans is righteousness—being in a right relationship with God. In the first section, Paul shows that Jews and Gentiles are sinners, under God's wrath, in great need of the righteousness God offers (Rom. 1:18–3:20). In section 2, Paul emphasizes justification—right standing or position in our relationship with God. Justification is God's proclamation that true believers are free from the penalty of sin. This is possible through faith in the death and resurrection of Jesus Christ (Rom. 3:21–5:21). Section 3 of Paul's gospel emphasizes sanctification—righteous and holy living. Sanctification includes transformation into the image of Christ. This is a process that spans from regeneration and adoption to glorification at Christ's returns. Righteous and holy living is possible as we turn from evil desires of the flesh, and submit to the enabling power of the Holy Spirit (Rom. 6–8). Section 4 of Paul's gospel focuses on Israel in God's plan of salvation (Rom. 9–11). In section 5 of Paul's gospel of salvation, the apostle shows that a right relationship with God affects our relationships on earth (Rom. 12–16). Paul's gospel is powerful and dynamic. His message of salvation includes a righteous relationship with God and others.

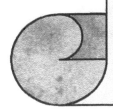

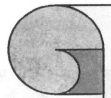

In Chapter 9 you will discover that Romans 12 is a key chapter. As you study the gospel in daily living we will help you to:
- *Contrast the sacrifice demanded in Romans 12:1 with the Old Testament sacrifices.*
- *Explain and illustrate how our response to God's mercy is personal, logical, and spiritual.*
- *Explain the negative and positive sides of our response to God's mercy (Rom. 12:2).*
- *Identify the result of presenting our bodies as living sacrifices to Christ (Rom. 12:1-2).*
- *Contrast the general and specific will of God for believers.*
- *Explain three factors that help us measure ourselves accurately.*
- *Analyze and illustrate seven examples of spiritual gifts in Romans 12:3-8.*
- *Summarize and illustrate the moral nature of agape love (Rom. 12:9).*
- *Explain principles on how love relates to others, even strangers (Rom. 12:10, 13).*
- *Clarify how we renew and refuel our love (Rom. 12:11).*
- *Analyze some aspects that strengthen the toughness of love (Rom. 12:12).*
- *Illustrate ways that love empathizes (Rom. 12:15).*
- *Give illustrations to show that love crosses social boundaries (Rom. 12:16).*
- *Illustrate ways that love is passive at times and active at other times (Rom. 12:17-19, 21).*

In Chapter 10 we find that Paul's gospel includes righteous relationships beyond the church. In Romans 13:1–15:13 you will discover how to:
- *Summarize at least three attitudes toward the government in Paul's day.*
- *Explain four reasons why believers must submit to government (Rom. 13:1-5).*
- *Summarize seven reasons why God may allow an evil government.*
- *Identify some debts that believers owe as citizens (Rom. 13:1-7).*
- *Explain: A believer is always in debt (Rom. 13:8-10). Illustrate this.*
- *Explain and illustrate three aspects of walking in love (Rom. 13:11-14).*
- *Summarize the background of Romans 14:1–15:13.*
- *Identify three types of matters believers face (Rom. 14:1–15:13).*
- *Explain the reason why believers should accept and not judge one another (Rom. 14:1-12; 15:7).*
- *Describe four types of people in or around the church.*
- *Explain how love avoids tripping or trapping a brother (Rom. 14:13-23). Give illustrations.*
- *Give examples of how a strong believer can carry the weaknesses of a brother (Rom. 15:1-6).*
- *Summarize the result when believers accept, love, and carry each other (Rom. 15:6).*

Congratulations! You have reached the final chapter of our study. As you work through Romans 15:14–16:27 we will guide you to:
- *Give evidence in Romans that shows Paul was sensitive to others.*
- *Summarize Paul's ministry as a priest. Apply this to us.*
- *Explain and illustrate: "Paul was Cristo-centric."*
- *Illustrate the fact that Paul depended on the Holy Spirit for his ministry.*
- *Explain and illustrate how Paul felt about hard work.*
- *Give examples to show that Paul valued planning ahead with hope.*
- *Summarize Paul's two prayer requests in Romans 16.*
- *Summarize the importance of prayer in your ministry.*
- *Identify four ways that Paul uses Old Testament quotes in Romans.*
- *Summarize a lesson we can learn from Paul's list of greetings in Romans 16.*
- *Explain the eternal story linked to Romans 16:20, and the warning just before it.*
- *Identify the two "bookends" of Romans, and terms common to both.*
- *Paraphrase the doxology of Romans 16:25-27.*

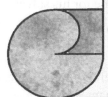

Chapter 9:

Relationships—Part 1

(Romans 12)

Introduction

Q 1 ✎ *What must we have to live Romans 12–15?*

John Wesley lived from 1703 to 1791. He started the Methodist Church. Some estimate that he led 250,000 people to trust in Christ as their Savior. But for about 20 years, Wesley thought he could be saved by his own good deeds. Here are some insights based on what Wesley wrote about himself:

Figure 9.1
John Wesley, founder of the Methodist Church

- At the age of 10 he thought that the only way to be saved was through keeping all of God's commandments.

- At the age of 16 he hoped to be saved for three reasons. *First,* because he was not as bad as some. *Second,* because he had a sincere desire for religion. *Third,* because he read the Bible, went to church, and said his prayers.

- From about 16 to 22 years old, he studied at the university. During this time he said public and private prayers, read the Scriptures, and read commentaries on the New Testament. Yet he was aware of sins he committed. He took communion three times a year, and repented at these times. But he had no knowledge of inner holiness.

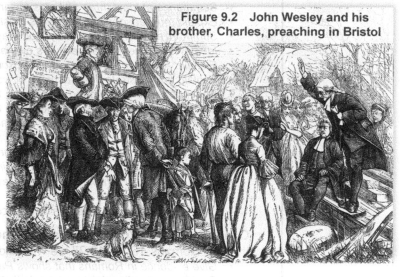

Figure 9.2   John Wesley and his brother, Charles, preaching in Bristol

- At the age of 22 he began to understand that true religion centers <u>in the heart</u>. He realized that God's law should govern our thoughts, as well as our actions. Still, he trusted in his own efforts.

- At the age of 27 (1730 A.D.) he began to visit prisons and to help the poor and the sick in town. He used his time and money to assist others. He tried to resist all sin. But after 2 to 3 years of self-denial, he had no inner comfort— no assurance that God accepted him. Although living for others, he remained empty inside.

- At the age of 28 he left England to be a missionary in Savannah, Georgia. On the boat, he talked with a group of 20 Moravians (a type of Evangelicals). They testified of finding peace with God through faith in Christ alone. But Wesley felt more educated than them and rejected their witness. He continued to be a slave of sin.

- At the age of 29 (May 24, 1738) he attended a meeting where someone was reading Martin Luther's preface about Romans. The leader was describing the change that God works in our hearts by *faith* in Christ. Suddenly, John Wesley felt his heart strangely warmed. He trusted in Christ alone for his salvation. At once God gave him the assurance that his sins were taken away, and he was free from the law of sin and death.[1]

Wesley tried to live Romans 12–15 for nearly 20 years. Then he discovered that we cannot please God until He saves us from our sins. As we begin to study Romans 12–15, let us remind ourselves that *before* we can *behave,* we must *believe* and *belong* to God. This is the reason why Paul wrote Romans 1–11 *before* he wrote Romans 12!

The Relationship of Believers to God (Rom. 12:1-2)

Goal A: *Contrast the sacrifice demanded in Romans 12:1 with the Old Testament sacrifices.*
Goal B: *Explain and illustrate how our response to God's mercy is personal, logical, and spiritual.*
Goal C: *Explain the negative and positive sides of our response to God's mercy (Rom. 12:2).*
Goal D: *Identify the result of presenting our bodies as living sacrifices to Christ (Rom. 12:1-2).*

The Relationship of Believers to Each Other (Rom. 12:3-8)

Goal A: *Contrast the general and specific will of God for believers.*
Goal B: *Explain 3 factors that help us measure ourselves accurately.*
Goal C: *Analyze and illustrate 7 examples of spiritual gifts in Romans 12:3-8.*

Nine Principles of *Agape* Love—Part 1 (Rom. 12:9-13)

Goal A: *Summarize and illustrate the moral nature of agape love (Rom. 12:9).*
Goal B: *Explain principles on how love relates to others, even strangers (Rom. 12:10, 13).*
Goal C: *Clarify how we renew and refuel our love (Rom. 12:11).*
Goal D: *Analyze some aspects that strengthen the toughness of love (Rom. 12:12).*

Nine Principles of *Agape* Love—Part 2 (Rom. 12:14-21)

Goal A: *Illustrate ways that love empathizes (Rom. 12:15).*
Goal B: *Give illustrations to show that love crosses social boundaries (Rom. 12:16).*
Goal C: *Illustrate ways that love is passive at times and active at other times (Rom. 12:17-19, 21).*

Key Words

living sacrifice—the daily giving of our bodies, desires, and thoughts to worship God, serving Him and others

worship—in Romans 12–15 the way we respond to God's mercy. Our worship is spiritual as the Spirit leads us. It is logical as we give our bodies as living sacrifices in response to the mercy God has given us.

will of God—includes the general plan of God for all believers to become like Christ; and the specific will of God to use the gifts He gives to serve others and live in love toward all

spiritual gifts—the various forms of grace and faith that God gives each believer to serve Him and others

love—to love is to imitate and reflect God—His values, attitudes, feelings, thoughts, and actions.

The Relationship of Believers to God (Rom. 12:1-2)

Lesson 34

Goal A: *Contrast the sacrifice demanded in Romans 12:1 with the Old Testament sacrifices.*
Goal B: *Explain and illustrate how our response to God's mercy is personal, logical, and spiritual.*
Goal C: *Explain the negative and positive sides of our response to God's mercy (Rom. 12:2).*
Goal D: *Identify the result of presenting our bodies as living sacrifices to Christ (Rom. 12:1-2).*

Setting

All of Paul's letters connect right theology and right living. In some letters, like Corinthians and Philippians, Paul integrates or mixes theology and practice. In other letters, Paul puts theology first, and practices second (Gal. 4:12–6:10; Eph. 4–6; Col. 3–4).[2] In Romans, Paul mixes theology with some practical application. For example, in Romans 6–8, Paul wrote about how we must live—dead to sin, alive in Christ, led by the Spirit, not the flesh. Still, even in Romans 6–8, the focus was theological—emphasizing what we believe. But in Romans 12–15, Paul turns to emphasize the practical application.

Q 2 ⬉ *Complete Figure 9.3 by summarizing what Paul teaches in each of the five parts of Romans.*

Romans	Your summary of what Paul emphasizes
1:18–3:20	
3:21–5:21	
6–8	
9–11	
12–15	

Figure 9.3   Practice summarizing what Paul emphasizes in the five units of Romans.

Romans 1–11 presents right theology as the basis for right living (Rom. 12–15). Early in Romans, Paul showed that all of us have sinned. We need God to forgive us and restore us to a right relationship with Him (Rom. 1:18–3:20). Through Christ's sacrifice on the cross, God has saved us from the *penalty* of sin (Rom. 3:21–5:21). And through the Spirit within, God saves us from the *power* of sin, and transforms us into the likeness of Christ (Rom. 6–8). Paul has written that, by faith in Christ, Jews and Gentiles are able to live in a right relationship with God (Rom. 9–11). Now, in Romans 12–15, Paul explains the way a person who believes in Christ lives, by the power of the Spirit. The righteous do not merely believe, and then live like sinners. We cannot separate righteous standing from righteous living. Rather, the righteous *live* by faith (Rom. 1:17). James wrote that *"faith without deeds is dead"* (James 2:26). Likewise, Paul believed that justification without holy living is fiction.[3]

A. Our response to God's mercy is the way we live (Rom. 12:1).

*Therefore, I urge you, brothers, **in view of God's mercy**, to offer your bodies as living sacrifices, holy and pleasing to God* (Rom. 12:1a).

Q 3 ⬈ *How does the mountain peak of Romans 11 help us in the valley of duty?*

Romans 11 closes on top of a mountain. There, Paul exalts God as the One who is all wise—He who seeks counsel from no one. Paul praises God and sings that *all things* are *from* Him, *through* Him, and *to* Him. He worships God who deserves the glory of all the ages (Rom. 11:36). This mountain of glory inspires us in the valley of duty that follows (Rom. 12–15). The glorious heights of Christian doctrine enable us to rejoice on the lower plane of daily living.[4]

Q 4 ⬈ *What are the 2 ways that people respond to God?*

God acts; people react—either to reject or accept God's mercy.[5] This is a huge theme in Scripture. God acts because He loves people. He desires all to be saved and to enjoy eternity in His house (2 Pet. 3:9). People react to God in two ways: Some rebel against His love and mercy. Others of us rejoice. We overflow with thanksgiving by offering ourselves as *living sacrifices.

Q 5 ⬉ *Do words of praise have meaning without actions of praise? Explain.*

The proof of our response to God is in our actions, not just our words. Many Scriptures emphasize that our words are important (Matt. 12:36-37; John 1:9). In regard to salvation, Paul has emphasized faith in the *heart*, and confession with the *mouth* (Rom. 10:9). But in Romans 12:1-8, Paul teaches that *walking* must accompany *talking.* There are always more who *say* they believe in Christ than those who *show* it. As Paul wrote, *"They claim to know God, but by their actions they deny him"* (Titus 1:16). James wrote that faith without actions is dead and useless (James 2:17). Godly actions show that words about God are genuine. *"Everyone who confesses the name of the Lord must turn away from wickedness"* (2 Tim. 2:19). Our confession is vital. But actions always speak louder than words (see Matt. 7:21-23; 25:14-46). Talk is cheap. And mere words are empty— like clouds without water. Sabio says, "Many know the recipe; show me the pudding!"

Q 6 ⬈ *What reason for worship does Paul give in Romans 12:1?*

The Scriptures give many reasons why we *worship and serve God. But in Romans 12:1, God's mercy is the reason why Paul urges us to worship and serve God. *"Therefore, I urge you, brothers, **in view of God's mercy**, to offer your bodies as living sacrifices, holy and pleasing to God"* (Rom. 12:1a).

God's mercy is a big theme in Romans. God has redeemed us, and now we are saints—God's holy people. Romans 1–3 emphasized that all of us were guilty. God was angry and outraged with us. As sinners, we were objects of God's wrath. But even when we were sinners, God showed His love and mercy as Christ died for us (Rom. 5:8). His mercy freed us from the *penalty* of sin. And His mercy imparts the Spirit to free us from the *power* of sin (Rom. 6–8). Likewise, the word *mercy* appears seven times in Romans 9–11. And mercy is like a big banner over Romans 11:25-32. Every blessing we enjoy depends on God's mercy for us in Christ. So mercy is the big reason Paul gives as he exhorts us to offer our bodies as living sacrifices. Paul insists that we love God *because* of the merciful way that He first loved us (compare 1 John 4:19-20).

God's power may cause people to hide. Even Moses trembled when God revealed His power on Mount Sinai (Heb. 12:21). People may fear as they see the lightning, hear the thunder, or hear the loud trumpet announcing the King's return (Rev. 6:15-17). Likewise, God's holiness may shine so bright that no one dares to approach it. And His wrath may frighten people away—or cause them to shake. But His mercy draws us to worship and serve Him. The love He has poured into our hearts causes us to cry *"Abba, Father"* (Rom. 5:5; 8:15).

Paul says, *"Therefore, I urge you, brothers, **in view of God's mercy**, to offer your bodies as living sacrifices, holy and pleasing to God"* (Rom. 12:1a). These words from Paul are not just a suggestion. Paul is not being timid or polite. He is not saying *"Please, give yourself to God completely."* Rather, Paul is saying that God's mercy *demands* our total commitment to Him. Our complete surrender to God is a theological necessity! The story of God's dealings with mankind always follows the same pattern: God acts; people react. God acts because He is merciful and gracious. Then, people react. We either reject or accept God's mercy. The only fitting response to God's mercy is to offer our bodies as living sacrifices.[6] We do not offer ourselves to God to earn His acceptance. Rather, as the gospel teaches, we offer ourselves to God as a response—*because* He has already accepted and adopted us.[7]

Q 7 *Why does Paul urge us to offer our bodies to God?*

B. Our response to God's mercy is personal and intimate (Rom. 12:1; 7:6).

God has shown us amazing mercy. Through Christ, God has forgiven our sins and welcomed us into His family. <u>Therefore</u> (Rom. 12:1), Paul says: "Here is what I want you to do:[8] Offer your body as a living sacrifice."

Earlier in Romans Paul wrote that *"we have been released from the law so that we serve in the new way of the Spirit, and not in the old way of the written code"* (Rom. 7:6). And in Romans 7–8 Paul contrasted life under the Law with the new way of the Spirit. In Romans 12:1-2 Paul continues the contrast between life under the Law and life by the Spirit. Worship under the Law required *less* than worship in the Spirit (Rom. 12:1). Each person responded to God by obeying the Law. But under the old covenant, there were those *between* the common people and God. Moses and all the Levites stood between God and the Israelites. And there was a veil between most of the priests and God. Of all the priests, *only* the high priest came directly into God's presence, and this priest entered the Holy of Holies *only once* a year (Heb. 9:7, 25). Under the Old Testament, seeing God at a distance did *not* encourage people to draw closer to Him. Recall how the writer of Hebrews contrasts those under the New Testament and those under the Old Testament:

Q 8 *How is relationship with God different under the new covenant?*

> [18]*You have not come to a mountain that can be touched and that is burning with fire; to darkness, gloom and storm;* [19]*to a trumpet blast or to such a voice speaking words that those who heard it begged that no further word be spoken to them,* [20]*because they could not bear what was commanded: "If even an animal touches the mountain, it must be stoned."* [21]*The sight was so terrifying that Moses said, "I am trembling with fear"* (Heb. 12:18-21).

What a contrast between those under the Law and us! Under the New Testament, God reveals Himself as our Heavenly Father and welcomes us directly into His presence as His children! No longer do we depend on priests, prophets, and scholars to learn about God. All believers can enjoy close, personal fellowship with our Heavenly Father through our Lord Jesus Christ. We still appreciate the teachers that God gives to the Church. But under the new covenant, the Holy Spirit is available to teach each person, from the least to the greatest (Heb. 8:10b-11).

Q 9 *How is the sacrifice God requires under the New Testament more personal and more demanding than sacrifice was under the Old Testament?*

Under the New Testament, our relationship with God is closer, more intimate, and more personal. Life under the Law required worshipers to offer animal sacrifices. In contrast, life in the Spirit requires a worshiper to offer *himself* or *herself*. Under the Law, a worship event focused on a dead animal on an altar. But under the Spirit, worship *begins* as we offer ourselves as living sacrifices. And worship continues as we daily present ourselves as *a living sacrifice—holy and acceptable to God*. The privilege of belonging to God brings personal responsibilities.[9] Life in the Spirit requires more from us than life under the Law. But in return, God gives more of Himself to us. Under the Old Testament, God's presence was in a pillar of fire, a cloud, a tabernacle, and a temple. But under the New Testament, our bodies are the temple of God—as we offer them as a holy, living sacrifice to Him.

Q 10 *Why is the sacrifice God requires under the New Testament more personal and more demanding than sacrifice was under the Old Testament?*

There were two types of sacrifices in the Old Testament—some for sin and some for thanksgiving. Jesus has already become our sacrifice for sin. But we offer ourselves as sacrifices of thanksgiving. The problem with a living sacrifice is that it can get up and walk away! So day by day we must choose to offer ourselves to God.

Worship involves our bodies. False teachers in Paul's day and in ours teach that worship is spiritual and what we do with the body does not matter. But Paul focuses on the body as a major part of worship. Everything we do as humans involves our bodies. It is impossible to serve God without presenting our bodies to Him. We cannot send our spirits to school or church and leave our bodies at home. We cannot send our spirits to witness, teach, or help a neighbor. Whatever we do requires our bodies. In the story of the Good Samaritan, the person who helped was the person who committed his body to the task. He used his feet to walk over to the wounded man. He used his hands to lift him up. Likewise, to serve God we must use our bodies. At water baptism, we allow our bodies to go into the water and then be raised anew with Christ. And then, unlike those under the Law, we offer our bodies as a living sacrifice, living holy day by day.[10]

A sacrifice costs something. Jesus sacrificed His life on a cross. And He says that to follow Him, we must take up our cross and die to selfish desires (Matt. 16:24-27). Being a living sacrifice involves self-denial. This includes turning away from fleshly desires, lusts, and activities that dishonor God. Presenting our bodies as a living sacrifice includes presenting holy, healthy bodies to God. This includes proper exercise, proper rest, and a healthy diet. God expects us to avoid foods, drinks, drugs, or activities that harm the body. Offering our bodies as a living sacrifice means using our bodies to serve God and others, *not* sin, self, or the world. We will explore this subject of using our bodies to worship and serve as we study Romans 12:2-8.

Q 11 *In your own words, summarize what each passage in Figure 9.4 teaches about offering our bodies to God as a living sacrifice.*

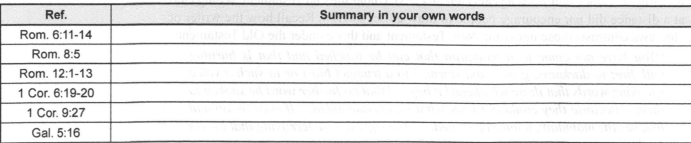

Ref.	Summary in your own words
Rom. 6:11-14	
Rom. 8:5	
Rom. 12:1-13	
1 Cor. 6:19-20	
1 Cor. 9:27	
Gal. 5:16	

Continued on next page

Eph. 5:3		
Col. 3:5-6		
1 Tim. 2:20-21		

Figure 9.4 Passages that teach us to offer our bodies to God as a living sacrifice

C. Our response to God's mercy is logical and spiritual (Rom. 12:1; 7:6).

*Therefore, I urge you, brothers, in view of God's mercy, to offer your bodies as living sacrifices, holy and pleasing to God—**this is your spiritual act of worship*** (Rom. 12:1).

Scholars debate what Paul means by *spiritual* (Greek: *logiken*). Does the apostle mean *spiritual* or *logical*? Paul does not use this Greek word *logiken* anywhere else in his letters. *Logiken* often means "logical, rational, or reasonable." So some scholars think *logiken* means "logical" in Romans 12:1. Other scholars prefer to translate *logiken* as "spiritual." It is true that offering our bodies to God is spiritual, in contrast to the fleshly ways some offer their bodies to serve sin. But other scholars think that if Paul meant "spiritual," he would have used the Greek word *pneumatikos,* which he used in Romans 7:14. So it is likely that Paul is emphasizing worship and service that is logical and appropriate.[11]

Q 12 *In what sense is offering our bodies to God a spiritual response?*

Worship is more than an hour on Sunday. Attending church services and activities is important. As we gather together, our prayers and songs rise like incense to the throne of God. But Paul emphasizes worship as a lifestyle. In church we *say* we are thankful. The rest of the week we *show* we are thankful. We worship by living for God seven days a week (Rom. 12:1). The road to heaven is 24/7.

Q 13 *Explain: Worship is a lifestyle—a way of life, not just an intersection.*

> SPIRITUAL WORSHIP IS A ROAD ON WHICH WE LIVE—A *WAY* OF LIFE, NOT JUST AN INTERSECTION CALLED CHURCH.

Our logical response to God's mercy is to offer our bodies as a living sacrifice—holy and pleasing to Him. If God had given less or forgiven less, a lesser response from us might be fitting. But God gave his Only Son to redeem us. And He forgave *all* of our sins. Therefore, the only response that matches God's action is a reaction from us that commits *all* to Him.

Q 14 *Why is offering our bodies to God a logical response?*

When two people marry, their commitments match. The vows of the husband mirror the vows of the wife. It would be illogical and unreasonable for one spouse to make a big commitment, and the other spouse to make a small commitment. Imagine a spouse who pledged, "I will be faithful to you, *part* of the time." Nonsense! A marriage relationship cannot be based on partial commitments. Rather, both spouses pledge to be *completely* faithful and loving to each other. Romans and other letters of the Bible compare our relationship with Christ to a marriage (Rom. 7:1-6; 2 Cor. 11:2; Eph. 5:22-33). Jesus did not give an animal sacrifice for us. He gave His own body as a sacrifice (Heb. 10:5-10). Therefore, it is reasonable that He requires us to give our bodies to Him (Rom. 6:11-14). Partial sacrifices to God are unreasonable. Half-hearted commitments to Him are illogical, unspiritual, and unacceptable. But offering our bodies as a living sacrifice is acceptable and pleasing to God (Rom. 12:1). We are bought with a great price, therefore we must glorify God with our bodies (1 Cor. 6:20). Our commitment to Him must be worthy of His commitment to us.

God's total commitment to us inspires and compels our total commitment to Him. When we consider the mercy God has given us, offering our bodies to God is a *reasonable* response (Rom. 12:1). As an old hymn says: "Love so amazing, so divine, demands my soul, my life, my all."[12] So in gratitude to God for all He has done for us, let us offer our bodies to Him as a living sacrifice.

D. Our response to God's mercy has two sides: a "do not," and a "do."

On the cross, Jesus paid the price for our salvation. In response, to show we are thankful, Paul teaches us what to do. In Romans 12:2-8 Paul explains how to offer our bodies as a living sacrifice. Paul gives us two keys—a negative and a positive.

Q 15 *What is the "negative" side of offering our bodies to God?*

1. Negative: *"Do not conform any longer to the pattern of this world"* (Rom. 12:2a). Phillips Bible says *"Do not let the world squeeze you into its mold"* (Rom. 12:2a).[13] The values, attitudes, and actions of the world center on self. Here are some sayings that reflect the world's point of view:[14]

- Life is all about me. How much can I own? How much fun can I have? How comfortable can I be? How important can I be? How much power can I have?
- My happiness is the most important thing.
- I will use money, sex, and power to satisfy myself.
- This life is all there is. I want to eat, drink, and enjoy myself as much as possible.

The world's point of view is I, me, mine, and myself. In contrast, as we will study in Romans 12–15, God's will is for us to be concerned about others. His law is for us to love our neighbor as ourselves. The world says, "Life is about me." But the follower of Christ says, "Life is about all of us."

Before we met Christ, we followed the standards set by the world. But Paul insists: *"Do not conform any longer..."* (Rom. 12:2). Our attitudes and actions must change for us to follow Christ.

The world squeezes people into its mold. It squeezes through pressures from society, family, and friends. The world presses and impresses people through print and media advertisements. It squeezes through entertainment via radio, television, Internet, other electronic devices, and in public. To avoid being squeezed into the world's pattern, we must set boundaries on what we watch, read, listen to, and think about. The price of freedom is living on guard, moment by moment, as aliens and strangers in the world. The more people eat from the world's menu, the more they live and act like people of the world. A tailor uses a pattern to shape a suit or a dress. And Satan uses the pattern of the world to shape his followers. In contrast, followers of Christ know that those who love the world do not love the Father.

Q 16 *Summarize God's counsel to believers in 1 John 2:15-17.*

[15]*Do not love the world or anything in the world. If anyone loves the world, love for the Father is not in him.* [16]*For everything in the world—the lust of the flesh, the lust of the eyes, and the pride of life—comes not from the Father but from the world.* [17]*The world and its desires pass away, but whoever does the will of God lives forever* (1 John 2:15-17, NIV 2011).

Do not conform any longer to the pattern of this world (Rom. 12:2a).

Q 17 *What is the "positive" side of offering our bodies to God?*

2. Positive: *"[Do] be transformed by the renewing of your mind"* (Rom. 12:2b). The mind is the battleground for the soul. To avoid being formed by the world's mold, Paul says to be *transformed* by renewing our minds. In other words, an important part of victorious living is mental. When we followed the ways of the world, our patterns of thought were selfish. Our thoughts included greed, lust, covetousness, unforgiveness, hate, and revenge. From our earliest years we learned to think selfish thoughts. These thought patterns became habits.

Q 18 *Is being renewed in our minds an event, a process, or both? Explain.*

As followers of Christ, we must learn to think in new ways. Renewed thinking *begins* with an event, the new birth. But learning to think from God's point of view is also a *process* for all of life. Believers start out as babes in the faith. We must learn how to live differently than those of the world. Growing takes time (Rom. 8:13; 2 Cor. 3:18; Phil 2:12-13; 1 John 3:3). There are victories and defeats. But as we mature, we learn to walk in God's will without stumbling or falling. God transforms a caterpillar into a butterfly over a period of time. Likewise, God transforms us, little by little, to have the mind of Christ—that is, to think like Christ thinks about things (Rom. 8:29; 2 Cor. 3:18; Eph. 4:11-16). After birth, there must be growth. Even the renewed mind continues to need instruction and reminding.[15] So apostles like Paul and Peter *reminded* believers to practice wholesome thinking (Phil. 4:8-9; 2 Pet. 3:1). Likewise Jude *reminded* believers to contend for the faith and press forward. As we grow in grace, we make our calling and election certain (2 Pet. 1:10-11). And by going forward, thinking in a spiritual way, we avoid the danger of going backward and falling into judgment (Jude 5).

How does God help us renew our minds? Here are some ways we cooperate with God to think right:

Q 19 *What are 5 ways that we cooperate with God to renew our minds?*

- **God's Spirit** imparts power and strength, enabling us to think in new ways as we submit to Him and refuse to be led by sinful, fleshly desires (Rom. 8:9; Gal. 5:16). The Spirit guides us to turn away from evil thoughts. And He urges us to think of ways we can glorify God and help others. The more the Spirit fills us, the less the flesh leads us. The more the Spirit renews our mind, the less the world squeezes us into patterns of sinful thinking.
- **God's Word** is also a major power to influence our minds. When we read the Word, we are thinking God's thoughts. His Word shines light on our attitudes and values. The Bible coaches us in the right directions. The Spirit uses the Word to shine light on the path where we should walk (Ps. 119:105). Paul wrote:

  Let the word of Christ dwell in you richly as you teach and admonish one another with all wisdom, and as you sing psalms, hymns and spiritual songs with gratitude in your hearts to God (Col. 3:16).

  Scripture is a powerful force that the Spirit uses to renew our minds (Ps. 119:11, 148; John 8:31-32; 15:7; 17:17).[16] Likewise, Scriptural songs can be a major key to inspire our thoughts.

  Q 20 *How did Juan cooperate with the Spirit to renew his mind?*

  Juan was wrestling with temptation. Softly, an inner voice whispered to him, "Do not be deceived: God cannot be mocked. A man reaps what he sows. The one who sows to please his flesh, from that flesh will reap destruction; the one who sows to please the Spirit, from the Spirit will reap eternal life." Juan recognized these words from Galatians 6:7-8. As he submitted to the Spirit and God's Word, he turned away from the temptation—and it soon disappeared like fog vanishes in the sunshine.

- **Prayer and worship** in a known tongue or unknown tongue renews our mind— for when we fellowship and commune with God, we become like Him. A person who spends time working in a flower garden smells like the flowers. And as we spend time in God's presence, we enjoy the fragrance of His influence in our character, thoughts, and actions.
- **Meeting together** with other believers, such as in church or home groups, helps renew our minds. Listening to sermons or biblical teachings, testimonies, and even the struggles of other believers helps us form habits of thinking spiritual thoughts.
- **Godly activities** such as enjoying wholesome entertainment, walks to admire nature, or having fun as a family guide the mind in the right direction.

The best way to keep the wrong things out of a bucket is to fill it with good things. Likewise, the best way to keep evil out of our minds is to fill it with godly, holy, healthy thoughts. (For more help, see Lesson 42 "Spiritual Thinking" in the *Faith & Action* book *First and Second Corinthians*).

Paul urges believers, *"Offer your bodies as living sacrifices, holy and pleasing to God"* (Rom. 12:1a). Then he gives two keys to obey this guideline from God
- *"Do not conform any longer to the pattern of this world"* (Rom. 12:2a).
- *"[Do] be transformed by the renewing of your mind"* (Rom. 12:2b).

So what is the result of obeying Romans 12:1-2b?

Q 21 ⬈ *What is the result of obeying Romans 12:1-2b?*

E. Result: Offering our bodies as living sacrifices enables us to discern and do God's will (Rom. 12:1-2).

Paul has given us two principles, like two sides of a coin, to offer ourselves as living sacrifices. The negative command is: *Do not* be conformed to the pattern of the world any longer. The positive is: *Do* be transformed by the renewing of our minds. <u>What is the benefit of obeying these two principles</u>? Paul answers this question in the last part of Romans 12:2.

> *Do not conform any longer to the pattern of this world, but be transformed by the renewing of your mind.* ***Then*** <u>***you will be able to test and approve what God's will is—his good, pleasing and perfect will***</u> (Rom. 12:2).

Q 22 ⬈ *How does Romans 12:1-2 relate to Romans 12:3–15:13?*

The result of not conforming to the world, but being transformed by a renewed mind, is knowing and proving God's will (NASB). As we turn away from the world's attitudes and actions, we turn from serving self to serving God and others. As we are transformed by a renewed mind, we discern God's will. Paul has a lot to say about knowing and doing God's will in Romans 12:3–15:13. These chapters are the result and application of obeying Romans 12:1-2.

Lesson 35 | **The Relationship of Believers to Each Other (Rom. 12:3-8)**
Goal A: *Contrast the general and specific will of God for believers.*
Goal B: *Explain 3 factors that help us measure ourselves accurately.*
Goal C: *Analyze and illustrate 7 examples of spiritual gifts in Romans 12:3-8.*

Q 23 ⬈ *What is the general will of God for all believers (Rom. 8:29)?*

Obeying Romans 12:1-2 enables us *"to test and approve what God's will is—his good, pleasing and perfect will"* (Rom. 12:2). The **will of God* for believers includes a *general* and a *specific* will. Paul has already written about God's **general will** for all believers:

> *For those God foreknew he also predestined to be conformed to the likeness of his Son* (Rom. 8:29a).

Hallelujah! God's will reveals a glorious plan for all believers. What a marvelous destiny—to become more and more like Jesus, God's Son. How wonderful that God's will is for us to become brothers and sisters of Jesus—*"that he might be the firstborn among many brothers"* (Rom. 8:29b). Can you imagine a better plan for humans? In Genesis we read that *"God created man **in his own image"*** (Gen. 1:27). And in Romans we read that God's will is to finish what He started—to conform us *"to the likeness of his Son."* This is the **general will** of God for all believers. And it becomes a reality as we present our bodies as a living sacrifice, turning away from the world, and being transformed through a renewed mind.

In Romans 12:3-8, Paul begins talking about the **specific will** of God. Although God's *general will* is the same for all believers (Rom. 8:29), His *specific will* differs for each person, especially as we relate to each other in the body of Christ. Let us take a closer look at God's specific will.

The song "Lifesong" is based on Colossians 3:17.[17]

A. God's specific will for us believers is to fulfill our role in the body of Christ (Rom. 12:3-8).

Q 24 ⬈ *In Romans 12:3-8, what does Paul say about the specific will of God for believers?*

It is important to see the connection between Romans 12:1-2 and Romans 12:3-8—and the rest of Romans 12–15. Romans 12:1-2 describes our response to the mercy God has shown us. In and through Christ, God has forgiven our sins, declared us righteous, and adopted us as His children. Our reasonable and spiritual response is to present our bodies as a living sacrifice, day by day. This includes two principles. *First,* we do not let the world squeeze us into its mold of selfishness. *Second,* we submit to the Spirit and the Word of God to renew our minds daily. As we practice this response to God, there is a beautiful result. We discover God's will—how to do our part as members of the Church, the body of Christ.

Christianity is a religion of relationships. Believers are all part of one family. Scripture compares us to members of one body. Note this emphasis in Romans 12:4-5.

> [4]*Just as each of us has one body with many members, and these members do not all have the same function,* [5]*so in Christ* we who are many form one body, *and each member belongs to all the others* (Rom. 12:4-5).

God's plan is for people to be born into families. God wants each baby to have a dad, a mom, brothers and/or sisters. Likewise, at the new birth we are born again into God's family. Like physical babies, spiritual babies need care and attention or they will die. In families, people need each other to live, learn, grow, and prosper. Families provide fellowship and relationship—give and take. Each member of a family gives and receives. Families eat together, play together, work together, laugh together, and cry together. The Church is a family.

So God expects us to care about each other and help each other.

There is a big difference between a group and a family. At a soccer game, a group of people gathers. Most of them do not know each other. They come to sit and watch players on a field. At a soccer game, it does not matter who is behind us, beside us, or in front of us. People just come to watch. In contrast, members of a church must build strong relationships. We must learn the names of others. God calls us to love each other. We are to *"carry each other's burdens"* (Gal. 6:2). We are to *"rejoice with those who rejoice; mourn with those who mourn"* (Rom. 12:15). Romans 12:3-8 emphasizes the relationship and responsibilities of believers to each other. God gives each believer gifts and talents to help others. A group of people at a soccer match does not care about each other. But in the Church, we are brothers and sisters of the same family, so we love one another. At a soccer match, people come to sit and watch. But in the Church, each believer has something to do.

In the human body, each member has a role. The eyes, ears, feet, and hands all have tasks to do. The mouth, nose, heart, and lungs each have a job. Likewise, in the body of Christ, each believer has a special task to make the body successful.

What is your task in the local church? How do you help your church be what God wants it to be? What is your part? To help you discover your personal ministry, we will examine two principles, B and C.

B. Let your measure of self be accurate—not too tall (Rom. 12:3-6).

> *For by the grace given me I say to every one of you: Do not think of yourself more highly than you ought, but rather think of yourself with sober judgment, in accordance with the measure of faith God has given you* (Rom. 12:3).

In Romans 12:3-8, Paul writes about *spiritual gifts (Greek: *charismata*). Our gifts and abilities can be a source of pride and division. Recall that Paul wrote to the Romans from Corinth. Some Corinthian believers felt proud because they spoke in tongues. Fleshly people compare themselves with others. But Paul steers believers away from feeling taller or shorter than other believers. Whether a person is Jew or Gentile, rich or poor, a prophet or a deacon, we should all be humble. It is true that we have different spiritual gifts. But our gifts should never be a source of pride.

Paul is a good example of a humble person. God gave him great gifts and a fruitful ministry. Paul stood tall among the apostles. Yet recall the way Paul referred to himself

Q 25 *What attitude of Paul should we have (Eph. 3:8)? Explain.*

and his ministry. *"Although I am less than the least of all God's people, this grace was given me: to preach to the Gentiles the unsearchable riches of Christ"* (Eph. 3:8). Picture Paul, with his hands upon his chest, as he says, "Unto **me** this grace was given! Unto **me**—although I am *less than the least!*" The least is the most unworthy—the last on the list. But Paul felt even lower than this. So he made up a new word (Greek: *elaxistoteros*). This Greek word appears only once in the New Testament. As Paul looked back on his past, he felt sorry for the way he had persecuted the Church. He was ashamed of his past sins. Of all people in the Church, he felt the least worthy to be given grace. Yet God chose him to preach the unsearchable riches of Christ. Imagine the riches, treasures, and blessing in Christ—broader than an ocean, too wide to search. The wealth in Christ is unsearchable—spread out without boundaries beyond the universe. Whom shall God choose to preach these vast riches? Who is worthy of such an honor? God chose Paul. And He has also chosen you and me to share these riches in Christ with others. So let us be humble and faithful with this great honor God has given us. Imagine—God has chosen **us** to share these unsearchable riches with the lost! One man asked a preacher, "Why did God choose Judas?" The preacher answered, "That is a hard question. But I can ask you an even harder question: Why did God choose me?"[18]

Q 26 *How are grace and faith a source of humility?*

> PAUL WARNS US NOT TO BE TOO TALL IN OUR OWN EYES (OR TOO SHORT).

Paul warns us not to be too tall in our own eyes (or too short). Rather, when we measure ourselves, we should keep **three things** in mind.

- **Grace.** *First,* we should recall that whatever we have comes through the *grace* God gives us. Paul emphasizes this when he, an apostle, says: *"By the grace given me I say to every one of you: Do not think of yourself more highly than you ought"* (Rom. 12:3). Note Paul's emphasis on grace. Paul was an apostle by the grace of God. Earlier Paul wrote about himself, "We received grace and apostleship" (Rom. 1:5; also 15:15-16). These words remind us of another passage Paul wrote,

For who makes you different from anyone else? What do you have that you did not receive? And if you did receive it, why do you boast as though you did not? (1 Cor. 4:7).

Since all spiritual gifts come by grace, none of us can brag about the gifts we have. *"We have different gifts, according to the grace given us"* (Rom. 12:6).

Q 27 *How is our faith like the light of the moon?*

- **Faith.** *Second,* Paul emphasizes that it is God who gives us a *measure of faith.* *"Do not think of yourself more highly than you ought, but rather think of yourself with sober judgment, in accordance with the measure of faith **God** has given you"* (Rom. 12:3). God gives grace and God gives faith. Scholars differ on the meaning of *measure of faith.* Some think that in Romans 12:3 *measure* (Greek: *metron*) *of faith* means that God gives every believer the same amount of faith.[19] Others note that some have more faith than others (1 Cor. 13:2; Matt. 8:10). These cite Romans 14, which contrasts the weak in faith with the strong in faith. But the main point in Romans 12:3 is not the *amount* of faith a believer has, but rather the *source* of faith, God. Whatever faith we have, God gave it to us. Therefore, let us exalt Him, rather than ourselves. The moon has no light of its own but only *reflects* the sun. Likewise, the only grace and faith we have are what God gives us.

Q 28 *How does our relationship to the body of Christ humble us?*

- **One body.** A *third* guide to humility is our relationship in the body of Christ. In a human body, all of the members depend on each other. The eye needs the foot, and the hand needs the head. Paul taught this in 1 Corinthians 12. And he uses this illustration of a body in Romans 12:3-8. In a body, the members need each other and belong to each other. A body needs feet to walk, eyes to see, ears to hear, teeth to chew, lungs to breathe, a heart to pump blood. There is diversity in a body, but there is unity. Whether the body is physical or spiritual, we need each other and belong to each other. Therefore, let each of us have a humble attitude, appreciating others and ourselves. A body has no war between members.[20]

Paul urges us not to be too tall in our own eyes. Let us not be like the common house cat that looked in the mirror and thought it was a lion. Let us not resemble the donkey that thought the crowds were cheering for him, rather than Jesus who rode him. Let us not be like the rooster who thought its crowing caused the sun to rise. Remember that even the best athletes on a team will fail without other players to help them. And the best students are taught everything by someone. Cooks depend on farmers, and farmers depend on cooks. Men depend on women, and women depend on men. We need each other. *"For by the grace given me I say to every one of you: Do not think of yourself more highly than you ought, but rather think of yourself with sober judgment, in accordance with the measure of faith God has given you"* (Rom. 12:3).

As long as King Saul was humble in his own eyes, God could use him (1 Sam. 15:17). But the day that he became proud of his gifts, God picked someone else to be king (1 Sam. 13:13-14). Young preachers must guard against pride. Or they *"may become conceited and fall under the same judgment as the devil"* (1 Tim. 3:6).

Application: Is there a job to do in the church? Do not feel like you are too good to do it. Is there a class of children to teach? Do not feel so proud that you will not help. Is there a poor family in the church or neighborhood? Do not feel too wealthy or too educated to sit by them or talk to them.

No believer should look down on another believer. Everyone has a gift from God. And each gift is important to the health of the church. Thus, believers should never think that they are better than other believers. And believers should never think that they are less important than other believers are.[21] This is what it means to *"think of yourself with sober judgment"* (Rom. 12:3).

C. Identify your spiritual gift—your way of serving in the church (Rom. 12:3-8).

None of the lists of Ephesians 4, 1 Corinthians 12, or Romans 12 names every gift (Figure 9.5). (In the *Full Life Study Bible,* see three resources: the chart, The Gifts of the Holy Spirit; the article, "Spiritual Gifts for Believers;" and the article, "The Ministry Gifts of the Church.") There are many different kinds of gifts. Wise leaders guide believers to identify and use their gifts.

Rom. 12:6-8	1 Cor. 12:8-11	1 Cor. 12:27-31	Eph. 4:11-12
Prophecy	Wisdom	Apostles	Apostles
Service	Knowledge	Prophets	Prophets
Teaching	Faith	Teachers	Evangelists
Encouragement	Healing	Workers of miracles	Pastors
Giving	Miracles	Those with gifts of healing	Teachers
Leadership	Prophecy	Those able to help others	
Mercy	Discernment	Those with gifts of administration	
	Tongues	Those speaking in tongues	
	Interpretation	Those who interpret tongues	

Figure 9.5   Four lists of gifts in the New Testament

Paul's writings contain four lists of gifts. But each list is from a different point of view. Ephesians lists people—gifts whom Christ gives to the Church (Eph. 4:11-12). First Corinthians 12 has two lists. The first list is manifestations of the Holy Spirit (1 Cor. 12:8-11). These nine gifts are not people, and people do not own these gifts. Rather, the Holy Spirit reveals Himself through people He chooses. The second list in

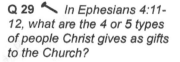
Q 29   *In Ephesians 4:11-12, what are the 4 or 5 types of people Christ gives as gifts to the Church?*

Q 30 *How do the four lists of gifts in Ephesians 4, 1 Corinthians 12, and Romans 12 differ?*

1 Corinthians 12 focuses on people God gives to serve the Church (1 Cor. 12:27-31). Likewise, the list in Romans 12 emphasizes seven ways people minister. This list in Romans 12 is broad. Some call the gifts in Romans 12 *motivational gifts, or gifts that inspire and guide us to serve in certain ways.

An electrician puts wires in a house so electricity can flow through the wires. We say that a house is "wired" in a certain way. But the wiring is not the electricity. 1 Corinthians 12 emphasizes the electricity or power of the Spirit that flows through people, rather than the way people are made or "wired." In contrast, Romans 12 emphasizes the way people are wired—the way God made them to respond, as well as the power of the Spirit that flows through them. Except perhaps for the gift of prophecy, the gifts of Romans 12 are woven into a person. So your gifts of Romans 12 are not just what you do, but who you are.

Q 31 *How does the illustration of the family help explain gifts in a local church?*

Imagine a family eating dinner together. The youngest child spills his milk. Family members will respond in various ways. These responses illustrate the spiritual gifts of believers.

- The dad may say, "Son, spilling your milk is what happens when you are not careful!" We may say that the dad's response represents the gift of prophecy—to strengthen, exhort, and correct. One who prophesies seeks to correct what is wrong, so it will become right. A dad might smile and whisper, "Pay attention to the dishes when you eat."
- The mother at the table may represent the ministry of service. She may say, "Let me help you clean up the milk." Her response, impulse, and motivation is to help meet a need.
- A brother might say, "I know why the milk fell. The glass was too close to the edge of the table." This person represents the gift of a teacher—looking for a lesson to learn.
- A sister might say, "I know this was an accident. Let us try to do better in the future." This response represents the gift of encouragement—to inspire and support.
- Another brother might say, "I am happy to share part of my milk." His response represents the gift of giving.
- A sister at the table might say, "Get the mop. Help me pour some more milk." Her response represents the gift of leadership. She analyzes a problem, makes a plan to help, and takes steps toward a solution.
- Another family member might say, "Do not feel badly. Accidents can happen to anyone." This response represents the gift of mercy—feeling and showing concern for someone in need.

So we see that within a family, people respond in different ways, according to the way God has created them. The Church is like this. There are many gifts and ministries. Paul is saying, "Do not try to be someone else in the body of Christ. Be whom God has called you to be." If you were in the family when the milk spilled, what would your first response be? Thinking about how you respond to needs helps you identify your gifts.[22]

God gives every believer at least one gift (compare 1 Cor. 12:11; 1 Pet. 4:10). Together the many believers make up one body. Each member is necessary to the whole.

[17]If the whole body were an eye, where would the sense of hearing be? If the whole body were an ear, where would the sense of smell be? [18]But in fact God has arranged the parts in the body, every one of them, just as he wanted them to be. [19]If they were all one part, where would the body be? [20]As it is, there are many parts, but one body (1 Cor. 12:17-20).

In the parable of the talents, the master gives each servant at least one talent (Matt. 25:14-30). Also in the parable of the minas, the nobleman gives ten of his servants one mina each. *"Put this money to work,"* he said, *"until I come back"* (Luke 19:11-27).

Every believer is part of the body of Christ. Each member of the body has a gift and a job to do. As you study this part of the lesson, identify your gift. And if you are a leader, use this study to help other believers discover their gifts and use them. Paul lists seven gifts in Romans 12:6-8. We will examine each gift, although Paul does not explain them. He only lists them. His goal is not instruction or explanation. Rather, Paul's goal is exhortation. Paul lists a few gifts. But his main point is: Whatever your gift is, use it!

1. Prophecy is at the top of Paul's list of gifts. The NIV has *"If a man's gift is prophesying, let him use it in proportion to his faith"* (Rom. 12:6). But the Greek has *"If prophecy, according to the proportion* [Greek: *analogian*] *of the faith."* Recall that Paul emphasized the gift of prophecy to the Corinthians (1 Cor. 14). Paul stressed prophecy because it builds up the whole church. Likewise, in Romans 12:3-8, Paul is emphasizing the need for believers to edify each other. So we would expect the gift of prophecy to be at the top of Paul's list. Note that prophecy or prophet is the only gift that is on all three of Paul's lists of gifts (Figure 9.5).

Prophecy is a sudden, supernatural message from the Spirit of God through a believer. Few are prophets, but all may prophesy (1 Cor. 14:31). Recall that Philip the evangelist had four daughters who prophesied (Acts 21:8-9). The purposes of prophecy are to strengthen, encourage, comfort, or instruct.

Prophecy may come in three forms:

- Prophecy may be *foretelling*—about the future. For example Agabus prophesied there would be a famine in Judea. This encouraged believers to send help to believers there (Acts 11:27-28).

- Most of the time prophecy is *forth-telling*—declaring the conditions and promises of being in a covenant relationship with God. Forth-telling may include emphasizing characteristics of God, such as His holiness, love, mercy, righteousness, and faithfulness. Likewise, prophetic forth-telling may emphasize God's promises, such as the Second Coming, the resurrection, a new body, and eternity in heaven with God. Or prophetic forth-telling may emphasize our responsibilities to repent, turn from sin, believe and obey Christ, accept forgiveness, forgive others, be baptized, pray, study the Scriptures, abide in Christ, and be led by the Spirit.

- A third form of the gift of prophecy is *heart-telling*. Through the gift of prophecy, Nathan revealed that King David committed murder and adultery (2 Sam. 12). Through the eyes of a prophet, Jesus often revealed the secrets of the heart, such as the woman at the well (John 4), Peter's thoughts about taxes (Matt. 17:24-27), the Pharisees' objections to forgiving sin (Matt. 9:2-4), and the sins of Judas (Matt. 26:20-25).

The gift of prophecy is at the top of Paul's list. He desires for all believers to prophesy (1 Cor. 14:1, 5). Although this gift is supernatural, it should be common in the church and in the lives of believers. As we live filled with the Spirit, we should overflow with fresh and sudden messages from God to encourage, strengthen, and comfort ourselves, other believers, and the whole church.

Prophecy is the number one gift Paul emphasizes. But note the guideline that comes with this gift: *"If prophecy, according to the proportion* [Greek: *analogian*] *of the faith."* In Romans 12:3 Paul mentioned that we all have a *measure* [Greek: *metron*] of faith. But in regard to prophecy, he says it must be *in proportion to the faith*. The Greek word translated *proportion* is *analogian*. It means "in proportion to, in relationship to, or analogous to." In other words, prophecy must always be in line with Scripture. Prophecy is a welcome gift. But it can also be dangerous. Those who prophesy claim to be inspired

Q 32 *What is the gift of prophecy? Explain it.*

Q 33 *What are 3 forms of the gift of prophecy? Explain each.*

Q 34 *In 1 Corinthians 14:29, why did Paul emphasize the need to "weigh" a prophecy?*

by God. This gives great freedom to speak with authority. So Paul insists that Scripture, *the faith,* or the whole of what we believe must rule over prophecy.[23]

Q 35 In 1 Thessalonians 5:19-22, what 5 things does Paul say about prophecy?

Q 36 In 2 Thessalonians 2:2, how were some people abusing prophecy?

Note: For a thorough study on the gift of prophecy, see the *Faith & Action* course on *First and Second Corinthians,* Lesson 24: The Gift of Prophecy (1 Cor. 14:1-32).

The Greek word *analogian* appears only once in the New Testament (Rom. 12:6). But this verse has had an important role in Church history. In the Middle Ages and the Reformation, church leaders built on this phrase of Romans 12:6, *"the analogy of faith."* They used this phrase to emphasize the principle of hermeneutics: We must interpret Scripture in the light of other Scripture.[24] They taught that as the gift of prophecy must relate to the whole of the faith, likewise the interpretation of one verse must relate to the whole of the faith, which the whole Bible reveals. In our *Faith & Action* courses on Hermeneutics we illustrate this in a diagram of six circles. This emphasizes the analogy of faith—the proportion, balance, and relationship of one Scriptural insight to others. In our diagram of the six circles, the sixth and biggest circle contains the other five circles, and represents the whole of Scripture.[25]

Q 37 Which Greek word is translated "service"?

2. Serving. *"If it is serving, let him serve"* (Rom. 12:7). Serving translates the Greek word *diakonia,* which is a role of ministry that supports. The English word *deacon* is based on this Greek word *diakonia.* The early church quickly recognized the need for people to help serve. Recall that the church in Jerusalem chose seven Spirit-filled servers (deacons) to provide care for the widows. This enabled the apostles to focus on prayer and preaching (Acts 6:1-6). Likewise, servers in the church today enable church leaders to focus on prayer and preaching. But remember that servers/deacons may also preach. Stephen and Philip were two of the first deacons, and they were outstanding preachers. Likewise, many deacons today begin in a ministry of service, and soon become pastors. Paul explains the qualifications for deacons in 1 Timothy 3:8-13.

Q 38 For what type of service are you known in your church? Explain.

Few today serve as deacons. Yet believers may serve in many ways. Figure 9.8 lists about 200 different ways that believers in one church serve. *Service* is a broad word that may include all gifts. Jesus, our example, came into this world to serve others (Mark 10:45). Your area of service may be as *big* as the ministry of Philip, a deacon who preached in a new place (Acts 8). Or it may be as *small* as the ministry of Dorcas, a woman known for kind deeds to widows, such as sewing clothes (Acts 9:36-42). Whether your service is big or small, be known for some type of service!

Figure 9.6
Dorcas was known for her gift of service, before and after Peter raised her from the dead.

A believer named Linda is known for her cooking. Time after time she bakes bread, or cookies, or a cake and serves it to someone. In heaven, Linda will be as famous for her cooking as Dorcas was for her sewing. Likewise, Linda's husband, John, is known for his building. Once he and a group of men helped repair a widow's house. Another time they built an extra room on a house. In heaven many will testify of the way he helped them through building projects.

Q 39 What are some formal ministries of teaching?

3. Teaching. *"If it is teaching, let him teach"* (Rom. 12:7). Teaching, like service, is a gift for every believer. Some with the gift of teaching hold official, formal positions. Examples of these are teachers over groups in a church—teaching adults, youth, or children. Others may be teachers in a school. Let us be sure that some of the best teachers are with children, the youngest of students. Why? Because children can learn very fast, and very well, <u>if</u> they have good teachers. In contrast, adults learn more slowly than children, and forget faster!

Some teach in formal positions, but the Scripture calls all to teach. Recall the Great Commission. Jesus commands us:

Q 40 ➘ *In what way should all believers teach?*

> [19] *"Therefore go and make disciples of all nations, baptizing them in the name of the Father and of the Son and of the Holy Spirit,* [20]*and **teaching** them to obey everything I have commanded you"* (Matt. 28:19-20).

The Great Commission commands <u>all</u> believers to teach. So remember that this is one of your callings, and that God has given you a gift to teach someone. You should have at least one student—someone you are helping disciple. Parents teach their children. And every believer is commissioned to teach someone to learn and obey the commandments of Jesus (Matt. 28:19-20). Mentor, coach, and teach someone. Teach another to pray, to have devotions, to worship, to tithe, to witness. Teach someone to persevere in trials, to relate better to others, to think on good things, to encourage themselves, and to make godly decisions. On the one hand, we all continue to learn as students throughout our lives. But even the youngest believer has learned something to teach someone else. Whatever you learn in church, go teach it to someone else. Teaching is a gift and a calling God has for every believer.

4. Encouraging. *"If it is encouraging, let him encourage"* (Rom. 12:8).

Q 41 ➘ *What are some ways that believers can encourage others?*

Many believers have the gift of encouragement (Rom. 12:8). Encouragers comfort the discouraged and strengthen the weary. They help lift up tired hands that hang down. Every person needs a word of encouragement once in a while. Even great prophets like Elijah and John the Baptist had their valleys (1 Kings 19:1-4; Matt. 11:2). The sick, the sorrowful, and the sour need encouragement. Believers with the gift of encouragement do not flatter people, but they comment on people's strengths. And encouragers use the Bible. These believers know how to mention the right verses to encourage others.

The name *Barnabas* means "Son of Encouragement." And Barnabas practiced the gift of encouragement (Acts 4:36-37; 9:27). He was a friend to Paul when others doubted him. Encouragement strengthens the heart, soul, mind, and emotions. This practical gift includes words and actions. It may express itself in ways such as a smile, a handshake, a helping hand, a meal, a gift, a kind deed, a shoulder under a load, a letter, a friendship, or a compliment. All of us believers can practice the gift of encouragement as we train ourselves to think about and notice others.

5. Giving. *"If it is contributing to the needs of others, let him give generously"*

Q 42 ➘ *How does the gift of giving vary in the church?*

(Rom. 12:8). Giving is one of the gifts that applies to all believers. Some are famous givers. Joseph of Arimathea was a rich man who gave his tomb for Jesus. Barnabas was known for giving the money he got from selling a piece of land (Acts 4:36-37). Mary, the sister of Lazarus, is known throughout history, all over the world, for her gift. She gave a pound of expensive perfume to anoint Jesus for His burial. It was worth a year's wages! Wow, what a big gift! And yet Scripture also records very small gifts. A widow is famous for giving two pennies (Mark 12:41-44). A little boy is known for sharing his lunch of fish and bread (John 6:5-8). God keeps a record of even the smallest gifts we give in His name—even a cup of cold water (Matt. 10:42). Believers at Macedonia were very poor. But as love filled their hearts, they gave to help those who were even poorer. Recall what happened when the Macedonian Christians heard about the Jerusalem saints who were suffering from famine and persecution. Paul uses the generosity of the Macedonians to inspire the Corinthians to give—and to inspire us to give.

> [1]*And now, brothers, we want you to know about the grace that God has given the Macedonian churches.* [2]*Out of the most severe trial, their overflowing joy and their extreme poverty welled up in rich generosity.* [3]*For I testify that they*

gave as much as they were able, and even beyond their ability. Entirely on their own, ⁴they urgently pleaded with us for the privilege of sharing in this service to the saints. ⁵And they did not do as we expected, but they gave themselves first to the Lord and then to us in keeping with God's will. ⁶So we urged Titus, since he had earlier made a beginning, to bring also to completion this act of grace on your part. ⁷But just as you excel in everything—in faith, in speech, in knowledge, in complete earnestness and in your love for us—<u>see that you also excel in this grace of giving</u> (2 Cor. 8:1-7).

We are talking about the grace (Greek: *charis*) God gives as spiritual gifts (*charismata*). The Corinthians excelled in spiritual gifts like tongues and the other gifts of 1 Corinthians 12. But Paul emphasized that they, like us, should *also* excel in the *grace of giving*. Because of what we know, we can afford to be generous.

Q 43 *What are some guidelines for the gift of giving?*

Scriptures give several guidelines for giving. Let us not give in a way that promotes laziness (2 Thess. 3:6-15). Let us give with joy (2 Cor. 9:7). Let us give to those with real needs (Acts 6:1-7; 1 Tim. 5:3-16). Let us give without favoritism (James 2:1-9) . Let us give with simplicity—pure hearts, and not to gain favors (Rom. 12:8). Let us never give to impress people, like the hypocrites, the Pharisees, and like Ananias and Sapphira gave (Matt. 6:1-4; 23:5; Acts 5:1-11).[26]

Giving is the mother tongue of love. *"God so loved the world that he gave his one and only Son"* (John 3:16). When we give, we are like God. Recall how Paul begins this practical section of Romans 12–15. He urges us to *give* our bodies to God as living sacrifices (Rom. 12:1-2). The more we love, the more we give ourselves to God and others.

Our attitude toward possessions reflects our relationship with God.
- When the Lord appeared to Abraham, he cooked a calf and set it before Him (Gen. 18:1-8).
- When the angel of the Lord visited Samson's father, he sacrificed a goat from his flock (Judges 13:15-20).
- Zacchaeus climbed a tree to see Jesus. This encounter led him to give half of his goods to help the poor (Luke 19:1-9).
- At Pentecost, the Holy Spirit filled believers. The result? They sold their possessions to help poor believers (Acts 2:41-45).

Giving is one of our most basic spiritual responses—an overflow of our relationship with God. Before Christ, we live for ourselves. Then we meet God. Before we know it, we are cooking the best calf in our herd JUST FOR HIM. And this is just the beginning![27]

Did you ever see a nest of baby birds? When the parent bird comes with food, the mouths of the baby birds open wide—so wide that the mouth is about all you can see. Perhaps all baby believers are like baby birds. In their earliest days, babies have nothing to give. But baby birds grow up, build nests, and feed others. And it is God's plan for baby believers to grow up and give to others. God forbid that we should just sit around like babies, crying and waiting for someone to take care of us. Let each of us practice a life of giving.

Q 44 *How are baby believers like baby birds?*

John Wesley said to give as soon as possible when the Holy Spirit warms and opens our heart. Otherwise, warned Wesley, the human heart is prone to grow cold and close, turning its thoughts from others to self.

Q 45 *What is the ministry of a leader? Give an example.*

6. Leadership. *"If it is leadership, let him govern diligently"* (Rom. 12:8). We have reached the sixth gift on Paul's list. The Greek word *proistemi* is often translated *leadership*. It means "to set before" or "to set over." This Greek word identifies a leader, but also a guardian—one responsible for those under his or her care.[28] Within a church there are many small groups, such as families, widows, orphans, youth, men, women, children, new believers, and visitors. Each of these groups needs believers who are guardians—people who will shoulder responsibility. For example, a father is a leader/guardian of his family. A teacher of children should be a guardian of the students in his or her class. There are too many people in a church for the pastor to care well for all of them. The church needs many "lesser leaders" to care for groups of believers in the church. Otherwise, peoples' needs will be neglected. Recall that the widows in the Jerusalem church were neglected until the church chose seven men full of the Spirit to care for them. Likewise, there will be many groups of people neglected in a church until believers become *guardians* to care for them. Be a leader or guardian of others, even if the group under your care has only one or two people in it. Show concern for the needs of others. Help someone besides yourself. Be a member of the body of Christ, not just a spectator.

Someone Else. The church was sad this week, because a person named "Someone Else" died.

Someone Else's passing creates a hole that will be hard to fill. This faithful person named "Someone Else" was with us for years. And for all those years, Someone Else did a big share of the work. Whenever we needed a leader or guardian, we looked to this wonderful person to help. Everyone said, "Someone Else can do that job." When there was a job to do, a need to meet, or a place of leadership, one name always arose: "Someone Else." Everyone in the church knew that the biggest giver of love, time, and money was "Someone Else." Whenever there was a task, everyone assumed that Someone Else would fulfill the responsibility. Now Someone Else is gone. We wonder what we are going to do. No longer can we say, "Let Someone Else do it." If it is going to be done, one of us will have to do it.[29]

7. Mercy. *"If it is showing mercy, let him do it cheerfully"* (Rom. 12:8). We have reached the final gift, mercy, in Paul's list of seven. Mercy is giving people what they *need*, instead of what they *deserve*. Synonyms of mercy are kindness, compassion, and love. Mercy includes giving forgiveness to those who hurt us (Matt. 18:33), giving compassion to those who despise us (Luke 10:37), and giving love to those less fortunate than us (James 2:14-16; 1 John 3:17). As some stars shine brighter than others, some believers will shine brighter with mercy than others (Rom. 12:8).[30] Still, all believers must practice using the gift of mercy. For without mercy, we will not enter heaven. Sabio says: "Beware if you think the gift of mercy is only for Someone Else to practice."

Q 46 Can you name a part of the human body that does not do something for the body? Apply this to the body of Christ.

Q 47 Look at all the groups of people that Figure 9.8 includes. Which group will have you to depend on as their leader/guardian? Or will you leave all the responsibility to Someone Else?

Q 48 Do you know someone who excels in the gift of mercy? Give an example.

Q 49 In Figure 9.7, summarize what each verse says about mercy.

Reference	Summary about mercy
Matt. 5:7	
Matt. 9:12-13	
Matt. 18:33	
Matt. 23:23	
Luke 10:37	
Gal. 5:22	
James 2:13	
1 John 3:17	
Rom. 12:8	

Figure 9.7 The Bible emphasizes that all believers must show mercy.

God gives the gift of mercy to help the sinful, the sick, the poor, the imprisoned, the suffering, the old, the abused, the widows, and orphans (Matt. 25:31-46; Gal. 2:10; James 1:27). Sometimes, the gift of mercy is more personal than giving.[31]

We have studied seven gifts in Romans 12:3-8. As we noted, these are just a few examples of the many gifts God gives. Each believer may have one main gift, but several lesser gifts. Paul does not spend over a half a sentence explaining each gift. The point is: Whatever your gift is, use it! The question is not whether you attend church, worship, or raise your hands. Rather, the question is: What is your gift to the rest of the body? What do you do to help others?

As we use our gifts, we need to guard our attitudes. Prophets can become too harsh. Servers can begin to feel sorry for themselves, or become too busy. Teachers can become dull. Administrators can be too strong-willed. Givers can try to control. And those given to mercy can refuse to make hard decisions. Each gift requires discipline and balance. Let all of us not think too highly of ourselves (Rom. 12:3). And let us practice being led by the Spirit, offering our bodies as a living sacrifice as we serve one another (Rom. 12:1-8).

Q 50 How many different gifts or ministries are possible in one church?

Anna visited a neighbor who was sick. As they prayed together, Anna placed her hand on the woman's head. After the prayer, the woman said, "I know it was your hands, but I felt God touch me." Anna replied, "It was my hands and God's hands too. Christ will use any hands we offer to serve Him."[32]

Some ministries of believers in a church	
Community service	Missionettes—girls program in the Assemblies of God
Ministry to the poor (food, clothes)	Royal Rangers—boys program in the Assemblies of God
Home for abused women	College students (campus and church)
Crisis telephone line	Young adult ministry (younger)
Literacy—reading classes for the illiterate	Single adult ministry (older)
Skills (for jobs, marriage, society, and such)	Single mothers ministry (help and fellowship)
Prison ministry	Senior adult ministry
Recovery Through Christ—addictions	Women's Ministry
Deaf culture ministry	Men's Ministry (includes Honor Bound—Men of Promise)
Soul winning—training and practice	Student ministries—evangelism and discipleship
Street evangelism—special events and tracts	Youth Alive—secondary school program
Athletes ministry—outreach and discipleship	Youth discipleship
Adopt-an-Area—praying for and visiting every home	Youth Bible Quiz
Ministry to the handicapped	Youth drama
Ministry to the terminally ill	Youth choir
Hospital visitation ministry	Speed the Light—youth missions fundraising
Comforting Touch ministry (funerals, sickness, and such)	Youth leadership training
Counseling/Marriage ministry	Master's Commission—1-2 year training program
Widows and orphans ministry	Adult choir
Foreign language ministry	Musical instruments ministry
Health ministry—Basic health teachings and clinics	Worship team
Sidewalk Sunday School (Saturday outreach)	Evangelistic music—outreach team
Children's meeting or rally—for children outside the church	Drama—acting, costumes, and support
Camps for children and youth	Special events/productions—holiday and evangelistic
Sunday School for all ages	Illustrated sermons
Children's Church—for church children	Fine Arts—using art talents to bless others
Children's choir	Art and design for church needs
Junior Bible Quiz (children)	Helping hands ministry for church tasks
Weddings—coordinating	Small groups—home fellowships; Bible studies
Welcome center ministry	Prayer ministries (including prayer chain)
Communion—prepare and clean up	Follow-up ministries for visitors and converts

Figure 9.8   Some churches have as many as 200 different ministries that church members are doing![33]

Conclusion: Romans 1–11 reveals that God offers love, mercy, forgiveness, and grace to all who have sinned. The Heavenly Father opens His arms and invites us into His family through a living relationship with Jesus Christ. As we accept His offer, He puts His Spirit within us to guide us in all of our ways and conform us to His likeness.

Jews and Gentiles, rich and poor, educated and illiterate, great and small—God welcomes all to become His children in Christ. Wow! The love and mercy of God are deeper than the ocean and broader than the heavens.

So Romans 1–11 leads us to the only reasonable and fitting response. We offer our bodies to God as living sacrifices. We resist selfish, worldly patterns of thought, and allow God's Word and Spirit to renew our minds. These spiritual decisions and powers enable us to live a holy life and to fellowship with the Holy God. As a result, we discover and practice God's will for us to serve in the church. God gives each of us a primary gift, as well as secondary gifts. With joy and diligence, let us use our gifts to serve others. For this is the greater part of our true and spiritual worship. We say thank you to God through the ways we serve others. Whatever your gifts are, use them!

Lesson 36

Nine Principles of *Agape* Love—Part 1 (Rom. 12:9-13)

Goal A: *Summarize and illustrate the moral nature of agape love (Rom. 12:9).*
Goal B: *Explain principles on how love relates to others, even strangers (Rom. 12:10, 13).*
Goal C: *Clarify how we renew and refuel our love (Rom. 12:11).*
Goal D: *Analyze some aspects that strengthen the toughness of love (Rom. 12:12).*

Setting

Romans 1–11 summarizes the mercy God has shown us in Jesus Christ. Our response to God's mercy is to offer our bodies as a living sacrifice (Rom. 12:1-2). Being a living sacrifice means using our gifts to serve others in the church (Rom. 12:3-8). Likewise, being a living sacrifice means walking in love (Rom. 12:9-21).

Q 51 *What is the connection between Romans 12:1-2 and Romans 12:3-8?*

Paul puts *love as a banner over Romans 12:9-21. True love (Greek: *agape*) is sincere, that is without hypocrisy (Rom. 12:9a). *Agape* love is real. It does not pretend. It is never like an actor on a stage.[34]

Q 52 *How does Romans 12:9-21 relate to Romans 12:3-8?*

In 1 Corinthians 12, Paul lists various gifts for serving the body of Christ. Then in 1 Corinthians 13, he emphasizes love as the path to walk on as we serve. Likewise, in Romans 12:3-8, Paul lists gifts God gives us so we can serve. And in Romans 12:9-21, Paul emphasizes that love is the path we must walk on as we serve.

First Corinthians 13 lists 10 characteristics of love. Likewise, Romans 12:9-21 lists 12 traits of love. These qualities are short and practical. They show us what love looks like in daily life—among believers and unbelievers. As a rainbow has different colors, love appears in different ways. Let us look at each of these beautiful qualities of sincere love.

Q 53 *Which passage in Romans is parallel to 1 Corinthians 13?*

A. Love is more than a feeling or a daydream—it has a moral backbone (Rom. 12:9).

Love must be sincere. Hate what is evil; cling to what is good (Rom. 12:9).

Q 54 *How can we recognize biblical love? Explain.*

Paul steers us away from linking love to a mere feeling or emotion. Love includes feelings, but love is more than a feeling. Feelings are fickle—like leaves in the wind. They may be the first to go, and the last to return.[35] Feelings are like a vapor that appears for a moment, and vanishes with the sun. Unlike a vapor, love has substance and fiber. As the spine supports the body, morality is the backbone of love. We can recognize biblical love by its moral nature—love hates what is evil, and clings to what is good. *Agape* hates darkness and loves light. It despises wrong, and is married to right. Paul is not just telling us to hate evil and love good. Rather, he is describing the nature of love. Paul is saying that love is pure *only* as it hates evil and clings to good.[36] Let us look more closely at these two sides of biblical love.

Q 55 ➤ *What are some things that love hates?*

Love hates! Consider the paradox of putting love and hate side by side. They seem like strange companions. Yet the Bible teaches that love hates—it hates what is evil. Some think of love only as a tender, kind emotion toward what is right. But Romans 12:9 reveals that love has a fiery side to it—like an enraged hen protecting her chicks. The normal Greek verb for hate is *stugeo*. But in Romans 12:9, Paul uses *apo-stugeo*, which intensifies hate, and means to "hate violently"—or "hate greatly, exceedingly."[37] Romans 12:9 describes *extreme hate*. Love does not just refrain from evil. Love rejects evil with an intense, fiery passion.[38] *Agape* is angry at evil. It has zeal *for* what is right, and zeal *against* what is wrong. Jesus showed furious love for God's house when He cleansed the temple. Likewise, the love of God in us causes us to reject and speak out against evils such as child abuse, pornography, abortion, homosexuality, and all forms of sin (see Rom. 13:9).

Paul wrote Romans from Corinth. Paul uses the strong Greek *poneros* for evil, rather than the less severe Greek word *kakos*. In the Greek New Testament, *ho poneros* often refers to Satan, the evil one (Matt. 5:37; 6:13; 13:19; John 17:15). Likewise, *poneros* refers to this evil age and evil generation (Gal. 1:4; Eph. 5:16).[39] The evil person must face God's judgment (1 Cor. 5:13). In contrast, Romans guides us not to be conformed to this evil world, but to be transformed—having a renewed mind (Rom. 12:2), hating evil, loving good. As Paul wrote Romans from Corinth, no doubt he recalled the evils in the Corinthian church, such as divisions, sexual sins, hypocrisy, selfishness, and pride.[40]

Q 56 ➤ *Do believers you know hate evil as they should? Explain.*

Love is not uncertain or undecided about evil. Love is not double-minded toward sin. It does not love evil at home, but hate evil in public. Whenever love meets evil, it detests it, despises it, abhors it, and rejects it. Love hates what God declares is wrong.

Love is not neutral toward evil. It is not passive or lukewarm toward things that are sinful. Love is a fiery enemy of evil. Love is not like the church members of Thyatira who tolerated Jezebel, an evil woman in the church (Rev. 2:20). Rather, love is like the attitude of believers at Ephesus. God commended them: *"But you have this in your favor: You hate the practices of the Nicolaitans, which I also hate"* (Rev. 2:6). Love feels toward evil what a father feels toward someone who wants to kidnap his child.

Q 57 ➤ *What is the greatest deception of this generation? Explain.*

Love is not attracted to evil. Because candy is sweet, we like to turn it over and over in our mouths. Likewise, some temptations are sweet to the flesh. We may be tempted to befriend or indulge "sweet" thoughts about lust, vengeance, greed, or pride. Paul shines a light on such sloppy, fleshly thinking. In Romans 6–8 he exposed sin for what it is—a law unto itself; rebellion against God's law. And in Romans 12:9, Paul guides us to see life through the eyes of God. The Word of God and the Spirit of God train us to hate what is wrong. We must beware of being at ease or comfortable with evil. We must refuse to let evil entertain us. We must abhor letting evil befriend us. Love does not flirt with evil. It does not pet what is sinful. Reject an evil thought from your mind like you would spit out a bitter seed. Love hates evil, as a man hates a poisonous snake about to strike. The world is immoral. It says, "Follow your heart." But the Bible says, "Hate what is wrong and cling to what is right." God is love. But the greatest deception of this generation is the notion that love can enjoy short walks with God between the times we fellowship with evil. To be friends of God, we must be enemies of evil.

Jesus warned that in the last days, because evil will abound, the love of most would grow cold (Matt. 24:12). As water puts out fire, evil can quench biblical love. So let us train ourselves to have the proper attitude toward evil—hating what is wrong. This is the first side of love that Paul mentions in Romans 12:9. As we hate evil, we fellowship with God.

Let those who love the LORD hate evil, for he guards the lives of his faithful ones and delivers them from the hand of the wicked (Ps. 97:10).

Love clings! Love is not one-sided. Rather, love is like a coin—it has two sides. The second side of love is that it *clings* to what is good. The Greek word for *clings* (*kollaomai*) appears in Paul's writings only with reference to sexual relations (1 Cor. 6:16-17; see also Matt. 19:5).[41] Paul guides us to cling to what is good as a man marries, unites with, and cleaves to his wife. Love embraces what is right, just as much as it hates what is wrong.

Love cleaves to what is right as Ruth clung to Naomi. With a continuous, steadfast attitude, love holds on to what is pure, just, and righteous. As Christ is committed to the Church, love hugs, holds tight to, and fastens itself to righteousness.

Practicing Romans 12:9 is a key to God's favor and blessing. For as we hate evil and love good, we imitate and fellowship with God. This enables God to conform us to His likeness and fulfill all of His will for us. Practicing Romans 12:9 was a key to the exaltation of Jesus. Recall Hebrews 1:9.

You have loved righteousness and hated wickedness; therefore God, your God, has set you above your companions by anointing you with the oil of joy (Heb. 1:9; compare Ps. 97:10).

Do yourself a favor: follow the footprints of Jesus. Practice sincere, consistent love—hate evil and cling to good (Rom. 12:9; 1 Thess. 5:20-22; Heb. 1:9; Ps. 97:10).

Q 58 *What are the 2 sides of love?*

Romans	Nine Principles of *Agape* Love
12:9	**A.** Love is more than a feeling or a daydream—it has a moral backbone.
12:10	**B.** Love puts others first.
12:11	**C.** Love fuels its fire from the source—the Holy Spirit.
12:12	**D.** Love is tough—it perseveres through hard times.
12:13	**E** Love shares with believers in need, even when they are strangers.
12:15	**F.** Love empathizes—it laughs and cries with others.
12:16	**G.** Love crosses social boundaries.
12:17-19	**H.** Love never hits back—it leaves vengeance to God.
12:14, 20-21	**I.** Love overcomes enemies with good deeds.

Figure 9.9   Nine principles about sincere love (Rom. 12:9-21)

B. Love puts others first (Rom. 12:10).

Q 59 *Explain how love shines through 3 circles (Rom. 12:9-21).*

Be devoted to one another in brotherly love. Honor one another above yourselves (Rom. 12:10).

Paul put *agape* love as a banner over Romans 12:9-21. In these verses, love shines outward in three expanding circles: 1) love for believers, 2) love for strangers, and 3) love for enemies (Figure 9.10).[42]

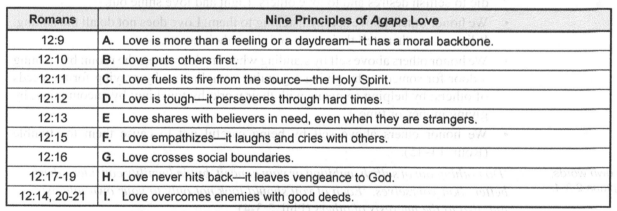

Figure 9.10   Three circles of love in Romans 12:9-21. Note that love begins with believers we know, then extends to strangers, and even to enemies who persecute us.

1 —> Love for brothers we know, Romans 12:10a
(Greek: *philadelphia*, brotherly love; and *philostorgos*, devotion/family love)

2 —> Love for strangers, Romans 12:13 (Greek: *philoxenia*, love for strangers; translated as hospitality)

3 —> Love for enemies who persecute us, Romans 12:14, 17-21
(Compare Matt. 5:44-48, which has a Greek form of *agape*.)

Q 60 ⬈ *What paradigm shift does God's love cause in us?*

Love begins at home, in the family of God. Family love is the tender love between a husband and wife. This is the tender love that fathers and mothers have for their children. It is the love of brothers and sisters for each other. Paul is teaching that in the family of God, we believers should have tender love for each other.

Romans 12:10b emphasizes that love has a respect and regard for others—putting them first. Other verses of the New Testament teach us to love others *as* we love ourselves. God expects us to be concerned about our own needs. But in Romans 12, Paul is emphasizing relationships and our orientation in life. The lesson is that the love of God frees us from loving *only* ourselves. God's love teaches us to be concerned about the needs of others. Biblical love gives us a change of perspective—a paradigm shift. God's love enables and inspires us to look away from the mirror and through the window at others.

Q 61 ⬊ *What are some ways you honor others above yourself?*

Application: What are some ways that we regard and honor others above ourselves?

- We use our gifts to honor others above ourselves. As we serve others, we put them first. Paul wrote about this in Romans 12:3-8. We look for ways to prophesy, edify, serve, teach, encourage, share, lead, and show mercy. Using our spiritual gifts is a way of life—a way to honor others above ourselves. Jesus modeled this by washing feet. And yet foot washing was just an example of His lifestyle. Almost everything Jesus did was for someone else. A fruit tree does not eat its own fruit. It lives to bless others. Likewise, as we follow Jesus, He teaches us to die to selfish desires and to love others. Light and love shine out.

- We honor others above self by listening to them. Love does not do all the talking. It listens as others tell their story and share their hearts.

- We honor others above self by standing when an elder enters the room; by opening a door for someone; by giving a genuine compliment; by praying for the needs of others; by helping someone with their work; by touching; by encouraging; by giving money or time.

- We honor others above self by being careful not to cause them to stumble (Rom. 14–15).

Q 62 ⬊ *In your own words, summarize Philippians 2:3-4.*

3Do nothing out of selfish ambition or vain conceit, but in humility consider others better than yourselves. 4Each of you should look not only to your own interests, but also to the interests of others (Phil. 2:3-4).

C. Love fuels its fire from the source—the Holy Spirit (Rom. 12:11).

The Need: *"Never be lacking in zeal, but keep your spiritual fervor, serving the Lord"* (Rom. 12:11).

The Greek text has: *"In diligence, not lazy; in the Spirit, zealous; in the Lord, serving"* (Rom. 12:11).

One scholar translates this: *"In zeal, do not be lazy. Be set on fire by the Spirit. Serve the Lord."*[43]

The word for *zeal* means "boiling over." Our love for God should be red hot, like the love of Apollos, who *"spoke with great fervor"* (Acts 18:25).

Q 63 ⬊ *What are some examples of love that has become lukewarm or cold?*

The Problem: Jesus was not happy with the lukewarm love of believers at Ephesus. He told them, *"Yet I hold this against you: You have forsaken your first love"* (Rev. 2:4). Likewise, Jesus warned believers at Laodicea: *15"I know your deeds, that you are neither cold nor hot. I wish you were either one or the other! 16So, because you are lukewarm—neither hot nor cold—I am about to spit you out of my mouth"* (Rev. 3:15-16).

Q 64 ⬊ *What warning did Jesus give about the love of most (Matt. 24:12)?*

A great concern in the modern church is her lack of zeal. So many believers have cooled off. The passion that marked the church in revival days is gone in some places.

Joshua showed zeal for God when he challenged the Israelites (Josh. 24:15). David showed zeal for God when he killed Goliath (1 Sam. 17:26). Isaiah showed zeal for God when he said, *"Here am I. Send me!"* (Isa. 6:8). Paul's love was hot when he wrote:

> ²*I have great sorrow and unceasing anguish in my heart.* ³*For I could wish that I myself were cursed and cut off from Christ for the sake of my brothers, those of my own race,* ⁴*the people of Israel* (Rom. 9:2-4).

The Solution: Read Romans 12:11 again, and notice that God gives us some responsibility. He tells us not to be lazy. God expects us to keep our love hot. But how can we keep the fire burning?

Earlier, in Romans 8, over 20 times, Paul emphasized depending on the Spirit. The hot love that Paul describes comes from a combination of two things: personal diligence (zeal without laziness, Rom. 12:11) and the Spirit's fire (1 Thess. 5:19; Eph. 5:18; Acts 1:8).[44]

The love Paul is writing about is neither natural nor human. Loving others instead of self, loving strangers, loving our enemies—this is impossible in our own strength! But with God all things are possible. As the Spirit of God fills us, we have the resources of heaven to live on earth.

> **AS THE SPIRIT OF GOD FILLS US, WE HAVE THE RESOURCES OF HEAVEN TO LIVE ON EARTH.**

Q 65 *What are 3 keys to keeping our zeal for God hot?*

How do we maintain our zeal and love for God? This question takes us back to the beginning of Romans 12:1. Day by day we must remember the mercy God has shown us. His love inspires us. We love Him because He first loved us (1 John 4:19). The Holy Spirit makes this love ever new, always real to us. God has poured out His love into our hearts by the Holy Spirit, whom He has given us (Rom. 5:5). As we are filled with the Spirit, we are filled with zeal and hot love for God. And to be filled with the Spirit daily, we must take time to enjoy God's presence in prayer, worship, and Bible study. Likewise, we must avoid being conformed to the world. The sinful influence of the world is a serial killer of love for God. Jesus prophesied that the world's increasing sinfulness will cause the love of most to grow cold (Rom. 12:2; Matt. 24:12). Take a few minutes to review Lesson 33, point D, near the beginning of this chapter. The key to keeping our love for God hot is to live filled with the Holy Spirit.

> **THE SINFUL INFLUENCE OF THE WORLD IS A SERIAL KILLER OF LOVE FOR GOD.**

D. Love is tough—it perseveres through hard times (Rom. 12:12).

Recall that Romans 12:9-21 is about qualities of sincere, genuine love. In Romans 12:11 Paul emphasized that love is zealous. It serves with fervor and passion. Note the trio that follows zeal: *"Be joyful in hope, patient in affliction, faithful in prayer"* (Rom. 12:12).

Paul puts zeal, joy, patience, and faithfulness side by side. These four faces of love befriend each other. They work together and strengthen each other.

Also note the setting of zeal's three friends. As a picture in a frame, joy is in hope, patience is in affliction, and faithfulness is in prayer. Let us take a closer look at each.

Be joyful in hope. Love rejoices in hope. In other words, love looks ahead. Sometimes the circumstances of our love are dark and gloomy. Everyone and everything around us may be frowning. But God's love reminds us to look ahead. Victory is as certain as the cross and the resurrection of Christ. Jesus has gone to prepare a place for us. God has promised to give Himself to us forever. A time is coming when there will be no more pain, no more sorrow, no more sin, no more night. Jesus promised He would come back and take us to be with Him forever. This Blessed Hope fills us with joy. Love is tough—it is joyful in hope. It sings about things unseen.

Q 66 *How does hope encourage our love for God?*

Be patient (persevere) in affliction. Love is patient in afflictions. Love endures trials. Love *"always trusts, always hopes, always perseveres"* (1 Cor. 13:7). Love is tough. You can knock it down, but it will get up. You can beat love and lock it in prison, but it will still sing (Acts 16). You can nail love to a cross and bury it. But it will rise again. Love never fails. The early believers lost their family members, their friends, their possessions, their freedom, and their lives (Heb. 10:32-34). But love enabled them to endure all these afflictions. Patience and endurance are qualities of love. As a star shines in the night, endurance glows in affliction.

Be faithful in prayer. Love manifests itself in prayer. Because a husband loves his wife, he wants to talk with her. If a young woman loves a man, she wants to share life with him. Likewise, our love for God draws us to Him. The God of the universe is our friend. He has given His Son to redeem us. He has adopted us into His family. He has put His Spirit within us. He has filled our hearts with His love. He has captured our hearts. And He has opened the door to us to talk with Him on any and every occasion. As a magnet attracts metal, God's love draws us to Him. Throughout every day, let us enjoy His presence. May our thoughts and our words be a prayer to please Him. May we offer our actions as a prayer to Him. May we offer our bodies to God as a prayer and a living sacrifice of worship. In prayer let us share with Him every heartache and every song— every trial and every victory. Let us be faithful in prayer. For sure, there must be times of private prayer when we are alone with God. But let our lives also be a constant prayer. Let us pray without ceasing (1 Thess. 5:17). Lord, let my life be a prayer. Teach me to live in unbroken communion with You. Like Watchman Nee, let us practice the presence of God.

John Wesley was a great preacher. For many years he began every day with 2 hours of prayer and Bible study. And he continued to pray throughout the day, whatever he did. As he went from place to place, he often greeted people with the question: "Do I meet you praying?" Likewise, prayer became such a habit for John Fletcher that he did not stand up without praying. General "Stonewall" Jackson said that prayer was so much a part of his life that he did not even raise a glass of water to his lips without praying as he did it.[45] Charles Spurgeon testified that in the hours he was awake, there was never a period of 15 minutes that He was unaware of God's presence. Brothers and sisters, prayer is our greatest privilege. Let us be faithful in prayer!

Love for God helped Jacob wrestle with an angel and receive a blessing (Gen. 32:24-29). Caleb and Joshua entered the land of promise because of their love for God (Num. 14:24, 38). The early church stood firm in times of trouble. *"They devoted themselves to the apostles' teaching and to the fellowship, to the breaking of bread and to prayer"* (Acts 2:42).

The love of God is tough. It is *"joyful in hope, patient in affliction, faithful in prayer"* (Rom. 12:12).

E. Love shares with believers in need—even when they are strangers (Rom. 12:13).

"Share with God's people who are in need. Practice hospitality" (Rom. 12:13).

Sharing is another word for *giving*. Recall that we studied the gift of giving in Lesson 34, section D., point 5. Take a couple of minutes to review the paragraphs about giving (Rom. 12:8). Giving is one of the ministry gifts that applies to all believers.

Love gives. We can give without loving, but we cannot love without giving. Giving is the mother tongue that love speaks. It is the proof of our relationship with God. We measure length with a ruler, and we measure love with giving. The more we love, the more we reflect the image of God.

Paul emphasizes that sharing begins with the family of God. *"Share with God's people who are in need"* (Rom. 12:13). Believers should share with all, but especially other believers. *"Therefore, as we have opportunity, let us do good to all people, especially to those who belong to the family of believers"* (Gal. 6:10). In the parable of the sheep and the goats, Jesus stressed sharing with *the least of His brothers*—believers in the family of God (Matt. 25:31-46). Paul collected offerings from believers for the poor saints in Jerusalem (1 Cor. 16:1-4). The hands we raise to God must be the same

Q 67 — *What are some forms of prayer in which we practice faithfulness?*

Q 68 — *How much of your life each day is a form of prayer?*

Q 69 — *Give an example of a believer with whom you shared, or one who shared with you.*

hands that reach out to share with believers in need.[46] Otherwise, our life song is out of tune, like the person who sang in one key while playing a guitar in another. Our deeds must match our words. Otherwise, we are like the person who wore a boot on one foot and a sandal on the other.

Believers of all ages face hard times. Some lose their possessions due to persecution (Acts 8:1-3; Heb. 10). In the early church, wherever believers scattered, they looked for any work they could find to get money for food. But rich employers often stole from poor believers (James 5:1-6). Likewise today, many oppress the poor. Employers often cheat the illiterate. Other human causes of poverty include war, political fighting, weak economies, lack of education, poor farming methods, over-population, addictions, unwise health practices, and foolish spending. Likewise, poverty often results from disasters of nature, such as drought, famine, earthquakes, hurricanes, tsunamis, and tornadoes. As Jesus said, we have the poor with us always—for many reasons. Sincere love guides those with more to share with those with less.

Romans 12:13b says, *"Practice hospitality."* The Greek word for hospitality is *philoxenia,* and means "love of strangers."[47] Review Figure 9.10. Love begins with believers we know, and then extends to believers who are strangers. The early church needed to practice hospitality, because many hotels and inns had a bad reputation.[48] Some inns were very dirty. Other inns were houses for prostitution. So the first missionaries and evangelists had few places to stay, except with other believers. Aquila and Priscilla were hospitable to Apollos (Acts 18:26). In so doing, they made him a better preacher. And John commended Gaius for showing hospitality to traveling preachers (3 John 5-8). Hebrews 13:2 says to help strangers, *"for by so doing some people have entertained [helped] angels without knowing it."*

Application: Today, there are more hotels, and yet many believers still appreciate staying in homes when they travel. Last week, some friends of ours traveled several hundred miles to see their daughter graduate from college. They were thankful to stay in our home, saving the expense of a hotel and meals. And we enjoyed the fellowship. Likewise, we have won many unbelievers to Christ after they have eaten in our home several times. And we have discipled many believers for Christ in our home. In times of fire, disasters, and unemployment, many people need a roof over their heads. *"As we have opportunity, let us do good to all people, especially to those who belong to the family of believers"* (Gal. 6:10). Many have entered the kingdom of God through the door of a believer's home. And many have grown in Christ in home meetings.

Share with God's people who are in need. Practice hospitality (Rom. 12:13).

Lesson 37 · Nine Principles of *Agape* Love—Part 2 (Rom. 12:14-21)

Goal A: *Illustrate ways that love empathizes (Rom. 12:15).*
Goal B: *Give illustrations to show that love crosses social boundaries (Rom. 12:16).*
Goal C: *Illustrate ways that love is passive at times and active at other times (Rom. 12:17-19, 21).*

In Lesson 36 we covered the first five principles of *agape* love. Now, in Lesson 37 we continue with the last four principles, F–I.

F. Love empathizes—it laughs and cries with others (Rom. 12:15).

Rejoice with those who rejoice; mourn with those who mourn (Rom. 12:15).

Jesus rejoiced at the wedding in Cana and mourned at the tomb of Lazarus.[49] Which is harder, to rejoice with those who rejoice or to mourn with those who mourn? Most of us can cry with those who are crying. But sometimes it is difficult to share the joy of others. Envy asks, "Why am I not blessed in that way? Why did I miss the financial increase? Why did I not receive healing—the church prayed for both of us?"

Q 70 In your culture, do people celebrate the successes of others, and mourn their defeats? Explain.

Group societies find it easier to obey Romans 12:15. There are at least two types of society: individual and group. America is an example of a society that focuses on the individual. English is the only language that capitalizes the letter "I". Too often, some Americans live life alone, or in very small groups. So these Americans may have difficulty sharing the victories and sorrows of others. Still, it is not possible to judge all people by the nation in which they live. Many Americans feel what others feel. But perhaps, in their culture, these Americans are like a fish swimming upstream. In contrast, in group societies it is common for people to share life as a group. In this way, what one person feels, all in the group feel. Believers of the first century lived in a group society. They ate together, prayed together, suffered together, and worshiped together. Note that whenever Paul writes about the spiritual gift of *one person,* the context is always *a body* of Christ. Whatever a person's culture is, in Christ, God teaches us to laugh and cry *together* with our brothers and sisters.

Q 71 What are some examples of times that believers should laugh or cry together?

David mourned over the death of Saul and Jonathan (2 Sam. 1:17-27). And Jesus mourned at the tomb of Lazarus (John 11:35). Naomi's friends rejoiced with her at the birth of her grandson (Ruth 4:14-15). And the neighbors of Elizabeth rejoiced with her when John the Baptist was born (Luke 1:58; compare 1:39-45). Job's friends mourned in silence with him for 7 days (Job 2:11-13). In the three parables of Luke 15, those rejoicing invited others to celebrate. And all of heaven celebrates when one sinner comes to Christ. Heaven is a group society. And on earth, believers are members of one family. We laugh and cry with each other.

G. Love crosses social boundaries (Rom. 12:16).[50]

Q 72 What are the 4 commands of Romans 12:16?

Live in harmony with one another. Do not be proud, but be willing to associate with people of low position. Do not be conceited (Rom. 12:16).

> HUMILITY IS THE OIL THAT KEEPS RELATIONSHIPS FROM SQUEAKING.

The four commands in this verse go together. Paul is writing about relationships. Please read Romans 12:16 again, noting the four commands. Note that the last three commands tell us how to fulfill the first command of Romans 12:16. What is the key to living in harmony with others? Do not be proud. Befriend the lowly. Do not be conceited. Sabio says, "Humility is the oil that keeps relationships from squeaking."

Fleshly people like to stand close to "big shots." We humans want to be in photos with the world's heroes. We seek the signatures of the rich and famous. We like to have our names linked to the biggest and the best. As one man said, "You are truly famous when someone brags about sitting beside you in primary school." Humans crave relationships with people of power and influence. This is human nature.

Q 73 Give examples of "Love feels at home with little people."

In contrast, love feels at home with little people. Jesus is love's greatest example of humility. Paul wrote:

> [3]*Do nothing out of selfish ambition or vain conceit, but in humility consider others better than yourselves.* [4]*Each of you should look not only to your own interests, but also to the interests of others.* [5]*Your attitude should be the same as that of Christ Jesus:* [6]*Who, being in very nature God, did not consider equality with God something to be grasped,* [7]*but made himself nothing, taking the very nature of a servant, being made in human likeness.* [8]*And being found in appearance as a man, he humbled himself and became obedient to death—even death on a cross!* (Phil. 2:3-8).

Paul guides us to imitate the attitude of Jesus. He left a throne in heaven to come and serve us! Imagine how many stairs He came down. Consider how Love put Himself last, and put us first. There is a great contrast between a king and a beggar. But ponder the distance between God and us! Love is not proud. It is *"willing to associate with people of low position"* (Rom. 12:16).

In Bible times, befriending the lowly was the opposite of what culture taught. But sometimes the love of heaven challenges the customs of earth. Recall what Jesus taught about inviting people for a meal:

> Then Jesus said to his host, [12] *"When you give a luncheon or dinner, do not invite your friends, your brothers or relatives, or your rich neighbors; if you do, they may invite you back and so you will be repaid.* [13] *But when you give a banquet, invite the poor, the crippled, the lame, the blind,* [14] *and you will be blessed. Although they cannot repay you, you will be repaid at the resurrection of the righteous"* (Luke 14:12-14).

Love reaches across fences. It crosses social boundaries. Jesus talked to the woman at the well (John 4:4-26). Recall that she was a Samaritan, and a sinful one. And Jesus was a Jew. Jews did not talk with Samaritans. Yet He talked with her. And in one of His parables, the good Samaritan was the hero (Luke 11:29-37). Love crosses social boundaries. Jesus touched a leper (Matt. 8:1-4). He helped a Roman centurion (Matt. 8:5-13). Imagine this. The Romans conquered the Jews, but Jesus healed the servant of a Roman. Likewise, He ministered to tax collectors and prostitutes, and delivered the daughter of a Canaanite woman, a social outcast of Israel (Matt. 15:22-28). The apostles felt above helping children. But Jesus took time to bless these little ones (Matt. 19:13-15). And His genealogy includes women from several nations (Matt. 1). Jesus showed us that love crosses social boundaries.

Q 74 *What are some ways that the love of Jesus crossed social boundaries?*

Application: Love crosses social boundaries. It reaches to befriend those with less education or money. Love shakes hands with those across ethnic and tribal boundaries. When love rules, Jews and Gentiles, rich and poor, employers and employees, black and white, brown and yellow, red and brown sit side by side at the same table. In your setting, if you sit beside the lowly, who is beside you? Who is the Samaritan that love wants you to talk with? Who is the poor person that love invites to your home for a meal? Who are those lower than you that love wants you to befriend, encourage, and bless?

Q 75 *What are some ways that your love can cross social boundaries?*

Some nations have a *caste system of social levels. In a caste system, the worth of people is thought to be unequal. A caste system allows little change in social position. Only birth and ancestors determine a person's future. Caste systems are found in many parts of the world (see Figure 9.11). There is no caste system in the kingdom of God. In Christ, a rich master and a slave become members of the same family, with the same Father (Philemon). In God's kingdom *"there is neither Jew nor Greek, slave nor free, male nor female, for you are all one in Christ Jesus"* (Gal. 3:28). Spain established a caste system to control society (Figure 9.11). A caste system stirs up resentments. It makes the upper class feel proud, and the lower classes feel bitter. But when love rules, it stretches its arms around all people and unites them into one family, as children of God the Father.

Upper Class
Judges
Top traders

Middle Class
Traders
Noble Indians
Mayors

Lower Class
Poor Spaniards | Mestizos
Indian people | Free people
| Castas

Slaves

Figure 9.11   This shows a caste system of four social levels in Peru when Spain conquered the Americas (1492–1898.)[51] The four levels were: Upper Class of judges and top traders; Middle Class of traders, noble Indians, and mayors; Lower Class of poor Spaniards, Indian people, *mestizos (a mixture of European and indigenous), free people with dark skin, and the castas (mixed race); Bottom, slaves.[52]

H. Love is passive—it never hits back, but leaves vengeance to God (Rom. 12:17-19).

[17]Do not repay anyone evil for evil. Be careful to do what is right in the eyes of everybody. [18]If it is possible, as far as it depends on you, live at peace with everyone. [19]Do not take revenge, my friends, but leave room for God's wrath, for it is written: "It is mine to avenge; I will repay," says the Lord (Rom. 12:17-19).

When others offend us, we are tempted to return evil for evil. But when someone is rude to us, our first reaction is often wrong. The flesh wants to curse those who persecute us. Paul forbids this reaction. Rather, he commands us *"do not curse"* those who persecute us—whether they are Christian or unchristian (Rom. 12:14). Again Paul says, *"Do not repay <u>anyone</u> evil for evil"*—in the church, or in the world (Rom. 12:17). Love does not hit back. It does not punch those who do evil. Jesus says the same thing. *[39]... "If someone strikes you on the right cheek, turn to him the other also. [40]And if someone wants to sue you and take your tunic, let him have your cloak as well. [41]If someone forces you to go one mile, go with him two miles"* (Matt. 5:39-41).

> THOSE WHO FIGHT FIRE WITH FIRE BURN EVERYTHING UP.

Those who return evil for evil disobey Romans 12:17. These are doing what is wrong in the eyes of everybody. These ruin their witness for Christ. They give the church a bad name. Sabio says, "Those who fight fire with fire burn everything up."

At an intersection, a car stopped and was slow to move ahead. The driver behind the slow car became furious. He honked his horn, yelled harsh words, and made angry signs with his hand. Just then, the angry driver heard a noise on his car window and looked into the face of a police officer. The policeman ordered the man to get out of the car and put his hands up. Then he took the angry driver to the police station. There they took his fingerprints, his photo, and locked him in a cell. After 2 hours, the policeman returned, opened the door, and freed the prisoner. The policeman said, "I'm sorry for this mistake. I pulled behind your car while you were blowing your horn, swearing, and making angry signs at the driver in front of you. I noticed that on the bumper of your car you had three stickers. One said: What Would Jesus Do? Another said: Follow Me to Sunday School. The third sticker was the Christian fish symbol. So I assumed you had stolen the car."

Q 76 *How can we avoid or end many quarrels?*

Paul does not say we can be at peace with everyone. Sometimes peace is impossible. So Paul says, *"If it is possible, as far as it depends on you, live at peace with everyone"* (Rom. 12:18). We cannot control the attitudes or actions of others. But Paul says we are responsible for our own thoughts and deeds.

> FIRE COOLS DOWN AND GOES OUT WHEN NO ONE ADDS WOOD.

Those who refuse to fight back gain respect and influence, even outside the church. *Ghandi won the respect of the world. When the British ruled India, Ghandi led his people in passive resistance. In time, this attitude led to freedom. Those who choose not to hit back are not weak. The nonviolent are strong. The nonviolent have great power to change others. This teaching is a key to solving conflicts. Someone must choose not to "hit back." The nonviolent response opens the door to peace. Refusing to return evil for evil decreases most personal conflicts. Sabio says, "Fire cools down and goes out when no one adds wood."

Saul tried to kill David at least twice (1 Sam. 18:11; 19:10). But David refused to strike back. Jesus did not hit back when members of the Sanhedrin slapped His face (Matt. 26:67; 1 Pet. 2:23). He was like a lamb led to the slaughter. Neither did Paul hit back when the guard slapped his jaw (Acts 23:1-3).

Love lets God even the score (Rom. 12:19). Refusing to hit back does not mean justice will not come. For God is the judge of all evil. *"Do not take revenge, my friends, but leave room for God's wrath, for it is written: 'It is mine to avenge; I will repay,' says the Lord"* (Rom. 12:19). So when we refuse to hit back, we are refusing to sit on the throne that belongs only to God. Revenge does not belong to us. God says, *"It is mine to avenge; I will repay"* (Rom. 12:19). Those who take vengeance into their own hands are proud, acting like they are God. So let us walk in humility, and let God be God. He will repay, just as Deuteronomy 32:35 promises (see also Luke 18:7). Only God is qualified to avenge. He knows all the facts of every case. Humans who take revenge stoop to the level of their enemies.[53] They assume God's position. Sabio says, "Two wrongs never make one right."

All of us may feel like striking back when others abuse or persecute us. But the Scriptures assure us that the Judge of all the earth will do right (Gen. 18:25). And when we cool down, let us look on our enemies with pity and mercy. And let us pray that our enemies will repent and turn from the terrible wrath of God that is coming. For the eternal judgment of God is severe. As His love is greater than ours, His wrath is also greater. Picture your worst enemy. Summarize all this person has done to you. In return for this, would you like for this person to suffer the fires of hell forever and ever? Is your life so important that you would wish for your personal enemies to suffer in the flames of hell forever? And yet, those who have offended believers have offended One of much greater importance, worth, and power. And He WILL repay them. So let us pity these offenders, and pray that they will turn from the wrath of God before it scalds them forever in eternal darkness. May even our worst enemies receive the forgiveness that we have received.

> [6]*God is just: He will pay back trouble to those who trouble you* [7]*and give relief to you who are troubled, and to us as well. This will happen when the Lord Jesus is revealed from heaven in blazing fire with his powerful angels.* [8]*He will punish those who do not know God and do not obey the gospel of our Lord Jesus.* [9]*They will be punished with everlasting destruction and shut out from the presence of the Lord and from the majesty of his power* [10]*on the day he comes to be glorified in his holy people and to be marveled at among all those who have believed* (2 Thess. 1:6-10).

> *"Do not seek revenge or bear a grudge against one of your people, but love your neighbor as yourself. I am the LORD"* (Lev. 19:18).

Love is passive. It never hits back, but leaves vengeance to God (Rom. 12:17-19).

I. Love is active—it overcomes enemies with good deeds (Rom. 12:20-21).

> [20]*On the contrary: "If your enemy is hungry, feed him; if he is thirsty, give him something to drink. In doing this, you will heap burning coals on his head."* [21]*Do not be overcome by evil, but overcome evil with good* (Rom. 12:20-21).

When love is passive, refusing to hit back, it wins only half of the victory. It is not enough to refrain from returning evil for evil. The goal of love must be to overcome evil with good.[54] Believers do not fight fire with fire. Instead, we spray the flames of evil with the waters of kindness.

Paul quotes Proverbs 25:21-22 to make his point. The coals of fire may refer to an ancient custom. In Egypt, to show repentance, a person carried a pot of burning coals on his head. This was a sign of repentance. So Paul may be referring to this old custom (Prov. 25:22).[55] In other words, deeds of kindness toward an enemy may make the person feel ashamed, leading to repentance. The best way to get rid of enemies is to make them into friends.[56]

Q 77 *Does refusing to hit back mean sinners will not be punished? Explain.*

Q 78 *What encourages us to pity our enemies rather than to seek revenge?*

Q 79 *Is there someone you need to forgive and to commit to God's justice?*

Q 80 ↖ *In your own words, summarize what each passage in Figure 9.12 teaches about returning good for evil.*

Reference	Your summary
Gen. 42:21	
Gen. 50:19-21	
Matt. 5:43-45	
Luke 23:34	
Acts 7:59-60	
Rom. 12:14	
Rom. 12:20-21	

Figure 9.12　Practice summarizing verses about returning good for evil.

In Egypt, Joseph could have taken revenge against his brothers. They deserved punishment for what they had done to him (Gen. 42:21). But Joseph did not seek revenge. Instead, he chose to overcome evil with good (Gen. 50:19-21). Christ could have called for thousands of angels to fight on His behalf (Matt. 26:53). But He did not. Christ overcame the worst evil of all time with good.

God tries to overcome evil with good. *"Do you show contempt for the riches of his kindness, tolerance and patience, not realizing that God's kindness leads you toward repentance?"* (Rom. 2:4). Let us imitate our Father.

Q 81 ↖ *Is it possible to obey the nine principles of love in Romans 12:9-21? Explain.*

Conclusion:　When we ponder these nine characteristics of love, we may be tempted to turn away, saying, "I can never love like this." But recall that Paul is not asking how much we can bring to the table. He wrote Romans 1–11 to summarize all that God has done for us. Our Father has forgiven our sins, and adopted us into His family. He has poured out His love in our hearts, and filled us with His Spirit. And the lesson of Romans 12 is that, because of all that God has done for and in us, we can obey Romans 12. He has freed us from sin and filled us with the power to love, as we walk in the Spirit.[57] By ourselves, we are not able to love as Romans 12:9-21 teaches. But this is possible as we surrender ourselves to God as living sacrifices. It may be natural to curse those who mistreat us. But it is supernatural to bless those who persecute us.

Test Yourself: Circle the letter by the **best** completion to each question or statement.

1. Why does God require greater sacrifice under the New Testament?
a) He wants us to give more of ourselves.
b) Worship under the New Testament is more expensive.
c) He offers us more of Himself.
d) We have more to give under the New Testament.

2. Why is sacrifice under the New Testament more personal?
a) A human body is more personal than an animal.
b) Under the Old Testament some sacrificed grain.
c) Jesus is more personal than an Old Testament high priest.
d) There were many Levites, but only one Savior.

3. What is the negative side of responding to God?
a) Do not covet your neighbor's property.
b) Avoid the appearance of evil.
c) Do not conform to the world.
d) Be transformed in your mind.

4. What is the general will of God for believers?
a) Repent and be saved from sin.
b) Go into all the world and preach the gospel.
c) Love your neighbor as yourself.
d) Be conformed to the image of Christ.

5. Which helps us measure ourselves accurately?
a) Praying while looking in the mirror
b) Considering the body of Christ
c) Remembering our past, present, and future
d) Using a measure that is spiritual

6. Which is a spiritual gift of Romans 12:3-8?
a) Administration
b) Love
c) Mercy
d) Evangelists

7. Which is TRUE of biblical love?
a) It serves on the basis of feelings.
b) It requires no conditions for fellowship.
c) It treats all people the same.
d) It hates things that are wrong.

8. What is the key to refueling our love?
a) Turning away from our enemies
b) Living far from evil
c) Being wise about who we love
d) Staying close to the source

9. Which of these does love cross?
a) Social boundaries
b) The line between good and evil
c) The cross of Calvary
d) The distance to eternity

10. Which best describes love?
a) Love is active
b) Love is passive
c) Love is both active and passive
d) Love is active, but never passive

 Essay Test Topics: Write 50-100 words on each of these goals that you studied in this chapter.

- Contrast the sacrifice demanded in Romans 12:1 with the Old Testament sacrifices.
- Explain and illustrate how our response to God's mercy is personal, logical, and spiritual.
- Explain the negative and positive sides of our response to God's mercy (Rom. 12:2).
- Identify the result of presenting our bodies as living sacrifices to Christ (Rom. 12:1-2).
- Contrast the general and specific will of God for believers.
- Explain 3 factors that help us measure ourselves accurately.
- Analyze and illustrate 7 examples of spiritual gifts in Romans 12:3-8.
- Summarize and illustrate the moral nature of *agape* love (Rom. 12:9).
- Explain principles on how love relates to others, even strangers (Rom. 12:10, 13).
- Clarify how we renew and refuel our love (Rom. 12:11).
- Analyze some aspects that strengthen the toughness of love (Rom. 12:12).
- Illustrate ways that love empathizes (Rom. 12:15).
- Give illustrations to show that love crosses social boundaries (Rom. 12:16).
- Illustrate ways that love is passive at times and active at other times (Rom. 12:17-19, 21).

Chapter 10:
Relationships—Part 2
(Romans 13:1–15:13)

Introduction

In Romans 12–13, Paul emphasizes the teachings of Jesus. As you begin this lesson, fill in the chart of Figure 10.1.

Q 1 ⬍ *Complete Figure 10.1 by filling in the third column.*

Gospels	Teaching of Jesus	Teaching of Paul	Rom.
Luke 6:28	*Bless those who curse you.*		12:14
Matt. 5:39	*Do not resist an evil person.*		12:17
Matt. 5:9; Mark 9:50	*Blessed are the peacemakers. Be at peace with each other.*		12:18; 14:19
Luke 6:27; Matt. 5:44	*Love your enemies, do good to those who hate you.*		12:20
Mark 12:14, 17	*Is it right to pay taxes to Caesar or not? ... Give to Caesar what is Caesar's, and to God what is God's.*		13:7
John 13:34-35	*Love one another.*		13:8
Matt. 22:37-40	*Love the Lord your God. ... Love your neighbor as yourself. All the Law and the Prophets hang on these two commandments.*		13:8
Matt. 7:12	*Do to others what you would have them do to you, for this sums up the Law and the Prophets.*		13:9
Luke 12:56	*How is it that you don't know how to interpret this present time?*		13:11a
Mark 13:36 Luke 21:28	*Do not let him find you sleeping. Your redemption is drawing near.*		13:11b, c

Figure 10.1   Practice chart comparing teachings of Jesus and Paul (Rom. 12–13).[1]

Lessons:

Living as a Citizen of Two Worlds—Part 1 (Rom. 13:1-7)
Goal A: *Summarize at least 3 attitudes toward the government in Paul's day.*
Goal B: *Explain 4 reasons why believers must submit to government (Rom. 13:1-5).*
Goal C: *Summarize 7 reasons why God may allow an evil government.*
Goal D: *Identify some debts that believers owe as citizens (Rom. 13:1-7).*

Living as a Citizen of Two Worlds—Part 2 (Rom. 13:8-14)
Goal A: *Explain: A believer is always in debt (Rom. 13:8-10). Illustrate this.*
Goal B: *Explain and illustrate 3 aspects of walking in love (Rom. 13:11-14).*

The Weak and the Strong on Debated Matters—Part 1 (Rom. 14:1–15:13)
Goal A: *Summarize the background of Romans 14:1–15:13.*
Goal B: *Identify 3 types of matters that believers face (Figure 10.8, Rom. 14:1–15:13).*
Goal C: *Explain the reason why believers should accept and not judge one another (Rom. 14:1-12; 15:7).*

The Weak and the Strong on Debated Matters—Part 2 (Rom. 14:1–15:13)
Goal A: *Describe 4 types of people in or around the church (Figure 10.9).*
Goal B: *Explain how love avoids tripping or trapping a brother (Rom. 14:13-23). Give illustrations.*
Goal C: *Give examples of how a strong believer can carry the weaknesses of a brother (Rom. 15:1-6).*
Goal D: *Summarize the result when believers accept, love, and carry each other (Rom. 15:6).*

libertine—a person who claims too much freedom. This person teaches holiness with few or no laws.

legalist—a person who emphasizes what we *cannot* do. Legalism tries to *command* holiness.

disputable (debatable) matters of faith—*not* essential matters of Christianity, such as the timing of the Millennium

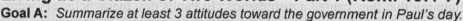

Lesson
38

Living as a Citizen of Two Worlds—Part 1 (Rom. 13:1-7)

Goal A: *Summarize at least 3 attitudes toward the government in Paul's day.*
Goal B: *Explain 4 reasons why believers must submit to government (Rom. 13:1-5).*
Goal C: *Summarize 7 reasons why God may allow an evil government.*
Goal D: *Identify some debts that believers owe as citizens (Rom. 13:1-7).*

Background and Setting

In Romans 12 Paul wrote about relating to people in the church and the world. He emphasized that love is the key in all our relationships. In Romans 13 Paul continues writing about relationships—to the government (Rom. 13:1-7), and to our neighbors and society (Rom. 13:8-14). Again, we will see that Paul emphasizes love as the key.

This world is not our home, we're merely passing through. Jesus said to Pilate, *"My kingdom is not of this world"* (John 18:36). And followers of Christ are *not of the world* any more than Christ was *of the world* (John 17:14). We are *in the world*, but not *of the world* (Rom. 12:2; John 15:19; 17:14; James 1:27; 4:4). *"Our citizenship is in heaven"* (Phil. 3:20). We are aliens and strangers on earth (1 Pet. 2:11). We are like Abraham who was *"a stranger in a foreign country; he lived in tents, as did Isaac and Jacob, who were heirs with him of the same promise. ¹⁰For he was looking forward to the city with foundations, whose architect and builder is God"* (Heb. 11:9-10). We use the things of this world, but we are not engrossed in them. *"For this world in its present form is passing away"* (1 Cor. 7:31).

Q 2 *In what sense are believers citizens of two worlds?*

Yet, for now, we live in this world as we wait for our full salvation. Jesus has gone to prepare a place for us. And He will return to take us unto Himself (John 14:1-4). But until He returns, we are citizens of two worlds: heaven and earth. As citizens of earth, yet bound for heaven, Paul emphasizes some principles that Jesus taught.

In Paul's day the *Zealots and others terrorists plotted to overthrow Roman rule in Judea. These Jewish rebels carried swords. They murdered Romans, and even Jews who did not share their beliefs. Paul did not want government to link Christianity with rebels like the Zealots. Rather, Paul wanted the gospel and the Church to have a good name on earth—especially in Rome, the capital of the Roman kingdom that ruled the world in Paul's day. Elsewhere Paul wrote:

Q 3 *What happened to Theudas and the 400 rebels who followed him (Acts 5:36)?*

> ⁹*Teach slaves to be subject to their masters in everything, to try to please them, not to talk back to them, ¹⁰and not to steal from them, but to show that they can be fully trusted, so that in every way they will make the teaching about God our Savior attractive* (Titus 2:9-10).

Also, Paul wrote that believers are an open letter, *"known and read by all men"* (2 Cor. 3:2, NASB). Let us always remember that people accept or reject the gospel on the basis of how believers live. We are either a stepping-stone for people to come to Christ, or a stumbling block. So the Spirit led Paul to discuss how believers must relate to government (Rom. 13:1-7), to neighbors (Rom. 13:8-10), and to society, as citizens of earth (Rom. 13:11-14). In this lesson we will study four principles to help us give the gospel a good name in this world.

A. First Command: Everyone must submit to the governing authorities (Rom. 13:1-5).

Q 4 ➤ *What are 2 reasons why Peter wants believers to submit to every authority (1 Pet. 2:13, 15)?*

Romans 13:1-7 is Paul's most thorough teaching on relating to government. Why did Paul write so much on this topic to Roman believers? Recall that Rome was the capital city of the Roman Empire. Paul wrote Romans in A.D. 57. Earlier, in A.D. 49, the Roman *Emperor Claudius had expelled all Jews from Rome. Aquila and Priscilla were among the Jews who left Rome (Acts 18:2). Claudius ordered all Jews to leave Rome, claiming that they caused a disturbance.[2] In Paul's day, many believers were attending house churches in Rome. No doubt the Christians in Rome were tempted to resist paying taxes or to complain about them. Such negative actions and talk would give the gospel a bad name and stir up unnecessary persecution,[3] and perhaps cause the Emperor Nero to expel believers from Rome. We cannot avoid some persecution. But rebels *"bring judgment on themselves"* (Rom. 13:2). So Paul emphasized to Roman believers that in God's plan all people must submit to government.

Q 5 ➤ *What were some reasons why believers in Rome might have had a bad attitude toward the government?*

There is a second reason why Paul may have written about relating to government. Perhaps some believers felt super-spiritual. Paul wrote from Corinth, and some there felt more spiritual than the apostles (1 Cor. 1:12; 2 Cor. 10–11). And Paul had written, *"Do not conform any longer to the pattern of this world"* (Rom. 12:2). Some might have used this as a reason to rebel against leaders, or an excuse to avoid paying taxes. So Paul clarified this matter. He wrote: *"Everyone must submit himself to the governing authorities"* (Rom. 13:1a). Everyone—believers and unbelievers—must submit to the authorities that govern.

Q 6 ➤ *What does "submit" mean? Give some examples of submission.*

The word *submit* is a key word in Romans 13:1-7. *To submit* means "to accept one's place in earth's levels of authority." Citizens submit to government. Employees submit to employers. Wives submit to husbands. Children submit to parents. God commands us to yield to authority, rather than to rebel against it. In most cases, submitting to authority means to obey. So Paul guides believers to obey government laws. However, God is the greatest authority. At rare times, the laws of an authority may conflict with the laws of God. At such times, believers should obey God rather than man. There have been thousands of government laws on earth. Of these, Scripture records only a few that contradict the laws of God. Here are some examples:

Q 7 ➤ *Give some examples of submission to authority, without obedience to that authority.*

- Hebrew midwives refused to kill the baby boys (Exod. 1:17);
- Shadrach, Meshach, and Abednego refused to worship the image of gold (Dan. 3);
- Daniel prayed in spite of the law passed against it (Dan. 6);
- The apostles preached after the Sanhedrin forbade them to do so (Acts 4:18-20; 5:17-42).[4]
- Believers in the Great Tribulation will refuse to accept the mark of the beast or bow to His image (Rev. 13:16-17).

Note that in most of the above cases, people submitted to authority, even though they did not obey. Daniel did not try to kill those who put him in the lion's den. He submitted, although he did not obey. Peter and John did not fight against the Sanhedrin. They submitted to the penalty for not obeying the law against preaching. When believers cannot obey a law that dishonors God, we can still submit to authority—and accept the penalty.

Q 8 ➤ *Did Dietrich Bonhoeffer submit to the government? Explain.*

In 1945 the German government hung Dietrich Bonhoeffer, a Lutheran pastor. What was his crime? He preached against the actions and laws of Hitler and the German government. Was Bonhoeffer guilty of rebellion against civil authorities? Was he in rebellion against God? No, Bonhoeffer was not like the Zealots, or like Theudas

(Acts 5:36). He did not lead a rebellion against the government. Still, he stood firm on his biblical convictions. All pastors have a responsibility to preach the truth. Pastor Bonhoeffer submitted to the penalty of death. He did not try to overthrow the government. He submitted to the penalty that came with his choice. But he died faithful to his conscience and his God.

Read Romans 13:1-5. As you read, underline the reasons you see for submitting to government.

> ¹*Everyone must submit himself to the governing authorities, for there is no authority except that which God has established. The authorities that exist have been established by God.* ²*Consequently, he who rebels against the authority is rebelling against what God has instituted, and those who do so will bring judgment on themselves.* ³*For rulers hold no terror for those who do right, but for those who do wrong. Do you want to be free from fear of the one in authority? Then do what is right and he will commend you.* ⁴*For he is God's servant to do you good. But if you do wrong, be afraid, for he does not bear the sword for nothing. He is God's servant, an agent of wrath to bring punishment on the wrongdoer.* ⁵*Therefore, it is necessary to submit to the authorities, not only because of possible punishment but also because of conscience* (Rom. 13:1-5).

Q 9 In Romans 13:1-5, underline the 4 reasons Paul gives for submitting to the authorities who govern.

Paul gives four reasons to submit to authorities that govern:

1. We should submit to authorities <u>because</u> God is the one who establishes all authority. *"There is no authority except that which God has established"* (Rom. 13:1). All authority flows down from God to earth. As Daniel said, *"He changes times and seasons; he sets up kings and deposes them"* (Dan. 2:21). There are and have been many forms of government on the earth. Earth has been ruled by Pharaohs, Kings, Queens, Emperors, Presidents, Dictators, Czars, Prime Ministers, Generals, Chiefs, Elders, and a hundred other types of government. And Paul teaches that God establishes, ordains, and appoints all authorities. As Jesus told Pilate, *"You would have no power over me if it were not given to you from above"* (John 19:11). Likewise, John the Baptist said, *"A man can receive only what is given him from heaven"* (John 3:27). God is the source of all authority—in heaven and on earth.

Q 10 What is the first reason why we should submit to authority?

2. We should submit to authorities <u>because</u> whoever rebels against authority rebels against God, and will be punished. *"He who rebels against the authority is rebelling against what God has instituted, and those who do so will bring judgment on themselves"* (Rom. 13:2). The judgment of God and of government will come down on rebels. We do not want to displease God, or suffer any judgment. *"But if you do wrong, be afraid, for he does not bear the sword for nothing. He is God's servant, an agent of wrath to bring punishment on the wrongdoer.* ⁵*Therefore, it is necessary to submit to the authorities"* (Rom. 13:4-5). In Paul's day, authorities used swords to hurt or kill people. God has given this power. Today, police may use clubs, swords, or guns. Wise people submit to authority, so they will not be punished!

Q 11 What 2 types of judgment will come down on those who rebel against government? Explain.

3. We should submit to authorities <u>so</u> we will have a conscience free from guilt and a heart free from fear. *"Do you want to be free from fear of the one in authority? Then do what is right and he will commend you. ...*⁵*It is necessary to submit to the authorities, not only because of possible punishment but also because of conscience"* (Rom. 13:3, 5).

Q 12 How does one's attitude toward government affect conscience?

4. We should submit to authorities <u>because</u> they are God's servants to do us good. Governments may provide many blessings, such as order, safety, justice, punishment for criminals, education, hospitals, roads, utilities, a climate for business to succeed, and even removal of garbage. Truly, the authorities that govern are God's servants to do us good. And as one preacher said, a bad government is better than

Q 13 Why does Paul tell us to pray for those in authority (1 Tim. 2:1-2)?

Q 14 What are some good things that government does for people?

no government. If you do not believe that, imagine what life would be like with no government for one month. At first, you might rejoice—no taxes, no police, no laws to obey. But after a few days, you would want to leave. Why? Because government exists to restrain evil. When a government falls, criminals steal, rape, and murder. We do not take vengeance into our own hands. But when government does its job, it restrains evil and rewards the good. So even a bad government is better than no government. Without government, evil rules. God has established three entities in society: the family, the church, and the government. These meet the needs of people. But how would the family and the church exist without government? It is true that some governments persecute the church. But without government, things might be even worse. Paul knew government could be unjust (2 Cor. 11:23-24). But government also saved his life a few times (see also Acts 16:35-39; 18:12-17; 19:23-41; 21:27–28:31). Many blessings come through the authorities who govern.

Moses formed a government in the desert so people could have order (Exod. 18:12-26). Then God gave him 70 elders to help him in that work (Num. 11:16-17). Joshua laid plans for a government after his death (Josh. 24:1). Later the Sanhedrin, under the rule of the Roman Empire, made laws to govern the land of Israel (John 18:28-32). From the beginning of time, God has formed governments to serve people. Otherwise, evil and chaos rule.

Q 15 Whose idea was government?

Every Christian must deal with authority in the home, church, workplace, and the government. Submission to authority is a matter of the heart. And it is close to the heart of God. In fact, it is impossible to submit to God until believers first submit to the authorities. When believers learn submission, peace and right relationships follow.

Q 16 What are some examples of submission at various levels?

The book of Esther illustrates that government restrains evil and rewards good. King Xerxes hanged Haman, his wicked official, for trying to kill the Jews (Esther 7). But he promoted Mordecai, because of his loyalty, to second in rank to himself (Esther 10). And in the end, God used the government to give the Jews victory over their enemies.

Symbols	7 Reasons Why God May Allow Evil Rulers	Example
	1.	
	2.	
	3.	
	4.	
	5.	
	6.	
	7.	

Figure 10.2   Practice explaining seven reasons why God may allow evil rulers.

Symbols	7 Reasons Why God May Allow Evil Rulers[5]
	1. Sometimes God allows a ruler who represents the evil desires of most people—the immoral majority. In other words, as Romans 1 teaches, God abandons those who abandon Him. In Israel's history, the kings and the judges illustrate this principle. The evil rulers were as disobedient to God as the common people.
	2. God may establish bad government to bring judgment on another nation or country. God raised up Assyria to bring judgment on the Northern Kingdom of Israel. And He raised up Babylon to conquer Judah because they had disobeyed Him.
	3. God may raise up evil leaders so He can judge them, and glorify Himself. *"For the Scripture says to Pharaoh: 'I raised you up for this very purpose, that I might display my power in you and that my name might be proclaimed in all the earth'"* (Rom. 9:17; Exod. 9:16).
	4. Sometimes God may permit an evil government to reveal the true character of evil. When evil rules, we recognize how vile sin is (compare Rom. 7:13). For example, when Hitler murdered 6 million Jews in this century, most liberal theologians stopped dreaming about a human who would bring world peace. Likewise, at the end of this age, God will allow the Antichrist to rule. Evil will parade its vileness, until the true Christ chains Satan and slams him into the abyss for a thousand years.
	5. God may exalt an evil government to fulfill His purposes. He raised up the evil Greek kingdom that united much of the world in one language. This made preaching much easier. Then God raised up the Roman government to continue preparing the world for Christ. The Roman government built roads and made them safe. This paved the way for the gospel preachers to travel from one place to another. Likewise, the Roman Caesars brought the peace of Rome—*Pax Romana*. God can use a small, rebellious group like the Sanhedrin to crucify Christ on the exact day the Passover lamb was to be slain. And He can use a corrupt world empire like Rome to prepare the world to receive the gospel of Jesus Christ.
	6. God may use evil rulers to glorify and show our loyalty to God. The Almighty used Satan to reveal Job's loyalty to God. The faithfulness of Shadrach, Meshach, and Abednego shone like stars in the dark night of Nebuchadnezzar's reign. Likewise, Daniel's loyalty to God blazed like the sun in the darkness of Nebuchadnezzar's kingdom.
	7. God may institute an evil government to remind people that He alone is on the throne of the universe. Israel danced on the shore of the Red Sea when God drowned the entire army of Egypt. God used Gideon and his 300 men with trumpets and pitchers to defeat an army of 135,000 Midianites (Judg. 8:10-12). And God exalted Himself when He used Cyrus, a pagan king of Persia, to finance the rebuilding of the temple in Jerusalem (Neh. 1:7-9). *"The king's heart is in the hand of the Lord; he directs it like a watercourse wherever he pleases"* (Prov. 21:1). The history of the world is in God's hands. Every time we see an evil government, we remind ourselves that God is greater than evil

Figure 10.3   Seven reasons why God may allow evil rulers

B. Second Command: Pay your debts (Rom. 13:6-7)

Q 17 *What are some reasons why believers should pay taxes to the government?*

God requires Christians to be responsible citizens on the earth. A person who is not a responsible citizen is not a good Christian. The Bible teaches that as Christians we do our part in society. Followers of Jesus pay their debts. The first debt Paul mentions is taxes to the government.

³This is also why you pay taxes, for the authorities are God's servants, who give their full time to governing. ⁷Give everyone what you owe him: If you owe taxes, pay taxes; if revenue, then revenue; if respect, then respect; if honor, then honor (Rom. 13:6-7).

In the eyes of God, even an ox that grinds grain deserves to be rewarded for his labor (Deut. 25:4, Figure 10.4). To a greater extent, *"the worker deserves his wages"* (Luke 10:7; 1 Tim. 5:18). *"The Lord has commanded that those who preach the gospel should receive their living from the gospel"* (1 Cor. 9:14). Preachers are paid by those they serve. Likewise, God's servants who govern are paid by taxes from those they serve (Rom. 13:6-7). For officials to work full time, someone has to pay their wages. Citizens pay taxes to the authorities so they can take care of the citizens.

Figure 10.4

One of the oxen in this photo is muzzled. In contrast, Scripture forbids muzzling the ox that grinds the grain. A muzzle prevents the ox from eating some of the grain it grinds.

The Pharisees tried to trap Jesus. Paying taxes is one of the ways we submit to authority (Rom. 13:6-7). Refusing to pay taxes is a sign of rebellion against authority.

Q 18 ➴ *What did Jesus teach about paying taxes to the Roman government?*

Q 19 ➴ *How does the 20/80 rule apply to tithing and taxes?*

16"Teacher," they said, "we know you are a man of integrity and that you teach the way of God in accordance with the truth. You aren't swayed by men, because you pay no attention to who they are. 17Tell us then, what is your opinion? Is it right to pay taxes to Caesar or not?" 18But Jesus, knowing their evil intent, said, "You hypocrites, why are you trying to trap me? 19Show me the coin used for paying the tax." They brought him a denarius, 20and he asked them, "Whose portrait is this? And whose inscription?" 21"Caesar's," they replied. Then he said to them, "Give to Caesar what is Caesar's, and to God what is God's" (Matt. 22:16-21).

Jesus taught that taxes belong to the government. Likewise, Paul reminds us that we owe taxes, and must pay them.

The 20/80 rule states that 20% of the people pay 80% of the bills. Many who call themselves Christians refuse to pay tithes. These people want a nice church to attend, with good seats, good worship, and good preaching. They want a place for their sons and daughters to marry, and a preacher to perform the marriage ceremony. They want someone to encourage them in their hard times, and visit them when they are sick. And when there is a death in the family, they want the funeral to be in the church, and the pastor to preach the sermon. Yet many of these same people who want all the blessings of the church refuse to tithe. They want others to plant the crops, hoe the rows, reap the harvest, grind the grain, bake the bread and serve it, so they can eat fresh, free, hot bread. At the end of life, God will judge these selfish people. It is not God's plan for us to have something for nothing. He requires us to help pay the bills. Likewise, the benefits of government are not free. God's Word instructs us to pay our tithes and our taxes.

In Romans 13:6-7, the first debt Paul mentions is taxes. But notice that Paul goes on to say,

<u>Give everyone what you owe him</u>: If you owe taxes, pay taxes; if revenue, then revenue; if respect, then respect; if honor, then honor (Rom. 13:7).

True Christians pay their debts. Some who claim to follow Jesus do not pay their rent or their bills. These bring shame on the name of Jesus. They ruin the name of the church. They dishonor God. Elsewhere, Paul wrote about people like this. *"They claim to know God, but by their actions they deny him"* (Titus 1:16).

Jesus taught that we can recognize His followers by the fruit of their character and actions, such as honesty in paying debts.

18"A good tree cannot bear bad fruit, and a bad tree cannot bear good fruit. 19Every tree that does not bear good fruit is cut down and thrown into the fire. 20Thus, by their fruit you will recognize them. 21Not everyone who says to me, 'Lord, Lord,' will enter the kingdom of heaven, but only he who does the will of my Father who is in heaven. 22Many will say to me on that day, 'Lord, Lord, did we not prophesy in your name, and in your name drive out demons and perform many miracles?' 23Then I will tell them plainly, 'I never knew you. Away from me, you evildoers!'" (Matt. 7:18-23).

Q 20 ➴ *Besides taxes, what other debts do believers owe in society? Give examples.*

> A PERSON WHO
> REFUSES TO PAY HIS
> DEBTS IS A THIEF
> WITHOUT A MASK.

Do you claim to follow Jesus? Then live by the teachings of the Lord and His apostles. Pay your debts in society. A person who refuses to pay his debts is a thief without a mask. Honor your father and mother. You owe them a debt of respect. Honor your elders. This is a debt that you owe in society. Stand up when a person with gray hair enters the room (Prov. 16:31; 20:29). Pay respect and honor to your teachers. This is a debt you owe. If your rent is due, pay it. You owe it! If you buy something on credit, make your payments until the debt is paid. Pay your taxes, your tithes, and every other debt you owe in society. Those who expect to be citizens in heaven are good citizens on earth.

Lesson 39

Living as a Citizen of Two Worlds—Part 2 (Rom. 13:8-14)

Goal A: *Explain: A believer is always in debt (Rom. 13:8-10). Illustrate this.*
Goal B: *Explain and illustrate 3 aspects of walking in love (Rom. 13:11-14).*

Paul uses the idea of paying debts as a bridge, a transition. He moves from paying our debts to the government, to paying the debt we owe our neighbors. Paul says we owe one another a debt—the debt to love each other.

Q 21 *How does Paul use the idea of "paying debts" as a bridge or transition?*

C. Walk in love: Make daily payments to others on a continuing debt of love (Rom. 13:8-10).

⁸Let no debt remain outstanding, except the continuing debt to love one another, for he who loves his fellowman has fulfilled the law. ⁹The commandments, "Do not commit adultery," "Do not murder," "Do not steal," "Do not covet," and whatever other commandment there may be, are summed up in this one rule: "Love your neighbor as yourself." ¹⁰Love does no harm to its neighbor. Therefore love is the fulfillment of the law (Rom. 13:8-10).

Q 22 *Are all debts bad? Explain.*

Scripture is not against credit or debts. In the Old Testament, Jews loaned money. But the law of Moses forbade Jews charging Jews interest (Exod. 22:25; Deut. 23:19-20). Jesus recognized that there are times when people need to borrow. He told a parable of a man who borrowed three loaves of bread from a friend. This was a small loan, but it was a loan. It is wise to borrow as little as possible. Wise people learn to live on what they have, rather than borrowing to live from day to day. Credit cards have ruined many families.

Q 23 *Which debt lasts from birth to death?*

The Bible commands us to be honest—to pay our debts. *"The wicked borrow and do not repay"* (Ps. 37:21).

Many buy a home on credit. The value of the home protects the lender and the borrowers. In such cases, the "debt" people owe is the monthly payment. When people buy a home, they may need to make payments for 15 to 30 years. Thirty years is a long time to make payments. But Romans 13:8 describes a debt that lasts from the cradle to the grave. Paul says we owe a debt of love to others, from the womb to the tomb. In our relationships with others, we should live as though we are making payments of love every day.

It is one thing to borrow money from a bank, but quite different to borrow money from a friend or a relative. We can see a bank, and it does not bother us that we owe it something. We just make our payments. But if we borrow from a family member or friend, every time we see him or her we recall, "I owe this person some money." Often, we remind ourselves, "I am in debt to this person." Paul says that the feeling we get toward someone we owe money is like the feeling we should have toward everyone we meet. We should not feel like an island—all by ourselves, owing no one anything. But rather, we should feel in debt to each person. Our debt is not just to those who look good, or to those we like, or to those who can do something for us. Our debt is to everyone, regardless. And the special debt that we owe is our debt to love them.⁶

Wow! Consider how practicing love guides us. Paul explains that *"he who loves his fellowman has fulfilled the law"* (Rom. 13:8). Earlier, in Lesson 23, we studied the relationship of believers to the Law. Jesus did not come to destroy the Law, but to fulfill it (Matt. 5:17-20). God's law is neither over, under, or behind us—His law is in us. Under the new covenant, God writes His law in our hearts. As Paul stated in Romans 8:4, as we deny the flesh and submit to the Spirit, we fulfill the righteous requirements of the Law. The Spirit enables us to live with justice and righteousness as we relate to others.

In Romans 12:9-21 and 13:8-10, Paul focuses on how we live in the church and the world. When Paul says we owe a *debt*, he means we have an obligation, a responsibility, a duty to *believers, neighbors,* and *fellowman* (Rom. 13:8-9). The first half of the Ten Commandments summarizes how we should relate to God. But Paul is on the topic of relating to people, so he refers to the second half of the Ten Commandments, which summarizes our debt to mankind—our duty to live rightly with others.[7] God has not saved us to ignore others, and just live as individuals who care *only* about ourselves. God loves and cares about <u>all</u> people. To follow Christ, we must be just in the way we relate to others. Paul says that we do not need a list of laws to know how we should relate to people. For as we walk in love, we pay all our debt to society.

> [8]*Let no debt remain outstanding, except the continuing debt to love one another, for he who loves his fellowman has fulfilled the law.* [9]*The commandments, "Do not commit adultery," "Do not murder," "Do not steal," "Do not covet," and whatever other commandment there may be, are summed up in this one rule: "Love your neighbor as yourself."* [10]*Love does no harm to its neighbor. Therefore love is the fulfillment of the law* (Rom. 13:8-10).

LOVE BEHAVES ITSELF. Love behaves itself. It does no harm to neighbors. Love does not commit adultery or murder. Love does not steal or covet. God expects us to love our neighbors as we love ourselves. Walking in love prevents us from exalting what we want, and trampling on the rights of others. Love is fair. It balances personal desires with the rights and needs of others. Those who follow Jesus walk in love, for this is the path He walked on. And as we love one another, all people know we are His disciples. God has delivered us from slavery to sin, and freed us to become slaves of doing right (Rom. 6:11-19). We used to walk in lust. But now we walk in love.

Talk is cheap. We preach Jesus Christ, *whispering* with our words, but *shouting* with our actions. We *point* to heaven with a 2-minute witness, but *lead* the way with a life of love. A good sermon takes 20 years.

Some believers were witnessing to a tough soldier name Rocky. He rejected their words and told them to leave. One believer named Miguel continued to share about Jesus. Suddenly, Rocky knocked him to the ground. Miguel's nose began to bleed. Rocky warned, "If you ever mention Jesus to me again, I will hurt you even worse." Miguel replied with tears, "But I cannot help it. Jesus loves you, and I love you." This stunned Rocky, who asked "How can you love me when I just made you bleed?" Miguel answered, "Because I serve the One who loved you when He was bleeding on the cross. And if He loves you, how can I help but love you?" This is the kind of love we need so that we can pay our debt to those we meet.[8] This is the love of God we need in us.

A young woman asked a pastor, "How much will it cost me to be a Christian?" "Hmmm," said the pastor, "That is a very good question. On the one hand, being a Christian is free. Jesus paid the price for us to be forgiven. But on the other hand, following Jesus means being in debt and making payments your whole life."[9] Like Paul, those who follow Jesus live in debt to all (Rom. 1:14). Yet, Jesus so fills our lives with His presence that we feel like the richest people in the world. What a paradox: Living in debt, but overflowing with riches!

In the final paragraph of Romans 13, Paul adds encouragement for paying our debt of love—fulfilling our duty to society.

Q 24 ✎ [13]*You, my brothers, were called to be free. But do not use your freedom to _____ the sinful nature [flesh]; rather, serve one another in _____.* [14]*The entire law is summed up in a single command: "_____"* (Gal. 5:13-14).

Q 25 ✎ As followers of Jesus, what debt does God require us to pay others?

Q 26 ✎ How does living in love fulfill the second half of the Ten Commandments?

Q 27 ✎ In our relationship with God, what is "the only thing that counts" (Gal. 5:6)?

Q 28 ✎ How much does it cost to be a Christian—a follower of Jesus? Explain.

D. Walk in light: Wake up, clean up, dress up (Rom. 13:11-14).

In Romans 13:8-10, Paul emphasized that we need to walk in love. Then, in Romans 13:11-14, he exhorts us to walk in light. Let us look at three aspects of walking in light: wake up, clean up, and dress up.

1. Wake up: [11]*"And do this, understanding the present time. The hour has come for you to* **wake up** *from your slumber, because our salvation is nearer now than when we first believed.* [12]*The night is nearly over; the day is almost here"* (Rom. 13:11-12a).

In New Testament times there was no electricity. People went to sleep early, soon after sundown. And they got up early, before sunrise. Paul writes that we need to discern *the present time.* We are living in that last hour of night, just before the dawn. This is the hour to wake up! Paul compares this present age to one night. And he likens the coming age to the dawn.

> SCRIPTURE OFTEN CONTRASTS DARKNESS AND LIGHT.

Scripture often contrasts darkness and light. *Night* represents this present age of sin and rebellion. *Day* represents the coming age, when Jesus returns for us (Rom. 13:12).

Q 29 *In Romans 13:12, what do "night" and "day" refer to?*

Paul says our salvation is nearer than when we first believed. Salvation includes three tenses: past, present, and future. As John Wesley said, "I *was* saved. I *am being* saved. And I *will be* saved." God has saved us and transferred us from the kingdom of darkness to the kingdom of light (Col. 1:13). He continues to save us as we follow after holiness and grow in grace. And when Christ returns, our salvation will be complete. At that glorious sunrise, we will receive a new body, and live face to face with the Lord forever. The night is nearly over. Every day brings us closer to the dawn of His coming. It is time to *wake up*—to be alert and ready to meet Him (Rom. 13:11-12a). The day of His coming is almost here!

Q 30 *Why does Paul say it is time for us to "wake up"?*

Q 31 *What does Paul mean by "wake up"?*

Q 32 *How does the parable of the ten virgins illustrate Romans 13:11-12a?*

Q 33 *How does Mark 11:32-37 illustrate Romans 13:11-12a?*

2. Clean up: *"So let us put aside the deeds of darkness and put on the armor of light.* [13]*Let us behave decently, as in the daytime, not in orgies and drunkenness, not in sexual immorality and debauchery, not in dissension and jealousy"* (Rom. 13:12b-13).

Paul refers to *putting aside the deeds of darkness,* like a person would take off pajamas. When we sleep, our clothes get wrinkled and ruffled. The clothes we sleep in are for the night. They are not fit for the day. Imagine how foolish someone would look if he went to work in pajamas. Paul compares our nightclothes to the sinful deeds of darkness. As a person would take off a pair of pajamas, Paul tells us to take off three pairs of sins.

Q 34 *As we wake up and clean up, what do we put aside?*

- The *first* pair of sins to take off is *"orgies and drunkenness."* Orgies were night parties, known for sinful behavior. Drunkenness is a common sin linked with night. Paul says Christians must put aside these sins, like a person lays aside old clothes.

Q 35 *What are 3 pairs of sins Paul commands us to "take off" like old clothes to throw away?*

- The *second* pair of sins to take off is *"sexual immorality and debauchery."* Sexual immorality includes all forms of sexual sins, from lust and pornography to any sex before marriage. Debauchery is literally the term *bed.* In its context, Paul is referring to *forbidden bed.*[10] *"Marriage should be honored by all, and the marriage bed kept pure, for God will judge the adulterer and all the sexually immoral"* (Heb. 13:4).

- The *third* pair of sins to take off is *"dissension and jealousy."* Debating is acceptable at times. But Paul is referring to sins of division, quarreling, arguing, and gossip. Proverbs 6:16-19 listens seven things that God hates, and number 7 is *"a man who stirs up dissension among brothers."*

Brothers and sisters in Christ, the sunrise of Christ's coming is near. Let us live as children of the light (Eph. 5:8-20). Let us take off the deeds of darkness as we would take off dirty clothes. Jesus warned those in the church at Sardis to wake up. He said that those who wear soiled clothes will not walk with Him when He returns (Rev. 3:2-4).

Q 36 ✎ *Complete Figure 10.5 by filling in the second column.*

Reference	Your summary of what Scripture commands us to "clean up"
Eph. 5:8-18	
Col. 3:4-9	
James 1:27b	

Figure 10.5   Practice summarizing biblical passages on clothes to take off or avoid.

3. Dress up: *"Rather, clothe yourselves with the Lord Jesus Christ, and do not think about how to gratify the desires of the sinful nature"* (Rom. 13:14). Each believer has two choices: to satisfy the flesh, or submit to the Spirit. Paul contrasted these two lifestyles in Romans 6–8. Again, in Romans 13:14, Paul contrasts the flesh and the Spirit. Note that this verse has a "do" and a "don't"—a positive and a negative.

Q 37 ✎ *How does Paul say we should respond to evil desires of the flesh that come from time to time?*

The Negative (Do Not).   In Romans 13:14, he tells us *not* to think about how to fulfill the sinful desires of the flesh. These desires arise in believers from time to time. But we are to turn away from them and not pay any attention to them. We should not take seriously the temptations that come to us. We should not give temptations a second thought, but rather, toss them into the trash and move on. You can't keep a bird from flying over your head. But you can keep it from building a nest in your hair! Wave an arm toward heaven, and the bird will fly away!

Q 38 ✎ *What does Paul mean by "clothe yourself with the Lord Jesus Christ" (Rom. 13:14)?*

The Positive (Do!).   In contrast to satisfying the flesh, Paul tells us to dress up. He says: *"Clothe yourselves with the Lord Jesus Christ"* (Rom. 13:14). Wear Jesus! Paul means for us to be in Christ, and have Christ in us. Paul wants us to clothe ourselves with the qualities, attitudes, and values of our Jesus, the Lord of our lives. As he told the Colossians, *"Clothe yourselves with compassion, kindness, humility, gentleness and patience. ¹³Bear with each other and forgive whatever grievances you may have against one another. Forgive as the Lord forgave you. ¹⁴And over all these virtues put on love, which binds them all together in perfect unity* (Col. 3:12-14).

In Romans 13:14 Paul gives the solution to the battle between flesh and Spirit. He says we should not think about how to fulfill occasional temptations of the flesh. Rather, let us turn our thoughts and energy to enjoying life in the Spirit. Paul likes to emphasize the solution—using the new life and resources God makes available through the Spirit.

Q 39 ✎ *Complete Figure 10.6 by filling in the second column in your own words.*

Reference	Your summary of what clothes to put on and wear
Col. 3:12-14	
Eph. 6:10-18	
Rev. 3:4	

Figure 10.6   Practice summarizing verses that describe the clothes to put on and wear.

Notice that Paul says *"clothe yourselves with the Lord Jesus Christ"* (Rom. 13:14). Ponder the last three words of Romans 13:14.[11]

Q 40 ✎ *What does each of these 3 words emphasize: Lord Jesus Christ (Rom. 13:14)?*

- **Lord** emphasizes a ruler; One to whom we submit our thoughts, words, deeds. Paul says to clothe ourselves with His lordship—to invite Him to rule over us.
- **Jesus** means "Savior." The angel told Joseph, *"You are to give him the name Jesus, because he will save his people from their sins"* (Matt. 1:21). As we clothe ourselves with Christ, we trust in His power to save us from all our sins and weaknesses. Paul wrote to the Roman Christians about putting off the deeds of darkness. He described three pairs of sins to take off. These Roman believers were mature. But Paul still reminded them to live holy lives. Every believer can be tempted. We all need to wrap Jesus around us and live in Him. He will keep us safe from sin as we abide in Him.

- **Christ** means "the anointed one." Jesus depended on the anointing of the Holy Spirit. With the Spirit's power Jesus resisted evil, and practiced good. May God give us this same anointing as we clothe ourselves with the Lord Jesus Christ. He makes us fruitful in every good way.

A young man named Gus was empty. He had tried various things on the world's menu. Like the prodigal son, he had rejected godly values and had wasted his life in sinful living (Luke 15). But the pleasures of sin left him lonely, guilty, and unhappy. In desperation, he went to a garden, seeking help from God. Just then he heard a child singing the words, "Take and read, take and read." This was a new song to Gus. He had never heard it. He wondered, "Could the Lord be calling to me through this child's song?" So he went and found a Bible, which was laying on a table, opened to Romans 13. The first verse he read was, *"Clothe yourselves with the Lord Jesus Christ, and do not think about how to gratify the desires of the sinful nature"* (Rom. 13:14). At once saving faith came to Gus as he opened his heart and soul to this verse and surrendered his life to God. This young man's full name was Augustine. He became one of the greatest leaders in Church history.[12]

 Q 41 *Which famous person did Romans 13:14 influence?*

There is power in the Word of God. Let us open our hearts to these verses. The night is nearly past, and the sunrise is at hand. Let us awake, clean up, and dress up—clothing ourselves with the Lord Jesus Christ. Amen.

Lesson 40 ## The Weak and the Strong on Debated Matters—Part 1 (Rom. 14:1–15:13)

Goal A: *Summarize the background of Romans 14:1–15:13.*
Goal B: *Identify 3 types of matters that believers face (Figure 10.8, Rom. 14:1–15:13).*
Goal C: *Explain the reason why believers should accept and not judge one another (Rom. 14:1–12; 15:7).*

Background

Romans 14:1–15:13 is Paul's pastoral response to a problem in Rome. The Emperor Claudius expelled all Jews from Rome in A.D. 49. Why? When the gospel reached Rome, there were several synagogues there. Some accepted and some rejected teachings about Jesus. This led to clashes between the synagogues. As a result, Claudius forced thousands of Jews to leave Rome—including Christians and non-Christian Jews. Jews were allowed to return 5 years later when Nero began to rule in A.D. 54.[13] As Jews returned, they became part of the various communities of believers in Rome. When Paul wrote Romans in A.D. 57, he showed great concern for Jews re-entering the churches in Rome, where Gentiles were the majority. Paul's words in Romans 14:1–15:13 echo Romans 11:17-21. Gentiles, who have been grafted in, should not be arrogant toward Jews.[14]

Q 42 *Why did the Emperor Claudius expel all Jews from Rome?*

Tensions rose as Jewish and Gentile believers mixed in communities and home churches. Their backgrounds, traditions, and culture were different. Jews grew up following the law of Moses. Jews divided all food into two categories: clean and unclean (Lev. 11:1-47). For example, some meat, such as pork, was always *unclean,* because although the pig had a split hoof, it did not chew the cud. Other meat, such as beef or lamb, was clean *if* it was killed in the right way, and cooked with *clean* hands in *clean* pots. People who had touched unclean animals were unclean until purified. Likewise, a pot that a lizard fell into was *unclean,* and had to be broken (Lev. 11:33). So a Jew might lack a clear conscience to eat meat, if he was uncertain of how the meat was slaughtered or cooked. In contrast, most Gentiles did not grow up with rules about eating. They felt free to eat whatever, wherever. Therefore, when Paul mentions believers who are *strong in faith,* he is referring to Gentiles. Their faith was not affected by rules about eating. In contrast, Jewish believers lacked faith to eat meat from the market. Their faith was troubled by the command, *"You must not eat meat that is unclean for you"*

Q 43 *As Jewish believers returned to Rome, why did some of them not eat meat?*

(see Lev. 11:8). In Babylon, *"Daniel resolved not to defile himself with the royal food and wine"* (Dan. 1:8). In Babylon, Gentiles would have stood in line to get free meat and wine from Nebuchadnezzar's palace. But Daniel and his three friends refused to eat it. Their consciences protested. For even the best of food was *unclean* if prepared by unclean hands, or in unclean dishes. For Jews, food that was *clean* and *kosher (fit) had to pass the test of Leviticus 11. Likewise, Jewish believers had "weak faith" about certain days, such as the Sabbath and feast days. In contrast, a Gentile conscience did not regard one day holier than another.

Q 44 ⬉ *In Rome, which 3 issues did Jewish and Gentile believers debate?*

Rom.	Strong Gentile Believers	Weak Jewish Believers
14:1-3, 6, 14, 20-21	Ate meat from various sources	Refused meat, and ate only vegetables (see Dan. 1:8-20)
14:21	Some drank wine.	Some abstained from wine.
14:5	Regarded all days the same	Regarded the Sabbath day and feast days as holier than other days

Figure 10.7   Gentile and Jewish believers in Rome debated three issues: meat, holy days, and wine (Rom. 14:1–15:13).

Q 45 ⬈ *What had mature Jewish believers, like Paul, learned about eating meat?*

Conscience judges on the basis of what it has been taught. Some Jews, like Paul, had a conscience that had learned more than others. As Paul grew in knowledge and faith, God taught him that *"no food is unclean in itself"* (Rom. 14:14). Elsewhere Paul wrote that under the new covenant, all foods may be eaten, for they are made holy *"by the word of God and prayer"* (1 Tim. 4:5). Paul grew in knowledge to understand the Lord's teaching, *"What goes into a man's mouth does not make him 'unclean,' but what comes out of his mouth, that is what makes him 'unclean'"* (Matt. 15:11). In contrast, some Gentile converts to Judaism and many Jewish believers still had a conscience taught by Moses. These believers had not yet discovered that in Christ, lower laws are replaced by higher laws. In this lesson, we will explore this further.

Q 46 ⬉ *What are the 3 types of issues that believers face (Figure 10.8)?*

As we prepare to study Romans 14:1–15:13, it is important to discern three types of issues. Take a minute to study Figure 10.8. Then we will briefly examine these three types of matters that believers face.

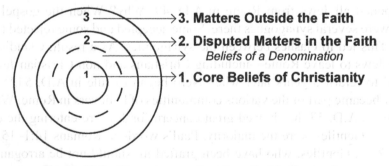

Figure 10.8   Three types of matters that believers face

Q 47 ⬈ *What are some examples in Circle 1, core beliefs of the faith?*

- **Circle 1—Core beliefs of the faith** are the essentials of Christianity. In Romans 1–8, Paul deals with some of the basic matters of the faith.[15] Examples of topics in **Circle 1** are: the inspiration of Scripture, the One True God, the deity of Christ, the lost-ness of man (Rom. 1–3); salvation through faith in Christ, who died for our sins and rose for our justification (Rom. 4–5); the ministry of the Holy Spirit for holy living (Rom. 6–8; 13:11–14); water baptism, communion, the Church and its mission, the second coming of Christ, the final judgment. If we deny any of these basic doctrines, we deny the faith. In Galatians 1:6-9 Paul condemns those who preach *"a different gospel."* The gospel is in **Circle 1**. It is not something we dispute or debate. Rather, the gospel is part of the core of Christianity. Some in Galatia were teaching that our salvation is based on obeying the Law. These Judaizers taught that we earn points with God and win His favor with our deeds (Gal. 3:1-14). Trusting in deeds we do is futility and heresy. In contrast, Paul emphasizes that offering ourselves as a living sacrifice is the way true believers respond to God's gift of salvation in Christ

(Rom. 12:1-2). Likewise, Paul warned believers in Colosse to let no one judge them on matters of eating, drinking, or special days (Col. 2:16-19). False teachers at Colosse were basing *salvation* on works and human experiences. In contrast, the issues among Roman believers were in **Circle 2**, not **Circle 1**.

- **Circle 2—Debated matters of the faith** are *not* essential matters of Christianity. By debated matters of faith, we mean matters on which true believers have different opinions. Even sincere, mature, godly, Spirit-filled believers do not agree on all matters of faith. In Romans 14:1–15:13, these debated matters included eating meat, drinking wine, and honoring one day above another. Unity on topics in **Circle 2** is not necessary for salvation. And subtracting them does not reduce Christianity. Today, matters in **Circle 2** include choices people make about hair, dress, and music. And they include beliefs that mark a particular denomination or fellowship. For example, most of us Pentecostals teach the baptism in the Holy Spirit, with the outward evidence of speaking in tongues. We emphasize that being filled with the Spirit increases power to witness, victorious living, godliness, and perseverance. Still, we believe that it is possible to be born again and reach heaven without being baptized in the Spirit. Other topics in **Circle 2** are: the age of the earth, the time of the Rapture, and views on the Millennium.

  Q 48 ⤢ *What are some examples in Circle 2, matters that believers debate?*

  Note that a dotted line divides **Circle 2** into two parts. The inner part of **Circle 2** refers to beliefs of a denomination or group of churches. Some of the beliefs of a denomination may be debated, especially *outside* the denomination. For example, in Bretal, members of Denomination A believe in the baptism in the Holy Spirit, with the evidence of speaking in tongues. So in Bretal, in Denomination A, this topic is seldom debated. It is a standard belief for membership. In contrast, members of Denomination B in Bretal do not embrace this belief. So in Bretal, we can say that the baptism in the Holy Spirit is a debated topic *between* members of different denominations. It is good for believers to search the Scriptures and become members of a denomination they can support. When believers in a denomination agree on doctrines and priorities, they have unity and strength. Still, let us remember that there are true believers in various denominations. So if we debate or discuss biblical topics with believers from different denominations, we should not be judgmental. Rather, let us show love and respect to sincere believers who interpret the Bible differently than we do. And let us *speak the truth,* as we see it, *in love* (Eph. 4:15). As Paul wrote, *"Each one should be fully convinced in his own mind"* (Rom. 14:5). It is not necessary for us to persuade everyone to believe *exactly* as we do. We may fellowship with believers from various denominations *if* we agree on the matters of **Circle 1**. Some err by insisting that fellowship depends on agreement about topics in **Circle 2**. But the main things are the plain things in **Circle 1**.

  Q 49 ⤡ *What does the inner part of Circle 2 refer to? Give an example.*

  Q 50 ⤡ *Why should believers in a local church agree on doctrines?*

- **Circle 3—Matters outside the faith** are non-religious topics, such as math, the sciences, government, health issues (like vaccinations and circumcision), and technology. Note that forms of government and political parties are not matters of faith. These are *not* a part of Christianity. However, our relationship to government *is* a matter of faith, which Paul wrote about in Romans 13:1-7.

  Q 51 ⤡ *What are some topics in Circle 3, matters outside the faith?*

We have reviewed the background of Romans 14:1–15:13. These verses apply to **Circle 2**—debated matters of the faith. Now let us examine three principles (A, B, and C) for relating to each other on matters in **Circle 2**.

A. Accept one another (on debatable, *disputable matters in the faith)— do not judge (Rom. 14:1-12; 15:7).

In a local church, members agree on matters of **Circle 1**. And church members agree on specific beliefs of their local church. We do not try to control what those outside the church believe. But each local church must have beliefs that its members agree on. In the

Q 52 ⤡ *Which circle does this lesson on Romans 14:1– 15:13 relate to the most?*

Q 53 ⤡ *Why did Jewish believers in Rome lack faith to eat meat?*

outer half of **Circle 2, *Debatable Matters,*** Paul guides us to accept one another without judging. These disputed topics are *less important*—matters of personal interpretation and personal conviction. For example today, within the same local church, believers might have different opinions on sports, television, hair styles, music, clothing, or food. On such matters, Paul exhorts us to accept and respect each other, instead of judging.

Q 54 ↗ *Did Jewish believers in Rome who refused to eat meat have a weak commitment? Explain.*

> WEAK IN
> FAITH ≠ WEAK IN
> COMMITMENT.

Read Romans 14:1. Paul tells strong believers to *accept* those with weak faith on **disputable matters*—instead of judging them. Discern that "weak in faith" does *not* equal "weak in commitment." In Romans 14, those "weak in faith" are Jewish believers who refused to eat meat. This was a *strong* commitment! These Jewish believers probably enjoyed eating meat. But they refused to eat it because conscience objected. For many years they had obeyed the rule to avoid unclean food (Lev. 11). These Jewish believers had *weak faith* toward eating meat from the market. But they had a *strong commitment* to God and His Word. Those we call weak in faith are often strong in their commitment to God.

Paul first tells those strong in faith to accept the weak in faith (Rom. 14:1). But he quickly shifts to the weak in faith, and tells them not to condemn those who eat everything. In other words, Paul does not want either group of believers to judge the other group (Rom. 14:3).

Q 55 ↗ *Why does Paul say believers should not judge each other on debatable matters?*

Paul gives *one big reason* why we should not judge one another.

The reason: <u>God is the judge of all believers</u>, and He has accepted us all (Rom. 14:3).

Judgment is a *vertical* activity on *non-essential, debatable, secondary* matters of faith. In **Circle 2**, God is the only judge of believers. On debatable matters of **Circle 2**, God forbids believers from judging each other. In Romans 13, Paul reminds us that God appoints rulers to judge people on government matters such as taxes. But in Romans 14, Paul reminds us that *God alone* is the judge of believers on disputable matters of the faith. The strong must not judge the weak. And the weak must not judge the strong. Rather, on matters in **Circle 2**, both should accept each other, knowing judgment belongs to God alone.

In Romans 14:1-12, Paul emphasizes that **God**, not any of us, is the judge of all believers. Paul hammers this point more than 10 times. Over and over he stresses this one principle: **God is the judge of believers.** An employer may criticize his own employees. But Paul asks, *"Who are you to judge someone else's servant?"* (Rom. 14:4). Those who judge and criticize believers on matters of **Circle 2** are trying to take over God's throne. Read Romans 14:1-12 slowly. As you read, underline every reference to God, master, and Lord.

Q 56 ↖ *How many times does Paul use the words 'God' and 'Lord' in Romans 14:1-12? What is the point?*

Q 57 ↖ *Why should each person be fully persuaded that what he or she does pleases God (Rom. 14:5)?*

¹Accept him whose faith is weak, without passing judgment on disputable matters. ²One man's faith allows him to eat everything, but another man, whose faith is weak, eats only vegetables. ³The man who eats everything must not look down on him who does not, and the man who does not eat everything must not condemn the man who does, for God has accepted him. ⁴Who are you to judge someone else's servant? To his own master he stands or falls. And he will stand, for the Lord is able to make him stand. ⁵One man considers one day more sacred than another; another man considers every day alike. Each one should be fully convinced in his own mind. ⁶He who regards one day as special, does so to the Lord. He who eats meat, eats to the Lord, for he gives thanks to God; and he who abstains, does so to the Lord and gives thanks to God. ⁷For none of us lives to himself alone and none of us dies to himself alone. ⁸If we live, we live to the Lord; and if we die, we die to the Lord. So, whether we live or die, we belong to the Lord. [9]For this very reason, Christ died and returned to life so that he might be the Lord of both the dead and the living. [10]You, then, why do you judge your brother? Or why do you look down on your brother? For we will all stand before God's judgment seat. [11]It is written: " 'As surely as I live,' says the Lord, 'every knee will bow before me; every tongue will confess to God.' " [12]So then, each of us will give an account of himself to God (Rom. 14:1-12).

Q 60 ↖ *Where you live, what are some topics in Circle 2?*

Q 61 ↖ *What is modesty? Does it vary with locations and generations? Explain.*

George grew up in a small, rural, Pentecostal church. The women there dressed plain. They did not braid their hair or wear jewelry. George recalled the pastor once preaching on 1 Timothy 2:9 and 1 Peter 3:3. These Scriptures emphasized modesty, unbraided hair, and no jewelry. After graduating from high school, George moved to a big city to attend college. In a local Pentecostal church, he noticed that some women had braided hair and jewelry. Others looked more modest and plain. George was confused. He wondered if some of these women in the city were saved. If you were George's pastor, what could you say to help him?

All of his life, Peter had obeyed the Jewish laws about avoiding unclean food. Then one day he had a vision that changed his life.

[9]About noon ... Peter went up on the roof to pray. [10]He became hungry and wanted something to eat, and while the meal was being prepared, he fell into a trance. [11]He saw heaven opened and something like a large sheet being let down to earth by its four corners. [12]It contained all kinds of four-footed animals, as well as reptiles of the earth and birds of the air. [13]Then a voice told him, "Get up, Peter. Kill and eat." [14]"Surely not, Lord!" Peter replied. "I have never eaten anything impure or unclean." [15]The voice spoke to him a second time, "Do not call anything impure that God has made clean." [16]This happened three times, and immediately the sheet was taken back to heaven (Acts 10:9-16).

As Peter wondered about the vision, messengers arrived from the household of Cornelius, a Roman centurion. Soon these Gentiles would be filled with the Spirit. And Peter would learn that under the New Testament, God accepts people with different backgrounds, different languages, and different beliefs. In Christ, this great God, the Creator of all humanity, adopts people of every nation and race into one family. Our beliefs are as different as our languages and the colors of our skin. But we all become accepted in Christ, the Beloved (Eph. 1:6; Rom. 8:17). May God help us never to call each other impure or unclean. We are all washed by the same blood.

Believers have different beliefs about what pleases God. These days, as believers move from place to place, there is a great need to study and obey Romans 14:1–15:13. Especially in urban churches, like Rome of Paul's day, there is great cultural diversity among believers.

Q 58 ↖ *If Jesus is the Lord of both dead and living believers, whom does that leave for us to judge on disputable matters (Rom. 14:9)?*

Q 59 ↖ *What is the good news and the bad news in Romans 14:12?*

Q 62 ↖ *Is it possible that two believers with different opinions can both please God? Explain.*

Q 63 ↖ *Who do you think has the greatest need to study Romans 14:1–15:13 today: rural or urban believers? Explain.*

> IN CHRIST, THIS GREAT GOD, THE CREATOR OF ALL HUMANITY, ADOPTS PEOPLE OF EVERY NATION AND RACE INTO ONE FAMILY.

Lesson 41

The Weak and the Strong on Debated Matters—Part 2 (Rom. 14:1–15:13)

Goal A: *Describe 4 types of people in or around the church (Figure 10.9).*
Goal B: *Explain how love avoids tripping or trapping a brother (Rom. 14:13-23). Give illustrations.*
Goal C: *Give examples of how a strong believer can carry the weaknesses of a brother (Rom. 15:1-6).*
Goal D: *Summarize the result when believers accept, love, and carry each other (Rom. 15:6).*

We are studying relationships between strong and weak believers. In Romans chapter 14 through half of chapter 15, Paul emphasizes three principles to guide us (Figure 10.10).

Q 64 How does a libertine differ from a legalist? Give examples.

Q 65 In your church, which problem is greater: too much freedom or too many rules? Explain.

Overview: The church must beware of two dangerous people: the *libertine and the *legalist (Figure 10.9). The libertine claims too much freedom. This person teaches holiness with few or no laws. In contrast, Paul wrote that, in Christ, the Spirit enables us to *fulfill* the Law as we practice love. Opposite the libertine is the legalist. He emphasizes what we *cannot* do. Legalism tries to *command* holiness. It has too many rules and too little freedom. As we must avoid too much freedom, we must also avoid too many rules. The Scripture guides us to a balance of liberty, law, and love. The truth is often in the middle, between two extremes. Figure 10.9 summarizes four types of people, ranging from the libertine to the legalist.

Four Types of People

Topic	The Libertine	The Strong Believer	The Weak Believer	The Legalist
Explanations and examples:	*"All things are lawful for me"* (NASB) 1 Cor. 6:12a; 10:23a; 15:32a	Jesus; Paul Matt. 15:10; Rom. 14:14, 21; 1 Tim. 4:4-5	Immature believers; new converts Rom. 14–15; 1 Cor. 3:1-3; Gal. 4:19-21; Heb. 5:11-14;	Do not _____! Pharisees (Matt. 23); Judaizers (Gal. 2:11-16)
Authority sources:	Selfish desires + Scripture	Scripture	Scripture + tradition	Tradition + Scripture
Characteristics:	Freedom without holiness; trying to use grace as a coat to cover a life of sin (Rom. 6:15)	A balance of freedom, holiness, and love; Righteousness, joy, and peace in the Spirit	False guilt from things Scripture does not condemn; Righteousness, joy, and peace in the Spirit	Holiness without freedom or joy
Dangers:	Eternal judgment	Pride; Ridiculing others; Destroying others; Abusing freedom	Pride; Criticizing others; Falling because of others	Eternal judgment

Figure 10.9   Four types of people in and around the church[16]

In Romans 14:1–15:13, Paul gives us three principles, A–C, on relationships between strong and weak believers. In Lesson 40 we studied **Principle A: Accept one another (on debated matters in the faith)—do not judge** (Rom. 14:1-12; 15:7). Now, in Lesson 41, we will look at Principles B and C.

Paul begins with Principle A, the easiest principle, and ends with Principle C, the most difficult. A wise person can lead people to live three levels above where they are. But he will not ask them to jump to the top level at once. Rather, he will lead them in three steps. Likewise, the Spirit guided Paul to use this three-step method in Romans 14–15. Each of his three principles, A–C, decrease our freedom and increase our responsibility.

Principle A was something like: live and let live. Paul said we are free to please conscience, but urged us not to judge others. Principle A does not ask for sacrifice. It accepts our beliefs. And it guides us to accept the beliefs of others on disputable matters.

Figure 10.10
Paul gives three principles for strong and weak believers. These principles guide relationships on disputed matters in the faith (Rom. 14:1-15:13).
In these three principles, A–C, Paul moves from the easiest to the hardest; from the least restrictive to the most demanding.

C. Carry one another's weaknesses, as Christ carried ours—Do not please yourself.

B. Love one another— Do not trip or trap.

A. Accept one another— Do not judge each other.

Q 66 How many principles will we study on the relationships of strong and weak believers (Rom. 14:1–15:13)?

Principle B is a step up from Principle A. In Principle B, Paul moves from *accept* others to *love* others. Let us take a closer look at this principle.

B. Love one another—do not trip or trap[17] (Rom. 14:13-23).

[13]*Therefore let us stop passing judgment on one another. Instead, make up your mind* [Greek: judge this] *not to put any **stumbling block** or **obstacle** in your brother's way.* [14]*As one who is in the Lord Jesus, I am fully convinced that no food is unclean in itself. But if anyone regards something as unclean, then for him it is unclean.* [15]*If your brother is distressed because of what you eat, you are no longer acting in **love**. Do not by your eating destroy your brother for whom Christ died* (Rom. 14:13-15).

Romans 14:13 is a bridge or transition. Paul summarizes the first principle of relationships on disputed matters in the faith. He says: *"Therefore let us stop passing judgment on one another"* (Rom. 14:13a). Then Paul moves on to the second principle: *"Do not put any **stumbling block** or **obstacle** in your brother's way."* In the Greek, we see two word pictures: stumbling block and obstacle. Paul used these same two Greek words earlier in Romans 9:33. There, Paul quoted Isaiah 8:14, which referred to Christ as *"a stone* [stumbling block] *that causes men to stumble and a rock* [obstacle] *that makes them fall"* (Rom. 9:33). The Jews stumbled over Jesus. They were offended at Him. Those who stumbled over Christ rejected God's plan of salvation, and fell away from God forever. Paul wrote about this terrible tragedy in Romans 9:33. And in Romans 14:13, he urges the strong not to be a stumbling block or an obstacle for other Jews.[18]

- **A stumbling block** is a rock in the path that causes someone to stumble and fall. Imagine a person putting a rock or stone, bigger than a soccer ball, on a path. When the light becomes dim, along comes a brother walking on the path. Unaware of the stumbling stone, this brother trips and falls, injuring himself. Whoever put the stone on the path is responsible for hurting his brother. Paul urges us not to *trip* our brother by doing something that puts a stumbling stone in his path.

- **An obstacle** (Greek: *scandalon*) gives a worse picture than *to trip*. Originally, the Greek word *scandalon* (obstacle) referred to a *trap*, and specifically to the trigger of a trap.[19] Throughout history, people have used *traps* to cause the downfall and ruin of animals. Often a trap has a trigger that holds the bait. Figure 10.11 shows a trap used in some nations to catch a mouse. Someone puts a small piece of cheese or food on the trigger, and then sets the trap. When the mouse tastes the food or bait, the trap snaps shut and kills the mouse.

Paul urges believers to neither *trip* nor *trap* another believer. As humans we *enjoy* many things, such as favorite foods, special clothes, and entertainment. These things we enjoy may bring us a good feeling within—a brief moment of satisfaction, fun, or pleasure. So long as these things are not sinful, they are matters of personal choice and freedom. But Paul reminds us that on things we enjoy, there is more at stake than our freedom. There is more involved than our good feelings. The eternal soul of our brother may be at risk! Do I feel so important that I value a bite of meat more than my brother's eternity? Am I so selfish that I would drink a glass of wine, even if it led my brother to become a drunkard? Am I so in love with myself that I have no concern with how my actions affect my weaker brother? Shall I follow the example of Lamech, who felt ten times more important than his father (Cain), and killed a young man who injured him (Gen. 4:23-24)? How highly do I think of myself? How tall do I think I am in relation to others (Rom. 12:3)? If I were introducing myself to preach, what would I say about myself?

How can a strong believer trip or trap a weaker brother or sister? Paul explains:
- *"As one who is in the Lord Jesus, I am fully convinced that no food is unclean in itself. But if anyone regards something as unclean, then <u>for him it is unclean</u>"* (Rom. 14:14).

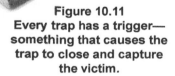

**Figure 10.11
Every trap has a trigger—something that causes the trap to close and capture the victim.**

Q 67 ➤ *In Romans 9:33, what causes Jews to stumble?*

Q 68 ➤ *Which 2 things does Paul urge us to avoid doing to another believer?*

Q 69 ➤ *How much did Jesus give up for your brother (Rom. 14:15)? How much will you give up for him?*

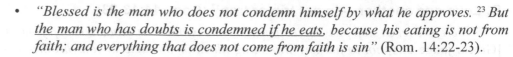

- *"Blessed is the man who does not condemn himself by what he approves. [23] But the man who has doubts is condemned if he eats, because his eating is not from faith; and everything that does not come from faith is sin"* (Rom. 14:22-23).

Q 70 *To live by faith, why must each believer obey conscience?*

Within each person, God has put an inner judge—a voice we call *conscience*. Conscience is not always an accurate judge, because it judges on the basis of what it has learned. And often, what we have learned is incomplete, or unbalanced. However, even though conscience is not always accurate, it is a helpful friend. Some light is better than no light. Paul teaches that conscience and faith work together. Walking by faith to please God means being true to what we have learned. Walking by faith is living in the light that we have. So when a person believes that a path is right, but walks instead on a path he or she believes is wrong, this person has stopped living by faith, and is living in sin (Rom. 14:23). Earlier Paul wrote: *"Each one should be fully convinced in his own mind"* that the Lord approves his actions (Rom. 14:5). Paul emphasized that whatever we do, we do as unto the Lord. We belong to Him. And at the end of our days, each of us will *"give an account"* unto God (Rom. 14:5-12). As we yield to the Holy Spirit, and live with a clear conscience, we are at peace with God. But those who violate conscience lose peace, cease to live by faith, and condemn themselves (Rom. 14:22-23).

Q 71 *Explain the process by which Norman tripped Laurence.*

Conscience plays a vital role in the life of a believer. Laurence believes that eating **pomanoc* is wrong. But Norman, a fellow believer, thinks believers are free to eat *pomanoc*, and he eats it in front of Laurence. In time, Laurence begins to feel social pressure. Then one day, a group of believers eat dinner together at a café. Norman and others order *pomanoc*. Laurence orders *walokia*. But soon, Norman puts some *pomanoc* on a plate and offers Laurence a *free* taste. Embarrassed, Laurence takes a bite, as his conscience whispers "No". To his surprise, Laurence enjoys the taste of the *pomanoc*. He smiles thinking, "Well, lightning from heaven did not strike me. His eyes are opened to a new experience. Later that night, on his bed in the dark, Laurence feels guilty—like he has betrayed his parents and his Lord. He feels like he has violated the beliefs of his pastor and his church. The next day Laurence is confused. As he reflects on eating the *pomanoc*, he thinks, "Perhaps eating *pomanoc* is ok. Maybe my parents and my pastor were wrong." As time goes by Laurence eats *pomanoc* several times. After a year, he no longer feels guilty when he eats it. His heart has hardened a little. His hearing is less sensitive to the voice of the Holy Spirit. And *pomanoc* becomes one of his favorite foods. It makes him feel happy. But with this new freedom comes new doubt. Laurence has questions like, "If my pastor was wrong about *pomanoc*, maybe he is wrong about other things, like pornography, or even sex before marriage. Several of my friends who eat *pomanoc* enjoy entertainment that my church disapproves." The tempter's voice whispers to Laurence, "Try this activity that the church forbids. These people are outdated and old fashioned. And you will discover new freedom that you enjoy even more than *pomanoc*." Five years later, Laurence is addicted to *pomanoc*, no longer attends church, and is dying from a sexual disease. He has been trapped by sin and Satan. The trigger was a brother named Norman.

Paul urges us to walk in love. *"If your brother is distressed because of what you eat, you are no longer acting in love"* (Rom. 14:15). *"Love does no harm to its neighbor"* (Rom. 13:10). *"It* [love] *is not self-seeking"* (1 Cor. 13:5). Paul will have more to say about walking in love, in point C.

Q 72 *Where you live, have some believers caused others to fall? Explain.*

Paul warned that in the last days people would fall in love with themselves. He said sinners would be void of *agape* love—*"without self-control, ...lovers of pleasure rather than lovers of God"* (2 Tim. 3:2-4). In contrast, let us believers bear the Spirit's fruit of *"love, joy, peace, patience, kindness, goodness, faithfulness, [23]gentleness and self-control"* (Gal. 5:22-23). Let us live in love, judging our choices, and limiting our freedom—lest we trip or trap a brother (Rom. 14:13). The kingdom of God is our inheritance. It contains wealth and riches beyond measure. But God's kingdom is spiritual, not physical. And it is eternal, not just for now. So let us not allow the earthly choices we make to be near-sighted. Let us be alert, walking in love. And may the choices we make in this brief life on earth never be the downfall of others (Rom. 14:16).

[17]For the kingdom of God is not a matter of eating and drinking, but of righteousness, peace and joy in the Holy Spirit, [18]because anyone who serves Christ in this way is pleasing to God and approved by men. [19]Let us therefore make every effort to do what leads to peace and to mutual edification. [20]Do not destroy the work of God for the sake of food. All food is clean, but it is wrong for a man to eat anything that causes someone else to stumble. [21]It is better not to eat meat or drink wine or to do anything else that will cause your brother to fall (Rom. 14:17-21).

Figure 10.12
In Romans 14:13-21, Paul arranges his thoughts in the form of a *chiasm, based on the Greek letter Chi, (pronounced Kai, and written: X).[20]
A chiasm is a literary device used in the Old and New Testaments. Its form is the > shape—the left half of the Greek letter X.

A
 B
  C
  C¹
 B¹
A¹

Q 73 *What is a chiasm?*

Biblical writers used the top half of a chiasm, such as A, B, C—to develop a truth, and in the bottom half, A¹, B¹, C¹—restated the thought in reverse order. In a chiasm, the main point is at the point (middle)—which is C and C¹ above. Also note that since A and A¹ are parallel thoughts, they help explain each other; likewise B and B¹ clarify each other; and C and C¹ shine a light on each other.[21]

IN A CHIASM,
THE MAIN POINT IS
AT THE POINT.

Q 74 *Where is the main point of a chiasm?*

Q 75 *In a chiasm, how do parts like A and A¹ help explain each other?*

A Do not trip or trap your brother (Rom. 14:13b).
 B No food is unclean in itself, but... (Rom. 14:14a).
  C Do not destroy your brother for whom Christ died (Rom. 14:15b).
  C¹ Do not destroy the work of God for the sake of food (Rom. 14:20a).
 B¹ All food is clean, but... (Rom. 14:20b).
A¹ Do not do anything that will cause your brother to fall (Rom. 14:21).[22]

Figure 10.13   Romans 14:13-21 is a chiasm.

Q 76 *In the church at Rome, how would it have affected a weak Jewish brother to eat meat?*

Before moving on, Paul says to the strong: On disputed matters, keep your beliefs between you and God. Do not flaunt what you feel free to do. And do not lobby or try to persuade the weak to follow your example.[23] Blessed is the person whose conscience does not condemn what he approves (Rom. 14:22.)

Q 77 *Fill in the blanks in Figure 10.14.*

Topic	The Libertine	The _____ Believer	The _____ Believer	The _____
Explanations and Examples:	"_____" 1 Cor. 6:12a; 10:23a; 15:32a	_____, Matt. 15:10; Rom. 14:14, 21; 1 Tim. 4:5	_____, Rom. 14-15; 1 Cor. 3:1-3; Gal. 4:19-21; Heb. 5:11-14;	_____! _____ (Matt. 23); _____ (Gal. 2:11-16)

Continued on next page

Continued from previous page

Authority sources:	_____ + _____		Scripture + _____	_____ + _____
Characteristics:	Freedom without _____; trying to use _____ as a coat to cover a life of sin (Rom. _____)	A balance of freedom, holiness, and _____; _____, _____, and _____ in the Spirit	False _____ from things Scripture does not _____; _____, _____ and _____ in the Spirit	_____ freedom or joy
Dangers:	_____	_____; _____ others; _____ others; _____ freedom	_____; _____ others; _____ because of others	_____ _____

Figure 10.14   Practice recognizing four types of people in and around the church.

C. Carry one another's weaknesses, as Christ carried ours—do not please yourself (Rom. 15:1-13).

The chapter division at Romans 15:1 makes it seem that Paul has changed subjects. But Romans 14:1–15:13 is on the same topic: relationships between strong and weak believers on disputed matters of the faith.

Paul's gives three principles for the strong to relate to the weak. These principles are like three steps, each with a higher commitment. Principles A–C rise from *accept* (do not judge), to *love* (do not trip or trap), to *carry* (do not please yourself)!

Principle C tells us to *carry* the weaknesses of our weak brothers and sisters in Christ. This verb *carry* (Greek: *bastazo*) means to lift up or bear. Here are some verses in the New Testament that use a form of this verb:

- John said he was not worthy *to carry* the shoes of Jesus (Matt. 3:11).
- Jesus took our infirmities and *carried* our sicknesses (Matt. 8:17).
- We do not *carry* the root [Israel], but the root carries us [the Gentiles] (Rom. 11:18).
- The strong ought *to carry* the weak faith of the weak (Rom. 15:1).
- Believers should *carry* one another's burdens, and thus fulfill the law of Christ (Gal. 6:2).

Q 78 *What are some sacrifices that love delights to make for others?*

A woman watched a little girl carrying a boy on her back. The boy being carried was almost as big as the sister doing the work. The woman walked up to the little girl and asked, " Is the boy you are carrying heavy?" The little girl smiled and replied, "Oh, no, he is not heavy—he is my brother!"[24]

When love is little, sacrifice seems big. Do you feel like God is asking too much of you to forgive someone? Is it too big a sacrifice for you to accept someone from a different culture? Are you being asked too much to miss a movie that contains pornography or profanity? Is the price too expensive if you are asked to join in singing someone else's favorite song, instead of your favorite song? Do you often object at denying yourself? If the answer is *yes* to any of these questions, then it is time to check your love level. When love is low, we think mostly of self. But where love abounds, we hardly notice what we give up for others. *"Jacob served seven years to get Rachel, but they seemed like only a few days to him because of his love for her"* (Gen. 29:20).

Figure 10.15   In some countries, a family member often carries a sister or brother who is less mature.

In a poor family with several children, there was seldom enough food for everyone. But once a month they all looked forward to sharing a chicken at the meal. Each time the pattern was always the same. The mother cut the chicken in pieces, cooked it, and then set the plate of chicken in the center of the table. The family prayed, thanking God for the special meal. There was one piece of chicken for each person. But before anyone chose a piece, the mother always said, "The back is my favorite piece of chicken. Would anyone mind if I take it first?" The children always agreed that mother could have her favorite piece. It was years later, after they grew up, that they realized the back of a chicken is the worst piece. It has almost no meat on it. Then they realized that their mother's love made it a joy for her sacrifice for them. Love delights in putting others ahead of self.

Three daughters were raised in a strict Jewish home. So they never ate ham, bacon, or pork. After they grew up and married, none of them continued to follow the Jewish customs about food. The oldest daughter, Miriam, lived in a big home. From time to time, she invited her two sisters, papa, and mama over for a meal. Miriam always served *kosher* food for papa and mama. But for the others, she cooked a big pork roast. Papa and mama never objected to the pork on the table. Yet the most sensitive sister, Rachel, knew their feelings were hurt. So Rachel said to Miriam, "Please do not serve pork when our parents are at the table." Miriam replied, "Hmm! When our parents are not here, we eat pork in this house, and they know it. So why be a hypocrite? Besides, this is *my* home, and I have the right to serve whatever *I* want." The third sister, Hannah, joined in and said, "Miriam, you are being unkind and disrespectful. Papa and mama know that you are your own boss now. They realize that you can do anything that pleases you. But you do not have to shove pork in their faces to prove that you have freedom." This story illustrates the point of Romans 14–15. Paul did not hide his beliefs. He wrote in Romans that he believes all food is clean. But on disputable matters of the faith, for the sake of love and unity, Paul urges us to accept others, not to trip or trap them, and not to please ourselves.[25]

Q 79 How did Miriam show a lack of love for her parents?

The supreme example of living for others is Christ.

²Each of us should please his neighbor for his good, to build him up. ³For even Christ did not please himself but, as it is written: "The insults of those who insult you [God] have fallen on me [Christ] (Rom. 15:2-4; Ps. 69:9).

Q 80 What are some ways that Jesus denied Himself to edify others?

On the cross, Jesus did not please Himself. He could have called 10,000 angels to deliver Him. Instead, He thought of us—the weak. The sinful words and deeds of mankind were an insult to God. Every sin is an insult to God—an act of rebellion against Him. But on the cross, Jesus became the target of man's rebellion. He was the Lamb of God who came to bear and take away the sins of the world (John 1:29). Calvary was not about Jesus eating His favorite food, celebrating His favorite day, or having the most fun. Jesus did not live to please Himself. He did not die to please Himself.

Paul wrote on behalf of Onesimus, a slave who had run away from his master. Paul led this slave to Christ, and loved him. Paul wrote to the slave's owner, *"If he has done you any wrong or owes you anything, charge it to me"* (Philemon 18). In other words, Paul said, "Put my brother's debts on my bill." Love bears the burdens of others.

On the cross, Jesus was saying, "Father, in whatever ways these sinners have insulted, offended, and sinned against You, put their crimes on My shoulders. Let Me be nailed to a cross to bring peace between You and them. Let Me carry their weaknesses." Consider the reason why Jesus endured the pain and shame of the cross.

---

⁴Surely he took up <u>our</u> infirmities and carried <u>our</u> sorrows,
yet <u>we</u> considered him stricken by God, smitten by him, and afflicted.
⁵But he was pierced for <u>our</u> transgressions, he was crushed for <u>our</u> iniquities;
the punishment that brought <u>us</u> peace was upon him, and by his wounds we are healed.
⁶<u>We all</u>, like sheep, have gone astray, <u>each of us</u> has turned to his own way;
and the LORD has laid <u>on him the iniquity of us all</u> (Isa. 53:4-6).

If you can read these verses without crying, please read them again. Read them and meditate upon them, over and over—until the lesson of these verses softens your heart. Read them until tears blur your eyes. When you cannot see the words clearly, ask yourself this question: "If Jesus gave up everything for me, what am I willing to give up to edify, protect, and shepherd my brothers and sisters?"

Q 81 *What are areas in which you can give up some of your freedom, to carry the weaknesses of others?*

Sarah studied hard and was doing well in a class. After school, she looked forward to doing some things she enjoyed. But then Sarah noticed that Beth, a new girl in school, was failing. Thinking of Romans 15:2, Sarah decided to give up some of her freedom in order to help Beth study. As a result, Beth passed the class, and the two girls became friends. Following the example of Christ means thinking of others—looking for ways to help them, rather than just living to please ourselves.

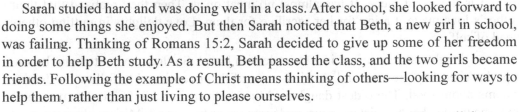

A young man was sitting on a bus when an elderly woman got on. Since all the seats were full, he got up and gave her his seat. She smiled and thanked him. He felt like this was a small way he could think of someone else, and not just please himself.

The Result: The goal and big picture.   This section of Romans 14:1–15:13 ends by focusing on the goal—unity that glorifies God in the church. Paul has given us three principles, A–C, that tell us *what* to do. Now he emphasizes *why* believers must practice these three principles.

> *⁵May the God who gives endurance and encouragement give you a spirit of unity among yourselves as you follow Christ Jesus, ⁶so that with one heart and mouth you may glorify the God and Father of our Lord Jesus Christ. ⁷Accept one another, then, just as Christ accepted you, in order to bring praise to God* (Rom. 15:5-7).

Paul sees the parts as well as the whole. He sees each member of the church—the strong and the weak. He is concerned about each believer. He does not want the weak to be destroyed. Nor does he want the strong to be judged for destroying the weak. Paul cares about each person—the parts of the body. But Paul also sees the whole—the big picture, the mission of God.

- In Romans, Paul first emphasized that *all* have sinned. Both Jews and Gentiles need the righteousness that only God can provide (Rom. 1:18–3:20).

- Next Paul showed that, in Christ, God provides the righteousness we need. As we put our trust in Christ, we receive the righteousness that God provides (Rom. 3:21–5:21). Abraham is the father of *us all*—Jews and Gentiles—who live by faith in Christ (Rom. 4:17).

- As we daily respond to the Spirit, God transforms us into His image. He produces in us the righteousness that Christ has made possible (Rom. 6–8).

- There is only one plan for Jews and Gentiles—to believe in Christ and be led by the Spirit (Rom. 9–11).

- All of us, Jews and Gentiles, are to respond to God in the same way. We are to present our bodies as living sacrifices—no longer conformed to the world, but living with a renewed mind (Rom. 12:1-2). Living with a renewed mind includes honoring government and walking in love (Rom. 13). And this new way of thinking guides us with three big principles. We accept others rather than judge them. We love others, and do not trip or trap them. We carry others, following the example of Christ, and do not please ourselves (Rom. 14:1–15:13).

- The result? Jews and Gentiles live together in love as the people of God. We agree to disagree on secondary matters of faith. With *one* heart and *one* mouth we glorify the God and Father of our one Lord Jesus Christ (Rom. 15:6). Note that Paul emphasizes *one*, not two! There is no division in the church! Hallelujah! When we obey God's principles, God fulfills His glorious plan of the ages!

In Romans 15:7-12, Paul emphasizes the big plan of God—for Jews and Gentiles.[26] Jesus came to fulfill what God planned from the beginning. Recall God's promise to Abraham. God promised to make him the father of many nations. And He promised that through Abraham's seed (Christ), all the nations of the earth will be blessed. Jesus became the servant of the Jews to confirm the promises to Abraham and the patriarchs (Rom. 15:8). Why? *"So that the Gentiles may glorify God for his mercy"* (Rom. 15:9; Gal. 3:14). And surely, as we Gentiles glorify God for His mercy, we will show love and respect to the Jews, to whom and through whom our Savior came.[27] As Paul says later, Gentiles who share in the spiritual blessings of Jews owe them a debt (Rom. 15:27).

Romans 15:9-12 emphasizes God's plan for saving the Gentiles. Paul quotes from the Torah, the Writings, and the Prophets to prove this point[28] (Figure 10.16).

Q 82 *Complete Figure 10.16 by filling in the third column.*

Old Testament	Rom.	Summary, in your own words, of what this passage teaches
2 Sam. 22:50	15:9	
Deut. 32:43	15:10	
Ps. 117:1	15:11	
Isa. 11:10	15:12	

Figure 10.16 Practice summarizing passages about God's love for people in all nations.

Paul closes Romans 14:1–15:13 with two prayers. The first prayer is in Romans 15:5-6. The final prayer of this section is:

May the God of hope fill you with all joy and peace as you trust in him, so that you may overflow with hope by the power of the Holy Spirit (Rom. 15:13).

When we follow the three principles of Romans 14:1–15:13, the kingdom of God manifests itself among us. We have righteousness, joy, and peace as we live in unity. And the Holy Spirit empowers us to overflow with hope even now, as we look forward to eternity in the family of God.

Test Yourself: Circle the letter by the *best* completion to each question or statement.

1. Why did some disobey the Roman government?
a) They were citizens of another world.
b) The emperors were not Christians.
c) The Romans conquered other nations.
d) All of the above.

2. Why must believers submit to government?
a) Governments are stronger than people.
b) Governments depend on submission.
c) Submission makes weak governments better.
d) God establishes all government.

3. God may allow an evil government because
a) it reminds us that time on earth is short.
b) it makes good government look better.
c) it represents the evil desires of the majority.
d) it is not a spiritual concern of His plan.

4. Which is a debt that believers owe?
a) Obedience to the government
b) Taxes to the government
c) Agreement with government policies
d) Participation in government wars

5. Which is true about a believer's debt?
a) We should avoid all debts on earth.
b) Debt is neutral—neither good nor bad.
c) There is one debt we always owe on earth.
d) Debt is evil, and is a form of sin and bondage.

6. Romans 13:8-10 emphasizes that love fulfills
a) the first half of the Ten Commandments.
b) the second half of the Ten Commandments.
c) neither half of the Ten Commandments.
d) both halves of the Ten Commandments.

7. Whom does Romans 14:1–15:13 address?
a) Gentiles and Jews
b) Sinners and saints
c) Those caught in a sin
d) The unconverted

8. Which is an example of a legalist?
a) Lawyers
b) Epicureans
c) Antinomians
d) Judaizers

9. Which does Romans urge us to avoid?
a) Exploiting a believer
b) Trapping a believer
c) Enlisting a believer
d) Using a believer

10. What is the goal of obeying Romans 14:1–15:13?
a) Unity that glorifies God
b) Conversion of the lost
c) Discipleship of the found
d) Transformation of the earth

Essay Test Topics: Write 50-100 words on each of these goals that you studied in this chapter.

- Summarize at least 3 attitudes toward the government in Paul's day.
- Explain 4 reasons why believers must submit to government (Rom. 13:1-5).
- Summarize 7 reasons why God may allow an evil government.
- Identify some debts that believers owe as citizens (Rom. 13:1-7).
- Explain: A believer is always in debt (Rom. 13:8-10). Illustrate this.
- Explain and illustrate 3 aspects of walking in love (Rom. 13:11-14).
- Summarize the background of Romans 14:1–15:13.
- Identify 3 types of matters that believers face (Figure 10.8, Rom. 14:1–15:13).
- Explain the reason why believers should accept and not judge one another (Rom. 14:1-12; 15:7).
- Describe 4 types of people in or around the church (Figure 10.9).
- Explain how love avoids tripping or trapping a brother (Rom. 14:13-23). Give illustrations.
- Give examples of how a strong believer can carry the weaknesses of a brother (Rom. 15:1-6).
- Summarize the result when believers accept, love, and carry each other (Rom. 15:6).

Chapter 11:
Closing of Romans
(Romans 15:14–16:27)

Introduction

This final chapter includes a study on some values of Paul, such as prayer.

Famous Quotes On Prayer
(Continued in Figure 11.10)

🖎 *"You can never do more than pray until you have prayed."* A. J. Gordon

🖎 *"God does nothing except in response to believing prayer."* John Wesley, who prayed 2 hours each day

🖎 *"If I fail to spend two hours in prayer each morning, the devil gets the victory through the day. I have so much work, I must spend three hours daily in prayer."* Martin Luther

🖎 *"Men may reject our message, oppose our arguments, and despise us as persons, but they are helpless against our prayers."* Sidlow Baxter

🖎 *"Satan does not care how many people read about prayer if only he can keep them from praying."* Paul E. Billheimer

🖎 *"Don't pray only when you feel like it. Have an appointment with the Lord and keep it. A person is powerful on his knees."* Corrie ten Boom

🖎 *"No learning can make up for the failure to pray. No earnestness, no diligence, no study, no gifts will take its place."* E. M. Bounds

🖎 *"The little value we put on prayer is seen from the little time we give to it."* E. M. Bounds

🖎 *"Prayer is not overcoming God's resistance, but laying hold of His willingness."* Martin Luther

🖎 When asked how much time he spent in prayer, George Muller replied, *"Hours every day. But I live in the spirit of prayer. I pray as I walk, when I lie down, and when I arise. And the answers are always coming."*

🖎 *"The biggest concern of the devil is to keep Christians from praying. He fears nothing from prayerless studies, prayerless work, and prayerless religion. He laughs at our labor, and mocks our wisdom, but he trembles when we pray."* Samuel Chadwick

🖎 *"I would rather teach one man to pray than ten men to preach."* Charles Spurgeon

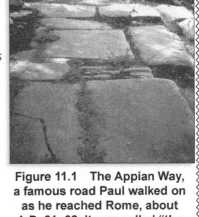

Figure 11.1   The Appian Way, a famous road Paul walked on as he reached Rome, about A.D. 61–62. It was called "the Queen of the long roads."[1]

Figure 11.2   Famous quotes on prayer (Continued in Figure 11.10)[2]

Lessons:

Conclusion: Seven Values of the Apostle Paul—Part 1 (Rom. 15:14–33)

Goal A: *Give evidence in Romans that shows Paul was sensitive to others.*
Goal B: *Summarize Paul's ministry as a priest. Apply this to us.*
Goal C: *Explain and illustrate: "Paul was Christocentric."*
Goal D: *Illustrate the fact that Paul depended on the Holy Spirit for his ministry.*

Conclusion: Seven Values of the Apostle Paul—Part 2 (Rom. 15:14–33)

Goal A: *Explain and illustrate how Paul felt about hard work.*
Goal B: *Give examples to show that Paul valued planning ahead with hope.*
Goal C: *Summarize Paul's two prayer requests in Romans 16.*
Goal D: *Summarize the importance of prayer in your ministry.*

The Vital Gospel (Rom. 16:1-27)

Goal A: *Identify 4 ways that Paul uses Old Testament quotes in Romans.*
Goal B: *Summarize a lesson we can learn from Paul's list of greetings in Romans 16.*
Goal C: *Explain the eternal story linked to Romans 16:20, and the warning just before it.*
Goal D: *Identify the two "bookends" of Romans, and terms common to both.*
Goal E: *Paraphrase the doxology of Romans 16:25-27.*

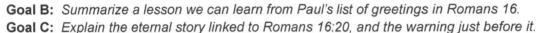

Key Words

doxology—words of praise to God. Sometimes believers sing a doxology at the end of a church service.

Conclusion: Seven Values of the Apostle Paul—Part 1 (Rom. 15:14–33)

Lesson
42

Goal A: *Give evidence in Romans that shows Paul was sensitive to others.*
Goal B: *Summarize Paul's ministry as a priest. Apply this to us.*
Goal C: *Explain and illustrate: "Paul was Christocentric."*
Goal D: *Illustrate the fact that Paul depended on the Holy Spirit for his ministry.*

Setting

Romans 14:1–15:13 is the final part of the practical section (Rom. 12:1–15:13). Then, from Romans 15:14 through chapter 16, Paul is closing the letter. Romans began with an overview of Paul's plans to visit Rome (Rom. 1:8-15). Likewise, as Romans ends, Paul once again mentions his desire to meet Roman believers (Rom. 15:14-33). So there are quite a few verses in Romans that refer to his travel plans. This shows us that Paul's visit to Rome was one of the reasons why he wrote to the Romans.

Paul desired to visit Rome for several reasons. He wanted to preach to the Romans and impart to them some spiritual gift (Rom. 1:11, 15). Some of what Paul hoped to do in person, he has done through his letter to the Romans. Paul also hoped the Romans would partner with him in ministry—giving finances, praying, and perhaps sending people with him to Spain. Paul often traveled with other ministers such as Barnabas, Silas, Timothy, Luke, and Trophimus. Paul had never been to Spain. Perhaps there was a brother or two in Rome who knew about Spain and would go with him.[3]

Q 1 ⟩ *What were some reasons why Paul wanted to visit Rome?*

Looking back at history, we are not sure that God enabled Paul to travel to Spain. We do know that when Paul arrived in Rome, he was a prisoner in chains. A few think Paul went on to Spain, but this is uncertain. Still, these are precious verses about Paul's travel plans to Rome and Spain. As we study Romans 15:14-33, we can identify seven values of Paul the apostle (A–G). We will state these values as principles that can help guide all believers.

Q 2 ⟩ *Looking over this lesson, how can you quickly identify the values of Paul?*

Q 3 🢤 *Which 3 compliments does Paul give to Roman believers? Why?*

A. Paul was sensitive to the feelings of others (Rom. 15:14-16).

¹⁴I myself am convinced, my brothers, that you yourselves are full of goodness, complete in knowledge and competent to instruct one another. ¹⁵I have written you quite boldly on some points, as if to remind you of them again, because of the grace God gave me ¹⁶to be a minister of Christ Jesus to the Gentiles (Rom. 15:14-16a).

Paul was as rough and rugged as any man who ever lived. Review the partial list of his sufferings in 2 Corinthians 11:1–12:10. Paul was as tough as a boot. Five times he received 40 lashes, less one. Many men died the first time they were flogged with 39 lashes. Three times Paul was beaten with rods. He survived being stoned. He made it through three shipwrecks—once spending all day and night in the open sea! He was robbed, imprisoned, and exposed to death *"again and again"* (2 Cor. 11:23). And if all these experiences were not his thorn in the flesh, then add the pain of the thorn to the list. History records that Paul was a small man. But pound for pound, he was as wiry as they came and as tough as the leather tents he sewed.

Paul was tough inside and out. He could rebuke a great apostle like Peter face to face (Gal. 2:11). He could call down blindness on an enemy of the gospel (Acts 13:9-11). Or he could call down a curse on those who perverted the gospel (Gal. 1:8-9).

Yet there was a sensitive side to Paul. He valued the feelings of others. Paul could be *"gentle...like a mother caring for her little children"* (1 Thess. 2:7). He hurt when the weak hurt. He cried when believers sinned (2 Cor. 11:28-29). And Romans 12–15 reveals his concern for righteous relationships between the strong and the weak.

Q 4 🢤 *What do the many questions in Romans reveal about Paul? Explain.*

Although Paul was tough, he was sensitive to the feelings of others. Recall the many questions in Romans. The Spirit led Paul to write these questions as he asked himself, "What will the Romans be thinking and feeling as they read my letter to them?" Paul practiced thinking from the viewpoint of his readers and listeners.

Q 5 🢤 *How did Gideon use a compliment to turn an angry enemy into a smiling friend (Judges 8:1-3)?*

The three compliments in Romans 15:14 reveal Paul's sensitivity to the feelings of others. Paying a sincere compliment is words well spent. The Roman church was strong, perhaps 25 years old, and had a good reputation for its faith (Rom. 1:8). Paul does not want these mature believers to feel like first graders in primary school. He has written them a long, bold letter—covering the A,B,C's of the faith. So he takes the time to compliment them. He reassures them that he is only *reminding* them again of what they already know. As the proverb says, "Men must be taught as if you taught them not, and things unknown proposed as things forgot."⁴ Like Paul, let us value the thoughts and feelings of others. Let us practice thinking from our listener's point of view. An important skill we need for relating to others is learning to think from their point of view.⁵

Q 6 🢧 *Did Jesus value the thoughts, needs, and feelings of others? Give examples.*

Jesus practiced thinking about the needs and feelings of others. He noticed when people were hungry or thirsty. He cared when people were sick or had physical problems. He perceived when people were sad, discouraged, angry, or afraid. He looked behind actions and understood why people did and said things. Jesus was sensitive and perceptive to the thoughts, desires, and feelings of others. And this value helped Him lead others, minister to them, and relate to them. As we practice thinking from the viewpoint of others, we are following our Master's example.

Q 7 🢤 *Why should every pastor practice seeing life through the eyes of others?*

 Sabio says: "All of us spend a lot of time thinking about what we want. But the wise become more fruitful as they practice discerning what others want, think, and feel."

After complimenting Roman believers three times, Paul adds that his long letter flows from his calling to the Gentiles. In other words, the long letter was *not* due to a lack of understanding among Roman believers. This polite explanation would make Roman readers feel more secure. And it reveals that Paul was thinking from the viewpoint of his readers. Let us follow his example. Even the roughest, toughest person can practice being sensitive to the feelings of others.

B. Paul treasured his calling as a priest to win and disciple the lost—especially the untold (Rom. 15:15b-16, 20-22).

¹⁵*I have written you quite boldly on some points, as if to remind you of them again, because of the grace God gave me* ¹⁶*to be a minister of Christ Jesus to the Gentiles with the priestly duty of proclaiming the gospel of God, so that the Gentiles might become an offering acceptable to God, sanctified by the Holy Spirit* (Rom. 15:15-16).

The practical section of Romans 14:1–15:13 ends by quoting four passages. These emphasize that God's plan of salvation includes the Gentiles. These four passages serve as a bridge to the closing of Romans—which focuses on Paul's ministry to the Gentiles. The Greek word for *Gentiles* is *ethnos,* which means "ethnic groups or nations." Sometimes in the New Testament, we see a contrast between Jews and Gentiles—a contrast between the Jews and all of the other ethnic groups or nations of the world. For example, Galatians 2:6-9 contrasts Peter's ministry to the Jews, and Paul's ministry to the Gentiles, all non-Jews.

Q 8 *What does the word "Gentiles" mean?*

Paul's calling was a delight to him. He saw his ministry as a *priestly* duty. The Greek word for *priestly* is *leitourgos* (Rom. 15:16). Every priest had a *holy offering*. Note that the Gentiles were Paul's holy offering. For as Paul proclaimed the gospel of Jesus Christ to the nations, it changed people's lives. And they became an *"offering acceptable to God, sanctified* [made holy] *by the Holy Spirit"* (Rom. 15:16).

Q 9 *As a priest, what was Paul's offering?*

Some live from pleasure to pleasure—from one thrill to the next. Instead of eating to live, they live to eat. But for Paul, life was not about eating his favorite meat. He could be just as happy eating vegetables. Nor did Paul care much about celebrating his favorite day. He did not live to be entertained. And he never argued about what songs to sing at church. Paul lived to win the lost to Christ, and to disciple them. This was his passion, his heartbeat, his calling, his life.

Q 10 *For what do you live? Is Jesus the Lord of your desires?*

> NOTE THAT PAUL ALWAYS LINKED EVANGELISM WITH DISCIPLESHIP.

Note that Paul always linked evangelism with discipleship. His ministry was *"leading the Gentiles to obey God"* by his words and deeds (Rom. 15:18). Paul links **faith and obedience** from the beginning (Rom. 1:5) to the end (Rom. 16:26) of his gospel. As fire and heat are always together, faith and obedience are impossible to separate. Wherever there is biblical faith, there is obedience. For as the body without the spirit is dead, faith without works of obedience is dead (James 2:14-17). In Romans, faith is the root of salvation, and obedience is the fruit.

Q 11 *Why must we always link evangelism and discipleship?*

The teachings of Jesus taught Paul and the other apostles to link faith and obedience. Matthew 5–7 contains some famous teachings of Jesus. The Master teacher closed with this story that linked faith and action:

> ²⁴*"Therefore everyone who hears these words of mine and puts them into practice is like a wise man who built his house on the rock.* ²⁵*The rain came down, the streams rose, and the winds blew and beat against that house; yet it did not fall, because it had its foundation on the rock.* ²⁶*But everyone who hears these words of mine and does not put them into practice is like a foolish man who built his house on sand.* ²⁷*The rain came down, the streams rose, and the winds blew and beat against that house, and it fell with a great crash"* (Matt. 7:24-27).

Q 12 *Is the goal of the Great Commission evangelism or discipleship (Matt. 28:19-20)? Explain.*

Paul lived and breathed to disciple people—to lead them to obey the teachings of Jesus. And he especially looked for those who had never heard the gospel.

Q 13 *Should anyone hear the gospel twice, before everyone has heard it once? Explain.*

²⁰It has always been my ambition to preach the gospel where Christ was not known, so that I would not be building on someone else's foundation. ²¹Rather, as it is written: "Those who were not told about him will see, and those who have not heard will understand." ²²This is why I have often been hindered from coming to you (Rom. 15:20-22).

This great apostle liked to build new foundations. He was a pioneer—a missionary and priest to the untold.

Today, in a world of 6 billion people, 3 billion have not yet heard a clear communication of the gospel. If Paul were alive today, he would be trying to reach the unreached.

All of us live around people who need Christ. May each of us see ourself as a priest. May we witness in our family, neighborhood, place of work, or school—and even distant places. For the promise of Acts 1:8 is that as the Spirit fills us, we will receive power to witness for Christ, in Jerusalem, Judea, Samaria, and the ends of the earth.

Justin was born a Gentile to pagan parents in Palestine. He received a Greek education, and spent many years studying music, astronomy, and geometry, and especially the philosophy of Plato. But the hundreds of hours of higher education left Justin empty. One day, in an effort to be alone to meditate, he went walking along beside the sea, probably near Ephesus. Along the seashore he met an old man. The old man listened as Justin emphasized the importance of much education and praised Greek philosophy. We do not know the name of the old man, or whether he had much education. But he is famous for asking Justin a simple question. The question was something like, "Who is more qualified to talk about God, the philosopher who has never met God, or the prophets who lived in God's presence?" This simple question from a common old man pierced the heart of Justin. At once he felt the desire to study the prophets of the Bible, to see what they could teach him about God. In time, the prophets led Justin to the manger, and then the cross. Justin was converted and grew strong in the faith. He moved to Rome and opened a school, defending Christian beliefs and leading many Gentiles to Christ. He became one of the most famous apologists, or defenders of the faith, in Church history. Today we know him as Justin Martyr, who was martyred or beheaded for his testimony for Christ in A.D. 165. Be encouraged that this highly educated sinner was brought to Christ by a common old man who dared to ask one question for Christ. Wherever you are, ask the Spirit to guide your words. A simple question from a common Christian may unlock the gate to heaven for someone.[6]

**Figure 11.3
Justin Martyr**

Q 14 *What does "Christocentric" mean?*

Q 15 *Should we see more T-shirts today that display Jeremiah 9:24? Explain.*

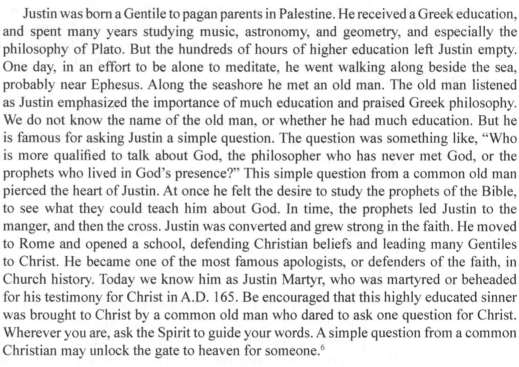

Jeremiah
9:24

Figure 11.4   Paul's motto was Jeremiah 9:24.

C. Paul was Christocentric—he kept the focus on Christ, not himself (Rom. 15:17-18).

¹⁷Therefore I glory in Christ Jesus in my service to God. ¹⁸I will not venture to speak of anything except what Christ has accomplished through me in leading the Gentiles to obey God by what I have said and done (Rom. 15:17-18).

We live in a day of superstars, famous athletes, and actors. The world exalts its celebrities—the big wheels, the fat cats, and the high flyers. Even some preachers and Christian singers today call attention to themselves by the way they dress and act. In contrast, Paul did not glory in himself. His education was the best of the day under Gamaliel, but he did not glory in it (Acts 22:3). His ancestors were 100 percent Jewish, but he did not mention them (Phil. 3:4-5). He worked harder than all the apostles, performed more miracles, had more visions, and suffered more—but he did not like to talk about these things. Paul's motto was, *"Let him who boasts, boast in the Lord"* (Jer. 9:24; 1 Cor. 1:31; 2 Cor. 10:1). If Paul wore a T-shirt today, it would display Jeremiah 9:24. Paul gloried in Christ, not himself. His favorite subject was *"what Christ has accomplished through me in leading the Gentiles to obey God by what I have said and done"* (Rom. 15:17-18).

Application: Do we follow Paul's example, or are we trying to make a name for ourselves? Suppose someone recorded our conversations and played them for us. What would we hear? Would we be talking about Christ or about ourselves? On the day when we give account for our words, will the Lord approve or accuse us (Matt. 12:36-37)? Lord, help us to rejoice in You and all You do for us day by day. May our conversations be filled with praise for You.

D. Paul depended on the power of the Holy Spirit for his supernatural ministry—words and deeds (Rom. 15:18-19).

Q 16 ↖ Does God still want to give signs and miracles today?

[18]I will not venture to speak of anything except what Christ has accomplished through me in leading the Gentiles to obey God by what I have said and done— [19]by the power of signs and miracles, through the power of the Spirit (Rom. 15:18-19a).

The Holy Spirit is *the* source of a fruitful ministry. The New Testament records that the preaching of the gospel came with miracles to confirm it. John's gospel is built around seven or more signs (miracles) that Jesus did (John 20:30-31). Likewise Luke emphasizes that miracles seized the attention of the listeners as the apostles and deacons preached the gospel (Acts 2:5-41; 3:1–4:4; 4:29-30; 5:12-16; 6:8; 8:13; 13:9-12; 14:3, 8-18; 15:12; 16:25-34; 19:11-20). Among people who did not know which religion to believe, miracles were signs that pointed in the direction of the one, true God.[7] It is true that signs and wonders often occur in regions where people first hear the gospel. But it is also true that God still answers prayer today. Let us have the faith to pray for the sick we meet. Prayer gives God an opportunity to reveal Himself. Even though much of the world has heard the gospel, healings and miracles in the name of Jesus still shed light on the right path. One picture is worth a thousand words. And one miracle can still turn a multitude toward Christ. Biblical sermons are not a substitute for signs and wonders, by the power of the Holy Spirit.

Q 17 ↖ How did the power of the Spirit transform Pastor Li's ministry?

Pastor Li (not his real name) in Northern Asia is frustrated. The groups of believers he pastors are small, and not growing. They meet each week, and share the gospel whenever they can. But few people are accepting Christ and being added to the fellowship. Also, it seems that believers are not becoming strong disciples and are not bearing fruit. Growth has stopped. Something powerful and supernatural needs to happen in the network of their house churches. Then one evening, Pastor Li comes home and finds his wife translating lessons for the new *Faith & Action* course *Acts of the Holy Spirit*. Looking over her shoulder, Li begins reading her translation. He usually feels tired when he comes home, and just wants to rest. But this evening he feels drawn to read this lesson on Acts. He leans forward and studies the lesson for several minutes. His heart beats faster and faster. The lesson comes alive to him. He feels the Holy Spirit speak to him in a powerful way. Pastor Li says to his wife, "These are wonderful teachings." He grabs some of the pages, lifts them up and says, "These are perfect! I can preach from these!" Not long after this Li preaches his first sermon on the power of the Holy Spirit. He describes what the book of Acts records. The *Spirit* enabled disciples to testify, preach, and pray for the sick in their communities. As Pastor Li preaches, the Lord anoints him. Revival breaks out in the house churches. Many are filled with the Spirit and begin to speak in tongues. This is the first time such a thing has happened in Pastor Li's network of house churches. Things begin to change rapidly. Those who are filled with the Spirit start to go out and share Jesus with others, using their new gifts and power of the Holy Spirit. As a result, many new people are added to the house churches. The revival continues for months, and even today. Later on, Pastor Li receives many invitations to preach the same message in other networks of house churches. So he begins to travel from place to place, preaching about the power of the Holy Spirit. As the message of the Spirit spreads, revival breaks out in new house churches. In fact, Pastor Li is becoming known in his area of China as "Pastor Acts." His life and ministry were transformed by the power of the Holy Spirit.[8] It is still God's desire *today* to equip believers for ministry with the power of the Holy Spirit.

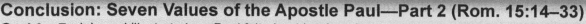

Conclusion: Seven Values of the Apostle Paul—Part 2 (Rom. 15:14–33)

Lesson 43

Goal A: *Explain and illustrate how Paul felt about hard work.*
Goal B: *Give examples to show that Paul valued planning ahead with hope.*
Goal C: *Summarize Paul's two prayer requests in Romans 16.*
Goal D: *Summarize the importance of prayer in your ministry.*

We are studying seven values of the apostle Paul. In Lesson 42 we studied values A–D:

A. Paul was sensitive to the feelings of others (Rom. 15:14-16).

B. Paul treasured his calling as a priest to win and disciple the lost—especially the untold (Rom. 15:15b-16, 20-22).

C. Paul was <u>Christo</u>centric—he kept the focus on Christ, not himself (Rom. 15:17-18).

D. Paul depended on the power of the Spirit for his supernatural ministry—words and deeds (Rom. 15:18-19).

Now, in this lesson, let us look at three more of Paul's values.

Q 18 ⚒ *Did the anointing of the Spirit eliminate the need for hard work in Paul's ministry? Explain.*

E. Paul valued hard work (Rom. 15:17-20, 23).

So from Jerusalem all the way around to Illyricum, I have fully proclaimed the gospel of Christ (Rom. 15:19b).

*But now that there is no more place for me to **work** in these regions ...* (Rom. 15:23).

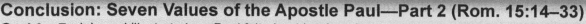

Figure 11.5   Paul *"fully proclaimed the gospel"* from Jerusalem to Illyricum.

Paul depended on the power of the Spirit. But the Spirit does not replace the need for hard work in ministry. Paul's travels were in the shape of an arc, from Jerusalem to Illyricum, which is called Yugoslavia today. Paul had planted churches in all the key cities of this entire region, which was a big area. Today, you can ride a train for 30 hours over just *part* of this area. Thirty hours, by train! So imagine how long it took Paul on a ship, or on foot. We know of three missionary trips that Paul took in this area of ministry. His first missionary trip was from Antioch, Syria in A.D. 48. And he wrote to the Romans from Corinth in A.D. 57. So Paul spent about 10 years spreading the gospel from Jerusalem to Illyricum. During those times he battled sickness, climbed mountains, crossed seas, and endured much persecution. By the power of the Spirit, with blood, sweat, and tears, Paul led the Gentiles to be an offering to Christ. The apostle Paul valued hard work.

Q 19 *Complete Figure 11.6, famous Proverbs about laziness.*

Reference	Your summary of the proverb
Prov. 19:15	
Prov. 20:4	
Prov. 20:13	

Figure 11.6   Famous proverbs about laziness and work

Here are some quotes about work:[9] No pain no gain. No dream comes true, until you wake up and go to work. Just over the hill is a beautiful valley, but you must climb the hill to see it. God gives us what we need for daily bread, but He expects us to bake it. The church needs people who talk less and work more. Families that pray together stay together; and families that work together eat. Good luck often has the odor of perspiration. A person's work is a portrait of self. *"Where there are no oxen, the manger is empty, but from the strength of an ox comes an abundant harvest"* (Prov. 14:4). The worst fear is fear of work.

Q 20 *Complete Figure 11.7, statements Paul made about work.*

Reference	Your summary of what Paul wrote about work
Rom. 12:12	
Rom. 16:6	
Rom. 16:12	
1 Cor. 9:24-27	
1 Cor. 15:10	
Col. 3:23	
2 Thess. 3:10-12	
1 Tim. 5:8	
2 Tim. 2:15	

Figure 11.7   Paul's life and writings emphasize the value of hard work.

F. Paul valued planning ahead—with hope (Rom. 15:23-26).

Q 21 *What evidence shows that Paul planned with hope?*

[23]*But now that there is no more place for me to work in these regions, and since I have been longing for many years to see you,* [24]*I **plan** to do so when I go to Spain. I hope to visit you while passing through and to have you assist me on my journey there, after I have enjoyed your company for a while.* [25]*Now, however, I am on my way to Jerusalem in the service of the saints there.* [26]*For Macedonia and Achaia were pleased to make a contribution for the poor among the saints in Jerusalem* (Rom. 15:23-26).

Paul lived with a calendar, a map, and a list of goals. It did not just happen that he preached in all the key cities from Jerusalem to Illyricum. Paul planned his ministry. Paul was intentional. He wrote to the Romans from Corinth. His plan, Lord willing, was to deliver an offering to the poor saints at Jerusalem. This offering was the result of a plan he had followed for several years. After he delivered the offering to Jerusalem, Paul planned to visit the Romans, on his way to Spain (see Figure 11.5). Some who claim to be spiritual do not plan or set goals. These refuse to plan. We are not sure what tomorrow will bring. So we must plan in hope, depending on God. Still, failing to plan is planning to fail. Spiritual people value planning.

Q 22 How would you respond to someone who said that planning is unspiritual?

God had a plan when He created the world. He planned day and night, land and sea, heaven and earth. His plan included animals, fish, birds, and humans. And in each of the thousands of species, God planned male and female. He planned the human body so that all of the parts work together. He has planned hell for all who rebel against Him, and heaven for those who obey Him. Those who value planning share a value of Paul, and of God.

G. Paul valued prayer support (Rom. 15:30-33).

Figure 11.8
Paul was often in prison because of enemies of the gospel. He asked Romans believers to pray that he be rescued from unbelievers in Judea (Rom. 15:31).

30I urge you, brothers, by our Lord Jesus Christ and by the love of the Spirit, to join me in my struggle by praying to God for me. 31Pray that I may be rescued from the unbelievers in Judea and that my service in Jerusalem may be acceptable to the saints there, 32so that by God's will I may come to you with joy and together with you be refreshed (Rom. 15:30-32).

Paul wanted more than admiration, applause, or spectators. He urged people, *"Join me in my struggle by praying to God for me"* (Rom. 15:30). Note that this verse mentions all three members of the Trinity. Paul was planning to go to Jerusalem. And he knew there would be a spiritual struggle there—a spiritual wrestling match with humans and demons. So Paul pleaded for the most powerful help available, prayer!

History depends on the prayers of God's people. When Aaron and Hur held up the hands of Moses toward God, Joshua defeated the Amalekites. If the Israelites had prayed and trusted God instead of fearing the giants of Canaan, God would have defeated Israel's enemies. But because the people magnified their problems instead of magnifying the Lord, a generation lost their inheritance and died in the wilderness (Num. 14). God could have even used hornets to drive out Israel's enemies (Exod. 23:28). But they refused to believe and pray. In contrast, the government chained Peter in prison and assigned 16 guards to keep him there. But the church prayed. As a result, the chains fell off, the gates opened, and Peter joined the prayer meeting!

Q 23 What were Paul's 2 prayer requests? Explain each.

Paul valued prayer. He urged believers in Rome to join in his struggles by praying to God for him (Rom. 15:30). The word *urge* reveals that Paul is very concerned about what will happen when he reaches Jerusalem.[10] Paul urged prayer for two urgent requests.

- *First,* Paul urged: *"Pray that I may be rescued from the unbelievers in Judea"* (Rom. 15:31a). Recall that in Jerusalem, the *unbelievers* included his enemies, who had tried to kill him (Acts 9:29-30). Paul's journey to Jerusalem was a matter of life and death. He urged Roman believers to pray for him.

- *Second,* Paul urged prayer *"that my service in Jerusalem may be acceptable to the saints there"* (Rom. 15:31b). Earlier Paul explained: *"I am on my way to Jerusalem in the service of the saints there. 26For Macedonia and Achaia were pleased to make a contribution for the poor among the saints in Jerusalem"* (Rom. 15:25-26). So his *service to the saints in Jerusalem* referred to delivering an offering from Gentile believers to poor Jewish believers. This offering or *collection for the saints* has a long background. In Galatians 2:9-10, Paul mentions that Jewish leaders in Jerusalem, including James, Peter, and John, affirmed Paul's ministry to the Gentiles. But they asked him to *"remember the poor,"* that is, the poor saints in Jerusalem. So delivering this offering from Gentile to Jewish believers was very important to Paul. The offering showed that Gentile believers felt a debt of love toward Jewish believers (Rom. 11:18; 15:27). And the offering, when received, would show that Jewish believers appreciated the love and faith of Gentile believers. In other words, the offering showed that Jews and Gentiles loved and appreciated each other. The offering was a practical symbol of unity in the body of Christ.[11] But Paul was not sure how Jewish believers in Jerusalem might feel about the offering from the Gentiles. Some Jewish believers resented Paul's ministry to the Gentiles. In fact, recall that when Paul does arrive in Jerusalem, church leaders told him:

20 *"You see, brother, how many thousands of Jews have believed, and all of them are zealous for the law.* 21 *They have been informed that you teach all the Jews who live among the Gentiles to turn away from Moses, telling them not to circumcise their children or live according to our customs"* (Acts 21:20-21).

So before traveling to Jerusalem, Paul urged the Romans to pray with him about this offering. Perhaps some Jews in Jerusalem would say, "Do not receive this offering from the Gentiles. Paul is a traitor to our Jewish traditions. Now he is trying to buy our favor. He is trying to bribe us into accepting his ministry. Let his money perish with him." Paul knew that the feeling for religious traditions is strong. But as the letter to the Romans shows, Paul did not try to persuade Jewish brothers to reject their traditions. Rather, he urged the Gentiles to respect and accept Jewish believers for their beliefs about clean foods, and honoring certain days—so long as these matters were viewed as secondary, disputed, and not vital to salvation. So as Paul prepares to travel to Jerusalem with the offering he has collected, he urges prayer that it be received in the same spirit of love that the Gentiles sacrificed to share it. Wow! This was an important offering. It could serve as a monument of unity between Jewish and Gentile believers.

Paul urged believers to pray that he would be delivered from unbelievers in Judea, and that the offering would be received well. If these two prayers were answered, Paul would come to the Romans *by God's will, with joy,* and *be refreshed* (Rom. 15:32). Looking back, we know that Paul's enemies did not kill him in Jerusalem. But the letter Paul sent to the Philippians was written from a prison cell in Rome (Phil. 1:12-18). In these verses, we see Paul encouraging himself that his prison experience encouraged some to preach. Thus he practiced the principle of Romans 8:28—seeing God at work for good in all things.[12]

Q 24 ✎ *Do you pray at least an hour a day? If not how much do you pray? When?*

Prayer connects us to God, the ruler of the universe. The Bible, the word of God Almighty, reveals the privilege and power of prayer. (Complete Figure 11.8 to review the value of prayer.)

Q 25 ✎ *Complete Figure 11.8 on biblical insights about prayer.*

Reference	Your summary of what God's Word teaches about prayer
Exod. 14:13-22	
Exod. 17:10-16	Because the hands of Moses were lifted up to the throne of the Lord, _____
2 Kings 6:8-20	
2 Chron. 7:11-14	
2 Chron. 14	
2 Chron. 20:1-29	
Dan. 2:17-18	
Dan. 6:4-24	
Matt. 7:7-11	
Mark 11:22-24	
Luke 11:5-13	
Luke 18:1-8	
John 15:7	
Acts 12:5, 12	
Phil. 4:6-7	
James 5:13-18	
1 John 3:21-22	
1 John 5:14-15	

Figure 11.9 Practice reviewing a few examples of what the Scriptures reveal about prayer.

At age 18 Hudson Taylor wandered into his father's library and read a gospel tract. He could not shake off its message. Finally, falling to his knees, he accepted Christ as his Savior. Later, his mother, who had been away, returned home. When Hudson told her the good news, she said, "I already know. Ten days ago, the very date on which you tell me you read that tract, I spent the entire afternoon in prayer for you. I prayed until the Lord assured me of your salvation." [Hudson Taylor (1832-1905) was a famous missionary in China. He was founder of the China Inland Mission which, at his death, included 205 mission stations with over 800 missionaries, and 125,000 Chinese Christians. He spent 51 years in China].[13]

Dwight L. Moody, a famous evangelist, was better at praying than at preaching. Often he faced problems that seemed impossible to solve. But he knew the way to overcome all difficulties. He believed in the depths of his soul that nothing is too hard for the Lord, and that prayer helps makes possible what God desires. Like Paul, he valued prayer as the key to victory.[14]

Famous quotes on prayer
(Continued from Figure 11.2)

✎ *"One should never begin anything until it is soaked with prayer."* Author unknown

✎ *"Prayer does not prepare us for the greater work; prayer is the greater work."* Oswald Chambers

✎ *"It is not enough to begin to pray, nor to pray rightly; neither is it enough to pray for a while; but we must be patient, believe, and continue in prayer until we receive an answer."* George Müller

✎ *"We are too busy to pray, and so we are too busy to have power. We have a great deal of activity, but we accomplish little; many services but few conversions; much machinery but few results."* R. A. Torrey

✎ *"Prayer is not learned in a classroom but in a closet."* E. M. Bounds

✎ *"Prayer is not monologue, but dialogue. Prayer is talking to God and listening to him."* Andrew Murray

✎ *"Each time, before you pray, be quiet first, and worship God in His glory. Think of what He can do, and how He delights to hear the prayers of His children. Think of your place and privilege in Christ, and expect great things!"* Andrew Murray

✎ *"If you want power in prayer, you must remain in loving, living, lasting, conscious, practical, abiding union with the Lord Jesus Christ."* C. H. Spurgeon

Figure 11.10   Famous quotes on prayer[15]

The God of peace be with you all. Amen
(Rom. 15:33).

The Vital Gospel (Rom. 16:1-27)

Lesson 44

Goal A: *Identify 4 ways that Paul uses Old Testament quotes in Romans.*
Goal B: *Summarize a lesson we can learn from Paul's list of greetings in Romans 16.*
Goal C: *Explain the eternal story linked to Romans 16:20, and the warning just before it.*
Goal D: *Identify the two "bookends" of Romans, and terms common to both.*
Goal E: *Paraphrase the doxology of Romans 16:25-27.*

Review and overview: Throughout Romans, Paul often *refers* or *alludes* to the Old Testament without quoting it. These references (without quotations) to the Old Testament include such concepts as gospel, promise, faith , calling, son of God, Holy Spirit, the fall of humanity, and human response to the law of God.[16] In addition to the allusions, Paul quotes and uses Old Testament passages in various ways—such as *historical citation, verification, comparison, and application.[17] Figure 11.11 gives an overview of the 60 passages in Romans that cite the Old Testament. As you read through these passages, think about which of the five parts of Romans each quote is in. And analyze how Paul used the passage.

Q 26 ✎ *What are 4 ways that Paul uses Old Testament quotes?*

Q 27 ✎ *Why do you think 30 of the 60 Old Testament quotes in Romans are in Romans 9–11?*

Rom.	Quote	Old Testament
1:17	*"The righteous will live by faith."*	Hab. 2:4
2:6	*"God will give to each person according to what he has done."*	Ps. 62:12
2:24	*"God's name is blasphemed among the Gentiles because of you."*	Isa. 52:5
2:29	*A man is a Jew if he is one inwardly; and circumcision is circumcision of the heart, by the Spirit, not by the written code.*	Deut. 30:6
3:4	*"So that you may be proved right when you speak and prevail when you judge."*	Ps. 51:4
3:10-12	*[10]"There is no one righteous, not even one; [11]there is no one who understands, no one who seeks God. All have turned away, they have together become worthless."*	Ps. 14:2-3
3:13a	*"Their throats are open graves; their tongues practice deceit."*	Ps. 5:9
3:13b	*"The poison of vipers is on their lips."*	Ps. 140:3
3:14	*"Their mouths are full of cursing and bitterness."*	Ps. 10:7
3:15-17	*[15]"Their feet are swift to shed blood; [16]ruin and misery mark their ways, [17]and the way of peace they do not know."*	Isa. 59:7-8
3:18	*"There is no fear of God before their eyes."*	Ps. 36:1
4:3	*"Abraham believed God, and it was credited to him as righteousness."*	Gen. 15:6
4:7-8	*[7]"Blessed are they whose transgressions are forgiven, whose sins are covered. [8]Blessed is the man whose sin the Lord will never count against him."*	Ps. 32:1-2
4:9	*Abraham's faith was credited to him as righteousness.*	Gen. 15:6
4:17	*"I have made you a father of many nations."*	Gen. 17:5
4:18	*"So shall your offspring be."*	Gen. 15:5
4:22-23	*"It was credited to him as righteousness."*	Gen. 15:6
7:7	*"Do not covet."*	Exod. 20:17
8:36	*"For your sake we face death all day long; we are considered as sheep to be slaughtered."*	Ps. 44:22
9:7	*"It is through Isaac that your offspring will be reckoned."*	Gen. 21:12
9:9	*"At the appointed time I will return, and Sarah will have a son."*	Gen. 18:10
9:12	*"The older will serve the younger."*	Gen. 25:23
9:13	*"Jacob I loved, but Esau I hated."*	Mal. 1:3
9:15	*"I will have mercy on whom I have mercy, and I will have compassion on whom I have compassion."*	Exod. 33:19
9:17	*"I raised you up for this very purpose, that I might display my power in you and that my name might be proclaimed in all the earth."*	Exod. 9:16
9:20	*"Shall what is formed say to him who formed it, 'Why did you make me like this?'"*	Isa. 29:16; 45:9
9:25	*"I will call them 'my people' who are not my people; and I will call her 'my loved one' who is not my loved one."*	Hos. 2:23
9:26	*"It will happen that in the very place where it was said to them, 'You are not my people,' they will be called 'sons of the living God.'"*	Hos. 1:10

Continued on next page

Continued from previous page

9:27-28	"Though the number of the Israelites be like the sand by the sea, only the remnant will be saved. For the Lord will carry out his sentence on earth with speed and finality."	Isa. 10:22-23
9:29	"Unless the Lord Almighty had left us descendants, we would have become like Sodom, we would have been like Gomorrah."	Isa. 1:9
9:33a	"See, I lay in Zion a stone that causes men to stumble and a rock that makes them fall,"	Isa. 8:14
9:33b	"and the one who trusts in him will never be put to shame."	Isa. 28:16
10:5	Moses describes in this way the righteousness that is by the law: "The man who does these things will live by them."	Lev. 18:5
10:6-8	"Do not say in your heart, 'Who will ascend into heaven?'" (that is, to bring Christ down) "or 'Who will descend into the deep?'" (that is, to bring Christ up from the dead). But what does it say? "The word is near you; it is in your mouth and in your heart."	Deut. 30:12-14
10:11	"Anyone who trusts in him will never be put to shame."	Isa. 28:16
10:13	"Everyone who calls on the name of the Lord will be saved."	Joel 2:32
10:15	"How beautiful are the feet of those who bring good news!"	Isa. 52:7
10:16	"Lord, who has believed our message?"	Isa. 53:1
10:18	"Their voice has gone out into all the earth, their words to the ends of the world."	Ps. 19:4
10:19	First Moses says, "I will make you envious by those who are not a nation; I will make you angry by a nation that has no understanding."	Deut. 32:21
10:20	And Isaiah boldly says, "I was found by those who did not seek me; I revealed myself to those who did not ask for me."	Isa. 65:1
10:21	But concerning Israel he says, "All day long I have held out my hands to a disobedient and obstinate people."	Isa. 65:2
11:3	...Elijah—how he appealed to God against Israel: "Lord, they have killed your prophets and torn down your altars; I am the only one left, and they are trying to kill me."	1 Kings 19:10, 14
11:4	And what was God's answer to him? "I have reserved for myself seven thousand who have not bowed the knee to Baal."	1 Kings 19:18
11:8	"God gave them a spirit of stupor, eyes so that they could not see and ears so that they could not hear, to this very day."	Deut. 29:4; Isa. 29:10
11:9-10	And David says: "May their table become a snare and a trap, a stumbling block and a retribution for them. May their eyes be darkened so they cannot see, and their backs be bent forever."	Ps. 69:22-23
11:26-27	"The deliverer will come from Zion; he will turn godlessness away from Jacob. And this is my covenant with them when I take away their sins."	Isa. 59:20-21
11:34	"Who has known the mind of the Lord? Or who has been his counselor?"	Isa. 40:13
11:35	"Who has ever given to God, that God should repay him?"	Job 41:11
12:19	"It is mine to avenge; I will repay," says the Lord.	Deut. 32:35
12:20	"If your enemy is hungry, feed him; if he is thirsty, give him something to drink. In doing this, you will heap burning coals on his head."	Prov. 25:21-22
13:9a	"Do not commit adultery," "Do not murder," "Do not steal," "Do not covet."	Exod. 20:13-17; Deut. 5:17-21
13:9b	"Love your neighbor as yourself."	Lev. 19:18
14:11	For we will all stand before God's judgment seat. It is written: "'As surely as I live,' says the Lord, 'every knee will bow before me; every tongue will confess to God.'"	Isa. 45:23
15:3	For even Christ did not please himself but, as it is written: "The insults of those who insult you have fallen on me."	Ps. 69:9
15:9	"Therefore I will praise you among the Gentiles; I will sing hymns to your name."	Ps. 18:49
15:10	Again, it says, "Rejoice, O Gentiles, with his people."	Deut. 32:43
15:11	And again, "Praise the Lord, all you Gentiles, and sing praises to him, all you peoples."	Ps. 117:1
15:12	And again, Isaiah says, "The Root of Jesse will spring up, one who will arise to rule over the nations; the Gentiles will hope in him."	Isa. 11:10
15:21	"Those who were not told about him will see, and those who have not heard will understand."	Isa. 52:15

Figure 11.11   In Romans, Paul quotes over 60 passages from the Old Testament Scriptures.

Q 28 ➤ *Which key words are in both bookends of Romans?.*

Setting: The two "bookends" of Romans (1:1-7 and 16:17-25) emphasize Paul's gospel to the nations: believe and obey Christ (Figure 1.18). Take time to read the verses of these two "bookends," at the introduction and conclusion of Romans. Notice the words and thoughts that are in both. Note that a form of the Greek word *ethnos* is translated *Gentiles* in Romans 1:5, and *nations* in Romans 16:26. So if you can read Greek, you will notice a form of *ethnos* in both bookends.

You might think that Romans 16 is only a dessert after a steak. But we will study two grand truths in this final chapter of Romans.[18]

A. Through the gospel we are part of one eternal family (Rom. 16:1-16; 20b-24).

Paul mentions at least 35 people or groups of people. The greetings in this section are not just about keeping in touch. These greetings strengthen the connections Paul has with believers and house churches in Rome.[19] Note that these names are in two parts. In the *first list,* Romans 16:1-16, Paul names 27 people he knows in Rome. The apostle Paul had never been to Rome. But he had many friends there. This was long before there were post offices, e-mail, cell phones, or Facebook! Imagine how many friends Paul would name if he were writing Romans today.

Q 29 ➤ *How do the two lists of Romans 16 differ?*

Q 30 ➤ *How many people or groups does Paul mention in Romans 16?*

The *second list* of believers is in Romans 16:21-24. Paul names eight brothers who sent their greetings to Roman believers. In Paul's day, sending greetings was a common and beautiful custom. In some parts of the world, there is still a strong emphasis on the relationships of friends and family. In other places, people are more distant, closed, and self-centered. In the place where you live, do people take time to greet each other? In your church, is a greeting just a social form, or do people really care about each other?

Q 31 ➘ *How important are greetings where you live? Explain.*

Q 32 ➘ *In Figure 11.12 summarize what Paul says as he commends co-workers and friends.*

Paul's list of names:

Names/Group	Rom.	Your summary of Paul's commendations
Phoebe	16:1-2	
Priscilla and Aquila	16:3-4	
The church that meets…	16:5	
Epenetus	16:5	
Mary	16:6	
Andronicus and Junias	16:7	
Ampliatus	16:8	
Urbanus and Stachys	16:9	
Apelles	16:10	
Aristobulus	16:10	
Herodian	16:11	
Household of Narcissus	16:11	
Tryphena and Tryphosa	16:12	
Persis	16:12	
Rufus and his mother	16:13	
Asyncritus, Phlegon, Hermes, Patrobas, Hermas, and the brothers with them	16:14	Probably a house church
Philologus, Julia, Nereus and his sister, Olympas, and all the saints with them	16:15	Probably a house church
Timothy	16:21	
Lucius, Jason, and Sosipater	16:21	
Tertius	16:22	
Gaius	16:23	
Erastus	16:23	
Quartus	16:23	

**Figure 11.12   In Romans 16 Paul names at least 35 Christians or groups.
He sends greetings to at least 27 believers or groups, and sends greetings from 8 more.**

The long list of names in Romans 16 emphasizes that each believer is part of an eternal family. We believers are not eternal. But the family is eternal, for the Father, Son,

Q 33 ➘ *Since people have a beginning, how can God's family be eternal?*

and Holy Spirit are eternal. Throughout human history, God has been *adopting* children into His family (Rom. 8:17)—and God's family will live forever.

We have all been brought into God's family through the same gospel (James 1:18). We are all God's children. We have one Father. We all obey one Savior and Lord. We all enjoy and submit to the same Spirit of God within us (Rom. 8).

Q 34 ⬧ *Is "in Christ" more than just a belief? Explain what "in Christ" means.*

Believers are all family members in Christ. Note the number of times Paul emphasizes this in Romans 16.[20]

- Romans 16:1-2 *Receive her* (Phoebe) **in the Lord**.
- Romans 16:3 *Greet Priscilla and Aquila, my fellow workers **in Christ Jesus***.
- Romans 16:5 *Greet my dear friend Epenetus, who was the first convert **to Christ** in the province of Asia.*
- Romans 16:7 *Greet Andronicus and Junias...they were **in Christ** before I was.*
- Romans 16:8 *Greet Ampliatus, whom I love **in the Lord**.*
- Romans 16:9 *Greet Urbanus, our fellow worker **in Christ**,*
- Romans 16:10 *Greet Apelles, tested and approved **in Christ**.*
- Romans 16:11 *Greet those in the household of Narcissus, who are **in the Lord**.*
- Romans 16:12 *Greet Tryphena and Tryphosa, those women who work hard **in the Lord**.*
- Romans 16:12 *Greet my dear friend Persis, another woman who has worked very hard **in the Lord**.*
- Romans 16:13 *Greet Rufus, chosen **in the Lord**,*
- Romans 16:16 *All the churches **of Christ** send greetings.*
- Romans 16:22 *I, Tertius, who wrote down this letter, greet you **in the Lord***

Through the gospel, we are all members of an eternal family—**in Jesus Christ, our Savior and Lord**! To be *in Christ* means "to believe in Him, abide in Him, obey Him"—we live, move, and have our being in Him (Acts 17:28).

Q 35 ⬧ *What are some ways that God strengthens us through family members?*

God uses family members to strengthen each other. Romans 16:25 begins with *"to him who is able **to establish** you by my gospel."* We will study this verse more later. But for now, notice the word *establish,* which means "strengthen, confirm, set firmly, support."[21] God establishes and strengthens us through the gospel—the gospel which Paul explains in Romans 1–16. By this gospel God brings us into His family, where we establish, strengthen, and support each other. Through obeying the gospel, Gentiles and Jews, the strong and the weak, men and women strengthen each other. The Greek verb (*sterizo*) translated *establish* appears at the end of the Romans (Rom. 16:25). In Romans, this same verb occurs only one other time, at the beginning of the letter (Rom. 1:11). Paul wrote:

[11]*I long to see you so that I may impart to you some spiritual gift **to make you strong** [establish you]—* [12]*that is, that you and I may be mutually encouraged by each other's faith* (Rom. 1:11-12).

As Paul wrote elsewhere,

From him [Christ] *the whole body, joined and held together by every supporting ligament, grows and builds itself up in love, as each part does its work* (Eph. 4:16).

Romans 16 gives many examples of believers who *strengthened* Paul. God used Sister Phoebe to strengthen the apostle Paul. And she was a great help to many others (Rom. 16:2). She is one of seven women in Romans 16 whom Paul commends for being a blessing, an encouragement—a source of strength for others in the faith. Some Bible versions refer to Phoebe as a *servant,* but the Greek word in Romans 16:1a is *diakonon*— usually translated *deacon* or *deaconess*. Phoebe is also called a *great help* (Greek: *prostatis*). It appears that she had wealth, influence, and a heart to help as many believers as she could. Phoebe is an example of special people our Father gifts and raises up in the church to strengthen, enable, support, and encourage others in the family of God.

Priscilla and Aquila were not relatives of Paul. They did not share the blood of an earthly father or mother. But they were members of the same family through the blood of Christ. After this married couple was chased from Rome, they first met Paul in Corinth, where they sewed tents side by side and preached the gospel together. The bond of love became strong between this married couple and Paul—so strong that they risked their lives for him. Perhaps this was during the riot mentioned in Acts 19:23-41. Later, this couple hosted a church in their home when they returned to Rome

Q 36 *In Rome, in the family of God, who was like a mother to Paul (Rom. 16:13)?*

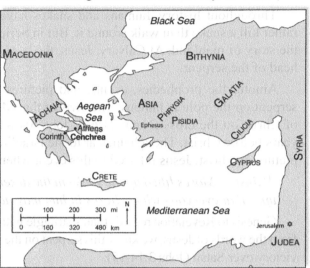

Figure 11.13
Phoebe is one of seven women Paul commends. She was from Cenchrea, a port city near Corinth.

(Rom. 16:5). Wherever they went, they were a source of strength to God's children—whether to Apollos (Acts 18:26), Paul, or others.

Through the gospel we are part of one eternal family. We strengthen and encourage one another. Parents nurture their children in the Lord. Believers use their gifts to strengthen and serve other believers in Christ (Rom. 12:3-8). The strong and the weak love and accept each other. The strong carry the weakness of the weak (Rom. 14:1–15:13). All believers practice bearing one another's burdens (Gal. 6:2). Older believers help disciple new converts. Older women train younger women (Titus 2:3-5). Mature disciples lead new believers into the fullness of the Spirit, as Priscilla and Aquila strengthened Apollos (Acts 18:26). Pastors shepherd God's people. At home, and wherever we travel, we meet members of God's family who are eager to help and strengthen us. And we ourselves always look for ways to strengthen others in the family of God. Read Paul's list of friends again. Isn't it awesome to belong to the family of God? Take a few minutes to worship God and to thank Him that you are part of His eternal family.

B. Through the gospel we are part of one eternal story (Rom. 16:17-20).

The God of peace will soon crush Satan under your feet (Rom. 16:20).

Q 37 *All believers are a part of what big story?*

Each of us has his or her own story. And we strengthen each other. But together, we are all part of one eternal story. The story began sometime in eternity past, before God created the earth or any member of the human race. As God thought about the story, the Trinity counted the cost. Way back then, God decided that the center of the story would be Jesus Christ, *"the Lamb slain from the foundation of the world"* (Rev. 13:8 KJV). Having planned the story, in time God created the heavens and the earth. As the summit of His creation, *"God created man in His own image, in the image of God He created him; male and female He created them"* (Gen. 1:27 NASB). God placed them in a garden called Eden. It was a paradise where God came and walked with them in the cool of the day. All went well for a time. Then Satan worked through the serpent and led Adam and Eve into sin. The story went bad in a hurry. God expelled Adam and Eve from the garden. And He said in anger to the serpent:

14 *"Cursed are you above all the livestock and all the wild animals! You will crawl on your belly and you will eat dust all the days of your life.* 15 *And I will put enmity*

*between you and the woman, and between your offspring and hers; **he will crush your head**, and you will strike his heel"* (Gen. 3:14-15).

Throughout history, humans and snakes have been enemies. Many people would rather kill a snake than walk around it. But in Scripture, the serpent is a *symbol* of evil in the story of mankind. At Calvary, Jesus, the seed or offspring of a woman, crushed the head of the serpent.

Among the prophecies, events, and pictures of Christ in the Old Testament, the serpent on the pole is famous. The serpent that Moses lifted up on a pole was a picture of Christ on the cross (Num. 21:6-9; John 3:14-15). This event happened about 1400 years before Christ. Though unclear to the Israelites at the time, today it gives us a clear picture of Christ. Jesus referred to this event when he said:

[14] *"Just as Moses lifted up the snake in the desert, so the Son of Man must be lifted up,* [15]*that everyone who believes in him may have eternal life"* (John 3:14-15).

Genesis to Revelation records man's struggle with the *"ancient serpent"* (Rev. 12:9). And from the words of Jesus, we know this serpent on the pole was a type of Christ—showing His victory over Satan (John 3:14-15).

Martin Luther compared the brazen serpent to Christ in two helpful ways.[22] *First,* the serpent lifted up on the pole was a *sign of triumph*. The snakes on the ground were alive, moving, and poisonous. But the brass snake on the pole was dead, stiff, and harmless. So the snake on the pole was lifted up as a sign of conquest and victory. *Second,* receiving healing through the snake on the pole required faith. Only those Israelites lived who believed God and obeyed by looking at the dead, harmless serpent. Likewise, if we want to be delivered from the sin and death that come through the bite of the *old serpent,* we must look with faith at Christ, lifted up on the cross.

Q 38 ✎ *In what sense will God soon crush Satan under the feet of believers?*

The Israelites took the brazen image of the serpent to Canaan. Hundreds of years later, King Hezekiah broke the brazen serpent in pieces because the Israelites were worshiping it and presenting offerings to it (2 Kings 18:4). Like the Israelites, we must remember that there is no value in worshiping forms—whether they are images of a snake on a pole, or images of a Savior on a cross. For eternal life only comes to us through a living relationship of faith and obedience to Christ Himself. And through our union with Christ by faith and obedience, we will share in the victory of the eternal story. For as God has promised in Romans 16:20, *"The God of peace will soon crush Satan under your feet."* Already, God has judged the serpent through Christ's death on the cross. But at the Second Coming of our Lord, we will reign with Him. Our gracious Lord delights to share the victory with *us!* It is *our* feet that will stand upon the head of the serpent! We all have our own small stories. But together, we are part of a great, eternal story. In Christ we are fighting a war that we know we are predestined to win.[23]

Q 39 ➚ *What warning does Paul give in Romans 16:17-19?*

Warning: *"Watch out for those who cause divisions and put obstacles in your way that are contrary to the teaching you have learned. Keep away from them.* [18]*For such people are not serving our Lord Jesus Christ, but their own appetites. By smooth talk and flattery they deceive the minds of naïve people"* (Rom. 16:17-18). These troublemakers had not yet made it to Rome. But they would arrive there.[24] Discord, dissension, and factions are works of the flesh (Gal. 5:20). These false teachers sometimes sound like true ministers. They use *smooth talk*—including twisted Bible verses and stories that they make up to exploit people (2 Pet. 2:3). Likewise, they use *flattery*—they tell people about their "rights" as children of God. They tell people what they want to hear.

Q 40 ✎ *Explain this riddle: Paul wants us to be naïve about some things, but not naïve about others (Rom. 16:17, 19).*

Paul tells *who* false teachers will deceive: the *naïve*. A *naïve* person is simple, simple-minded, innocent, childlike, unsuspecting, unsuspicious, over-trusting, gullible, foolable; green, immature, unseasoned, lacking experience, uninformed.[25] Trusting is good, but Paul warns that we should not trust everyone. Paul wants us to be *naïve* or *innocent* about evil (Rom. 16:19). He wants believers to be experts in what is right, but have little knowledge about sinful things.

Q 41 ✎ *Do you know a naïve person who was deceived? Give an example if possible.*

In contrast, Paul does not want us to be *naïve* about false teachers. The Israelites were led astray various times by:

- grumblers (like the ten spies), and those who caused God to send the deadly snakes to bite them,
- those who caused divisions (like Korah),
- the Gibeonites (who flattered and deceived them), and
- by their own fleshly appetites.

Q 42 ✎ *What can happen to those who do not watch out for false teachers? Give examples.*

These are the same Israelites who were children of Abraham, members of God's family, and delivered from the bondage of Egypt. They were baptized in the Red Sea, ate manna, and drank from the rock that represented Christ. These were the same Israelites whom God promised to give Canaan. But this entire generation of Israelites lost their inheritance and died in the wilderness, falling short of the Promised Land (1 Cor. 10:1-12; Heb. 3:16-19). *"Everything written in the past* [Scriptures] *was written to teach us"* (Rom. 15:4). So Paul warns us that we have a responsibility to *"watch out."* For false teachers will *"deceive the minds of naïve people"*—some of God's children! These are the type of false teachers who, to serve their own bellies, ruin *"whole households by teaching things they ought not to teach—and that for the sake of dishonest gain"* (Titus 1:11). They distort the truth to cause division, and draw away disciples after themselves (Acts 20:30). They are like *"savage wolves"* who will not spare the flock of God (Acts 20:29).Through the gospel we are part of an eternal family and an eternal story. But Paul warns us lest we be deceived by false teachers. *"So, if you think you are standing firm, be careful that you don't fall!"* (1 Cor. 10:12). Child of God, *"be on your guard!"* (Acts 20:31). *"Watch out"* (Rom. 16:17). The God of peace will soon crush Satan under our feet, as we remain alert and remember that we are in a spiritual war.

Concluding *Doxology: Glory to God through Jesus Christ, whom Paul's gospel proclaims (Rom. 16:25-27).

Q 43 ✎ *Underline the words or thoughts in Romans 16:25-27 that appear in the other "bookend" of Romans (Rom. 1:1-7, see Figure 11.14).*

25Now to him who is able to establish you by my gospel and the proclamation of Jesus Christ, according to the revelation of the mystery hidden for long ages past, 26but now revealed and made known through the prophetic writings by the command of the eternal God, so that all nations might believe and obey him— 27to the only wise God be glory forever through Jesus Christ! Amen (Rom. 16:25-27).

Q 44 ✎ *What are some truths that Paul's doxology summarizes?*

As we noted earlier, the two bookends of Romans are 1:1-7 and 16:17-25. In these passages that introduce and conclude his letter, Paul mentions the gospel he preaches. And in between these passages, Paul explains the gospel he preaches. This is why many refer to Romans as *the gospel according to Paul*. Romans shows us what Paul means by "the gospel." For Paul, the gospel is the good news about Jesus Christ—past, present, and future. Paul explains his gospel in the five parts of Romans. Review these five parts in the outline of Romans (Figure 1.12). Some refer to the gospel as the *Christ event*—the life and ministry of Christ on earth.[26] In contrast, for Paul the gospel is especially about the Christ *relationship* made possible by the Christ event and the Holy Spirit—the Spirit of Christ (Rom. 8:9)! Paul's five-part gospel of Romans emphasizes the work of Christ, past, present, and future:

Q 45 ➚ *What are the 5 big parts of the gospel Paul preached?*

- Sinners need a right relationship with God (Rom. 1:18–3:20).
- We can have a right relationship with God through faith in the death and resurrection of Jesus Christ (Rom. 3:21–5:21).

- We live victoriously in a <u>right relationship</u> with God, free from sin's power, as we submit to the Holy Spirit. Sons of God are led by the Spirit, not the flesh (Rom. 8:13). We depend on Him to fill, empower, and guide us to our glorification, when Christ returns (Rom. 6–8).
- Everyone, Jews and Gentiles, can live in a <u>right relationship</u> with God through faith in Jesus Christ. He is the Cornerstone of our salvation (Rom. 9–11).
- Both strong and weak believers live in a <u>right relationship</u> with God and each other—as we respond to God's mercy by offering our bodies as a living sacrifice to God, submit to the Spirit, and walk in love (Rom. 12–15).

These five big parts of Romans explain the gospel Paul preached.

Q 46 ⚒ *What is a doxology?*

Paul does not want to end Romans with a *warning* (Rom. 16:17-19), or a *greeting* from those with him (Rom. 16:21-24). Rather, the Spirit leads Paul to close Romans with a *doxology*. The Greek word *doxology* means "words of praise." Sometimes churches today sing a doxology at the end of a church service. Some scholars think that Romans 16:27 might have been said or sung by believers, at the end of Paul's letter.

This *doxology* of Romans summarize some great truths about the gospel:[27]
- Through the gospel, God establishes and strengthens believers in His family (Rom. 16:25);
- God commissioned Paul to preach the gospel (Rom. 1:1; 16:25);
- The gospel proclaims Jesus Christ as our Savior and Lord (Rom. 1:3-4; 16:25);
- The gospel was a mystery for ages past—hidden in the plan of God (Rom. 16:25-26; Eph. 3:2-12);
- The gospel was made known through the Old Testament Scriptures (which Romans refers to over 60 times, Figure 11.11);
- God has commanded that the gospel be preached to *all nations* (Jews and Gentiles), so they will believe and obey (Rom. 1:5; 15:18; 16:26). For Paul, the faith that saves is the faith that obeys. God has one plan for all nations—faith and obedience in Jesus Christ. This was the big theme of Romans 9–11. Recall the doxology at the end of that section:

[33]*Oh, the depth of the riches of the wisdom and knowledge of God! How unsearchable his judgments, and his paths beyond tracing out!* [34] *"Who has known the mind of the Lord? Or who has been his counselor?"* [35] *"Who has ever given to God, that God should repay him?"* [36]*For from him and through him and to him are all things. To him be the glory forever! Amen* (Rom. 11:33-36).

Likewise, Paul's summary of the gospel at the end of Romans leads him to a burst of praise:

To the only wise God be glory forever through Jesus Christ! Amen (Rom. 16:27).

The glorious gospel of Romans calls us to praise God—in our words and deeds—through Jesus Christ, and say "**Amen**"!

Thank you for studying our *Faith & Action* course on *Romans & Galatians*. May God bless you.

Q 47 *Fill in the blanks in Figure 11.14.*

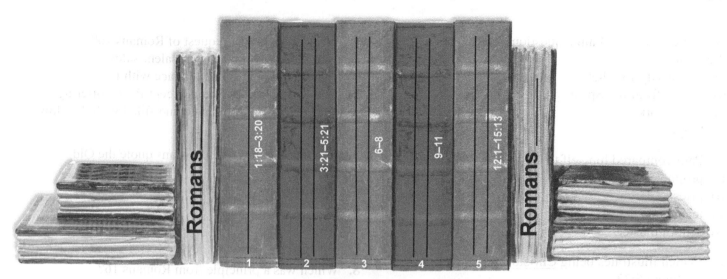

Figure 11.14 Practice identifying the bookends and five units of Romans.

Test Yourself: Circle the letter by the **best** completion to each question or statement.

1. Which value do Paul's questions in Romans illustrate?
a) Sensitivity to others
b) Power from the Spirit
c) Hard work
d) Prayer

2. Paul compared himself to a
a) prophet.
b) priest.
c) teacher.
d) school master.

3. Which illustrates being <u>Christo</u>centric?
a) Matthew 6:33
b) Psalms 32:1-2
c) Romans 4:3
d) Jeremiah 9:24

4. Which statement is TRUE?
a) We need sermons and miracles.
b) The day of miracles is past.
c) Miracles are a substitute for sermons.
d) Sermons are a substitute for miracles.

5. Paul preached from Jerusalem to Illyricum for
a) 2 years.
b) 5 years.
c) 10 years.
d) 20 years.

6. What was a prayer request of Romans 16?
a) That Paul would reach Jerusalem safely
b) That Paul would finish his race with joy
c) That Jewish saints would accept Paul's offering
d) That Jews would be saved and filled with the Holy Spirit

7. How many times does Romans quote the Old Testament?
a) 20
b) 60
c) 100
d) 200

8. Which was a principle from Romans 16?
a) Paul greeted at least 35 people.
b) God knows the names of His sheep.
c) Greetings may begin or end a letter.
d) We are part of an eternal family.

9. The two bookends of Romans emphasize:
a) Evangelism and discipleship.
b) Believe and obey.
c) Signs and miracles.
d) Prayer and fasting.

10. How does Romans end?
a) With a warning
b) With a greeting
c) With a doxology
d) With a promise

Essay Test Topics: Write 50-100 words on each of these goals that you studied in this chapter.

- Give evidence in Romans that shows Paul was sensitive to others.
- Summarize Paul's ministry as a priest. Apply this to us.
- Explain and illustrate: "Paul was <u>Christo</u>centric."
- Illustrate the fact that Paul depended on the Holy Spirit for his ministry.
- Explain and illustrate how Paul felt about hard work.
- Give examples to show that Paul valued planning ahead with hope.
- Summarize Paul's two prayer requests in Romans 16.
- Summarize the importance of prayer in your ministry.
- Identify 4 ways that Paul uses Old Testament quotes in Romans.
- Summarize a lesson we can learn from Paul's list of greetings in Romans 16.
- Explain the eternal story linked to Romans 16:20, and the warning just before it.
- Identify the two "bookends" of Romans, and terms common to both.
- Paraphrase the doxology of Romans 16:25-27.

Definitions

The right-hand column lists the chapter in the textbook in which the word is used. **Chapter**

Abba—Aramaic for father. We are God's children and He is our Father. 7

advocate—lawyer, intercessor, mediator, legal friend, defender 5

antinomianism—lawlessness; anti-law; rebellious and against law 5, 7

arbitrary—random; done by chance, without fairness or logic 8

Buddha—the common name for a prince in India; he is known as the founder of a world religion called 2
Buddhism. This religion seeks to escape from suffering. Buddha died from eating poisonous toadstools
that he thought were mushrooms.

called—God wants all to be saved. The *called* are those who respond and agree to God's invitation, conditions 7
of salvation, and Lordship of Jesus.

caste system—the level of society that a person is born into, as in India; in such a system, levels of society 9
are seen as either inferior or superior to each other

chiasm—a literary device named for the Greek letter "X" (chi, pronounced kee). There are four parts of a 10
basic chiasm: A, B, and B^1, A^1 (Figure 7.2).

condemnation (a judicial term)—a judgment that comes down from the court of heaven. God *condemns* 6, 7
those who practice sin.

contaminates—defiles, corrupts, pollutes, spoils, dishonors 5

disputable (debatable) matters of faith—*not* essential matters of Christianity, such as the timing of the 10
Millennium

doxology—words of praise to God. Sometimes believers sing a doxology at the end of a church service. 8, 11

election—choosing for a purpose, whether service or salvation; God elects all who choose and obey Jesus 8
to be saved.

Emperor Claudius— Roman ruler of the fourth- to third century B.C., who built the first aqueduct and began 10
construction of the Appian Way.

Evangelicals—those who believe at least three things: 1) the Bible, in the original autographs, is the 3
authoritative, inspired, infallible, inerrant word of God for faith and practice; 2) to reach heaven, a person
must be born-again, and follow Jesus Christ as Savior and Lord); 3) following Jesus includes sharing our
faith with those who do not know Christ.

faith—trusting in Jesus Christ, believing in Him; shown by obeying the gospel and submitting to the Holy 1, 3
Spirit

favoritism—partiality; preference; showing favor to one over another 2

finite—having bounds, limits, or restrictions 7

flesh—the human enemy of the Spirit. Fleshly life is pursuing one's own desires, independent of God or His 5, 6
law, not submitting to Jesus as Lord, and hostile to the Holy Spirit. Living in the flesh is pleasing self,
ignoring God, and rebelling against Him (Rom. 8:1-15; Gal. 5:16–6:10).

foreknew—knew in advance, before something happened — 7

foreknowledge—knowledge *before* something happens. God *foreknows* the events of earth and the choices of people. He knows in advance what will happen. — 7

Galatians—probably refers to those in the southern towns of the province of Galatia, such as Lystra — 1

Gentiles—ethnic groups or nations that are all non-Jews — 1, 2

Ghandi—a famous leader of India; he led them to political freedom, and died in 1948. — 2, 9

glorified—restored to the glory, honor, and destiny that God intends for us. Glorification begins at regeneration, increases as we grow in grace, and reaches a new height when Jesus returns for us. — 7

glory of God—the glory God intends for us (Rom. 3:23) — 3

gospel—the good news that Jesus died on the cross, arose from the dead, and ascended to the Father to deliver us from the penalty and power of sin, and restore us to a right relationship with God; He will come again to judge sinners, and rapture those of us who love Him so that we may live together with God forever. — 1

grace—the love, mercy, kindness, and favor God shows us in Christ — 3

---

hermeneutics—the study of principles for interpreting the Bible — 3

historical citation—a reference in an ancient book or manuscript — 11

horizontal wars—between two nations on the earth. — 4

---

immorality—sin, evil, wickedness, corruption, depravity; sexual misconduct — 2

imparted—given or bestowed; Isaac imparted his blessing to Jacob; Jesus imparted the Holy Spirit to believers at Pentecost; teachers impart knowledge to students. God imparts righteousness and holiness at regeneration, and these qualities increase as we are transformed into the image of Christ, day by day. — 1, 3

imparted righteousness—holiness we experience (sanctification) as we partake of the nature of God at regeneration, and as we grow in the likeness of Christ (Rom. 8:29). — 3, 5

imputed—credited, attributed, reckoned to, accounted to; the righteousness of Christ is imputed or credited to believers, apart from any works of their own, as we believe in Christ as Savior and Lord. — 3

imputed righteousness—right standing (justification) that God credits to us as we trust in Jesus as Savior and Lord — 3, 5

infinite—without bounds, limits, or restrictions — 7

Israel—sometimes refers to physical descendants of Abraham; other times refers to spiritual descendants of Abraham, that is, those who live by faith — 8

Jews—descendants of Abraham — 2

Judaizers—born-again Jewish believers who were Pharisees. They accepted Jesus, but still taught that all believers must obey the law of Moses. Thus they emphasized circumcision for Gentiles. — 1

justice—righteousness; fairness; that which is due, as a reward or a punishment — 3

justification—a legal term that means right standing with God; righteousness that God provides for us and credits to us through the Cross as we believe and abide in Christ (Rom. 3:21–5:21) — 1, 3, 5

justified—credited as righteous by faith in Jesus Christ; forgiven and brought into a right relationship with   3, 7
    God; declared righteous, holy, and not guilty through faith and obedience to Jesus Christ

karma—in Hinduism or Buddhism, a person's fate or destiny   4

kosher—conforming to strict, Jewish rules of dietary foods; ritually pure   10

law of gravity—is too complicated to define well in this course. But it explains why an apple or mango falls   7
    to the ground when it is loosed from the tree. And the law of gravity explains why people stay on the earth
    and do not float away into space

law of sin—the authority or rulership of sin. Being a prisoner of the law of sin means that sin is a person's   6
    master or lord.

law of sin and death—the rule, authority and power of sin and death; being under these laws means that a   7
    person is a slave of sin, under the sentence of physical and spiritual death.

law of the Spirit—the authority, rule, or power of the Holy Spirit. The power of the Spirit sets us free from   7
    the powers of sin and death.

legalist—a person who emphasizes what we *cannot* do. Legalism tries to *command* holiness.   10

libertine—a person who claims too much freedom. This person teaches holiness with few or no laws.   10

living sacrifice—the daily giving of our bodies, desires, and thoughts to worship God, serving Him and   9
    others

love—to love is to imitate and reflect God—His values, attitudes, feelings, thoughts, and actions.   9

mercy—kindness, love, and compassion that God desires to give each and every person   8

mestizos—people of mixed racial ancestry, especially of mixed European and Native American ancestry.   9

motivational gifts—abilities, talents, and interests that God gives each person to guide and enable service   9
    in the body of Christ

omniscient—all knowing   7

patriarch—Abraham, Isaac, Jacob, and his sons; the founders of Israel   8

personification—compares a deed, action, idea or *thing* to a person. Example: "The mountains and hills will   6
    burst into song before you, and all the trees of the field will clap their hands."

phylacteries—small boxes some Jews wore on the forehead and left arm (Deut 6:8; 11:18). These boxes   2
    contained Scripture verses. Likewise, the Jews wore small *tassels. (See below.)

pomanoc—an imaginary word to represent something questionable, or of doubtful value and morality   10

predestination—tells us about the ship's destination and what God has prepared for those who remain on it   8

predestined—planned for a destiny. Those who choose Christ, God predestines or plans to become like   7
    Christ.

Protestant Reformation—a religious movement in the 16th century. *Protestant* was the name given to   1
    followers of Christ who protested against the unbiblical doctrines and practices of the Roman Catholic
    Church. Today, the three major groups of Christianity are Protestants, Roman Catholics, and Eastern
    Orthodox Protestants teach that we are justified by faith and that the Bible is a higher authority than
    tradition or the pope.

redemption—buying back a slave; making him or her free by paying a ransom 3

remnant—those physical descendants of Abraham whom God saved, as they chose to live by faith 8

righteousness—justice; a right relationship with God 1, 2, 3

Romans—people who lived in Rome, the capital of the Roman Empire 1

sacrifice of atonement—Jesus offering Himself to pay the penalty for our sins and to remove them 3

salvation—deliverance from the penalty and power of sin, and restoration to a right relationship with God 1

sanctification—right living; holiness of position, actions and condition; freedom from the power of sin as we are set apart to serve God through the power of the Holy Spirit 1, 3, 5

sewer—a place that is polluted with human bodily waste 1

simultaneous—occurring at the same time 5

sin—disobeying God; following the evil desires of the flesh, and resisting the Holy Spirit 5

sinful nature—the flesh (Greek: *sarx*); the human enemy of the Spirit. Fleshly life is pursuing one's own desires, independent of God or His law, not submitting to Jesus as Lord, and hostile to the Holy Spirit. Living in the flesh is pleasing self, ignoring and rebelling against God (Rom. 8:1-15; Gal. 5:16–6:10). 7

sinned—disobeyed God's Law or commands (Rom. 3:23) 3

sola fide—a Latin saying that means by faith alone 3

spiritual gifts—the various forms of grace and faith that God gives each believer to confirm the gospel, to assist in the ministry, and to serve God and others as we build up the body of Christ 1, 9

substitute—a person, animal, or thing that takes the place of another 3

under grace—being under the new covenant 6

under law—being under the old covenant 6

vertical war—a conflict between earth and heaven 4

will of God—includes the general plan of God for all believers to become like Christ; and the specific will of God to use the gifts He gives to serve others and live in love toward all 9

worship—in Romans 12–15 the way we respond to God's mercy. Our worship is spiritual as the Spirit leads us. It is logical as we give our bodies as living sacrifices in response to the mercy God has given us. 9

wrath—vengeance, punishment, judgment for sin 2

zealots—members of a Jewish movement in the first century A.D. who fought against Roman rule in Palestine. 10

Scripture List

Bibliography

Allen, Roland. *Missionary Methods: St. Paul's or Ours?* Grand Rapids, Michigan; Wm. B. Eerdmans Publishing Company, 1962.

Arndt, William F. and F. Wilbur Gingrich. *A Greek-English Lexicon of the New Testament and Other Early Christian Literature.* Chicago, Illinois: The University of Chicago Press, 1957.

Arrington, French L. and Roger Stronstad, eds. *Life in the Spirit New Testament Commentary.* Grand Rapids, Michigan: Zondervan Publishing House, 2003.

Barclay, William. *Daily Study Bible – Romans.* Grand Rapids, Michigan: Zondervan Publishing House, 1975.

Barker, Kenneth. gen. ed. *The NIV Study Bible.* Grand Rapids, Michigan: Zondervan Publishing House, 1985.

Barrett, C. K. *The Epistle to the Romans.* New York City, New York: Harper and Row, 1957.

Barrett, David. *International Bulletin of Missionary Research,* (January 2000), p. 25.

Barth, Karl. *The Epistle to the Romans,* 6th ed. [trans. Edwyn C. Hoskyns]. London: Oxford University Press, 1965.

Beale G. K. and D. A. Carlson. *Commentary on the New Testament,* "Use of the Old Testament." Grand Rapids, Michigan: Baker Book House, 2007.

Bernard, David K. *The Message of Romans.* Hazelwood, Missouri: Word of Flame Press, 1987.

Brown, Colin. *The New International Dictionary of New Testament Theology,* Vol. I. Grand Rapids, Michigan: Zondervan Publishing House, 1975.

Brown, Michael B. "God Loves Like a Persistent Mother," not published but available from www.PreachingToday.com

Bruce, F. F. *The Epistle of Paul to the Romans: An Introduction and Commentary.* Grand Rapids, Michigan: Wm. B. Eerdmans Publishing Company, 1963.

Bruce, F. F. *The New International Commentary on the New Testament, The Epistle to the Hebrews* Grand Rapids, Michigan: Wm. B. Eerdmans Publishing Company, 1964.

Carnegie, Dale. *How to Win Friends and Influence People.* New York, New York: Simon and Schuster, 1966.

Carter, Tom. *Spurgeon At His Best.* Grand Rapids, Michigan: Baker, Book House 1988.

Casting Crowns, "Lifesong," Lyrics: http://www.azlyrics.com/lyrics/castingcrowns/lifesong.html

Cocoris, G. Michael. "Full Pardon Refused," *Evangelism: A Biblical Approach.* Chicago, Illinois: Moody Press, 1984. www.bible.org, under the reference "John 1:12."

Cranfield, C. E. B. *International Critical Commentary, Romans 9-16.* New York, New York: Continuum International Publishing Group, 1979.

Cranfield, C. E. B. *Romans: A Shorter Commentary.* Grand Rapids, Michigan: Wm. B. Eerdmans Publishing Company, 1985.

Curtis, Eastman. "Embarrassed to Witness," *Raising Heaven-Bound Kids in a Hell-Bent World.* Thomas Nelson Publishing House, 2000. Quoted in *Men of Integrity* (July/August 2001). www.PreachingToday.com, under the word "Boldness."

Douglas, J. D. *The New Bible Dictionary.* Grand Rapids, Michigan: Wm. B. Eerdmanns Publishing Co., 1962.

Fee, Gordon D. *New International Biblical Commentary, 1 and 2 Timothy, Titus.* Peabody, Massachusettes: Hendrickson Publishers, 1988.

Fee, Gordon. *God's Empowering Presence: The Holy Spirit in the Letters of Paul.* Peabody, Massachusetts: Hendrickson Publishers, 1994.

Franzmann, Martin H. *Romans: A Commentary.* St. Louis, Missouri: Concordia Publishing House, 1968.

Galli, Mark. "Nero Betrays Mother to Please Mistress," adapted from Michael Grant, *The Roman Emperors: A Biographical Guide to the Rulers of Imperial Rome, 31 B.C.–A.D. 476.* New York, New York: Scribner, 1985. www.PreachingToday.com, "Romans 1:28-31."

Gilbrandt, Thoralf, ed. *The Complete Biblical Library, The New Testament Greek-English Dictionary, Pi-Rho.* Springfield, Missouri: World Library Press, 1991.

Gilbrandt, Thoralf, ed. *The Complete Biblical Library: The New Testament Greek-English Dictionary, Alpha-Gamma.* Springfield, Missouri: World Library Press, 1994.

Gilbrandt, Thoralf, ed. *The Complete Biblical Library: The New Testament Greek-English Dictionary, Delta-Epsilon.* Springfield, Missouri: World Library Press, 1990.

Gilbrandt, Thoralf, ed. *The Complete Biblical Library: The New Testament Greek-English Dictionary, Sigma-Omega.* Springfield, Missouri: World Library Press, 1991.

Godet, Frederic Louis. *Commentary on Romans.* Grand Rapids, Michigan: Kregel Publications, 1977.

Greathouse, William M. and Willard H. Taylor, eds. "Romans," in *Beacon Bible Expositions*, Vol. 6. Kansas City, Missouri: Beacon Hill Press of Kansas City, 1975.

Greathouse, William M. *Romans, Beacon Bible Commentary*, Vol. 8. [Eds. A. F. Harper, et al] Kansas City, Missouri: Beacon Hill Press of Kansas City, 1968.

Gundry, Stanley N., Series Editor. *Counterpoints: Five Views on Sanctification.* Grand Rapids, Michigan: Zondervan Publishing House, 1987. [Stanley M. Horton, Pentecostal View]

Guthrie, Donald. *The Pastoral Epistles, Tyndale New Testament Commentaries.* London: The Tyndale Press, 1967.

Harris, Ralph W., ed. *The Complete Biblical Library: The New Testament Study Bible, Galatians–Philemon,* Vol. 8. Springfield, Missouri: World Library Press, 1989.

Harris, Ralph W., ed. *The Complete Biblical Library: The New Testament Study Bible, Romans–Corinthians,* Vol. 7. Springfield, Missouri: World Library Press, 1989.

Hastings, James. *The Speaker's Bible, Romans.* Grand Rapids, Michigan: Baker Book House, 1978.

Heil, John Paul. Paul's *Letter to the Romans: A Reader-Response Commentary.* Eugene, Oregon: Wipf and Stock Publishers, 1987.

Hodge, Charles. *Romans.* [ed. Alister McGrath and J. I. Packer] Wheaton, Illinois; Crossway Books, 1993.

Horton, Stanley M. *What the Bible Says About the Holy Spirit.* Springfield, Missouri: Gospel Publishing House, 1976.

Howard, R. E. *Beacon Bible Commentary; Galatians through Philemon,* Vol. 9. Kansas City, Missouri: Beacon Hill Press, 1968.

Johnson, Van. *Life in the Spirit New Testament Commentary: Romans.* Grand Rapids, Michigan: Zondervan Publishing House, 2008.

Jowett, J. H. "Life in the Heights" New York: The Christian Herald, 1925.

Jowett, J. H. *The Passion for Souls.* London, England: Fleming H. Revell Company, 1905.

Keil, C. E. and F. Delitzsch. *Commentary on the Old Testament in Ten Volumes:* Volume 1, *The Pentateuch:* "Numbers." Grand Rapids, Michigan: Wm. B. Eerdmanns Publishing Co., 1976.

Kingsley, Stephen "Black Light Exposes Stains," not published but available from www.PreachingToday.com

Macchia, Frank D. *Justified in the Spirit: Creation, Redemption, and the Triune God, Pentecostal Manifestos.* Grand Rapids, Michigan: William B. Eerdmans Publishing Company, 2010.

Maddox, Eugene A. "When Mom Was My Hero," www.PreachingToday.com, "Prejudice."

Mathewson, Steve. Sermon on Romans 12:1-8, "Give Your Life Away to Someone Who Can Use It!" http://www. crosslifeefc.org/avms.asp?seriesid=9

Mathewson, Steve. Sermon on Romans 12:9-21, "Genuine Love." http://www.crosslifeefc.org/avms.asp?seriesid=9

Mathewson, Steve. Sermon on Romans 16:1-27, "The Gospel Really IS the Power of God." http://www.crosslifeefc.org/ avms.asp?seriesid=9

McGarvey, John B. "Prayers of the Spirit," not published but available from www.PreachingToday.com

McGhee, Quentin and Carl Gibbs. *General Principles for Interpreting Scripture—Hermeneutics 1,* 2nd ed. Springfield, Missouri: Faith & Action Team, 2011.

McKenzie, E. C. *Mac's Giant Book of Quips and Quotes.* Grand Rapids, Michigan: Baker Book House, 1980.

Menzies, William W. and Stanley M. Horton. *Bible Doctrines.* Springfield, Missouri: Gospel Publishing House, 1993.

Meyer, F. B. *Great Verses Through the Bible.* Grand Rapids, Michigan: Zondervan Publishing House, 1966.

Moo, Douglas. *The New International Commentary on the New Testament: The Epistle to the Romans.* Grand Rapids, Michigan: Wm . B. Eerdmans Publishing Company, 1996.

Morris, Bill. "Freedom of the Air," not published but available from www.PreachingToday.com

Murray, John. *The Epistle to the Romans: The English Text With Introduction, Exposition and Notes.* Grand Rapids, Michigan: Wm. B. Eerdmans Publishing Company, 1965.

Murray, John. *The Epistle to the Romans,* Vol. 2. Grand Rapids, Michigan: Wm. B. Eerdmans Publishing House, 1968.

Nicholson, Dick. "Communique," April 2007.

Orr, James. gen. ed. *The International Standard Bible Encyclopedia,* Vol. II. Grand Rapids, Michigan: Wm. B. Eerdmans Publishing Company, 1974.

Orr, James. gen. ed. *The International Standard Bible Encyclopedia,* Vol. III. Grand Rapids, Michigan: Wm. B. Eerdmans Publishing Company, 1956.

Orr, James, gen. ed. *The International Standard Bible Encyclopedia,* Vol. IV. Grand Rapids, Michigan: Wm. B. Eerdmans Publishing Company, 1956.

Peterson, Eugene H. *The Message* [Bible]. Colorado Springs, Colorado: NavPress Publishing Group, 1993.

Phillips, J. B. *The New Testament in Modern English.* New York, New York: HarperCollins Publishers, 1962.

Phillips, John. *Exploring Romans.* Neptune, New Jersey: Loizeaux Brothers, 1969.

Plumber, Alfred. *International Critical Commentary, 2 Corinthians.* Edinburgh, Scotland: T & T Clark, 1975.

Robertson, A. T. *Word Pictures in the New Testament,* Vol. IV: *The Epistles of Paul.* Nashville, Tennessee: Broadman Press, 1931.

Rupprecht, A. "Slave, Slavery," *Dictionary of Paul and His Letters.* Downers Grove, Illinois: Intervarsity Press, 1993.

Simmons, William. *Life in the Spirit New Testament Commentary: Galatians.* Grand Rapids, Michigan: Zondervan Publishing House, 1999.

Simpson, E. K. and F. F. Bruce. *New International Commentary on the New Testament, The Epistles to the Ephesians and Colossians.* Grand Rapids, Michigan: Wm. B. Eerdmans Publishing Company, 1977.

Stamps, Donald C. gen. ed., and J. Wesley Adams, assoc. ed. *The Full Life Study Bible.* Springfield, Missouri: Life Publishers International, 1992.

Stott, John R. W. *The Message of Romans: God's Good News for the World.* Downers Grove, Illinois, InterVarsity Press, 1994.

Tidwell, William Moses. "Sin: The Chains of Sin," from "Pointed Illustrations," www.Elbourne.org

Tucker, Ruth. "William Carey's Dream," *From Jerusalem to Irian Jaya: A Biographical History of Christian Missions.* Grand Rapids, Michigan: Zondervan Publishing House, 1983. Submitted by Mark Galli, managing editor of *Christianity Today,* www.PreachingToday.com, under the word "Calling."

Watts, Isaac. "When I Survey the Wondrous Cross," Lyrics: http://library.timelesstruths.org/music/When_I_Survey_the_Wondrous_Cross/

Wesley, John. *Wesley's Notes on the New Testament,* Vol. 2. Grand Rapids, Michigan: Baker Book House, 1983.

Whedon, Daniel D. *Commentary on the New Testament: Intended for Popular Use,* Vol. 3, *Acts-Romans.* New York, New York: Nelson & Phillips, 1892.

Wiersbe, Warren B. *The Bible Exposition Commentary: New Testament,* Vol. 1. Colorado Springs, Colorado: Victor, 2001.

Williams, Morrris. *Declare His Righteousness.* Springfield, Missouri, Gospel Publishing House, 1975.

Witherington, Ben III. *Paul's Letter to the Romans, A Socio Rhetorical Commentary.* Grand Rapids, Michigan: Wm. B. Eerdmans Publishing Company, 2004.

ALL George O. Wood sermons can be found on the website http://georgeowood.com. Then look under Expositional Sermons, New Testament, and choose Romans or another book.

Wood, George O. Sermon on Acts 3, "Suffering for Doing Right."

Wood, George O. Sermon on Romans 7:13-25, "The Struggle Within."

Wood, George O. Sermon on Romans 8:5-17, "In the Flesh or in the Spirit?"

Wood, George O. Sermon on Romans 8:18-25, "The Agony and the Ecstasy."

Wood, George O. Sermon on Romans 8:31-39, "How to Be a Failure."

Wood, George O. Sermon on Romans 9, "The Freedom of God."

Wood, George O. Sermon on Romans 12:1-2, "A Call to Commitment."

Wood, George O. Sermon on Romans 12:3-5, "Know Yourself."

Wood, George O. Sermon on Romans 12:8, "The Gift of Exhortation."

Wood, George O. Sermon on Romans 13:1-7, "God and Government."

Wood, George O. Sermon on Romans 13:8-14., "Walking in Love and Light."

Wood, George O. Sermon on Romans 14:13-23, "When Christians Disagree—Part 2."

Wood, George O. Sermon on Romans 15:1-13, "When Christians Disagree—Part 3."

http://answers.yahoo.com/question/index?qid=20080106181835AA6w0Hw

http://bhpca.mypublicsquare.com/view/lt-general-thomas

http://en.wikipedia.org/wiki/Appian_Way

http://en.wikipedia.org/wiki/Boeing_747

http://en.wikipedia.org/wiki/File:PiraSocVirreinatoPer% C3%BA.jpg

http://en.wikipedia.org/wiki/George_Boardman_the_Younger

http://en.wikipedia.org/wiki/Herod%27s_Temple#Herod.27s_Temple

http://en.wikipedia.org/wiki/Justin_Martyr

http://en.wikipedia.org/wiki/Spanish_colonization_of_the_Americas

http://gracethrufaith.com/selah/holidays-and-holy-days/the-feast-of-first-fruits/

http://quotationsbook.com/quote/10741/

http://scienceblogs.com/notrocketscience/2008/06/parasitic_wasp_turns_caterpillars_into_headbanging_bodyguard.php

http://thinkexist.com/quotation/men_must_be_taught_as_if_you_taught_them_not-and/146854.html

http://thinkexist.com/quotes/with/keyword/holiness/

http://www.abideinchrist.com/messages/jn14v6.html

http://www.aviewoncities.com/rome/colosseo.htm

http://www.christian-prayer-quotes.christian-attorney.net/

http://www.churchsociety.org/crossway/documents/Cway_102_Slavery1.pdf

http://www.cubroundtable.com/assets/pdf-sundry/Not-My-Job.pdf

http://www.docstoc.com/docs/4675409/Paul-s-Epistles-and-Letter-Writing-in-the-Graeco-Roman-World-the-New-Testament-the-church-Apostle-Paul-St-Paul-Paul-s-epistles-Epistles-Of-Paul-2-CORINTHIANS-Pauline-Epistles-the-Bible

http://www.fourth-avenue.org/chapters/17

http://www.google.com/search?q=John+Wesley%27s+father+told+him+to+seek+the+inner+witness&rlz=1I7DLUS_en&ie=UTF-8&oe=UTF-8&sourceid=ie7

http://www.graceteaching.com/notes/paulsuseofot.pdf.

http://www.hccentral.com/gkeys/chiasm.html

http://www.howjsay.com/index.php?word=chiasm

http://www.jewishjournal.com/world/article/in_world_of_7_billion_demographers_struggle_to_ascertain_the_number_of_jews/

http://www.lyricsmania.com/no_more_night_lyrics_david_phelps.html

http://www.lyricsmode.com/lyrics/h/hillsong_united/#share

http://www.orthodoxyouth.org/romans/print/introexpulsionjews.htm

http://www.preceptaustin.org/holiness_quotes.htm

http://www.puritanfellowship.com/2008/05/charles-spurgeon-imparted-righteousness.html

http://www.ringsurf.com/online/1936-pantheon_ita.html

http://www.rome.info/colosseum/

http://www.sing365.com/music/lyric.nsf/Forever-lyrics-Michael-W-Smith/A27059E93435AE7E48256C69000D957B

http://www.whatisthegospel.org.uk/gospelbasics.html

Endnotes

Cover Photo Description
[1] http://www.aviewoncities.com/rome/colosseo.htm

[2] http://www.rome.info/colosseum/

Chapter 1
[1] Story by Assemblies of God World Missionary Willard Teague.

[2] http://www.ringsurf.com/online/1936-pantheon_ita.html

[3] http://answers.yahoo.com/question/index?qid=20080106181835AA6w0Hw

[4] http://www.churchsociety.org/crossway/documents/Cway_102_Slavery1.pdf

[5] C. E. B. Cranfield, *Romans: A Shorter Commentary* (Grand Rapids, Michigan: Wm. B. Eerdmans Publishing Company, 1985), p. 2.

[6] Van Johnson, *Life in the Spirit New Testament Commentary: Romans* (Grand Rapids, Michigan: Zondervan Publishing House, 2008), p. 693.

[7] F. F. Bruce, *The Epistle of Paul to the Romans: An Introduction and Commentary* (Grand Rapids, Michigan: Wm. B. Eerdmans Publishing Company, 1963), p. 12.

[8] William M. Greathouse and Willard H. Taylor, eds., "Romans," in *Beacon Bible Expositions*, vol. 6, (Kansas City, Missouri: Beacon Hill Press of Kansas City, 1975), p. 22.

[9] http://www.docstoc.com/docs/4675409/Paul-s-Epistles-and-Letter-Writing-in-the-Graeco-Roman-World-the-New-Testament-the-church-Apostle-Paul-St-Paul-Paul-s-epistles-Epistles-Of-Paul-2-CORINTHIANS-Pauline-Epistles-the-Bible

[10] Roland Allen, *Missionary Methods: St. Paul's or Ours?* (Grand Rapids, Michigan; Wm. B. Eerdmans Publishing Company, 1962), pp. 12-17.

[11] G. Michael Cocoris, "Full Pardon Refused," *Evangelism: A Biblical Approach* (Chicago, Illinois: Moody Press, 1984), pp. 83 and following, www.bible.org, under the reference "John 1:12" [accessed November 24, 1999].

[12] Donald C. Stamps, gen. ed., and J. Wesley Adams, assoc. ed., *The Full Life Study Bible* (Springfield, Missouri: Life Publishers International, 1992), "Special Features," p. 1706.

[13] Cranfield, p. 7.

[14] Stamps, *The Full Life Study Bible,* "Faith and Grace," article on Romans 5:21, pp. 1720-1721.

[15] John R. W. Stott, *The Message of Romans: God's Good News for the World* (Downers Grove, Illinois, InterVarsity Press, 1994), p. 53.

[16] Ruth Tucker, "William Carey's Dream," *From Jerusalem to Irian Jaya: A Biographical History of Christian Missions* (Grand Rapids, Michigan: Zondervan Publishing House, 1983), pp. 114-115; submitted by Mark Galli, managing editor of *Christianity Today*, www.PreachingToday.com, under the word "Calling" [accessed January 7, 2003].

[17] Compare F. F. Bruce on six basic elements of the gospel, http://www.whatisthegospel.org.uk/gospelbasics.html, p. 2.

[18] Eastman Curtis, "Embarrassed to Witness," *Raising Heaven-Bound Kids in a Hell-Bent World* (Thomas Nelson Publishing House, 2000), quoted in *Men of Integrity* (July/August 2001), www.PreachingToday.com, under the word "Boldness" [accessed January 9, 2003].

Chapter 2
[1] Stott, p. 69.

[2] Stamps, *The Full Life Study Bible,* Romans 1:18 comments, pp. 1708-1709.

[3] Cranfield, pp. 28-29.

[4] William M. Greathouse, *Romans, Beacon Bible Commentary*, vol. 8, [eds. A. F. Harper, et al] (Kansas City, Missouri: Beacon Hill Press of Kansas City, 1968), p. 50.

[5] Johnson, p. 708.

[6] Ralph W. Harris, ed., *The Complete Biblical Library: The New Testament Study Bible, Romans–Corinthians,* vol. 7 (Springfield, Missouri: World Library Press, 1989), p. 35.

[7] Johnson referring to Kasemann, p. 708.

[8] C. K. Barrett, *The Epistle to the Romans* (New York City, New York: Harper and Row, 1957), p. 39.

[9] Ben Witherington III, *Paul's Letter to the Romans, A Socio Rhetorical Commentary* (Grand Rapids, Michigan: Wm. B. Eerdmans Publishing Company, 2004), p. 69.

[10] Harris, *The Complete Biblical Library: The New Testament Study Bible, Romans–Corinthians,* vol. 7, p. 132.

[11] Stamps, *The Full Life Study Bible,* Romans 1:24 comment, p. 1709.

[12] Karl Barth, *The Epistle to the Romans*, 6th ed. [trans. Edwyn C. Hoskyns] (London: Oxford University Press, 1965), p. 51.

[13] Mark Galli, "Nero Betrays Mother to Please Mistress," adapted from Michael Grant, *The Roman Emperors: A Biographical Guide to the Rulers of Imperial Rome, 31 B.C.–A.D. 476* (New York, New York: Scribner, 1985), www.PreachingToday.com, "Romans 1:28-31" [accessed February 28, 2003].

[14] Johnson, p. 713.

[15] Johnson, p. 714.

[16] Johnson, p. 714.

[17] Johnson, p. 715.

[18] Douglas Moo, *The New International Commentary on the New Testament: The Epistle to the Romans* (Grand Rapids, Michigan: Wm . B. Eerdmans Publishing Company, 1996), p. 202.

Chapter 3

1 Johnson, p. 715.

2 Adapted from D. L. Moody.

3 Moo, p. 226.

4 Moo, p. 221.

5 Thoralf Gilbrandt, ed., *The Complete Biblical Library: The New Testament Greek-English Dictionary, Sigma-Omega* (Springfield, Missouri: World Library Press, 1991), 4375-5457, *charis,* p. 490.

6 Thoralf Gilbrandt, ed., *The Complete Biblical Library: The New Testament Greek-English Dictionary, Alpha-Gamma* (Springfield, Missouri: World Library Press, 1994), 1-1131, *apolutrosis,* p. 387.

7 Johnson, p. 717.

8 Lyrics and music by Gordon Jensen.

9 Johnson, p. 718.

10 Thoralf Gilbrandt, ed., *The Complete Biblical Library: The New Testament Greek-English Dictionary, Delta-Epsilon* (Springfield, Missouri: World Library Press, 1990), 1132–2175, *dikaiosune,* p. 138.

11 http://www.abideinchrist.com/messages/jn14v6.html

12 Tom Carter, *Spurgeon At His Best* (Grand Rapids, Michigan: Baker, Book House 1988), p. 115.

13 Carter, p. 200.

14 Johnson, p. 717.

15 Moo, p. 223.

16 Carter, p. 251.

17 Lyrics by Augustus M. Toplady.

18 F. F. Bruce, *The New International Commentary on the New Testament, The Epistle to the Hebrews* (Grand Rapids, Michigan: Wm. B. Eerdmans Publishing Company, 1964), p. 173.

19 Moo, p. 245.

20 Frederic Louis Godet, *Commentary on Romans* (Grand Rapids, Michigan: Kregel Publications, 1977), p. 185.

21 Moo, p. 243.

22 Johnson, p. 720.

23 Eugene A. Maddox, "When Mom Was My Hero," www.PreachingToday.com, "Prejudice" [accessed April 4, 2003].

24 J. H. Jowett, "Life in the Heights" New York, New York: The Christian Herald, 1925, pp. 11-12.

25 Johnson, p. 723.

26 Moo, pp. 289-290.

27 Dick Nicholson, "Communique," April 2007.

Chapter 4

1 Johnson, p. 724.

2 Johnson, pp. 723-724.

3 Moo, p. 298.

4 William Barclay, *Daily Study Bible – Romans* (Grand Rapids, Michigan: Zondervan Publishing House, 1975), p. 72.

5 Moo, p. 394.

6 Johnson, p. 724.

7 Moo, p. 295.

8 Johnson, p. 725.

9 Gordon Fee, *God's Empowering Presence: The Holy Spirit in the Letters of Paul* (Peabody, Massachusetts: Hendrickson Publishers, 1994), p. 497.

10 Moo, p. 311.

11 Johnson, pp. 724-726.

12 Charles Hodge, *Romans*, ed. Alister McGrath and J. I. Packer (Wheaton, Illinois; Crossway Books, 1993), p. 146.

13 Johnson, p. 727.

14 Johnson, pp. 726-727.

15 Stamps, *The Full Life Study Bible,* Genesis 3:4 comment, p. 11.

16 Johnson, pp. 727-728.

17 Moo, pp. 335-339.

18 Warren B. Wiersbe, *The Bible Exposition Commentary: New Testament,* vol. 1 (Colorado Springs, Colorado: Victor, 2001), p. 54.

Chapter 5

1 http://www.puritanfellowship.com/2008/05/charles-spurgeon-imparted-righteousness.html

2 Johnson, p. 729.

3 Johnson, p. 729.

4 James Orr, gen. ed., *The International Standard Bible Encyclopedia,* vol. IV (Grand Rapids, Michigan: Wm. B. Eerdmans Publishing Company, 1956), p. 2682.

5 Stanley N. Gundry, series editor, *Counterpoints: Five Views on Sanctification* (Grand Rapids, Michigan: Zondervan Publishing House, 1987), Stanley M. Horton [Pentecostal View], p. 116.

6 Stanley M. Horton in *Counterpoints,* referring to Myer Pearlman, p. 114.

7 Stanley M. Horton in *Counterpoints,* p. 116.

8 Kenneth Barker, gen. ed., *NIV Study Bible* (Grand Rapids, Michigan: Zondervan Publishing House, 1985), Romans 6:22 comment, p. 1716.

9 James Orr, gen. ed., *The International Standard Bible Encyclopedia,* vol. III (Grand Rapids, Michigan: Wm. B. Eerdmans Publishing Company, 1956), p. 1403.

10 Orr, *The International Standard Bible Encyclopedia,* vol. IV, p. 2685.

11 http://www.preceptaustin.org/holiness_quotes.htm

12 Stanley M. Horton, *What the Bible Says About the Holy Spirit* (Springfield, Missouri: Gospel Publishing House, 1976), p. 258.

13 William W. Menzies and Stanley M. Horton, *Bible Doctrines* (Springfield, Missouri: Gospel Publishing House, 1993), p. 149.

14 Stanley M. Horton in *Counterpoints,* p. 116.

15 P. C. Nelson quoted in *Bible Doctrines,* p. 103.

16 http://thinkexist.com/quotes/with/keyword/holiness/

[17] Diagram adapted from Morrris Williams, *Declare His Righteousness* (Springfield, Missouri, Gospel Publishing House, 1975), p. 50.

[18] Carter, p. 354.

[19] Alfred Plumber, *International Critical Commentary, 2 Corinthians* (Edinburgh, Scotland: T & T Clark, 1975, p. 212.

[20] Jowett, p. 48.

[21] Orr, *The International Standard Bible Encyclopedia,* vol. IV, p. 2685.

[22] Johnson, p. 732

[23] Greathouse and Taylor, p. 104.

[24] Johnson, pp. 732-733.

[25] Johnson, p. 731.

[26] Johnson, p. 734

[27] Harris Franklin Rall, in *The International Standard Bible Encyclopedia,* vol. IV, p. 2085.

[28] A. Rupprecht, "Slave, Slavery," *Dictionary of Paul and His Letters* (Downers Grove, Illinois: Intervarsity Press, 1993), p. 881.

[29] Johnson, pp. 735-736.

[30] Donald Guthrie, *The Pastoral Epistles, Tyndale New Testament Commentaries* (London: The Tyndale Press, 1967), p. 130.

[31] Gordon D. Fee, *New International Biblical Commentary, 1 and 2 Timothy, Titus* (Peabody, Massachusettes: Hendrickson Publishers, 1988), p. 47.

[32] http://www.whatisthegospel.org.uk/gospelbasics.html

[33] Johnson, p. 736.

[34] John Wesley, *Wesley's Notes on the New Testament,* vol. 2 (Grand Rapids, Michigan: Baker Book House, 1983), commentary on Romans 6:17.

[35] http://en.wikipedia.org/wiki/George_Boardman_the_Younger (quote of Rev. George Dana Boardman, pastor).

[36] Harris, *The Complete Biblical Library, The New Testament Study Bible, Romans–Corinthians,* vol. 7, p. 103.

[37] Bruce, *Romans,* pp. 142-143.

[38] William Moses Tidwell, "Sin: The Chains of Sin," from "Pointed Illustrations," www.Elbourne.org.

Chapter 6

[1] Johnson, p. 737.

[2] R. E. Howard, *Beacon Bible Commentary; Galatians through Philemon,* vol. 9 (Kansas City, Missouri: Beacon Hill Press, 1968), p. 65.

[3] Ralph W. Harris, ed., *The Complete Biblical Library: The New Testament Study Bible, Galatians–Philemon,* vol. 8 (Springfield, Missouri: World Library Press, 1989), pp. 55-57.

[4] Johnson, pp. 737-738.

[5] Johnson, p. 739.

[6] Moo, p. 451.

[7] Gilbrandt, *The Complete Biblical Library: The New Testament Greek-English Dictionary, Alpha-Gamma* 1-1131, p. 509.

[8] Johnson, p. 740.

[9] http://scienceblogs.com/notrocketscience/2008/06/parasitic_wasp_turns_caterpillars_into_headbanging_bodyguard.php

[10] Moo, p. 443.

[11] Johnson, p. 742.

[12] Moo, pp. 461-462.

[13] Moo, p. 445.

[14] Colin Brown, *The New International Dictionary of New Testament Theology,* vol. I (Grand Rapids, Michigan: Zondervan Publishing House, 1975), p. 674.

[15] William F. Arndt and F. Wilbur Gingrich, *A Greek-English Lexicon of the New Testament and Other Early Christian Literature* (Chicago, Illinois: The University of Chicago Press, 1957), pp. 750-752.

[16] Brown, p. 681.

[17] George O. Wood, "In the Flesh or in the Spirit?" Sermon on Romans 8:5-17. http://georgeowood.com/?TargetPage=E43E3DB9-F4F8-4AE5-9B56-A2F2718D24F1

[18] George O. Wood, "The Struggle Within," Sermon on Romans 7:13-25. http://georgeowood.com/?TargetPage=E43E3DB9-F4F8-4AE5-9B56-A2F2718D24F1

[19] A. T. Robertson, *Word Pictures in the New Testament,* vol. IV: *The Epistles of Paul* (Nashville, Tennessee: Broadman Press, 1931), pp. 370-371.

Chapter 7

[1] Moo, p. 468.

[2] Johnson, p. 744.

[3] Stamps, *The Full Life Study Bible,* Ephesians 1:1 comment, p. 1823.

[4] Johnson, p. 745.

[5] F. B. Meyer, *Great Verses Through the Bible* (Grand Rapids, Michigan: Zondervan Publishing House, 1966), p. 369.

[6] Adapted from Greathouse and Taylor, pp. 119-120.

[7] http://en.wikipedia.org/wiki/Boeing_747 (970,000 lb (439,985 kg)

[8] Bill Morris, "Freedom of the Air," n.p.; available from www.PreachingToday.com, [accessed 7 August 2003].

[9] Interview with Steve Benintendi, creator of the program "Look Away."

[10] Moo, p. 468.

[11] Johnson, p. 908.

[12] Jowett, p. 107.

[13] http://www.google.com/search?q=John+Wesley%27s+father+told+him+to+seek+the+inner+witness&rlz=1I7DLUS_en&ie=UTF-8&oe=UTF-8&sourceid=ie7

[14] "Amazing Grace (My Chains Are Gone)," Words and music by Chris Tomlin and others. http://www.lyricsmode.com/lyrics/c/chris_tomlin/amazing_grace_my_chains_are_gone.html http://www.youtube.com/watch?v=Jbe7OruLk8I&feature=related

[15] E. K. Simpson and F. F. Bruce, *New International Commentary on the New Testament, The Epistles to the Ephesians and Colossians* (Grand Rapids, Michigan: Wm. B. Eerdmans Publishing Company, 1977), p. 269.

16 Harris, *The Complete Biblical Library: The New Testament Study Bible, Galatians–Philemon,* vol. 8, p. 85.

17 William Simmons, *Life in the Spirit New Testament Commentary: Galatians* (Grand Rapids, Michigan: Zondervan Publishing House, 1999), p. 1014.

18 This insight is from a sermon by George O. Wood on Acts 3, "Suffering for Doing Right." http://georgeowood.com/?TargetPage=FC7FDACE-85D6-47F3-AFD5-332304D265FD

19 *NIV Study Bible,* Galatians 6:1 comment, p. 1788.

20 Ralph Waldo Emerson via http://quotationsbook.com/quote/10741/

21 French L. Arrington and Roger Stronstad, eds., *Life in the Spirit New Testament Commentary* (Grand Rapids, Michigan: Zondervan Publishing House, 2003), p. 1015.

22 Adapted from http://www.fourth-avenue.org/chapters/17

23 George O. Wood, "The Agony and the Ecstasy." Sermon on Romans 8:18-25. http://georgeowood.com/?TargetPage=E43E3DB9-F4F8-4AE5-9B56-A2F2718D24F1

24 John Paul Heil, Paul's *Letter to the Romans: A Reader-Response Commentary* (Eugene, Oregon: Wipf and Stock Publishers, 1987), p. 87.

25 Greathouse and Taylor, p. 136.

26 http://gracethrufaith.com/selah/holidays-and-holy-days/the-feast-of-first-fruits/

27 Morris, p. 327.

28 John Phillips, *Exploring Romans* (Neptune, New Jersey: Loizeaux Brothers, 1969), p. 133.

29 Fee, *God's Empowering Presence: The Holy Spirit in the Letters of Paul,* pp. 575–586.

30 John B. McGarvey, "Prayers of the Spirit," n.p.; available from www.PreachingToday.com, [accessed 15 August 2003].

31 "No More Night," Words and music by Walt Harrah.
No more night. No more pain.
No more tears. Never crying again
And praises to the great "I AM."
We will live in the light of the risen Lamb.
http://www.lyricsmania.com/no_more_night_lyrics_david_phelps.html
http://www.youtube.com/watch?v=w0uTPWlDk6k

32 Gilbrandt, *The Complete Biblical Library: The New Testament Greek-English Dictionary, Delta-Epsilon,* 1132-2175, p. 146.

33 Gilbrandt, *The Complete Biblical Library: The New Testament Greek-English Dictionary, Delta-Epsilon,* 1132-2175, pp. 134-146.

34 Gilbrandt, *The Complete Biblical Library: The New Testament Greek-English Dictionary, Delta-Epsilon,* 1132-2175, p. 138.

35 Harris, *The Complete Biblical Library: The New Testament Study Bible, Romans–Corinthians,* vol. 7, p. 137.

36 Arndt and Gingrich, p. 223.

37 James Hastings, *The Speaker's Bible, Romans* (Grand Rapids, Michigan: Baker Book House, 1978), pp. 173-174.

38 George O. Wood, "How to Be a Failure," Sermon on Romans 8:31-39. http://georgeowood.com/?TargetPage=E43E3DB9-F4F8-4AE5-9B56-A2F2718D24F1

39 David Barrett, *International Bulletin of Missionary Research,* (January 2000), p. 25.

40 Hastings, pp. 176-177.

41 "Still," Words and music by Hillsong
When the oceans rise and thunders roar,
I will soar with You above the storm.
Father you are King over the flood.
I will be still and know You are God.
http://www.lyricsmode.com/lyrics/h/hillsong_united/#share
http://www.youtube.com/watch?v=Qk8horRi3_E

Chapter 8

1 Adapted from Stamps, *The Full Life Study Bible,* Article on "Election and Predestination," p. 1825.

2 Daniel D. Whedon, *Commentary on the New Testament: Intended for Popular Use,* vol. 3, *Acts-Romans* (New York, New York: Nelson & Phillips, 1892), p. 443.

3 Wiersbe, p. 101.

4 Greathouse, *Romans, Beacon Bible Commentary,* p. 197.

5 Johnson, p. 756.

6 Gilbrandt, *The Complete Biblical Library: The New Testament Greek-English Dictionary, Delta-Epsilon,* 1132-2175, pp. 341–350.

7 Meyer, p. 416.

8 Meyer, p. 416.

9 George O. Wood, "The Freedom of God," Sermon on Romans 9. http://georgeowood.com/?TargetPage=E43E3DB9-F4F8-4AE5-9B56-A2F2718D24F1

10 Johnson, p. 758.

11 Michael B. Brown, "God Loves Like a Persistent Mother," n.p.; available from www.PreachingToday.com, [accessed 22 October 2003].

12 http://www.sing365.com/music/lyric.nsf/Forever-lyrics-Michael-W-Smith/A27059E93435AE7E48256C69000D957B (http://www.youtube.com/watch?v=G7Bh0b3-JAg)

13 http://en.wikipedia.org/wiki/Herod%27s_Temple#Herod.27s_Temple

14 *NIV Study Bible,* Romans 9:32 comment, p.1722 .

15 Johnson, p. 759.

16 *NIV Study Bible,* Isaiah 52:13–53:12 comment, p. 1087.

17 Stephen Kingsley, "Black Light Exposes Stains," n.p.; available from www.PreachingToday.com, [accessed 3 November 2003].

18 Wesley, commentary on Matthew 13:13

19 Gordon Fee, *New International Biblical Commentary, 1 and 2 Timothy, Titus* (Peabody, Massachusettes: Hendrickson Publishers, 1988), p. 51.

20 James Orr, gen. ed., *The International Standard Bible Encyclopedia,* vol. II (Grand Rapids, Michigan: Wm. B. Eerdmans Publishing Company, 1974) p. 1232.

21 Barclay, p. 148.

[22] http://www.jewishjournal.com/world/article/in_world_of_7_billion_demographers_struggle_to_ascertain_the_number_of_jews/

Chapter 9

[1] http://www.forthegospel.org/articles/the_conversion_of_john_wesley

[2] Johnson, p. 767.

[3] Compare Frank D. Macchia, *Justified in the Spirit: Creation, Redemption, and the Triune God, Pentecostal Manifestos* (Grand Rapids, Michigan: William B. Eerdmans Publishing Company, 2010), p. 67.

[4] Harris, *The Complete Biblical Library: The New Testament Study Bible, Romans–Corinthians,* vol. 7, p. 191.

[5] Johnson, p. 767.

[6] Johnson, p. 769.

[7] Steve Mathewson, sermon on Romans 12:1-8, "Give Your Life Away to Someone Who Can Use It!" http://www.crosslifeefc.org/avms.asp?seriesid=9

[8] Eugene H. Peterson, *The Message* [Bible] (Colorado Springs, Colorado: NavPress Publishing Group, 1993), Romans 12:1.

[9] Harris, *The Complete Biblical Library: The New Testament Study Bible, Romans–Corinthians,* vol. 7, p. 191.

[10] George O. Wood, "A Call to Commitment," Sermon on Romans 12:1-2. http://georgeowood.com/?TargetPage=E43E3DB9-F4F8-4AE5-9B56-A2F2718D24F1

[11] Johnson, p. 768.

[12] Isaac Watts, "When I Survey the Wondrous Cross," Lyrics: http://library.timelesstruths.org/music/When_I_Survey_the_Wondrous_Cross/ Performed: http://www.youtube.com/watch?v=4tUZrxqAzeA&feature=related

[13] See J. B. Phillips, *The New Testament in Modern English* (New York, New York: HarperCollins Publishers, 1962).

[14] Steve Mathewson, Sermon on Romans 12:1-8, "Give Your Life Away to Someone Who Can Use It!" http://www.crosslifeefc.org/avms.asp?seriesid=9

[15] David K. Bernard, *The Message of Romans* (Hazelwood, Missouri: Word of Flame Press, 1987), p. 215.

[16] Stamps, *The Full Life Study Bible,* Romans 12:2 (4) comment, p. 1736.

[17] Casting Crowns, "Lifesong," Lyrics: http://www.azlyrics.com/lyrics/castingcrowns/lifesong.html Performed: http://www.youtube.com/watch?v=vaia32TsPq0

[18] J. H. Jowett, *The Passion for Souls* (London, England: Fleming H. Revell Company, 1905), pp. 9-23.

[19] Moo, pp. 760-764.

[20] Harris, *The Complete Biblical Library: The New Testament Study Bible, Romans–Corinthians,* vol. 7, p. 193.

[21] Harris, *The Complete Biblical Library: The New Testament Study Bible, Romans–Corinthians,* vol. 7, p. 193.

[22] Adapted from a sermon by George O. Wood, "Know Yourself," on Romans 12:3-5. http://georgeowood.com/?TargetPage=E43E3DB9-F4F8-4AE5-9B56-A2F2718D24F1

[23] Johnson, pp. 769-770.

[24] Moo, p. 765.

[25] Quentin McGhee and Carl Gibbs, *General Principles for Interpreting Scripture—Hermeneutics 1,* 2nd ed. (Springfield, Missouri: Faith & Action Team, 2011), p. 64.

[26] John Murray, *The Epistle to the Romans,* vol. 2 (Grand Rapids, Michigan: Wm. B. Eerdmans Publishing House, 1968), p. 126.

[27] Illustration by Larry Hatfield.

[28] Johnson, p. 770.

[29] Adapted from http://www.cubroundtable.com/assets/pdf-sundry/Not-My-Job.pdf

[30] George O. Wood, "The Gift of Exhortation," Sermon on Romans 12:8. http://georgeowood.com/?TargetPage=E43E3DB9-F4F8-4AE5-9B56-A2F2718D24F1

[31] Murray, vol. 2, p. 127.

[32] Greathouse and Taylor, pp. 183-184.

[33] This list is adapted from Phoenix First Assembly of God, which has over 200 ministries by church members.

[34] Moo, p. 775.

[35] Steve Mathewson, sermon on Romans 12:9-21, "Genuine Love." http://www.crosslifeefc.org/avms.asp?seriesid=9

[36] Godet, p. 434.

[37] Moo, p. 776.

[38] C. E. B. Cranfield, *International Critical Commentary, Romans 9-16* (New York, New York: Continuum International Publishing Group, 1979) p. 631.

[39] Thoralf Gilbrandt, ed., *The Complete Biblical Library, The New Testament Greek-English Dictionary, Pi-Rho* (Springfield, Missouri: World Library Press, 1991), 3665-4374, pp. 258-259.

[40] Johnson, p. 771.

[41] Moo, p. 776.

[42] Godet, p. 436.

[43] Moo, p. 769.

[44] Johnson, p. 771.

[45] bhpca.mypublicsquare.com/view/lt-general-thomas

[46] Johnson, p. 772.

[47] Harris, *The Complete Biblical Library: The New Testament Study Bible, Romans–Corinthians,* vol. 7, p. 197.

[48] Johnson, p. 772.

[49] Harris, *The Complete Biblical Library: The New Testament Study Bible, Romans–Corinthians,* vol. 7, p. 197.

[50] Steve Mathewson, sermon on Romans 12:9-21, "Genuine Love." http://www.crosslifeefc.org/avms.asp?seriesid=9

[51] http://en.wikipedia.org/wiki/Spanish_colonization_of_the_Americas

[52] http://en.wikipedia.org/wiki/File:PiraSocVirreinatoPer%C3%BA.jpg

[53] Harris, *The Complete Biblical Library: The New Testament Study Bible, Romans–Corinthians,* vol. 7, p. 201.

[54] Godet, p. 438.

[55] *NIV Study Bible,* Proverbs 25:22 comment, p. 974.

[56] Bruce, *Romans,* p. 230.

[57] Steve Mathewson, sermon on Romans 12:9-21, "Genuine Love." http://www.crosslifeefc.org/avms.asp?seriesid=9

Chapter 10

1 Stott, pp. 317-319.

2 Greathouse, *Romans, Beacon Bible Commentary*, p. 248.

3 Johnson, p. 773.

4 Stott, p. 342.

5 George O. Wood, "God and Government," Sermon on Romans 13:1-7. http://georgeowood.com/?TargetPage=E43E3DB9-F4F8-4AE5-9B56-A2F2718D24F1

6 George O. Wood, "Walking in Love and Light," Sermon on Romans 13:8-14. http://georgeowood.com/?TargetPage=E43E3DB9-F4F8-4AE5-9B56-A2F2718D24F1.

7 Godet, pp. 446-447.

8 Wood, "Walking in Love and Light," Sermon on Romans 13:8-14.

9 Adapted from an illustration by Larry Hatfield

10 Wood, "Walking in Love and Light," Sermon on Romans 13:8-14.

11 Wood, "Walking in Love and Light," Sermon on Romans 13:8-14.

12 Wood, "Walking in Love and Light," Sermon on Romans 13:8-14.

13 http://www.orthodoxyouth.org/romans/print/introexpulsionjews.htm

14 Johnson, p. 777

15 George O. Wood, "When Christians Disagree—Part 2," Sermon on Romans 14:13-23. http://georgeowood.com/?TargetPage=E43E3DB9-F4F8-4AE5-9B56-A2F2718D24F1.

16 George O. Wood, "When Christians Disagree—Part 3," Sermon on Romans 15:1-13. http://georgeowood.com/?TargetPage=E43E3DB9-F4F8-4AE5-9B56-A2F2718D24F1.

17 Wood, "When Christians Disagree—Part 2," Sermon on Romans 14:13-23.

18 Johnson, p. 781.

19 Gilbrandt, *Complete Biblical Library, The New Testament Greek-English Dictionary, Sigma-Omega, 4375-5457,* p. 59.

20 http://www.howjsay.com/index.php?word=chiasm

21 http://www.hccentral.com/gkeys/chiasm.html

22 Adapted from Moo, p. 850.

23 Johnson, p. 784.

24 Wood, "When Christians Disagree—Part 3," Sermon on Romans 15:1-13.

25 Adapted from Wood, "When Christians Disagree—Part 3," Sermon on Romans 15:1-13.

26 Moo, p. 875.

27 Johnson, p. 786.

28 Johnson, p. 786.

Chapter 11

1 http://en.wikipedia.org/wiki/Appian_Way

2 http://www.christian-prayer-quotes.christian-attorney.net/

3 Johnson, p. 787.

4 Alexander Pope, English Poet, 1688-1744, http://thinkexist.com/quotation/men_must_be_taught_as_if_you_taught_them_not-and/146854.html

5 Dale Carnegie, *How to Win Friends and Influence People* (New York, New York: Simon and Schuster, 1966), p. 43.

6 http://en.wikipedia.org/wiki/Justin_Martyr

7 Johnson, p. 789.

8 This story courtesy of LIFE Publishers, September, 2011.

9 E. C. McKenzie, *Mac's Giant Book of Quips and Quotes* (Grand Rapids, Michigan: Baker Book House, 1980), pp. 563-564.

10 Johnson, p. 791.

11 Johnson, pp. 790-791.

12 Johnson, p. 791.

13 http://www.christian-prayer-quotes.christian-attorney.net/

14 http://www.christian-prayer-quotes.christian-attorney.net/

15 http://www.christian-prayer-quotes.christian-attorney.net/

16 G. K. Beale and D. A. Carlson, *Commentary on the New Testament,* "Use of the Old Testament" (Grand Rapids, Michigan: Baker Book House, 2007), p. 607.

17 http://www.graceteaching.com/notes/paulsuseofot.pdf.

18 Steve Mathewson, adapted from a sermon on Romans 16:1-27, "The Gospel Really IS the Power of God." http://www.crosslifeefc.org/avms.asp?seriesid=9

19 Johnson, p. 792.

20 Steve Mathewson, sermon on Romans 16:1-27, "The Gospel Really IS the Power of God." http://www.crosslifeefc.org/avms.asp?seriesid=9

21 Gilbrandt, Complete Biblical Library, The New Testament Greek-English Dictionary, Sigma-Omega, 4375-5457, p. 117.

22 C. E. Keil and F. Delitzsch, *Commentary on the Old Testament in Ten Volumes:* Volume 1, *The Pentateuch:* "Numbers" (Grand Rapids, Michigan: Wm. B. Eerdmanns Publishing Co., 1976), pp. 141-142.

23 Johnson, p. 794.

24 Martin H. Franzmann, *Romans: A Commentary* (St. Louis, Missouri: Concordia Publishing House, 1968), p. 278.

25 MasterWriter Professional computer program.

26 J. D. Douglas, *The New Bible Dictionary* (Grand Rapids, Michigan: Wm. B. Eerdmanns Publishing Co., 1962), p. 484.

27 Greathouse, *Romans, Beacon Bible Commentary*, p. 288.

God's Plan of Salvation

1. Introduction: God is holy, good, and pure—completely righteous. *"God is light; in him there is no darkness at all"* (1 John 1:5).

2. The Problem: Our sins have separated us from God. Because we have sinned—done things we know are wrong—we cannot fellowship with God. Our sins make us too dirty to come into God's holy presence. As we cannot enter a clean room with muddy shoes, we cannot come into God's presence with our sins. *"All have sinned"* (Rom. 3:23). The wages for our sin is death—spiritual death—which is separation from God, now and forever. Those who reject Jesus will die in their sins. They will spend eternity tormented in the flames of hell, away from the presence of God.

3. God's Solution: God loves us so much that he sent Jesus to rescue us. Jesus said, *"I am the way and the truth and the life. No one comes to the Father except through me"* (John 14:6). His name is Jesus, which means Savior, because He saves us from our sins (Matt. 1:21). Jesus saves us from both the penalty and the power of sin–now and forever. Jesus, the Son of God, became a man and lived a perfect, sinless life (John 1:14; Heb. 4:15). He died on the cross as our substitute—He took the penalty for our sins (Rom. 6:23; 2 Cor. 5:21; 1 Pet. 2:24-25. Those who submit their lives to Jesus—God declares to be forgiven, clean and righteous (Rom. 5:1-2).

4. God's Invitation: Jesus says, *"Here I am! I stand at the door (of your heart) and knock. If anyone hears my voice and opens the door, I will come in"* (Rev. 3:20). God's favorite word is "Come". He wants to come to all people, and He wants them to come to him. *"The Spirit and the bride say, "Come!" And let him who hears say, "Come!" Whoever is thirsty, let him come; and whoever wishes, let him take the free gift of the water of life"* (Rev. 22:17). Accept God's invitation. Come to Jesus. Repent of your sins, that is, turn away from what you know is wrong. Put your trust in Jesus as your Savior and Lord. Believe that He died to save you from your sins. Ask Him to forgive your past sins and free you from being a slave to sin. *"If we confess our sins, He is faithful and just and will forgive us our sins, and cleanse us from all unrighteousness"* (1 John 1:9). Welcome Jesus into your life and He will enter. To all who receive Him, He gives the right to become God's children (1 John 1:12).

5. Your Commitment: Welcome to the family of God! God's plan of salvation has a beginning, a middle, and a completion–when we reach heaven. By walking through steps 1-4 above, you have begun to follow God's plan of salvation. Your name is now written in God's book of life (Phil. 4:3; Rev. 3:5; 20:12). The middle part of God's plan is following Jesus as we live on earth. As a child of God, seek to obey the teachings of Jesus in the Bible (Matt. 28:19-20). As you follow Him, He will lead and strengthen you in your relationship with God. As a baby grows into an adult, you will grow from a new child of God into to a mature family member. Be baptized in water (Matt. 28:19; Acts 8:36-38; Rom. 6:4; Mark 16:16). Become part of a local church that preaches and teaches the Bible (Acts 2:41; 9:31). Seek to be filled with the Holy Spirit (Acts 1:8; 2:4; 4:31; 8:17; 10:44-46; 19:1-7; Eph. 5:18-20). Learn to walk in the Spirit, so you can overcome sinful desires that come through the flesh (Rom. 8:5; Gal. 5:16). Grow in grace, and in the knowledge of our Lord and Savior Jesus Christ, and in maturity (2 Pet. 3:18; 2 Pet. 1:5-18). Fellowship with other believers who will encourage you. Share your testimony with others, and lead them to Jesus (John 1:40-42; 4:39). The completion of salvation occurs when Jesus Christ returns. At that time, He will give you a new body, and complete His glorious plan of salvation in your life (Rom. 8:18-25; 1 Cor. 15:20-58; 1 Thess. 4:13-17). We do not know the exact time Jesus will return. For now, enjoy the presence of God, and His Spirit in you, as you grow in grace. You have been saved from your past sins. You are being saved daily, as you abide and grow in Christ. And your salvation has a glorious completion ahead.